The Plymouth and DeSoto Story

By Don Butler

Editing and Design by George H. Dammann

Crestline Publishing

1251 NORTH JEFFERSON AVE.
SARASOTA, FLA. 33577

THE PLYMOUTH and DeSOTO STORY

By Don Butler

Copyright © By Crestline Publishing Co. Inc.

Library of Congress Catalog Number 77-93182
ISBN Number 0-912612-14-2

Typesetting by Colonial Cold Type, Glendale Heights, Ill.
Printed in U.S.A. by Wallace Press, Hillside, Ill.
Binding by The Engdahl Co., Elmhurst, Ill.
Cover Design by William J. Hentges, Warren, Mich.

Published By: Crestline Publishing Co., Inc.
1251 North Jefferson Ave.
Sarasota, Florida 33577

All rights to this book are reserved. No part of this book
may be reproduced in any manner whatsoever without the
express written permission of the publisher. For further
information, contact Crestline Publishing Co. Inc., 1251
North Jefferson Ave., Sarasota, FL 33577.

In Appreciation

This book could not have been so extensive in coverage and detail without the contributions of many. I am most grateful to the Chrysler Historical Collection, which revealed much information of absolute authenticity. Clifford C. Lockwood, who founded the Collection in 1966, introduced me to its fascinating content. Upon Cliff's retirement in 1971, John F. Bunnell became corporate historian. Constant growth required an archivist, and H. Donald Schaerer was given that task. These men gave me every possible courtesy and privilege, as did young C.R. (Rob) Cheney, who took over after John and Don retired. After my status was changed from stylist to retiree, I was engaged by Michael M. Ducody, administrator of the Collection, to work with Rob for a limited time. D. L. Davis, now the main link with the public, has always been generously helpful. Also kindly providing information were Denise Heppler and Madryn Johnson, librarians in the newly reorganized contents. To all associated with the Collection, I am deeply grateful.

Rob Cheney eventually transferred to Chrysler's Engineering Standards and Data department, and has supplied specific information I needed — just as his boss, Ed Vosburgh, had been doing for years. Also, much general information was gained from my perusal of many publications in the Chrysler Engineering Library, where librarian Phyllis Sears was most helpful.

Special thanks also go to Jeffrey I. Godshall of the Chrysler Design Office. Stylist Jeff, an auto historian and author during his free time, added the DeSoto Diplomats and their captions to this history, besides providing detail information for use elsewhere. Inadvertently contributing in a very unusual manner were Donald H. Beyreis and Robert Grove, immediate superiors during the last years of my styling career, who never admonished me for using countless portions of styling time for indulgence in historical interest. Dean Clark, son of original 1924 Chrysler designer Oliver Clark, gave of the 43 years of knowledge gathered since he started in Chrysler's art and color section in 1931. Many other Chrysler folks directly or indirectly gave to this history during my employment and association with the corporation.

James J. Bradley, Curator of the vast National Automotive History Collection in the Detroit Public Library, deserves special thanks for the services and privileges extended to me. He and his staff made my researching of many reams of published matter more pleasant, and easier. And library staff member George Risley, now retired, has earned extra thanks for patiently and absorbedly listening, and often uttering constructive comments, as I related the book's procedures and problems during many long dinner periods.

Fellow Crestline author James K. Wagner's knowledge of trucks was especially useful, and he aided in many other ways. Other friends made sales literature and advertisements available, among them Dave Collier, Warren, Mich., and William Coombe, St. Clair Shores, Mich., who are fellow officers in the Autoenthusiasts International literature club. Also Charles and Gertrude Bohman, Dexter, Mich.; Robert Gale, West Bloomfield, Mich.; and Tod Kelly, Goshen, Ind. Many Plymouth 4 & 6 Cylinder Owners Club members were helpful, especially Jim Benjaminson, Cavalier, N.D.; Wilbur O. Burkett, Ida, Mich.; and Andrew G. Weimann II, of Torrington, Conn. Adding much in a special way was parts specialist and merchant Robert Burchill, of Port Huron, Mich.

Much of the photographic material is from the Chrysler Historical Collection, which is supplied by the Chrysler Corp. Photographic Services, on whose staff is Mary Borchard. I am grateful to Mary for heeding my plea for old and new views not found in the Collection's files. She obligingly made trips to the storage "morgue" in search of rare old negatives which I had found listed in records opened to me by Paul Serratoni, then the department boss. Some members of the Plymouth 4 & 6 Cylinder Owners Club and the DeSoto Club of America sent pictures of their cars and are credited where used, but many were not of suitable quality for publishing. The National Automotive History Collection was another source. Sales literature, periodicals and other printed matter also yielded many illustrations. Most of the camera-copy work was done by Crestline Publishing, but a sizable portion is the work of William L. Bailey, Royal Oak, Mich.

Don Butler
May, 1978

**Note: Prices quoted for the various models are factory retail prices for vehicles at the place of manufacture, except that imported models of 1971 and later were priced at the shipping port of entry. All prices apply to vehicles with standard equipment only, and do not include taxes and charges incidental to sale and delivery. As a general guide, dealer retail prices varied from 10% to 20% more than factory retail. Weights are dry weight, without fuel, oil or coolants, and are for vehicles with standard equipment only. Prices and weights sometimes varied within model years and in relation to the geographic location of manufacture. Each figure, quoted from authentic sources, is typical of the model it relates to and is offered primarily for interest and reference.

FOREWORD

It was said long ago that Walter P. Chrysler should have placed the Chrysler name and seal-like medallion on the car he introduced in 1928 as the Plymouth. This feeling was based on the fact that the car looked very much like a scaled-down replica of the 6-cylinder 1929 Chrysler 65, which teamed with the yet larger Chrysler 75 for their share of attention when all three were first shown on the same day. After all, the Chrysler name had served well on the earlier 4-cylinder cars, and the new one had justifiable reasons to bear it, too. To further support this contention, it was pointed out that the Chrysler 65 and 75 succeeded the 1928 models 62 and 72, respectively, and the new 4-cylinder car should have been the Chrysler 55, successor to the 1928 Chrysler 52.

Not that there was any dislike for the Plymouth name — it was meaningful, highly respected and well-known in the annals of Early American history — but it was felt that the magnetism of the Chrysler name could not possibly be matched by any other. Exceptional success had accompanied use of the Chrysler name on all of the company's cars, and why risk public acceptance of a car without it?

Apparently, Walter P. Chrysler felt there was little risk, for he sought new names for the 4-cylinder car and a new light six closely linked to it. He had corporate expansion in mind, and certainly some new names were needed. It was the thing to do. General Motors had introduced the Pontiac as Oakland's companion car in 1926 and given Cadillac the LaSalle in 1927, and maybe Mr. Chrysler had heard that the Viking would come from Oldsmobile in 1929 and Buick would produce the Marquette in 1930. Studebaker already had the Erskine, Marmon's Roosevelt was about ready, and John N. Willys had added the Falcon-Knight and was about to sever the Overland name from the more popular Whippet. Ford, who had the Lincoln, didn't get involved in product expansion and further name-gathering until several years later.

There are signs, however, that Mr. Chryler's new 4-cylinder baby was regarded as a Chrysler, not a Plymouth, until shortly before it was placed in production. Perhaps it was then that a decision was made to reserve the Chrysler name for larger cars. But when the Plymouth name was chosen, it was not used alone. Nameplated and advertised as the Chrysler Plymouth, there are hints that the car was regarded as a sub-series Chrysler, similar to the Chrysler 55 idea. But it seems more likely that the Chrysler name was prefixed simply to add strength to the new Plymouth name, which probably was expected to support itself within a short while. Also, the car was to be sold only by dealers who sold Chryslers, and that probably was another reason for the name combination. And it could have been a compromise with fears of little success without it.

Success was immediate, and the car paraded through its first several months so strongly that the Chrysler name was shed early in 1929. The Plymouth name quickly won acclaim around the world, and has stood on its own merits ever since. Adversity overtook the car only 16 months after it was introduced, when the devastating economic disaster struck the nation and hurt all automakers and eveything else. For 20 months, Plymouth gradually lost strength, then began a vigorous recovery that showed all other automakers how to pull out of a depression. That spurt lasted almost seven years, when a temporary recession slowed the pace, then it raced on to World War II and a proud record of war goods production.

Following a good post-war period of several years, Plymouth's pattern was one of ups and downs, mostly of short duration in either direction. New heights of popularity were successively attained, and the 1973 model year was by far the most rewarding of all. Up to the present time, probably more than 23 million Plymouths have been built in North America, plus perhaps many hundreds of thousands built in foreign countries. The Plymouth name means much to many, and it has given us a fantastically immense succession of models to write and read about.

The DeSoto story is distinctively different. Some have wondered why the DeSoto was created, because there seemed to be no logical reason for it. They say that Mr. Chrysler had a wide range of Dodge sixes in the lower medium price market, therefore the DeSoto was not needed, and in fact was a misfit in the overall Chrysler product layout. Similar feelings have been expressed about the Fargo truck and commercial car line. Those contentions have no factual basis, as factors prevalent during the period will show.

Walter Chrysler first tried to buy the Dodge

Brothers company in 1926. He wanted the manufacturing facilities and huge dealer network, and could expand his corporation's size and market coverage with the highly respected Dodge Brothers car and truck lines. But Dodge wasn't then willing to sell out to anyone. Deciding to expand anyway, he laid out some new plans. They called for a new light 6-cylinder car to sell between a new 4-cylinder car and the smallest Chrysler, and a new commercial car and truck line was on the schedule, too. So the then nameless Plymouth and DeSoto development program was begun in 1926, interlocking because the two cars were to share nearly all parts in order to keep costs down and allow low retail prices. The truck program was linked to that operation as a sort of sideline activity so that it could gain all possible advantages.

Plymouth and DeSoto were about to go into production in 1928 when Dodge's owners finally decided to sell their company. But by then, Dodge had discontinued the 4-cylinder cars and had a spread of sixes in three market brackets. The Chrysler purchase put DeSoto almost in line with the smallest Dodge, but priced about $30 less and with some popular models not offered by Dodge. DeSoto remained just below Dodge until 1933, when an upgrade in size and price placed it between Dodge and Chrysler, and it generally stayed there from then on.

Mr. Chrysler would have planned his 1929 product line differently in 1926 if he had found good reason to suspect that Dodge would eventually be made available to him. Had he thought so, it is likely that the DeSoto would not have come about, and certainly not the Fargo line. Fargo production for the domestic market lasted about two years, but like DeSoto, the name is still used today on commercial vehicles built in Turkey. Fluctuating DeSoto popularity was registered in production totals, which show that DeSoto out-produced corresponding higher-priced Chrysler models in only 11 of its 30 model years. That fact is a basis for this question: Why was the DeSoto car retained so long?

A single total reason for DeSoto's continuance has never been spelled out, and it probably could not be contained in one statement. But there are several possible reasons. Certainly its rebounds to heights above Chrysler, after pre-1958 sags that only once exceeded two years, was encouragement for carrying on. Likely another factor was the vast number of buyers who chose DeSotos because they were

DeSotos, and it could not be assumed that all or most of them would buy Chryslers or Dodges if DeSotos were not available. Then there is General Motors, regarded by many as the "bell cow" of the industry, whose line-up of cars Chrysler must challenge in all basic areas — car line for car line. Facing GM's Chevrolet, Pontiac, Oldsmobile, Buick and Cadillac were Plymouth, Dodge, DeSoto, Chrysler and Imperial, in that order. Certainly Chrysler Corp. had no desire to reduce its spread of car lines, which the public might misinterpret as a shrinkage of corporate size and vitality.

Perhaps there were other reasons to justify DeSoto's presence so long, but whether or not it was ever justified, DeSoto traced an interesting course through the years. At first very popular, it struggled through the depression and was swatted down by the Airflow design. Redeeming itself, it swept into the war years and won glory in the making of war goods. The first 12 years of peacetime were much more rewarding, but also more eventful. Sometimes daring, sometimes moderate, DeSoto wove a tapestry of colorful history that is offered for study and pleasure in these pages.

Plymouth and DeSoto are combined in this book because they were developed together, introduced in the same year, and remained closely related. Domestic Fargo models were included for similar reasons. The primary purpose was to cover domestic Plymouth and DeSoto models, but DeSoto Diplomats were added at the insistence of some of my colleagues. A single book can show only a few foreign cars in a 50-year range embracing two car lines, especially when the objective is to illustrate and basically describe every body model of every U.S. series in every model year. However, some models are not shown because acceptable photographic material was not available, or because no pictorial record of them was found. The extensive coverage of car lines left relatively little opportunity to report activities and operations of the Plymouth and DeSoto divisions and Chrysler Corp.

Every effort has been made to report all models, engines, vital specifications and notable new features

each year, especially as regards cars offered to the public. But some details undoubtedly escaped me, or were not satisfactorily justified for inclusion. Generally, these would probably be in-production changes, special engines or devices. Accuracy was the keynote for the book's entire content. In adherence to this, research was never-ending. Sometimes, late-found information relating to earlier models was uncovered. The printing preparation process required that quantities of completed chapters be released to the publisher so that his work could progress while later chapters were being written. But when I found bits felt necessary for insertion in released chapters, I submitted them anyway. Certainly the publisher must have found this a bit disturbing. Though truth was foremost, conjecture was sometimes employed, and it is recognizable as such wherever it was useful in examining a point.

The facts within this book originated within Chrysler Corp., where many of them are on record in the Chrysler Historical Collection. Fortunately, I had direct access to the Collection's material for a number of years. During that time, contributions intermittently arrived from donors, adding more information. Official directives and letters, plus publications for employees, dealers and the Chrysler public, tell of many decisions and actions through the years. Some former assumptions have been proved wrong, others right, and surprises have been uncovered.

Elsewhere, many trade publications yielded background and specific information. The most utilized were Automotive Industries, Automotive News, Automotive Topics, Automobile Trade Journal, Branham Automobile Reference Books, Commercial Car Journal, Motor (U.S.), Motor Age, Motor Vehicle Monthly, National Automobile Dealers Association Used Car Guides, and Ward's Automotive Reports and Yearbooks. Company periodicals most often used were the Chrysler News, Chrysler Motors Magazine, Chrysler War Work Magazine, DeSoto Retailer, and the Chrysler-Plymouth Spectator.

Preparing and writing this book has been a new and deeply involved experience for me. Previously, my familiarity with books consisted of reading and studying those authored by others. Always a daydreamer, I had dreamed of doing many things, most of which were beyond my scope, and a book was among the "impossible" visions. Untrained as a typist and journalist, I had no aims at such a venture, but had researched and written a magazine article or two.

Then I met George H. Dammann, of Crestlin Publishing Co., in the Chrysler Historical Collectio while he was gathering material for his 70 YEARS O CHRYSLER book. Then a stylist at Chrysler, I spen lunch periods and "borrowed" time with George in th Collection, helping him in whatever ways I could Later, he asked me for research and editing aid in th pre-1943 portion of THE DODGE STORY. As tha was getting under way early in 1974, I was approach ed about writing this Plymouth and DeSoto book Secretly I was delighted, but also scared of the im mense work and my doubts of ability to accomplish i properly. After repeatedly delaying an answer while weighed the factors, George persisted, and initia work on the book began.

One reason for my hesitation in accepting the boo proposal was my previous promise to Georg Slankard, publisher of Cars & Parts magazine, that would begin writing articles for him after retiring fror Chrysler. Therefore, early in 1975 that ongoing wor was launched, and in many ways it has complemente and added a measure of proficiency to the concurren work on this book. But its work/time requirement delayed the book's completion, which allowed th bonus addition of Plymouth's 50th-year vehicles – the 1978 models. Many readers have waited muc longer for this book than they expected to, and t them I apologize.

This experience has taught me a lot about "doing" book. Though I tried hard to preclude them, ther must be mistakes, and I invite correction as well a criticism. I enjoyed every minute and the settin down of every word, even though finding various an interesting ways of reporting standard ingredients i picture captions was a constant problem that usuall was unsolved. Preparing the book has expanded m knowledge of these cars, which were fascinating t study through all of their years. And I sincerely hop that you will find like enchantment on the pages tha follow.

As a finishing touch, eight examples of my artwor were selected to follow the final chapter. They wer drawn in 1968-69 at the insistence of a friend who wa the editor of the bulletin published by the Plymouth & 6 Cylinder Owners Club. Primarily intended to i lustrate identifying details of the earliest Plymout models, they have appeared in various matter publish ed by the Club. They are owned by me, however, an each one has my mark, stylized "db" letters framed b a vertical rectangle. The details shown will serve t enhance the definition of cars in correspondin chapters.

In summary, the book is a factual reference inco porating 50 years of cars in such a manner tha favorites can easily be found or the total arra surveyed. Though necessarily brief in comment about individual models, I hope readers will find it t be a good record.

Don Butler
P.O. Box 28130
Detroit, MI 48228

Pre - Chrysler Era

Many of the countless hundreds of thousands of people familiar with Plymouth and DeSoto automobiles might expect a history of these makes to begin with their introduction by Chrysler Corporation almost fifty years ago. Such expectancy is logical, but a history must include at least a summary of the background from which the principal subjects emerged. In this case the background extends well beyond the days when the public first became aware of Chrysler as an automotive name. Only Plymouth can claim such far-reaching lineage, since it is a direct descendant of the Maxwell, which is therefore our starting point.

Jonathan D. Maxwell was a machinist and engineer who helped in the development of several early automobiles before starting his own project. Elwood Haynes, Elmer and Edgar Apperson, Ransom E. Olds, Roy Chapin and others benefited from his knowledge and skills, which aided the launching of successful manufacturing ventures in the first budding of what was to become a vast automobile industry. While employed with the Olds Motor Works, which was by far the most prosperous of the new auto companies, Mr. Maxwell decided to depart and become more personally involved in the design and manufacture of another car. Fellow Olds employee Charles B. King joined with him in developing the car. A Mr. W. T. Barbour entered the team and they organized the Northern Manufacturing Company in Detroit in 1902. The fruit of that effort was a lightweight one-cylinder car known as the Northern, but larger cars were turned out before company operations ceased in 1909. Mr. Maxwell did not remain with the Northern company that long, however, as he now had ambitions to design and manufacture an automobile to bear his own name.

The new car was developed while Jonathan Maxwell was associated with the Briscoe brothers, Benjamin and Frank, who had enjoyed a successful metal stamping business since 1897. The Briscoes also owned a 97% interest in the fledgling Buick Motor Company, which was already floundering. So they withdrew from Buick and provided the initial financial resources necessary to form the Maxwell-Briscoe Motor Company in 1904. Further financing was realized from preferred and common stock, while half of the latter was divided between Maxwell and the Briscoes. The investment firm of J.P. Morgan in New York added a tidy sum, and production of automobiles was begun in November, 1904.

The new car bore the singular name of Maxwell, but it was often called the Maxwell-Briscoe because of the company name. It was built in Tarrytown, New York, in a factory that was slow in meeting demands of the instant sales success. Within a year, another model was added to the original, and another plant was acquired at Pawtucket, Rhode Island, for necessary extra facilities. Public acceptance of the need for motorized vehicles was growing slowly but steadily, and Maxwell-Briscoe prosperity grew along with it. Early in 1906, a midwest plant was opened in Chicago to assemble cars built with parts made in the eastern plants, but it remained in operation only two years. During the first months of this midwestern operation, the company decided they could manufacture and distribute more advantageously if they established production facilities in Indiana, and the city of New Castle soon became the focal point.

A new plant was erected at New Castle, turning out parts at first, but car assemblies began in 1908 after a delay caused by the economic panic that gained headway across the country in 1907. The growing company was by now operating four plants, making mostly the popular 2-cylinder models while increasing production of its desirable new 4-cylinder car. After a temporary slowing in 1907, the company surged ahead.

The company was materially aided by the reputation of its products, but its successes were due in large part to the daring and drive of Benjamin Briscoe, who was dominant in his position as president. Mr. Maxwell was vice-president while serving quite capably in directing engineering and manufacturing activities. Frank Briscoe was younger than Benjamin, and always overshadowed by him. However, Frank displayed daring of his own when he entered into partnership with Alanson P. Brush and formed the Brush Motor Car Company in Detroit late in 1906. This venture had the blessing of big brother Ben, but the Brush never came into the Maxwell-Briscoe organization, although it became a fringe relative later when they both were involved in a huge merger of many companies.

During the economic problem period of 1908, Buick's president William C. Durant approached Benjamin Briscoe, Henry Ford, officials from Cadillac, Oldsmobile and others with a proposition to combine their companies into one unit as a solution to industry complexities and difficulties of the time. Mr. Ford demanded a huge cash settlement in exchange for his agreement, and Briscoe quickly echoed the demand. The cash demands became so great that they

First production Maxwells were 1905 models announced late in 1904. The line was comprised of the Model L 2-passenger Tourabout and Model H 5-passenger Touring Car. The 2-cylinder 8-horsepower Tourabout had a 72-inch wheelbase. At introduction it was priced at $700, but was increased to $750 within a few months. Price changes also happened to the Touring Car shown, but in a different direction. At first it listed at $1,550 but later was cut to $1,400. The Touring Car was the larger of the two models, having a 2-cylinder, 16-horsepower engine and an 84-inch wheelbase. As was typical of early open cars, no doors were provided to the front seat. Some cars had no side doors to the rear seat either, while others offered rear entrance by means of a hinged center seat section which swung as a door. Maxwell featured side-entrance rear doors as standard equipment. Doors were arched across the top — a line that would be straightened out flat for next year. Another identifying though small mark on both of this year's Maxwell models was the oval-shaped feature on the side panel below the front seat.

could not be met, and Durant's effort to include them failed. However, he did manage to use an exchange of stock as the means for bringing Buick, Oldsmobile and Oakland together in forming the General Motors Company, known today as General Motors Corporation. Cadillac joined the family in 1909, and Chevrolet did not yet exist. There would never have been a Chevrolet Division if Ford had entered the combine, and likely not if Maxwell-Briscoe had joined without Ford.

Briscoe, awed by the magnitude of the new General Motors Company, was now eager to pack more parties into a bigger package than Durant had assembled. Using his sound and solid Maxwell-Briscoe company and the parts-making Briscoe Manufacturing Company as a foundation, much like Durant had used Buick, he went looking for structural components to build upon it. By manipulations and an exchange of stock, seven companies merged with the original two, forming the United States Motor Company. Of course, Benjamin Briscoe was president, and counted among the eight vice-presidents were Jonathan Maxwell in charge of Maxwell plants, and Frank Briscoe as head of engineering.

The passenger car makes involved were Brush, Columbia, Maxwell and Stoddard-Dayton, while Sampson was the only truck. The Gray Motor Company, makers of stationary and marine engines, and Providence Engineering Works, which made engines and drive train components, teamed with the Briscoe parts firm to complete the merger group. The Thomas automobile and plants were added a year later.

Organized in 1910 with headquarters in New York City, the new company soon bought land in Highland Park, Michigan, a Detroit suburb. Plants built on this site ultimately produced Maxwells, small Chryslers, and early Chrysler-built Plymouths and DeSotos. In fact, the area has expanded and become the general headquarters, engineering, research and styling complex of the Chrysler Corporation today.

Unwise acquisitions, unwieldy combinations and unprofitable operations caused the collapse of the United States Motor Company late in 1912. A series of reorganizing maneuvers resulted in departure of the Briscoe brothers and J. D. Maxwell, and the discontinuance of all vehicles except the Maxwell. Since it had a good reputation and salability, Maxwell was the nucleus around which salvagable elements of the defunct combine were gathered to create the successor Maxwell Motor Company, Inc. early in 1913. Leadership now centered in Detroit, and production of the newly-designed Maxwell 25 began at Highland Park in the summer. The new car restored respect for the Maxwell name after suffering from the stigma of unfortunate circumstances for three years. Prosperity and eventless years were enjoyed until the American involvement in World War I.

While highlighted events were taking place in the ancestral lineage, some unrelated sidelights flickered feebly and flopped. Their sparks rate recognition here because of the sameness of names: Plymouth and de Soto (with small d and divided name). Though their point in time was within the era of the Chrysler forebears, they were not akin to any, or to each other.

The earliest Plymouths were commercial vehicles built at Plymouth, Ohio. The Commercial Motor Truck Company was formed at Toledo, Ohio in 1906, and built an experimental truck before moving to Plymouth in November of that year. In 1909, the name was changed to Plymouth Motor Truck Company, which remained in existence until 1914. During that period a wide variety of vehicles were offered. Among them were one-half to one-ton delivery wagons, 1½ to 3-ton stake and sideboard trucks, 2 to 3-ton covered vans, 20 to 24-passenger bus types, and sightseeing vehicles of 20 to 40-passenger capacity. Known engine sizes were 2 to 4 cylinders and 24 to 55 horsepower, mounted on wheelbases ranging from 96 to 146 inches. Never a volume producer, there are indications that production did not exceed 200 units for the company's entire life span.

Their most unusual feature was a double friction drive utilizing a system of two revolving discs (one for forward and one reverse) against which two friction-driven wheels were compressed when road movement was desired. Each friction wheel operated a chain drive to a road wheel. This

This brand-new 1906 Maxwell Model L Tourabout posed before starting out on the first of the famed Glidden Tours in July 1905, with Johnathan D. Maxwell at the wheel. The Tourabout's specifications, price and general design did not noticeably change for 1906. Glidden Tours were inaugurated to prove and promote the capability of motor cars for pleasure. Of the 44 tour entrants, six were Maxwells, two of which were Tourabouts. Entrant No. 19 completed the 12-day, 883-mile trip from New York City to Bretton Woods, N. H., and return, but not without some breakdowns that cost it a place among the award winners. In its peak performance on the tour, a speed of almost 20 mph was reached, and a fuel consumption of nearly 14 mpg was recorded. The other Tourabout dropped out after bumping into a wagon on the first day. Of the four Model H Touring Cars entered, one was driven by Benjamin Briscoe, who received one of the 22 "First Class Certificate" awards for completing the tour without delays at overnight stops. Another Model H driver got a "Second Class Certificate" for failing to make one or more control points on time, though he did finish the trip. All of the tour Maxwells were 1906 production models. The best record of the Maxwell entries was achieved by a Model H, which won one of five "Perfect Score" awards for meeting all conditions with no mechanical trouble. One of the top five scorers, Percy Pierce, drove his Great Arrow with such competence and courtesy that 15 competitors voted for him. That was twice as many votes as any other driver got, and the Tour Commission named him the overall tour winner.

concept was an elaboration of the friction power-transfer principle used by a minority of makers, but the chain drive itself had been featured by almost every company at one time or another. However, by 1908 many had advanced to the drive train consisting of transmission, driveshaft and differential, and earlier methods were doomed to oblivion.

A Plymouth passenger car was also made by the truck maker, appearing about midway in the company's life span. There is no proof of production reality, but at least one experimental car was built before the company released details and specifications to the press, indicating intent to manufacture. The model publicized for 1910 featured the double friction and chain drive mechanism, but protected it with enclosures. The 5-passenger touring car body was known as a "torpedo" design, which treated the front seat area as a compartment with cowling and doors, thereby combining it with the rear seat into an integrated body appearance. The "torpedo" style was then used by few manufacturers, but it quickly caught on like wildfire and remained throughout the existence of open cars. The car's general appearance was not as advanced as the body, and was marred by an obnoxious domed turret on top of the hood. The turret dome included an 8-inch filler cap sufficient for use of a 3-gallon bucket in pouring gasoline to the enclosed fuel tank which gravity-fed the engine. The manufacturer regarded this novel location of the fuel tank as an advanced and more practical gravity-feed application, but it was never exactly copied. Best-known and most acceptable was Ford's unobtrusive adaptation for 1926-31 models, in which the tank was neatly concealed within the body cowl.

The first de Soto was announced by the new de Soto Motor Car Company, Auburn, Indiana, in June of 1913. At first, it was an L-head 6-cylinder of 55 horsepower with 130-inch wheelbase mounting a 5-passenger touring body only. While using mostly common components, the car did have some unique features. Engine oil was circulated through a sight-feed glass on the dash. A novel arrangement included the engine's rear support on a bolt-attached frame cross-member to which the forward end of the torsion tube was connected by the use of a hinged yoke device. This was claimed to facilitate removal of the transmission without disturbing the engine and axle, as well as freeing the universal joint from driveshaft weight. A pneumatic cranker was available for engine starting, and the rear-located gasoline tank was suspended in an unusual manner. Front compartment legroom was exceptional, due to locating the center-mounted gearshift lever well forward and omission of a hand lever for the parking brake, which was operated by a foot pedal. Another pedal actuated both the clutch and service brakes.

The de Soto continued into 1914 as substantially the same car, but reported a 132-inch wheelbase and a unique sub-frame to support the engine within the chassis frame. Bodies of 2, 4, 5 and 7-passenger size were offered, the 7-passenger being factory-priced at $2,185, which was an expensive car in those days. The company did not wholly depend upon the big car for support, which it demonstrated by entering the extreme lower end of the price scale with a cyclecar. A brief craze for these cheap lyweight vehicles reached its height by 1914, and the de Soto cyclecar was calculated to reap a golden harvest from the crop of crazed consumer-candidates. The mini-model de Soto carried two passengers in tandem at speeds up to 40 miles an hour and boasted of getting 35 to 50 miles per gallon of gasoline. The $385 factory price was competitive, but there was no parade of purchasers to the showrooms. The flagging de Soto company's big 6-cylinder car became the Zimmerman, and production was continued in Auburn, Indiana by the Zimmerman Manufacturing Company. Indicators point to the probability that Zimmerman also built some cyclecars before the flyweight

Arriving in midsummer 1906, the first 4-cylinder Maxwell was destined to father several more generations of fours to come in the next 19 years, the mainstay of the major portion of Maxwell's existence. The 1907 Model M was an impressive 40-horsepower machine built to carry five passengers on a 104-inch wheelbase. Buyers paid $3,000 a copy and could choose from red, maroon and black paints.

Not actually related to Maxwell yet, the Chalmers-Detroit line would eventually become a branch of the family tree. In 1908, Hugh Chalmers and backers bought the Detroit properties of E. R. Thomas Motor Co., including the Thomas-Detroit 4-40 car line. A name switch made it the 1909 Chalmers-Detroit 40. Then the smaller 30, shown here, was added. Its 4-cylinder, 30-horsepower, 110-inch wheelbase chassis carried 2, 3 or 4-passenger runabout bodies, this 5-passenger touring type, or a 7-passenger limousine. The runabouts and touring car sold for $1,500 without tops, and the limousine went for $2,500.

fad faded out. Both names, de Soto and Zimmerman, vanished from vehicle rosters either before or during 1916.

The Maxwell's journey toward the inevitable meeting with Mr. Chrysler and a linkup with his Plymouth was hampered but not halted by obstacles created by World War I and an almost immediate world economic recession. The war cut car-making sharply, and several new branch assembly plants which opened during the past few prosperous years were disposed of. Parent plants devoted

most of their productive effort to war contracts, but more space was needed. It was found only a few miles away, where the Chalmers Motor Company had some to spare because of slumping sales since 1916.

In September of 1917, Maxwell secured a 5-year profit sharing lease of all Chalmers business and assets, and moved its car assembly and some other operations in with the Chalmers activity. Each company retained its separate organization identity while sharing the work, including administrative direction and functions. Disputes arose over procedures and results, inflicting serious injury to mutual accord so necessary to successful teamwork. Financial strength weakened as the weight of Chalmers liabilities increased. Automobile output was low, but even though the factories hummed with war goods production, no profit was realized from the effort. It was hoped and expected that the war's end would bring an immediate consumer business boom and replenish the company coffers, but the hopes were not destined to be fulfilled

Inadequate federal government planning slowed industry's return to full peacetime production, and by the time full capacity was in sight a sharp resurgence of consumer demand was receding with an economic decline. Labor and material costs shot upward and the profit potential was shot down. By early 1920, Maxwell's ledger entries were using more red ink than black. Many new cars long in inventory met with buyer resistance caused by economic uncertainty, but also because of a widespread rumor that the cars were mechanically unsound. The rumor was true — Maxwells had a rear axle weakness due to incorrect design. This formidable accumulation of adversities, and the recession growing into a full-scale depression, was forcing the company into a nosedive toward bankruptcy. To avert the disaster, help was sought by the banking syndicate to whom Maxwell was so deeply indebted. They turned to a man who they felt was capable of accomplishing the miracle. Fortunately for themselves and for him, he was persuaded to accept. That man was Walter P. Chrysler.

Preceding Chrysler's Plymouth by 22 years, the 1907 Plymouth truck was built in Ohio, and was not a forebear of any Chrysler-built vehicle. This huge stake truck was available in 2 or 3-ton payload capacities, and was one of 6 basic models. All were powered by a 4-cylinder, 40-horsepower water-cooled engine with 5 x 5 inches bore and stroke, and all rode on a 144-inch wheelbase. An unusual mechanical feature was a double friction drive system; enclosed within the drumlike case ahead of the rear wheels, it drove each wheel separately by means of sprocket chains. Front and rear tread dimension was adapted to streetcar tracks. Tires were solid rubber, with duals used at the rear. Radiators were made by the Briscoe Manufacturing Co. in Detroit, and engines came from the Western Motor Co. in Logansport, Ind. This was the only line of Plymouth trucks for 1907.

For 1908, a smaller Plymouth truck line was introduced. Featuring the friction drive system used in the bigger jobs, this model carried a 2-ton payload on a 103-inch chassis with 56-inch tread. The engine was a 4-cylinder, 4-cycle, water-cooled type with 4.75 x 5 inches bore and stroke, said to deliver 40 horsepower. Solid rubber tires were used, with 34 x 3½ singles in front and 36 x 2½ duals on the rear. Ready for the road and with no load, this 3,800-pound stake rack model sold for $2,250, including three oil lamps, a horn and tools. Several truck models were listed, plus open sightseeing and enclosed bus types. Not all of them placed the driver above the engine.

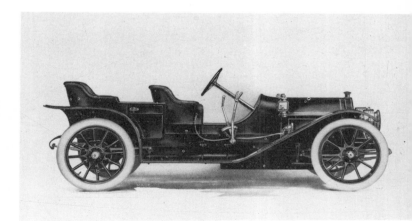

The 1910 Chalmers-Detroit 30 and 40 were announced in August 1909, with new 115 and 122-inch wheelbases, respectively. About February 1910 they dropped the secondary name "Detroit" and continued simply as Chalmers cars. The breadwinner was the 30 series, which offered five body types. This racy-looking 30 was advertised as the Pony Tonneau at $1,600.

Pre - Chrysler Era

11

The Plymouth truck makers publicized this Plymouth 5-passenger touring car for 1910, but it is doubtful that any reached the market. The smaller truck's 4-cylinder engine and double friction drive were used, but the drive mechanism with its twin chains was completely encased in the low-hanging undersides. The body design was advanced for its time, and was called "torpedo" because of the fully enclosed sides with doors in front as well as at the rear. The repugnant dome suggests a turret, but it housed the gasoline tank which fed the engine by gravity. Its location was obviously unsafe, impractical and unattractive. The 112-inch wheelbase car had pneumatic tires and a $2,500 price tag, including windshield, top, and all equipment.

Bearing the name "de Soto," this big and handsome car was in no way related to the Chrysler. Made in Auburn, Ind., it was announced in mid-1913. The 6-cylinder, 55-horsepower car was first said to have a 130-inch wheelbase, but 132 was reported by year-end. Bodies of 2, 4, 5 and 7-passenger capacity were offered. The 5-passenger touring car shown weighed 3,500 pounds and cost $2,185. In size, power and price it was above the Cadillac touring car of its day, and it is likely that the production total was very low. Just catching on in the industry, electric lights were featured, but the engine was started by a pneumatic "cranker." For 1914, the de Soto Six became the Zimmerman Model B-6 by just changing names.

The de Soto Six boasted several unique features. A test chassis shows the fuel tank suspended by brackets hinged to a frame cross-member, and the battery was located for front seat accessibility. The driver's compartment discloses the 3-speed transmission's stick shift, which was more forward than in other cars, and the fuel tank hand-pressure pump just ahead of the seat. One of the two foot pedals projecting from the left actuated both the clutch and service brakes, and the other was for the parking brake. A large stowage pocket was part of the door trim panel.

Maxwell, now a division of the United States Motor Co., gave its cars new and smarter characteristics for 1912. Names were given to each of the four series, rather than letter designations as before. This was the last year for a 2-cylinder model, which would give way to the rising popularity of fours. Shown is the Mascotte, smallest of the 4-cylinder models. The 25-horsepower, 4-passenger Touring Car was on a 104-inch wheelbase and listed at $980 without top and windshield. Color was blue-black with battleship gray wheels. A Roadster completed the Mascotte line.

The newly-designed 1914 Maxwell 25 was announced in April of 1913 but did not reach production until about three months later. It became a popular little car and restored faith in the marque after a mauling in the United States Motor melee. The 4-cylinder engine developed 25-horsepower and the wheelbase was 103 inches. Increasing sales were attracted by the new lower price for this size Maxwell. The popular Touring Car listed at $750, and there was a 2-passenger Roadster at $725. Some Touring Cars had an embossed panel outline between the doors; this one does not. A new type for Maxwell was a 6-passenger Town Car on the stock chassis. Often used as a taxi, it sold for $950.

Looking much like the 1913 de Soto Six, Maxwell's 50-6 for the same year was also very similar in many other respects. As 50-6 indicates, the 50-horsepower engine was a 6-cylinder. This 7-passenger Touring Car was the only body type, and it rested on a 130-inch wheelbase. The $2,350 price included electric lighting. The 50-6 and the 118-inch wheelbase 40-6 were formerly 1913 Flanders sixes, and the old name-change trick was replayed to make them Maxwells about February 1st, when a reformed Maxwell company emerged from the bankrupt USMC. The unexpected addition of these sixes came about when the Flanders Motor Co. was absorbed during the Maxwell reorganizing process in order to get the dynamic Walter Flanders as president for Maxwell. The 4-cylinder Flanders 20 had previously been bought by Studebaker to become its 1913 Model 20.

During 1917, Chalmers was first linked to Maxwell by a lease for sharing properties and operations. Also during that year, Chalmers had two model ranges, both advertised as the 6-30. Shown is the first series, which was a 1916 carryover announced about July 1, 1916. The 45-horsepower, 5-passenger Touring Car was mounted on a 115-inch wheelbase and billed at $1,090. On March 1, 1917 it was succeeded by the slightly refined second series. Chalmers design then remained substantially unchanged until 1920.

The mid-door sedan was on its way out of the 1918 Maxwell 25 lineup when it posed for this photo, looking very much like a Model T Ford. It was known as a convertible type by virtue of removable windows and door posts which made it an early hardtop. An honest 4-door sedan replaced it during this model year. Maxwell had been making only the Model 25 since 1914, and the engine remained basically unchanged, but the considerably re-designed 1918 line lengthened the wheelbase to 109 inches. Prices ranged from $745 for the Roadster and Touring Car to $1,195 for the Sedan. Maxwell would change little during the next three years.

Early Chrysler Era

Walter P. Chrysler began his working life as a teen-age apprentice machinist for a railroad, and progressively made his way through the ranks of labor and supervision, serving three railroads as he went. He next entered the American Locomotive Company in Pittsburgh as superintendent, and his efficient methods earned him a promotion to works manager. While there, his extraordinary capabilities impressed a director of the company, who was also chairman of the finance committee of General Motors. GM needed a new works manager in the Buick Division, which was ripe for a general overhauling of operations. This was a happenstance that was to change the course of Walter Chrysler and direct him to certain destiny as an automotive giant.

After 19 years with the railroads, Mr. Chrysler welcomed the chance to get into automobile manufacturing and, aside from new experiences in another industry, he did not suspect it would bring much change into his life. At this point he had no dreams of his own auto empire, or even a car with his name on it. He had much to learn about the auto industry when he was hired by Buick's president Charles W. Nash, with whom a meeting was arranged by the GM finance chairman, James J. Storrow. He regarded the change as a challenge he must meet, even with a penalty of 50% less income to start. Beginning as works manager in 1911, he advanced to the Buick presidency in 1916, three years after Mr. Nash became GM president. In only five years Mr. Chrysler had demonstrated outstanding ability in automaking and management. Having a reserve capacity for much greater responsibility, he was elevated to a GM vice-presidency in charge of production in all units, which proved to be a stepping stone to the office of executive vice-president. Now he worked closely with W. C. Durant, GM's creator who had lost and regained control of it, and he became increasingly distressed by Durant's methods and billowing corporate expansion program. Tolerance reached its limit, and Mr. Chrysler resigned in 1919. Wealthy by now, he intended to retire and enjoy his family, but eight years of acceleration in the auto world could not be brought to a dead stop.

By 1920 the energetic 45-year-old Chrysler was discontented with little to do, and he welcomed a summons to save the stricken Willys-Overland business from bankruptcy. He would not again approach an inactive state until his last days. The summons to activity came from the bankers to whom W-O was heavily indebted. They expected he would salvage their investment, if indeed anyone could. He demanded and got full authority, then proceeded to examine, assess and rearrange things in the W-O household. While scrutinizing all areas of activity he discovered a new Willys Six under development, to be built in a huge new plant under construction in Elizabeth, New Jersey.

He agreed with John N. Willys that a new model was needed, but felt that this one was not new enough. A better car must be designed, and he put a trio of sharp consultant engineers to work on it. That is how he first met Zeder, Skelton and Breer, who would accompany him to fame later on. W-O people vetoed the car as a Willys because of the advanced design, especially of the engine, so it was named the Chrysler Six. This was actually the first use of the Chrysler name for an automobile. In the fall of 1920 the Chrysler Motor Co. was formed as an entity within W-O, and based in the Elizabeth plant where production was also to be. Three cars were prepared and used primarily for engine testing, but production was repeatedly delayed while methods of rebuilding W-O continued. The ultimate fate of the first Chrysler would come later.

While diagnosing the W-O sickness in 1920, another bunch of bankers beckoned Mr. Chrysler to prescribe a panacea for the Maxwell Motor Co., which was critically ill from a complication of diseases. With Willys' consent, he eagerly accepted the call, while still committed to cure the cramps of W-O. By this acceptance, he unwittingly set the stage for what was to be the first act in his finest performance: Creating and building the Chrysler Corporation.

Offered to a declining market caused by the depression following World War I, the 1920 Maxwell still had 25 horsepower and a 109-inch wheelbase. Changes included new fenders, radiator shell and hood louvers. The claim of 22 miles per gallon of gasoline was attributed to weight-saving design. Weighing 2,130 pounds, the Touring Car listed at $985.

Chalmers got this new design at the first of the year, 1920. It obsoleted the earlier 1920 model which was a carryover from 1919. Specifications did not change much, with six-cylinders delivering 45-horsepower and wheelbases of 117 and 122 inches. The 7-passenger Touring Car shown used the long chassis.

Early Chrysler Era

Mr. Chrysler explored the Maxwell-Chalmers inter-company operations and found such a distasteful mess that he doubted a rehash could ever make it palatable to him. In fact, he questioned the wisdom of associating himself with it for long, but a close friend convinced him that this company was what he needed. He agreed to tackle it but only on his own terms. Maxwell's banker-owners then gave him complete control by naming him chairman of the reorganization and management committee, which included everything. To begin with, operating cash was needed, so he beseeched the balky bankers and got it. Faulty Maxwell cars were recalled and corrected, and financial fusing patched up a broken dealer organization. A plan to reorganize Maxwell and merge Chalmers with it was submitted to stockholders in the fall, and was approved. To carry out the combined plan, a receivership was instituted and the Maxwell Motor Co. went on the auction block in May, 1921. W. C. Durant, John Willys, Cletrac's Rollin White, the Studebakers and some eastern brokers pushed the bidding to where Mr. Chrysler had to bid an unexpected high of almost 11 million to buy it for the account of the reorganization committee. At this time he was not certain that this purchase would ever be important to his automotive plans, which still were coupled with Willys-Overland. The auction was followed in May by formation of the new Maxwell Motor Corp. to facilitate the remedies and merger, but the two companies continued to identify themselves separately.

Meanwhile, the shifting winds at Willys-Overland had brought a change in climate. The specter of receivership loomed, and swathed the W-O Chrysler car plans in a shroud. The engineers and their staff moved out and set themselves up as the Zeder-Skelton-Breer Engineering Corp. in the neighbor city of Newark. Mr. Chrysler was somewhat distressed by the stalling of his car, but his insight into matters pertaining to W-O served him well, as later events would prove, in foretelling that the car would not make it to the market place. He was convinced that the country was waiting for a better car than had yet been offered it, and he was determined that somewhere and somehow he would build it. So he commissioned the Zeder group to design a newer car with a more advanced engine. He would get what he wanted, and would pay for it out of his W-O salary. This was the beginning of what was to become the 1924 Chrysler, the product foundation of the Chrysler Corp. of today, and an ancestor of the Plymouth and DeSoto.

Willys-Overland was placed in receivership late in 1921, and the vacant Elizabeth plant, with rights to the W-O car planned as a Chrysler, would have to be sold. Rights to the Chrysler name would not be included, and the infant Chrysler Motor Co., with no further purpose, would be dissolved. The sprawling New Jersey building and its unborn car were offered at auction on June 9, 1922. Mr. Chrysler, whose W-O stewardship had ended three months earlier, could have bought the 14-million-dollar package for Maxwell at a much lower figure, but didn't. He sent a representative to the auction with authority to bid just over five million, but this was not enough. Among the bidders was the ever-shopping W. C. Durant, who had lost his second hold on GM in 1920, hurriedly launched his new Durant Motors, Inc., and already had the Durant 4-cylinder car near production in Long Island, N.Y. Characteristically, he had extravagant plans to build a giant corporation with products to challenge GM — and worry Ford. He topped bid after bid to buy the Elizabeth package at a bargain for just over 5-and-a-half million. He wanted the plant for production of the low-priced Star car, and the former W-O Chrysler would be the basis for his medium-priced Flint. He wanted the Flint to compete with the Buick Six, and he got Zeder's engineers to beef up the engine to 70 horsepower, 20 more than Buick's. Since he had his eye on the high-priced luxury Locomobile, and would eventually get it as flagship for his fleet, the W-O car was redesigned to resemble it in appearance. Therefore, the Flint was definitely another automobile, and not the W-O Chrysler with a different name. The car was so-named because it would be built in Flint, Mich., a city beloved by Durant since his early days with Buick, which is still built there.

A completely new look was given to Maxwell for 1922, and the 5-passenger Touring Car was the best seller. Many refinements were incorporated in the chassis, which continued the familiar 4-cylinder, 25-horsepower engine and 109-inch wheelbase. The $885 model shown was one of five standard body types. Maxwell policy was never based on the model-year plan, and advertising did not proclaim a specific year for any model. Cars were changed whenever the company felt it necessary. Carryover models did not always have even minor appearance changes to distinguish them from former models. This standard 1922 model continued unaltered the next year, and got only new-design disc wheels two years later.

Looking like a bigger Maxwell, the all-new 1922 Chalmers did not register nearly as much sales appeal as its teammate. Chalmers was fast losing public respect, and this model did nothing to restore it. Like Maxwell, it was new in appearance only. Under the new skin was the same old 45-horsepower six and wheelbases of 117 and 122 inches, though minor changes were incorporated. When introduced, five body types ranged from $1,345 to $2,295. The 5-passenger Touring Car shown was priced at $1,395. The Chalmers continued practically unchanged for another year, when it gave way to the new Chrysler Six.

The severe depression of 1920-21 wiped a large number of car names from the slate and brought worries to most of the survivors. At the low point, Maxwell fixed up its defective cars, began "The Good Maxwell" advertising pitch midway of the 1921 model, and sales began a modest rise. General business was emerging from the slump by fall, when Maxwell brought out the brand-new 1922 model and enjoyed prosperity during its last three years. In contrast, weak sister Chalmers continued to fall back even though it had a new 1922 model that looked like a scaled-up Maxwell. Willys-Overland came out of its receivership as a smaller and sounder company, upon which John Willys proceeded to build another booming empire. The recovery of Maxwell and W-O proved once more that Walter Chrysler, the former machinist, was an expert at putting broken pieces back together for a strong and efficient unit.

An interesting sidelight appeared while the Zeder-Skelton-Breer Engineering Corp. was working under commission to design Mr. Chrysler's newest car. The Zeder Motor Co. was incorporated in Ohio, to manufacture a new car known as the Zeder in a plant of the Cleveland Tractor Co. in Cleveland. The news broke in March, 1922, with a report that Fred M. Zeder of Z-S-B was formulating the organization, and denying rumors that efforts were under way to buy rights to the inert Chrysler Six from W-O, which was then in receivership. (Apparently, legalties would prohibit sale of the rights without the Elizabeth plant, anyway). Reports followed that the car was being designed by Z-S-B in Newark, experimental models would be built in Cleveland, and completion of development was yet several months away. Mr. Zeder said that the car would in no sense be a copy of any previous design, adding that it would be a 6-cylinder to sell for about $2,000. Financing was to come from certain interests in Cleveland and New York (incidentally, Walter P. Chrysler had N.Y. offices at that time). Among the known backers were two prominent names: Studebaker and White. Clement Studebaker, Jr. invested heavily, and Col. George M. Studebaker also got involved. Both Studebakers had left their family's company in South Bend. Rollin H. White was president of the Cleveland Tractor Co., which intended to manufacture the Zeder car. Rollin was one of the White family of auto pioneers who had built cars and trucks for many years, but was better known for the latter. He wanted to make a new car, and after the Zeder car plan failed he fathered the 4-cylinder Rollin made in 1924-25 by the Rollin Motor Co. in Cleveland.

As the Zeder Motor Co. proceeded with organization it acquired another important member of the tractor firm. E. E. Allyne ranked so highly that the new company's name was changed to Allyne-Zeder Motors Co. The whole plan slipped from sight by midsummer 1922. At one time during the planning of the car, the name "White-Zeder" was considered as the product name. Through all of the aborted Cleveland project, the main effort of the Z-S-B group in Newark was concentrated on the Chrysler-inspired program, which also was known as the "Zeder" car. Few original design drawings are known to exist, but they reveal the Zeder name on scuffers (presumably for running boards or door sills), and the letter Z was predominant on radiator medallion design proposals. One of the proposals was handcrafted and affixed to a prototype car.

By 1923, Maxwell's reorganization was shaping up well and the future was brightening. Chalmers was the usual heavy loser, so production stopped and the subsidiary was written off the records early in the year. Walter Chrysler's car went into high gear when the Maxwell board of directors approved purchase of the Zeder-Skelton-Breer Engineering Corp. and its Zeder automobile. Z-S-B moved into the renovated Chalmers plant and took charge of Maxwell engineering, a just reward to the trio Mr. Chrysler fondly called "the Three Musketeers." The Zeder car became a prototype 1924 Chrysler by simply changing the radiator medallion and other parts that had name identity. Having worked closely with Z-S-B in developing his car, Mr. Chrysler had moved it into its proper home and was now in the enterprise with all his heart and soul. He got a shocking jolt, however, when Maxwell's financiers suddenly wanted to sell to the Studebaker Corp. of America, which was anxious to buy. Fortunately, the deal was dropped, and the Chrysler Six appeared in January, 1924.

The Chrysler name was well-known within the auto industry, but not familiar to the general public. In those days, radio was not yet available to most households, and the spoken word required much travel time to be heard by the masses. The printed word was the means of broad communication, and it was found that many readers of Chrysler's earliest advertising mispronounced the name. Shortly, advertising began underlining its banner line, "The Chrysler Six," with this small-print instruction: "Pronounced as though spelled Cry-sler." But regardless of how it was spoken, the name and the car were already acclaimed by the public.

This prototype of the 1924 Chrysler Six exists today and is owned by Chrysler Corp. Often mistaken as the No. 1 production car, it was one of six prototypes built in 1923, programmed as "Experimental B Cars." The group of six included three touring cars, a roadster, brougham and sedan. This prototype and one other touring car were painted black. The other four cars were finished in Ditzler Marine Blue, with black fenders, chassis sheetmetal, and upper structure of closed bodies. Walter Chrysler personally selected colors and all details for these cars, which appeared in Chrysler's premiere showing in New York City's Commodore Hotel and the New York Auto Show. The cars had many advanced features, but a unique small detail was the tiny parking lamp shown between the doors. Headlamps had no provision for this function, so touring cars and roadsters placed them amidships.

Production gained steadily in the former Chalmers plant, and an anxious buyer waited for every Chrysler built. Maxwell sales climbed slowly, but the marque was losing respect to the magnetic name of Chrysler. Soaring profits and a bright future did not ease the insecure feelings of Maxwell's bankers, who still wanted to be free of the company. They became insistent, and Mr. Chrysler took steps to prevent a possibility that the company might be swept into a financial whirlwind. He bought their stock, and the Chrysler Corp. was formed on June 6, 1925 to acquire all Maxwell properties and business. At about this same time, the last automobile to bear the Maxwell name was built.

To replace Maxwell in the 4-cylinder field, the Chrysler Four was introduced about July 1, 1925 as a 1926 model. Companion to the Chrysler Six, it was the ancestral link between Maxwell and Plymouth, getting only minor changes during the connecting process. The Four entered production at Highland Park, where Plymouth and DeSoto

A proud Walter P. Chrysler smiled broadly as he stood beside his prototype Chrysler Six Brougham before it was shown in New York City. The Brougham had a trunk rack at the rear, so the spare tire was moved to a left front fender well. Conventional cowl lamps were used on closed bodies. Mr. Chrysler priced his cars from $1,335 to $1,895, intentionally competitive with Buick. Bumpers were not yet considered essential, and cars were often seen without them. However, they were offered as extra-cost options.

The last Maxwell model built was the 1925 series, of which this example is a standard 5-passenger Touring Car. At $895, it was the most popular model. Maxwell dressed up a bit for its departure. Radiator shells were plated, modified headlamps were ornate, cowl lamps were added, a subtle belt line extended through the body and hood of open cars, and closed bodies were given new touches. Under it all was the long-used 109-inch wheelbase, but the 4-cylinder engine cranked out 38.5 horsepower. Maxwell survived many bumps in its 20-year ride since the 1905 Glidden Tour, but it could not endure the impact of the Chrysler name.

would do likewise three years later. While Chrysler's parade of 1926 models really began with the Four, two new units were added and the entire procession took on a fresh model designation format. Dawning of the calendar year revealed the all-new Imperial 80, and the company proclaimed the Four and Six to be the 58 and 70, respectively. Announced in May was a new light six Model 60, selling between the 58 and 70. Walter P. Chrysler now had models in four market segments, but that was not good enough coverage. His Maxwell-based 58 was larger and correspondingly higher-priced than Ford and Chevrolet, and the 60 was in the next higher bracket. He would work to bring the cost of these two down during the next two years, but would accomplish little. Aware of that probability, in 1926 he ordered design work to begin on two new lines of cars aimed at the lower cost limits. They eventually became known as Plymouth and DeSoto.

For 1927, the Imperial 80 looked down upon a Finer 70, a 60 with a bit lower price tag, and a 50 of slightly less size, power and price than the 58 it replaced. The 1928 line-up was headed by a redesigned Imperial 80, followed by the 72, 62, and the 52 at a few dollars less than its predecessor 50. The 52 was the last 4-cylinder Chrysler sold in the USA. Mr. Chrysler had not succeeded in bringing it into the lowest-price field, but it did cost less than the Dodge fours, which realized one of his goals.

Foreseeing an ever-expanding market and the needs it would generate, Mr. Chrysler had wisely projected the two brand-new car lines to take advantage of it. He also had prepared a new line of commercial cars and trucks for entry in that growing area, but an unforeseeable event would soon alter the hopes for this venture. This ambitious expansion of product lines would apply more pressure to current manufacturing facilities. Also, the corporation's lack of foundries and parts-making shops would restrain efforts to keep production costs low and retail prices competitive. Nevertheless, vehicle development was completed and plant tooling already under way when Fate walked in with welcome news on a spring day in 1928. The prosperous Dodge Brothers corporation, with all the goodies Mr. Chrysler needed, was offered to him by the banker-owners who didn't want to have an automaking business anymore. After two months of dickering and bickering, a stock exchange plan was agreed on and the Dodge purchase became effective on July 31st. Chrysler didn't really need the Dodge cars, but the plants and splendid dealer network were especially desirable, and the truck business proved to be a good acquisition.

The year 1928 was an eventful one for Chrysler Corp. The new 4-cylinder car, descendant of the Maxwell and Chrysler fours, was named "Plymouth" and offered to the public 24 days before the Dodge purchase. The light 6-cylinder car, which had not come by way of a direct descendancy, was christened "DeSoto" and placed on sale only four days after the Dodge deal. The new commercial and truck line, which also had no direct ancestor, became "Fargo" and began deliveries about the time the established Dodge truck business was acquired, which would quickly restrict the purpose of Fargo.

Having amassed the necessary ingredients, Walter P. Chrysler proceeded with characteristic aggressiveness to whip his corporate mix into contention with Ford and General Motors, and cause them to become collectively known as "The Big Three."

Mr. Chrysler seemed about to say, "This is my new 4-cylinder car. Get in and I'll show you how good it is." It was indeed a 1926 Chrysler Four, later known as the 58. Though its appearance was distinctly Chrysler, it was a refined Maxwell underneath. Basic specifications and dimensions of the Maxwell were retained. The Touring Car price was also like Maxwell at first, but coincident with the 58 designation in January the price dropped to $845. Other 58 models were cut as much as $100 to place them below the Dodge range, whose cake Chrysler wanted a piece of.

Announced as a 1926 model, the Chrysler 60 answered the need for a light six in the family. In many respects it was almost a direct ancestor of the coming DeSoto, which was now beginning its initial planning stage. The 60's 109-inch wheelbase would be used by DeSoto, and its 54-horse-power was about equal but the engines differed. Also, the 60 weighed about 200 pounds more and averaged $230 above corresponding figures DeSoto was aimed at. The 60 was clearly a harbinger that lighter sixes would come. The 5-passenger, 2-door sedan, called a Coach, was now becoming important in the preference of closed cars over open types. The $1,195 price of this Coach did not place it in contention with Essex and Pontiac sixes which were of similar size but up to $500 less. The 60 shared many parts with the 58.

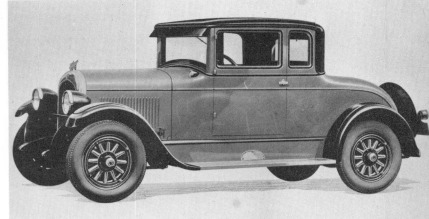

While first lines were being drawn for what would become the Plymouth, its forebear 1927 Chrysler 50 was presented in August 1926. Looking little changed from the former 58, it was actually a slightly smaller car. Cost-cutting slashed three inches from the wheelbase, making it 106. The modified engine had less stroke but still reported 38 horsepower. About January 1927, all closed bodies were given the short and smart "cadet" windshield visor. The late-model 4-door sedan shown listed at $830. The 50 now averaged $130 less than Dodge, but $170 more than Chevrolet and $350 above Ford.

The Chrysler 60 received changes during its 1927 season. Early models were a continuation of those announced in May 1926, but modifications came with the 1927 calendar year. Cadet visors and window reveals were added to closed bodies, and all models got smaller wheels and larger tires in addition to other items. Basic specifications and price range continued as before. The late Coupe is shown.

Continuing nearly all characteristics of the 60, Chrysler gave the 62 modified drum headlamps and omitted cowl lamps to identify it for 1928. Though power and wheelbase were still about equal to the unborn DeSoto, weight and prices remained well above DeSoto's targets. Initial price of the 4-door Sedan was $1,245, but January found it reduced to $1,175. The 62 would be succeeded by the 1929 Chrysler 65, slightly longer and more powerful but of about equal weight and price. It is obvious that Chrysler had not intended the name to be borne by a smaller car.

Chrysler Corporation proudly presented its new Plymouth and DeSoto automobiles in midyear 1928, and regarded them as 1929 models. Continuing the practice of Maxwell and many other automakers, Chrysler corporate policy was flexible in regard to the timing and dating of models. It was not based on the model-per-year plan, but instead permitted new models whenever desired. The general public had not yet come to demand models identified with specific years, and distinctly different annual models were not necessary. Regardless, each new car sold required designation of an identifying year for titling and licensing purposes. This was done by various means, since there was no one authority for guidance.

States used differing methods for affixing a particular year to a car, and the calendar year was generally used as a basis. Two means were most widely employed: Year of manufacture and/or year of titling. Thus, many early Plymouths and DeSotos were titled as 1928 models. However, many states had laws requiring a model year for titling, and they relied on the manufacturer for designation. In line with its policy, Chrysler did not advertise any model as being for a specific year, but it had to meet the needs of states requiring direction. For this purpose, definite model years were assigned and necessary starting points selected.

July 1st of each year was the nominal point at which a car line then in production began registration as the next year's model. In some instances the starting date was shifted slightly, especially when a distinctly new car was introduced. In any case, states, key trade agencies and the sales organization were informed of the date on which the model year advance would be effective. The name and/or code of the model, plus beginning serial and engine numbers, were also specified. The advisory cautioned that the designation was for registration purposes only. Chrysler Corp. thusly defined its models when clarification was needed in the early years. Its definitions are regarded as conclusive, and are the key to model and year relation-

ships in this book.

The Plymouth name was selected because the car typified the endurance, ruggedness and determination of the Pilgrims who settled Plymouth and were among the first American Colonists. The first production Plymouth was built on June 11, 1928 in the Highland Park, Mich. plant where its predecessor 1928 Chrysler 52 had just ended assemblies. Formal announcement followed on July 7th, and the public swarmed into more than 5,000 Chrysler dealerships to see it and the 1929 Chrysler 65 and 75, which also were being shown for the first time. Only Chrysler dealers were authorized to sell Plymouths, and they were quite busy doing it. By the end of 1928, more than 58,000 had been shipped to them, and they wanted larger and more frequent shipments.

Soon after starting up, Plymouth shared Highland Park production with DeSoto, and Fargo followed shortly, but sales success required that a new factory be built quickly. During the winter of 1928-29 a huge plant was erected on Lynch Road in Detroit for the sole purpose of Plymouth production. It was completed in only six months, but manufacturing was under way long before it was finished.

Chrysler had spread its wings wide and fast by forming three new divisions and acquiring a fourth with the Dodge purchase. DeSoto Motor Corp. became a reality in May, 1928, and Fargo Motor Corp. came four months later. Plymouth Motor Corp. existed by midyear 1928, but seldom advertised the fact, contrasting with the other three who often stated their divisional corporate names.

DeSoto was named for the 16th century Spanish explorer Hernando de Soto who discovered our Mississippi River. His name symbolized travel, pioneering and adventure, and his family coat-of-arms was chosen as the automobile's emblem. The new light six was so eagerly anticipated that 500 prospective dealers, without seeing a prototype, took franchise options and went to Detroit at their own expense to get their first look. Over 95% of them signed franchises on the spot, the first of 1,500 dealers by the end of 1928. DeSoto dealers were exclusive, selling no other makes of passenger cars.

The final link between Maxwell and Plymouth was the last 4-cylinder Chrysler, 1928 Model 52. No alterations were made in the principal engine and chassis dimensions of the former 50, but "Red-Head" cylinder heads were now available for adding pep to all Chryslers. The late 60 shared bodies with the 52 and gave them to the new 62. The 52 4-door Sedan was first offered at $795 in August 1927, but in January it was cut to $720. The entire body range now averaged $125 more than Chevrolet. Early in 1928, Chrysler vigorously denied rumors that its 4-cylinder car would be replaced by a new light six. The rumors were not altogether incorrect.

The first Plymouth was officially known as "Chrysler PLYMOUTH," which appeared on the cars and in advertising. Two consecutive series were built this year, first of which was the Model Q. Developed from many of the mechanical components of Chrysler 4-cylinder cars, the 109.75-inch wheelbase reflected back to 1926. Six body types were borne by this chassis, which stretched to a 169-inch overall length with bumpers. Shown is the Model Q Roadster, which at first listed no rumble seat and a price of $670. Within one month it included a rumble seat, weighed 2,210 pounds, and carried a $675 price tag from then on. It was the lightest model and, with rumble seat, was the lowest-priced.

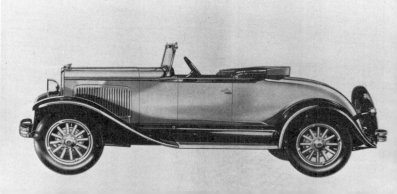

At Bakersfield, Calif., a new Plymouth DeLuxe Coupe stopped for a picture to show the steep maximum grade on Tice Hill. On the same day, two stock Plymouth Touring Cars unfalteringly negotiated the 840 feet to the summit in low gear. 5,000 people saw the climbing test up an average 54% grade rising to 76% near the summit. The rumble seat was a standard feature of the DeLuxe Coupe, which carried 4 passengers. Although looking like a convertible, the top was not a folding type. Weighing 2,345 pounds, this type of Model Q first appeared at $720, but dropped to $695 as a Model U.

This type was fast losing popularity in the salesrooms of all automakers. The comfort of enclosed bodies was now a major preference. The Plymouth Model Q Touring Car carried 5 passengers, and is the only body having a 2-piece windshield. It was a 2,305-pound car, and the $695 price remained unchanged. Smart styling featured a unique slender profile radiator shell and gracefully sweeping "Air wing" fenders. Lockheed hydraulic 4-wheel brakes and artillery-type wood wheels with 29 x 4.75 tires were standard equipment, but bumpers and spare tire were optional. The succeeding Model U Touring Car was unchanged in weight and price.

The DeSoto Six was formally introduced on August 4, 1928, and more than 80,000 were sold within the next 12 months. This was a record for a car in its first year, and it would not be broken for 30 years. Instant success of the smartly-styled car was due in large part to its inherent value. It offered much for a low-priced six, having the cost-cutting advantage of sharing many parts with Plymouth. In fact, these two cars were so closely related, especially from development through the early production years, that they deserved to be chronicled in one book. Their striking similarities in the formative years would prove to be a boon to both. They entered the market in a prosperous year, and 1929 went on to boom proportions that would not burst until late in October. A record 4,794,898 cars and 826,817 trucks were built in the USA during the calendar year.

The Fargo line was named for William G. Fargo, who with Henry Wells formed the famed Wells, Fargo & Co. in 1852 to provide banking facilities and an express route for California gold miners. Another of Mr. Fargo's namesakes was the city of Fargo, N.D., where DeSoto president J. E. Fields came from — probably a factor in the trunk naming. The first Fargo vehicles were delivered to dealers in October, 1928.

They were sold by selected Chrysler-Plymouth and DeSoto dealers, while independent truck dealers were chosen for some areas. When it entered the game, Fargo already had one strike against it: The competitive and well-known Dodge truck line. A second strike was quickly delivered by the devastating depression, which also threw the third strike two years later. Fargo was a good sport, bred of champion stock, but much too young to face such formidable opponents.

This restored example of a Plymouth Model Q 2-door Sedan was shown at a 1965 meet in Highland Park. Two identifying features typical of Model Q cars are visible here. Bumper impact bars had two longitudinal grooves, and one vertical plate was located at the center. Hub caps on artillery wheels had a hexagon shape projected on the outer surface. A third feature not recognizable here was "Chrysler PLYMOUTH" on the radiator medallion. This car does not have the winged radiator filler cap typical of Plymouths this year. The car scaled at 2,485 pounds and first sold at $690. Prices of all four Model Q enclosed cars rose slightly within a month after introduction.

Rear passenger area of the Plymouth 4-door Sedan seated three in conservative style. Trim style of the front seat was like that of the rear. A pull-down roller curtain above the rear window was a feature of both sedan types. It was claimed that softness and richness of the upholstery was unusual in a low-cost car.

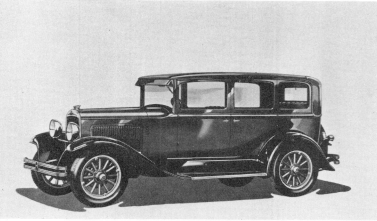

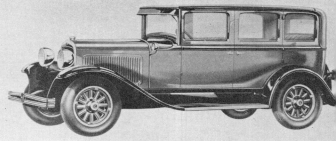

A scaled-down replica of the Chrysler 65, the Plymouth Q was purposely planned to bring uncompromised medium-price styling into the low-price field. This was intended as a selling advantage, as well as for prestige and Chrysler family identity factors. Introduced on the same day and in the same salesrooms alongside the 65, Plymouth's exterior differed only in minor detail (other than obviously smaller size). Bumpers and hub caps had distinctive touches, and Plymouth lacked cowl lamps and a surcingle molding. Probably derived from a photograph of a prototype car, this early illustration shows door handles below the belt, and scrutiny of the original revealed a round or elliptical radiator medallion. Plymouth was advertised as America's lowest-priced full-size car. The 2,510-pound 4-Door Sedan was the heaviest Model Q. Introduced at $725, it was also the highest priced. Q-series of all types totalled a production of 62,444 units. The last Q was built February 4, 1929, bearing motor number Q242482 and serial number RH-977-H.

Comparison of this 1929 Chrysler 65 with the Plymouth clearly illustrates the sameness of pattern. While general styling of the body, fenders, headlamps and radiator shell are also like DeSoto, Plymouth went further. It also used the undivided expanse of hood louvers and straight tie-bar between the headlamps. The 65 weighed 450 pounds more, cost $420 more, and was 4 inches longer than the comparable Plymouth. The larger Chrysler 75 also was introduced and marketed with the 65 and Plymouth.

The Plymouth 2-door Sedan front compartment was austere by today's standards, but was quite acceptable in its day. Front seats used an absolute minimum of trim, but the rear seat was like the 4-door model. Side trim lacked any decor, and arm rests were not yet considered necessary. The simple instrument cluster included speedometer, oil gauge and ammeter elements. Throttle, horn button and light controls were at hand in the steering wheel center. At center on the flat floor was the parking brake lever and stickshift for the 3-speed selective sliding gear transmission.

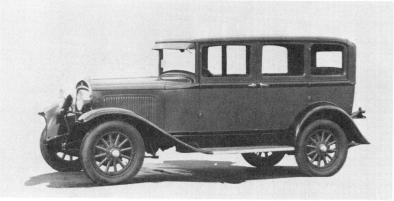

Plymouth went after the taxicab trade with this adaptation of the Model Q 4-door sedan. A vertical divider is visible behind the front seat. Bumpers, a $15 extra for all models, had not yet been fitted to this car. All Model Q cars were powered by the Silver Dome L-head 4-cylinder engine with 3-5/8 bore and 4-1/8 stroke and displacement of 170.3 cubic inches. Called a high-compression powerplant, it was rated at 21.03 horsepower but developed 45.

Succeeding the Model Q was the Model U. This restored Plymouth U Roadster is shown when it visited its birthplace in 1965. The roadster was a sharp-looking car, especially when equipped with optional wire wheels and forward-mounted spares as shown. All models could be ordered with this option, which included a folding trunk rack at the rear. A rumble seat was standard in all roadsters, making it a 4-passenger car. The Model U Roadster, in standard form, equalled the Model Q in weight and price. Vaguely discernible is the I-beam front axle. Teamed with a semi-floating rear axle, it was common to all Plymouths this year.

Known simply as the Plymouth Coupe, this Model U was a 2-passenger business type with stowage compartment in the deck. The interior was normally done in leather, but mohair was available at extra cost. Exterior rear quarter of the cab was steel on this practical coupe. Starting as a Model Q, the Coupe cost $670, but dropped to $655 for the lowest-priced U body. All Q and U cars featured semi-elliptic front and rear springs, and shock-absorbing spring compensators helped smooth the ride. Also, an innovation was the body impulse neutralizer, which was said to prevent engine vibrations from being transmitted to the body.

This Plymouth Model U 2-Door Sedan illustrates distinctions identifying it from its Q counterpart. Bumper impact bars had smooth surfaces, and 2 vertical plates were used. Artillery wheels had slightly larger diameter hub caps of ornamental design which placed the hexagon on the surface facing the wheel. A radiator medallion proclaiming only "Plymouth" is not noticeable here. These points were typical of cars built during the Model U production run, and they were incorporated at intervals during a period of several weeks. Model U was not publicly announced — it just evolved as a refined continuation of the Q. The first car with a U-series engine, number U-999, was completed January 7, 1929, bearing serial number RR-120-P. Though it preceded the final Q car by 28 days, it was actually the beginning of the Model U series. Approximately 68,000 were shipped from U.S. and Canadian plants by mid-1929. Minor technical changes and a 4.75/20 tire size came with the U, but basic Q components and specifications were retained. The 2-Door Sedan was a 5-passenger model weighing 2,485 pounds and listing at $675 beginning in February with full U-series production.

Plymouth was promoted by various means, but this endurance run was perhaps the most convincing demonstration of its capabilities. The Model U broke the world's endurance record by running nonstop for 632 hours and 36 minutes. It ticked off 11,419 miles, and when voluntarily stopped, was operating perfectly. All servicing functions are shown being accomplished while the car was in motion.

The Model U Silver Dome engine was mostly a new design, but in keeping with the fundamentals of the Q powerplant. A heavier crankshaft, new crankcase reinforcement webbing and altered oil pan shape were notable changes. The stroke was increased to 4¼ inches and connecting rods were longer. Horsepower output remained at 45. Many other changes improved efficiency and serviceability.

The famed Plymouth Rock, now cracked and patched, was the stepping stone to religious freedom for the Pilgrims. They landed on it in 1620 and established a settlement now known as Plymouth, Mass. In 1920 it was enshrined in this classic structure erected by the National Society of the Colonial Dames of America. The Pilgrims came to the new continent aboard the little ship "Mayflower," which has served as a symbol for the Plymouth automobile. The Model U 4-Door Sedan accommodated 5 passengers and scaled at 2,510 pounds. From February on it had a new low price of $695. It was the heaviest U-series model, but its price was the same as two other models.

DeSoto was consistently Spanish in the naming of its body types. This was the Roadster Espanol, and with optional wire wheels, fender wells and folding rear trunk rack it was a classy car. A rumble seat was standard in all roadsters. With only standard equipment, this 4-passenger was the lightest model at 2,350 pounds. At $845, it was one of 4 models having the lowest-price figure. A deluxe package option included 6 wire wheels, fender wells, fenders and chassis sheetmetal in body-color lacquer, chromed headlamp tie-bar, finer grade upholstery and other appointments.

Known as Model K. DeSoto shared bodies, fenders, hoods (with different louver pattern), chassis dimensions and many components with Plymouth. Called the Faeton, this 5-passenger model was the only body with a 2-piece windshield. In standard form it listed at $845 and tipped the scales at 2,445 pounds. This example is equipped with an extra-cost option of 5 wire wheels, the spare being mounted at the rear. Parked on the grounds of a Hollywood movie company, a pretty starlet is at the wheel. DeSoto often used movie stars for promotion, as they were so adored by the public.

The DeSoto Cupe Business was a practical 2-passenger car with the rear deck devoted to luggage carrying. It is shown with all standard equipment. As such, it weighed 2,465 pounds and posted a price of $845. All DeSotos had a wheelbase of 109.75 inches and overall length of 169 inches with bumpers. Wood artillery wheels with 5.00 x 19 tires were standard, and a spare tire and rim were carried at the rear. Lockheed hydraulic 4-wheel brakes and semi-elliptic front and rear springs were other characteristics.

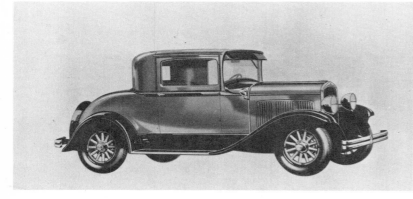

One of the smartest models in the smart DeSoto line was the Cupe de Lujo (translated as Coupe de Luxe). It looked like a convertible, but wasn't. The fixed top was designed and covered to appear foldable, and the landau irons were dummies. The 2-passenger rumble seat brought accommodations up to 4. With standard equipment shown, it weighed 2,525 pounds and asked a list price of $885. Born with an engineering heritage, DeSoto stressed style. The narrow-profile radiator shell was its most innovative styling idea. Light fleetness conveyed by the "Air-wing" fenders is quite evident.

In the springtime, the convertible-like Cupe de Lujo was replaced by this version using the same name. Upper rear quarters were of steel, giving it a businesslike appearance. The rumble seat was continued, as was the price. The optional wire wheels lent a sporting air to this car. The standard fender and chassis sheetmetal finish was black enamel, regardless of body color.

Because of being the same size as the Plymouth, and looking so much like that 4-cylinder car, DeSoto advertising proclaimed its distinction as the "DeSoto Six." The Sedan Coche (Coach) was a 2-door, 5-passenger type of 2,580 pounds weight and $845 price. Though all options were available, this model was most often seen with standard equipment as shown.

Silver Dome engines powering all K-series DeSoto Sixes were, like Plymouth, manufactured by Chrysler Corp. The standard compression ratio was 5.2 to 1, called high-compression in those days. The L-head design had a bore and stroke of 3 x 4-1/8, displacement of 174.9 cubic inches, was rated at 21.6 horsepower but delivered 55. Four main bearings supported the crankshaft, and the engine rested on rubber mountings. A Red-Head higher-performance cylinder head, requiring use of high-test fuel, was an extra-cost option available for any model. The only transmission offered was a 3-speed selective sliding-gear type.

Secondary name for the Model K was "Conquerer," a moniker seldom used. Simply called the Sedan, this 5-passenger, 4-door model weighed 2,645 pounds and was a good buy at $885. All models utilized an I-beam front axle and semi-floating rear axle with 4.7 to 1 gear ratio. Obvious exterior differences from the Plymouth are an arched headlamp tie-bar, triple-grouped hood louvers, cowl lamps integrated with a surcingle molding, and one vertical plate on the front bumper. All of the cars shown are typical for this year, but minor exterior refinements appeared intermittently, beginning in the spring. Collectively, they will become typical of a carryover model. DeSoto, like Plymouth, incorporated changes whenever they were felt necessary.

Top-of-the-line was the DeSoto Model K Sedan de Lujo. It outweighed the Sedan by 10 pounds to claim the heaviest model title, and at $995 it was by far the most costly model in the line. With the entire optional deluxe equipment group shown, it cost even more. To the casual observer on the street, the Sedan de Lujo with standard equipment seemed the same as the lower-cost Sedan, but it had a fancier interior with more appointments.

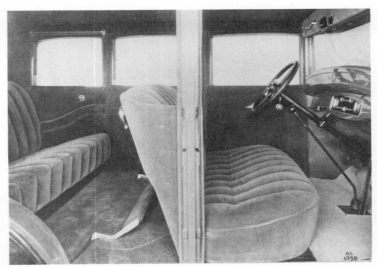

The DeSoto Six Sedan interior was quite acceptable for its price class. The rear seat area had side arm rests, and door trim panels included useful pockets. In the front compartment, speedometer, ammeter, oil gauge and fuel gauge were grouped in the center of the instrument panel. Like Plymouth, the body sat high enough to clear the drive train below and have flat floors.

The new Fargo line of commercial cars were stylish in their own right, coming by it naturally. Collectively, they adapted many parts from Plymouth, DeSoto and the Chrysler 65. The manufacturer said they were built to provide passenger car comfort and performance. Shown is the Packet, smallest of the two lines offered this year. It was based on a 109.75-inch wheelbase and used the chassis frame, transmission, springs and brakes of Plymouth. Power was provided by the Plymouth Model Q 4-cylinder, 45-horsepower engine. DeSoto's rear axle of 4.7 to 1 ratio was borrowed. All Packets were ½-ton payload class. The Panel, in standard form shown, weighed 3,050 pounds. Base price was $795, with bumpers and spare tire extra.

This brand-new Packet Canopy Delivery shows its Plymouth fenders, lamps and bumper, but the thin profile radiator shell and hood were not used. With standard equipment, this model weighed 3,045 pounds and cost $895. A Screen Delivery model used the same body with screened sides, and had Canopy weight and price figures. A chassis with cowl-only cost $545. Some buyers required special bodies not offered by Fargo. Packets included only the driver seat in the base price, a right-side seat costing extra. Some additional options were right-side fender well with spare rim and lock (as shown), wire wheels and special body colors. Standard tires were 6-ply 4.75 x 20 at front and rear.

This model would be popularly regarded as a suburban or station wagon, but Fargo called it the Sedan. The Packet shown, owned by Chrysler Motors, is equipped with optional full seating, providing capacity for up to 9 persons. The Sedan had one door on each side and two at the rear. Passenger entrance and exit was awkward, at best. Packet supplied another version of this body, called the Commercial Sedan. Instead of seats, the rear compartment was a carrying space for supplies, sample cases, etc. For this purpose it could be equipped with display panels for side windows, and shelves or pull-out drawers in the compartment. In basic form the Sedan listed at $895 and weighed 3,050 pounds. A total of 1,063 Packets of all types were built as this year's model.

Dressed up with 6 wire wheels, chromed headlamps and tie-bar, the Fargo Clipper Panel could serve the snobbiest shops. All of these items were supplied at added cost. Clipper's option list was the same as for the Packet. In addition to Packet chassis features, Clippers had Lovejoy hydraulic shock absorbers, rubber shackles and a 100-ampere-hour battery.

News traveled in class when it was carried by the Fargo Clipper. The Panel, as were other Clipper bodies, was interchangeable with the smaller Packet. Clippers had a 3-quarter ton payload capacity, and were based on Chrysler 65 components. Even the 65 engine and 112.75-inch wheelbase were used. The Panel tipped the scales at 3,475 pounds and sold at the factory for $975. Bumpers and spare tire were extra-cost options.

Fresh from the factory, the screened adaptation of the Panel has protective curtains enclosing the cargo area. This Clipper has the optional right-side fender well and tire. The standard wood artillery wheels and optional front bumper were contributed by the Chrysler 65. The 65 tire size of 5.50 x 18 was duplicated, but for Clipper's use they were 6 ply. In standard form this model sold for $1,075. A canopy variation sold at the same price.

1929

The Commercial Sedan promoted the use of window displays as one of its advantages. The cargo-carrying area measured 72.75 inches long, 49 inches wide and 47¼ inches high. All bodies had wood framework reinforced with iron at critical points. Though it adapted passenger car styling to commercial proportions, the Clipper used the Packet design for its radiator shell and hood. The Commercial Sedan listed at $1,075 and weighed 3,475 pounds in basic Clipper form.

Nine solemn persons in this Clipper Sedan seem to indicate it was slightly crowded, but the 4 standees were sober-faced, too. All of them, possibly excepting the driver, must have felt sorry that this desirable vehicle was not theirs. A similar Sedan, without the optional seats, could have carried the luggage for all 13 people. Without people and options, this model weighed 3,475 pounds. It could be purchased, sans extras, for $1,075 at the factory.

Another example of special bodywork on a Fargo chassis is this Clipper with a familiar name on the door. Body craftsmen literally "raised the roof" of the regular panel delivery body, then cut the side openings and inserted windows. This vehicle was built at a time when silent movies were just beginning to give way to the new sound-recorded films.

An illusion is created by this panel body. Extra height and about 10 inches more body length at the rear causes the Clipper wheelbase to appear shorter than its 112.75 inches. The body would carry 5-foot shrubs upright. The Clipper chassis was supplied only with cowl, weighed 2,475 pounds, and was delivered on receipt of $725.

Built on a chassis perhaps 20 inches longer than standard, this Fargo Clipper was an impressive vehicle. The Chrysler 65 engine powering all Clippers was a Silver Dome L-head 6-cylinder with bore of 3-1/8 inches and stroke of 4¼ inches. Cubic inch displacement was 195.6, rated horsepower was 23.43, and developed horsepower was 65. The heavily counterweighed crankshaft was supported by 7 main bearings. It seems safe to say that the long panel body shown was not available for the Packet series. There is evidence that a pickup body was offered on the Packet and Clipper, but no records to confirm it as a fact.

The nation, and in fact the entire world, was sliding into the economic depression as this year began. Most of Chrysler's plans had been laid well before the slide began, and were carried out regardless. The first important move took place in March, as scheduled, when Plymouth Motor Corp. became a full-fledged Division of Chrysler Corp. Also happening in March was a sweeping move that probably was hurried by the economic situation. Plymouth's marketing, previously restricted to dealers handling only Chrysler cars, was extensively broadened by adding Dodge and DeSoto dealers to the sales force. This immediately swelled the Plymouth dealer structure to more than 7,000 outlets, and the total would continue to grow. At the same time, more sales punch was added when Plymouth Model U prices were reduced by $65 to $75. This brought the 4-door Sedan to $100 less than the corresponding Model Q when announced in 1928. Walter P. Chrysler said that the reductions now brought Plymouth into the lowest-priced automobile market.

Plymouth began this model year on July 18, 1929 by advising certain states concerned that current Model U cars should be titled as 1930 models beginning on that date. Other states using their own methods for recording model years on titles simply continued to do so. Typical of policy, advertising did not attach a given year to this carryover model, but it was generally bannered as "The Improved Plymouth." It was not marked by any visible changes in appearance, but a number of minor technical improvements were incorporated. A new DeLuxe 4-Door Sedan was added to the 6 body types already offered. A total of 108,350 Model U cars were built in the U.S. and Canada during the 1929-1930 model run. The last one came off the assembly line on April 5, 1930.

Since DeSoto was almost a carbon copy of Plymouth, and they were begun in the same plant, a similar model-run policy prevailed. But in DeSoto's case the one-year update did not occur until August 15, 1929. Like Plymouth, no public announcement was made because it was not actually a new model. Basically unchanged from last year, the Model K received some minor appearance changes about the time it assumed the 1930 registration status. This model included the 100,000th DeSoto, which was built in the latter half of the 1929 calendar year. The total number of 1930 K's built is not known, but volume production ended in April. The last 50, of unknown body type, were dribbled through the next 8 months, during production of the succeeding model.

Generally regarded as the only 1930 Plymouth model, the new 30-U was announced to the public on May 10, 1930. Proclaimed as the "New Finer Plymouth," it was not quite totally new. The 4-cylinder Silver Dome L-head engine was continued, but with a ¼-inch increase in piston stroke which added 3 more horsepower for a total of 48. Wheelbase of 109.75 inches, and most chassis components remained basically unchanged. Hydraulic shock absorbers were added to the option list. New Safety-Steel bodies were constructed mainly of large stampings welded into a unit. For the first time, radios were available, but in closed bodies only. Fenders looked like those of the previous model, but were actually a bit heavier in design. In fact, most models weighed a little more than the corresponding types they replaced, but prices did not go up. Plymouth prices were still not quite competitive with

Ford and Chevrolet, and sales were slipping, but theirs were too. Model 30-U was on the market only 2½ months when its maker sent out word that the breaking point for advancing the model year designation had come. In its 14-month production run, 75,510 units were built. About 55% were built before the year-switch point.

Again getting most of its parts from Plymouth, DeSoto put together a new 6-cylinder car, the Model CK. Heralded as the "Finer DeSoto Six," it went to market in May. Popularly regarded as the only 1930 DeSoto 6, it was largely a new model. The carryover Silver Dome engine was upgraded to 60 horsepower by increasing the cylinder bore 1/8 inch, adopting a new fuel system with larger carburetor, and rounding the corners of new mani-

Beginning on July 18, 1929, Plymouth regarded the Model U as a 1930 model. Continued without visible change, it included mechanical improvements which dubbed it the "Improved Plymouth." Most important of the changes was a new crankshaft, which increased piston stroke to 4.5 inches. The standard version 4-Door Sedan shown was priced at $695 before it and all other models got a price cut in March. Locality of this scene was Novi, a village northwest of Detroit.

A DeLuxe 4-Door Sedan was added to the Improved Plymouth line in October 1929. On the exterior it was identified by bracketed cowl lamps and a bright cowl surcingle molding, which came with this model. Interior trim was of better quality than the standard version. The only new addition to the Improved series, it weighed 2,590 pounds and cost $745 before the price cut. Bumpers were extra-cost equipment on all Model U cars.

olding. Chassis components were given only minimal efinement, and dimensions of wheelbase and overall length vere unchanged. New bodies were like Plymouth's 30-U xcept for details, and were advertised as having Steelweld onstruction. Fenders and chassis sheetmetal were orrowed from Plymouth. Weight was a bit higher than he Model K, but prices were from $10 to $35 lower. \pproximately 56% of the 8-month 12,200-unit roduction run was built before the registration model-year hange took place.

The trend to straight-eight engines was now gaining nomentum in the industry. Packard was most famous in hat field, but Auburn, Hupmobile, Marmon and Stude-aker were the best-known of about 18 or 20 others. Chrysler had not yet joined the trend, but would do so vith its 1931 models. Only one, the Marmon-built Roosevelt straight-8, had managed to bring the factory rice below $1,000. Even at $995 the Roosevelt was not uccessful, but that did not alter Chrysler Corporation's lan to put a light straight-8 squarely into that price racket. They did it with the brand-new DeSoto Eight, sting at up to $30 less than the Roosevelt. At the same ime, Chrysler introduced the Dodge straight-8, but it vas priced a notch above DeSoto. These were the first -cylinder cars offered by Chrysler Corp.

The new DeSoto Eight was announced to the public in January of this year. Called the "World's Lowest-Priced Eight," it is on the records as Model CF. Its performance in acceleration and hill-climbing was claimed to surpass, often by a wide margin, that of straight-eights costing twice its price. In appearance, the new Eight was un-mistakably DeSoto, but differed from the CK Six in execution of body details. Though built in the Highland Park plant alongside the K and CK Sixes and the small Chryslers, it borrowed few parts from them. Instead, its engine and many chassis parts were shared with the Dodge Eight, which was built in the Dodge factories a short distance away.

The chassis of the CF Eight was of conventional design, with semi-elliptic springs at front and rear, an I-beam front axle and semi-floating rear axle. The wheelbase was 114 inches and overall length with bumpers measured 177 inches. Lockheed 4-wheel hydraulic brakes had 11-inch drums, and tire size was 5.25 x 19.

In 12 months of production, DeSoto turned out 20,075 of the CF eights, 373 of them as stripped chassis. About 88% of the total was built by July 1st. During the 1930 calendar year, the industry produced 2,910,187 passenger cars and 599,991 trucks. In the same period, Plymouth's total was 67,658 and DeSoto tallied 34,889 for 8th and 13th positions, respectively. Fargo Division added the 1-ton Freighter to its Packet and Clipper lines, but steadily lost sales ground.

The New Finer Plymouth was the 30-U, which replaced the Model U. The Sport Roadster, at 2,280 pounds, was the lightweight of the family of 6. Its $610 price tag included the rumble seat, which all of this model had. A roadster without rumble seat was not available. 12-spoke wood artillery wheels with 4.75 x 19 tires were standard on all 30-U cars. A folding windshield was optional on roadsters and phaetons.

Lowest-priced of the Plymouth 30-U line was the Coupe, at $590. It carried 2 passengers, and hauled their luggage or sample cases in the rear deck compartment. This car was ideal for business and professional people. Weighing 2,420 pounds, it was 40 pounds heavier than its Model U counterpart. All Safety-Steel closed bodies featured a military front with new visor, and French-type roof side panels of steel extended from the windshield to the rear quarters.

The 30-U Phaeton was a 5-passenger model, and was the only body type with a 2-piece windshield. This, like the Sport Roadster, was truly an open car, with detachable side enclosures. The 2,340-pound Phaeton sold poorly at $625, which would also buy the comforts of the sedan.

The 30-U Coupe with Rumble Seat replaced the Model U DeLuxe Coupe, but its steel upper quarters lacked the sporty flavor of the fabric-topped earlier model. Like the Sport Roadster and Convertible Coupe, the rumble seat accommodated 2 people, making each model a 4-passenger car. The Rumble Seat Coupe weighed 2,510 pounds and cost $625.

Plymouth's first convertible offering was the 30-U Convertible Coupe. The fully-collapsible fabric top had the sporty look of the former Model U DeLuxe Coupe's non-folding top. At $695, the 2,450-pound car was the highest-priced 30-U model. The rumble seat was standard equipment, but the 6-wheel package was not. Among other options, the 30-U list included bumpers, wire and disc wheels, front fender wells and wheelmounts, folding rear rack with trunk, cowl lamps, cowl molding, and chromed headlamps. Wire wheels were a new design with larger hubs and caps concealing the security nuts.

The 4-Door Sedan was the heaviest 30-U model, weighing 2,595 pounds. The 5-passenger car cost $625 with standard velour upholstery. The Sedan was not offered as a DeLuxe model, but leather upholstery was optional in this and the coupe types. The new wide-side radiator shell of the Plymouth 30-U seemed like a conventional design, especially after the slender profile used before. The oval rear window was characteristic of most 30-U bodies made in the first few months, though a rectangular opening was used in some. The rear window shape was not optional to the buyer. Bodies with rectangular windows were scattered through the production run, becoming much more prevalent in the later months (see 1931). Minor details changed from time to time as parts supply or production facility necessitated or permitted. The 30-U shared much with the DeSoto CK Six and Chrysler CJ Six, and a smaller share with the Dodge DD Six. This may have influenced some of the irregularities.

Plymouth had little interest in commercial vehicles at this time, as this field was well covered by the Dodge and Fargo Divisions. The example shown was not actually a Plymouth, as the chassis was a Dodge, confirmed by radiator and hub-cap name identity. The chassis frame was stepped down behind the transmission, at the forward edge of the door. The driver's seat was suspended over the depressed floor in such a manner that it was removable to allow the driver to stand while driving. The vehicle was probably a prototype built for evaluation purposes, as there is no evidence that Plymouth offered the type even in limited numbers.

DeSoto gave the original Model K a 1930 registration status by August 15, 1929. Seven body types were continued, of which the Cupe de Lujo (DeLuxe Coupe) is shown. Prices remained unchanged, but several minor technical details were reworked. All changes in chassis and appearance did not come at one time, but were spread over a period during which the model-year advance occurred. Some new exterior details were generally related to the 1930 range. Wood wheels had slightly larger hubcaps, and wire wheels featured much larger hubs with caps concealing the wheel attachments. On the hood, dummy unslotted "louvers" replaced 3 functional louvers, one in the middle of the center group and one at the outer end of each flanking group. A new radiator filler cap had a "mini-fin" through the center.

The 100,000th DeSoto came out of the factory late in the summer of 1929, just 14 months after production began in 1928. This was a record-breaking achievement for a brand new make of automobile. The milestone car, a Model K, is shown as its significance brought smiles and a congratulatory handshake from company officials. Leaning against the car is L.G. Peed, DeSoto's general sales manager. Sharing the shake is J.E. Fields, DeSoto's president, who also was Chrysler Corporation's vice-president in charge of sales. Just off the assembly line, the car did not yet have bumpers.

1930

Modified from the 2-door sedan body, this is a rare DeSoto Model K commercial sedan. Side window areas were paneled, and the rear end had an access door. This example was a prototype. Records of production are not available, but some must have been built. One was seen in the Pacific Northwest in 1956.

The Finer DeSoto Six, Model CK, replaced the K. Though it was a new model, styling did not differ much from the previous car. The narrow-profile radiator shell was replaced by the new wide-side design, and cowl lamps were moved to the front fenders. Bumpers and wire wheels continued as options, and chromed lamps were now optional. The smart-looking Roadster was supplied only as a rumble seat model, which made it a 2 or 4-passenger car. Weighing 2,385 pounds, it was the lightest CK, and at $810 it was the least expensive. 1,086 CK Roadsters were built.

Shown in absolutely standard form, the DeSoto Six Phaeton was offered at $830. The 5-passenger 2,475-pound car was alone in the use of a 2-piece windshield. Seen here in a painted finish, chrome-plated windshield frames were optional for the Phaeton and Roadster. Lack of popularity held CK Phaeton production to 209 units.

The Business Coupe was known as a personal car because it accommodated only 2 persons. There was generous storage space under the rear deck. Shown in strict business-like standard form, it could be ordered with dressy options. A rumble seat option was not offered for this model. In the form shown, this model cost $830 and weighed 2,515 pounds. DeSoto turned out 858 of them. Common to all CK closed bodies was the new military front with its snug visor artistically embossed at the center.

The first convertible type on a DeSoto Six chassis was this Model CK Convertible Coupe. It was the most expensive CK body type, priced at $945, and its 184-unit production figure was the lowest of all CK models. A rumble seat was standard, and the car scaled at 2,540 pounds. Fender wells, wire wheels and folding rear trunk rack were optional. The black-painted headlamp and parking lamp shells were standard items for all CK Sixes.

The DeLuxe Coupe in the Finer DeSoto Six line was an attractive car. Its rumble seat expanded the passenger capacity to four. Anyone with $860 could buy the 2,585-pound car, and 1,521 buyers had that much to spend. All CK interiors had a new instrument panel with single-button choke control, and a new 3-spoke steering wheel. All closed bodies now had adjustable front seats.

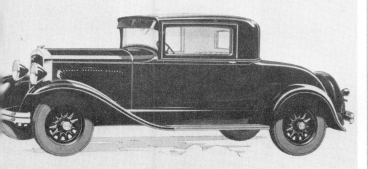

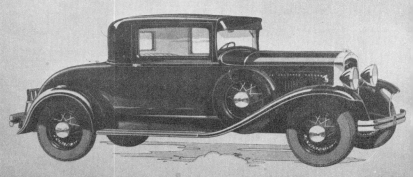

With optional fender wells and 6 wire wheels, the Finer DeSoto Six 4-Door Sedan took on an expensive look. Without the extras, it was in the lower-middle price class at $875. It weighed more than any other standard CK, pressing the scales to 2,705 pounds. This 5-passenger car was the most popular CK model, as 8,248 buyers made it so. A DeLuxe 4-door version was not offered; neither was a 2-door sedan in any form. Steelweld closed bodies featured the new French-type roof with steel on the curved section above the drip rail. All bodies had a rectangular rear window. DeSoto CK chassis were used for other than the factory bodies, as evidenced by the fact that 94 units were assembled.

DeSoto's first 8-cylinder car ushered in this New Year with all the exuberance of Youth. In the 8-cylinder thrust toward the lower-medium price field, it brought the smoothness of the 8 to many buyers who could not get it before. The Roadster was a sleek-looking car, especially with the top folded and the stock folding windshield flattened. With the rumble seat in use, it carried 4 passengers. With standard equipment, this model was priced at $985, and it was the lightest-weight DeSoto Eight at 2,720 pounds. Standard trim for Roadsters and Phaetons included painted windshield frames and lamp shells. Bumpers, wire wheels and fender wells were extra-cost items available for all models. Roadster production totalled 1,457 units.

The DeSoto Eight Phaeton was a 5-passenger open model with detachable side enclosures. More options shown here are chromed lamps and windshield frame, and a folding rack with trunk. All Phaetons had folding windshields. In standard form, this model cost $1,035 and scaled at 2,800 pounds. The least popular Eight, only 179 were built.

The Phaeton with top raised was still a sharp-looking DeSoto Eight. This one was built for export, probably to a country with consistently warm climate. At this time, most Phaetons were shipped to such places. Note the steering wheel and tail lamp on the right-hand side. This car had no cowl lamps, but the wire wheel equipment and folding trunk rack are the same as those available for domestic models.

The Business Coupe was DeSoto Eight's answer to those who wanted only a 2-passenger car. In the standard form shown, it weighed 2,835 pounds and cost $965, which made this model the lowest-priced 8-cylinder car in the world at that time. 1,015 of this model came off the assembly lines. The first DeSoto Eight was known as Model CF. It did not share much with the DeSoto Six CK and Plymouth 30-U.

1930

Factory-fresh and ready for one of the 524 persons who bought this type, this DeSoto Eight Convertible Coupe poses with its rumble seat open. The 4-passenger body was completely convertible. The 2,845-pound car is equipped with 12-spoke wood artillery wheels with 5.25 x 19 tires, standard items for all Eights. Priced at $1,075, it was the most expensive CF model.

The CF Eight DeLuxe Coupe was normally known as a 4-passenger car, carrying 2 inside and 2 in the rumble seat. This car has 3 persons inside. Without any extra equipment, this model was priced at $1,025 and swung the scale pointer to 2,875 pounds. Production sheets tallied up 2,735 units. CF bodies were called "Mono-piece," and were said to be all-steel construction. Typical closed body features were a slightly sloped windshield with snug visor.

This demonstrates how steeply the DeSoto Eight would tip without tipping over. The body is the Sedan, a 4-door, 5-passenger type with standard trim and equippage except for the bumpers. While all Eights had bumpers, they were extra-cost items, as were spare tires. The standard-type Sedan was listed as weighing 2,965 pounds and costing $995. 9,653 orders for this car were filled. All CF closed cars featured adjustable front seats. This view effectively shows the new French-type roof, which was a step toward the one-piece steel roofs DeSoto and Plymouth would get in another 7 years. The roofside contours of steel were definitely superior to the former method of bringing the top fabric down to the drip rails.

The DeSoto Eight DeLuxe Sedan used the same 4-door, 5-passenger shell as the standard sedan version, but it had richer upholstery and added luxury appointments. With the optional equipment shown, it looked more costly than it was. Without options it had an asking price of $1,065. It was the heaviest of the Eights, weighing 2,975 pounds. 4,139 were built, making it second to the standard Sedan in popularity. The new Eight looked typically DeSoto, though its hood louvers, body belt and window treatment were of different styling.

The Silver Dome engine of the DeSoto Eight was relatively clean in appearance. Having 8 cylinders in a row, the L-head powerplant's length limitation dictated an exceptionally small cylinder bore of 2-7/8 inches. Piston stroke was 4 inches, and displacement was 207.7 cubic inches. A 5-bearing crankshaft with torsional impulse neutralizer gave smooth performance to the engine, which rested on 4 points with rubber in the rear pair. 70 horsepower was delivered at 3,400 RPM. That is low horsepower by today's standards, but not bad for such an engine of its time. This was known as a high compression engine. Routing power toward the rear was a clutch of single dry-plate type and a transmission of 3-speed selective sliding gear design. The entire power package was of conventional concept.

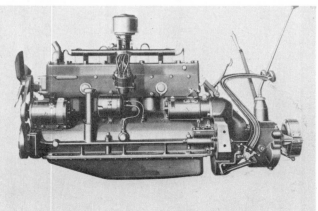

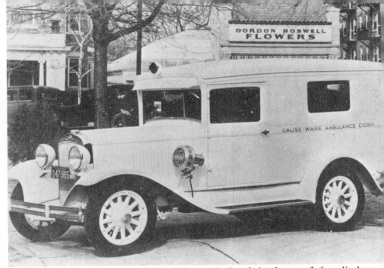

Visible differences between Fargo Packets and Clippers were not easy to distinguish. They were of equal wheelbase and had a general look-alike appearance, though Clippers were 3-quarter tonners. Clipper wheels, with 5.50 x 18 tires, were one inch smaller than CK-powered Packets. Means of model-year identity were clouded by the inter-mixing of parts. Fargo production was very low and the future of the product line was in grave doubt, a combination which contributed to the conditions just previously mentioned. The Clipper shown with convertible driver's compartment was an exceptionally dressed-up version. Note the chrome-plated disc wheels.

1930

The Fargo Packet dropped the 4 in favor of 6 cylinders this year. The DeSoto K 57-horsepower engine was used from August 1929 to May 1930, when DeSoto's CK engine of 60 horsepower replaced it. Wheelbase of 109.75 inches was unchanged, and the model continued as a half-ton carrier. Early sixes had a 4.75 x 20 tire size, and later models used 5.00 x 19. The ambulance shown was converted from a Panel body. The chassis was priced at $595, Panel at $845, and Canopy or Screen Delivery at $945. Commercial Sedan and Pickup types were also offered. Fargo production records are generally not adaptable to model-year breakdowns. However, they do record that 2,059 K-engined and 110 CK-engined Packets were built up to November 1930.

The smaller Fargo Clipper had a 109.75-inch wheelbase, which was 3 inches shorter than last year. The 6-cylinder engine now delivered 62 horsepower, 3 less than before. This engine compared in size and output with the 1930 Chrysler CJ passenger car, from which it was probably borrowed. Shown is the Panel, which weighed 3,195 pounds and cost $975. A bare chassis weighed 2,340 pounds and cost $725. With Canopy or Screen Delivery bodies, the Clipper weighed 3,230 pounds and was priced at $1,075. Other available types were a Commercial Sedan and Pickup. Clipper production ended in March, 1930. Total production of all Clipper types built since August 1928 was 1,424.

This view is of the Fargo Freighter with wood type "T" gravity dumper. It looks much like the Freighter with hydraulic hoist and C-4 body that is also illustrated. Both were fitted with the squarish commercial-design cab. The natural finish artillery wheels, similar in appearance to those used on passenger cars, seem far out of character for a hard-working truck. Pressed steel wheels were not yet common to trucks of one ton or less capacity. Front brake drums were 1-¾ inches wide and of 14-inch diameter. Rear drums were of 2-inch width and 15-inch diameter. The semi-floating rear axle was housed in a steel casting, and had a gear ratio of 5.67 to 1. The frame had a "kick-up" over the rear axle. Those features apply to Freighters in general.

The cab on this Fargo Freighter chassis is of the "passenger car styling" design, but with a high roof. The top of the door opening was at the roof drip rail. Since a standard-size window glass was employed, the height of the door necessitated a few inches of sheetmetal across the top of the door panel. Note that dual rear windows were featured, and the "swelled" side belt treatment was not continued across the rear of the cab, since later installation of a utility body would partly or completely obscure design characteristics. Many Fargo Freighters left the factory in this form. They were shipped to commercial body-building companies, where various types of bodies were mounted. Then they went to Fargo dealers for delivery to buyers.

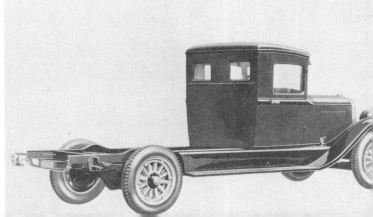

Making its first appearance in June 1929, the new Fargo Freighter was classified as a one-tonner. It was powered by the same engines as used in this year's Packets, with the DeSoto K plant being replaced by the CK late in March 1930. The wheelbase of all models was an adequate 133 inches. The Screen Delivery weighed 3,660 pounds and was factory-priced at $1,055.

The Fargo Freighter Panel Delivery was of the same dimensions and basic structure as the screened version. Weighing 3,820 pounds, this model was priced at $1,145. Though sharing general styling characteristics with the Packet and Clipper, the Freighter necessarily required adjustment of them to its larger proportions. Fender design and contour was not shared with the other two series.

A wide variety of bodies were offered for the Freighter. This panel job differs completely in design. The cowl molding does not take a sweeping upward curve in front of the windshield, and the cowl unit is butted against the "A" pillar. Two parallel belt moldings are narrow and widely separated. A window behind the door, flat body side panels and square corners are other characteristics.

Not listed among the Freighter body offerings, this body seems to be similar to Commercial Sedans of the Packet and Clipper series. Side doors service only the front compartment, and rear-end doors provide commercial access. The body probably had removable passenger seats, making it useful as a bus or delivery car. This is a photo of an actual vehicle, and it is reasonable to assume that some of these were built.

The Freighter Express is shown with additional sideboards and endboard attached, providing greater hauling capacity. The cab of this and some other models was quite squared, with flat panels and narrow belt moldings spaced well apart. The 3,590-pound Express was called a Weatherproof model, and was priced at $1,010. A similar model listed as a Grain Truck weighed 3,715 pounds and cost $1,045.

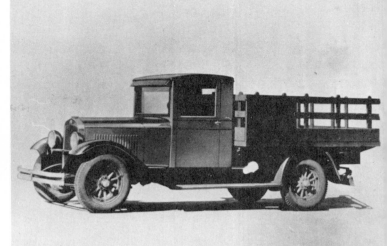

This is the Fargo Freighter with wood type hydraulic hoist and C-4 body. Weight and price of this model are not available. Also offered was another model much like this, but with G-1 hoist and J-1 body. All Freighters used a new design 4-speed transmission with standard S.A.E. shift pattern having a latch out for reverse backward and to the right of high gear position.

Known as the Weatherproof Stake, this Freighter also has the squarish cab. All Freighters were as commercially useful and serviceable as they looked, but they could not meet the competition and survive the depression years. Dodge and other established truck makes were just too much to cope with, especially in difficult times. The Stake tipped the scales at 3,790 pounds and carried a $1,045 price tag.

The Freighter shown in this factory photo has the cab which featured what Fargo called "passenger car styling." Note the cowl side molding which branches into an arching sweep across the cowl top, and exhibits its main strength in the wide "swelled" horizontal treatment through the cab side. The crowned roof begins with a "chopped" military front and visor of conforming line. Cab side panels are curved, mating smoothly with the cowl sides. Some chassis were sold with this cab and no cargo body. This platform is equipped with high stakes, and no rear fenders were used. A Freighter chassis with cowl (no cab) was priced at $795 and weighed 2,725 pounds.

Farmers could haul a lot of hay, sacked grain, or produce in this Freighter. Listed as the Farm Truck, it pressed the scales to 3,815 pounds and was price-tagged at $1,045. It was photographed on the factory grounds in Highland Park, Mich., a city within the city of Detroit. The large building in the background was the center of operations for Chrysler Corporation's extensive research and engineering activities.

A special kind of Freighter was this panel job. A drastic revision of basic dimensions and proportions creates a much different vehicle package. Compared with the regular Freighter panel body, the roof was several inches higher, while the dimension from windshield to rear end was shorter by a similar amount. Doors were wider and, like the body side panels, extended downward to the higher-than-normal running boards. The wheelbase was perhaps 6 inches shorter, and the radiator sat well forward of the front axle. Headlamps were removed to the cowl, fenders were not stock Freighter, and wheels were pressed steel. This may have been an experimental vehicle, or one of a small lot built for market testing.

Fargo Freighters were adaptable to heavier hauling tasks than they were normally known to handle. This one is carrying four new 1930 Pontiacs to their dealership destination. One of the earliest types of motor transport for shipping new cars, this was an unusual scene in the days when most new ones were driven from factory to market. This truck has wood artillery wheels in front and duals at the rear.

A special body on the standard Freighter chassis, this creation used flashy trim details to give it class. The roof had fabric covering and chrome-plated landau quarter irons. Chromed tubular side rails extended to the step below the gateless rear end. Standard Freighter wheels were wood artillery type with spokes in natural finish. Tire sizes were 5.50/20 in front and 32 x 6 at the rear, both interchangeable on common 20-inch rims.

Gulf Refining Company's products were toted by this hard-working Freighter. Heavy pressed steel wheels were more adequate for the job. There are no known records to indicate how many Freighters were built for extra heavy hauling, or for what specific purposes they were built. Available records place the Freighter only in the one-ton class, but it is certain that modifications were necessary for the heavyweight haulers.

The Freighter did its bit for the railroads, too. The diminutive "Tom Thumb," one of the first American-built steam locomotives, was carried as a platform display. The ancient steamer's actual service on the rails lasted about as long as Fargo's short production run. In its heyday, the little locomotive raced a horse from Baltimore to Ellicott Mills and returned. The horse's performance is not known, but the engine completed the trip of perhaps 25 miles under its own power. The time required for the race eludes research, but this particular Freighter with its DeSoto K engine could easily have carried the Tom Thumb over the equivalent 1929 motor route in one-quarter of the time.

Responding to fire alarms was another of Fargo's many capabilities. Boyer Fire Apparatus Co., Logansport, Ind., outfitted this one for dedication to its purpose. Many observers must have been awed at sight of this able-looking fire-fighting Freighter. Wheels and rims got special treatment to complement the typical fire engine decorative theme. All of the varied functions for which Fargo trucks were built will never be known.

The depression economy continued its unalterable downward drift, bringing production and sales of all kinds of products down with it. Of all industries, the automobile manufacturers and their supplier companies were among the hardest hit. Competition was exceptionally keen as each maker's sales forces summoned all resourcefulness and persuasive ability to convince the public that the best buying opportunities in decades were now at hand. Products now offered much more usefulness and durability, and retail prices were plummeting. Better values had never before been available. But the general scarcity of financial resources, which was the one factor that generated these values, was also the factor that prohibited taking advantage of them. The fact was that the average man had little money to spend after providing his daily essentials, and ever-increasing numbers were becoming destitute for the simplest means of living.

The chaos wrought by the overwhelming depressive forces did not cause a realignment of sights on one of the big guns of the auto industry: Chrysler Corporation. Walter P. Chrysler had always been an exceedingly optimistic man, and he now gave the impression that a world financial disorder did not exist. Characteristically, he pressed research and engineering facilities for new ideas, and would this year introduce a sensational new feature for controlling engine vibration in cars to be designated as next year's models. He also pulled the throttle wide open on development and planning programs for the first 6-cylinder Plymouth, a 1933 model. Another idea that captured some interest this year was the streamlined body concept Carl Breer had been experimenting with on a small scale. Mr. Chrysler gave encouragement to Breer, and the work began to assume the proportions of a program to develop the concept for the DeSoto Division. Eventually, the unique design so fascinated Walter Chrylser that he ordered it also for the Chrysler 8-cylinder models. They all culminated as the 1934 Airflow cars. All of these actions were typical of the dynamic man whose vision was toward the future, and whose courage and optimism sustained him well in times of distress.

Though Mr. Chrysler did not harbor thoughts of depression, his corporation was very busy at coping with conditions. Chrysler, Dodge and DeSoto Divisions all were given newly-tooled models for 1931, but Plymouth did not fare alike. Tooling costs for the new designs were enormous, and tight money conditions dictated that they carefully be disbursed at selected intervals. Chrysler Eights went to market in midsummer last year, only two months after the 1930 Plymouth 30-U and DeSoto CK. Chrysler's new Six and the new-style Dodge and DeSoto lines came at the first of this calendar year. The next new model was the Plymouth PA, which had to wait until the middle of this year, causing it to miss designation as this year's car. This set of circumstances left the 30-U in position as the only company-designated 1931 Plymouth, though the designation was acknowledged as for registration purposes only.

The 30-U had been on the market only 7 weeks when it quietly assumed 1931 status on July 1, 1930. Less than a month afterward, a 2-Door Sedan was added to the line, and was followed a month later by the Roadster without rumble seat. Plymouths were now sold by more than 10,000 Chrysler, Dodge and DeSoto dealers. Advertising claimed that they had "Chrysler Performance, Dodge Dependability, DeSoto Smartness." No important technical changes took place, and the only change in prices was a $25 cut for the 2-passenger Coupe. Minor appearance changes occurred at various times, chief of which was the intermittent shuffling of rear window shapes. On June 8th this year the last 30-U was built, the 75,510th unit turned out during the long 14-month production run of this model. Because of a poor market, 30-U sales failed to match the success of Plymouth's earlier models. Though an overall decline was registered up to mid-year, the succeeding Model PA lifted Plymouth to third place in the industry by the end of this calendar year, taking the position away from Buick. The rise to third spot was partly due to a drastic reduction in Ford demand, which now rated second to the top spot Chevrolet. Total industry production fell by about one million units this year.

The Plymouth Model 30-U Roadster was a 2-passenger car primarily intended for commercial use, having only stowage space under the deck lid. Its $535 price was the lowest figure the company had ever asked for a car. The 2,245-pound car was the lightest of the 8 models available this year, and its 169-unit production total made it the least popular. Hydraulic shock absorbers were an extra-cost option for all models of early 30-U cars, but became standard equipment at no extra cost in August, 1930, about the time this Roadster was added to the line.

The Sport Roadster was supplied only with rumble seat, classifying it a 2 or 4-passenger car. In the standard form it weighed 2,280 pounds and cost $610. 2,884 of these were turned out during the entire 30-U production run. A folding windshield with chrome-plated stanchions was available at extra cost. A number of minor technical changes were made in the 30-U series at about the time it became the 1931 Plymouth. Among them was introduction of a water pump and reduction of water capacity from 3½ to 2 gallons.

DeSoto's Six and Eight, CK and CF respectively, got 1931 status on July 1, 1930. No discernible changes took place as they continued in production to the end of last year. Neither of them was an outstanding sales success. The CK Six did not live up to the selling reputation of its predecessor Model K, which had the advantage of more prosperous times. The Eight, doing full-year battle with Hudson's 8 and a latter-half clash with Buick's small 8, failed to make headway against them.

With the dawning of this year two new DeSoto series were announced, a Six and an Eight. As was typical of Chrysler Corp. no-annual-model policy, they were not factory-advertised as 1931 models. Today, however, they are generally regarded as the only 1931 DeSotos. The Model SA Six, though new in design, strongly resembled former DeSoto Sixes. With a longer hood and slightly less overall height, they looked like longer cars. The radiator sat well ahead of the front axle, adding the extra hood length.

The 6-cylinder engine was given an improved vibration damper, longer pistons with 4 rings, and a 1/8-inch larger cylinder bore. Displacement was increased 8% to 205.3 cubic inches, and horsepower went up to 67. A new counter-weighted crankshaft later replaced the original, and a 5th engine mount was added in May. The 3-speed transmission was continued, but the rear axle ratio changed to 4.3. The new chassis frame was of double-drop design, and the wheelbase measured 109 inches. Enclosed bodies were of Steelweld structure, and they shared much with this year's new Chrysler Six, Model CM. Plymouth did not use these bodies until its new Model PA came in mid-year. DeSoto SA production was moved to the new plant Plymouth had occupied since early 1929. Previously, all DeSotos were assembled in the Highland Park plant where earliest Plymouths were born. The SA Six was in production about 12 months, totalling 28,356 units. About 5% of them were built before the series got the usual mid-year designation change. All SA models were lower-priced than those of the previous CK Six, with reductions ranging from $15 for the Roadster to $120 for the Convertible Coupe.

The new DeSoto Eight did not have as many new parts as the new Six. Designated the Model CF*, it continued the bodies, fenders and basic chassis of the previous Model CF. New radiator trim, hood, and frontal tie-bar were

styling changes. Enclosed bodies, now called Unisteel, rode on the 114-inch wheelbase chassis, which now included minor improvements. Most technical change was in the straight-8 engine in which the piston stroke was increased ¼ inch, displacement went up to 220.7, and developed horsepower rose to 77. A heavier crankshaft was adopted, the engine ran 6% slower, and a new 4.6 rear axle ratio was used. The clutch hub was given a new rubber composition center, but the transmission remained as before.

A total of 4,224 of the new Eights were built in its production span of approximately 12 months. About half of the total had been turned out when the company advanced the model year. Volume shipments continued through November, then dropped to more modest numbers monthly through May 1932. The price range of former models was generally held by the new series. In May of this year a host of deluxe features were added to the CF* body line, but the chassis, bodies and sheetmetal were like the earliest models. The difference was in fancier exterior trim and superior quality interiors with more luxurious appointments. Prices of all models remained unchanged.

Fargo's last fling at general marketing on the domestic scene was made with last year's Packet and Freighter models, which became one year newer on July 1, 1930. They did not stick around long after that. Packet specifications, body types and prices were unchanged, and production was finished by November 1930. The Freighter was also unchanged in all respects, and it was terminated one month earlier than the Packet. Total Freighter production since its inception in June 1929 is unknown, but 855 of the DeSoto CK-powered vehicles were assembled from March 1930 to the end. Fargo was not finished in 1930, however, as the Fargo Division eventually took on new responsibilities in certain fleet sales and export operations.

The Plymouth 30-U Coupe carried 2 passengers in its snug interior and had room for their luggage in the deck compartment. $565 was asked for the 2,420-pound car. In the overall 30-U manufacturing program, 9,189 of this model were assembled. The restored Coupe shown is owned by Michael Chila of Girard, Ohio. Its horn position and rear window shape are typical of the 1931 range. The 30-U series began its 1931 status on July 1, 1930 with a car bearing serial number 1530245. Many and varied minor changes were given to the 30-U at different times during its production span. A few of these made their appearance in an erratic and seemingly unscheduled manner.

Now called the Sport Phaeton, this was the former Phaeton with a classier name. There was no lower-cost version of this open type. In standard form as shown, it cost $625 and gave a weight reading of 2,340 pounds. It was again the only body with a 2-piece windshield glass. Total 30-U production of this 5-passenger touring-type body was 632. Note the position of the round horn at center front. Its top is barely higher than the bottoms of the headlamps. This position was used for early 30-U cars, but gradually phased out during '31-status production. An improvement Plymouth added to all 30-U models by mid-July was a fuel pump, which replaced the former vacuum tank.

The Coupe with Rumble Seat was continued in its previous
form. The 2 or 4-passenger car weighed 2,510 pounds and
was priced at $625. Access to the rumble seats of all models
having them was by means of steps at the lower rear body
sill and on top of the rear fender on the curb side. Entry and
exit was awkward, and was not appreciated by many women.
On total 30-U production records, 5,850 of this model were
recorded.

The lady in the rumble seat of this Convertible Coupe leans
over for a look at the lilies available for Easter this year.
This was the highest-priced passenger car offered by
Plymouth in the 1931 model series, being factory-tagged at
$695. The 2 or 4-passenger car pressed the weight scale to
2,450 pounds. In all 30-U production, 1,272 convertibles
were registered. Leather interior trim was an extra-cost
option for convertibles. The car shown has one of the 30-U
hood variations. All louvers on this hood were the functional
slotted ventilating kind, having 15 in the forward group
separated from the group of 14 by the flat surface of the
hood side panel. A different version added 3 "dummy"
unslotted louvers, placing one in the division area and one at
the end of each of the groups. The latter version was inter-
mixed with the other in the 1931 range. A set of 5 wire
wheels became optional at no extra cost at the beginning of
this calendar year. 6 wire wheels, front fender wells and a
folding trunk rack were also available for any 30-U, but for
an extra sum. Wire and wood wheels now had hub caps
with the Plymouth name on them, and they all had 4.75 x 19
tires.

New to the 30-U series, the 2-Door Sedan came soon after
the start of the model year. In the standard form it
weighed 2,497 pounds and listed at $565. 7,980 of these
sensible-looking cars left the factory. Leather upholstery
was available for this model, accompanied by an extra
charge. This body type was also modified and sold as a
Commercial Sedan. As such, the rear side window areas
were panelled, rear seat omitted, and a door was installed
in the rear end. Upon arrival it was priced at $750, but soon
was reduced to $675. The price cut did not help sales,
as only 80 were built.

The most popular 30-U model was the 4-Door Sedan, which
chalked up a total of 47,152 built during the entire production run. It weighed 2,595 pounds and bore a price of
$625 when standard-equipped. The fender well with tire
and rim were optional extra-cost items. This car probably
had the same equipment on the opposite side. Single
forward spare mounts were on the right-hand side only.
A DeLuxe version of the 4-door body was not available.

Wearing a new 1931 license plate is this just-as-new 30-U. The horn almost sits on top of the headlamp tie-bar, placing its top about on a level with the headlamp centers. This position was most common with the 1931-designated models, though advertising art often did not reflect the change. Compare this photo of an actual car with the artwork of the Sport Phaeton. Plymouth was not very fussy about artwork for the 30-U.

The Convertible Coupe is loaded with some of the options Plymouth had for the 30-U. Chrome plating embellished the headlamp shells and the tie-bar they sat on. Cowl lamps were mounted on the sheetmetal near the cowl surcingle molding bordering the hood cut. Six wheels and sidemount spares completed the equipment ensemble. Body and fenders in matching color was available on special order. Standard paints included a different color for each body type, and these were changed on most types from time to time. The 2-Door Sedan is shown with pure standard finish which included color only on the hood and lower body, with black on all other parts. A milestone in options came with the announcement that closed bodies with factory wiring for radio were available on special order. Philco Transitone radios could then be immediately installed elsewhere.

Though an oval rear window was used in many bodies throughout the production run, this rectangular shape was given its most extensive use during the 1931 portion of 30-U manufacture. The rectangle used in open and convertible bodies was of different proportions and smaller size. Artwork often did not show the rectangle, either. The spare wheel without a tire was common to brand-new cars, since spare tires cost extra.

Plymouth was giving serious attention to the taxicab market, a move that was destined to reach major proportions in the future. This fleet of about 150 cabs was built for the Red Top Cab Co. of San Francisco, Calif., who paid for them with one check written for $120,000. Delivery was made about March 1st this year. Bodies were stock 4-door sedans with special paint jobs and interior details.

The DeSoto Six, Model CK, was continued with a 1931 designation beginning on July 1, 1930. The first car's serial number was 5006933 and its engine number was CK8444. The CK had not been in production long when the model shift occurred. Less than half of total CK production came within this model year. The line of 6 bodies, and their prices, did not change. Neither did the styling and most specifications. The 4-Door Sedan with standard equipment is shown. A 2-Door Commercial Sedan which shared its body with Plymouth's 30-U was announced in the fall of 1930.

DeSoto gave its Model CF Eight a 1931 registration status on the same date as the CK Six. Only about one-eighth of the production total was built after that date. The new registration began with serial number L-172-PR and engine number CF19389. No noticeable mechanical changes were made, and the full line of 7 bodies was carried through with no readjustment of prices. No little earmarks appeared to provide clues for identification as this year's model. The illustration of the Coupe is from an advertisement which appeared in August, 1930.

Awaiting shipment from the factory, this new DeSoto Six Business Coupe did not yet have bumpers. The 2-passenger model was a good choice for people who needed to carry things in the rear deck compartment. The snug Coupe cost $740 and weighed 2,630 pounds. Of total SA production, 1,309 were this model. All new Sixes had cowl lamps mounted to the sheetmetal. The car shown has chrome-plated headlamps, tie-bar and cowl lamps, all optional extras. Note the absence of an exterior sun visor, that function now handled by a new foldaway type inside. The visorless appearance was typical of many SA enclosed bodies.

The Convertible Coupe of the new Six line was singled out for photo work while waiting for departure from a shipping point. Missing bumpers would be mounted before the car was delivered to a proud buyer. This model accounted for 638 units of total SA production. Passenger accommodations were provided for 4, including 2 in the rumble seat. The factory listed it at $825, a figure shared with one other model. It tipped the scales at 2,630 pounds. The arched support arm for the tail lamp was used on all early SA cars, but was replaced by an unattractive standard attached to the chassis frame. That change began about June 1st, and it was typical of the policy of making changes at any time throughout the manufacturing span of the new DeSoto Six.

Peter De Paolo, famous race driver, smiled broadly as he sat in the new DeSoto Six Roadster. This Model SA looked pretty sharp with its windshield and top folded. Optional 6-wheel equipment and fenders painted body color added much to its appeal. The model listed at $795 and weighed 2,520 pounds in standard form. This was the lightest-weight car in the SA line. A rumble seat accommodated 2, bringing the total passenger capacity to 4. 1,949 were built during the entire SA production period. Comparison of production figures for individual SA body types and corresponding CK models reveals a substantial SA increase, with but one exception. The gain was not due to better sales demand, but only because the SA was in production a few months longer than the former CK.

The only Model SA body type that did not register more production than its CK counterpart was the Phaeton. Instead, it mustered less than half as many as the model it replaced. Only 100 of these unpopular cars found buyers, making this the least desirable model of the new Six. At $795, the 5-passenger Phaeton cost more than the 4-Door Sedan. The 2,645-pound car is shown with standard equipment. The folding windshield was not optional on this and the new Six Roadster.

The new DeSoto Six Coupe with Rumble Seat is shown with standard trim, even the lamp shells were not chromed. The optional spare tire was not yet installed. The 4-passenger car was factory-priced at $775 and scaled 2,685 pounds when weighed. 2,663 of these came off the assembly lines. SA radiator shells could best be called radiator trim, since the design was a "ribbon" concept. This was similar to the narrow-profile shell of the original Model K, but more abbreviated. All SA radiators were equipped with built-in vertical shutters. The thin trim on the radiator, which was positioned well ahead of the front axle, gave longer hoods to the SA Six. That feature, combined with the slightly lower Steelweld bodies, created the impression of a longer car than the model it replaced. They were approximately the same in overall length, however.

Announced late in May, the new DeSoto Six 2-Door Sedan was the first such body type offered since the original Model K. Its $695 price was not only the lowest of any SA body, but held an additional distinction as the lowest-priced 6-cylinder sedan yet offered by any Chrysler Corp. Division. The car weighed 2,715 pounds and chalked up a total of 2,349 built. Equipment and features included all items used by other bodies. All of the new 2-door models had exterior sun visors. Hydraulic shock absorbers were standard on all models of the new Six. Several technical improvements were made about the time the new 2-door appeared.

Shown in standard form is the new DeSoto Six 4-Door Sedan. It has the single-bar bumpers common to all Model SA cars. This was the most popular SA body, and it also scored the highest popularity of any kind of DeSoto made this year. Total production of this model was 17,866 units. At $775, the 2,745-pound car cost less than the Phaeton. Accommodating 5 passengers, it was a sensibly attractive car for family use. The frontal aspect of the "ribbon" radiator outline is notably evident, as is the medallion perched on the standard black-painted tie-bar. A stylish oval panel incorporated dials on the instrument boards of all SA body types.

This 4-Door Sedan is showing off its wood artillery-type wheels. The 12-spoke wheels had chrome rings surrounding the hubs to give them a larger look more consistent with the size of wire wheel hub caps. Though wood or wire wheels were optional at no difference in cost, wires were by far the most popular. The standard tire size for all wheels was 5.00 x 19. Six wire wheels and front fender wells with mounts were available at extra cost.

1931

A station wagon was not offered by DeSoto Division this year, and had never been. But DeSoto dealers could order stripped chassis from the factory and ship them to wagon builders for construction and mounting of the bodies. This SA Six was probably one of the 32 chassis shipped. Otherwise, a passenger car body could have been removed for conversion to the wagon. The owner of this restored vehicle is unknown. The body is a Cantrell Suburban, built by J. T. Cantrell & Co., Huntington, N.Y. They were well-known quality station wagon craftsmen whose products were mounted on various chassis.

The DeLuxe Sedan was added to the SA line on the same day as the 2-Door Sedan. A 5-passenger car, it was the first DeLuxe 4-door DeSoto Six since the original Model K. At 2,835 pounds it was the heaviest of the SA series. Its $825 price tag was equalled by the Convertible Coupe, and they shared the highest price position. DeSoto turned out 1,450 of the DeLuxe Sedans. The car had the same 67-horsepower engine and 109-inch wheelbase as other SA models, but was given special treatment in details and appointments. The radiator filler cap had a sculptured head and shoulders of Hernando DeSoto, the Spanish explorer for whom the automobile was named. Other exterior refinements included twin cowl-top ventilators, striped sun visor, and chrome plating on the windshield frame and fuel filler cap. A long list of niceties were featured inside. Seats had luxury springs, front seat risers were covered with body cloth, garnish moldings had aprons, and the right rear door had a pocket. Also, there were matching assist cords and robe rail cord, velvet carpets, a carpeted footrest, and the dome light switch was moved to the door post. Chrome plating enhanced the gearshift and handbrake levers, steering post brackets and scuff plates. Truly lots of extras, but these were not all.

The new DeSoto Eight was a facelift of the previous straight-8 series. A notable styling change was the use of "ribbon" radiator trim, which required a new and longer hood. Fenders and all body styling remained untouched, only a few details receiving attention. The new Eight was designated as Model CF*, the star meaning that the model was a slightly modified version of the former Model CF. The brand new Roadster is seen with no bumpers, possibly about to be shipped in the automobile freight cars. Many new cars were transported by rail, and they fitted into the freight cars better with no bumpers. The tail lamp of this car is mounted on an upright standard attached to the chassis. This mounting is one of two types used on the CF*, and it was shared with late SA production. All Roadsters had rumble seats and accommodated 4 passengers. With standard equipment, the Roadster was the lightweight CF* model at 2,825 pounds, and was factory-priced at $995. Only 73 of them were built. Production figures given for individual body types represent total CF* production, including cars sold as next year's model.

The Phaeton recorded the lowest production figure of any in the CF* line. Also, it ranked as the least desirable of any DeSoto Six or Eight body yet built. This record for lowest demand would not be broken by a DeSoto body type until 1936. Domestic demand for a 5-passenger open car was almost nonexistent, and overall sales of the Eight took a nosedive this year. Consequently, only 22 Phaetons were built. There is evidence indicating that none were built before July, which if true would place them in next year's category. Weight of the Phaeton is unknown, but its list price was $1,035.

Least costly of any new Eight, the Business Coupe was priced at $965. Weight was 2,935 pounds. A 2-passenger model, it had a spacious storage compartment in the rear. 102 of these practical cars came off the assembly line. The spare wheel carried forward on the right-hand side only was one of two forward-mount options; the other choice being dual forward mounts. All new Eights had carryover 2-bar bumpers, though they were optional. Cowl lamps were at first integrated with the surcingle molding, but later were mounted directly to the cowl sheetmetal. All enclosed bodies were Unisteel construction, featuring French roofs and exterior visors. Front end styling of the new Eight was like the 1929 Chrysler 75, with the thin radiator outline and an arched tie-bar with gracefully diverging ends. The radiator featured vertical built-in shutters, and all lamps were fully chrome plated.

Styling character of the carryover coupe body itself is plainly evident in this illustration. It differed from the similar model of the SA Six, and from the previous CK Six as well. Main areas of unlikeness were the belt treatment and windshield post attitude. The catalog artwork shows carryover hubcaps, but the new design employed on the SA Six was also used on the new Eight. This model is the Coupe with Rumble Seat, sporting an optional forward sidemount. In standard form it weighed 2,970 pounds and listed at $995. On production records the 4-passenger car accounted for 486 units. The riding comfort of all CF* cars was aided by hydraulic shock absorbers. These were a boon in the days of semi-elliptic leaf springs at front as well as rear.

The smiling gentleman is Peter De Paolo, who put this car through its paces on a cross-country test trip. The stylish automobile is a Model CF* DeLuxe Sedan. With basic equipment, it weighed 3,115 pounds, which earned it the distinction of being the heaviest DeSoto of any kind offered thus far. The price tag was $1,065, but it is not known how many buyers were attracted. The 4-door body used the same shell as the standard version, but it seated 5 passengers in a better-class interior. This particular car was built during the early months of CF* production, before DeSoto added more class to the series. In an effort to encourage greater demand, all 7 models were given a dose of deluxe treatment, which meant an extra dose for the DeLuxe Sedan, and at no increase in prices. The niceties were added in May, and the CF* cars having them were sometimes called the "DeLuxe Eight." They were outwardly distinguished by an ornate Hernando DeSoto head and shoulders on the radiator cap, fenders in body color, a striped visor, and chrome on the windshield frame and fuel tank cap. Interiorwise, all enclosed cars got luxury seat springs, wider upholstery pleats, seat fabric on sidewalls, better carpets, and carpeted cowl panels. Sedans had draw shades at quarter windows, lights in rear quarters, and smoking sets. All interiors featured screened cowl side ventilators, and chrome plating was applied to gearshift and handbrake levers, door sill plates and rearview mirror bracket. No new mechanical innovations were added at this time. Shipments of the CF* series continued well into next year.

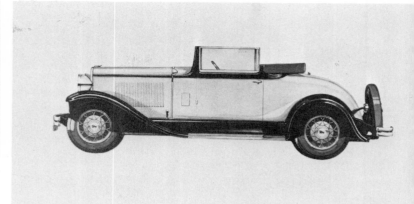

The new DeSoto Eight Convertible Coupe is shown in strictly standard form, even to the spare wheel carried at the rear. Five wire wheels were standard for all CF* models. Side glass could be lowered into the doors in true convertible manner. With rumble seat in use, the car easily carried 4 passengers. When equipped with 6 wire wheels it was the most expensive new Eight, carrying a price of $1,110. Also in that form it weighed 2,970 pounds. Perhaps none were delivered without 6-wheel equipment. A mere 48 of these classy cars came out of the factory. The arched tail lamp support shown, which was attached to the fender, was one of two types employed. All body types continued the use of side cowl ventilators, a feature the new Six did not have. Another convenience was adjustable front seats in all bodies but the Roadster.

Known simply as the Sedan, the standard 4-door, 5-passenger model weighed 3,025 pounds and cost $995. The production total of 3,490 includes all sedans in both standard and deluxe trim versions. Therefore, the 4-door sedan drew more buyers than any other CF* model. Wood artillery 12-spoke wheels were optional, and their availability was not restricted to this body type. The spare tire and its cover were also optional. Standard tire size for wire and wood wheels was 5.25 x 19. Sedan body styling of DeSoto Eights, both CF and CF*, strongly resembled that of this year's Chrysler CD Eight sedan, but they were not the same body. Other DeSoto Eight bodies bore much less likeness to Chryslers. When these cars were designed, Chrysler Corporation's "styling staff" was but a very few men who worked under engineering direction. They were generally known as artists, not stylists, but they did a good job in the pioneering days of styling. Given basic dimensions and interchangeability requirements, they created functional designs with artistic taste. Engineering personnel then developed approved concepts.

1932

For this calendar year the auto industry recorded the lowest production since 1918 when production was cut back because of World War I. This was the worst year of the depression, and the industry total at year-end was about 75% less than the all-time high in 1929 when the depression began. During the same period, the combined Chrysler Corp. loss was about 46%, much less than it would have been if Plymouth had not held it up. Individually, approximate losses were 73% for Chrysler cars, 76% for Dodge, while DeSoto fell 67%. For that overall period, Plymouth was not in the loss column. In fact, it was the only car in the industry to register a gain, which was a healthy 26%. After a drop in 1930, Plymouth rebounded with vigor in 1931, taking the industry's third place. A further rise of 14% held the position this year. Plymouth could not touch the Ford and Chevrolet heights, who respectively held second and first.

Plymouth's phenomenal rise in the latter half of the 1931 calendar year was due to the all-new Model PA and aggressive sales promotion. The smart new car was publicly announced in national advertising on July 11, 1931. Production had been under way 10 weeks, even though

The Plymouth Model PA Thrift series was a late addition about February 1st. It comprised only 2 body types and was of austere trim, being directed at low-income buyers. The engine and chassis were basically the same as for fancier models. At first, Thrift models were painted solidly in black, including the grille and headlamp tie-bar, with body striping to match the wheel color. Only wood artillery wheels were used, and the radiator filler cap was simply functional, not ornamental. The early 4-Door Sedan shown weighed 2,655 pounds and factory-listed at $575. Its later counterpart weighed 2,745 pounds.

Beginning April 4th, all Thrift models were equipped with wire wheels, and the grille was in a color to match them. Free Wheeling, not available on the earlier Thrift, was also added. Shown is the late Thrift 2-Door Sedan which, at $495 list, was the lowest-priced PA model. It weighed 2,690 pounds, while the same model in earlier form scaled 70 pounds less. In all, a total of 4,894 Thrift cars were built.

assemblies of the 1931 30-U would continue another 3 days, so that the huge dealer network would be ampl supplied by announcement day. From that running star PA sales picked up speed as the car's qualities becam known and the sales campaign hammered away relentlessl

From its beginning, the Model PA was regarded by it makers as a 1932 model, and they so informed the state and agencies concerned. Customarily, the company did nc publicly identify the car with a year designation, but th PA was the last model to be so treated. Much of the publi did not care about the car's model year — it was wante regardless of dating. The main concern of many was: Ho\\ can I afford it and how soon can I get it? They wanted ı because it had a brand new "Floating Power" engin suspension method said to give its 4-cylinder engine "th smoothness of an eight." They also liked other technic; features and the same interior room as some Chrysler-buil sixes. Also, there was perky performance and good ridin qualities — all for a low price. Dealers pressed the factor for cars to satisfy the demand.

Though the PA was an all-new Plymouth, much of was taken from 1931 DeSoto SA and Chrysler CM sixe which had already been on the market 6 months. But was the first complete change made by Plymouth. Ne\\ lowness of 67 inches made the car look longer than i overall 169 inches, while the wheelbase remained at 10 inches. Basic size of the previous 30-U engine w; retained, but developed horsepower was claimed to be 5(By far the most outstanding feature of the PA, Floatin Power was touted as the auto industry's most significar engineering advance in a decade. Conceived and develope by Chrysler, it resulted from 5 years of research. Plymout was the first to adopt it, and would use it in various forn through more than two decades. Other important featur were Free Wheeling and Easy-Shift silent second-ge; transmission.

On the average, the PA weighed almost 200 pounds mo than last year's 30-U, but the overall price range was $2 less. Despite the exceptional sales success of the PA, th new Model PB went into production within 8 month after the PA went to market. Concurrent with PB start-u was the addition of PA Thrift models which continue into September. Total PA assemblies amounted to 105,09 units, which included 131 basic chassis.

Introduced early in April, the new Plymouth Model P was given a new kind of sales promotion. Walter Chrysl appeared in many advertisements, spreading the Plymou gospel and inviting the public to compare it with the oth two lowest-priced cars. Before the year was out, he w advising "Look at All Three," a slogan that would popular next year. The PB was another all-new mode made larger so it could use much from the new DeSo SC. The engine was the PA Silver Dome refined to deliv 65 horsepower, and an optional Red Head cylinder he; provided a few more horses. Of course, the engine w supported by Floating Power mountings, which by no were incorporated in all Chrysler Corp. cars. Free Wheelir was continued, and a vacuum-operated automatic clutc was optional. With the latter gimmick, the clutch w; engaged by pressing the accelerator pedal, disengaged l withdrawing pressure. Also new was a steering shoc eliminator on the left front spring, designed to relieve tl steering wheel of road shock. Many other refinements we added.

1932

Model PB was the first Plymouth to be publicly identified with a specific year, as advertising clearly proclaimed it as a 1932 model. Furthermore, Chrysler Corp. informed dealers on June 9th that the customary practice of changing models in midsummer was now abandoned, and that current models were established as 1932 series whether shipped before or after June 30th. However, the practice of making improvements at any time during the model year was continued. Another note of interest about the PB is that it was the last domestically-sold 4-cylinder car bearing the Plymouth name until 1971.

In production only 7 months, the PB totalled out at 81,010 units, including 159 varied chassis. As a sales-getter it rivalled the PA, contributing a major share of the gain for this calendar year. Body for body, it was a better-than-PA value, averaging 90 pounds more car for $27 less cost.

DeSoto's pseudo-1932 models, the SA Six and CF* Eight, silently stepped into that rank on July 1, 1931. The only changes noted were a new Easy-Shift transmission and Free Wheeling, the latter being optional for $20 extra. DeSoto's star for this year was the brand new Model SC, which proudly and sophisticatedly made its debut at the beginning of the year. Heralded as having exceptionally smart styling appeal, it was launched in a grand manner, aided by endorsements from people of the arts, cultures and professions. Headline Hunter Floyd Gibbons, famed artist-illustrator James Montgomery Flagg, and "Believe It or Not" Robert Ripley were among those who boasted of it on radio and paper. Race driver Peter DePaolo put an SC through a gruelling 10-day 3,000-mile cross-country run that ended with a sizzling 300-mile track sprint at near-80 speeds, proving it had plenty of enduring "go."

The new SC was longer and heavier than the SA, having a chassis shared with Plymouth's PB, including all basic features except the engine. The Silver-Dome 6-cylinder L-head powerplant developed 75 horsepower, smoothing it out with DeSoto's first use of Floating Power mounts. The transmission was of silent-shift constant-mesh design, and Free Wheeling was now a standard item.

With the SC, DeSoto offered the broadest range of body types since its beginning, and they were available in Standard and Custom treatments. A comparison of SA and SC standard bodies indicates that the SC averaged 224 pounds heavier and cost $32 less. Considering all qualities and aspects of the SC, it should have been an excellent seller, but it failed to match the SA in salesability. Only 24,413 cars and 83 chassis were built. Perhaps the dealers were satisfied to concentrate mostly on selling the very popular Plymouth. Regardless of reasons, DeSoto ended up in the industry's ninth position at the end of this calendar year. That was an improvement from fourteenth spot a year before, but it resulted from the shifting of other companies. Mostly it was caused by the severe drops of Oldsmobile and Willys from loftier heights.

Undaunted by what was happening to DeSoto on the sales scene this year, the visionary Walter Chrysler became more than casually interested in development of the revolutionary "streamlined" DeSoto. Given a demonstration ride in a prototype, he was so impressed that he decided the design should be fully engineered for production feasibility. Also, he reasoned that the concept should be applied to the Chrysler car lines as well. It all reached fruition in 1934 as the Airflow cars.

A Model PA Sport Phaeton was favored by Franklin D. Roosevelt, who became President of the U.S.A. in 1933, stepping up from the New York state governorship. Crippled by polio, the car was specially equipped with manual controls so he could drive it. He apparently got it while serving as Governor. The windshield folded, and the top could be folded much lower and neater. In basic form, the Sport Phaeton weighed 2,545 pounds and the price was $595. Plymouth turned out 528 of them. There was no standard version of the Phaeton.

Plymouth Roadster

The Roadster was a 2-passenger car with a rear compartment for carrying luggage or whatever. At 2,440 pounds, it was the lightweight of all Plymouths this year. In standard form its price was factory-listed at $535. The Model PA was the first Plymouth to have a built-in radiator grille, which in standard practice was painted to match the body, except as noted for the late Thrift models. The non-folding windshield stanchions and frame were painted, and the glass could be swung open at the bottom. Only 200 Roadsters were built, making this the least popular Plymouth passenger car this year.

Looking every bit the part, the Sport Roadster was for fun-loving people, and 2,680 buyers could not resist having one. The 2 or 4-passenger car had a rumble seat, and the folding windshield's metalwork was chrome-plated. With standard equipment, it listed at $595 and scaled 2,470 pounds. All PA cars had 5 wire wheels and blackwall tires, with rear-mounted spare, as basic equipment. Bumpers were optional on all, as also were wood artillery wheels except as noted for early Thrift models. Another PA option was the chromed screen grid attached to the grille. The snappy PA could accelerate from 0 to 40 in 9.7 seconds and hit 65-to-70 mph, not bad for a light car of its time.

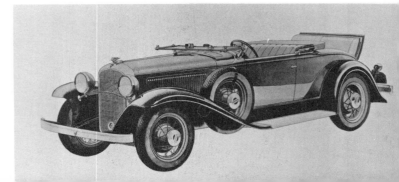

The Coupe of the PA line was ideal for salesmen and professional people. It accommodated 2 passengers and had room in the rear deck for whatever they carried. Its basic cost was $565 and it weighed 2,600 pounds. 12,079 buyers got this model, and one of them was a relative of H. Ray Mark, Centre Hall, Pa., who now owns this fine example. It sports a chrome-plated grille, which was an option not available for Thrift sedans. Plymouth called the grille "radiator louvres."

1932

The Coupe with Rumble Seat was a neat personal car that could seat 2 passengers inside and 2 extras outside in what often was called the "mother-in-law" seat. The folding trunk rack on the rear was part of the forward-mounted spare wheel option. This Model PA, without options, cost $610 and weighed 2,645 pounds. Plymouth built 9,696 of them. The PA had a new double-drop chassis frame, enabling lower overall height. A carburetor air intake silencer and vacuum-actuated automatic spark control were standard. Gear ratio was 4.3 to 1, and tire size was 19 x 4.75. All enclosed bodies were of Safety-Steel construction, and were factory-wired and equipped with radio antennae at no extra cost. Other body types were so-equipped only on order and for a price. Radios were the popular Philco-Transitone, another extra-cost item.

Gathering more popularity was the Convertible Coupe. 2,783 of this PA type rolled out of the Plymouth-DeSoto plant. Its price was $645 and it weighed 2,615 pounds in basic form. With its standard rumble seat open it could carry 4 passengers. Specially dressed up, this car has more of the many options available for all but the Thrift. Chromed headlamp shells, cowl lamps to match, and a chromed cowl molding at the hood were nice touches. Leather interior upholstery was an extra in this and any enclosed body.

For the high-powered launching of the Model PA sales drive, dealers got these flamboyant cars. They were painted flame red and equipped with glass newly developed in Europe, having a mirror appearance outside but having transparency from the inside. As the cars were driven about, they incited interest and created the impression that they were automatically controlled. Some of them had sound broadcasting equipment. Dealers paid list price for them, and when the showmanship was over they were repainted in stock colors and given standard window glass. Bodies were the standard 4-Door Sedan which, as made for the market, cost $635 and weighed 2,730 pounds in the basic. Drawing more buyers than any other Plymouth this year, assembly lines rolled off 49,465 of these and the Thrift 4-door models.

When compared with the 1931 DeSoto SA Six, it is obvious that the Plymouth PA was almost a carbon copy in appearance. General proportions, body and fender styling, and radiator well ahead of the axle are proof of the almost total sharing of parts. The window poster was not quoting the price of this 2-Door Sedan, which was $575. Without extras, this model weighed 2,650 pounds. 23,038 2-door types were built, including Thrifts. The 5-passenger 2-door ranked second to the 4-door in demand.

The PA is shown while on display with some of its team-mates near the first of the year. In succession, the 1932 models beyond it were a Dodge DK Eight, Dodge DL Six, and DeSoto SC Custom. The Plymouth is a DeLuxe Sedan, a 5-passenger, 4-door model added to the line during the previous autumn. The DeLuxe was distinguished by a more sumptuous interior which included rear window roll shades with pendants, assist pulls on rear pillars, and other luxuries and conveniences. In basic form it was priced at $690, which was higher than any other PA model. Its weight was 2,795 pounds without extras. 4,384 buyers got the luxury car. Special body colors could be ordered on any except Thrift models, and fenders and chassis sheetmetal were also available in colors. The metal spare tire cover shown was another option.

At least one 7-passenger sedan was built as Plymouth pondered whether to manufacture the type for marketing. A Model PA chassis was stretched approximately 9 inches, which was enough to accommodate 2-door sedan doors in place of the front doors of a 5-passenger 4-door. The roof, running boards and scuff aprons were lengthened, and many unseen details were altered. The oval rear window was common to all sedans and coupes, and some convertibles had it.

Walter P. Chrysler declared that Floating Power was "The Fourth Milestone," after the electric self-starter, enclosed body and 4-wheel brakes, in that order. Milestone or not, it was an outstanding contribution to engine operating smoothness and the pleasure of driving. It resulted from a 5-year program during which over 1,000 engine mounting ideas were developed. Simply stated, the unique method employed only 2 mounts, one under the cooling fan shaft and the other at the rear of the transmission, each liberally cushioned in rubber. In principle, an imaginary line drawn between the mounts and through the engine center of gravity (shown by dotted lines) was the axis of the running engine's rocking motion. Cradled in this manner, the engine might have oscillated from its mountings if a stabilizing spring had not been incorporated between the bell housing and the rightside rail of the chassis frame. The patented method amazingly restricted vibration from transmission to the car and its occupants. Before announcement day, mayors of major cities were blindfolded and given rides in the PA and other 4-cylinder cars. Asked if they thought any was an 8-cylinder car, a great majority guessed Plymouth to be an 8. The same test, given to automotive experts, drew like results.

Louis B. Miller, 57-year-old salesman for Chrysler in San Francisco, and the car that proved to the nation that the PA had both performance and stamina. Not a professional race driver, he demonstrated that the car would deliver its fullest potential for a long and punishing period of time. He and a relief truck driver asked more of this car in 5½ days than an average owner would have expected of a similar model during his ownership. The eastward coast-to-coast trip was made in 65 hours and 33 minutes. One hour and a quarter later the return trip was begun. Running against winds from the west was no deterrent, as 9 minutes were shaved from the easterly record. During the 6,287-mile trip, the car averaged 47.52 miles per hour and 1,140 miles per day. A previous S.F.–N.Y. roundtrip record was bettered by almost 36 hours, and 9½ hours were cut from the best prior cross-continent record. High-powered expensive cars with professional drivers made the earlier runs. The record-smashing Plymouth 4-Door Sedan was specially-equipped with extra roadlights and a rear-mounted spare wheel in addition to forward-mounts.

For 3 years, advertising had promoted Plymouth as the full-size car in the lowest-priced field, implying that Ford and Chevrolet were not full-size. If the PA 7-passenger sedan had gone to market, the ad agency might have called it "extra full-size." The auxiliary seats folded snugly into the front seat back when not in use. General design of the interior was like the standard 5-passenger model, but this one had rear seat armrests and the smaller car had a footrest on the rear floor.

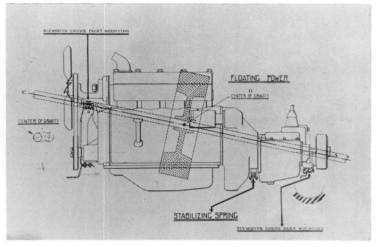

Not all PA demonstrator cars were the mirrored "mystery" kind. Most were entirely practical, like this one at W.D. Bonner, Inc., a Los Angeles dealership. The little dancer performed without a disturbance of rhythm, while the engine ran at a speed equal to 33 miles an hour. This was only one of various clever ingenuities employed to emphasize and prove the freedom from vibration. The Silver Dome of the engine is clearly visible in this view. Mr. Chrysler felt that low-cost cars should and could have no more than 4 cylinders, and should run as smoothly as an 8. Later events proved that he would accept compromise.

The Plymouth PA Taxicab placed the driver in a special compartment. At the right of the driver was a rear-facing seat, and another was directly behind the compartment, on the left side. Thus, there was room for 5 passengers. Not yet much concerned with the taxicab market, Plymouth turned out only 112 PA cabs. The 2,785-pound cab was priced at $665.

The PA 2-Door Sedan was easily adapted to ambulance use. Plymouth would give more attention to that purpose within the next few years, as it also would to other particular needs. There is evidence that some commercial or utility sedans were built on the PA chassis, but no known surviving records substantiate them.

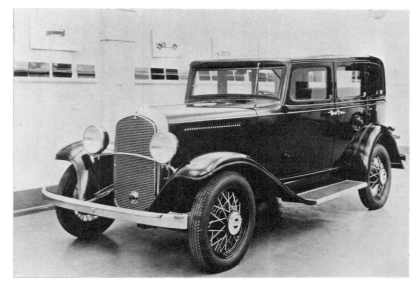

Designed and built by the Edw. G. Budd Mfg. Co., of Philadelphia, Pa. in 1931, this prototype was obviously a proposal for 1932. Briggs Mfg. Co., in Detroit, was supplying Plymouth with coupe, sedan and convertible bodies, and Budd wanted the business. Budd occasionally built proposals directed to various automakers. This car was based on the PA chassis, and retained PA fenders, headlamps and tie-bar. The PA radiator shell was made taller for conformity with a higher hood, cowl and body beltline. The slanted windshield had a smoothly-rounded steel header with no visor. The two parallel belt moldings, as treated on this car, were strikingly similar to the belt styling on popular General Motors cars in 1931-32.

The new Model PB was another all-out styling change, but still characteristically Plymouth in appearance. A larger car, it rode on a 112-inch wheelbase. The Business Roadster was a 2-passenger car with ample storage space in the rear. Its utilitarian purpose was exemplified by more conservative coloring and details than the others had. In the standard form shown, it was the least-heavy PB at 2,545 pounds, and its factory price of $495 made it the least costly. The price was equal to the PA Thrift 2-Door Sedan. Only 325 buyers took advantage of its kind of practicality.

The PB was the first Plymouth that did not have headlamps mounted on a tie-bar. New one-piece front fenders curved a bit more toward the bumper. Fender wells and forward-mounts were extra-cost items when ordered for most PB models. The Sport Roadster featured a folding windshield and a rumble seat. With standard equipment it weighed 2,595 pounds and was priced at $595. 2,163 were built, and one of them eventually wound up as the well-restored example shown, owned by Frank Kleptz, Terre Haute, Ind. It is seen while on display at the huge flea market and old car show at Hershey, Pa.

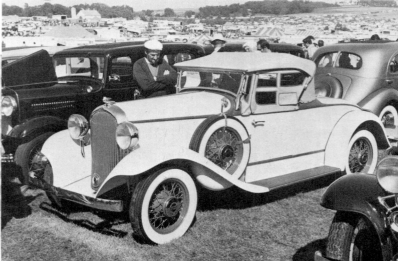

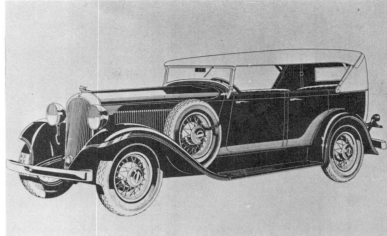

The last phaeton type offered by Plymouth in the U.S.A. was the Model PB Sport Phaeton. Logically, it registered a lower demand than any other in the PB line, and only 259 were built. Without extras, the 5-passenger 2,655-pound car was available for $595. Truly open cars were out of favor because they lacked weather protection.

The Collegiate Special was added in May as a PB Sport Roadster special-order car. It was aimed at the college market, perhaps intended to spark a youth market 30 years before that buyer category assumed recognizable proportions. Its only distinction was its paint job, which was in school colors, regardless of what they were. The Sport Roadster production total did not indicate how many of these Specials were built. The special college colors cost $40 extra, the same as asked for special paint jobs on other PB models. The distinctive curvature of the PB grille, increasing toward the bottom, is evident. 1932 was the last year Plymouth offered a roadster of any kind in the U.S.A.

Built on the new 121-inch wheelbase inaugurated for extra passenger capacity, a PB 7-passenger Phaeton posed for its picture. Possibly this type was sold on foreign markets, but it was not available in the U.S.A. The rear doors opened from the rear, while those of the Sport Phaeton were front-opening. For this model, a DeSoto Phaeton body was lengthened by inserting wider sections between the doors. The usual type of folding auxiliary seats were utilized.

The Coupe with Rumble Seat continued to be a fairly popular model, requiring production of 8,159 to meet the demand. Without extras, weight was 2,750 pounds and price was $610. The more pronounced slant of PB windshields was a definite advance, as was the smoothly-contoured visorless header. Bodies were again known as Safety-Steel, and Duplate safety glass continued as an option. The ornate winged-woman radiator filler cap, new for the PA, was also used on the PB. Though most cars came out of the factory with the fancy cap, it was an extra-cost item, as also were bumpers.

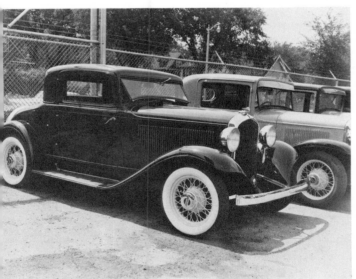

This restored Model PB Business Coupe shows that the windshield could be swung open, a feature of all PB coupes, sedans and convertibles. Chromed headlamp shells were optional on this model, as the standard specification was paint. Whitewall tires were extra-cost on all PB models. The 2,695-pound car carried a $565 price tag. The 2-passenger capacity with a storage compartment proved desirable to 11,126 buyers.

The 2-Door Sedan trailed introduction of the main PB line by a few weeks. A family-size car of modest price, it cost $575. The 2,825-pound model did not win much more popularity than the Business Coupe, as the production sheets recorded 13,031 built. Standard PB wheel equipment included 5 wire wheels and 18 x 5.25 tires, with the spare mounted on the rear. 18-inch wood-spoke wheels were an option, and could be had in painted or natural wood finish. Another choice was 17-inch wire or wood wheels with 5.50 tires. In all cases, spare mounting could be on the rear or in one or both front fenders.

Best seller of the PB line was the 4-Door Sedan for 5 passengers. The convenience of 4 doors was regarded as necessary by most buyers of family cars. The restored example shown was one of 38,066 new ones built. Standard-equipped, the model weighed 2,870 pounds and listed at $635. Chromed headlamp shells were standard on all PB models except the Business Roadster and Business Coupe. Painted grilles were standard, but chrome could be ordered at extra cost.

Interested in marketing cars with extra passenger capacity, Plymouth introduced its first long wheelbase with the Model PB. Of 121 inches, its primary purpose was to accommodate the 2,179 7-passenger Sedan bodies that were built. Weighing 3,075 pounds, the big car was heavier than any other PA or PB model offered for sale. The asking price was a reasonable $725.

Plymouth's first practice of opening doors from the forward pillars, rather than being hinged to them, came with the Model PB. All bodies included the feature. The new hood was cut on an angle approximating that of the door, and extended over the cowl to near the windshield. The cowl-covering hood idea originated in Europe, and was intended to give an impression of greater length from the radiator to the windshield, which in turn was to suggest a powerful engine. In Plymouth's application, twin cowl vent doors were flush-mounted in the top. A slenderly attractive movie star posed with a Convertible Coupe on the movie company's lot in Hollywood, Calif. The car, like all of its kind, had a rumble seat. At $645, the 2,730-pound convertible was a smart buy. 4,853 of them were built.

A masked beauty smilingly waved as she leaned on a Convertible Sedan. Plymouth's first offering of this body type, it was also the last until 1939. A close-coupled 5-passenger body, it had only 2 doors. The sporty model was available only with dual forward-mounts, and a removable trunk rode on a stylish fixed platform at the rear. At $785, this was the highest-priced of all PA and PB models. Weight was 2,920 pounds. The model was sought and bought by 690 buyers. The vertical-standing tail lamps shown on PB models were standard equipment, mounted on the left side only. Optional dual tail lamps projected horizontally from the rear fenders, and were the chromed style used on DeSoto SC Customs. Other PB extras included chromed dual horns for the front, windshield wiper for right side, radio antenna for open cars and convertibles, and leather interiors in convertibles, coupes, and 4-door sedans.

For the PB Taxicab, Plymouth retained the basic interior layout used for the similar PA model. Built on the 112-inch wheelbase chassis, the 4-door vehicle had room for 5 passengers and baggage, plus the driver. Price, weight and production data for this model is not available. Plymouth constantly looked for specialty markets to which it could readily adapt. Some specialty manufacturers looked to Plymouth, too, as a means of broadening their market potential. Among them were two builders of wooden station wagon bodies, a type not yet widely accepted. Each offered what was called a "Suburban" body on the PB 112-inch wheelbase. The unique vehicles were ordered and sold by a very few Plymouth dealers, the Plymouth factory having little to do with it but the assembly of chassis. Cantrell, of Huntington, N. Y., asked $347 for the body, including mounting, and another $8 for a gas tank filler pipe extension. The completed vehicle cost approximately $800. U.S. Body and Forging Co., Tell City, Ind., supplied a mounted body for $375, and the finished vehicle listed at $830.

At least 2 PB Limousines had interiors entirely done in leather, but differing in minor details and fittings. Each had a half-seat for the driver, and utilized the righthand side of the compartment for carrying luggage. These practical vehicles probably were used as commercial limousines, courtesy cars, or even taxicab service. Another version was done in the true limousine tradition, having a driver's compartment with full-width seat and all-leather trim, and the passenger compartment tastefully upholstered and trimmed with fabric. Ornate garnish moldings and appropriate details completed the luxury look.

A Plymouth PB 112-inch wheelbase chassis posed for a picture of mechanical beauty. The X-member center bracing, new with the PB, provided greater frame stiffness. The I-section front axle is visible, as are the semi-elliptic front and rear springs. The rear axle was semi-floating, with 4.33 to 1 gear ratio. The air cleaner was perched much higher than the engine's Silver Dome cylinder head. Use of a stick-shift transmission is obvious. Chassis could be purchased with or without cowl/windshield assemblies at prices ranging from $410 to $445. 159 chassis were shipped, but probably not all of them were this length.

Not offered to the public, a 7-passenger Limousine type was built on the PB 121-inch wheelbase. Production records do not list limousines, but there is evidence that at least several were built. The partitioning wall behind the driver's compartment was exceptionally high, and had upper panels at each pillar. Divided partition glass could be moved sidewise in parallel channels. The front doors of this body were the same as used for the 2-Door Sedan. Not all limousines had forward-mounted spare wheels.

The previous DeSoto Six, Model SA, assumed a 1932 status on July 1, 1931 with serial number 5030807 and engine number SA20306. Appearance, weights and prices continued unchanged, but some specifications and equipment differed slightly. The most important change was the adoption of the Easy-Shift silent second-gear transmission. A significant new option was Free Wheeling, which cost $20 extra. The DeLuxe Sedan is shown. Approximately 25% of total SA production was turned out during the 1932 registration period.

Also designated a 1932 model for registration purposes, the DeSoto Model CF* Eight slipped into it without public notice. It became a later model on the same day as the SA Six, and did so with serial number L192EW and engine number CF*24309. No discernible changes took place in appearance, weights and prices. Specifications as of May, 1931 were retained, with the exception of the transmission, which was replaced by the new Easy-Shift design. An addition was the new $20 Free Wheeling option. Shown is the DeLuxe Sedan, which bore the same appearance as its earlier CF* counterpart. Of total CF* production, about 50% were built after the pseudo-1932 change took place. This was the last DeSoto 8-cylinder car until 1952.

1932

The all-new DeSoto Six, Model SC, was the first DeSoto to be related to a specific model year in company advertising. It also was the first DeSoto that was not associated with dual year designations. A different kind of dual representation, at least for DeSoto, was in the offering of two car lines under one series. The Model SC family was comprised of a Standard line and a Custom line, each having several body types and minor points of difference. The Phaeton was offered only as a Standard model. The 5-passenger car was factory-priced at $775, and was the least popular SC model. A mere 30 of them were built, and never again would DeSoto make the type available in the U.S.A. Wheel equipment of the car shown caused a needless addition to its proper name. The 6-wheel option package automatically added "DeLuxe" to the end of the proper name of any body type. Therefore, this car was properly called the Standard Phaeton DeLuxe. A Phaeton was not offered in the Custom line. All Standard cars had single tail lamps mounted on an unattractive upright support, as shown.

The Standard Coupe was a 2-passenger model intended for business people who needed toting space in the rear deck. The Custom line did not include this body type. The handy SC semi-utility car weighed 2,843 pounds, cost $695 and drew 1,691 buyers. One of the means of identifying Standard models was the absence of trumpet horns on the front. A single windshield wiper was another Standard mark. All Standard cars were fitted with 18 x 5.25 tires and, when ordered in basic form, were equipped with 5 wire wheels, including a rear-mounted spare. Chromed or painted radiator shells (not grilles) were optional on all SC models, and chromed headlamp shells were used for all.

Another body available only in the Standard line was the 2-Door Sedan. It tipped the scales at 2,903 pounds and carried a $695 price tag. DeSoto turned out 3,730 of these practical 5-passenger cars. Hailed as a car of striking beauty, most notable SC newness was in the grille, and in the longer hood that extended to the slanted windshield. Also new were doors that latched to the windshield pillars instead of being hinged to them, and one-piece front fenders of slightly heavier appearance.

The DeSoto SC grille design bore a striking resemblance to that of the famed Miller front-wheel-drive race cars, causing reports that it was copied from the Miller. Since it actually was very similar to, but not a copy of, one can reasonably assume that the Miller inspired it. For this scene at the Indianapolis Motor Speedway in May, 1930, a Miller was "buddy" to a new DeSoto Eight Roadster. The Roadster was owned by Jones-Maley, a DeSoto agency in Indiana, who sponsored the Miller for the annual Memorial Day 500-mile racing classic. The racer was driven by Dave Evans, who averaged 92.571 mph and finished in 6th place. That position was somewhat behind the usual Miller finish.

The car that won more demand than any other SC was the Standard 4-Door Sedan for 5 passengers. 8,924 buyers regarded it as most suitable for their needs. The factory asked $775 for the 2,993-pound model. All SC bodies of 5-passenger or less capacity were mounted on the 112-inch wheelbase chassis shared with Plymouth's PB, but the DeSoto engine was a 75-horsepower six. Windshields of all SC models were flat-across with a vertical divider at the center, and were framed in chrome.

An attractive car was the Custom Coupe with Rumble Seat, especially when equipped in the DeLuxe manner. It weighed 2,913 pounds and cost $790. Also offered by DeSoto was a Standard Coupe with Rumble Seat, which weighed 2,888 pounds and was priced at $735. Total Standard and Custom production of this body type was 2,897. Engines in the Custom car line were the same as those in the Standard cars.

The 7-passenger Sedan was a Standard line exclusive, and was the only catalogued model utilizing a 121-inch wheelbase. The engine was the same as any other SC had. Conforming to SC practice, this body was also shared with the Plymouth PB. 221 of these 3,148-pound cars were built, and they sold for $925 a copy. When equipped as shown, this model was the Standard 7-passenger Sedan DeLuxe. Most Standard cars had fenders and chassis sheetmetal painted black regardless of body colors, as that was the basic specification. But the black could be replaced with color on special order.

The Custom 5-Passenger Sedan was a handsome luxury vehicle that could make any family proud. Its 4 doors opened to an exquisite interior with extra conveniences. It caught the eyes and captured the hearts of 4,791 buyers. The 3,028-pound SC model was priced at $835. The DeLuxe equipment offered a choice of wheels, one of which was the artillery type shown. All Custom cars were fitted with 17 x 5.50 tires. Additional Custom-identifying marks were twin trumpet horns, twin windshield wipers, and twin tail lamps projecting horizontally from the rear fenders. Available for all Standard and Custom models, Duplate safety glass and a radio were extra-cost items. All enclosed bodies were factory-wired and antenna-equipped for radio.

Usually DeLuxe-equipped, a Custom Roadster is shown with optional Goodyear Air Wheels. The sport-flavored car featured a rumble seat and folding windshield. A boot was supplied for covering the top when folded down. In basic form this model weighed 2,738 pounds and was priced at $775. A Standard Roadster, which had no rumble seat, was also available. It weighed 2,720 pounds, and its $675 price made it the lowest-cost SC. Total Standard and Custom Roadster production was 894 units. Contrary to an industry trend toward pointed V-shaped grilles, DeSoto introduced a smartly rounded grille on the Model SC. That feature distinctly set DeSoto apart from all other automobiles.

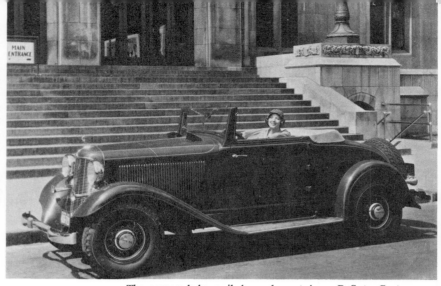

The most expensive DeSoto offered to the public this year was the Custom Convertible Sedan DeLuxe. The 2-door, 5-passenger beauty was priced at $975. With a smartly styled trunk, it was offered only with DeLuxe equipment and was the heaviest SC production model, weighing 3,175 pounds. 275 of the swanky Custom models were built, there being no Standard version. This was the first convertible sedan offered by DeSoto, who advertised the entire SC line as "America's Smartest Low-Priced Car."

1932

The young lady smiled as she sat in a DeSoto Custom Convertible Coupe. Perhaps she had just heard on the radio that the campaigning Franklin D. Roosevelt was promising prosperity for everyone if he were elected to the U.S. presidency in November. The rumble-seated convertible was priced at $845 and weighed 2,858 pounds in basic form. 960 of them were built. The Standard line did not include this body. The twin cowl vents, an SC feature, were open on a warm day sometime after May, when the fat Goodyear Air Wheels became an SC option. DeSoto was the first automaker to offer the soft low-pressure tires. Nicknamed "Doughnut" and "Jumbo," they were size 7.50 by 15. They were claimed to give a sort of "floating ride" which would complement driving pleasures already derived from the vibrationless Floating Power of the DeSoto engine.

In July, a DeSoto SC Custom Town Car was shown, and there is evidence that at least 2 were built, each with interior detail differences. Identity of the coachbuilder is unknown, but they probably were built by Chrysler's custom body shop, which was in operation from 1931 to 1935. Limousine bodies were reworked and mounted on 121-inch chassis. Wheel discs were used, covering the spokes. Relating to SC models in general, the painted radiator shell made the long hood look even longer, but the curved bumper design did not make its protective purpose more effective.

Town Car passenger compartments were luxuriously upholstered and appointed. The automobile shown had this interior. The seat had a folding center armrest, tiny pockets were below and ashtrays just above the side armrests. A vanity compartment, mirror pocket and quarter lamp are also shown. Pillows, lap robes and soft wedge-shaped footrests were included. All was in keeping with the finest town car tradition.

The program for development of a revolutionary car produced this road test prototype this year. It was a forerunner of the 1934 Airflow. Because Chrysler maintained tight secrecy about the program, the car bore no Chrysler or DeSoto identification. It needed a name for license and registration purposes, so it was registered as the "Trifon Special" by consent of Demitrion Trifon, a mechanic and driver in the road test garage. This car was demonstrated to Mr. Chrysler, and he was highly elated about it. The unique automobile had many major and minor features and a sumptuous interior. Somehow, it escaped usual prototype wrecking, and survives to this day.

For the automobile industry, and for the nation, this year marked the beginning of economic recovery from the effects of the severe depression. Franklin D. Roosevelt was inaugurated as President of the U.S.A. in January, sweeping a wholly new administration in with him. Drastic measures were instituted to start business and employment on an upswing, and they worked. The gradual return of buying power pushed passenger car production to a 37.5% gain by the end of this calendar year. Plymouth production soared to a 110% gain for the same period, second only to Dodge's fantastic 300% rise, and 25% more than third best gainer Pontiac. This was by far the best production year in Plymouth's short history, but it did not move up from its position as the industry's third largest producer because Ford and Chevrolet picked up gains, too. Chrysler cars scored a 19% increase, but DeSoto suffered a loss of almost 31% which dropped it to twelfth position in the industry ranks. Of the 32 makes of cars on the market, most of the industry's gain was registered by the higher-volume producers. At least half of the companies built fewer than they did in 1932. But the tide was turning toward more business, and it would continue to rise in the years to come, though it would not save several weak companies.

The financially strong Chrysler Corp. emerged from the tight money period with ample resources to forge ahead. Always optimistic, Walter P. Chrysler prepared for the resurgence of business while the slump was worsening. He never cut research and engineering budgets, even in bad times. Planning for the future could not be influenced by conditions of the present, he reasoned. The Airflow development program was accelerated toward completion by the end of this year. Another area of concentrated activity was the planning of a new Plymouth. While sincerely believing that a 4-cylinder engine was best for any car in the low-priced field, Mr. Chrysler conceded as early as 1931 that it soon would be competitively doomed. Chevrolet began exclusive use of a 6-cylinder with its 1929 model, and there were strong indications that Henry Ford would place a V-8 in his cars in 1932. Chrysler had no alternative but to invest in a new Plymouth. Retooling the plants cost $9,000,000, a huge sum to lay out during the worst depression year which had brought Chrysler Corp. its first financial loss.

The new Plymouth Six was the Model PC, placed on the market in the autumn of 1932. An extensive advertising campaign again urged the public to "Look at All Three," claiming that popular opinion regarded the Plymouth as "America's Next Number One Car." The new Six had the distinction of being launched by means of a special radio broadcast. Walter Chrysler and other executives aired a business meeting for 75,000 Chrysler employees and a nationwide listening audience. Actual public response to the PC was somewhat less favorable than Plymouth had been accustomed to. The car was smaller than the former PB, having a wheelbase 5 inches shorter and averaging 297 pounds less weight. Though overall length was only 1.5 inches less than the PB, many people thought the PC Six looked more like a 4-cylinder car than the PB did. First PC prices averaged $60 less than corresponding PB models, and an average reduction of $15 in mid-December did little to encourage increased sales. By that time, plans were already afoot to rectify the situation.

A crash program was begun in January to prepare the new and larger DeLuxe Plymouth, Model PD. Based on the popular 1933 Dodge Model DP 6-cylinder 111¼-inch wheelbase, it caused Dodge to lengthen its own Six to 115 inches in order to maintain the size differential between itself and Plymouth. The DeLuxe Plymouth, more pleasing than the PC in every respect, caught the public's fancy when introduced in April, and resumed a rising sales pattern. Concurrent with the preparation of the DeLuxe was the modification of the PC package to become the Standard Plymouth Six, coded as Model PCXX. Sold to fleet buyers and those who could get along with a lower-cost car, the Standard was downgraded from the PC in price and detail. Plymouth's problems this model year caused the introduction of three different series within five months, which was quite a penalty. In addition, numerous changes were made in the original PC Six during its short production run, either in response to dealer requests or for reasons unknown. Combined demand for the new Standard and DeLuxe cars was partly met by the opening of a branch assembly plant in Los Angeles on June 15th.

DeSoto had its own set of circumstances this year. For the first time since its beginning, it did not share most of its parts with Plymouth. Instead, it was closely allied with the 1933 Chrysler Six and Royal Eight, Models CC and CT respectively. The new Model SD was heralded as "Smart in Style" and "Smart to Buy," and it invitingly suggested "Let's Go Places." As the production totals show, it didn't go as far as the previous Model SC. The SD was the fourth newly-tooled DeSoto in as many years, which required large expenditures during lean years. Of course, much of the cost was shared by whatever sister make DeSoto was teamed with.

Compared with the SC, the SD averaged 216 pounds more and cost about the same at the first of the year. Its wheelbase was two inches longer and its general appearance gave an impression of being larger and heavier than it actually was. The distinctive rounded grille concept was retained, and more tastefulness was applied to interiors. For the first six months, the L-head Silver Dome 6-cylinder engine delivered 79 horsepower. When equipped with the optional Red Head high compression cylinder head, horse-

The Plymouth Six Business Coupe was the lowest-priced car in the Model PC line, being factory-listed at $495. Weighing 2,418 pounds, it was the lightweight PC. 10,853 of these were built, some of them being delivered to fleet buyers. The snug, 2-passenger economy car is shown with a simple low-profile ornament on the top of the radiator shell. The winged ornament seen on other models was optional in all cases, but most cars were equipped with it. The ornament was not a radiator filler cap, as Plymouth adopted the new idea of placing the filler under the hood. The PC standard finish for the grille, headlamp shells and fenders was black.

1933

The Coupe with Rumble Seat was chosen by 8,894 buyers. In basic form, the 2-4-passenger model weighed 2,473 pounds and listed for $545 when the PC bowed in November 1932. A $20 cut followed in mid-December. The example shown had body color fenders, headlamps, and 6.00 x 16 Goodyear Airwheels. These were on the option list, which also included dual exterior trumpet horns, dual tail lamps, and windows of Duplate safety glass. Early PC hood louvers were progressively more slanted from front to rear, as shown by this photograph.

Added to the PC line in February was the 2-Door Sedan. Without extras, it was priced at $505 and weighed 2,498 pounds. Optional Goodyear Airwheels are shown. Only 4,008 of these 5-passenger models were built. The hood of this car had all louvers slanted parallel with each other, having a constant angle from front to rear. It was one of three louver layouts used for the PC, and was the pattern that most cars had. The 2-Door Sedan body was mounted on the Rigid-X double-drop chassis frame which was a PC feature. New technical details included shockless cross steering and Chrysler Oilite discs between spring leaves.

power was increased to 86. With a bore and stroke of 3.25 x 4-3/8, displacement was 217.8 cubic inches. The engine was suspended on Floating Power mountings. New exhaust valve seat inserts were said to nearly eliminate the need for valve grinding. An automatic choke and automatic manifold heat control were among the features. In June, horsepower was raised from 79 to 82 at no extra cost to the buyer.

Additional features common to all SD DeSotos were a coincidental starter and accelerator pedal, thermostatically controlled cooling system, and an all-silent 3-speed transmission. Flex-Beam headlighting allowed the left headlight beam to be directed downward when another car approached, while the right headlight beam remained steady to illuminate the roadside. This feature was in addition to the normal means for depressing beams in the city, and dimmers for parking. Free Wheeling was standard equipment, as was the Duplate safety glass windshield. Among extra-cost options were an automatic clutch and Duplate window glass.

The month of June was a time of change for DeSoto. Assembly operations were moved from the Plymouth plant to the Chrysler plant on Detroit's East Jefferson Ave. This was a sensible move, because the SD was Chrysler-shared rather than Plymouth-shared. The relocation also allowed Plymouth to devote all of its facilities to take advantage of its capacity of 40,000 units monthly. Coincidental with the move was the SD change to the 82-horsepower engine, which was almost the same as the Chrysler Six was using. At the same time, a number of items common to the Custom line were included on the Standard cars at no increase in prices. Eight new body colors were added to give extra selectivity and more appeal to buyers. Despite the "free" offering of goodies and a midyear price cut averaging $60 across the board, DeSoto finished the year in a worse position than before. However, the midyear changes did bring a spurt in sales, as factory shipments were substantially higher in July, August and September.

DeSoto was not the only well-known make to continue the decline this year. Buick, Nash, Hupmobile, Reo, and the Hudson-Terraplane duo were counted among the losers. Of those, Nash, Hupmobile, Hudson and Terraplane had models competitive with DeSoto. Perhaps there simply was not enough buyers in that particular class to go around. But in DeSoto's case, it is probable that sales were lost to the revised Dodge Six, which could be bought for roughly $165 less than DeSoto. In size, its wheelbase compared favorably with DeSoto's 114-3/8 inches, and it averaged 524 pounds less weight. With 75 horsepower, Dodge had a better power-to-weight ratio than DeSoto, therefore snappier performance. Peter DePaolo, the race driver who did much testing and sales promotion for DeSoto, said the SD would hit 85 miles per hour, but acceleration was not boasted.

People in the rumble seat of this Plymouth Model PC Convertible Coupe got a cold ride in the wintertime. This 2,483-pound model was first priced at $595 and given a $30 cut later. The factory turned out 2,034 of them. More PC options were a vacuum-operated automatic clutch, radio, and leather upholstery in convertible and enclosed bodies. A chromed grille was also optional, but the chromed radiator shell was a PC standard for that part.

1933

Shown as standard-equipped with 5.25 x 17 tires on wire wheels is the 4-Door Sedan of the Plymouth Six PC line. The car shown was an early model. The 5-passenger car was the most popular Model PC, and the factory built 33,815 of them. It weighed 2,553 pounds and was priced at $575 before it received a $30 reduction. Only the Convertible Coupe had a higher price, but the 4-Door Sedan was the heaviest. Optional chromed headlamp shells and tail lamp assemblies could have been used on this car, as well as any other PC model.

When the Plymouth PC Six was placed on the market it had a 107-inch wheelbase. Also, forward-mounted spare wheels were not offered. But dealers began to ask for the forward-mounts to add attractiveness to the cars. Since fender wells would not quite allow enough room for front wheel jounce, wheels were moved forward just enough for adequate clearance. That move increased the wheelbase to 108 inches, and the forward spares became available early in January. At about the same time, hood louvers appeared in a vertical attitude, rather than slanted, and similar to those of the succeeding Standard Plymouth PCXX. The car shown had vertical louvers and an accessory trunk as well as the cramped forward spares.

Plymouth's new 6-cylinder engine is shown in a Model PC. The Silver Dome powerplant was an L-head with 3-1/8 x 4-1/8 bore and stroke, displacement of 189.8 cubic inches, and a developed horsepower of 70. With optional Red Head it produced 76 horsepower. New T-slot aluminum alloy pistons had four rings each. A downdraft carburetor was equipped with an air cleaner and intake silencer. The engine rested on Floating Power mounts. Free wheeling and an easy-shift 3-speed transmission complemented the performance. The vacuum-operated automatic clutch actuator is shown at lower right. At upper left is the radiator filler inlet cap. Plymouth was the first Chrysler Corp. car to feature the under-hood location, but it was not continued on succeeding 1933 models. This engine powered 59,604 cars and 396 stripped chassis.

The Model PC 4-Door Sedan is shown in full body color, which was also applied to the radiator shell. A painted shell always had a chrome grille. The full color treatment could be had on any PC model. This car had Goodyear Airwheel tires on artillery wheels that were painted, but chrome could have been had. Wheels were available in 16 and 17-inch sizes, either of wire or artillery type, with the latter made of wood or steel. A natural wood finish was also used on 17-inch wood wheels. For the national automobile shows, Plymouth engaged the nationally-known industrial and stage designer, Henry Dreyfuss, to design the displays and settings.

The PC Plymouth had an attractive wood-grained instrument panel with dials and controls grouped in an oval area of engine-turned finish. The optional glove box was Plymouth's first offering of that convenience. Broadcloth was the standard interior upholstery. 4-Door Sedans had silk braided robe cords on front seat backs, and chrome-plated footrests for rear seat passengers. Front seats of all models were adjustable.

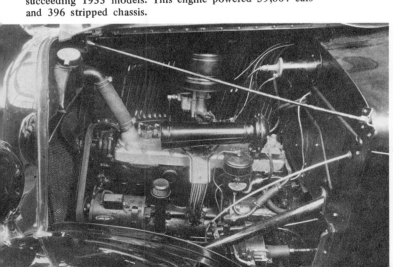

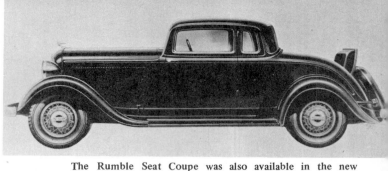

The Standard Plymouth Six, Model PCXX, arrived in the spring to replace the original PC. While it used most of its predecessor's parts, it was stripped of many frills for its role as a complete economy series. The radiator shell and grille assembly was new, as were the headlamps. The shell was painted body color and the grille had a light finish, while black was used for fenders, chassis sheetmetal and lamps. Full color treatment was not available to the public. Unlike the PC, the radiator was filled at the top of the shell. Shown is the basic-equipment filler cap, but the winged version was optional. The 2,353-pound Business Coupe was the lightest-weight Plymouth this year, and at $445 it was the least expensive. 9,200 of these practical cars were built.

1933

The Rumble Seat Coupe was also available in the new Standard Plymouth line. 2,497 of these $485 cars were built. The weight was 2,423 pounds. The Standard Six retained the basic engine and chassis specifications of the last production PC models, including the 70/76 horsepower choice and the 108-inch wheelbase. Standard tires were 5.25 x 17, and on wire wheels only. Airwheel tires with wire or wood wheels were extra-cost. In August, 20-inch wheels and special springs were offered on the Standard. For domestic rural areas and export to undeveloped countries, the special model provided 9.75 inches of road clearance.

Proud of her new Standard Plymouth Six was Ann Lee Doran, a motion picture actress. She is shown in a 4-Door Sedan which, at $510, was the highest-priced Standard model. Weighing 2,523 pounds, it was the heaviest of the economy series. Plymouth produced 13,661 of them. The PCXX chassis was available for special bodies, too. Production records show that 309 unbodied chassis were built. Some PCXX passenger cars were built for the Fargo fleet and export division. As such, they carried the Fargo name and identification in place of Plymouth identity.

Contrary to the usual overwhelming popularity of 4-door models, the 2-Door Sedan drew the most favor in the Standard Plymouth line. It attracted 17,736 sales, cost $465 and weighed 2,443 pounds. The Standard had a more vertical grille than the former PC, but retained the vertical hood louver style used on some PC cars. The radiator shell of the Standard could be ordered in chrome-plate finish. The new headlamps were a cone-like shape rather than the bowl style of before. This model was priced only $15 above the Ford 4 Standard Tudor, $35 under the similar-bodied Ford V-8, and $10 more than the Chevrolet Standard Six Coach. Plymouth had at last attained a competitive price position with the "biggest two."

The new DeLuxe Plymouth Six, Model PD, was an April response to public feeling that the original PC Six was too small. Based on the early 1933 Dodge Six frame, the DeLuxe had a 112-inch wheelbase, which was the same dimension used for the 1932 Plymouth PB. Body shells of the PC were also used for the new PD. The DeLuxe Six Business Coupe was the lightest weight and least costly model of the PD line. It scaled at 2,485 pounds and was priced at $495. The 2-passenger car with utility carrying space in the rear brought a total of 30,728 sales.

The DeLuxe Six was indeed a smart-looking car, an asset that could not have been attained without using the longer chassis. The added length was forward of the windshield, providing a longer hood. Other newness was in the radiator shell/grille assembly, bullet-shape headlamps, front fenders and running board aprons. The Rumble Seat Coupe was factory-priced at $545 and weighed 2,545 pounds. 20,821 of these came off the assembly lines. An accessory spare tire cover of metal is shown. Regular tire size was 5.25 x 17, on wire or wood wheels. Airwheel tires were an extra-cost option.

1933

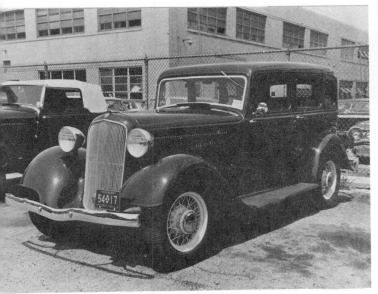

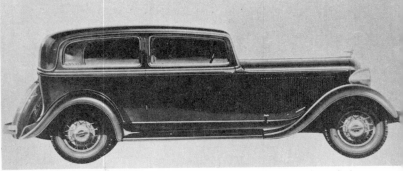

The 2-Door Sedan in the DeLuxe series was listed at $525 and had a weight of 2,560 pounds. It mustered enough sales to require the building of 49,826 of them. The DeLuxe line was powered by the 70/76-horsepower PC engine. An all-silent 3-speed transmission was a new item for the PD. The longer chassis continued the features associated with the PC.

Clearly the most popular model of all 1933 Plymouths, the DeLuxe Six 4-Door Sedan was also the heaviest of all. 88,404 of these 2,645-pound cars were built. They were factory-priced at $575 each. This restored car was at one time owned by Louis De Simone, a Chrysler employee in Highland Park. The bumper used for the DeLuxe series had a slight dip at the center. Headlamps of all DeLuxe cars were chrome-plated. The DeLuxe had a body color radiator shell and chromed grille, but the opposite was optional. Most DeLuxe body colors were accompanied by black fenders, but two light colors included matching fenders.

The DeLuxe Plymouth instrument panel was attractively arranged and finished. The oval center feature included a clock-type speedometer flanked by ammeter, fuel, oil and temperature gauges. The door to the built-in glove compartment is seen on the passenger side, while at the far side a false panel of similar design included the light control knob. Interiors of enclosed models were trimmed in broadcloth or mohair, and added some niceties of appointments to those carried over from the earlier model.

Eleanor Roosevelt, the First Lady, smiled as she sat in her new DeLuxe Plymouth Six Convertible Coupe. It was a car anyone would be pleased with. Plymouth was not a stranger to she and President Franklin D. Roosevelt. This car was equipped with optional forward-mounted spare wheels and metal spare tire covers. Accessory twin trumpets, 5.25 x 17 whitewall tires and body-color fenders added a custom flavor. The folding windshield was a standard feature, but the winged lady filler cap was optional.

The most expensive 1933 Plymouth was the DeLuxe Six Convertible Coupe. The rumble-seated darling was listed at $595. 4,596 of the sporty 2,530-pound convertibles were built. The restored car shown is owned by John Coletti of San Rafael, Calif. It is equipped with twin trumpet horns, and the 6.00 x 16 tires complement the artillery wheels of natural wood finish. The owner painted the belt molding black, and added running board step plates and chrome wheel trim rings as personal touches.

Designed and built by an unknown Italian coachbuilder, this Plymouth was truly a custom-built creation. An original PC Six chassis was stretched to accommodate the sweeping length of line. The long-hood/short-rear package concept, with the severely raked windshield, would be common in the U.S.A. some 35 years later. The roof of the 4-door close-coupled body was exceptionally low. Skirted fenders were already a feature on some American cars, but were not yet adopted by Chrysler Corp.

The DeLuxe Plymouth Six lent itself quite pleasingly to custom bodywork. This Town Car by Derham positively conveyed an impression of class distinction. It appears that Derham tastefully adapted the Briggs town car body used by the Ford Model A. An obvious necessity was a new cowl, and the sill had to be reconstructed. The impression of unusual overall length indicates that the 112-inch wheelbase was stretched a few inches. Plymouth shipped 779 DeLuxe Six chassis which obviously received a variety of special-purpose bodies elsewhere.

The new DeSoto Six, Model SD, had sweeping fender lines and a heavier appearance. It actually was heavier than the previous model, as it was closely related to the Chrysler Six rather than to the Plymouth. The Standard Business Coupe weighed the least of all SD models, scaling 2,905 pounds. It shared the lowest SD price with another model, bearing a factory list figure of $695 at introduction and getting a $30 reduction at mid-year. Only 800 smart Business Coupes were built.

Simply stated, the Standard 2-Door Special Brougham was for those who wanted a 2-door sedan with frills. It borrowed twin trumpet horns, twin windshield wipers, twin tail lamps and a few other extras from the Custom equippage. The Special weighed 3,015 pounds and carried a $725 price tag. Headlamps of the Standard models did not have a vertical divider on the lens surface.

The Standard 2-Door Brougham shared the lowest DeSoto price with the Business Coupe. The 5-passenger car is shown in absolutely basic form. It swung the scale pointer to a reading of 2,995 pounds. DeSoto turned out 2,436 Broughams, including the Special version. The unusual shape of the bumper is especially obvious in this view.

The DeSoto Six Standard 4-Door Sedan ranked higher in demand, weight and cost than any other Standard model. The 5-passenger car totalled 7,890 sales, weighed 3,070 pounds and was priced at $765 until a mid-year price cut of $30. Early Standard cars used 17 x 5.50 tires on wire or wood wheels. All enclosed cars were factory-wired for radio. Early engines of the Model SD delivered 79 horsepower with a Silver Dome head, 86 with a Red Head. The wheelbase of catalogued models was 114-3/8 inches.

Standard DeSotos received many of the Custom features as standard equipment at no extra cost, beginning in June. The items included dual horns, wipers, tail lamps, etc., the same as previously standardized for the Special Brougham, and Airwheel tires on wood wheels became a Standard option. Also among the changes was an increase of horsepower to 82, which also applied to all Customs. The new one-piece fenders, which DeSoto called "Air-Flow" design, were joined at the car's center. The Standard cars seen here had 17 x 5.50 whitewall tires on wire wheels concealed by chrome wheel covers. L.G. Peed, DeSoto general sales manager, was about to apply a sticker as the car moved along the final inspection line in the Plymouth plant, shortly before DeSoto assembly operations were moved to the Chrysler facilities.

1933

Peter De Paolo, the racing driver and wordy DeSoto sales promoter, pondered the Goodyear Airwheel 7.00 x 15 tire on the sturdy artillery wheel. All Custom cars were Airwheel-equipped at no extra cost. A detail that identified the Custom series was the thin vertical divider on the lens surface. Shown is the Custom Coupe with Rumble Seat, which weighed 2,995 pounds and cost $790 before a mid-year reduction to $750. The Standard line also offered this body type, which in that form weighed 2,975 pounds and was priced from $735 down to $705. A total of 2,705 Standard and Custom versions were built. The body design was like that of the Standard Business Coupe.

Actress Dorothy McNulty, who later became Penny Singleton and was "Blondie" in a popular radio and television series, posed with her DeSoto Custom Convertible Coupe. With folded top and open rumble seat, it was a youthful car. In the basic form shown, it weighed 2,990 pounds and was first priced at $845. A severe slash of $70 came when other models were reduced. Overall price cutting, coupled with the upgrading of the Standard line, exemplified DeSoto's desperate attempts to reverse its sagging sales. Production of the Convertible Coupe totalled 412 units. The windshields on all SD convertible types were fixed, non-foldable. Unlike 1932 models, all Plymouths and DeSotos had but one cowl vent and the hood edge was forward of it. The vent on Dorothy's car was open.

All DeSoto Custom Convertible Sedans were fitted with forward-mounted spare wheels and a trunk at the rear as regular equippage included in the price. The model was a 2-door close-coupled type with exceptional smartness. As only 132 were built, it drew the least demand of any SD model. Its unknown weight was probably more than any factory-listed model, but its early price of $975 definitely was the highest figure quoted by its makers. In the later slashing action, it got a whopping $100 cut. President Roosevelt also got one of these, which Chrysler-DeSoto engineers converted to hand-operated controls for the leg-crippled chief executive.

This was the most-wanted Model SD, as the production total of 8,133 indicates. The Custom 4-Door Sedan accommodated five passengers and was priced at $835, which was reduced to $795 at mid-year. Forward-mounted spare wheels and the folding rear trunk rack were extra-cost items. In basic trim, its weight was 3,150 pounds. The interior was of sumptuous design and appointment. Garnish moldings were finished in a rich wood grain, and incorporated an inlaid effect. Door trim panels were fashioned in a square tufted pattern. Seats were upholstered in a luxurious French roll manner. Four ash receivers, mirrors on center door panels and many other niceties made it a car with luxury appeal.

Madam Ernestine Schumann-Heink, famed contralto of grand opera, theater and radio, smiled and waved as she was about to leave her Hollywood home for a ride in a DeSoto Custom 4-Door Sedan. The lovable and matronly woman was adored by hundreds of thousands of people in all levels of life. Through the years, DeSoto enlisted the endorsements of many people who were extraordinarily popular with the public. Stars of the movies, radio and sports were the most effective DeSoto promoters because they appealed to most of the population.

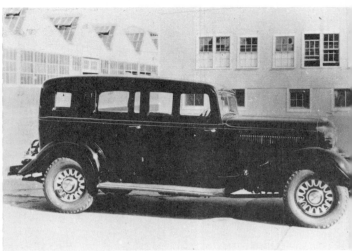

A DeSoto 7-passenger Sedan was not offered to the American public, but 104 of them were built. This example had a right-hand drive for export, but it is uncertain that all were built for export. The regular chassis was stretched, and extra body length was inserted between the windshield and "B" pillars by the use of Brougham doors at the front. This car was fitted in the Custom manner, with a duality of horns, wipers and tail lamps. However, the 6.00 x 17 tires were not according to the domestic Custom practice of Airwheel equipment. With a folding trunk rack at the rear, the spare wheel was carried at the left front side.

The interior of the DeSoto 7-Passenger Sedan was appointed much like the Custom 5-passenger model, but the trim was different. Seats were upholstered in accordance with the domestic Standard pattern, and rear seat armrests were not of the rolled form used in the smaller Custom. The 7-passenger cars were obviously built for a very limited clientele which could not be called a market. Production records list a total of 124 SD chassis shipped. Though of miscellaneous variety, they were not for the long sedan bodies.

The DeSoto Foursome was first shown at the Chicago Auto Show. Stating that it was the first American company to produce this type of body, DeSoto hoped that the innovative car would bring new and needed laurels. The smartly close-coupled sport sedan gave much emphasis to the slogan "DeSoto Sets the Style," but it did not start a trend. The pillarless 4-door car was a prototype based on the Custom chassis, but it did not have an engine. The body was designed and constructed in the coachbuilder's tradition. In profile, the rear swept downward and toward the bumper, resulting in a definite forward-leaning shape. The chassis was cloaked with an apron conforming to the fender sweep from the body to the bumper mounts. The spare wheel reclined in a rakish attitude on top of the apron. Burbank material covered the roof in chic fashion. Seriously intended for production, Foursome bodies were to be exclusively custom-built by an undesignated but well-known custom body-builder, and the automobile's list price was set at $925, with bumpers extra. Though dealers were strongly urged to place orders, nothing came of the effort, and the Foursome never reached production.

Ease of entrance and exit was the main asset of the Foursome, which was said to have startled the industry and thrilled the public. Planned as a 4-passenger personal car with emphasis on sport appeal of the highest class, it featured bucket-type front seats. Interior design was in accord with a motif of simplicity, and in a tailored luxury fashion. Door trim panels were of leather, seats were upholstered with Bedford cord, and overstuffed rear armrests provided armchair comfort.

The DeSoto instrument panel was a beautiful presentation of functional elements. The panel proper was smartly recessed, with the center portion subtly modelled upon it to provide relief for what otherwise would have been a flat panel. The dial cluster, detailed in a hunter's horn theme, was a centerpiece of meticulous design. A glove compartment was built into the right side, and the driver's side only appeared to have one. The panel was finished in a wood grained effect.

Advance publicity was directed to the Airflow principle of aerodynamics· in November when this modified DeSoto Custom was driven backwards from Michigan to New York City. Cruising at road speeds, the purpose of the trip was to dramatize the point that the blunt end of a moving object should face the direction of travel, thereby lessening resistance to the wind. The main benefits were to be realized by less required horsepower and much better fuel economy. Experience with the wrong-way car indicated that an increase of 20% in top speed was possible. The curious car was driven by Harry Hartz, well-known racing driver, who told the author about the car and the trip. To create even more curiosity than its disoriented direction evoked, the vehicle did not bear the DeSoto name or symbolic identity, nor did it give any lettered clue to a builder or sponsor. Wraparound "windshields," twenty years ahead of the industry, were installed in the rear quarters, and driving lights were mounted near the rear bumper. For this scene in New York's Central Park, driver Hartz was stopped and ticketed for going the wrong way on a one-way street. The incident was rigged for publicity coverage by four movie newsreel companies. The press was given demonstration rides around the City and its burroughs, and reported that the car had exceptional acceleration and good roadability. No other claims were made.

Driver Harry Hartz had to reorient himself in addressing the car to a desired direction before going anywhere. All facilities and controls necessary for driving were reversed within the front compartment. Remote controls were linked to the accelerator, clutch, transmission, brakes, etc. Steering linkage was to the normal front wheels, which in this case were behind the driver. Ring and pinion gears in the rear axle were reversed, as was the engine cooling fan. The unbelievable automobile was the work of Aero-Dynamics of New York City, in conjunction with Chrysler Corp. It did indeed alert the public to suspect that someone in the auto industry was about to spring a radical new "streamlined" model.

1933

DeSoto considered various styling and market possibilities, including a few probes in the direction of small cars. This 3-window coupe had a 100-inch wheelbase and was a full-scale wooden mockup. Doors were designed to be interchangeable for right and left side use. The little personal car was intended to have a rumble seat. This was an application of Airflow design principles to a coupe with a deck, a type never offered in any Airflow series. Obviously not planned as a true Airflow type, it retained conventional headlamp and grille design. The hood extended to the bottom of the grille, and the roof was designed to be made of steel. Hubcaps carried the DeSoto name, and DeSoto heavily influenced the headlamps and grille. The hood ornament was a Chrysler gazelle and wings, but that does not mean that the car might have been considered for the Chrysler car line. To make a mockup more complete, stylists often used minor parts from other cars if new parts were not yet made.

Another DeSoto design for an economy car was this 4-door sedan with a neat bustle at the rear. Using the basic concept of the 1932 Trifon Special, it had a more Airflow-like frontal form, but did not concede to recessed headlamps. Slotting of the lower hood surface for cooling was a low-cost substitute for a grille. The wood mockup had a DeSoto hubcap in front, but Chrysler donated one for the rear. This typified the intermix of the small group of designers and craftsmen who worked closely together on programs for four car lines. DeSoto sponsored most Airflow exploration, but it was subject to sharing with other members of the corporate family. Any concept could have become a Dodge or Plymouth, just as the Airflow design was eventually split with Chrysler.

RD-124-B

The body proper of this unpainted wood mockup was not unlike the production version to come, but much work was yet to be done to the mass from the windshield forward. Headlamps had become recessed and acquired oval-shaped lenses, but the front end profile was still not rounded enough. Skirted fenders were not a factor at this point, but fenders and running boards were wider.

By midsummer, the 1934 Airflow design was complete except for minor details. So also was a junior version of it, fashioned in clay as a fastback coupe. The 106-inch wheelbase full-scale model had stacked-rail bumpers propped in position for the picture. The ultimate Airflow shape discarded any semblance of a coupe rear deck, or even a bustle back. Enclosure of the rear wheels had come to be regarded as a necessary complement to the overall design. The Airflow DeSoto already committed for production was a larger car, but exploration of smaller sizes continued. Mr. Chrysler did not stop small car design work, as he believed that engineering and design ideas and effort should not be restricted. However, this year's Plymouth experience had already shown that the best-selling car must be a larger one.

This was a better year nationally, as general business conditions improved and employment rose. Most of the stronger automobile companies enjoyed sales gains, though some of the low-volume producers suffered losses. Most of the losers were so weakened by the depression that they would not last beyond a few more years. Total sales and production would have been even higher if the industry had not been hit by crippling labor strikes. Economic recovery was accompanied by a surging labor union movement to organize workers, who joined by the thousands. Pressure was then exerted on the companies to bring about closed shop agreements, which would guarantee that only union labor would be employed. Understandably, the revolutionary nature of the labor effort met with disapproval and resistance in the front offices of the manufacturers involved. The labor organizing effort did not engulf the industry in one sweeping action. The movement was selective and gradual, and would continue for several more years. Another complication this year was the struggle with the NRA (National Recovery Act) Merit clause. The NRA exercised extensive control over the operations of manufacturers and merchandisers, who conducted a running battle against such stringent action.

For this calendar year, the industry recorded a gain of % in passenger car production. All four Chrysler Corp. divisions held the same positions they had at the end of '33, and all but one of them registered gains. The lone loser was DeSoto, taking a 22% drop on top of last year's minus 31%. Despite its loss, and because of others shuffling about, DeSoto clung to twelfth position. Plymouth's substantial rise of 37% held it in third spot, which was not challenged by Dodge's 19% gain for retention of fourth. The Chrysler Six, which was the only Chrysler that was not an Airflow, accounted for that division's increase of 22% to hold it in tenth place. Plymouth began the year with prices generally higher than 1933. Increased labor and material costs forced prices up again on April 2nd, but they did not stay that high for long. Competitive position combined with restrictive NRA regulations and a new dealer sales agreement to bring June 5th reductions to a compromising level below the April rise. DeSoto prices, reflecting huge tooling costs for the radical new Airflow, were 22% higher than at year-end 1933. This placed DeSoto in a definitely higher price range, where it was stabilized for the year.

The New Year was ushered in with most exciting news from Chrysler Corp. Headlines proclaimed the beginning of a new era of automobile design. The new Airflow Chryslers and Airflow DeSoto had arrived. Publicity did its job, and at the big auto shows they were viewed and examined by many thousands of people. Some regarded them as exciting, and others thought they were curious cars. Many placed orders and wanted immediate or early delivery. In Chrysler's case, few cars came out of the factory before spring, but DeSoto did better by shipping 759 cars by March 1st. The fact was that dealers did not have cars to show or demonstrate at announcement time. The general populace across the nation could not see them for some weeks. DeSotos were built in the Chrysler plant, and unusual construction and assembly methods required by the radical design created many problems in getting both cars under way. Many early orders were cancelled because deliveries were not forthcoming. In addition, some minor mechanical problems developed in early cars already in use. To sum it up, the Airflow cars were not a market success. Less wind resistance, construction design and excellence of engineering were popularly held as commendable. Styling was the main stumbling block to popular acceptance. Most objectionable was front end design, which was regarded as being too rounded in profile and too smooth and unrelieved across the front. The roundness made hoods look too short, and fenders could have been longer. The body proper, defined as from the windshield rearward, was acceptable. Prospective buyers had little understanding of styling, but they had personal tastes and definite preferences. They were accustomed to more prominent front end features, and the Airflow was just too different in that respect.

The Airflow DeSoto, which would continue in production three years, was the most thoroughly different DeSoto in the entire 33-year history of the marque. With explicit faith in salesability of the Airflow, DeSoto offered only the radical car for 1934. That proved to be the wrong thing to do. Chrysler, in placing heavy emphasis on its various Airflow series, left its conventional 6-cylinder model in a relatively obscure corner. Regardless, the common six proved to be Chrysler's 1934 breadwinner, registering more than twice as many sales than its glamorous teammates could muster. DeSoto could have used a conventional companion car.

The Airflow DeSoto, coded as Model SE, was offered as one series only, there being no standard and custom differential. The unique bridge-like frame of the unit body and chassis utilized a 115.5-inch wheelbase. A tubular front

The Standard Plymouth Six, Model PG, was the only Plymouth series with an axle and leaf springs in front. As the economy line, it offered little more than essentials. The Coupe is shown in basic form, including the low-profile radiator top ornament. The 2-passenger car was the lowest-priced Plymouth this year, factory-listed at $485 when prices were stabilized in June. At 2,438 pounds, it weighed the least of all. 7,844 of them were built. Five wire wheels with 5.25 x 17 tires were basic PG equipment. Airwheel tires with wire or steel artillery wheels were a PG extra-cost option. For rural areas, a special 20-inch wheel package providing 9¾ inches of ground clearance could be ordered. Other PG extra-cost choices were chromed headlamp shells and a radiator mascot with the ship in a circle. The low-cost line featured hydraulic brakes and a Rigid-X double-drop chassis frame, as did all other series.

axle was employed, and semi-elliptic front and rear springs with Oilite inserts between the leaves were fitted with covers. The L-head 6-cylinder engine had a bore and stroke of 3-3/8 x 4.5 inches, displaced 241.5 cubic inches, and developed 100 horsepower. The engine was cradled in Floating Power mountings and coupled to an all-silent 3-speed manual-shift transmission. Free wheeling was incorporated as standard, and an automatic clutch was an extra-cost option. The rear axle gear ratio was 4.11 to 1. All mechanical components were of conventional design. The Airflow was only radical in appearance, structure, and placement of the wheelbase in relation to engine and passenger compartments.

Walter P. Chrysler continued to appear in Plymouth advertising, personally extolling its virtues in the manner of a common man talking to the public. Sales boomed, and the 1,000,000th Plymouth was among the 321,171 units that came out of the factories. First to appear were the Plymouth Six and the DeLuxe Plymouth, Models PF and PE, respectively. Formally announced late in January, they were among the first American production cars with independent front wheel suspension, which featured coil springs. Both series were powered by an L-head engine with bore and stroke of 3-1/8 x 4-3/8 inches. Displacement was 201.3 cubic inches, and standard horsepower was 77, with 82 delivered by an optional aluminum head. The radiator filler cap returned to an under-hood location which was not used on the second series 1933 models.

Floating Power mountings were employed, and the tran mission was an all-silent 3-speed type. Wheelbases were t most important of many differences, as the PF Six w based on 108 inches and the DeLuxe PE rode on 1 inches.

The Standard Plymouth Six, Model PG, was added abo April 1st. Answering the need for an economy mod suited to fleet use, rural areas and low-income buyers, borrowed basic specifications and dimensions from the P A major difference was in the use of an I-beam front ax instead of independent suspension. The PG, like the P had a 4.11 to 1 rear axle ratio. Lower-keyed than the F in trim, options and price, the PG served its purpose we Another series added for a special purpose was t Plymouth Special Six. Quickly prepared and placed on t market about June 1st, it enabled Plymouth to boast th the 4-door sedan, having hydraulic brakes and independe front suspension, cost only $5 more than the lowest-pric deluxe 4-door sedan (Ford) available, which didn't ha those important features. Also, it offered some of t DeLuxe items to those who preferred a smaller car at le cost. The Special Six was Model PFXX, which was simpl a PF in fancier dress, and with a Town Sedan added give it more variety of bodies. The Special was the thi series this year to make use of the 108-inch wheelbas which proved to be a salable size when given tasteful bod and hood proportions. The smaller of Chevrolet's tw 1934 series had a wheelbase of 107 inches, as did t corresponding model before it, but Ford stuck to 1 inches for both standard and deluxe models.

This well-restored Standard Six 2-Door Sedan is owned by Robert L. Brake, Thurmont, Md. This view illustrates the new forward lean of the rounder rear quarters. Also seen is the more generous sweep of sheetmetal concealing the chassis and fuel tank, and the rakish angle of the spare wheel. The 5-passenger car weighed 2,538 pounds and was mid-year priced at $510. Plymouth turned out 12,603 of these practical family cars. Though not catalogued or advertised, 62 Standard Six 4-Door Sedans were built. The PG stripped chassis was not in demand for special purposes, as only three were shipped. The PG series was built for anyone who wanted a low-cost car. It served families and business, farmers and mail carriers, fleets and the export market.

Simply known as the Plymouth Six, the Model PF served as the basis from which the PG and PFXX were derived. Body shells, sheetmetal, 77/82 horsepower engine and 108-inch wheelbases were common to all. The PF Six featured coil-sprung independent front wheel suspension, which was not shared with the PG Standard. The new Six was a step above the Standard in class and trim. While more popular with the public, it was also sold to fleets, businesses, etc. The Business Coupe of the Model PF line was cut to $540 in June, making it the lowest-priced of the series. It was the least-heavy PF, weighing 2,513 pounds. 6,980 rolled off the assembly lines.

1934

For those who wanted a bit better 5-passenger 2-door car than the Standard Six, the Plymouth Six 2-Door Sedan was the answer. 12,562 of the 2,603-pound cars were built. Its final list price was $560. Shown is the first of two radiator shell trim versions used on PG, PF and PE cars. At the base of the ship ornament on top, the chrome trim parted and curved toward each side. A triangle of body color emphasized the dividing point.

The Plymouth Six Rumble Seat Coupe rated the least demand of the four models in the PF line. 2,061 of the 2-4 passenger cars were produced. It tipped the scales at 2,573 pounds. Most Plymouth prices were higher than 1933 at the beginning of the model year, and were given a substantial boost in April. In June, they were reduced to a level between the January and April listings, and remained stabilized to the end of the year. The last factory-quoted price of the PF Rumble Seat Coupe was $570.

Heaviest of the PF series was the 2,693-pound 4-Door Sedan. Also, it was the most desirable PF, as shown by its production total of 16,789. As if not yet satisfied, it took more honors as the top dollar PF with a final list price of $600. Additional PF choices at extra cost were Airwheel tires and chromed headlamp shells. Most obvious styling newness of the PF Six and its borrowing brothers was in the pointed grille and skirted fenders. Subtle refinements were the slightly increased slant of the windshield, softer roof contours, modest forward lean of the upper rear quarters, and more rearward sweep of the lower rear sheetmetal. For the mounting of other kinds of bodies, 1,152 Model PF chassis were assembled.

Though Plymouth ceased offering purely open cars to the U.S.A. in 1932, they were continued in certain foreign countries. This Model PF Tourer, shown with detachable weather enclosures in place, is owned by Don B. Main of Victoria, Australia. Except for the body and right-hand drive, the car is like its American counterparts. The body was built by Holden, which manufactured bodies long before it became a foreign subsidiary of General Motors in the 1930's. Under GM, Holden also assembled U. S. and British GM products for the Australian market, and in 1948 began the manufacture of Holden automobiles.

The Special Six series was added in June to round out the Plymouth family. Coded as Model PFXX, it was a PF with fancier fittings. It had the second radiator shell trim, which was a minor change in the grille edge and a tiny chrome peak on top. The Business Coupe, lightest and lowest-priced PFXX, weighed 2,563 pounds and cost $560. One of the 3,721 built took many years to arrive at the home of Bob Prosser, Stone Mountain, Ga., who currently owns it. The Special had many DeLuxe niceties, and at no extra cost. Mr. Prosser's car shows off the valchrome grille, chromed headlamps and twin trumpet horns. Another Special touch seen on the 5-window car is the chrome-plated windshield frame.

An unidentified owner displayed this restored Special Six Rumble Seat Coupe at the annual meet at Hershey, Pa. It is one of 1,746 built. When new, it was priced at $590 and it weighed 2,600 pounds. Visible is the right-side unit of the PFXX dual tail lamp feature. Also regular equipment on the Special series were pressed steel artillery wheels and 5.25 x 17 tires.

1934

The Special Six 2-Door Sedan cost $580 and weighed 2,658 pounds. A total of 12,497 were built. Interiors of PFXX models featured a sun visor of improved design, an ash receiver and glove compartment in the instrument panel, and extra-padded seats upholstered in Bedford cord. All sedans had armrests, two ash receivers and a chromed footrest rail in the rear seating area.

As was usual with other series, the 4-Door Sedan was the most popular of the five Special Six models. The factories turned out 16,760 of the 2,708-pound cars. The desirable family-size car with deluxe appointments was modestly priced at $620. This view illustrates the sculptured character of the belt molding, which was not painted to match the fenders. The Special Six line also included a Town Sedan which rated the lowest PFXX production because only 574 were built. It weighed 2,783 pounds and carried a $655 price tag.

The DeLuxe Plymouth was the largest 1934 series. Excluding previous limited-demand 7-passenger models, it was the largest Plymouth offered up to its time. Its 114-inch wheelbase carried six catalogued models, of which the Business Coupe cost the least, bearing a final list price of $595. The 2-passenger car with a rear storage compartment weighed 2,668 pounds, making it the lightweight of the DeLuxe Model PE line. It rated good demand, as 28,433 were built to fill the orders. All DeLuxe cars had independent front wheel suspension and Airwheel 6.00/16 tires on steel artillery wheels.

DeLuxe

The Rumble Seat Coupe was a fairly popular DeLuxe model, as 15,658 of them were built to meet the demand. Weighing 2,733 pounds, it was last listed at $630. All DeLuxe Coupes had a rear axle ratio of 4.11 to 1. Free wheeling was standard equipment throughout the DeLuxe line, and an automatic clutch could be had at extra cost. Among other options were a radio and dual windshield wipers. Available for all four Plymouth series was Duplate safety window glass.

Of all catalogued DeLuxe models, the Convertible Coupe was at the bottom of the production list, as only 4,482 were built. Basic-equipped, it weighed 2,698 pounds and was final-priced at $685. Shown is a restored example owned by Harry Konieczka of Buffalo, N.Y. All convertibles had a rumble seat and 4.11 to 1 rear axle ratio. Forward-mounted spare wheels were an extra-cost option for any DeLuxe model.

By far the best seller of the DeLuxe series, and of the entire 1934 Plymouth line, the 4-Door Sedan accounted for 108,407 units of this year's total production. The 5-passenger car weighed 2,848 pounds and its list price was $660 from June onward. The 4-door car's ventilation system included pivoting quarter windows. Tail lamp support arms could be had in chrome, as shown. All DeLuxe sedans, 2-door and 4-door, had a rear axle ratio of 4.375 to 1. Plymouth Safety-Steel bodies were so strong that they defied total destruction. They were deliberately subjected to tumbles in demonstrating their structural strength. Cars were given punishing treatment in shows staged by the famous Hell-Drivers, in which well-known race driver Billy Arnold was a star performer. Barney Oldfield, long-time famous endurance and racing driver, also helped to promote Plymouth.

1934

On August 8th, the 1,000,000th Plymouth was driven off a Detroit assembly line by Walter P. Chrysler. The smiling chief of Chrysler Corp. happily shook hands with an executive as he was about to move the DeLuxe 4-Door Sedan out of the way of others to follow. The car was shipped to Chrysler's exhibit at the Century of Progress exposition in Chicago, where it was placed on display. Mrs. Ethel Miller of Turlock, Calif., who purchased the first Plymouth in 1928 and still owned it, wired Mr. Chrysler that she would like the one-millionth car to be reserved for her. He obliged, and she drove the first one to Chicago where it was traded for the milestone car early in September. The earliest Plymouth was then displayed at the exposition.

This restored DeLuxe Plymouth 2-Door Sedan is owned by Jim Benjaminson, Cavalier, N.D. Among other things, this photo shows that the ventilating vane could be lowered with main glass into the door. The new method of ventilation was a standard feature of the DeLuxe series, and was not available for others. With the window in raised position, the vane could be pivoted outward as desired. Also, the main glass could be fully lowered while the vane remained in the window opening. All DeLuxe cars had chromed headlamps of longer bullet shape with a tiny fin on top, and lenses were given a pronounced convex curvature. The DeLuxe hood louver layout was a combination of vertical slots and horizontal doors. Optional at extra cost were the ship radiator mascot, twin trumpet horns, bumper guards and wheel trim rings. As a new car in basic form, the 2-Door Sedan weighed 2,773 pounds and was listed at $610 during the latter half of the model year. Mr. Benjamin's car is one of the 58,535 that came out of the factories.

Plymouth's first official recognition of station wagon possibilities came this year. Wagon bodybuilders had offered their wooden wares on Plymouth chassis before, but the arrangement was with dealers rather than through the Plymouth company. Mr. Chrysler thought the utility body might have a good future potential, and encouraged collaboration with a wagonbuilding firm to adapt the type especially to the Plymouth chassis. The result was the Westchester Suburban on the 114-inch DeLuxe wheelbase. The smart woodcrafted bodies were built and chassis-mounted by the U.S. Body & Forging Co., Tell City, Ind. The 7-passenger body had removable rear seats, plate glass in front doors, and curtains for other openings. The 35 chassis upon which Westchester Suburbans were mounted were part* of the total of 2,362 Model PE chassis assembled.

The DeLuxe Town Sedan, added to the line in April, was the heaviest and most expensive catalogued Plymouth this year. Weighing 2,898 pounds, it was given a $695 price at mid-year. 7,049 of these luxury models were manufactured. The close-coupled 5-passenger 4-door body featured an integral trunk and different tail lamps. Upholstery and certain interior appointments were new, and buyers were given a choice of four body colors. Not catalogued was a DeLuxe 7-passenger Sedan, of which 891 were built. It was probably for special-purpose and export marketing.

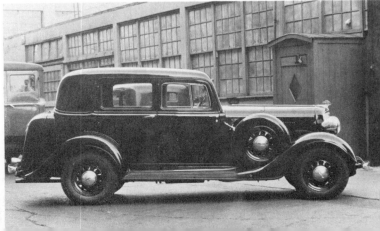

Shown in its native land is a Plymouth PF Roadster owned by Lester Cole of Victoria, Australia. The restored car has a body by Holden, as Chrysler did not have facilities for production of this type in the land "down under." Neither the Roadster nor the Tourer had windshields that would fold. According to the step on the rear fender, this car has a rumble seat. Detachable weather enclosures are necessary, since Australia has seasons similar to the U.S.A., though reversed in relation to the calendar.

1934

To satisfy an ambition to be the first cyclist to hit 300 miles an hour, Fred Luther, a Chrysler employee in California, built this Plymouth-powered supercycle in 1934. The next year he took it to the Bonneville salt falts where Sir Malcolm Campbell had just hit 300 in his fantastic Bluebird. Luther was clocked at 140 on his first one-way run, and in the return a rod busted when he reached 180 in second gear. That ended the record attempt, but Luther was satisfied that the machine could hit 300 if anyone was willing to ride it at wide-open throttle. Lying on his belly, Luther was smacked by terrific wind pressure, but he averaged 160.33 for the two-way trial. A cycle racer for Indian and Henderson, Luther was provided with a Plymouth PF engine and transmission by the factory. Engine horsepower was increased from 77 to a whopping 125 at 4,500 r.p.m. when tested in the shop of famed race car builder Harry Miller. It was fitted with three radiators and electric starting. Luther built the bike, starting by reworking the frame of a Henderson X. Remote steering was by chain mockup, braking was by skid shoes applied to the ground, and tires were special 8-ply 30 x 5. The completed machine was 130 inches long, weighed 1,500 pounds and cost about $3,000.

The revolutionary Airflow DeSoto was more often shown with streamlined trains than with airplanes. This model was first called the 2-Door 5-Passenger Coupe, but later was advertised as the 3-Passenger Coupe with enclosed rumble seats. The latter designation did not seem appropriate. Regardless of the name, its 3,323-pound weight was the same as another model, which shared a distinction as the least-heavy Airflows. All Airflow models were factory-priced at $995. 1,584 Coupes came out of the Chrysler plants.

The Airflow DeSoto Coupe was a true fastback, made sleek at the rear by enclosing the spare wheel in the rear compartment. This was one of the first production fastbacks in the industry. Though a businesslike version of the 1934 Airflow Coupe is not on record, it is obvious that the potential was investigated. Logically, the ultramodern car would attract attention to itself and to the product it advertised. Perhaps it was adapted to commercial use by omitting the "enclosed rumble seats" so as to utilize that area for carrying merchandise, sample cases, luggage, etc. In normal form as a 5-passenger car, the Coupe had two rear seats. They were hinged to the body sides, and could be folded against them or completely removed from the car. Airflow bodies were exceptionally wide, and the front seat of all bodies accommodated three adults. This was the beginning of the trend to 3-passenger front seats, which brought about 6-passenger sedans as normal.

DeSoto changed the name of this model, too. First known as the 2-Door 6-Passenger Sedan, it soon became the 2-Door 6-Passenger Brougham. Its weight and price were the same as given for the Coupe. Only 522 of these were built. The car shown was a pre-production sample, operational in every respect, and like the production counterpart except for the lack of proper ornamental detail on the rear fender shield. To the purchaser, the shields were an extra-cost option, but it is doubtful that any Airflow was without them. The 2-Door Brougham had a full-size rear seat and adequate rear headroom, which required that the roof not slope as gradually as that of the Coupe. Accordingly, this body had more expansive side windows for rear seat passengers. The spare wheel was carried on the rear of the body, and access to the luggage compartment was by means of raising the rear seat. This awkward and inconvenient process was required in other Airflow sedans.

Byron C. Foy, president of DeSoto Motor Corp. and son-in-law of Walter P. Chrysler, posed with the Airflow DeSoto 4-Door 6-Passenger Sedan. The scene was the Chrysler exhibit at Chicago's Century of Progress exposition, which was in its second and last year as what was popularly called a "world's fair." The modernistic building bears the name "Chrysler Motors," which was proper throughout the early 'Thirties. The $995 4-Door Sedan ranked as the most popular and heaviest Airflow, as 11,713 of the 3,378-pound cars were built. This model was fitted with five disc wheels. Forward-mounting of spare wheels could not be done on Airflows, as the fenders were too near the doors. Aesthetically, they would have been grossly unattractive and opposed to Airflow design. In contrast to conventional layout, the Model SE wheelbase was shifted 20 inches toward the rear, which placed the engine directly above the front axle instead of behind it, and the rear seat ahead of the rear axle rather than above it. The new distribution of weight combined with extra-long leaf springs to give what DeSoto called a "Floating Ride."

1934

The Airflow Town Sedan was the 6-window sedan body with blind quarters. Since only 119 were built, it was the least popular Model SE. The $995 car weighed 3,343 pounds. The illustrated car was a pre-production sample with improper decor on the rear fender shield, and the white-painted "DeSoto" on the hubcap was incorrect. The frontal roundness, coupled with the well-forward placement of the engine, necessitated a low radiator core. The recessed headlamps, also new to mass-production cars, were consistent with Airflow design. While boasting of its many new advanced features, most of which were of major importance, DeSoto also praised the styling leadership of the Airflow. In Europe, its aerodynamic styling won the coveted Grand Prix award in the Concours d'Elegance at Monte Carlo.

The structure of the unit body/frame of the Airflow was described as similar to a girder-trussed bridge. The mass was positioned well forward on the 115.5-inch wheelbase, centering the 100-horsepower engine over the front axle and placing the rear seat ahead of the rear axle. The hood assembly, which included the grille, provided engine access from the top and front only. To facilitate engine adjustments from the sides, removable front wheel housing panels were provided. The steering drag link was ahead of the axle, the column was fully adjustable, and the steering wheel attitude was more vertical than usual. The gearshift lever was in normal floor position, but the parking brake handle projected from the firewall near the body center and below the instrument panel. The interior was in keeping with the advanced nature of the Airflow. Upholstery utilized a Frieze material, a first for any car, and the headlining was washable.

Maybe these unidentified Hollywood movie people were wondering which way to go, or whether to go at all. With gasoline at 10.5 cents a gallon, the Airflow DeSoto could have taken them to San Francisco for $2.00. The car was capable of getting as many as 21.4 miles out of a gallon of fuel. The plain-tube downdraft carburetor was augmented by an automatic choke and an automatic manifold heat control. All Airflows had a rear axle ratio of 4.11 to 1. The car shown had its ventilating windshields open. They were individually crank-operated.

The Airflow was suitable as a taxicab, though DeSoto did not indicate that any were specially prepared for that particular kind of service. Outwardly, this car was a regular 4-door sedan except for the signs and a lamp above the windshield which had the Hills name on its lens. On that warm day the twin cowl vents were open and the rear quarter window was pivoted outward. The Airflow had a window ventilation system like the DeLuxe Plymouth. Steel artillery wheels and the disc type were available at no cost difference. Airwheel tires were 6.50 x 16 in both cases. DeSoto did not join the beginning trend to independent front wheel suspension, but it was not alone. Of 30 car makes listed, 19 employed the front axle exclusively, 6 had i.f.s. only, and 5 used both.

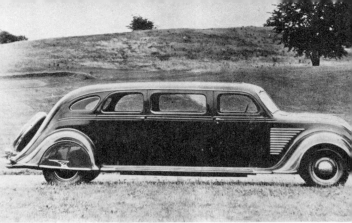

Muroc Dry Lake, near the Mojave Desert in California, was the scene of some record smashing by Airflow DeSotos. 32 new AAA speed marks were established by two cars. A Coupe set a new class record of 86.23 miles an hour for five miles. Breaking every stock closed car record in its class, a 4-Door Sedan averaged 86.2 miles per hour for one mile, 80.9 for 100 miles, 76.2 for 500 miles, and 74.7 for a 2,000-mile stretch. The cars were equipped with Goodyear G3 tires. Racing driver Harry Hartz, shown in the sedan, set an economy record in a cross-country trip from New York City to San Francisco. The sedan averaged 21.4 miles per gallon on the 3,114-mile journey, and the total fuel cost was only $33.06.

1934

The bridge-like frame and unit body construction of the Airflow discouraged custom body modifications and adaptation to special-purpose vehicles, especially if a longer wheelbase was essential. Regardless, the Knightstown Body Co., Knightstown, Ind., ambitiously converted a stock 4-door sedan to the extra-capacity needs of Frank Stanley, a funeral director in New Castle, Ind. The car was bisected at the "B" pillar and some 40 inches of framework and panels were fixed in midship position. The stretch job resulted in a wheelbase of 156 inches. Reinforcing understructure was lower than the long running board. Though the Airflow did not have a chassis in the normal sense, production records show that two chassis were assembled and shipped.

Chrysler Corp. was keeping itself prepared for any possible market demand for much smaller cars than were in production. In fact, the programs were directed to smaller cars than Chrysler had ever built. The basic design theme was based on the Airflow concept, which was revised to remove weight and production cost. The stylist's sketch proposed a Plymouth of about 100-inch wheelbase, which conceded that a more prominent hood and conventional grille attitude were needed for the Airflow body. Headlamps were behind the grille, and trailing ends of fenders were contoured under instead of curving toward the rear. Running boards were considered unnecessary as well as a cost penalty.

In looking for better fuel economy and other advantages through even less wind resistance, DeSoto superimposed new front and rear shapes on a stock 4-door sedan for testing. The sedan windshield and cowl can be seen behind the new panoramic panes, which extended forward so far that the hood surface was quite short. A small hatch provided reach-in room for servicing the engine. Headlamps were behind the upper portion of the grille, but holes in the fenders indicate that conventional lamps were sometimes mounted. Sheetmetal was wrapped under the front and extended to the rear, smoothly enclosing much of the vehicle's undersides in a belly sheath. The prow-like nose was found to be aerodynamically acceptable, and it would moderately influence succeeding Airflow design. When this vehicle was built, Chrysler already knew that the rounded front of the production Airflow was not popular with the public.

This clay proposal in full-size dimensions retained the Airflow roundness in front-end profile but gave more pleasing contours to the rear. Doors were to be hinged on the "B" pillar rather than latching to it. Fender skirts were snugly contoured under, and running boards were omitted. Headlamps were slightly projected, and the spare wheel was to be stored behind the rear seat. A part of DeSoto's program, the clay compact had a 100-inch wheelbase.

The automobile industry marched on with a faster
cadence, paced by the snappy music of a better business
wind. The snarls of NRA controls were straightened out
and almost all manufacturers scored higher sales and
production marks. By the end of this calendar year,
industry passenger car production was more than 49%
above 1934. Ford zoomed past Chevrolet to take first
place, squashing the GM division into second spot for the
first time since 1930. Plymouth climbed almost 26% and
held its third rank, which it now had for five years. Dodge
chalked up a huge gain of nearly 95%, holding fourth
place for three years in a row. Chrysler cars picked up
more than 35% and retained tenth position for the third
successive year. Thanks to its new Airflow models,
DeSoto was the star gainer of Chrysler Corp., registering
a fantastic increase of well over 116%. However, DeSoto
dropped a notch into thirteenth position because of
Packard's rise from sixteenth to ninth place on the wings
of its new Series 120. In total, Chrysler Corp. fared 44%
better than the year before.

By midyear, Chrysler was tooling a plant in Evansville,
Ind., to serve as a Plymouth branch assembly facility.
Adding it to the Detroit and Los Angeles operations
provided Plymouth with substantial production capacity.
The growing prosperity and the increasing popularity of
Plymouth would need the vast manufacturing capabilities.
The Chrysler factories in Detroit continued to turn out
DeSotos.

The big news was the addition of the new DeSoto
Airstream series. It was engendered as soon as the 1934
Airflow showed signs of not bearing the DeSoto banner
very well. The same Airflow disappointment happened in
the Chrysler Division, but the conventional 6-cylinder
model kept business strong. DeSoto took a cue from that

performance and came up with a copycat program. The
Airflow would be continued with a commonplace companion for support. The DeSoto Airstream was put
together with parts already developed for Plymouth, Dodge
and Airstream Chryslers. DeSoto styling distinction was
designed into the grille, hood louvers, interiors and
decorative details. The 116-inch wheelbase was the same
as Dodge, and the chassis frame was much like Dodge,
differing mainly at the front end for accommodation of
DeSoto's first use of independent wheel suspension.
The engine was the same as used for the Airflow, adapted
to the new chassis and sitting on Floating Power

Contrary to the usual rank as the most-demanded model of a
series, the Business 4-Door Sedan rated as the third-best
seller, with 15,761 built. Shown is the hood louver treatment
common to most Business series cars. The five rings that
were a "trademark" of most PJ models were omitted,
retaining only the three horizontal moldings. The ship-in-a-
ring ornament atop the radiator shell was an extra-cost
option available for all Business cars, as were the bumper
guards. A single front fender-mounted spare wheel was
an extra-cost availability for sedans and coupes, which had a
built-in radio antenna as standard at no cost difference. The
Business 4-Door Sedan weighed 2,720 pounds and cost $570,
which was the highest price of the three enclosed models.

Awaiting shipment to "Uncle Sam," part of a fleet of
Business 4-Door Sedans built for the U.S. Government is
seen in the Plymouth factory yard. They were consigned to
the Tennessee Valley Authority, created in 1933 to harness
the Tennessee River for hydroelectric power. All Business cars
had 5.25 x 17 tires as standard equipment, but 20-inch disc
wheels were available on special order. The latter provided
9-7/8 inches of road clearance, and cars built with them also
had a special rear axle ratio of 4.375 to 1. The standard
ratio was 4.125 to 1. The utilitarian Business series lacked
some minor mechanical features included in higher-priced
Plymouths.

A new Business series was added to the Plymouth line in
March. Somewhat austere in trim and equipment, this version
of the Model PJ was directed at the fleet and economy
market. Its 6-cylinder 82-horsepower engine and 113-inch
wheelbase were the same as all other PJ models had. It was
simply known as the Plymouth Business line. The Coupe was
the lightest-weight and lowest-priced of the line, and of all
Plymouths this year. The 2-passenger car weighed 2,526
pounds and was factory-priced at $510. 16,691 of them were
built. The simple ornament on top of the radiator shell was a
standard item on all models of the Business line. The black-
painted grille, headlamp shells and fenders were common to
all, regardless of body colors. Among the cars in the
background is a Business 2-Door Sedan, seen above the
coupe's radiator. The 5-passenger 2-door was the most
popular of the Business line, as 29,942 of the 2,670-pound
$535 cars were built. Business line models were added at
various times over a 30-day period.

mountings. Prices were sandwiched between Dodge and the Airstream Chrysler Six. This year's Airflow DeSoto was a facelifted version which retained basic specifications of the former model but dropped free wheeling and added an overdrive unit as optional. A 2-door sedan did not appear in the new line, but a business coupe was a new addition. Weights of the Airflow Model SG were slightly heavier and factory prices were $200 higher at first, but were reduced to only $20 more on February 7th.

Plymouth was an all-new design which shared basic styling and weight distribution principles with Dodge and the Airstreamsof DeSoto and Chrysler. One chassis served as the basis for the three Plymouth series, which were all coded as Model PJ. The new 113-inch wheelbase chassis did not feature independent front wheel suspension,

utilizing a tubular front axle and leaf springs with a so ride quality. The L-head 6-cylinder engine had the sar bore and stroke as 1934, but a new cylinder he increased horsepower. Among other features was calit rated ignition, a vacuum spark control which permitt advance to point of maximum economy without "ping Water circulation through the block was so directed as cool exhaust valve seats and the entire length of cylind walls. The powerplant was cradled in Floating Pow fashion.

Ride quality of the Plymouth was given the nar "Floating Ride." Semi-elliptic leaf springs at front and re were made of a new steel. Approximately the same weig was carried by each spring, and each had the sar frequency. Sidesway was reduced by a new torsion b across the front, below the springs. Weights of t 113-inch models averaged about the same as the 19. Plymouths, but factory prices were a bit higher. Plymou returned to catalogued 7-passenger cars this year, t first since the 1932 Model PB. The long body type w not included in the catalogued domestic line.

Plymouth this year took a deeper interest in vehicles for light commercial use. The Commercial Sedan in the Business series was a dual-purpose car that looked like the 2-Door Sedan except when the rear end could be seen. For family use, it had a 5-passenger interior of normal 2-door layout. When used commercially, the rear seat was removed and floor boards provided a level floor space of more than 18 square feet. The cargo area measured 40.5 inches from floor to headliner. Advertising panels were snap-fitted inside the rear side windows, serving also to protect the glass. The rear door dimensions were 34.5 by 42.5 inches. This model was painted solid black only, and carried the spare wheel at the right front as a standard feature. The dual-function car utilized the PJ 113-inch chassis, weighed 2,735 pounds and cost $635. The production total was 1,142.

The middle Plymouth series was comprised of only two body types, which hardly qualified it to be a series. But its trim, mechanical details and prices placed it between the low-line Business and high-line DeLuxe series, thereby giving it a slightly different caste than either of the other two. Formally announced with the DeLuxe line near the first of the year, it was the level from which the Business line began to descend two months later. Advertised simply as the "Plymouth," the factory called it the "Plymouth Six." The "Six" was one of the Model PJ "three." Easiest sight identification of the Six was afforded by the combination of 5-ringed hood louvers and painted headlamps. The grille, headlamps and fenders were in black. Windshield frames were generally in chrome. The PJ Six Business Coupe (not to be confused with the Business car line) cost $565 and weighed 2,665 pounds. 6,664 of them were built.

The Westchester Suburban body was again built by the U.S. Body & Forging Co., Tell City, Ind., and mounted on a slightly modified 113-inch chassis. According to production records, 119 of the wood-crafted cars were turned out, and only in the Business series. The example shown had a chromed windshield frame and a hood with side rings, not usually seen on the economy cars, but serving to dress up this handsome model. The 4-door vehicle could carry up to eight passengers, and rear seats were removable for carrying cargo. Station wagons were classified as commercial vehicles. Heavy duty front and rear springs, as well as the fender-mounted spare wheel, were standard equippage. The $415 chassis and $350 body added up to a $765 list price, making this the most expensive model in the entire PJ 113-inch series.

1935

The DeLuxe series of the Model PJ was the top-line Plymouth, with more attractions than the others. All DeLuxe models for 5 passengers or less were built on the 113-inch chassis. Shown is the DeLuxe Business Coupe, which was a 2-passenger car with luggage space in the rear. Placed in production in February, it accounted for 29,190 units built. It weighed 2,675 pounds, which was the least of any DeLuxe, and its $575 price made it the lowest-cost model of the series. The DeLuxe tire size was 6.00 x 16, and there was no wheel and tire option. Some of the options for all DeLuxe cars were a metal spare tire cover and lock, dual trumpet horns, dual tail lamps and dual windshield wipers.

The Plymouth Six had the same 82-horsepower engine and 113-inch wheelbase as the other two series. The car is shown with the 20-inch wheel option. Other extras, not all of which were available for its low-line companion, were twin trumpet horns, twin tail lamps, chromed headlamps, two forward-mounted spare wheels (not for 20-inch), Duplate safety window glass, mohair upholstery and Philco Transitone radio. With no options, the 2-Door Sedan was priced at $615 and weighed 2,670 pounds. The factories turned out 7,284 of these models. With 20-inch wheels, rear axle ratio was 4.375 to 1.

The Plymouth DeLuxe Rumble Seat Coupe was a 2,730-pound car with a $630 price tag. 12,118 rolled off the assembly lines. Side-mounted spare wheels were not included in the basics. The DeLuxe line offered some body colors which included matching fenders. Other colors could be ordered with fenders to match, but otherwise the fenders were painted black. All DeLuxe cars had Duplate safety glass windshields as standard, but it could be ordered for all windows as well.

The convertible body had its own X-braced frame which combined with like members of the chassis frame to eliminate twisting. The rumble-seated car entered production about April 1st, just as the warm weather season was beginning. The start-up of convertible assemblies at that time of the year was normal for most automakers. The DeLuxe Convertible Coupe weighed 2,810 pounds, cost $695 and marked up a production total of 2,308. All DeLuxe models had chromed headlamp shells and the hood louver treatment shown. They were standard ornamentation for the line. The ornament atop the radiator was optional at $3.50 extra, but no DeLuxe cars were built without one. Bumpers, bumper guards, spare tire and tube were extra-cost items for all three PJ series.

Assemblies of the DeLuxe 2-Door Sedan were begun in February. Production delay was not always for seasonal reasons, but a less popular body type was sometimes held up while initial manufacturing was devoted to the models most in demand. This model rated in the low-demand category. The 5-passenger car weighed 2,720 pounds and was priced at $625. Demand required the building of 12,424 of them. The trunkless model was found to be useful in promoting safety. Plymouth boasted of safety engineering, and it was appropriate that the Detroit Police Dept. got a fleet of them for use in its Public Safety Education program. The specially painted cars carried huge rooftop loudspeakers as part of their equipment.

A new trend to integral trunks was joined by Plymouth, who called this the DeLuxe 2-Door Touring Sedan. It was a popular model, as the production of 45,203 indicates. The price of the 2,780-pound car was $650. The rear quarters were a few inches more forward than those of the 2-Door Sedan, shortening rear passenger legroom, but necessary to accommodate the trunk within the car's length. The trunk door extended down to the bumper, affording liberal and convenient access. The spare wheel rested on the trunk floor under a luggage shelf. The body accommodated five passengers. This view illustrates the new "packaging" concept adopted for the PJ series. Compared to former practice, the engine was moved forward eight inches and the major body load was shoved ahead six inches. This resulted in a weight distribution which gave better ride qualities and other advantages. Though the forward movement was a spin-off from Airflow principles, the PJ did not incorporate Airflow unit body construction, but was of body-on-chassis design.

1935

The Plymouth DeLuxe 4-Door Sedan was a 5-passenger car weighing 2,790 pounds and priced at $660. The production lines rolled out 66,083 of them. All coupes and sedans had broadcloth interior upholstery unless optional mohair was chosen. A right-side visor was also available. Philco Transitone radio was an all-model option, but only enclosed bodies were factory-wired for it. An accessory add-on trunk was available for sedans, which increased rear overhang somewhat, especially if the spare wheel was mounted behind it.

Plymouth returned to the field of larger cars in April, offering two models on a 128-inch wheelbase. Powered by the 82-horsepower engine, they were primarily designed for export but were also made available to the American market. The DeLuxe 7-Passenger Sedan weighed 3,130 pounds, which probably was the heaviest Plymouth this year. It and the Traveler shared honors as the most costly PJ models, being priced at $895. 350 of the 7-passenger sedans were built.

The long-wheelbase DeLuxe Traveler Sedan was a 5-passenger car with a trunk. The rear quarters and integral trunk were patterned after the shorter touring sedans. This model was first known as the Voyager, but by production time that name was sunk. The Traveler drew the least demand of all PJ models, as only 77 were built. Though it is not illustrated with chromed headlamps, it was a DeLuxe model. Standard 6.00 x 16 tires were specified for both of the lengthy cars. Both models had interiors of the design used in the smaller DeLuxe sedans. Plymouth expected these big cars to appeal to morticians, taxicab companies, etc. Only 24 DeLuxe chassis, of undesignated length, were assembled. Apparently they were not in much demand for special bodies.

The DeLuxe 4-Door Touring Sedan was unchallenged as the most winsome Plymouth model this year, recording a total of 82,068 built. The 2,815-pound car attracted buyers with its $685 price tag. Like the 2-door counterpart, the rear passenger compartment was shortened because of the integral trunk which normally housed a spare wheel and luggage. Regardless, it was a 5-passenger car. Optional side-mounted spare wheels permitted use of the entire trunk for carrying miscellaneous items. The sidemounts could be ordered for both front fenders. When other than touring sedans were built with sidemounts, a folding trunk rack was included at the rear. All PJ models had one cowl vent and a windshield that could be cranked open. Gone was the window ventilating system of 1934. Instead, fully-raised front windows could be moved three inches rearward by a fraction-turn of the regulator crank, providing a narrow opening for drawing inside air to be expelled. This was augmented by ventilators at the base of the front seat.

Plymouth did not record any taxicabs built this year, but some of the 7-passenger sedans were apparently fitted for that purpose. These vehicles had larger tires than the 6.00 x 16 size prescribed for the big sedan. They are shown at the moment Plymouth turned them over to the cab company. Not much cab business would be done by Plymouth until 1937.

A poster in the rear door window boasted "Plymouth — the High-Speed Safety Car." For chasing dangerous criminals of the gangster era, the Perfection Windshield Co., Indianapolis, Ind., specialized in the armoring of cars. The car shown had a gun port in the windshield which, like the angled sidewings, had bullet-resisting glass. Closely meshed heavy screening protected the radiator, and armor plates guarded the front tires. Lightweight bullet-resisting steel innerlined the body and protected the fuel tank. The glass and armor would stop 45-caliber submachine gun bullets. Some cars had more gun ports. Over 200 police departments had Plymouths, and armored car demand was growing.

1935

Quite adaptable for the purpose, a Plymouth engine powered the "Plymacoupe" airplane. Chrysler's Amplex Division collaborated with the Fahlin Aircraft Co., Marshall, Mo., who built the 2-place dual-control monoplane. The craft weighed 1,078 pounds dry, and was planned to sell at a lower price than the average plane of its day. Whether it was placed in production is not known, but first informative news releases brought more than 4,500 inquiries. The 82-horsepower engine gave a weight/power ratio of about 5 to 1. The plane cruised at 100 miles per hour and reached a maximum speed of 120. Fuel consumption averaged 25 miles per gallon in flight. Some minor automotive parts were used in the plane's construction, and the cockpit had a Plymouth instrument panel with aircraft instrumentation. Interior furnishings were as similar to a car as airplane limitations permitted. Plymouth hood rings decorated the engine side cowling.

The Plymouth engine was selected for aircraft use because its full-length water jackets and full-pressure lubrication insured perfect operating conditions at sustained high speed. It was said that only minimum changes were necessary for conversion. The flywheel, electrical fittings and cooling fan were removed. An aircraft magneto, updraft carburetor and sheetmetal exhaust manifold were installed. An aluminum cylinder head was used to reduce weight and give 7 to 1 compression ratio. A reduction gear of 2 to 1 ratio was driven directly off the crankshaft and lubricated under pressure from the engine, spinning the propeller to a maximum of 1,800 revolutions per minute. The U.S. Bureau of Air Commerce, whose tests were only half as severe as the manufacturer's, approved the engine's performance and ordered one of the planes for its own use.

Wheelchair invalids could also enjoy a Plymouth ride. Bohman & Schwartz, well-known custom craftsmen in Pasadena, Calif., built this conversion. The seat, which was upholstered to match the interior, had six wheels, two of them fixed for sidewise movement. In car position, the seat rested in recessed tracks and was secured to the floor by hasps. For removal, U-section aluminum channel-ramps were connected to the tracks. The invalid accommodation required removal of the body "B" pillar and some reinforcement of body structure.

Plymouth quit building roadsters and touring cars in the U.S.A. in 1932, but they were continued in some foreign lands. This restored PJ roadster is owned by Ellis A. Baron, Victoria, Australia, who also owns a PJ tourer and a 1934 roadster in unrestored state. The body of the car shown was built by T.J. Richards & Sons, a Chrysler division in Australia. The Richards company began as carriage builders in 1885. When new, the car was shipped to Africa, and was returned to Australia at the outbreak of World War II.

Another interesting Plymouth that was built "down under" is shown in this recent photograph. It is owned by John Schuurman, Victoria, Australia. The commercial vehicle was a Coupe-Utility, which in Australian parlance is generally called a Coupe-Ute. In the U.S., this type is known simply as a pick-up. This vehicle appears to have utilized the DeLuxe chassis. The Ute box was well-integrated with the cab, merely extending the cab contours in a flush manner from the doors back. Even the creased beltline continued completely around the box.

1935

The Briggs Mfg. Co., a major supplier of bodies to Chrysler Corp., created this proposal for a 100-inch wheelbase Plymouth. Projected as a 1935 model, it was a wooden model built to full scale in 1933. The design had Airflow-like roundness in the hood, and the blending of the front fender into the door would be picked up by Chrysler in 1946. A severely angled windshield and absence of running boards were other features. The mockup had no interior fittings.

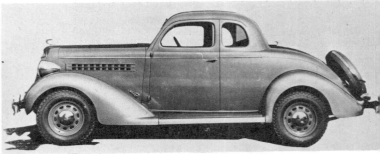

This view shows that the Airstream DeSoto, like Plymouth, located the grille, hood and passengers well forward in relation to the wheelbase. The new distribution of weight, combined with softer rear leaf springs and DeSoto's first use of independent front wheel suspension, gave a "Floating Ride" quality. Unlike Airflow unit construction, Airstream bodies were built separately, then mounted on the 116-inch wheelbase chassis. The Rumble Seat Coupe had a rear window which could be lowered to allow conversation with the outside passengers. It weighed 2,925 pounds, was priced at $760, and accounted for 900 units of total production.

The conventional styling of the new Airstream DeSoto was more acceptable to the public. Its slim and graceful grille combined with a high and lengthy hood to give it an impressive appearance. Chromed bullet-shaped headlamps perched upon struts on the catwalks. Fenders were long and generously contoured, their crowns curving toward the ground instead of trailing off toward the rear. Narrower bodies than the Airflow enhanced the overall image. The flat one-piece windshield of Duplate safety glass was pleasingly slanted. Those features, with exception of a slightly shorter hood and front fenders, also apply to the Plymouth. The Airstream series, Model SF, had seven body types, of which the Business Coupe was the lowest priced and lightest in weight. The 2-passenger car was factory-listed at $695 and weighed 2,840 pounds. 1,760 of them were built.

The Airstream DeSoto 2-Door Sedan was a 5-passenger model weighing 2,915 pounds and priced at $745. 1,350 of these cars were built. Airstream cars had the same kind of interior ventilation system as employed by Plymouth, which discarded "butterfly wings" in favor of a sliding front window glass. The engine of the Airstream series was an L-head 6-cylinder of 3-3/8 inches bore and 4.5 inches stroke. With a cast iron cylinder head and compression ratio of 6.0 to 1, 93 brake horsepower was developed. It was suspended by Floating Power mountings. The Syncro-Silent transmission was a 3-speed unit featuring quiet helical gears throughout.

Not in the line when the Model SF was announced at the first of the year, the Airstream Convertible Coupe was added in April. This body had a foundation X-braced frame of its own, further reinforced by crosswise members through the X. When this body was mounted on the chassis, its X-type bracing was directly upon like members of the chassis frame, providing rigidity needed to eliminate twisting action previously common to convertibles. This model included a rumble seat and a choice of Bedford cord or leather interior upholstery. It was the least-demanded Airstream, requiring production of only 226. But it was the highest-priced SF model, listing at $835. Weight was recorded as 3,035 pounds. The Airflow DeSoto never had a convertible body because engineers felt that framework through the upper structure was necessary to unit body construction. Also, an Airflow convertible with the top down would not have conformed to the prescribed Airflow "streamlined" shape.

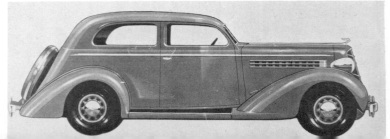

Trunks of the Airstream DeSoto were integral, designed to conform to the shape of the body. They were definitely superior to the storage space of trunkless sedans, which was between the rear seat and the rear body panel. The trunk provided for luggage on a shelf above the spare wheel, which laid flat on a track for easy removal. The trunk door opened from the lower body by means of unlocking two latches. Cars with optional front fender-mounted spare wheels left the entire trunk for luggage, in which case a shelf was not included. The 2-Door Touring Sedan was a 5-passenger car of 2,960 pounds weight. Priced at $775, it drew enough demand to require a production of 2,035.

1935

The rear quarter view of the Airstream 4-Door Sedan shows smooth contours and simplicity of design. This model cost $795 and weighed 2,990 pounds. 5,714 of these 5-passenger cars were built. All Model SF cars were equipped with pressed steel spoke wheels fitted with Airwheel 6.25/16 tires. The metal spare wheel cover was an extra-cost option. Among numerous other SF options were Duplate safety window glass, bumpers, bumper guards, and a radio. It can be noted that there was no hinged rear body panel to allow access to the luggage compartment of trunkless sedans.

Upper rear quarters of all trunk sedans were shorter than those of the trunkless variety, a fact not effectively illustrated by catalog artwork. The shortness moved the rear seat forward, and was necessary in order to provide spare wheel storage and not have a long body overhang. The Airstream DeSoto 4-Door Touring Sedan had 5-passenger capacity and, at 3,085 pounds, was the heaviest of the series. It was also the costliest and most popular SF, being priced at $825 and registering 8,018 units on the production records. SF enclosed body interiors offered a choice of Bedford cord or mohair upholstery. Another SF feature was the matching of colors on the body, fenders, wheels, etc., giving the cars a monotone effect. Special body colors could be had on special order.

This fleet of Airstream DeSotos was built for the Yellow Cab Co. They were 4-door sedans, specially painted and fitted according to cab company requirements. Interiors incorporated a partition and cab practicalities. Exteriors got special treatment in addition to the usual taxicab lights and signs. Bumpers and guards were neither DeSoto nor Plymouth parts, and the guards were placed well toward the bumper ends. Front fenders and running boards were fitted with sturdy bolted-on chrome-plated moldings. Production records do not indicate that any taxicabs were built, as they probably were included in the 4-door sedan total. The company was not yet a competitor in the taxicab market, but would be seriously involved the following year. Basic Model SF chassis were in moderate demand for special purpose bodies, as 781 of them were assembled. This was in contrast to the two dozen shipped by Plymouth.

DeSoto offered relief from the monotone Airstream colors by introducing a DeLuxe equipment package in June. The extra beauty treatment cost only $35 and featured two-tone colors, having fenders painted to harmonize with the body rather than match it. Included in the fittings were miniature lamps on the front fenders, twin tail lamps, twin trumpet horns, twin windshield wipers, wheel trim rings, chromed fender and running board moldings, a cigar lighter and carpeted front compartment. An added touch was a medallion at the forward end of the hood louvers. Whitewall tires complemented the dressed-up appearance of the 4-Door Touring Sedan shown. The DeLuxe equipment was in compliance with a growing demand for fancier features.

The Airflow DeSoto, Model SG, featured a more prominent hood and a slenderly attractive grille, relieving the roundness of before. New bumpers and side louvers were other obvious appearance changes. Mechanically, the Airflow continued much as before though free wheeling was dropped and optional overdrive was added. Independent front wheel suspension was not adopted, but a hypoid rear axle was employed. Prices announced at the first of the year were $1,195 for any Airflow model. A price reduction on February 7th cut them to $1,015 where they remained. The Airflow Coupe was offered in two versions. The Business Coupe was a 3-passenger, 3,390-pound car, of which 70 were built. The Coupe with Enclosed Rumble Seat was a 5-passenger model of equal weight, which recorded a total of 418 built. The rumble seat was in normal rear seat location. Both models shared the same coupe body shell.

The Airflow 4-Door 6-Passenger Sedan ranked as the most-demanded Airflow, scoring a total of 6,269 built. Its weight and price were the same as the coupes. A 2-door sedan was not offered. Interior design eliminated some of the chrome tubular front seat framing, and a soft headlining replaced the former washable material. The Airflow wheelbase remained at 115.5 inches. The engine was essentially the same as the Airstream powerplant, having like bore and stroke dimensions. The cylinder heads differed, however. The standard Airflow head was aluminum with 6.5 to 1 compression ratio providing 100 horsepower, while an optional head of 7.0 to 1 ratio added five horsepower. The clutch was now provided with ventilation.

The Airflow 6-Passenger Town Sedan drew the least demand of any Airflow and Airstream DeSoto model. Only 40 of this blind quarter type were built. At 3,400 pounds it was the heaviest DeSoto this year. Its price was the same as the other Airflow models. Weights and prices given for all Airflow models did not include the overdrive transmission, which added 55 pounds and $30. Again this year, an Airflow DeSoto was awarded the Grand Prix for aerodynamic automotive design in the Concours d'Elegance at Monte Carlo.

As did Chrysler, DeSoto offered its dealers a hood conversion to make 1934 Airflows resemble 1935. At dealer previews of the new models, DeSoto proposed that the hood/grille adaptation should be made available to customers for updating their 1934 cars. Unsold 1934 models could also look newer, making them more salable. Perhaps a possible added benefit would come from the public impression that many 1935 Airflows were on the road, therefore implying popular approval of the revolutionary car in the hope of spurring more sales. The conversion idea was not original, as Packard had used 1932 appearance features to update leftover 1931 models. A converted DeSoto is shown at the right, evidenced by the wider hood which got narrower to pass the headlamps. The updated car retained its original bumper as well as the louvers below the headlamps.

This cutaway Airflow was displayed at auto shows to reveal what the insides of the car really were. The uniqueness of the unit body construction was not shown to best advantage, but the angular strut in the cowl area was part of the bridge-like frame which arched through the roof to the lower rear. The thinness of the sill section, amply strong in combination with other members, allowed a low floor. The tilted attitude of the engine was clearly shown.

1935

An early stage of experimental Model AH is shown in unfinished full-scale clay form. Exploratory thoughts were still being applied to the front end of the compact model. Scribed outlines on the fenders may have been in contemplation of flush lenses for recessed headlamps instead of the conventional lamps shown. Full concealment would not have been within the production cost limits established for an economy car. The hood was planned to be hinged at the center and fully-opening at the sides. The four doors would latch at the "B" pillars but their handles would be located higher. Front end lines and contours would be adjusted as development progressed. The grille would also receive changes, mostly at the top. A bumper of unidentified origin was propped up for effect.

Ongoing experimentation with compact cars and Airflow design produced this DeSoto baby this year. Using 2.5-inch square tubing for Airflow-like framework, the front frame extension, which supported the engine, axle, steering, etc., was bolted to the body. The light 6-cylinder engine was of conventional design and rested on Floating Power mountings. A tubular front axle and semi-elliptic springs were employed. The 100-inch wheelbase car was road-tested for two years. The line wrapping over the sheetmetal from the grille to the fender was the edge of the hood, which latched at the lower sides to allow easy engine access. The four doors were hinged to the "B" pillars, and the rear shape was fastback fashion. The spare wheel stowed inside, behind the rear seat. The car was labeled AA in an extensive A-Series research and development program.

The experimental Model AH compact car in road-test form had headlamps much like the Airflow. Lamp lenses had a thin vertical chrome rib though the center, much like the 1933 DeSoto. The AH utilized a bolt-on front stub frame in the manner of the AA, but a square-tube front axle was used. Two AH cars were built, of which the one shown was a 6-cylinder. The other was an 8-cylinder, and tried two types of engines, the first of which was a Chrysler-designed small V-8. The experimental compact V-type did not prove satisfactory, so it was replaced by a very small-bore straight-8 marine engine acquired from a boat works. Adapted to automotive use, the straight-8 gave acceptable performance. Both AH cars looked alike except that the 8-cylinder car had smaller wheels and fatter tires. Most chassis components were commonplace, but a hydraulic clutch actuator was unusual. Approximate wheelbase and weight of the AH cars was 100 inches and 2,200 pounds. The nameless compacts were road-tested for two years, impressing their drivers so much that some asked to buy them after 30,000 miles of trials. Passers-by sometimes asked a driver where they could buy one like it. Engineering executives Zeder, Skelton and Breer, plus division heads and others in top management, were not of the opinion that small cars might be needed. Walter P. Chrysler did not share that view, and kept the projects alive.

Not so small was the experimental Model AG, which had a wheelbase of approximately 110 inches (three inches less than the 1935 Plymouth). Whether intended to be a Plymouth or DeSoto is not known, but the front end and certain parts of the rear were removed from a production Airflow DeSoto as a start. Claymodeling revamped the front end, windshield, roof, rear end and running boards. Built for testing, the car had much-modified bolted-on frame structure in the front. The side-opening hood sheltered a stock DeSoto engine, and a deck lid concealed the spare wheel at the rear. Independent headlamps were mounted on the short bases on top of the fenders. As shown, the production doors were not to be changed. This car was just one of several directions explored.

For the first time in its history, the National Automobile Show was held in November instead of January. Therefore, most 1936 models were introduced in November 1935, which shortened the selling span of 1935 models by two months. Advancing the date was calculated to take up the former slack in employment during the fall season, which was traditionally a long period of low production. The introduction of new models in the fall brought an easing of the employment slump, and sales spurted ahead at a lively pace. But the severe winter of 1935-36 partly erased the gains. An over-abundance of snow over much of the nation cut traffic of buyers to dealerships and hampered deliveries. Overall, this year was a continuation of the constantly improving prosperity pattern. Restrictions imposed by the federal government's NRA controls had subsided as President Franklin D. Roosevelt sought election for his second term, which he easily won.

Total industry passenger car production for the calendar year was about 13% more than for 1935, while total production of all Chrysler Corp. cars rose more than 25%. Plymouth retained its position as the industry's third-biggest producer and Chrysler's best-selling car, while it was the corporation's smallest gainer at about 19%. DeSoto's 54% increase was the greatest of all Chrysler divisions, an honor it now held for the second consecutive year. The repeat performance did not boost DeSoto's position among all makers, but held it in thirteenth place. Dodge scored a 30% gain to hang onto fourth spot, just below Plymouth. The Chrysler car lines went up about 43%, which was a better growth than 1935, but fell from tenth to eleventh position because of surging Studebaker and Packard popularity. At the top of the roster, Ford suffered a drastic loss and surrendered first position to Chevrolet. Ford would not regain that cherished position until 1959.

While this year's DeSotos continued to come from Chrysler assembly lines, growing popularity of the Spanish-named car, coupled with optimistic upward market forecasts, justified production facilities for DeSoto alone. Accordingly, a new stamping plant was built adjacent to Chrysler Corp. building on Detroit's far west side. The older structure was modernized and tooled for the assembly of 500 cars daily. These first exclusively DeSoto manufacturing operations began in September with 1937 models. While the new home was being prepared, DeSoto enjoyed the success of its 1936 Airstream models but phased out production of the Airflow. Though the Airflow Chrysler lingered until mid-1937, DeSoto elected not to keep its unique automobile in the line-up that long. Because unusual assembly methods were required, it had been necessary to manufacture all Airflows in one plant, namely Chrysler. With no Airflow ties, DeSoto would be free to manufacture elsewhere. The third and last model of DeSoto's "dream car" was dubbed the Airflow III. With little more difference than a minor styling facelift, the line was reduced to only two body types: a coupe and a sedan. Weight increased approximately 150 pounds and prices went up $80.

Again the shining star of DeSoto, the Airstream model reaped even more market rewards than before. The series was available in DeLuxe and Custom features and equipment on a full line of bodies. The chassis frame was one inch lower and twice as rigid as before. Wheelbase of the popular models was 117 inches, an increase of one inch, and a new 130-inch wheelbase was provided for luxury cars. The 6-cylinder L-head engine retained its 3-3/8-inch bore and 4½-inch stroke, and horsepower output continued at 93. An optional overdrive transmission cut engine speed 30% when car speed exceeded 40 miles per hour, effecting greater fuel economy and less engine wear. Weight of the popular-size models averaged 70 pounds heavier, and prices averaged $15 above those of 1935. Styling appeal was broadly advertised, claiming the Airstream as the "leader of the style parade." DeSoto said "Genuine Custom Designing" produced these cars. That statement was based on the fact that Ray Dietrich, famed

The Plymouth Business series, Model P-1, was especially intended for fleet buyers, but some individuals found it also suited their needs. The Coupe was just the thing for the traveling salesman, providing ample space for samples and luggage as well as a passenger. At 2,650 pounds, it weighed the least of all Plymouths this year. It was also the lowest-priced model, listing at the factory for $510. The price was equal to the Ford Standard 2-Passenger 5-Window Coupe and $15 more than the Chevrolet Standard Six comparable model. 26,856 Plymouth Business Coupes were produced. The fleet example is shown with a simple low-profile ornament on top of the radiator shell. The item was standard equipment on all Plymouths, but most cars sported the optional ornate design with a ship and teardrop motif.

The 2-Door Sedan was the most popular model in the Business series, chalking up 39,516 units built. The 5-passenger 2,720-pound car was priced at $545 with basic equipment. The car is shown with optional rightside windshield wiper and tail lamp, as well as fenders and headlamp shells in body color. Those items were available on any passenger car. Visual differences between the Business and DeLuxe lines were not easy to spot. The Business cars had bumpers of constant width and squared ends, no chrome bars on headlamp supports, painted windshield frames, simplified body belt stripe, and no stripe on the wheel rims.

1936

esigner of strictly custom coachbuilt bodies, was now hief of design for Chrysler Corp. Mr. Dietrich had reviously created many bodies for various luxury car nakes, and they are today regarded as notable examples f classic automotive design. Having teamed with Thomas Iibbard in the formation of LeBaron, Inc. in 1920, he ecame head of Dietrich, Inc. when it was organized in 925 as the custom subsidiary of Murray Corp. of America. About 1930, he left Murray to work for the hree Graham brothers in creating the 1932 Graham known s the Blue Streak model. After that car received styling cclaim at the auto shows, Walter P. Chrysler snapped him ip. Mr. Dietrich's interest in Airflow styling was only in he application of facelift touches. Conventional models eceived the benefit of his talent and taste for several years s he guided and coached the designers and clay modelers.

Plymouth was a substantially new car, though it was not eadily apparent to the casual observer. New bodies vere shared with Dodge and the DeSoto DeLuxe, and were one inch lower than 1935. The proven engine of the orevious year was continued, but with minor improvements. Retained was the 3-1/8-inch bore and 4-3/8-inch troke, and developed horsepower remained at 82. Popularize cars continued to use a 113-inch wheelbase, but the ong wheelbase was reduced three inches to 125. More than 10 improvements were incorporated in the overall autonobile. A Business and a DeLuxe series were offered. At first, both were coded as Model P-2, which was the orefix to all engine numbers. Two weeks after introduction, lowever, Plymouth advised its dealers that the Business ine would be known as P-1 regardless of the P-2 engine number. Some states had requested a model (not model vear) designation for purposes of registration and titling, ince the Business line was a distinct economy series apart from the DeLuxe. That eliminated a repetition of the 1935 confusion which resulted from having three series under a common PJ designation.

Across the board, P-1 and P-2 models averaged 74½ pounds heavier than the former PJ. Price average did not change, though some models were a bit higher and others lower. This year, the banner line "Plymouth Builds Great Cars" was inaugurated, and would endure for some years. Though engineering, reliability and low cost were heavily advertised, styling was sometimes boasted. Plymouth styling was also done under the supervision of Ray Dietrich. The new assembly plant at Evansville, Ind. began operations by turning out Plymouths, and would add the 1937 Dodge some months later. Combined with Detroit and Los Angeles facilities, Plymouth now had a large production capability.

The P-1 Business Coupe could be had with a utility box equipped with a dropgate. The spare wheel was normally carried behind the seat, but rightside or dual forward-mounted spares could be ordered for any P-1 model. Pressed steel spoke wheels fitted with 17 x 5.25 tires were standard, and 16 x 6.00 was optional on all. Spare tires and tubes were extra-cost items on all P-1 and P-2 cars, as were bumpers and bumper guards. Safety glass windshields were standard in all Plymouth passenger cars, and such protection could be had for all windows as well.

Without the men's weight on the rear bumper, the empty car would have appeared to pitch forward. Obviously the men were more convenient than straps for pulling the body closer to the rear axle in order to achieve a level appearance. The purpose was to photograph the level car so a retouch artist could paint out the men and the picture could be used for publicity. The intent of this illustration is to show the optional 20-inch wheels that could be ordered on P-1 and P-2 pleasure cars. Shown is a P-2 2-Door Sedan. The wheels of disc design provided a ground clearance of 9-7/8 inches, which was 1½ inches more than other Plymouth cars. Other special chassis features supplemented the wheels. Among them were a rear axle gear ratio of 4.375 to 1 and shock absorbers with longer links. This equipment was not available for Touring Sedans, 7-Passenger Sedans, and Commercial Sedans. Also, it could not be ordered with forward-mounted spares.

This illustration of the P-1 4-Door Sedan looks like a duplicate of the DeLuxe model, but close scrutiny will prove it is not. The 5-passenger Business model was the heaviest and highest-priced P-1 pleasure car, weighing 2,750 pounds and costing $590. Plymouth turned out 19,104 of them. No Touring Sedans were included in the Business line. Excepting commercial types, all Business models had a built-in radio antenna as standard, and a Philco Transitone radio cost extra. Two fuel economy package options were available. One consisted of a modified carburetor, special intake manifold and a 3.7 to 1 rear axle ratio (standard was 4.125 to 1). The other package added manifold heat shields and a hardened steel throttle stop to the other items. Plymouth boasted 18 to 24 miles per gallon, and this option was said to effect a maximum increase of 20%. Since economy exacts penalties, horsepower was cut over 20%, acceleration was up to 15% slower, and top speed was about 70 miles per hour.

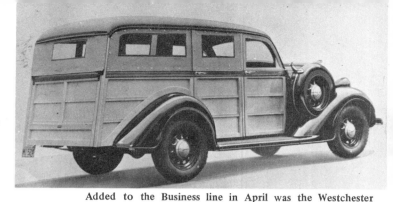

Unlike the 1935 2-door sedan commercial version with rear-end door and removable rear seat, the new Commercial Sedan body was especially developed for the purpose. It utilized front doors of the 5-passenger 4-door sedan dimension and devoted the entire space behind the driver's seat to commercial use. The spare wheel in fender well was standard for this model. 3,527 of these vehicles were built, and they were priced at $605. The 113-inch P-1 Business chassis served the purpose. This particular example was purchased by the Brown & Williamson Tobacco Co., whose products were Sir Walter Raleigh smoking tobacco, Raleigh cigarettes with coupons, and Wings cigarettes.

1936

Added to the Business line in April was the Westchester Suburban. The U.S. Body & Forging Co. of Tell City, Ind., builders of the body, listed it as a Semi-Sedan Suburban. Plymouth said it was an informal country car for a wide variety of uses. For the title and license registration, it was called a commercial car or truck. By whatever name, the 4-door vehicle had room for up to eight passengers. The center seat was not as wide as the others, allowing eight inches on the curb side for an access aisle to the rear seat. Center and rear seats could be removed to provide cargo space. The forward-mounted spare wheel and safety glass in the windshield and front doors were standard equipment. The detachable weather curtains were also standard. A rear bumper was not available. 309 of these utility cars were built. The body cost $350, chassis with standard 17-inch wheels was $415, adding up to a total of $765. The 113-inch chassis was especially adapted for the Suburban. For other special-purpose bodies, 1,211 P-1 bare chassis were assembled.

Shown with optional rightside windshield wiper and tail lamp is the Plymouth DeLuxe Rumble Seat Coupe. 9,663 of the 2,775-pound $620 cars were built. Spare wheel storage was behind the inside seat, which also was the location in the Business Coupe. Among options available for all DeLuxe models were dual or single (rightside) forward-mounted spare wheels, whitewall tires, dual trumpet horns below the head-lamps, and special body colors.

The Convertible Coupe went into production early in February. The flashy sport model drew the least demand of all DeLuxe models, and a modest total of 3,297 were built. It was priced at $725 and weighed 2,830 pounds. The spare wheel was carried on the rear and dual windshield wipers, standard on this model, were mounted on the cowl instead of above. A special X-braced frame was built into the body floor which, added to a similar bracing in the chassis frame, provided greater stiffness and prevented rattles and twisting common to convertibles. Special attention was given to the reduction of interior drafts. The rear curtain had a zipper instead of buttons, and soft rubber cups were fitted to the bases of foot pedals and hand levers. A felt pad was beneath the floor mat, and the back of the instrument panel was insulated with felt and fibre-board.

The Business Coupe in the Plymouth DeLuxe P-2 line was a 2-passenger car. At 2,705 pounds it was the lightweight of the DeLuxe line, and its $580 price was the lowest. The factories turned out a total of 54,601. Modest special touches identified all models of the DeLuxe line. Bumpers tapered narrower toward the ends, headlamp supports were ornamented with three small chrome bars, and windshields had brightwork frames. The body belt stripe was prominent, and wheel rims were also striped. Standard wheel equipment was pressed steel spoke design with 16 x 6.00 tires.

DeLuxe cars also served in various commercial ways. This 2-Door Sedan was owned by the Skelly Oil Co., Tulsa, Okla., and made regular trips to that company's 140 oil wells. The 5-passenger car carried the spare wheel on the rear. This practical model weighed 2,785 pounds and asked a price of $625 at the factories, which rolled out 6,149 of them. Plymouth's Safety-Steel bodies and Rigid-X chassis frame gave a ruggedness of character that was sought by those who wanted an economical car for hard use.

The DeLuxe 4-Door Sedan accommodated 5 passengers comfortably. It tipped the scales at 2,820 pounds and was factory-priced at $660. A production total of 10,001 was evidence of the rapidly declining popularity of trunkless passenger cars. The spare wheel was carried at the rear, on the outside. All DeLuxe enclosed cars (not the convertible) offered a choice of broadcloth or mohair interior upholstery fabric, and leather was an extra-cost option in passenger cars of the Business and DeLuxe series. A rightside interior sun visor was optional in both series, and a more deluxe steering wheel was available for DeLuxe cars. All DeLuxe enclosed cars were factory-wired for optional Philco Transitone radios.

1936

By far the most popular 1936 Plymouth was the DeLuxe 4-Door Touring Sedan. 240,136 of the 5-passenger models were turned out. The car weighed 2,850 pounds and was priced at $680. The rear of this body was four inches longer than all other P-1 and P-2 5-passenger sedans, and was mounted on the regular 113-inch wheelbase. The extra length provided full legroom for rear seat passengers, a luxury the comparable 1935 model did not have. The trunks of 2 and 4-door touring models housed the spare wheel and had space for luggage. The interior ventilation system of all 1936 Plymouths was essentially the same as that used for 1935. The windshield swung open by crank, front door glass moved back a trifle, and rear quarter windows swung outward in butterfly fashion.

With an O.K. tag tied to its ship ornament, a Plymouth DeLuxe 2-Door Touring Sedan's rear wheels were spun for engine starting at the end of the assembly and final inspection lines. Starting the new engine, for which initial gasoline must be pumped from the tank to the carburetor, was done more quickly and positively by the method shown. The car must spring to life and move on, as the next one behind was steadily moving toward it. This car was one of 99,373 of like model to come off the lines. It weighed 2,815 pounds and cost $645 at the place of manufacture.

The 5-passenger Plymouth DeLuxe 4-Door Touring Sedan was available as a three-way vehicle. It served as a pleasure car, hearse, or ambulance. Shown as the latter, a stretcher bears a "patient," whose head is seen inside while his legs extended through the trunk as he was being moved in or out. Folding runways are seen just above the car floor. They and the stretcher, plus a splint case, were stored in the trunk when not in use. The spare wheel was mounted up front in a fender well. Cars and equipment were ordered through Plymouth dealers. For ambulance use, cars were built with a split rear seat, of which the rightside half could be folded and secured to the headlining by straps. A section of the trunk partition was necessarily cut away. The remaining half of the seat remained fixed for accommodation of an attendant. The factory conversion added $40 to the regular car price. Plymouth Floating Power engine mounts and Floating Ride combination of balanced weight and spring action provided a smooth and vibrationless ride for patients. For hearse use, cars were built with the modified rear end and a 2-door sedan split-back front seat. The rightside seat back had to be removed to accommodate a casket. The hearse adaptation cost $65 more than car price. Special ambulance and hearse equipment cost was not included in the converted car price. For completely different special-purpose bodies built elsewhere, Plymouth assembled 2,775 stripped DeLuxe chassis.

The only long wheelbase Plymouth passenger car this year was the DeLuxe 7-Passenger Sedan. Though built with a rear trunk, it was not known as a touring model. It was the most expensive of all P-1 and P-2 models, and was the heaviest. The price was $895 and the scale reading was 3,155 pounds. A total of 1,504 were built, making it the least popular catalogued model. Built on a 125-inch wheelbase, the car had the same engine used in other models. The long body had wider doors than those of the 5-passenger variety.

The DeLuxe Airstream DeSoto Touring Brougham was the least popular DeLuxe body type, accounting for 2,207 units of the production total. The 2-door 5-passenger car weighed 3,051 pounds and carried a $770 price tag. On this and the 4-door model, the trunk opening was at bumper height, allowing easy access. The trunk housed the spare wheel horizontally on the floor, and luggage on a shelf above. DeLuxe models had a simplified interior ventilation system. All had a cowl ventilator, crank-operated windshield, and front door glass that slid back a trifle. In addition, the 4-door model had pivoting rear quarter windows. Windshield and quarter windows were of safety glass, which was optional for other windows. DeLuxe cars were more readily recognized by their one-piece flat windshields. That windshield type was also used on Custom convertibles, but the DeLuxe line had no convertible bodies.

De Soto

The Airstream series was again the darling of DeSoto. Offered in distinctly different DeLuxe and Custom versions, both were known as Model S-1. The lowest-priced of all DeSotos this year was the DeLuxe Airstream Business Coupe, which was factory-priced at $695 in basic form. It was also the least heavy DeSoto, tipping the scales at 2,941 pounds. The Chrysler factory turned out 2,592 of the 2-passenger cars. The chromed wheel covers were optional. The spare wheel was stowed vertically behind the seat, with a partition behind it. The deck lid extended downward to rear bumper level, providing easier loading and unloading of luggage. During the year, the medallion used two locations on the grille. First placed in the lower area, by early spring it was moved up to the location shown.

Shown near the end of the final inspection line is a DeLuxe Airstream Touring Sedan. This was the heaviest, highest-priced and most popular DeLuxe model. It weighed 3,111 pounds and cost $810. The 5-passenger 4-door type accounted for 13,093 units built. It featured a trunk, as DeSoto did not offer sedans without trunks this year. The car shown did not have an optional rightside windshield wiper. Distinctive grille features below the headlamps were horn housings. DeSoto assembled and shipped 99 stripped DeLuxe chassis for special-purpose bodies or other uses. DeLuxe and Custom cars of 117-inch wheelbase were powered by a 6-cylinder engine of 93 horsepower, said to be vibrationless through utilization of Floating Power mountings. The DeLuxe series had a helical-gear transmission as standard, while an overdrive type was an extra-cost option. When equipped with the latter, a hypoid rear axle was included. A spiral bevel gear axle was standard.

Truly a dual-purpose car was the Custom Airstream Rumble Seat Coupe. Salesmen and professional people found the smart S-1 model an asset to their business and pleasure activities. 641 of the $795 cars were manufactured. 940 Custom Airstream Business Coupes, priced at $745, were also built. In both models, the spare wheel was stowed behind the inside seat. All Airstream cars featured independent front wheel suspension, extra-long tapered-leaf rear springs, and a ride stabilizer to eliminate lurching and sidesway. Tires were Airwheel 6.25 x 16 on pressed steel spoke wheels. This total combination produced what was called the "Magic Carpet Ride."

The Custom Airstream DeSoto Touring Brougham was a 2-door model with comfort for five passengers. Each of the 1,120 built weighed 3,031 pounds and cost $825. The easiest means of identifying all Custom cars except convertibles was by the split "vee" windshield and divided rear window. Other Custom touches were chrome chevrons on front fenders, and the use of chrome moldings on headlamp tops, fender skirt bottoms, running boards and rear wheel shields. The illustration shows the first location of the Airstream front medallion, which was well down on the grille. The trunk of all Custom body types accommodated the spare wheel and luggage unless spares were mounted in front fender wells. In case of the latter, the trunk was totally useful for luggage.

Rating the most demand of any S-1 model was the Custom Airstream Touring Sedan. 13,801 of the 4-door models were built. Weighing 3,126 pounds and costing $865, this model accommodated five passengers in stylish luxury. Chair-height seats, contoured armrests, pleated door trim panels, tailored assist loops, silken robe cord, carpeted footrest, Circassian walnut paneling and Bedford cord or mohair upholstery were only some of the niceties typical of Custom interiors. Many of these were also included in the DeLuxe series. Another comfort and convenience feature was adjustable front seats in all. Interior ventilation of Custom closed cars was more elaborate than the DeLuxe had. The "vee" windshields were fixed in place but there was a cowl ventilator. Pivoting panes in front windows could be lowered with the main glass. Rear quarter windows of 4-door sedans were also pivoted.

1936

The stylish Airstream DeSoto is seen on display in a foreign land. The car is a Custom Touring Sedan. With spare wheels carried forward, it was a smart automobile. Forward-mounts were available on any DeLuxe or Custom model. Safety glass was standard in Custom windshields and front and rear vent panes, optional for windows. Windshield wipers on all Custom cars were located at the cowl. New for 1936 was a steel panel inserted in the top of the roof where fabric formerly was. It was insulated at the edges and served as a radio antenna.

Dealers wanted this kind of car long before the usual spring announcement time, so it was added early in February. The Custom Airstream Convertible Sedan was the most expensive catalogued S-1 model, costing $1,095. Regardless of its early introduction, only 215 were built. Like the Convertible Coupe, it had a one-piece windshield. Special engineering attention was applied to make this and the Convertible Coupe as draft-free as possible. Snug fittings at all floor openings, weatherstripping around doors and zippered rear curtains were standard. The body floor included an X-member frame of its own to provide convertible body strength. Rear wheel shields added style to the smart convertibles, but they were an extra-cost option on this and all other models.

The first long-wheelbase DeSoto for 1936 was the Custom Airstream 7-Passenger Sedan announced in February. Built on a 130-inch wheelbase, its engine produced 100 horsepower instead of the 93 which was sufficient for the shorter cars. Steering the heavy automobile was easy with DeSoto's shockless center-controlled steering, like that built into all other S-1 cars. The factory produced 208 of the big sedans and asked a price of $1,075 for each. The S-1 model that registered the lowest production total was the 130-inch wheelbase Custom Airstream Limousine, of which a tiny 10 were built. S-1 Custom chassis, probably of standard and long wheelbases, were sought for various purposes, and 460 of them were assembled.

The Convertible Coupe of the Custom Airstream line was a youthful car with a rumble seat. The weight of the car was 3,031 pounds and its price was $895. It did not spark much demand, as only 350 were built. Unlike the closed bodies, it had a flat one-piece windshield. The spare wheel was carried on the rear end unless fender well mountings were employed. An X-braced frame was built into the body floor to eliminate flexibility normally common to a convertible body. All Custom models were equipped with a silent 3-speed transmission as standard unless an optional type with automatic overdrive was specified. A hypoid rear axle was employed with the overdrive unit. With the gas-saving overdrive, DeSoto claimed that one out of every five miles was traveled at no cost.

Another long DeSoto was the Custom Airstream Traveler, which made its initial appearance in March. Of 5-passenger capacity, it utilized the 7-passenger body and had extra spaciousness for occupants of the rear seat. The generous floor space could be used for extra luggage without interfering with leg-stretch room needed by rear seat passengers. Embossed door panels, armrest ash receivers and individual footrests in the rear compartment were among the many interior appointments. The luxurious body was mounted on the 130-inch wheelbase chassis powered by the 100-horsepower engine. The factory asked $1,075 for the Traveler, and built 23 of them.

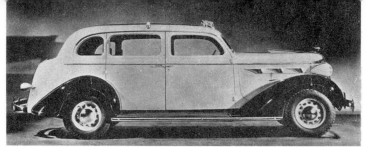

By now DeSoto was quite active in the taxicab market, building 2,951 Custom S-1 cabs. A 7-passenger "sample copy" is shown. Some were built for the Yellow Cab Co., having the name in large script style cut from metal and spread across the grilles before the vehicles left the factory. The example shows a number of special taxi touches used on Yellow Cabs and possibly others. A V-shaped wing-like sign light above the windshield, lights above the rear doors, a long chrome fin on the hood hinge, a guide light on the front fender and a heavy molding on the running board are visible. Another version was the Sunshine Cab built for service in New York City. Of total cab production, 2,200 were Sunshines. When placed, the order was the largest in taxicab history. The Custom 7-passenger bodies had DeLuxe one-piece windshields, European-type sliding roofs and many new cab features.

1936

Known as Airflow III and registered as Model S-2, it was the last DeSoto of this unique design to be manufactured. Only minor styling changes were applied to the exterior. New were a diecast grille, bumpers, louvers, body side moldings and tail lamps. Inside was a new instrument panel and a general redesign of seats and door panels. Mechanical details were not appreciably changed. The 100-horsepower engine and 115½-inch wheelbase were as before, and the spring and axle setup was not changed. The line was reduced to only two body types, of which the Coupe is shown. It retained the smooth fastback rear shape with no alteration. The rear seat of the 5-passenger body was called an auxiliary seat because it was removable. The Coupe weighed 3,535 pounds, cost $1,095 and registered a total of 250 built.

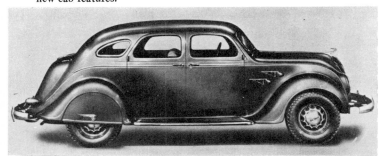

For the first time, Airflow sedans enclosed the spare wheel within the body. The popular trunk was integrated with the rear panel as a part of the body. The spare was laid flat in the bottom with a luggage shelf above it. The interior of the 4-door body accommodated six passengers quite comfortably. The Airflow III Sedan tipped the scales at 3,595 pounds and was factory-priced at $1,095. The Chrysler factory turned out 4,750 of them. For DeSoto, this was the final edition of the Airflow series, though the Airflow Chrysler continued for one more year. For 1934, 1935 and 1936, DeSoto's Airflow production was 13,940, 6,797 and 5,000, respectively. A total of 25,737 spread over a period of three years did not justify continuation of production. Nevertheless, many of its features were adopted by other cars.

A Plymouth is shown as it hurdled a truck as part of the carnival of crashes staged by "Lucky" Teter of the Hell Drivers exhibition team. Publicly demonstrating Plymouth ruggedness, cars were also rammed through flaming walls, rolled over and otherwise punished. The scene is from "Lucky Spills," a Grantland Rice Sportlight 2-reel thriller film released by Paramount Pictures, Inc. Narration was by Ted Husing, ace radio sports announcer of the time. Eighty million people went to movie theatres every week, and most of them saw this daredevil film during the year. Other hundreds of thousands saw the feats in live performances regularly staged across the country. This was excellent advertising for Plymouth.

Bouncing and hammering across railroad ties was one of the tortures Plymouth cars were given in tests and demonstrations. They were engineered and built for rugged service. Stiffness of the X-braced chassis frame resisted distortion, and the body was bolted to the frame by 36 bolts applied horizontally and vertically. That combination was said to be "unit body and frame" construction because of its rigidity. The tubular front axle and leaf springing withstood rigorous punishment. A sway eliminator located in front combined with easier shockless steering to maintain driver control.

Looking much like a 1937 Plymouth, this full-scale wooden mockup was completed this year. The design proposal featured a split "vee" windshield with wipers at the bottom, headlamps attached to horizontal stub struts, and no running boards. Bumpers were of 3-piece construction intended to provide flexible resistance under pressure. Proportional comparisons indicate that this was a slightly smaller car than the 1937 Plymouth turned out to be.

For the industry as a whole, passenger car production for this calendar year continued to gain, but not quite as much as 1936. Returning prosperity tapered off some, resulting in a modest increase of approximately 7%. Logically, the tapering was reflected in the combined production of Chrysler Corp. passenger cars, which advanced barely 8%. For the third consecutive year, DeSoto captured honors as Chrysler's best gainer, registering a whopping increase of more than 63%. That gain was largely responsible for DeSoto's elevation from 13th to 11th position among all automakers, but losses taken by Hudson-Terraplane and Studebaker helped some. The next-best plus-performance of Chrysler Corp. was scored by the Chrysler car division, whose rise of about 51% boosted it from 11th to 10th place. Dodge recorded a scant 6% margin over the previous year to hold 4th rank for five years in a row. Plymouth, hurt by work stoppages caused by labor strife, broke its long record of constant gains in production, a record that had become synonymous with the name. The loss was just over 2%, which was not enough to shake Plymouth from its position as the industry's No. 3 car, a perch it now occupied for the 7th straight year.

This year, Plymouth displayed even more aggressiveness than before by entering the light truck field. This action in itself was significant, but was made even more so by the fact that it was done when a huge sum of money was also spent for tooling and production of two almost totally new lines of passenger cars. The investment was not just for product improvement, but also to provide thrust for a deeper penetration of the market. The decision to tackle the commercial market on a broader scale was in response to the growing demands of American business for economy, durability and performance characteristics that rocketed Plymouth to third place in the passenger car field.

The new Commercial Car Line's most popular vehicle was the Pick-Up which, as built by Plymouth, was of half-ton payload capacity. When fitted with special bodies built by others, the chassis could accommodate payloads of up to one ton. The new Commercial Sedan was larger and more economical in relation to payload than its predecessor. The Westchester Suburban was included in the new line, since it was built on the commercial chassis and was registered as a commercial car or truck on titles and license applications as well as other records. The Commercial Line comprised only these three types.

Plymouth's new passenger car line boasted eight new features of design. For the first time, Plymouth had one-piece steel roof panels. Bodies were mounted on outrigger brackets utilizing live rubber to cushion body weight. Protection from weather temperatures, engine heat and car and road noises was provided by five new kinds of insulation. A hypoid rear axle, usually employed in higher-priced cars, was stronger than the former spiral-bevel type and was said to be longer-lived. The hypoid design placed the driveshaft lower, eliminating the need for a tunnel in the rear compartment floor. More interior room resulted from wider bodies, which were said to accommodate six full-size adults in cars of family size. Interiors were of safety design, with special attention given to the shape and location of controls and fittings. Better ride quality came with the use of airplane-type shock absorbers which used five times more oil and were of low pressure.

Plymouth's low line was the Business series, Model P-3. Popular with fleet owners, it also found favor with merchants, the trades, and just plain economy-minded individuals. The Business Coupe weighed the least of all Plymouth passenger cars this year, registering 2,771 pounds on the scales. It also was the least expensive model, asking $580 as an advertised delivered price (not an F.O.B. factory price as formerly used). This new pricing method quoted the delivered price at point of manufacture, and in Plymouth's case was up to $80 more than F.O.B. The method was employed throughout the industry, beginning with 1937 models. Demand for the Business Coupe drew 18,202 production orders. A fleet-ordered car is shown with rightside windshield wiper and tail lamp, which were extra-cost options. The single seat could accommodate three adults, but this was regarded as a 2-passenger car.

Again available were 20-inch wheels, which could be ordered on all Plymouth passenger cars but 7-passenger models. As shown on the Business Coupe, they were for rough roads and tough going. The hubcaps were a carryover from 1935-36 production. Road clearance was 9-7/8 inches, which was 1½ inches more than with standard wheels. The $15 option included a special rear axle ratio of 4.375 to 1, heavy duty shock absorbers and other chassis modifications. The equipment was especially useful to rural mail carriers, farmers, veterinarians, contractors and others who often did not have pavement or even good road surface to travel on. Another option, not related to the high wheels, was an economy setup offered in two versions to suit the nature of the terrain where cars were to be used. One for hilly country had a carburetor and intake manifold of special adaptation plus a 3.7 to 1 rear axle ratio, all at no extra cost when factory-ordered. The version for flatter country included those features plus a throttle stop and manifold heat shields for $3.75. Less horsepower, acceleration and top speed resulted, but hilly economy was up to 20% better and flatter driving realized a maximum 30% increase. The option was applicable to both the Business and DeLuxe series.

The wheelbase of popular-sized Plymouths was 112 inches, a reduction of one inch from the previous model. The tubular front axle and leafed semi-elliptic springs were continued as before. The 6-cylinder 82-horsepower engine with Floating Power was carried over, as was the 3-speed synchro-silent stickshift transmission. Styling was in character with the prevailing trend to a heavier appearance with more generous use of curves and contours. Though the wheelbase was an inch shorter, overall length was a bit longer than before, and the cars looked heavier than they actually were. Average weight went up 150 pounds and factory list prices averaged $15 more. The Business series, Model P-3, had three catalogued body types especially fitted for the needs of fleet and low-cost buyers. The DeLuxe line, Model P-4, offered eight catalogued body types, including a 7-passenger on a 132-inch wheelbase.

DeSoto began assemblies of its new Model S-3 in its new Detroit factory about October 1, 1936. After more than eight years of production, these were the first exclusively DeSoto manufacturing facilities. They included a renovated Chrysler property and a newly-erected stamping plant declared ultra-modern partly because of extensive use of glass to allow as much daylight as possible. Many DeSoto parts were still shared with other cars, however. DeSoto offered only one series this year, there being no DeLuxe, Custom, and Airflow. The 6-cylinder engine previously used received changes including a reduction of ¼ inch in the piston stroke, but developed horsepower remained at 93. The wheelbase of the regular series was reduced two inches to 116, but that of 7-passenger models was increased three inches to 133. The standard 3-speed transmission received detail changes and the optional overdrive type continued available. All rear axles were now of silent hypoid design which did away with the rear floor tunnel. Independent suspension of front wheels was retained as a desirable feature.

Bodywise, DeSoto had all of the ideas and advantages utilized by Plymouth. Styling, too, was of the same heavily-contoured concept. Ray Dietrich, Chrysler's chief designer, distinguished DeSoto from Plymouth mainly by applying bolder design to the grille and hood. The S-3 catalogued body line included ten choices, including two 7-passenger models. Compared with similar models of the previous Custom Airstream series, they averaged about 50 pounds heavier but factory prices averaged $50 less. Usually, increased weight is accompanied by higher prices, but the pattern was reversed in this instance because of a realignment of models and competitive adjustments.

The Plymouth 2-Door Business Sedan was the most-demanded P-3 car, accounting for 28,685 units of total P-3 production. It weighed 2,841 pounds and was priced at $620. Though front and rear seats were said to be adequate for three adults each, this was considered a 5-passenger car. Trunkless sedans now carried the spare wheel inside, accessible by means of a lid in the fastback rear of the body. Exterior identity of Business series cars was most difficult, to say the least. A painted windshield frame was evidence and, if front windows were up, absence of ventilating panes was another clue. Standard tire size was 16 x 5.50 but 16 x 6.00 was optional. All Plymouths were equipped with steel disc wheels.

The highest-priced model of the P-3 line was the 4-Door Business Sedan priced at $665. An even 16,000 of these 2,841-pound cars were built. The fastback design of the rear end concealed what was called a "luggage compartment" which also stored the spare wheel. All body types of the Business series now had safety glass in windshields and all windows as a standard feature. Unless ordered with fender colors to match the bodies, any Business model had black fenders regardless of body color. Plymouth continued to provide stripped chassis for other than its own bodies, and 1,025 with P-3 specifications were assembled for that purpose. All P-3 cars had a P-4 motor number prefix.

The lightest and lowest-priced Plymouth P-4 DeLuxe model was the Coupe, which weighed 2,839 pounds and cost $650. It was a fairly popular car, as shown by the total of 67,144 built. A 2-passenger car with luggage deck, it was a Business Coupe type, but the word "Business" was not used for this DeLuxe model, and confusion with the Business series counterpart was eliminated. All DeLuxe body types were standard-equipped with safety glass all around, and 112-inch wheelbase DeLuxe models were fitted with 16 x 6.00 tires as standard. Spare tires and tubes, bumpers and bumper guards were extra-cost items though all Plymouths were equipped with them.

The DeLuxe Rumble Seat Coupe was Plymouth's answer to buyers who wanted an enclosed personal car with provision for a couple of extra passengers. Each of the 6,877 built weighed 2,884 pounds and was priced at $700. All models of the DeLuxe line were identifiable externally by chromed windshield frames and front window ventilating panes. Not used since 1934, Plymouth reinstated the vent panes as part of the interior ventilation system on DeLuxe cars only. The vent panes and window glass could be operated independently, or lowered into the doors as a unit. Rear quarter windows of 4-door models were again fitted with pivoting panes. Complete ventilation was made possible by a cowl vent and crank-operated windshield. Common to all Plymouths was the abstract ship hood ornament, a $3.50 extra, but a plain design could be special-ordered at no charge.

Though costing only $715, the DeLuxe 2-Door Sedan was not a very popular car. The reason was its fastback luggage compartment, which was smaller by comparison with the trunk. Only 7,926 of them were built. The 5-passenger car weighed 2,899 pounds. All Plymouth bodies were mounted on the chassis frame by a new rubber-poised method. The frame had outrigger brackets upon which the bodies were "floated" by means of spool-shaped mountings of live rubber. This was said to prevent road shocks and noises from being transmitted to the body. In addition, five kinds of insulation were used in bodies, providing what Plymouth proudly advertised as a "hushed ride." The principle of balanced weight and balanced spring action, achieved by the forward location of engine and passengers in relation to wheelbase, was continued from previous years.

By far the most popular 2-door model offered by Plymouth was the DeLuxe 2-Door Touring Sedan. 111,099 of the 5-passenger cars were turned out. Touring Sedan trunks stored the spare wheel on the floor, with a shelf above it. Maximum dimensions of the luggage area were 52 inches wide, 18¼ inches high and 33 inches longitudinal depth. This $725 model weighed 2,914 pounds empty. Styling of the new Plymouths was in tune with the trend of the times. Lines were more curved and flowing, contours were rounder and more generous, and the general effect created an impression of more weight than the cars had. Considering all Business and DeLuxe models, average weight was 3,052 pounds. By comparison with the 1936 range, the new series averaged 150 pounds heavier.

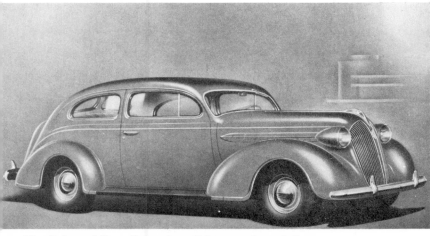

The DeLuxe 4-Door Sedan drew little more demand than the 2-door fastback, registering an even 9,000 on the production records. The 5-passenger 2,914-pound car was priced at $745. Options available on all DeLuxe models included a rightside windshield wiper and tail lamp, fenders in color to match the body, and special body colors. Unless color was ordered on fenders, they were painted black. Philco Transitone radios were available for all Business and DeLuxe models, for which the antenna was located on the underside of the cars.

With a runaway lead in popularity of any Plymouth body type up to its time, the DeLuxe 4-Door Touring Sedan scored a fantastic total production of 269,062. That was more than the total of all Plymouths built during the calendar year 1933. The car accommodated five passengers easily and weighed 2,914 pounds. Its delivered price at the factory was $755. The comparable model Ford DeLuxe V-8 cost $758 and Chevrolet's Master DeLuxe was tagged at $789, so Plymouth was in the competitive ball park. Again this year, this 5-passenger model was available with an ambulance conversion built by a company other than Plymouth.

E. DeLuxe FOUR DOOR SEDAN

Forward-mounted spare wheels were not available for 1937 Plymouth passenger cars. As this illustration shows, spares would have to be mounted quite high because there was not enough space between the front wheel and door to place them lower. The high spare simply was not attractive and would have drawn little demand. The new one-piece steel roof is clearly evident in this view. All enclosed bodies incorporated the feature. Also shown is the hood hinge. Contrary to DeSoto, Plymouth hoods were opened from the sides.

The Convertible Coupe was added to the DeLuxe line about March 1st. This was the only convertible type offered by Plymouth. The sporty car included a rumble seat and slanted rear floor with footrest. New for the convertible was the storage of the spare wheel inside the body, just behind the front seat. Standard equipment included dual windshield wipers and dual tail lamps. Whitewall tires were optional at extra cost. This was the most expensive and heaviest 112-inch wheelbase model, costing $830 and weighing 2,994 pounds. 3,110 were built, making this the least popular of the shorter models. The body had an X-braced floor frame of its own. The inside seat was upholstered in genuine leather, and the rumble seat was covered with a special tan moleskin material. Ventilating panes were standard, but some early production cars were not factory-equipped with them because they were not at first available. The car is shown without the rear curtain in place.

The Plymouth DeLuxe 7-Passenger Sedan utilized a long 132-inch wheelbase but was powered by the standard 82-horsepower engine. It entered the market in April at a price of $995. The largest car Plymouth had ever built, it weighed 3,333 pounds and measured 213 inches from bumper to bumper. It earned enough demand to require a production of 1,840. Although it had a trunk, it was not called a Touring Sedan. The car was fitted with larger tires of 16 x 6.50 size, and was said to be roomy enough for nine passengers without crowding. Auxiliary seats were wider and placed closer together than previous cars of this size had. The luxurious interior was offered in a choice of mohair, broadcloth or Bedford cord at no extra cost. 63 DeLuxe Sedan-Limousines were also built on the long chassis. At $1,095, this was the costliest Plymouth yet built.

The easy and quiet Plymouth ride qualities were advantageous for ambulance use. Stock DeLuxe 7-Passenger Sedans were purchased by the Yellow Cab Co. of Philadelphia, who had them converted for the purpose. In service, the mercy vehicles were given the name "Cabulance." The example shown looks even longer than the stock 7-passenger model.

When persons were stricken while at work, or an invalid needed transportation, a call to Yellow Cab's Philadelphia headquarters brought a "Cabulance." Note the curtain hanging from a rod between the invalid and the driver's seat. The "Cabulance" was originated by the Yellow Cab Co. For special-purpose bodies built by others, Plymouth built 1,729 stripped DeLuxe chassis of unknown lengths.

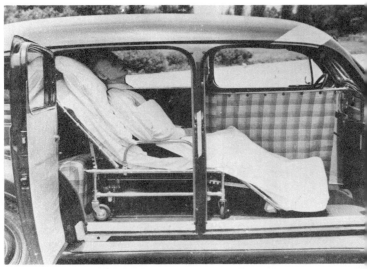

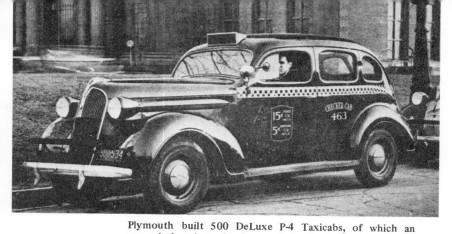

Plymouth built 500 DeLuxe P-4 Taxicabs, of which an example based on the 4-Door Sedan is shown. Though the sizes and body types built are unknown, this one was a 5-passenger 112-inch wheelbase model. It was part of a Checker Cab fleet of 194 Plymouths purchased for service in the city of Detroit. They were specially fitted to meet the Checker specifications. Among other things, note the front bumper guards turned bottoms-up and a special guard rail above. An accessory winterfront was fastened to the grille. Independent cab owners, usually in small cities and towns, often wanted regular passenger cars without cab interior fixtures to serve doubly for cab or family use. For them, a taxicab package consisting of specially-hardened transmission gears, a 10-inch clutch and heavier front springs were available on special order. Surviving records do not show many cabs of any kind built, but some were possibly recorded as passenger car production.

A Plymouth highlight was the Safety Interior, most exemplified in the instrument panel. The functional and attractive panel layout placed the primary dials in front of the driver for quick and easy reading. The safety design was effected by flat panel surfaces without projecting knobs and controls. Throttle, choke and light controls were of slide design fitted flush in the rounded panel bottom. Windshield wiper control buttons were of soft rubber and the windshield operating crank folded away. The switch key and other items were recessed. Door handles were designed to minimize hooking of clothing. Front seat backs had heavy padding across the top to protect rear passengers if they were thrown forward. A DeLuxe interior is shown. Buyers of DeLuxe closed cars had a choice of mohair, broadcloth or leather interiors, and a special steering wheel was available for all Plymouths.

1937

Plymouth was again selected by the Detroit Police for cruising the streets in the interest of public safety. The DeLuxe 4-Door Sedan was used by the Department of Safety Education. Besides a special paint treatment, the car was equipped with a radio and whip antenna, rooftop loud-speaker and special tail lamp. This view is a good example of the Plymouth fastback profile.

The 2,000,000th Plymouth, a 1937 DeLuxe model, was purchased by Mrs. Ethel Miller of Turlock, Calif., shown beside it. This was her third very special Plymouth. In 1928 she bought the first Plymouth new, which she traded on the 1,000,000th in 1934 after asking Walter P. Chrysler for the privilege. At that time she asked that the 2,000,000th be reserved for her. At the left is Plymouth vice-president H. G. Moock, and the other man is Verne Orr, sales manager of Chrysler Motors of Calif. Plymouth took just over six years to build its first million, and less than 28 months to produce the second million. No automaker had ever before built the first million in less than nine years. In fact, the whole industry required 12 years to reach the million mark.

A Plymouth DeLuxe happened to be the millionth vehicle produced by Chrysler Corp. in 1936. Walter P. Chrysler proudly drove the car away from the final inspection line late in the year. Chrysler had never before built a million in one year. Nearest the camera was B. E. Hutchinson, chairman of Chrysler's finance committee. Next was Fred Zeder, vice-president in charge of engineering, and leaning against the car was K. T. Keller, president of Chrysler Corp. A half-dozen other executives stood in the background. Mr. Chrysler was chairman of the board of directors of Chrysler Corp.

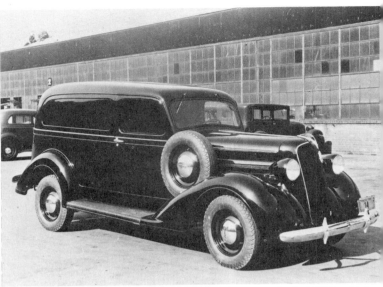

This year, the Westchester Suburban was based on Plymouth's new commercial chassis. The body was again built by the U.S. Body & Forging Co., which moved from Tell City to Frankfort, Ind. after suffering a destructive Ohio River flood in January. In standard form, the Suburban cost $740. 602 of them were built. Standard equipment included the forward spare wheel mounting, safety glass windshield and weather curtains for all doors and windows, but safety glass could be ordered in the latter, too. The 8-passenger body had four side doors, but a choice of rear-end openings was offered. Besides the usual tailgate with liftgate above, there was a combination of tailgate and two swinging doors above. Also, two full-length doors in the manner of a panel delivery were available.

The Plymouth Commercial Sedan was priced at $655, which included safety glass all around, bumpers and radiator ornament. A fairly popular model, 3,256 were built. The load compartment measured 78 inches long at the floor and 55-7/8 inches wide at the belt. A rear bumper was standard on this model only, optional on others. Available options for all commercials were bumper guards, leftside spare wheel and mount, rightside windshield wiper, chrome windshield frame, fenders and chassis sheetmetal in color, and other items. The Commercial Line was coded PT-50 and comprised of four bodied models and one chassis.

The Plymouth Pick-Up Truck had safety glass all around, front bumper and rightside spare wheel as standard features included in its $525 price. 10,709 of them were built. The cab (which in passenger car terms would be the body) had a very functional interior. The express body (pick-up box) was six feet long with a floor width of 47.5 inches. The PT-50 had the P-4 L-head 6-cylinder with a bore of 3-1/8 inches and stroke of 4-3/8 inches. Compression ratio was 6.7 to 1 and brake horsepower was 70 at 3,000 rpm, with a capability of 82 horsepower at maximum. The 3-speed transmission had silent helical gears in second speed.

Plymouth continued to experiment with compact-size cars, which might have been considered for production in foreign countries rather than the U.S.A. Road-tested this year was this little 4-door touring sedan on a wheelbase of approximately 100 inches. General styling was like 1937-38 regular-size cars, but the more vertical grille would come in 1938 with vertical rather than horizontal bars. Known as experimental model AW, the car had a tubular front axle, leaf springs, and probably had a 4-passenger capacity.

The PT-50 chassis with cab only cost $495 with equipment listed for the pick-up. 158 of these units were produced. A cabless chassis with flat face cowl was offered, but only 11 were built. The cabless unit was priced at $395. Rear fenders and long running boards were standard equipment on all chassis and models. As built by Plymouth, commercial vehicles were of half-ton payload capacity, but the chassis could carry one ton when bodied by others. Passenger car sheetmetal was not used for the commercials. The PT-50 chassis was of truck design with five frame cross-members and a 116-inch wheelbase. Tires were heavy duty 6.00 x 16. The rear axle was of hypoid design with standard ratio of 3.73 to 1, with 4.1 to 1 and 4.78 to 1 optional.

1937

For unknown reasons, DeSoto reinstated trunkless sedans after an absence of them in 1936. It could not have been for the purpose of offering family-size sedans at worthwhile savings in cost, as there was only $10 difference between these and the sedans with trunks. Perhaps it was because others in DeSoto's area of competition were offering fastback and trunk models, but they had a $20 to $25 price difference which gave some justification to having two types available. The DeSoto 2-door fastback was the Brougham, which cost $830 and weighed 3,123 pounds. Only 1,200 of the 6-passenger cars were built. DeSoto's interior ventilation system employed ventilating panes that could be lowered with front windows, while swing-type panes were used in quarter windows of 4-door models. Full ventilation was achieved by opening the cowl ventilator and crank-operated windshield.

DeSoto offered just one series, the S-3, with no DeLuxe and Custom differentiation. The Coupe with Rear Luggage Deck, popularly regarded as a business coupe, was the lightest and lowest-priced model. In the standard form shown, it weighed 3,038 pounds and had an advertised delivered price of $770 at the factory. The new pricing method included bumpers, bumper guards, spare tire with tube and safety glass in the windshield and all windows as standard equipment at extra cost. Simply stated, factory prices were adjusted upward to include formerly optional items now regarded as essential to the cars. Standard-equipped, the car shown did not have a rightside tail lamp. All coupe bodies had a one-piece rear window, but sedans featured a divided design. New bodies were wider, and one seat could accommodate three adults. 11,050 Coupes were manufactured.

The DeSoto Touring Brougham featured a trunk which concealed the sapre wheel and had ample room for luggage. Bucket front seats were not used. Instead, the divided front seat back was straight-across so that a center passenger could sit comfortably. 11,660 of the 3,148-pound $840 cars were built. The standard S-3 6-cylinder engine had a bore of 3-3/8 inches and stroke of 4¼ inches (¼ inch less than last year). The compression ratio was 6.5 to 1 and developed horsepower was 93 at 3,600 rpm. The standard transmission was a 3-speed unit, but an optional overdrive version was popular. Called the "Gas Saver Transmission," the overdrive was claimed to give one free mile for every four miles driven. Hypoid rear axles provided humpless floors for rear seat passengers. A wheelbase of 116 inches was utilized for all models of not more than 6-passenger capacity.

The other fastback version was the DeSoto Sedan, a 4-door model with a snug luggage and spare wheel compartment in the rear. This model attracted only 2,265 buyers, cost $870 and weighed 3,123 pounds. It is illustrated with optional chrome running board moldings and rear wheel shields which could be ordered for any model. Among other available items were an aluminum head, two Airtone horns and a booster vacuum pump. DeSoto boasted of 87 new standard features which gave a new kind of ride. This was claimed to be the safest and most fatigue-proof car ever built. With the engine cradled on Floating Power mountings, front wheels independently suspended and new airplane-type shock absorbers all around, a ride free of vibration and bouncing was assured, so it said. Much new insulation and Rubber Float body mountings combined to give a very quiet ride.

The DeSoto Coupe with Rumble Seat could accommodate five passengers. The car weighed 3,088 pounds, was priced at $820, and chalked up 1,030 units on the total production records. The example shown had an optional right-side windshield wiper and tail lamp. This view emphasizes the new position of the headlamps, which were moved rearward while the grille was projected much more forward. The purpose was to create a bolder grille effect and a more impressive hood length. The long hood was further accentuated by sweeping the top grille bars in an unbroken stretch toward the windshield. The hood was of the new one-piece type often called an "alligator" hood because it opened at the front and swung upward. The graceful hood ornament also served as a handle to secure and release the hood. Side panels were not attached to the hood top but were removable for access.

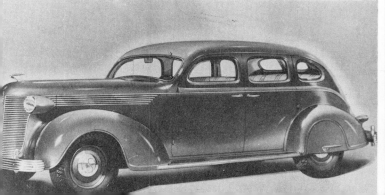

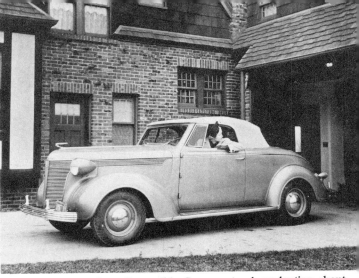

The new S-3 styling was oriented toward a heavy appearance by the use of curving lines and a liberal application of contours. The roundness of the grille harked back to 1932, but was relieved by a vertical divider in body color. The DeSoto name was vertically applied by separate gold-finish letters and, for the first time, there was no medallion on the front. There were no split "vee" windshields, either, but a one-piece steel roof was new. The Touring Sedan was not only the most popular S-3, but was by far the most-demanded DeSoto body type yet offered. Its total of 51,889 built was considerably more than the entire 1936 DeSoto production. Boasted as seating six passengers but generally recorded as a 5-passenger, the 4-door car weighed 3,148 pounds and cost $880. Its trunk, which can barely be seen, had 20% more luggage space than last year's trunk.

1937

The DeSoto Convertible Coupe entered production about January 1st, several months earlier than the usual spring season timing. Convertible weatherproofing technology had improved to such a degree that the type was no longer known as a summer car, but rather as an all-weather car. The smart new car had a rumble seat, weighed 3,225 pounds and was priced at $975. The price included such rightside extras as the windshield wiper, tail lamp and sun visor, as well as dual horns, door armrests and a cigar lighter, all of which were standard on this model. 992 of these cars were built. Wipers were located on the cowl rather than above. The floor was specially reinforced with X-type bracing to provide body rigidity. The top was made of duck material which could be had in tan or black. Interior trim was of leather, colored to blend with the choice of body colors.

The Convertible Sedan was the highest-priced DeSoto, costing $1,300. This body type had not been offered by DeSoto since 1933. The rear doors opened from the rear, unlike those of sedans which were front-opening. Only 426 of the 3,441-pound cars were produced. Standard equipment and option choices were the same as for the Convertible Coupe. Whitewall tires, slowly approaching prices acceptable for less than expensive cars, were available for any model. Though ventilator panes like those shown on the Convertible Coupe were specified, this car had a substitute type installed on some cars because of a shortage of the others. A sign letterer was applying finishing touches to this car, which was appropriately painted silver in accordance with the Silver Anniversary of the Indianapolis 500-Mile Memorial Day Race. The car was used by the Secretary of the AAA Contest Board as his official "office on wheels."

DeSoto began production of the 7-Passenger Sedan about February 1st. Employing an extra-long 133-inch wheelbase, it was powered by the regular 6-cylinder engine. Actually roomy enough for eight passengers, it weighed 3,451 pounds. 695 were manufactured, and the price was $1,120. The two auxiliary seats, each 23¼ inches wide, were not of the skeleton type but were well-padded and upholstered. Equipped with an integral trunk, it could have been called a Touring Sedan, but wasn't.

As a teammate on the long chassis, the Sedan-Limousine made its debut simultaneously with the big sedan. It rounded out DeSoto's factory-offered body line, bringing the total to ten. Registering the least demand of all S-3 factory models, it totalled only 71 built. Weight is unknown, but it probably was heavier than its teammate, which would rank it the heaviest S-3. At $1,220, it was a luxury car "steal." The front compartment, separated from the rear by a slanted partition glass, was completely upholstered in black grained leather. The rear compartment was done in fabric and fitted luxuriously. Standard tire size for the big jobs was 16 x 6.50 as compared with 16 x 6.00 for the smaller S-3 models. The car shown had wheels dressed up with optional chrome trim rings on the rims. They were popularly known as "beauty rings."

The Suburban was not a DeSoto factory offering. The woodcrafted 8-passenger body was mounted on the standard 116-inch wheelbase. Because the rear seats could be removed so it could carry cargo instead of people, it was necessarily classified as a truck. Therefore, it was DeSoto's only appearance, though unofficially, in the domestic truck field this year. The body was constructed and chassis-mounted by J. C. Cantrell & Co., well-respected station wagon builders in Huntington, L.I., N.Y. The vehicle shown had glass all around and four doors that were all hinged on the forward edge. It is not known how many were built, but certainly only a few at most. The chassis were ordered from the factory and shipped to Cantrell. DeSoto assembled 497 S-3 unbodied chassis. Probably most of them were destined for other bodybuilders.

1937

This version on a long chassis could properly be called a Formal Limousine because the quarter windows were replaced with blind quarters. However, it was actually a Sedan-Limousine with variation. The little front fender lamps could be ordered on any model. The chauffeur of this car was provided with an accessory side mirror. Whitewall tires smartened up the somber but sedate automobile. Fender wells with forward-mounted spare wheels were not offered for any S-3 model. The corrugated effect stamped into S-3 bumpers was triple-purpose because it increased bumper strength, gave an appearance similar to the grille bars, and tended to minimize scratches and scars that would be much more obvious and damaging on a plain surface. Guards were cleverly placed behind so as not to obstruct the horizontal bumper effect. Not necessarily related to the long-chassis models was DeSoto's production of 225 taxicabs this year.

The DeSoto instrument panel used in all S-3 cars featured safety design as described for Plymouth. Panel decor was not the same in all S-3 cars, however, as a change occurred by springtime of 1937. Shown is the late edition which featured a simulated woodgrain finish on the entire panel. Early cars had a metallic machine-turned effect on the long rectangular raised expanse within which the dial cluster and glove compartment door were placed, and simulated wood was used on the surfaces adjacent to it. Detail changes were made in other areas at about the same time. Shown is a deluxe steering wheel which was optional throughout the year. DeSoto interiors had all of the safety considerations Plymouth had, and both first had windshield defroster vents this year. DeSoto closed car interiors offered a choice of Bedford cord or mohair fabrics. Philco Transitone radios were available in all models.

Sliding roof panels with sunshine windows were looked into by DeSoto long before they became well-known to the general public. This adaptation was on a 7-passenger body. A section large enough to accommodate the window and hidden cover panel was removed from the roof. The removed section was then cut to provide the daylight opening. Probably the cutout piece was used for the cover panel. The window was divided into two panes. To complete the installation, the altered roof section was replaced in position and sealed around the edges. The sliding cover panel disappeared under the forward section to provide a sky view for rear passengers only. There is no indication that the glass could be moved forward.

The world's first 3-way radio system was installed in DeSoto squad cars of the Eastchester Police Dept. in Tuckahoe, N.Y. Developed by Charles Bodnar, a Tuckahoe engineer, it permitted message exchanges with headquarters and other cruising cars. The officer shown was holding a microphone while acknowledging a call from another DeSoto. The radio equipment and batteries were carried in the roomy DeSoto Coupe luggage compartment, while the transmitter and receiver were in the front compartment. Broadcasting was on a 5-meter band with 10-mile range. First radios in cars were home sets tried out in 1922, and the first one especially for car use came in 1926. A few automakers offered built-in roof antennas in 1929, and by 1934 most instrument panels were designed to accept radios. Steel roofs forced development of the whip antenna in 1936, and one-piece radio sets were first available in 1937.

After five years of steadily growing prosperity following the depression, a serious recession wiped out some of the gains this year. The slump actually began late in 1937, causing that year's growth to be somewhat less than the year before. The national economic decline was attributed to several factors. War clouds were gathering over Europe because of the hostility of Hitler and his build-up of the German war machine. At home, some said a scary stock market and an imbalanced wage-to-living-cost ratio were responsible. Others reasoned that recessions were a natural occurrence every few years, serving a necessary adjustment and balancing function, and there was no reason for alarm. For whatever reasons, general business suffered a slide.

For the 1938 calendar year, total industry production of passenger cars dropped almost 49%. Operations of the combined Chrysler Corp. divisions were cut by more than 52%. Plymouth remained the star performer of the Chrysler troupe by registering the smallest loss of any in the family. Its drop of 42% safely held its position as the

industry's 3rd largest producer, while No. 2 Ford slipp 51% and No. 1 Chevrolet declined almost 43.5%. Chrysle biggest loser was Dodge, which suffered a cut of almc 64% and dropped from 4th to 5th position. Buick got 4 spot because it lost less than 24%. The Chrysler car divisi took a 61.5% dive and sank to 11th position. DeSotc loss of more than 62% pushed it down to 12th plac Studebaker's drop of 43.5% was good enough to lift from 13th position and knock Chrysler out of 10t

The severe loss of sales brought about a wage-cutti trend after the model year began. Though factory-quo prices were higher than 1937, they remained stable throu the year despite the business slump, wage cuts, and lc earning and spending power. Most of the labor force in t industry was unionized by now, and short strikes scatter through the year hindered production to a modera extent. Huge stocks of used cars posed a monstrc problem for dealers, while manufacturers sought ways encourage both new and used car sales.

Plymouth's offering to prospective new car buyers wa: slightly facelifted model. In fact, the alteration was minor that dealers complained. Soon after introduction October, 1937, they said the car was not selling w because it looked too much like the previous mod Adding to the sales-retarding effect of the recession alrea under way meant that something had to be done. Chrysl decided to reposition Plymouth headlamps so they wou be more consistent with those of the corporation's oth cars, on which they were lower and further back. T Plymouth relocation, for appearance sake only, lowered t lamps and moved them approximately four inches towa the rear. Though the others mounted their lamps on tl fender sheetmetal, Plymouth retained the grilleside type mounting. The change was hurried into production k February.

The new Plymouth passenger cars, sometimes called tl Jubilee series in respect to Plymouth's 10th anniversar were introduced in two versions: Business and DeLux However, dealers advised the company that the "Busines name was no longer helpful in selling the line which w originally offered primarily for fleet buyers. The low-ke line had expanded in response to public demand, and i name should be more appropriate. Accordingly, deale were advised in mid-March that the new name "Roadking was being phased in as a replacement. Minor interic appearance changes came shortly afterward. The Busines Roadking line was Model P-5 and the DeLuxe was Mod P-6, but both had P-6 engine numbers. The 6-cylindc L-head engine with Floating Power mountings was carrie over from 1937. In standard form it delivered 82 hors power, but 86 was developed with an optional head. Clut improvements reduced required pedal pressure about 15% A new steering system providing quicker and easi response by means of roller bearings in the king pins and new 14.6 to 1 ratio. The chassis remained essentiall unchanged, even to wheelbase lengths. This was the la: Plymouth with a front axle and leaf-type front spring

Sales promotion concentrated on economy, engineerir and durability, and Plymouth advised buyers to invest i "The Car That Stands Up Best." Compared with 193 prices averaged $33 more but, surprisingly, weight average 38 pounds less. The commercial line was given minc appearance and mechanical changes, and average diffe ences were $52 more and 50 pounds less.

The Model P-5 Coupe was the lightest and lowest-priced Plymouth passenger car, weighing 2,739 pounds and costing $645. The P-5 series was known as the "Business" line until March, when it was named the "Roadking." 15,932 P-5 Coupes were built, of which some went to the Police Dept. of New York City in May. Used as radio patrol cars, they were painted in special colors to attract attention of motorists, reduce collisions and save policemen from injury or death while on emergency runs. White was applied above the beltline and on headlamp shells and the grille center. Green was used below the beltline, and fenders were painted black. This Roadking had an optional extra windshield wiper. Leather upholstery could be had in all P-5 models.

Extra carrying capacity was provided by an optional utility box for the P-5 Coupe. It is shown with the endgate open and deck lid removed for maximum usage. The deck lid could remain hinged and raised as a shelter for smaller loads. The box was available throughout the P-5 production run, but the car shown was built in the very early months as a Business model before headlamps were relocated. The right-side tail lamp was an extra-cost option that could be ordered on any P-5 body type.

DeSoto presented many changes this year, including nger wheelbases of 119 and 136 inches. Styling of the w S-5 series was an extensive facelift which utilized e former body shells. Continued with refinements was e 6-cylinder L-head engine and its Floating Power ounts. Horsepower remained at 93 with a standard head d 100 optional. The new chassis frame strengthened the evious X-braced design. Independent front wheel sus- nsion, semi-elliptic leaf-type rear springs and hypoid rear le were continued, but brake drums were 10% bigger d designed for longer lining life. A new steering echanism was mounted in rubber and the parking brake ntrol was moved from the floor to just below the in- rument panel. A choice of standard 3-speed or optional erdrive transmission was offered, both with floor- ounted stickshift.

The new DeSoto, like the Plymouth, was styled under e supervision of Ray Dietrich, the well-known custom car signer who continued as chief stylist for Chrysler Corp. n important DeSoto sales punch proclaimed it as America's Smartest Low-Priced Car," a line it had used fore. The cars were larger but they averaged about six unds lighter. Advertised delivered prices at the factory eraged $87 higher. Though buyers were hard to find, eSoto and Plymouth factory prices held steady through- t the model year. Much consideration was given to easures calculated to increase sales, but price reductions re ruled out because of the high cost of materials.

Again offered for all Plymouth passenger cars except 7-passenger models, 20-inch wheels were an $18 option. The price included tires with tubes, double-acting heavy-duty shock absorbers and a special hypoid rear axle with 4.3 to 1 gear ratio. Road clearance of 9-7/8 inches was 1½ inches more than with standard wheels. The extra clearance was an advantage on unpaved roads and areas with rough going. The car is a P-5 2-Door Sedan, which had a fastback luggage compartment. A total of 15,393 were built, including high-wheel models. With standard 16 x 5.50 wheels and tires, it weighed 2,764 pounds and cost $685 without options. 16 x 6.00 tires could aslo be had on any P-5. Shown as a Business model built in February, it looked the same as when later known as a Roadking. The hubcaps shown, unlike those used on standard wheels, were 1935-36 production.

The 2-Door Touring Sedan was added to the P-5 line in March when Plymouth changed the low-line series name from "Business" to "Roadking" for a better appeal to the public. Without options it weighed 2,779 pounds and cost $701. 16,413 were built. The body featured a trunk as standard. The car shown, owned by the Police Dept. of Detroit's suburban city of Grosse Pointe, had two extra-large bumper guards for grille protection. Coming with the change to the Roadking name was an upgrading of P-5 interiors. Paint on the instrument panel and garnish moldings was replaced with woodgrain, and the color of the steering column, gearshift lever and handbrake handle was changed. A bench-type front seat option was offered for 2-Door Sedans and Touring Sedans, which continued the bucket seats as standard.

This restored example of a Plymouth P-5 4-Door Sedan is owned by George Barnett, Salem, Ind. It was built in the early weeks of the Business series. This model was the least popular P-5, as indicated by a total of 6,459 built. In standard form it weighed 2,809 pounds and was factory-priced at $730. Like the 2-Door Sedan and Coupe, it was in production throughout the P-5 manufacturing span. A choice of several body colors was available on all passenger cars. P-5 cars were built with fenders in body-matching color at extra cost unless ordered with standard black fenders. All P-6 DeLuxe cars were built with fenders to match bodies at no extra cost, and could not be ordered otherwise. Special body colors could be ordered for both series. A gasoline economy option was again available for both series, giving better fuel mileage but reducing power and acceleration.

First to be added after the introduction of the Business series was the 4-Door Touring Sedan, which appeared early in February. It was the most popular, heaviest, and highest priced P-5. It cost $746 and weighed 2,824 pounds. A total of 18,664 were built. The car is shown here with the early production headlamp location, which was phasing out as this P-5 body type was phasing in. The model was continued under the Roadking name. Externally, there was no way to distinguish a car of the Business series from the same model of the later Roadking line. Details were exactly alike, and there were no series-identifying nameplates. For similar reasons, it was virtually impossible to differentiate the P-5 Business/Roadking cars from P-6 DeLuxe models unless windows were especially noticed. P-5 bodies did not have ventilator wings in front windows nor swing-out panes in the rear quarters, but P-6 models did. The P-5 chassis in stripped form was available for other purposes, and 1,586 of them were assembled.

Plymouth continued to offer fastback sedans because its competitors did. The DeLuxe 2-Door Sedan was the least popular of all Plymouth passenger cars on the 112-inch wheelbase. Only 1,222 were built, hardly enough to keep it in the P-6 line, especially when its P-5 counterpart sold at a ratio of almost 12 to 1. The DeLuxe model did not offer enough extra appeal to justify its $88 extra cost. It was priced at $773 and it weighed 2,874 pounds. All 112-inch DeLuxe models were fitted with 16 x 6.00 tires. DeLuxe closed bodies on both wheelbases offered a choice of broadcloth or mohair interiors at no cost difference, and leather was available for a price.

The DeLuxe Plymouth Coupe was a 3-passenger car with rear deck luggage compartment. Lightest and lowest-priced of the DeLuxe P-6 line, it weighed 2,804 pounds and cost $730. It accounted for 27,181 units of the year's production. A more vertical grille was the most dominant new feature of Plymouth styling this year. The high and more forward position of the headlamps was typical of P-5 and P-6 cars built during the early production months. All popular-size passenger cars utilized a standard 112-inch wheelbase. One engine was common to all cars regardless of wheelbase lengths. It had six cylinders of 3-1/8 inch bore and 4-3/8 inch stroke, developed 82 horsepower with standard head and 86 with an optional design.

Rumble seat models were losing popularity but would remain another year or so. The DeLuxe Rumble Seat Coupe tipped the weighing scale at 2,864 pounds and was priced at $770. Though it cost only $40 more than the Coupe without rumble seat, it drew only about 7% as many buyers. An even 2,000 built was enough to satisfy the meager demand. Plymouth again featured safety design in all interiors. The instrument panel was altered but it emphasized safety consideration in the placement of newly-designed controls. Windshields were now fixed in place, so there was no longer need for an operating crank. Also, the new fixed glass required no metal frame on the exterior.

The DeLuxe 2-Door Touring Sedan was a fairly popular model, as indicated by the total of 46,669 built. The 2,864-pound car was priced at $785 in standard form. The rightside windshield wiper and tail lamp were extra-cost options available for all DeLuxe closed cars. In P-5 and P-6 Touring Sedans, the spare wheel now stood upright behind the rear seat partition, eliminating the former shelf and providing more luggage space in the trunks. An ambulance interior conversion was offered for P-5 and P-6 sedans with trunks. All Plymouths had hoods four inches longer than previously. Hinged at the center, they opened at the beltline. Side panels were bolted in place.

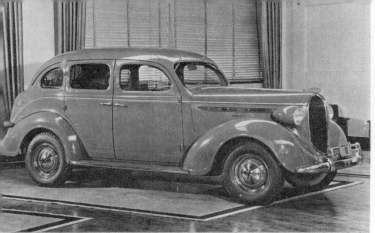

As usual, the Plymouth most in demand was the DeLuxe 4-Door Touring Sedan. The 6-passenger car recorded a total of 119,669 built. With standard trim and equipment it weighed 2,874 pounds and cost $815. The car shown was equipped with a new Custom Accessory Group which added $35 to the cost. Added in March, it was needed to attract buyers, and was available on any DeLuxe model. It embraced a host of luxury and dress-up items. On the exterior were a special dual-rail grille guard, chromed license plate frames, chromed dual windshield wipers, chromed wheel rim rings, chromed running board moldings, and an auxiliary tail lamp. The interior had pillow-type seat upholstery, special trim design on the front seat back and doors, lighter graining on the instrument panel and garnish moldings, instruments in contrasting color, a special color steering wheel with chrome horn ring, colored hardware escutcheon plates, a special gearshift knob, front armrests, carpeting at door bottoms, a glove box lock, cigar lighter and auxiliary sun visor. Dual Airtone horns were also included. It can be seen that this car had whitewall tires on the opposite side, but they were not part of the group option.

1938

The DeLuxe Convertible Coupe entered production about April 1st. This was the heaviest and most expensive Plymouth 112-inch wheelbase passenger car. It weighed 3,009 pounds and cost $850. 1,900 of these smart sport cars were produced. The manually-operated top was available in tan or black duck material. The interior was upholstered in genuine leather colored to harmonize with body colors, and the rumble seat was covered with a special moleskin material. Dual tail lamps and dual windshield wipers were standard for this model, which was the only Plymouth with wipers on the cowl. The underbody was reinforced with special framework for rigidity. When compared with the illustration of the DeLuxe Coupe, this car effectively shows the change in headlamp position which was given to all Plymouths early in the production run. The lamps were lowered about two inches and moved toward the rear approximately four inches, which clearly affected their relationship to the grille, beltline and hood louvers. The new position was more similar to DeSoto, as well as to Dodge and Chrysler.

With a production total little more than its 2-door sister model, the DeLuxe 4-Door Sedan also reflected public apathy toward trunkless sedans. The total of 1,446 built was less than 22% of the demand registered by the comparable P-5 model. It was priced at $803 and weighed 2,894 pounds. Not confined to the model illustrated, taxicab options were again made available. Though registered only in production totals for the DeLuxe series, of which 35 were taxicabs, they also could be had for the P-5 line. First announced in January was a package including heavy-duty versions of the transmission, springs and shock absorbers, plus an 11-inch clutch. Some cab operators did not want all of that, so in May another package was added. It omitted the heavy-duty transmission, had a 10-inch clutch and, when installed on Roadkings, supplied spring covers.

The DeLuxe Plymouth 7-Passenger Sedan could seat nine, according to its makers. The two auxiliary seats, which folded into the front seat back when not in use, were said to be wide enough for three persons. Though the body had a trunk, it was not called a Touring Sedan. The spacious 132-inch wheelbase car was placed in production in mid-April. It weighed 3,289 pounds and was priced at $1,005. A total of 1,824 were built. It was the lowest-priced 7-passenger model on the market, and its 214 inches of bumper-to-bumper overall length was 12 inches more than any comparable model in its price class. It was said to be for large families and others who may occasionally want to be chauffeured, but it undoubtedly was more useful to taxicab operators, funeral homes, airlines, etc. This model required 16 x 6.50 tires and a special rear axle ratio of 4.3 to 1. Smaller Plymouths had a 4.1 to 1 ratio.

Not a catalogued model, the DeLuxe Plymouth 7-Passenger Sedan-Limousine was a limited production car. The beginning date of production is not known, but the headlamps of the car shown indicate that it was built prior to February. This car may have been a pilot limousine model, however. Regardless, the car borrowed everything but the driver's compartment from the 7-Passenger Sedan, including the 132-inch wheelbase. At $1,095 it was the most expensive 1938 Plymouth passenger car, and its production total of only 75 made it the least-wanted of all. Its weight is not known, but it undoubtedly was heavier than the huge sedan.

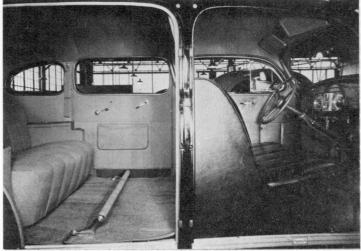

The Sedan-Limousine interior was tailored and fitted in the traditional manner and taste appropriate for a formal automobile. The chauffeur's compartment was trimmed in dark leather and separated from the rear compartment by a partition glass which was slanted to conform to the angle of the front seat back. For this view the auxiliary center seats were folded out of sight in the dividing partition. The carpeted footrest was hinged so it could be swung toward the rear seat when not wanted. Rear doors had large pockets, and long assist straps were hung on the "C" pillars. Among many options available for all Plymouths were Philco Transitone radios and hot water heaters, the latter offering a choice of three types.

The station wagon reverted to use of a passenger car chassis after going 100% commercial for 1937. Though still classified as a commercial vehicle, it was now getting closer to full recognition as a dual-purpose passenger car. Because of the growing market potential of this type, Plymouth placed it on the DeLuxe P-6 chassis to provide better handling, riding and comfort qualities. The U.S. Body and Forging Co., Frankfort, Ind., continued to manufacture the woodcrafted bodies. The bodymaker's identification plate spelled out "Westchester Suburban," but Plymouth simply called it the Suburban. The 4-door body was a new and larger design with wider doors, softer seats and better glass enclosures. Access to the rearmost seat of the 8-passenger body was provided by a narrow passway at the curb side of the center seat. Rear and center seats were removable. The spare wheel was carried on the outside of the tailgate. The car shown had safety glass in all windows including the rear liftgate, the ultra-option at $60. In standard form, safety glass was used in the windshield and front doors, and all other openings were fitted with windowed curtains. The cowl and windshield was similar to the Convertible Coupe, with cowl-mounted wipers and a chrome frame. Without options, the Suburban sold for $880 and weighed 3,039 pounds. Plymouth and USBF turned out 555 of these DeLuxe 112-inch wheelbase cars. 2,027 DeLuxe chassis without bodies were built for other purposes.

Shown in standard form is the Plymouth PT-57 Pick-Up, which sold for $585. A total of 4,620 came off the assembly line. It had a half-ton payload capacity. The chassis with cab only, priced at $560, was offered for those who wanted to mount special cargo bodies. In that case, the combined cab, body and payload allowance was one ton. Only 95 chassis/cab units were built. More options were available for commercial cars this year. Among them were a cowl with windshield, dual forward-mounted spare wheels, a rear bumper (for the Pick-Up), bumper guards, auxiliary tail lamp (Commercial Sedan only) and auxiliary windshield wiper. For dress up, chrome plating could be had on the radiator shell, headlamps and windshield frame, and a custom touch could be given to the Commercial Sedan by adding side-mounted coach lamps. Others were an oil bath air cleaner, engine speed governor, oil filter, double-acting hydraulic shock absorbers, metal spare tire covers and long-arm rear view mirrors. Normally painted black, the radiator shell, headlamps and brackets, fenders and splash shields could be ordered to match the six standard body colors other than black.

The Plymouth Commercial Line, Model PT-57, was not much different from the previous model. Most notable was the vertical grille, not so deep at the bottom, which related these vehicles to the passenger cars. No sheetmetal was borrowed from the cars, however. The 116-inch wheelbase commercial chassis was retained, including an I-beam front axle, hypoid rear axle with 4.1 to 1 ratio, semi-elliptic springs and Hotchkiss double U-joint drive. The L-head 6-cylinder engine had a bore of 3-1/8 inches and stroke of 4-3/8 inches, and developed horsepower was 70 at 3,000 rpm. A 3-speed transmission was standard, and a 4-speed was optional. Standard tires were 4-ply 16 x 6.00, with 6-ply optional. 20-inch wheels could also be had. A fuel economy option with modified carburetor and intake manifold plus a 3.73 rear axle ratio was offered. The Commercial Sedan, as shown with standard equipment except for an accessory grille guard, was priced at $695. 1,601 of them were built. A single rear door gave access to a load area which, measured in maximum inches, was 78 long, 45½ inches high and 55-7/8 wide. Only the driver's seat was supplied unless an auxiliary seat was ordered.

The DeSoto Coupe with Rear Luggage Deck accommodated three passengers and a large amount of travel necessities. It weighed the least of any DeSoto this year, tipping the scales at 3,039 pounds. Also, it was the lowest-priced model in the new series, listing at the factory for $870. Assembly lines rolled off 5,160 of these attractive and businesslike cars. The car shown was fitted with an optional auxiliary windshield wiper. All models now had wipers mounted on the cowl. A non-opening windshield was new this year, and enclosed bodies had no metal frame on the front side of the glass. That omission slightly increased the vision area. Not catalogued as one of the body line was a Coupe with Rumble Seat, but only 38 of them were built. Possibly they were a special order built for delivery in a specific sales area.

1938

The new series DeSoto, known as the S-5, was distinguished by its new front end styling. Sides of the vertical grille curved down to the front center, beneath which were five chevron-like louvers for extra cooling. Headlamps nestled on the fenders, well withdrawn toward the rear so that the grille projected boldly forward. The upright grille further enhanced appearance by resulting in a longer stretch of sheetmetal back to the windshield. Also new was the hood, which discarded the former one-piece alligator type for a two-piece design hinged at the center and opening from each side at the beltline. The louvered side panels were bolted in place. Shown is the Touring Brougham, a 2-door type with trunk. 5,367 of the 3,119-pound, $930 cars were built. Not catalogued was a Brougham without trunk, of which 11 were built.

The DeSoto Convertible Coupe was placed in production in March. Dual windshield wipers and dual tail lamps were standard equipment. The list price was $1,045 and the weight was 3,229 pounds. Only 431 of the sporty cars were built. The rumble seat compartment had a footrest built into the floor. A special framework in the underbody provided stiffness necessary to a body which had no roof and upper structure for strength. The folding top was of manual-operating design with a choice of tan or black duck material. The body was exceptionally well insulated, and special attention was given to means of making it weathertight. The interior leather trim was in colors to harmonize with a choice of six exterior hues. The car is shown equipped with rear wheel enclosure panels, an option which could be had on any S-5 model.

The most popular DeSoto was the Touring Sedan, a 4-door model with trunk. The 6-passenger car recorded a total production of 23,681. It weighed 3,139 pounds and was priced at $970. The auxiliary tail lamp shown was optional on all but convertible models. The S-5 interior ventilation system, in addition to the cowl ventilator, employed pivoting panes called "butterfly wings" in the front windows. Rear quarter windows of sedans also had them. Optional hot water heaters provided winter warmth. More luggage space in the trunk was obtained by mounting the spare wheel in a tilted upright position next to, and conforming to the angle of, the forward partition. Not catalogued as a regular offering was the Custom Touring Sedan, a 4-door type, of which 2,550 were built. Probably it was a dressed up version to attract more sales.

The DeSoto Sedan with Luggage Compartment was a 4-door fastback with a low popularity rating. Only 498 of them were built. A price of $958 was asked for the 3,134-pound model. All S-5 models of less than 7-passenger capacity were built on a 119-inch wheelbase, three inches more than the previous model. The S-5 engine was continued from 1937. With a bore of 3-3/8 inches and stroke of 4¼ inches, the six-cylinders developed 93 horsepower with a standard head having a compression ratio of 6.5 to 1. With a special head and 7.0 to 1 ratio it produced 100 horsepower. A 3-speed stickshift all-silent transmission was standard. An optional "Gas-Saver" transmission was actually a built-in part added to the standard type. It was fundamentally an overdrive which cut in at 35-40 miles an hour when accelerator pressure was momentarily relieved.

The DeSoto Convertible Sedan had all of the specialized construction and appearance features that were incorporated in its sister convertible model. The 6-passenger 4-door body had a built-in trunk. It weighed 3,394 pounds and cost $1,375. In relation to the S-5 family, it was the heaviest 119-inch wheelbase model and was the costliest offering regardless of size. A production of only 88 was recorded. This was the last convertible sedan built by DeSoto, at least in the U.S.A. Adding a bit of class, both convertible types had windshields framed in chrome, a touch not given to enclosed bodies. All 119-inch wheelbase cars were fitted with 16 x 6.00 tires as standard equipment. Styling and body package characteristics did not permit attractive forward-mounted spare wheels. DeSoto, like Plymouth, last offered them in 1936.

An impressive automobile was the DeSoto 7-Passenger Sedan. The S-5 long chassis was extended three inches, giving it a 136-inch wheelbase. It weighed 3,439 pounds and was priced at $1,195. The factories turned out 513 of these models. The huge interior, which featured all of the safety design considerations of other models, could actually seat nine adults. A choice of two upholstery materials was offered. DeSoto's "Cushioned Ride" qualities were multiplied by the size and luxury of this vehicle. The big jobs had a tire size of 16 x 6.50. The option list included a radio, which was available for all S-5 body types. This car probably entered production when the limousine did. Though not particularly confined to the large cars, DeSoto again offered specially-adapted models for the taxicab trade, and built a total of 372 of them.

The heaviest and most luxurious of all production DeSotos this year was the 7-Passenger Sedan-Limousine. The 3,524-pound car offered an imposing array of sumptuous trim, fittings and appointments. The body, which was mounted on the long chassis, could be had with rear quarter windows as shown, or with blind quarters. Trim in front and rear compartments could be selected from four combinations: Black leather in front and either cloth or mohair in the rear, or the entire interior could be in cloth or mohair. An extra-cost choice was seats in pillow style, special cushion springs, a folding center armrest in the rear seat and cigar lighters above the rear side armrests. The $1,285 car entered production in February. Only 81 of them were manufactured. All of the long-wheelbase DeSotos were equipped with the 100-horsepower engine, necessary for the size.

This conversion was publicized as an emergency ambulance and funeral car for transporting the sick and injured as well as pallbearers and mourners. It was designed specifically for funeral directors and funeral car rental agencies. Without lengthening, the DeSoto 7-Passenger Sedan was a good vehicle for such multi-purpose use. The front seat was divided so that the rightside half could be removed, and there was no rightside auxiliary seat. The center pillar was made removable by means of a pin and dowel at the sill and two thumb screws in a locking plate at the top. Those features provided ample accommodation for a stretcher patient and nurse. When used strictly for seating, it could carry six persons including the driver. Because of the omission of the auxiliary seat, a portable folding chair had to be used for a seventh person.

A 7-passenger chassis and body was the basis for this formal town car. The bodywork was done by Derham, well-known coachbuilders in Rosemont, Pa. The roof and quarters were padded and covered with a leatherlike material. A detail refinement was the rounding of the upper rear corners of the rear doors. Interestingly, the new windshield was made with less slant than stock bodies had. The partition glass behind the chauffeur's seat was divided at the center so that it could be opened by sliding sidewise. A protective canopy was provided for the front compartment. For special bodies and purposes, DeSoto built 413 chassis which probably included both lengths.

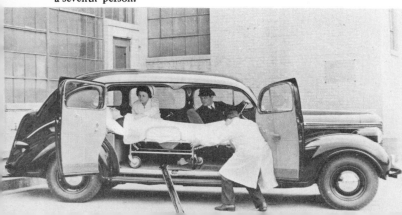

This was a year of recuperation from the effects of the 1938 recession, but full recovery was still ten years away. The recovery period might have been three and a half years shorter if a nasty world war had not butted in. More and more of Europe was taken over as Germany's aggression gained momentum during the year. The world grew increasingly uneasy as the threat of widespread involvement became more certain. In the U.S.A., automobile manufacturers and key companies in other important industries were quietly and thoroughly canvassed by the federal government to determine military product allocations, preparation requirements and potential production capacity of machines and material for national defense and foreign aid. Labor unrest continued as the unions sought more power. Hit by a strike late in the year, Chrysler Corp. plants were shut down eight weeks. Regardless of all, public confidence and buying habits were on the rebound, aided by a return to the wage scale that prevailed before the 1938 reductions in pay.

The auto industry, as usual, was a leader in reflecting the rise on the business barometer. At the end of the 1939 calendar year, it registered a gain of more than 43% over 1938, while the divisions of Chrysler Corp. collectively gathered a gain of 37.5%. Plymouth, the steadiest seller in Chrysler's store, was its smallest gainer at 17.5%. Normally, sales fluctuations were not so severe in the lowest-priced field, and the low gain did not mean a poor showing in relation to others. Plymouth easily retained 3rd position in the ranks of all automakers. Though Dodge's 75% boost was the best score chalked up by any Chrysler division, it did not surpass Buick and lift itself up from 5th place. The Chrysler car division earned an increase of over 63% but fell a notch into 12th spot because of the entry of Ford's new Mercury, which took 11th. DeSoto's gain of nearly 63% was about equal to Chrysler but its double drop to 14th place was because of Mercury and the rising demand for Nash. Some of the shuffling of the industry's passenger car production positions was due to a Studebaker spurt induced by introduction of its new low-priced Champion series. Of course, the Studebaker Champion was brand-new competition for Plymouth, but time would show that it was not a threat.

Flying a new banner which declared "This Year Plymouth's the Car," dealers showed the new Roadking and DeLuxe models to the public in mid-September, 1938. They were enthusiastically received. New styling was largely due to a wholly new front end treatment. The grille, fenders, hood and "vee" windshield were a complete departure from the former design. Gone were the traditional upright grille and independent headlamps, replaced by a triple layout of horizontal cooling louvers and fully-recessed headlamps. Rear fenders had tail lamps recessed within them. Except for the new windshield, exterior body styling was not new, but new design was applied to the interior.

The Roadking series was Model P-7 and the DeLuxe was Model P-8, but P-8 engine numbers applied to both series. The engine was a refined continuation from the previous year, but basic specifications were retained. The 6-cylinder plant had a bore of 3-1/8 inches and a stroke of 4-3/8 inches. With standard head and 6.7 compression ratio, 82 horsepower was developed, and with optional head and 7.0 ratio the horsepower output was 86. The wheelbase of the popular-sized cars was 114 inches, while 134 inches was used for the 7-passenger models, each being an increase of two inches. The Roadking was based on the short chassis only. A 117-inch wheelbase carried the DeLuxe Convertible Sedan only. This year saw Plymouth's return to independent front wheel suspension, after an absence of four years. Chassis frames were made stronger and many technical improvements were scattered throughout the cars. An important new feature was the remote control gearshift on the steering column of DeLuxe models. The new device made changing of speeds much easier but the 3-speed transmission remained basically unchanged.

The total weight of the Plymouth passenger car range averaged 37 pounds more than the previous models. The price average did not change, though nine models were as much as $15 less, one was $45 more and the others remained stable. The Commercial Line was divided into two categories. One was based on the P-7 and P-8 series, and consisted of passenger cars adapted for commercial use, plus the Panel Delivery (commercial sedan). The other was the new PT-81 light truck series which included the Pick-Up and a chassis offered for other bodies. The PT-81 was a drastic change from the former model but it held onto the 116-inch wheelbase and 70 horsepower engine while adding improvements in minor areas. Prices of the PT-81 averaged slightly less than its predecessor's.

DeSoto formally announced its new series S-6 late in October of 1938. The cars were almost totally new and, with Plymouth, required a good-sized chunk of the $15,000,000 Chrysler Corp. spent for tooling up all of its car divisions this year. DeSoto's completely new styling, developed under the direction of Raymond Dietrich, resulted from one of the most exhaustive studies of dealer opinion ever conducted by the company. A survey made use of questionnaires, personal interviews, field meetings and other means of finding out what the marketplace felt was required. The need for a new styling concept was fulfilled by creation of one of the most beautiful series of cars DeSoto had yet built. Smoothly flowing lines and contours were in step with the trend to more complete unity of design. Elements of function and form were brought together in graceful proportion to each other. Triple grilles were a transition from the former single vertical to the low horizontal type to come. Headlamps

The Roadking Coupe was the lightest and lowest-priced Plymouth passenger car of the year. It weighed 2,274 pounds and delivered at the factory for $645. A total of 22,537 were built. The businesslike car accommodated three passengers and had a spacious luggage compartment in the deck. The Roadking, coded as Model P-7, was popular with fleet buyers as well as the public. More austere than DeLuxe models, it continued to use the floor-mounted gearshift lever. Not included in the factory-offered list of body types was the Roadking Coupe with Rumble Seat, of which 222 were built.

were finally and completely engulfed by the fenders. The "vee" windshield, absent for two years, returned to split the wind as it rushed toward the tailored rear end. Gone was the trunk hump, which gave way to a sweeping fastback with greater luggage space for all sedan-type cars. Rear fenders curved slightly away from the body rear and sheltered tail lamps within them. Rear pillars of 4-door sedans were smartly arched forward like coupe pillars, and a subtle swelling at the beltline seemed to support the sweeping length of the bright molding. Lower body sides

For the first time, the name "Plymouth" appeared as chrome nameplates on the exterior. However, there was no similar means for distinguishing Roadking from DeLuxe models. The most notable Roadking exterior difference was the beltline trim. The bright molding which began at the center of the prow-like radiator shell swept around the sides and ended on the hood panels a few inches beyond the shell. Some did not have bright trim around the windshield but all DeLuxe cars did. Shown is the Roadking 2-Door Sedan, of which 7,499 were built. Its weight was 2,824 pounds and it cost $685.

The 2-Door Touring Sedan was the most popular Plymouth Roadking model, recording a total of 42,186 built. The 6-passenger car cost $699 and weighed 2,824 pounds. Standard Roadking tire size was 16 x 5.50, with 16 x 6.00 optional. Dual windshield wipers and tail lamps were optional for all Plymouths except convertibles. Fenders and wheels in colors to match bodies were standard specifications for any Roadking or DeLuxe. A special wheel color option for the two series, added as a spring dress-up at no extra cost, was Casino Red or Packard Ivory, each with a Silver stripe.

were slightly curved outward toward the running board hinting that the eventual enclosure of the latter was und consideration.

The new DeSoto line of bodies was simplified to a dealers in stocking cars. Sedan types were no longer offere with or without trunks, and all body types were availab in DeLuxe or Custom trim, a reversion to the double-lin setup of the 1936 Airstream. Also, convertibles were n offered, largely because the 1938 demand was so low th only 519 were built, which was not enough to warra building such specially-constructed cars. Compared wit similar models of the single 1938 series, the new DeLu line was priced the same but averaged 25 pounds heavi Body for body, Custom cars cost $53 more and were pounds heavier than those of the DeLuxe line.

Mechanically, DeSoto had many newly-designed featur but the basic chassis layout of 1938 was unchanged. Eve the wheelbase lengths of 119 and 136 inches were before. The previous 6-cylinder engine was continued, b with Chrysler's new "Superfinishing" method applied moving parts. Among parts receiving the super-slick trea ment were the crankshaft, camshaft, pistons, valve stem tappet heads, wrist pins and the flywheel. Surfaces we said to be smoother within a range of 3 to 10 milliont of an inch, resulting in smoother operations and long engine life. The engine bore and stroke was 3-3/8 4-1/4 inches, respectively. Horsepower was 93 with t standard 6.5 to 1 cylinder head and 100 with an option head and 7.0 to 1 compression ratio. New this year was t remote control gearshift on the steering column. Also ne was an optional overdrive unit with "Step-Down" featur Claiming the equivalent of five speeds forward, it operate in second and high gears. Engaging at 25 miles an ho instead of 35 as formerly, it was disengaged by pressu on the accelerator pedal and re-engaged by pedal releas The new unit reduced engine revolutions by one-third a gave greater economy by operating in city as well country driving.

The least popular Roadking in the Plymouth factory listing was the 4-Door Sedan, which reported a total of 2,553 built. The 2,839-pound car was priced at $726. No early production Roadkings had ventilating wings in the front windows. However, in response to widespread requests from dealers, they were made available in January. The special factory-installed option was offered for $10 and did not include wings to replace standard glass in sedan rear quarter windows. A taxicab package was offered for Roadkings, but there is no indication of how many were so-equipped.

The Plymouth Roadking 4-Door Touring Sedan was the highest-priced model in the economy series, costing $740. It pressed the weighing scale to a reading of 2,829 pounds. Assembly lines rolled off 23,047 examples of this 6-passenger family car. Normally upholstered in cloth, Roadking interiors could be ordered in leather. Roadking interiors included, as standard, some fittings that formerly were not available in the economy line. Rear armrests and ash receivers were among the items included. The P-7 chassis was available without bodies, and a total of 1,616 of them were assembled.

The DeLuxe Plymouth Coupe weighed and cost the least of any P-8 passenger car. The 2,789-pound model was priced at $725. The factories produced a total of 41,924 of the 3-passenger cars. Note the large hinges on the lid of the roomy luggage compartment. The engine that powered P-7 and P-8 cars developed 82 horsepower in standard form, while 86 was delivered when an optional cylinder head was employed. Two fuel economy options were again offered. A mileage increase of as much as 25% was claimed. Without such equipment, owners reported getting from 18 to 24 miles per gallon.

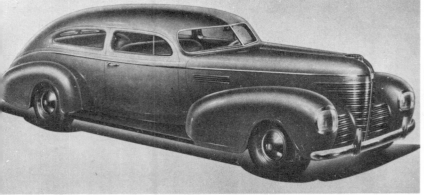

Fastback Plymouths rated very little buyer preference because the rear luggage compartment did not have as much space as a trunk. The DeLuxe 2-Door Sedan seated six passengers comfortably and was suitable for those who could do without so much luggage space, or did not want to pay $14 more for a trunk. 2,653 of these cars found owners. The price was $761 at the factory, and the weight was 2,889 pounds. Interiors of all DeLuxe closed bodies were more stylish than before. Door window garnish moldings, previously of simple functional design, received extra decoration.

DeLuxe Plymouths featured a bright beltline molding which swept from the front center of the car to the rear. Also, the windshield was brightly outlined. The windshield center divider strip was generally in body color, but some were of bright metal. The DeLuxe 2-Door Touring Sedan was a popular model, accounting for 80,981 units of this year's production. Its weight was 2,894 pounds and it cost $775. The trunk of all Plymouth Touring Sedan models provided 17.5 cubic feet of luggage capacity. The spare wheel stood in an upright tilted position behind the rear seat.

This was the last year Plymouth offered a rumble seat model of any kind, at least in the U.S.A. For many years the rumble seat was regarded as essential to the equipment of any rear-decked model intended as a sport-type automobile. The desire for personal comfort in closed cars gradually obsoleted the rear deck seat, which was always hard to get in and out of anyway. Though some comforts were built in, the wind, weather and dust could not be licked. The DeLuxe Coupe with Rumble Seat weighed 2,874 pounds and was priced at $755. 1,332 of them rolled out of the factories.

The DeLuxe Plymouth 4-Door Sedan was another fastback model with a low popularity rating, chalking up only 2,279 units on the production scoreboard. The factory delivered price of the 2,909-pound car was $791. DeLuxe models of not more than 6-passenger capacity were standard-equipped with 16 x 6.00 tires. Forward-mounted spare wheels were not available on strictly passenger car models. All Plymouth passenger cars but the Convertible Sedan and longer types had a 114-inch wheelbase. Unidentified as to body types, a total of only 12 DeLuxe Taxicabs were produced.

Drawing the most demand of any 1939 Plymouth was the DeLuxe 4-Door Touring Sedan. 175,054 of the 6-passenger cars were built. It recorded a weight of 2,919 pounds and asked a price of $805. Push-button radios were optional, and the car shown had an antenna under the running board. Also available was a whip-type antenna. Excepting convertibles, DeLuxe interiors offered broadcloth or mohair trim, and leather was extra-cost. New this year was the gearshift on the steering column of DeLuxe cars only, and a new "Finger Touch" power shifting option became available in January.

Again available were 20-inch wheels on all Plymouths except 7-passenger models. Still using 1935-36 hubcaps, they are shown on a DeLuxe 4-Door Touring Sedan. They were for the kind of rough traveling shown. Another option for cars to be operated under abnormal service conditions included double-capacity shock absorbers, stone shields for shock absorbers, commercial duty springs, and spring bumpers. All Plymouths had the handbrake operating handle at the driver's left. Also new on all was a lighted speed indicator that changed from green to amber to red as speed increased.

The DeLuxe Plymouth Convertible Sedan was the only such model offered by Chrysler Corp. this year. The first such Plymouth since 1932, it was also the last. Oddly, it had an exclusive 117-inch wheelbase. Only 387 of the 4-door 6-passenger cars were built. Costing $1,150, it included all of the Convertible Coupe equipment but the power top mechanism. Convertible Coupe options could also be had. The family-size convertible was also one of the "Sportsmen." Both convertibles had special underbody frames. The restored car shown is owned by Willis Schneider, Kitchener, Ont., Can.

Never before was there a Plymouth so large as the super-stretched cars of this year. Their 134-inch wheelbase bested the previous models by two inches. With center auxiliary seats in use there was adequate room for nine adult passengers. A special larger tire size of 16 x 6.50 was required. Illustrated is the DeLuxe 7-Passenger Sedan, which weighed 3,374 pounds and cost $1,005. A total of 1,837 were built. Its big teammate, the DeLuxe 7-Passenger Sedan-Limousine, was the least-wanted Plymouth passenger car this year, as only 98 were built. It was priced at $1,095.

New was a power-operated top on the DeLuxe Plymouth Convertible Coupe. It was a standard item on this model, which cost $895 in basic form. The rumble seat car, of which 5,976 were built, weighed 3,044 pounds. This unrestored example owned by Wilbur Burkett, Ida, Mich., was built with dual sidemounted spare wheels, normally not available. Also unusual were black instead of body color fenders. Plymouth simply used commercial car parts for this car. Looping bumper guards were regular extras. For sales appeal, this was one of three models occasionally advertised as Plymouth "Sportsmen."

1939

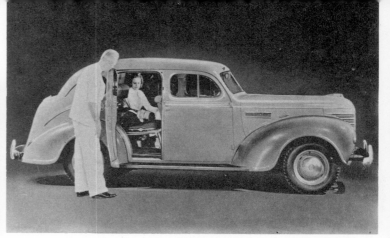

The Plymouth Ambulance Conversion was a Commercial Car offering. The conversion added $55 to the automobile list price and did not include the stretcher and other ambulance equipment. The right half of the rear seat folded upward and stretcher access was through the trunk. Shown is the DeLuxe 4-Door Touring Sedan. The conversion was also available for the similar Roadking model, as well as Roadking and DeLuxe 2-Door Touring Sedans. Ambulance equipment included a rollaway stretcher, a smaller auxiliary stretcher, leg splints and a carrying bag, all available through Plymouth dealers.

Still a commercial vehicle was the Suburban on the DeLuxe 114-inch wheelbase. The U.S. Body & Forging Co. wood-crafted the bodies for the 1,680 vehicles built. Shown with standard spare wheel mounting and optional safety glass, it weighed 3,189 pounds and cost $970. The 4-door body, larger than formerly, was still an 8-passenger. Advertising also named this one of the "Sportsmen." Not advertised to the general public was a similar model in the Roadking series, of which 97 were built. The DeLuxe chassis without body was also offered, and 935 of them were assembled.

The Commercial Car adaptations included a pick-up box for $23.95. Available for the Coupe in the Roadking and DeLuxe series, it is shown on the latter. The unit was short enough to store within the compartment and close the deck lid. Extended, it simply added to the compartment floor area, providing a floor length of 75.5 inches and a floor width of 37.5 inches at the tailgate. The unit had its own tail lamp and license plate attachment. The deck lid could be lowered and secured by a special latch on the tailgate, or could be detached for high loads. The box was easily removable.

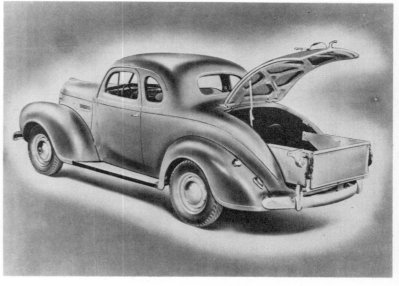

The Utility Sedan was a Commercial Car version of the 2-Door Sedan. The Roadking shown, of which 341 were built, cost $685 without the sliding screen behind the front seats. The fender-mounted spare wheel was standard. The right front seat could be fully tipped forward and propped up for curbside loading or unloading. Also, it was easily removable when full load space was needed. For conversion to a passenger car, a rear seat was an extra-cost option. Not advertised with this conversion was the DeLuxe Plymouth Utility Sedan, of which production records indicated 13 built.

Built only on the Roadking chassis was the Plymouth Panel Delivery, which recorded a production of 2,270 units. The price was $715, including a spare wheel on the curbside front fender and a driver's seat only. Two rear doors, with windows that could be opened, provided a dual opening 39 inches wide. Floor length behind the seat was 82.5 inches and total load space was 124.6 cubic feet. The P-7 Commercial Car chassis had heavier coil springs in the independent front wheel suspension, six additional leaves in rear springs, and special 2-way shock absorbers of low-pressure type.

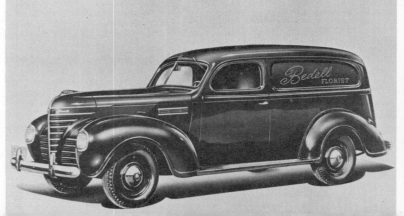

Though it was a new commercial design for Plymouth, the PT-81 light truck series borrowed almost everything from Dodge. In comparison with its 1938 counterpart, the cab was three inches further forward and the overall appearance was more trucklike. The Pick-Up was factory-priced at $575. 6,181 of them were manufactured. The pick-up box had a floor length of 78 inches, width of 48¼ inches and a half-ton payload capacity. Box sides were 14-3/8 inches high, and the floor was approximately 31¼ inches above ground level when empty. It would carry an object four feet wide flat on the floor.

The Plymouth PT-81 Chassis with Cab was a reasonable buy at $545. Various special cargo bodies were built and mounted by other companies. When so built, the combined cab, body and payload allowance was one ton. The PT-81 wheelbase was 116 inches and the engine developed 70 horsepower. Standard tire size was 16 x 6.00 and the spare wheel was carried under the frame at the rear end. The multitude of options as listed for 1938 were again available. Production of the Chassis with Cab amounted to 140 units. The special-bodied vehicle shown was built for a firm in Minneapolis.

On display at the New York World's Fair was this DeLuxe Plymouth with a transparent plastic roof. The Convertible Sedan body was chosen by John Tjaarda, chief of design research for Briggs Mfg. Co., to show off Briggs' newly-developed "Steelplast" material. Claimed to have about 18.5% more tensile strength than steel, the plastic was very tough and was not brittle. It could be painted without priming, and Briggs hoped to use it for building complete bodies, though the display body was of steel. They said the material could be used for engine blocks, axle housings and many parts.

Still under consideration as late as January, 1938 was this front-end proposal for the 1939 Plymouth. The full-size mockup indicates that Plymouth was to follow the theme used by Dodge, DeSoto and Chrysler production cars in 1938. Bullet-shaped headlamps were slightly countersunk in the fender sheetmetal. The grille would have been a stamping with cooling louvers ornamented in chrome, and there were no auxiliary side grilles. Wisely, the proposal was abandoned in favor of a more modern front, and the passenger cars were saved from a frontal appearance similar to the PT-81 light trucks.

This design development car is shown when the 1939 Plymouth was almost ready for production. A prototype car that could be driven, it was like production cars to follow except that headlamp "lenses" were solid mockups painted white or pale gray. It is probable that fully-recessed headlamps were not accepted for Plymouth until after all other styling was approved and released for tooling and manufacture. Last minute changes could be made if they were of a minor nature. Sometimes, however, more extensive styling alterations were made during the course of production.

1939

This illustration further exemplifies the late hour at which some decisions were made. Catalog artwork cannot be prepared until car design is given final approval for production, and this example shows the DeLuxe Convertible Coupe with a flat one-piece windshield. The production car had a "vee" windshield. Since the artwork includes recessed headlamps, the switch to a split windshield for the convertible was quite late. This model entered production five months after 1939 Plymouth assemblies began. It is unknown why the one-piece windshield was first approved.

DeSoto's new S-6 series was presented in DeLuxe and Custom versions. Looking exactly alike from the exterior point of view, the two lines differed in interior trim. The smart new styling added length to the hood, and fenders swept away from the wheels in a gesture of motion. Shown is the DeLuxe Coupe, lightest and lowest-priced model in the S-6 series. The 3-passenger car weighed 3,064 pounds and cost $870. 5,176 were built. The Custom Coupe weighed 3,069 pounds and was priced at $923. 498 Customs were produced. The deck housed the spare wheel and 48 cubic feet of luggage space.

Announced in January was the DeSoto Custom Club Coupe, a special edition not available in DeLuxe trim. The body was built by Hayes Body Co., Grand Rapids, Mich. The upper structure was longer and the deck shorter than the regular Coupe. Side windows were crisply accentuated by thin chrome frames with sharp corners, and pillars were narrow. A slight "vee" shape came off the roof to divide the rear window. Mounted on the 119-inch wheelbase, the stylish car weighed 3,164 pounds and was factory-priced at $1,145. Production, though not limited, only amounted to 264 vehicles.

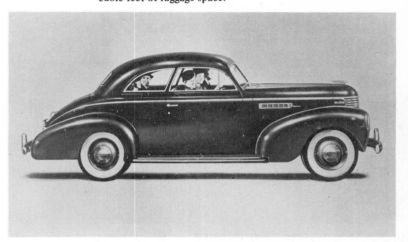

The interior of the DeSoto Custom Club Coupe accommodated five passengers in soft comfort. The rear seat was 42.5 inches wide, and cushions could be folded out of the way if extra space was needed for luggage. All seats had full luxury springs and the front seat cushion was padded with airfoam rubber. Parcel storage compartments were concealed within rear armrests. Upholstery was of blue or tan broadcloth, and carpeting as well as hardware was in matching colors. The large rear quarter windows could be swung open. Chrysler and Dodge also offered this special Hayes body.

The DeSoto Coupe with Auxiliary Seats replaced the 1938 rumble seat coupe. The 5-passenger interior had two folding seats behind the split-back front seat. The DeLuxe model shown, of which 2,124 were built, cost $925 and weighed 3,089 pounds. Priced at $978 and weighing 3,094 pounds was the Custom version, of which 287 were built. Except for 7-passenger models, all DeSotos were built on a 119-inch wheelbase and were equipped with 16 x 6.00 tires. The engine of the previous model was continued, offering a choice of 93 horsepower in standard form or 100 with optional head.

All DeSoto sedans had fastback styling which smartly concealed a luggage space of 23 cubic feet. Shown is the Custom 2-Door Touring Sedan which weighed 3,134 pounds and listed for $983. 424 of the 6-passenger cars were built. The DeLuxe 2-Door Touring Sedan, of which 7,472 were built, weighed 3,129 pounds and was priced at $930. Dual electric windshield wipers were standard equipment on all S-6 models. A new body paint called "Durasheen" was a glossy synthetic enamel with hard and durable qualities. Two-tone color combinations were not offered because there was too little demand.

The best seller in each of the two lines, and therefore the most popular DeSoto this year, the 4-Door Touring Sedan accounted for more than 67% of total production. One of the 31,513 DeLuxe models built is shown. It weighed 3,174 pounds, was priced at $970, and easily seated six passengers. Its Custom counterpart, of which 5,993 were assembled, tipped the scales at 3,179 pounds and asked a price of $1,023. DeSoto's serious competitors were the 8-cylinder Mercury, Pontiac and Oldsmobile. Also, some models of Hudson, Nash and Studebaker, mostly sixes, had to be dealt with.

DeSoto's advertising campaign placed much emphasis on the car's popularity with prominent persons in the motion picture industry. Spencer Tracy, beloved actor and star of many great films, is shown on a Hollywood movie lot with a Custom 4-Door Touring Sedan. Popular actress Myrna Loy, and animated cartoon perfectionist Walt Disney were among the leading personalities who proudly associated their names with DeSoto. In this view the stylish front end is shown to advantage. Whitewall tires, then white on both sides, and optional chrome wheel trim added much to the car's appearance.

A Custom 7-Passenger Sedan is shown with blind rear quarters. Optionally available for the big sedans and limousines, they lent a formal appearance but were not particularly attractive because of the extra mass resulting from the tapered fastback design. All long bodies had two auxiliary folding seats which faced forward, and nine passengers could be accommodated in the spacious interior. DeSoto's strongest competitors did not offer cars of more than 6-passenger size. The S-6 chassis without body was desirable for other applications, and 154 of them were assembled.

The DeSoto DeLuxe 7-Passenger Sedan was an impressive vehicle. The immense automobile weighed 3,454 pounds and was factory-priced at $1,195. 425 of them rolled off the assembly lines. The hood looked quite short in proportion to the extra-long body. In the Custom version, of which 30 came out of the factory, the huge car tipped the scales at 3,459 pounds and posted a price of $1,248 when purchased from the manufacturer. This body size was probably used for at least some of the taxicabs DeSoto built this year. Of undefined sizes, 1,250 S-6 taxicabs were manufactured.

1939

DeSoto developed a sedan skylight in 1937, but came up with a roof hatch this year because General Motors made it an option on some models of Cadillac, La Salle, Buick and Oldsmobile. The feature was also offered as an option for Chrysler cars this year. The clever idea found little acceptance and was discontinued. A Custom Coupe is shown with the manually-operated cover slid back to admit air. The innovation was intended to substitute for the lack of a convertible this year. With optional whitewall tires and chrome wheel discs, this was a smart-looking automobile.

The DeSoto DeLuxe interior, shown in the large illustration, was upholstered in a choice of blue-gray pile fabric or taupe Bedford Cord. A broadlace pattern decorated rear armrests and trim. The inset shows the Custom interior, which featured blue or tan broadcloth. The much darker colors of Custom interiors served to differentiate Custom and DeLuxe models, as there were no positive exterior means to identify one from the other. Six-passenger interiors are shown, but the billowy look of seats was typical of all. DeSoto said the seats were chair height and sofa-wide.

This interesting interior view of the opened roof hatch also illustrates other features typical of DeSoto front compartments. The smoothly-faced instrument panel had no projecting knobs or controls. New this year was the placement of the gearshift lever on the steering column, which cleared the floor for a center passenger's legs. The handbrake was moved to the driver's left to provide more passenger room free of obstructions.

The Custom 7-Passenger Sedan-Limousine was the heaviest, costliest and least popular DeSoto this year. As shown in standard form, it weighed 3,554 pounds and cost $1,338. Only five of the custom-trimmed cars were built. The DeLuxe model drew a trifle more demand, as 84 were produced. It weighed 3,549 pounds and listed at $1,285. Limousines offered a choice of four standard upholstery combinations plus special cloth and equipment variations. All 7-passenger cars were powered by the 100-horsepower 6-cylinder engine and rode on a 136-inch wheelbase and 16 x 6.50 tires.

An ambulance conversion was again offered by DeSoto. This view shows that the DeLuxe 7-passenger Sedan was quite adequate for the purpose. Instead of the standard front seat, two individual seats were used so that the rightside unit could be removed. The new steering post gearshift allowed a clear front floor for more stretcher room. The "B" pillar was easily removed and replaced. The big bodies had 1939 Dodge DeLuxe door window garnish moldings. The ride qualities of the heavy car, plus the vibrationless engine with Floating Power mounts, was good for ambulance use.

The economic climate continued to improve, but this year the upswing was due in part to production of weapons and material for national defense and war-stricken European countries. The urge to buy consumer goods grew stronger as employment increased and income swelled. However, the momentum built up last year in pulling out of the 1938 recession was now in slower motion. Production of automobiles was not encumbered by the manufacture of armaments as there was adequate space and materials for all. Considering all, this was a very good business year.

The year-end totals revealed that the auto industry produced almost 30% more passenger cars than it did in the year before. All divisions of Chrysler Corp. were stalled by a paralyzing 8-week labor strike at the start of new model production late in 1939, but went on to pile up a gain of more than 42% by the end of calendar year 1940. Plymouth popularity brought the major breadwinner a very respectable increase of 45.5% and assured retention of its rank as the nation's 3rd largest auto producer. A newcomer when compared to Ford, Plymouth came within 90,000 units of matching the No. 2 automaker's production this year. It possibly could have surpassed Ford if the crippling strike had not occurred. Never before had Plymouth come nearly that close to Walter P. Chrysler's goal of overtaking Ford. A gain of 72%, or 30% more than it registered, would have put Plymouth in the No. 2 spot. In the next 37 years of recorded history it would not again come so close in a full production year.

The calendar year was good for DeSoto, which scored a 57.2% increase. Its movement from 14th to 10th position put it past the low-gain Mercury and losers Hudson, Packard and Nash. The Chrysler car line recorded the corporation's biggest boost, a whopper of almost 71%, lifting it from 12th to 9th position. The climb was aided by those who also got out of DeSoto's way. Dodge turned out to be the corporation's smallest winner, reporting a plus of just under 21%. It could not keep ahead of the tremendous strides of Pontiac and Oldsmobile, who stepped up to tumble Dodge from 5th to 7th position. Competitive aggressiveness on the sales front combined with sporadic work stoppages in the plants to cause some of the shifting of manufacturers.

Plymouth presented its passenger car lines in mid-September, 1939. Two series were again offered, the Model P-9 Roadking and Model P-10 DeLuxe. This year the Roadking had its own P-9 engine numbers rather than sharing the DeLuxe prefix as before. The cars displayed totally new styling with a tastefully simple and uncluttered appearance. Lines and contours were blended into a harmonious mass. The front end, in tune with the trend sported twin groups of cooling louvers in the new low fashion. Fender crowns were molded in a horizontal attitude, the former sweep toward the ground now obsolete. Running boards, long considered so necessary now became optional as bodies became lower. Rear fenders were gracefully contoured into the fastback styling of sedan rear ends in an illusion of full integration. New one-piece curved glass rear windows were a modern touch on sedans. The entire styling form enveloped a wholly-new chassis layout. In relation to the engine, front wheels were four inches more rearward than previously, while rear axle and wheels were 7.5 inches further back than formerly. The new popular-size wheelbase was 117 inches and the 7-passenger wheelbase was 137 inches, each having received three inches more length. The new dimensions and shifting of mechanical components allowed relocating the rear seat several inches more forward to place it ahead of the rear axle, while the front seat advanced about one-third as much. The arrangement provided better weight distribution and more riding comfort. It was a further development of similar principles in use since 1935.

The engine of the Plymouth was the same 6-cylinder L-head of before, but with refinements. Vital parts were "Superfinished," a Chrysler process used last year by other divisions. The new finish contributed to operating smoothness and, with Floating Power mountings, resulted in even more vibrationless engine performance. Bore and stroke continued at 3-1/8 x 4-3/8 inches, respectively, but two more horsepower increased the developed total to 84 when the standard head with 6.7 to 1 compression ratio was used. Equipped with an aluminum head of 7.0 to 1 ratio, output was 87 horsepower, an increase of one. The transmission was a new all-helical gear design with 3-speed range. A steering post gearshift lever, featured on DeLuxe cars last year, was given to the Roadking this year. Hypoid rear axles had ratios of 3.9 to 1 for the Roadking, 4.1 for the 117-inch DeLuxe, and 4.3 for 7-passenger cars. Chassis frames were of stronger X-braced design required by the longer wheelbases.

The entire Plymouth passenger car range of 11 catalogued

Photographer's notes indicate only "1940 Plymouth Club Coupe" for this picture, taken at the 1977 antique car meet at Hershey, Pa. If correct, this is a very rare car indeed, being the Plymouth Roadking 4-Passenger Coupe, of which only 360 were manufactured. The production was so low that the car was not even included in the catalogued body line, and seldom appears in other reference sources such as dealer books, used car guides, etc. Lack of chrome beltline molding and brightwork around the windshield identify this as the Roadking model, though in its contemporary era it seems unlikely that the economy Roadking would be fitted with extra-cost whitewalls. The twin fog lights seem to be post-war units, as pre-war fog lights were usually much larger and more teardrop shaped.

The Plymouth Roadking Coupe illustrates that the passenger compartment was now placed further forward in relation to the wheelbase. This resulted in a longer luggage compartment. The 3-passenger business model, of which 26,745 were built, was the lightest and least expensive Plymouth passenger car this year. It weighed 2,769 pounds and cost $645.

models averaged 14.5 pounds heavier than the previous models. Contrary to the usual cost-per-pound formula, which in this case would have meant higher prices, most models retained last year's factory delivered price. Only three models were given a higher price tag.

The Commercial Car Line again had models on the passenger car chassis and the light truck chassis. The latter, known as the PT-105, was announced in December of 1939. It was the same vehicle as before, but horsepower was boosted to 79, which was an increase of nine. Almost no appearance changes were made, but weight and price went up 10 pounds and $10. The P-9 light commercials, based on the 117-inch passenger car chassis with modifications, were added in January. They quoted a maximum of $14 more.

The new DeSoto, known as the S-7, was every bit as new as Plymouth. The attractive styling concept was the same, which applied also to Dodge and Chrysler cars this year. The redistribution of weight by moving the engine and seats forward was just as advantageous to DeSoto. It had its own distinctions like die-cast grilles, special hood side decor, different crease lines on the fenders, and a host of other exclusive design details. Wheelbases were stretched 3.5 inches, providing 122.5 inches for popular models and 139.5 inches for the extra-big jobs. Not new, the 6-cylinder engine with bore and stroke of 3-3/8 x 4-1/4 inches continued the use of Floating Power mountings. Standard developed horsepower with a 6.5 to 1 compression ratio was now 100, a gain of seven. With optional aluminum 7.0 to 1 head, 105 horsepower was delivered, which was five more than last year's option. A new high-lift camshaft stepped up engine torque as much as 6.5%. Transmission and rear axle units received only detail changes, and the automatic overdrive option was continued. Chassis frames, new because of longer wheelbases and new body design, were stronger and lower for the same reasons.

DeSoto continued the practice of offering two series, DeLuxe and Custom. Both were S-7 models, but the DeLuxe did not have as many niceties as the Custom. From the exterior point of view, identifying a DeLuxe from a Custom was almost as difficult as was the case last year. However, this year's DeLuxe models had no brightwork framing on the windshield, rear window and side ventpanes, but Customs had the dressy trim. In addition, Custom cars had special chrome ornamentation strips

above and below the tail lamps. Interiors, too, provided a clue if they could be glimpsed. As before, Custom interiors featured seats in much darker color than DeLuxe cars had. All body types were not available in the DeLuxe series, but only two were reserved for the Custom only. Compared with 1939 models, the S-7 body line averaged nine pounds heavier but $36.50 less. All models were priced lower, with reductions ranging from $20 to $48. The lower price tags, especially on newly-designed cars of larger size, were mostly responsible for DeSoto's sales success and its rise to 10th position this year. Perhaps many buyers felt the way DeSoto hoped they would when it advertised itself as "America's Family Car."

Though early production of 1940 models was delayed by a long strike, Chrysler Corp. resolved the differences and went on to enjoy a successful year. But sadness fell upon the corporation, the industry and the business world when Walter P. Chrysler passed away on August 18th. Born on April 2, 1875, he grew up in the austere surroundings of a rural Kansas community. A poor boy at the start, hard work and dogged determination combined with good business and mechanical sense to make him an automotive giant. He had been chairman of the board of directors of Chrysler Corp. since it was formed in 1925. Without his vision and daring, Plymouth and DeSoto would not have been conceived.

All Plymouths could again be equipped with 20-inch wheels for more road clearance. Tire size was 20 x 5.25 and hubcaps were 1935-36 production. They are shown on a Roadking 2-Door Touring Sedan. The standard Roadking tire size was 16 x 5.50. From the exterior viewpoint, Roadkings were not easy to identify. A bold paint stripe, rather than a chrome molding, accentuated the beltline of the body and hood. Also, there was no bright outline on the windshield and rear window.

Of the 20,076 Roadking 4-Door Touring Sedans built, ten were for the New York World's Fair, which was reopened for another year. They are shown while awaiting shipment to their purchaser. In standard form this model weighed 2,689 pounds and was priced at $740, which made it the heaviest and highest-priced Roadking passenger car. Standard Roadking interiors offered no cloth options, but leather was available. The Roadking chassis with no body could be purchased, and 970 of them were shipped.

The Roadking 2-Door Touring Sedan weighed 2,834 pounds and delivered at the factory for $699. It was the most-demanded Roadking, accounting for 55,092 units built. All sedans were called Touring Sedans though the familiar extended trunk was gone. Ventipanes in front windows were an extra-cost option available for all Roadkings. New to all Plymouth passenger cars were concealed front door hinges and the offering of cars with or without running boards. The latter involved no cost difference.

The DeLuxe Plymouth Coupe was a 3-passenger businesslike car with plenty of space for carrying things behind the seat and within the rear deck. It was the lightest and lowest-priced DeLuxe model, weighing 2,804 pounds and costing $725. 32,244 of them came out of the factories. A new Plymouth feature this year was the hood top panels extended to the extreme nose of the car. All Plymouths of less than 7-passenger size were built on a new 117-inch wheelbase.

1940

Replacing the former rumble seat coupe was the new DeLuxe 4-Passenger Coupe. Two folding seats were located inside. The full-width seat back was hinged at the top so that it could be raised to allow folding the seat cushions away. That provision gave storage space behind the front seat as well as within the rear deck. This model, of which 22,174 were built, weighed 2,849 pounds and cost $770. It was one of three models advertised as a "Sportsman" group this year. Actually, five or six passengers could be accommodated. The passenger car engine was 84 horsepower in standard form, 87 optional.

This restored DeLuxe 2-Door Touring Sedan, owned by Jim Benjaminson of Cavalier, N. D., is one of 76,781 built. In standard form, this model sold for $775 and weighed 2,889 pounds when new. The accessory wheel trim shown is of a later period. Auxiliary driving lamps and Skyway radio antenna were available for the P-9 and P-10. DeLuxe Plymouth exterior trim featured full-length chrome beltline treatment and brightwork around the windshield and rear window. Not all had brightwork on the windshield center divider, however. New for all Plymouths this year were the round Sealed Beam headlight units, which were an industry-wide move for much better lighting. The new unit was only for road illumination, and the parking lamp was included in the upper tip of the headlamp assembly.

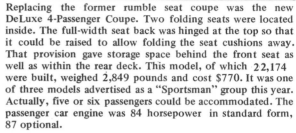

The best-selling Plymouth offered this year was the DeLuxe 4-Door Touring Sedan, of which 173,351 were produced. With standard equipment, the 6-passenger car sold for $805 and weighed 2,924 pounds. Whitewall tires were an extra-cost option. This car had no running boards, a choice not available for all DeLuxe body types. When so built, sub-titute lengths of sheetmetal, ornamented with chrome moldings, combined with rear fender stone shields to emphasize the omission. All 117-inch DeLuxe enclosed cars offered a choice of broadcloth or mohair upholstery, and all models on that wheelbase had 16 x 6.00 tires when standard-equipped. The new Plymouth body design permitted a straight rear door edge from the beltline down, eliminating rear fender intrusion of former models.

One of the "Sportsman" models was the DeLuxe Plymouth Convertible Coupe, of which 6,986 were built. It cost $950 and weighed 3,049 pounds. With no rumble seat, it could carry as many as six passengers by using the folding rear seats such as those in the 4-Passenger Coupe. The standard interior trim was tan leather, but combinations of whipcord and leather could be ordered. A gray or black top was a matter of choice. Standard accessory items included chrome wheel trim rings, whitewall tires and a glove box lock. A special underbody frame was employed in its construction. Because of added floor height in the rear area of this model, Plymouth recommended that all be equipped with running boards as an aid to entrance and exit of rear seat passengers. However, on special order, the car could be had without boards.

Not a commercial car anymore, the former suburban was now the DeLuxe Plymouth Station Wagon. The natural finish wood bodies continued to be crafted by the U. S. Body & Forging Co. The 8-passenger 4-door car, now accepted as a full-fledged member of the passenger car line, weighed 3,144 pounds and cost $970. 3,126 of them came out of the factories. The dual-purpose car was also advertised as a "Sportsman" type, and could not be had without running boards. Not catalogued and promoted was the Roadking Station Wagon, of which 80 were built.

1940

Again offered to a special kind of market was the DeLuxe Plymouth 7-Passenger Sedan. The big car was built on a 137-inch wheelbase and could carry nine adults. It weighed 3,359 pounds and cost $1,005. 1,179 of them were manufactured. As shown, this model also had a straight rear door cut. The DeLuxe 7-Passenger Sedan-Limousine was alike except for the glass-partitioned front compartment. The formal car was the highest-priced and least popular Plymouth, as it cost $1,080 and only 68 were built. The long-chassis cars had 16 x 6.50 tires and a 4.3 to 1 rear axle ratio. They were not offered without running boards. All Plymouth passenger cars carried the spare wheel in an upright position against the rightside wall of the trunk.

This DeLuxe Station Wagon was obviously a traveling display for Continental Coffee products. This illustrates just one of the several personalities this versatile vehicle could assume. For the particular role in this instance, it was given a two-tone glossy paint finish. Painting the wooden body surfaces was not recommended but could be done by special order. The sheetmetal and roof were normally in beige color to harmonize with the natural wood, but special colors could be ordered for those even though painting the roof covering material was not advised. An accessory 3-rail front guard is shown fitted to the bumper.

The Ambulance Conversion was again offered by Plymouth as part of the Commercial Car series. A Roadking is shown serving the purpose, but the DeLuxe could also be ordered with the adaptation. 2-Door and 4-Door Touring Sedan alteration included two basic changes. The rear seat was divided so that one side could be swung upward, and half of the partition back of it was cut away. Stretcher space was on the lefthand side this year so as not to disturb the standard spare wheel location on the opposite side. The Plymouth "Luxury Ride" was an asset to this kind of vehicle use. Year-around comfort was claimed when cars were equipped with Plymouth's optional All-Weather Air-control System. It drew fresh air from the cowl ventilator, forced it through ducts on each side of the front compartment and provided thorough interior circulation. Not an air conditioner, it served both heating and cooling functions. Simpler heaters were available.

No taxicabs were acknowledged in company production records, but Plymouth made two taxicab options available for the Roadking and DeLuxe. To replace former streetcar lines in Maywood, Ill., DeLuxe 7-Passenger Sedans were placed in service as trolley-taxis. Traveling main thoroughfares, they carried passengers anywhere within the town limits for only a nickel. The car shown had an extensive front-end guard fabricated from strap iron by a local shop. The DeLuxe chassis without body was available, and 503 units of unrecorded lengths were assembled.

An ice cream cabinet was easily carried in the deck compartment of a Plymouth Roadking Coupe. With the deck lid removed and a platform extension in place, there was no problem. The car could serve as a mobile product display or as a delivery vehicle. The Minneapolis maker of the cabinets found the car to be practical for these purposes.

1940

Receiving enough demand to be offered again this year, the Utility Sedan was an adaptation of the Plymouth Roadking 2-door model. The screen interior divider, of which the right side opened, was extra-cost. There was no rear seat and no rear partition, since the area from the driver's seat to the trunk lid was devoted to carrying space. By removing the right front seat, even more material could be carried. One of this car's advantages was that it was permitted on some boulevards where trucks were prohibited. The 2,769-pound car, of which 589 were built, was priced at $699 in basic form. Four DeLuxe Utility Sedans were also built.

The Panel Delivery continued to be a leader in the Plymouth Commercial Car Line. Based on the Roadking 117-inch chassis with minor commercial alterations, it cost $720 in the standard form shown. 2,889 of them were built. Unlike the Roadking passenger cars, it was not offered without running boards. The spare wheel location was new this year. Among many options were an auxiliary front seat, coach sidelamps and ventipanes in front windows. One DeLuxe Panel Delivery was built to fill a special order.

The Plymouth PT-105 differed from the previous light truck model only in minor features. Tiny parking lamps perched on top of the headlamps because they could not be incorporated in the new Sealed Beam headlamp lighting units. A decorative touch was in the use of three chrome bars on the top grille louvers. The smart vehicle shown had a special utility body built and mounted by someone other than Plymouth. For this purpose, the PT-105 Chassis and Cab was available for $555. 174 of the 2,610-pound units were built. A few of the regular options are shown. They include chromed headlamp shells and windshield frame, auxiliary windshield wiper and whitewall tires. The special fender lamps were from another source.

This year's light truck was known as the PT-105, of which the Pick-Up is shown. The vehicle, of which 6,879 were built, was priced at $585. Overall, the new model was not much different from the previous series. Unchanged was the 116-inch wheelbase, but horsepower was increased to 79. Sheetmetal and dimensions remained as before, but advertising boasted of "a new 3-man cab." The pick-up box was 78-1/8 inches long, 48-1/4 inches wide, and was rated at half-ton payload capacity.

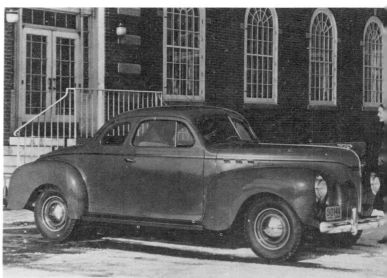

The DeLuxe line was the lower-priced of two DeSoto S-7 series. It was characterized by less exterior ornamentation and plainer interiors. There was no brightwork around the windshield and rear window, and side window ventipanes were not chromed. Also, no chrome trim was applied above and below the tail lamps. Shown is the DeLuxe Coupe, a 3-passenger car for business and pleasure. The 3,026-pound car, of which 3,650 were built, was the lowest-priced DeSoto model, listing at $845.

1940

The DeSoto DeLuxe 5-Passenger Coupe featured folding rear seats like the similar Plymouth model. Rear passengers now faced the front. Weighing 3,051 pounds, the car sold for $905. The assembly lines rolled out 2,098 of them. All S-7 DeSotos of less than 7-passenger capacity rode on a new and longer wheelbase of 122.5 inches. The new weight distribution, with engine and passengers further forward in relation to the wheelbase, helped measurably in providing what DeSoto called a "Floating Ride."

Forward placement of the body allowed a straight rear door cut from the beltline to the sill, eliminating the former obstruction of the rear fender. DeSoto bodies were made longer than Plymouth by adding length from the rear door back. The longer rear quarters included larger quarter windows. Front doors, like Plymouth, had concealed hinges. The 4-Door Touring Sedan was the most popular DeSoto DeLuxe model, accounting for 18,666 units built. The 6-passenger car weighed 3,111 pounds and cost $945.

The proportions of the DeSoto DeLuxe 7 Passenger Sedan body made the hood look rather short. This was the heaviest, costliest and least popular DeLuxe model. It weighed 3,515 pounds, cost $1,175 and recorded a total of 142 built. A limousine version was not offered in the DeLuxe line. All DeSoto 7-passenger cars, DeLuxe and Custom, were powered by the 105-horsepower engine. Not necessarily associated with the 7-passenger bodies were the DeSoto DeLuxe Taxicabs, of which 2,323 were built.

The DeSoto Custom Coupe was a 3-passenger model with interior luggage space to supplement that in the rear deck compartment. At $885, it was the lowest-priced Custom model. 1,898 of the 3,024-pound cars were built. The same body, featuring auxiliary folding seats in the rear of the interior, was known as the Custom 5-Passenger Coupe. The chummy club-type model, of which 2,234 were built, weighed 3,044 pounds and cost $945. Running boards were a Custom series option, and they were omitted from the model shown. A strip of sheetmetal with chrome molding was fitted to the body sill, and stone shields were applied to rear fenders. Weights quoted for Custom cars do not include running boards, which would add 25 pounds.

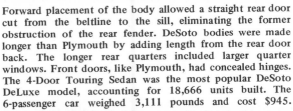

This view of the DeSoto DeLuxe 2-Door Touring Sedan illustrates the simplicity of the new styling. All bodies were wider and overall car height was lower. This model was factory-priced at $905. Weight of the 6-passenger car was 3,091 pounds. 7,072 of them rolled out of the factories. No model in the DeLuxe series was available without running boards. All DeLuxe interiors were available in Bedford Cord or mohair pile fabric, both in a neutral shade.

The 2-Door Touring Sedan of the DeSoto Custom line, of which 3,109 were built, weighed 3,084 pounds and cost $945. Interiors of all Custom closed bodies offered a choice of Bedford Cord or mohair pile fabric upholstery. Interior colors harmonized with exteriors and were darkish in tone. Seats were completely in color, and doors were given a 2-tone effect. A new All-Weather Air Control System was available for all DeSotos. Not an air-conditioner, it was a heating and ventilating apparatus which circulated fresh air by force. Also available were less elaborate units for heating only. All DeSotos of not more than 6-passenger capacity had a 122.5-inch wheelbase. Standard horsepower was 100, while 105 was optional. Wheels were fitted with 16 x 6.00 tires.

The Custom 4-Door Touring Sedan drew more demand than any other DeSoto model this year. The 6-passenger car rolled up a production total of 25,221. Weight was 3,104 pounds and price was $985. From the exterior point of view, Custom cars were identified by brightwork around the windshield and rear window, chrome on side window ventipane frames, and vertical chrome strips above and below the tail lamps. All sedans featured a larger trunk capacity. The bottom of the trunk lid was flush with the trunk floor, which was barely higher than bumper level. This facilitated easier handling of luggage and the spare wheel, which now stood upright at the righthand side.

The DeSoto Custom Convertible Coupe entered production in April. Sporting a price of $1,095, it weighed 3,354 pounds and chalked up a production total of 1,085 units. This body type was exclusive to the Custom line, and was DeSoto's re-entry of the convertible field after an absence of one year. It featured a power-operated top, and rear seat passengers now were accommodated within the interior. Its price included many items that were listed as options for other models. Note the chrome wheel trim and whitewall tires. All DeSotos were fitted with Sealed Beam headlighting units, an industry-wide advancement first introduced this year. Parking lamps were at the top of the headlamp assembly.

Added late in March was the DeSoto Sportsman, featuring 2-tone color treatment and a number of special touches. The Sportsman was in 4-Door Touring Sedan form only. This was DeSoto's first use of exterior 2-tones since 1935, though this time with a fresh approach. Three color combinations were offered, including 2-tone green, 2-tone gray, and blue with gunmetal. Interiors were in matching 2-tone fabrics augmented by special Sportsman niceties such as chrome strips on door panels, steering wheel in harmonizing color, and 2-tone graining on the instrument panel. Outside, the Sportsman option added chrome strips to the small louvers at the hood's nose, chrome "speedline" strips on the fenders, and a chrome center divider on the windshield. Regular features and some options of the Custom line were included as standard.

The costliest and least-wanted DeSoto was the Custom 7-Passenger Sedan-Limousine. Only 34 buyers were willing to spend $1,290 to get it. It is shown with optional guards which could be ordered for any model. Also in the Custom line was a 7-Passenger Sedan, of which 206 were built. It weighed 3,515 pounds and cost $1,215. All DeSoto 7-passenger models were on a new and longer 139.5-inch wheelbase and were equipped with 16 x 6.50 tires. The Custom chassis without body was offered for other purposes, too. Records indicate that 52 were assembled, but their wheelbase lengths were not defined.

This was a year of feverish national preparation for war. All industries were geared for the effort which turned out massive quantities of weapons and material. As usual, the automobile industry was a ringleader in an amazing demonstration of patriotism and ability to move swiftly and effectively. War production spurted upward as commitments to allied nations already in the conflict were met. The build-up of national defense evolved into an intensive arming for active participation in hostilities as it became increasingly apparent that the U.S.A. would be drawn into combat. By the time the official declaration came late in the year, the auto industry had turned out an enormous amount of war goods and shown that it was capable of much more. In addition to providing needed products for the national and world emergency, unrestricted production of vehicles for civilian consumption continued until the latter part of the year.

Scattered labor strikes hampered the flow of some parts at times, but production was not effectively interrupted. The imminence of war and a possible shortage of new cars did not create a rush to buy them. For the calendar year, industry production of passenger cars registered a gain of slightly more than 1.65% over the previous year. However, combined operations of Chrysler Corp. divisions suffered a loss of more than 6.6% for the same period. Plymouth, which usually showed the best results, lost almost 15.7% but held fast to its position as the 3rd biggest producer in the industry. Dodge was down nearly 4.5%, but easily remained in 7th spot. Chrysler cars advanced to 8th position, taking it away from Studebaker by earning a 2% gain. DeSoto rose about 2.6% but did not go above the No. 10 slot it held before.

Arriving at the marketplace late in September, 1940, Plymouth passenger cars were an instant hit. Boldly advertised as "The 'One' for '41," Chrysler's breadwinner was presented in three series. The lowest-priced line, simply called the Plymouth, was coded as Model P-11. The middle line was the DeLuxe Plymouth, which was a P-11 with dress-up trim. This intermediate model was not at first officially designated as a "DeLuxe" line, but simply as a P-11 with trim extras. By public announcement time, however, the company decided that this line was different enough to be marketed as a third series, so the "DeLuxe"

name was given to it. Some company records identify the DeLuxe as the P-11D. The top line was the Special DeLuxe Plymouth, Model P-12.

Increased labor and material costs forced Plymouth to introduce its new cars at higher prices, and elevate them again by June. At first, low-line P-11 factory delivered prices averaged $40 more than the former Roadking, but another $27.50 was later added. The DeLuxe P-11D began with an average of $9.50 more than comparable 1940 DeLuxe models, but later tacked on $28 more. The new Special DeLuxe series started at $40.50 above the 1940 DeLuxe, adding another $34 by June. For the 1941 model year, the grand average was an increase of $56.50.

Weightwise, Plymouths were again heavier than before. The P-11 averaged 30 pounds more than its Roadking predecessor, and the P-11D scaled 17.5 pounds above corresponding DeLuxe models of the previous year. The P-12 averaged 37.5 pounds above the 1940 DeLuxe line. The 1941 grand average increase was 30 pounds.

Continuing to inform the public that "Plymouth Builds Great Cars," the new models were developed to uphold that reputation. They boasted 10 major advancements. Among them were safety wheel rims to keep tires on when blowouts occurred, while rear springs had grooved leaves, rubber-insulated rear shackles and metal covers. The sedan rear axle ratio was changed from 4.1 to 4.3, and the coupe ratio went from 3.9 to 4.1. Transmission second gear ratio, formerly 1.55 to 1, became 1.83. The new ratios gave snappier acceleration and were said to make second and high gears sufficient for almost all driving, reserving first gear for difficult starts or uphill pulls. Powermatic shifting, a vacuum-operated device to aid normal hand-shifting, was a new option. The ignition distributor was protected against moisture, and the battery was located just behind the radiator.

The reliable 6-cylinder L-head Plymouth engine was continued with no change in bore and stroke dimension, but horsepower was upped from 84 to 87 by the use of higher lift cams and a new intake manifold design. Floating Power engine suspension was retained as a feature. The wheelbase of popular-sized cars remained at 117 inches, and 7-passenger cars kept the 137-inch length.

In respect to styling, the new Plymouths were a major modification of the previous package, with all sheetmetal but the body shells being changed. The front end received more alteration than any other area, and all fenders took on some new creases. Interiors were given their share of

The Plymouth Coupe was the lowest-priced passenger car in the company's line this year. The 3-passenger model, listed at $685 when announced, was increased to $720 some months later. The businesslike P-11 was also Plymouth's lightest model for the passenger trade, weighing 2,809 pounds. Production totalled 23,754 units. This body, when fitted with auxiliary rear seats inside, became a 4-passenger model. As such, 994 were mounted on the low-line P-11 chassis but not catalogued as part of the public offering. Nameplates on P-11 hood sides carried only the Plymouth name and varied in design.

One of the three P-11 models regularly offered was the Plymouth 2-Door Sedan, which was the most popular low-line car. 46,646 of the 2,859-pound cars were built. The model started out with a factory price of $739 and wound up at $769. This year no sedan was designated as a Touring Sedan. Trunks were large and the spare wheel stood upright at the right side. All P-11 and P-12 trunks now featured counter-balanced lids.

attention, which included a movement toward two-tones. Chrysler Corp. spent $15,000,000 to prepare all of its cars this year.

Plymouth's new Commercial Car Line went to market about a month after the passenger cars appeared. It again was comprised of models on a modified passenger car chassis, the P-11, and the light truck offering now known as the PT-125. This was the last year Plymouth would offer trucks and commercial cars on the domestic market until 1974. The P-11 commercials, on a 117-inch wheelbase, averaged $32.50 higher than 1940 when introduced. The PT-125 was not much different from the previous light truck. Several minor but distinct appearance changes were made. The 116-inch wheelbase was retained, but the 6-cylinder engine developed 82.5 horsepower, an increase of 3.5. It was initially priced an average of $37.50 more than 1940. By June, commercial prices were pushed up again.

The Plymouth 4-Door Sedan, of which 21,175 were produced, was the heaviest P-11 model. Weighing 2,889 pounds, it was also the highest-priced low-liner. First tagged at $780, it later went up to $800. It is shown with optional 18-inch wheels fitted with 18 x 6.00 tires, equipment which could be ordered on any car or truck when extra road clearance was desired. Standard wheel and tire size for P-11, P-11D, and P-12 cars except 7-passenger models was 16 x 6.00. P-11 windshields and rear windows had no bright trim, and front window ventipanes with painted frames were optional. Shown is another version of the P-11 side nameplate, which had "Plymouth" letters with no supporting feature. The low-line P-11 chassis was available with no body, and 676 were shipped.

The DeLuxe Plymouth 2-Door Sedan was the most popular P-11D model, accounting for 46,138 units. In standard form it weighed 2,899 pounds. Initially priced at $779, it rose to $809. Additional standard items on all P-11D cars were a vertical center guard and tapered end guards on the bumpers, dual chrome windshield wipers, dual sun visors, a driver's armrest, dual horns and a sway eliminator. The wheel trim bands, running board moldings and rear wheel shields were optional. The third DeLuxe model in the catalogued line was a 4-Door Sedan, of which 32,336 were built. Weighing 2,924 pounds, its price went from $820 to $845.

DeSoto formally presented its new S-8 series on October 5, 1940. The cars were almost totally new, with the previous engine carried over and upgraded in power. The new design gave an impression of more weight, and the cars were actually heavier. Though bodies and all sheetmetal were new, the most obvious appearance change was in the front end. A much bolder grille treatment bore no resemblance to the former model. The basic body concept was not new, but beltline design took on a more puffed character. Chrome trim was more lavishly used than ever before. The popular wheelbase was 121.5 inches, a reduction of one inch, but 7-passenger models continued to ride on a 139.5-inch wheelbase. Overall length was 5.5 inches longer, width was increased 2.25 inches and overall height was 1.5 inches lower.

The DeSoto 6-cylinder engine, supported by Floating Power mounts, received a number of refinements. Bore and stroke were unchanged, but a new 6.8 to 1 compression ratio increased horsepower from 100 to 105. The battery moved to a new location under the left fender shield. The standard 3-speed transmission had a numerically higher second gear ratio for faster acceleration and to allow start-ups without using low gear. New was an optional "Simplimatic" transmission coupled to the engine by "Fluid Drive." The new gearbox featured two forward ranges providing a low range for heavy pulling and a high range for acceleration and cruising. Shifting was automatically accomplished by increasing or relaxing accelerator pedal pressure. The revolutionary Fluid Drive coupling unit, introduced on Chryslers in 1939, softened the power flow to the transmission and drive train. A clutch pedal was necessary for manual shifting when starting out of parking.

DeSoto again offered two lines: DeLuxe and Custom. Compared with the previous year, weight for the two lines was up 121 pounds. Prices likewise moved upward. On introduction day, factory delivered prices averaged about $57.50 higher. By the following summer another $42.50 was added. As DeSoto's prices went up, its competitors also reflected the escalating production cost of labor demands and a booming wartime economy.

The DeLuxe Plymouth was the middle line this year. It was the P-11 line of three models, and was designated the P-11D. Standard equipment included brightwork around the windshield and rear window, chrome-framed ventipanes, a thin, auxiliary molding just below the windows, and other extras. Whitewall tires were not included. Shown is the DeLuxe Coupe, a 2,839-pound car. Early models were priced at $729, but the cost eventually became $760. 15,862 of the 3-passenger cars were built. Not listed among the DeLuxe offerings was a 4-passenger version, of which 204 were turned out. The simple nameplate which spelled out "Plymouth" only was replaced by a more detailed design with rounded ends. The new plate added "DeLuxe" below the Plymouth name and was decorated with orange color in the background.

For an unknown reason, but possibly because of a lack of parts when production started, some early Plymouths did not have the familiar vertical parking lamp housings. They were fitted with lenses of nearly flush design, further characterized by a pentagon-like outline. Also, the lens-retaining bezels did not extend as far up on the fenders as the production design did. They were not borrowed from any other car, but were fashioned to fit particular conditions. They are shown on a car owned by Wilbur Burkett, Ida, Mich. A Special DeLuxe 4-Door Sedan, it also differs in its original interior which was entirely done in neutral shade fabrics not in conformity with the "Fashion-Tone" treatment generally specified. Since this was not a special-order car, and there was no fabric option for Special DeLuxe interiors, it was built with substitutions.

The Special DeLuxe Plymouth 4-Passenger Coupe built up a production total of 37,352. Actually, it could seat five passengers. Tipping the scales at 2,934 pounds, its price went from $805 to $842 in a few months. It is shown without running boards, a no-cost-penalty option available for all Plymouth passenger cars of not more than 6-passenger size. The model was one of three production models often advertised as the Plymouth "Sportsman" group.

1941

A fairly popular model in the Special DeLuxe line was the 2-Door Sedan, of which 84,810 were built. It weighed 2,934 pounds and its price ranged from $810 to $845 during the year. Two-tone body colors were available for Special DeLuxe 2 and 4-door sedans only, and were an extra-cost choice. A new Plymouth option this year was direction signal lights. Also new to Plymouth was the one-piece "alligator" hood which was hinged at the rear. Released by a control under the instrument panel, it popped open a few inches to allow releasing a safety latch and opening it fully.

The top Plymouth line was the Special DeLuxe series, coded as the P-12. Shown is the Coupe, which was the lightest and lowest-priced P-12 model. First listed at $760, the 2,859-pound car later went up to $795. 23,851 were manufactured. As a personal car it accommodated three passengers, and for business use it had plenty of luggage room. All Plymouths of less than 7-passenger capacity utilized a 117-inch wheelbase. The standard 6-cylinder engine delivered 87 horsepower, and an optional head gave 92.

Mickey Rooney, then starring as teen-age Andy Hardy in a popular series of commonfolk movies, posed as if applying the finishing touch to the lettering on the four-millionth Plymouth. Looking on was Verne Orr, sales manager of Chrysler Motors of Calif. The Special DeLuxe Convertible Coupe was probably built in the Los Angeles assembly plant. One of the models advertised but not nameplated as a "Sportsman," it weighed 3,166 pounds. Initially priced at $970, it later escalated to $1,007. The price included many dressy niceties that were options on other models. 10,545 of the youthful cars were built. A specially-braced underbody resulted in a higher floor than other models had. For that reason, the factory advised dealers that all convertibles should have running boards, but the model could be built without them on special order only.

By far the most-demanded Plymouth this year, the Special DeLuxe 4-Door Sedan production total was 190,513. It is shown with standard equipment except for the 2-tone colors, bright reveal moldings in side windows, whitewall tires and rear wheel shields. Stainless steel running board moldings were standard P-12 items. Without options, this 2,959-pound model cost $840 before a midyear increase to $877. All Special DeLuxe models were publicized as having "Fashion-Tone" interiors which featured a band of blue fabric on the doors to contrast with the otherwise gray trim and upholstery. Not quite all of them had this combination, however, as some were given neutral substitutions for unknown reasons.

A huge Plymouth was the Special DeLuxe 7-Passenger Sedan. Built on a 137-inch wheelbase, it weighed 3,379 pounds. Costing $1,045 when announced, it went up to $1,078 in the general readjustment. This luxury model, which actually could seat nine persons, rolled up a total of 1,127 built. Its companion car, the Special DeLuxe 7-Passenger Sedan-Limousine, was the costliest Plymouth. First tagged at $1,120, its readjustment price is unknown. It also was the least-wanted model, as only 24 were built. The big cars had 16 x 6.50 tires and were not available without running boards. The sedan shown had an optional molding on the lower edge of the front fender. Though some P-12 models, apparently prototype or early production, had "Plymouth" side nameplates, the series was generally identified by plates which spelled out "Plymouth Special DeLuxe."

1941

Tremendous acceptance was won by this smart dual-purpose car, the Special DeLuxe Plymouth Station Wagon. A record total of 5,594 were built, by far the largest number this body type had yet reached. Built on the 117-inch wheelbase, it weighed 3,194 pounds and could carry eight passengers with plenty of baggage. The middle and rear seats continued the removable and interchangeable feature and the spare wheel was concealed in the back of the front seat. First offered at $995, it later cost $1,031. The U. S. Body & Forging Co. continued as builder of the wooden bodies, which now offered a choice of Honduras mahogany or white maple panels within the white ash framing. It could not be had without running boards. The handsome car was one of the production models advertised but not nameplated as a "Sportsman" type. Not publicized were 217 series P-11 wagons built.

Displayed at the auto shows, a press release called this "a new addition to the Sportsmen's line." The semi-custom Special DeLuxe Plymouth Phaeton was strictly an open car and was not among the factory's advertised offerings. There are indications that at least two were built. The basis for the conversion, built by Briggs, was the Convertible Coupe body. To provide more rear legroom and a phaeton appearance, the deck was shortened and the rear seat, which had a full-width cushion instead of the divided folding type, was moved back. The split-back front seat was retained, as this was a 2-door phaeton. The belt, above the beltline molding, was made pleasingly lower. The chromed windshield frame of cast construction was slanted at a sportier angle. Interior styling was a special 2-tone design, and padding was wrapped over the belt in cockpit fashion. Side curtains were provided, and the top was not power-operated. The 5-passenger body was mounted on the standard 117-inch chassis. The Special DeLuxe chassis with no body was available for other than stock Plymouth bodies, as indicated by a total of 321 built.

The Commercial Car Line again included a Utility Sedan. Offered on the Plymouth P-11 chassis, it was for small shops which did not need a larger delivery car. Without extras, it weighed 2,794 pounds, cost $739 at the beginning and increased to $760 later in the year. The car is shown with optional partition screen. Also available at extra cost was a rear seat assembly which was easily installed or removed. For use as a passenger car, the screen was also easily removed. Utility access was through the curbside door and the trunk opening. 468 of these catalogued models were built. Not catalogued were three other Utility Sedans built of which one was a DeLuxe P-11D and two were Special DeLuxe P-12 models, all probably built for special orders. Ambulance conversions for sedans were again part of the Commercial Line offering. Taxicab adaptations could be ordered but they were not part of the Commercial Line.

Continued with the body used the previous year was the Plymouth Panel Delivery. Built on the P-11 chassis, it was not available without running boards. As shown in basic form, early production was priced at $745 but the later price is unknown. A front passenger seat, window ventipanes and side coachlamps were among the available extras. The attractive delivery car, of which 3,200 were built, provided more than 124 cubic feet of load space. Double rear doors provided an opening 37.5 inches wide and 36 inches high, which allowed ample access to a floor more than seven feet long. The interior was completely lined across the top and on the sides. One was built as a P-12 Special DeLuxe.

The Plymouth light truck, now known as the PT-125, was a slightly changed version of the previous model. The wheelbase remained at 116 inches but horsepower rose from 79 to 82.5. No sheetmetal was of new design, but revised appearance details gave it new identity. The center grille sported a new vertical centerpiece and stainless steel moldings were applied to alternate horizontal louvers of the center and flanking grilles. Headlamps were moved outward to rest on the fender peaks, and bullet-shape parking lamps were mounted on the cowl sides. Plymouth nameplates were shifted to the hood sides, and the front bumper received a slight "V" at the center. Passenger car hubcap design completed the exterior alterations. Numerous useful and decorative options were available. The PT-125 was not offered without running boards. With basic equipment the Pick-Up, of half-ton payload capacity, was introduced at $625. 6,073 of them were built. The Chassis with Cab, for buyers who wanted to install special-purpose bodies, weighed 2,615 pounds and was initially priced at $590. Later PT-125 prices are not known.

The DeSoto DeLuxe 5-Passenger Coupe had a full-width non-folding rear seat cushion. First priced at $985, it escalated to $1,025 within a few months. The 3,219-pound car drew enough demand for the factories to build 5,603 of them. The example shown was fitted with optional chromed wheel trim rings. Wheels of all DeSotos now were painted in two colors, the rim being in contrast to the center. The tire size of other than 7-passenger models was 16 x 6.25.

An attractive car was the DeSoto DeLuxe 2-Door Sedan, of which 9,228 were produced. Introduced at $965, the 3,224-pound model later cost $1,008. All DeLuxe models, lacking some of the exterior and interior trim of the Custom series, were identified by a chrome script "DeLuxe" nameplate on each side, just below the beltline molding and near the rear of the hood. This year, both DeSoto and Plymouth finally recognized the need to identify each series by nameplate, eliminating much public guesswork done previously. In some DeSoto records, the two S-8 series were defined by listing the DeLuxe as S-8S and the Custom as S-8C. Not a DeSoto feature since 1937, the "alligator" hood returned this year. Hinged at the rear and with a safety catch at the front, it was released by a control in the driver's area. Forced out by higher fender crowns, there was no longer any trace of hood side louvers or ports.

The DeSoto DeLuxe Business Coupe was the least-heavy and lowest-priced car in the new S-8 series. Weighing 3,134 pounds, its price ranged from $898 on announcement day to $945 by midyear. 4,449 of the practical cars were built. Whitewall tires and rear wheel shields were not included in the prices. In January, bright moldings on the lower edge of front fenders became standard on all DeSotos not fitted with running boards. The compartment under the rear deck of this 3-passenger model was enormously spacious, and the deck lid was counter-balanced for easy opening action.

The new lowness of the DeSoto is readily apparent in this view of the DeLuxe 4-Door Sedan. The 6-passenger car was the most popular DeLuxe model, registering a total of 26,417 built. Weighing 3,254 pounds, it began at $995 and rose to $1,035. Interiors of all DeLuxe body types offered a choice of broadcloth or pile fabric upholstery, while leather could be ordered at extra cost in any DeSoto. The new bodies featured more room and luxury. As exterior body sides became cleaner in appearance, all door hinges but the lower rear were now concealed and door handles were in line with the belt molding. Advertising boasted of the new "Rocket" body styling. An exorbitant claim, it apparently was coined to counter Pontiac's "Torpedo" design.

An adequate vehicle for those who needed extra passenger capacity was the DeSoto DeLuxe 7-Passenger Sedan. Built on a 139.5-inch wheelbase, it was powered only by the 110-horsepower engine. The heaviest DeLuxe model, weighing 3,629 pounds, it could actually accommodate nine persons. It also ranked as the highest-priced and lowest-demand DeLuxe car. Launched at $1,255 and ascending to $1,270, this model was delivered to 101 buyers. Not available without running boards, the example shown had an extension molding on the front fender's bottom edge. The interior, as in all DeLuxe models, was upholstered in neutral monotone. All DeSoto sedan trunk lids were counterbalanced.

1941

Not offered by DeSoto since 1933, the blind-quarter 3-window coupe body returned this year. With the more forward location of seating and engine relative to the wheelbase, the short cab was almost midway of the vehicle's length. The configuration resulted in a long rear deck with large carrying capacity. Shown is the DeSoto Custom Coupe, a very personal 3-passenger car. Of all Custom models, it weighed and cost the least. Registering 3,144 pounds of weight, it entered the market at $945 and increased to $982. 2,033 buyers found it desirable. It is shown with extra-cost wheel trim rings. The Custom series was designated as S-8C in some company records.

In the Custom line, the coupe for five passengers was known as the Club Coupe. Without options it weighed 3,239 pounds and was first priced at $1,035, eventually going up to $1,080. It is shown with handle-like auxiliary front protection which the company classified as "fender guards." Like the wheel dress-up, they were extra-cost items. This chummy close-coupled model, of which 6,726 were built, had a short rear deck with counter-balanced lid. Like all popular-size DeSotos, it utilized a 121.5-inch wheelbase. The engine with standard head developed 105 horsepower, and for better performance an aluminum head providing 110 horsepower was available.

Shown is the DeSoto Custom Brougham, which was a fancier and more luxurious counterpart of the DeLuxe 2-Door Sedan. Included as standard were ventipanes for rear seat passengers. The 3,264-pound beauty sold for $1,020 until raised to $1,060 in midyear. It drew enough attraction to require the building of 4,609. In addition to Custom script nameplates on the forward sides, all S-8C models had vertical chrome strips above and below the tail lamps, and enclosed bodies had chrome reveal moldings around all windows. Note the much larger rear window which all of this year's enclosed DeSotos had.

Added to the Custom line in March was the DeSoto Sportsman Club Coupe. It featured an interior with seats and side panels of a design similar to the convertible. The seats were a combination of narrowly-tufted neutral whipcord with a wide band of leather across the upper back and forward edge of the cushion. The pattern was repeated on side panels. Armrests were included in the rear. A choice of four leather colors was offered. A special steering wheel had maroon spokes and a cream-colored centerpiece and rim. Unlike Plymouth, whose "Sportsmen" terminology was an advertising gimmick, DeSoto treated its Sportsman as a distinct model with special features.

The Custom 4-Door Sedan was the most popular DeSoto manufactured this year. Its production total was 30,876 units. Weight of the 6-passenger car was 3,269 pounds. Its announcement price of $1,045 was constant until midyear when a new $1,085 price tag was affixed. The example shown had a number of extra-cost items, among them a 2-tone treatment of body colors which was available for any other DeSoto enclosed type. For the entire S-8 line of two series, eight solid colors and four 2-tone combinations were offered.

After an absence of six years, the Town Sedan returned to DeSoto. Appearing only in the Custom series, it was a special body design. Doors were of special dimension, with rear doors cut well up along the rear fenders. Also, rear doors opened from the rear and included ventipanes in the windows. Blind rear quarters added distinction. This model and the Custom Brougham were the only DeSotos with a foldout center armrest in the rear seat. 4,362 of the 3,329-pound cars were built. Costing $1,095 at the start, the price eventually rose to $1,133. Important new options for DeSotos this year were the Fluid Drive coupling unit and Simplimatic transmission, which provided a smooth power flow and accelerator-actuated automatic shifting. In view of that offering, it is odd that a power-assist shifting unit was also available for the standard 3-speed transmission.

1941

The DeSoto Custom Convertible Club Coupe had a shorter rear deck than the Club Coupe because of provision for the top when lowered. In turn, the Club Coupe had a shorter deck than its 1940 counterpart because the rear seat was moved back to allow more legroom for rear passengers, an advantage which the convertible also had. The convertible was given rear quarter windows, a new feature for this body type. The standard upholstery was whipcord with leather trim, the latter offered in a choice of four colors. Whitewall tires and other dressy niceties were included in the list price, which ranged from $1,195 at first to $1,240 by midyear. Weighing 3,494 pounds, this model marked up a production total of 2,937. It is shown without running boards, a no-extra-cost option available for all DeSotos except 7-passenger cars. Without the boards, rear fender paint was protected from stone damage by the use of applied shields which extended up to the chrome molding. Though Plymouth did not recommend the boardless option for convertibles, DeSoto apparently felt there was no need for restriction.

Another of DeSoto's long wheelbase cars was the Custom 7-Passenger Sedan. The 110-horsepower car had an overall length of 225.75 inches. Tipping the scales at 3,649 pounds, it was initially priced at $1,295 and later joined the ranks of the price boosters by going up to $1,310. 120 were built and delivered to buyers who got a lot of car for their money. All three S-8 7-passenger models entered production about February 1st. Tires used on these big cars were size 16 x 6.50.

The lowest-production DeSoto model this year was the Custom 7-Passenger Sedan-Limousine, of which only 35 were built. It was also DeSoto's most expensive car, first appearing at $1,370 and later rising to $1,390. Mounted on the luxury 139.5-inch wheelbase, the body was partitioned in true formal tradition. The chauffeur's compartment was trimmed in black leather, while passengers enjoyed the comforting feel of high quality fabrics. Auxiliary seats folded snugly into a recess of the partition, as shown. Exquisitely appointed and built for a limited and fastidious clientele, this was a car for exclusive use. The "snob" appeal of this model was so respected that it was not made available to the public as a DeLuxe offering.

Except for its extra length and auxiliary seats, the DeSoto Custom 7-Passenger Sedan interior was typical of Custom treatment in all but the Sportsman and Convertible. Two-tone was the rule, with a choice of broadcloth or pile fabric of better quality than offered in the DeLuxe. Seats were luxuriously puffed in bolster-type fashion, and cushions were of Airfoam. Deep-pile carpeting was also used for scuff panels across the door bottoms. Garnish moldings were embellished with rectangular center accents, and other special touches expressed a look of expensiveness.

Again offering an ambulance conversion, DeSoto now pro-provided a hinged "B" pillar which swung up out of the way. The DeLuxe 7-Passenger Sedan served as the vehicle for this modification. The adapted cars were ordered through DeSoto dealers, who delivered them with stretchers and necessary items for the care of patients. For the conversion, front seats of the 2-door sedan were used, with provision for removing or installing the curbside seat as ambulance or passenger use of the car was desired. This car illustrates the neutral tones of upholstery and trim that were typical of all DeLuxe interiors.

Shown is the DeSoto chassis of 121.5-inch wheelbase. Gone was the X-braced frame which, except for Airflow models, was a touted feature since it began with the 1932 Model SC. Designed to permit lower bodies without sacrifices of interior headroom, the new frame had box-section side rails 4.25 inches deep, a reduction of 1.75 inches, but claimed to be stiffer because of the box section. Independent front wheel suspension and a ride stabilizing bar are obvious. Production records show that only one S-8C bare chassis was built, but the length was not defined. Perhaps it was the chassis shown.

While Plymouth was preparing for more serious involvement in the manufacture of war goods, 4-door sedans were specially built for the U. S. Army. Major Suttles of the Quartermaster Corps and Plymouth president D. S. Eddins, second from right, are shown as the first portion of a new 1,000-car order was accepted for shipment in April. Presumably for use as staff cars, they were completely painted in the Army's familiar olive drab. Among specified Army equipment were small bullet-shape lamps above the head-lamps. Regular parking lamps were the early production low-profile substitution.

DeSoto's instrument panel was an example of simple form with attractive finish. With dials and controls in orderly arrangement, it presented a relatively smooth facade devoid of projections for safety reasons. Reflecting the 2-tone trend, the depressed horizontal area was in rich wood grain while surrounding surfaces were finished in a harmonizing solid color. The 2-spoke steering wheel, fitted with a semi-circular horn bar, provided the driver with an unobstructed view of the dials.

DeSoto built 2,502 DeLuxe Taxicabs this year, but pro-duction records do not indicate their sizes. The example shown utilized the 7-Passenger Sedan-Limousine body, a type not offered to the public in the DeLuxe series. The Sky-View model featured a roof window over the rear compart-ment. Substantial protective moldings were bolted to the running boards. Directional signal lamps on the front fenders were not exclusive to taxicabs, but were a factory-installed option which any buyer could order on the DeSoto of his or her choice.

The model year and the calendar year were both turned topsy-turvy by the requirements and restrictions of the [wa]r. Most companies began production at least three [mo]nths before the U.S.A. formally entered the conflict [ea]rly in December, 1941. Placed on the market in late [su]mmer and early fall, the new models sold well. The U.S. [go]vernment hesitated to restrict production, but the war [for]ced allotments and drew some raw materials away from [th]e manufacture of automobiles. However, a reasonable [ra]te of assemblies was permitted until the beginning of an [in]evitable tapering off. Soon after the U. S. went to war, [ca]rs felt victim to the allocation of certain materials to [mi]litary needs. Substitutions were made where possible, [an]d some items were discontinued. Shortly after New [Ye]ar's Day of 1942, the severe pressure of the crisis began [th]e crushing of civilian vehicle production. The industry, [as] required by law, halted passenger car manufacturing on [Fe]bruary 9th, but some automakers had phased out days [ear]lier.

[T]his was so far short of a normal production year that [co]mparisons of this and the previous year are not feasible. [As]semblies ended approximately five months after they [be]gan, though Plymouth enjoyed about six months of [19]42 model production. The fluctuating rate of some [au]tomakers caused some odd shifting of positions in the [ran]ks of producers. For the period of January 1st to [Fe]bruary 9th, two Chrysler Corp. divisions were victims of [th]e changing pace. The Chrysler car division dropped from [9t]h to 12th place while DeSoto slipped from 10th to [11]th place. Plymouth was unshaken from its position as [th]e 3rd biggest producer in the industry, and Dodge was [no]t shoved out of 7th.

[W]ith an early production start, Plymouth placed its new [ca]rs on the market about September 1, 1941. Only two [se]ries were presented, DeLuxe and Special DeLuxe, coded [as] P-14S and P-14C respectively. A complete styling [ch]ange effected a heavier appearance, and more brightwork [wa]s employed for ornamentation than ever before. The [ca]rs were lower and wider than 1941 models, and overall

length was greater by 3/4 of an inch. Interiors got fresh treatment, including more detailing for the DeLuxe series and a liberal use of two-tone colors in Special DeLuxe models.

Retained was the former wheelbase dimension of 117 inches for popular-size cars, but the long chassis was not continued, there being no 7-passenger sedans this year. The new chassis frame had double-channel box-section side rails, eliminating the X-braced design featured by Plymouth since the Model PB of 1932. Many chassis components were of new design. The familiar 6-cylinder L-head engine with Floating Power mounts was given a 1/8-inch larger cylinder bore for a dimension of 3-1/4 inches, but the stroke remained at 4-3/8 inches. Piston displacement increased from 201.3 cubic inches to 217.8. Compression ratio was raised, with 6.8 to 1 replacing the former 6.7. Engine speed was reduced, as 95 horsepower was developed at 3,400 r.p.m. in contrast to the previous 87 at 3,800. The rear axle gear ratio, formerly 4.3 to 1, was cut to 3.9.

Plymouths looked heavier and more expensive this year, and they actually were. Compared with 1941 DeLuxe and Special DeLuxe models, they averaged 90 pounds heavier and cost $61.50 more. The increased prices were not only due to more weight, but also to rising labor and material costs in addition to the penalty of extensive new tooling. A commercial car line and light truck series was not offered this year, but a small number of commercial sedans were built on the DeLuxe chassis.

DeSoto unveiled its cars soon after Plymouth, showing DeLuxe and Custom lines coded as S-10S and S-10C respectively. The styling was a major application of new sheetmetal and features to the basics of the previous model. The new frontal design featured an unusual and daring innovation in the treatment of headlamps by concealing them behind retractable doors. Though the idea had been used on 1936-37 Cord front-wheel-drive cars, it was not proven satisfactory. DeSoto displayed exceptional courage by adopting the novel idea which was destined to be dropped until the middle 'Sixties when it

The Plymouth DeLuxe Coupe accommodated three passengers and had plenty of space in the deck for luggage or salesmen's sample cases. This model had the lowest price of any Plymouth this year, costing $812 at the factory. It also ranked as the model of lowest weight, tipping the scales at 2,930 pounds. 3,783 of them were built. It is shown with standard equipment except for end guards on the rear bumper. However, soon after introduction it was found that fleet buyers and some others wanted cars without certain items, and the equipment list was revised in mid-October 1941. Changed from standard to extra-cost were front window ventpanes, front bumper center guards, right-side windshield wiper and some other items, but no cars were built without them unless orders specified the omissions.

The Plymouth DeLuxe model which rated lowest demand was the Club Coupe, of which 2,458 were built. The 6-passenger car weighed 2,990 pounds and cost $885. The new ornamental fixture to which the license plate was attached now included the stoplight, which was in the deck lid handle assembly last year. The gravel shield between the bumper and body was introduced on the rear last year, and the feature was added to the front this year. The tapered end guards shown, and a vertical center guard not shown, were optional for rear bumpers only.

This model topped the DeLuxe line in popularity, weight and price. The 4-Door Sedan, of which 11,973 were built, weighed 3,025 pounds and cost $889. On the exterior, DeLuxe models were identified by "DeLuxe" nameplates on the sides and windshields had no brightwork trim. Interiors were in neutral monotone, and standard upholstery was pile fabric. Leather interiors were available on special order at extra cost. Typical of all Plymouths were the two vertical guards near the center of the front bumper, though they became a DeLuxe option early in the model year. The DeLuxe chassis without body was not in demand, as only one was assembled.

Plymouth built 9,350 DeLuxe 2-Door Sedans and asked a price of $850 for each of them. The practical 6-passenger family car weighed 2,985 pounds. Oddly, this model weighed and cost less than the DeLuxe Club Coupe. This year, Plymouth offered a 117-inch wheelbase chassis only, which was the same dimension used for last year's popular-sized cars. The refined engine boosted developed horsepower to 95, and there was no optional head for extra power.

would return with some measure of acceptance. The grille was a broad expanse of vertical bars with compound curvature. Lines and contours of the automobiles gave a general impression of more weight than previous models, and they were heavier by an average of 36 pounds for popular-size cars and about 34 pounds for 7-passenger models. Prices also escalated, averaging $70 more for those of less than 7-passenger size and $187.50 for the big ones. It is interesting that the large cars were given much greater price increases.

A businesslike car was the Plymouth Special DeLuxe Coupe. It was the lightest and least expensive model in the highline series, weighing 2,955 pounds and costing $855. The 3-passenger car was preferred by 7,258 buyers. This body type, whether in the DeLuxe or Special DeLuxe line, was not available with 2-tone paint treatment because the roof was curved into the deck, providing no crease for a suitable division of colors in the rear. A new feature was the auxiliary air scoop below the front bumper. Also new were the enclosed running boards, smartly concealed by the outward curvature of the doors. Hiding the boards was a definite advance in styling, and they were sensibly placed on a level with the interior floor. An advancement not new was optional Powermatic shifting, which Plymouth carried over from last year.

Horsepower of the DeSoto 6-cylinder L-head engine wa stepped up from 105 to 115. This was accomplished b increasing the piston displacement and valve diamete and by smoothing the contours of intake passages in th engine block. Cylinder bore was 1/16-inch larger, no being 3-7/16, while the stroke remained at 4-1/4 inche Displacement grew from 228.1 to 236.8 cubic inches, an engine speed was reduced by adoption of a 3.9 to 1 rea axle ratio to replace the former 4.1. Cast iron alloy pisto were used in the "Powermaster" engine, which wa suspended on Floating Power mountings. While chass components remained basically unchanged, numerous im provements in design and function were added. Whee bases of 121.5 and 139.5 inches were the same as for th previous year.

The war made this a year of successive and joltir restrictions. Following the cut-off of civilian car pr duction on February 9th came car rationing on March 2n Production of civilian trucks was halted on March 3r To conserve fuel, a national speed limit of 40 m.p.h. bega in May and was later cut to 35 m.p.h. Also in Ma gasoline supplies to 17 eastern states were cut 50%, prelude to nationwide rationing which began December 1 for the conservation of fuel and rubber.

Following the cessation of civilian work, Plymouth an DeSoto factories were 100% devoted to war productio Parts for airplanes, anti-aircraft guns and many other iten were produced in ever-increasing quantities as the pr ductive rate was stepped up. By year-end the divisions ha contributed much to the industry's arms productio which for this year alone amounted to the staggering su of $4,665,000,000. Total conversion to the national effo came after more than thirteen and one-half years of vehic production during which 4,333,444 were turned ou by Plymouth and approximately 653,000 were bui by DeSoto. The 1937 model year was best for both.

A new body type for Plymouth was the Club Coupe, which replaced the 4-Passenger Coupe of 1941. The rear seating area was roomier because the seat was further back, permitting more legroom. Gone were the former folding rear seat cushions, replaced by a full-width seat. It was a close-coupled 6-passenger body with a larger trunk than sedans. The longer interior layout necessarily resulted in a longer roof and shorter deck than the 3-passenger body had. These characteristics were typical of this body in either of the two series. Shown is the Special DeLuxe Club Coupe, of which 14,685 were built. It cost $928 and weighed 3,035 pounds. The roof of this model was abruptly terminated at the deck, creating a good division line for 2-tone body colors which were offered for this body and all sedans, whether DeLuxe or Special DeLuxe. Odd-shaped cutouts of the new fenders ignored wheel roundness and were especially unconformative to the rear wheels.

1942

Weighing and costing less than the Club Coupe was the Special DeLuxe 2-Door Sedan, which scaled 3,020 pounds and was priced at $895. Perhaps the difference in prices was simply because of the difference in weights. 24,142 of these sedans were built. The car shown had standard equipment. In solid dark color, and with no dress-up extras, it appeared rather somber. A wide range of colors and accessories was available. Various 2-tone colors in a choice of broadcloth or pile fabric gave special appeal to interiors of highline models, which were externally identified by "Special DeLuxe" nameplates on the sides. Interiors of leather could also be had in this series. All Plymouths were fitted with 16 x 6.00 tires unless optional 18-inch wheels were ordered. Whitewall tires became increasingly scarce in the early months and were removed from the available option list January 1st. Plymouth bumpers were slightly heavier in design, and the evolution of wraparound ends was begun.

Registering the highest demand of all 1942 Plymouths was the Special DeLuxe 4-Door Sedan, of which 68,924 were produced. Its weight was 3,060 pounds and its price was $935. The weighty and low appearance of the Plymouth is quite apparent in this view. The flare of lower body sides, concealing the running boards, emphasized the impression. The heavy horizontal grille and lower headlamps also served the effect. Parking lamps moved from above the headlamps to become part of the top grille member. Again this year, directional signals were available. Not offered this year were 7-passenger Plymouths. Continued was the offering of taxicab options.

Another new Plymouth body type was the Town Sedan, though it was only new in styling, proportions and engineering, since Plymouth had offered a car of this name and type in 1934. It was not made of the regular 4-door body shell. All doors were wider, and those at the rear extended well over the fenders. Also, rear doors opened at the rear and had ventpanes in the windows. Available only in the Special DeLuxe series, it weighed 3,085 pounds and cost $980. 5,821 of them were built. Side window reveal moldings of brightwork could be ordered for any coupe or sedan. Also shown is accessory chromed wheel trim, to which rim rings could be added. Two of the thousands of combat tanks built by Chrysler were suggestive of the ruggedness of the automobile.

The Special DeLuxe Convertible Coupe was Plymouth's offering to the young in heart. Its $1,078 price included a power-operated top and many items that were options for others. A pair of very attractive rear wheel shields was included. Production of the 3,255-pound car totalled 2,806 units. At least 60% of them had optional light-colored tops because of a shortage of the standard dark material. The rear passenger area was more roomy than before and a full-width rear seat replaced the former divided and folding type. The interior was of exclusive design, and leather upholstery was in standard red or optional blue or tan. The car shown had painted trim because of a ban on critical metals needed for war production. The ban affected all brightwork except bumpers and guards. Plymouth switched to color trim on December 15th.

The most expensive Plymouth this year was the Special DeLuxe Station Wagon, which cost $1,145. It also ranked as the lowest-production Plymouth passenger car, tallying 1,136 on the score sheet. With seating for seven or eight passengers, this was the largest 1942 Plymouth. The woodcrafted body, built by U. S. Body & Forging Co., was a new design. All four doors were wider, and were hinged at the front. Rear doors curved upward to fender height like those of the Town Sedan. A choice of mahogany or light maple was again offered for paneling. Beltline moldings extended from the hood through the body sides. Standard upholstery was a leatherette material, while genuine leather could be ordered at extra cost. For unknown pruposes, 10 Special DeLuxe chassis were shipped without bodies. Perhaps they were later equipped with special bodies.

The Plymouth Special DeLuxe 4-Door Sedan was adapted to commercial use, though the conversion apparently was not built in numbers. The example shown featured a special trunk lid extended to the rear window and was attached by exposed hinges. Extra rear spring leaves completed the conversion. The large trunk opening would have been desirable for an ambulance conversion, but such a package was not available this year. An adaptation that was offered, however, was a Utility Sedan in the DeLuxe series. Utilizing the 2-Door Sedan body, it was priced at $842 without options. Provided at extra cost were a removable rear seat and front partition screen. As only 80 were built, this was the least-wanted Plymouth.

Converted for utility use, the Special DeLuxe 4-Door Sedan served as a transport for mobile radial saw equipment on the job. Equipment was mounted on a special extending rack. The equipment manufacturer, J. D. Wallace & Co., Chicago, Ill., found this sales approach to be an effective means of expanding sales volume of saws. Plymouth caught the cue and urged its salesmen to demonstrate Plymouths to prospective buyers instead of just talking and showing. With no indication that salesmen were to sell the utility conversion also, it is obvious that the adaptaion was not available to sell.

Shown with further changes in line with the restrictions of wartime is a Special DeLuxe. Front fender moldings were shortened from full fender length to a point just above the wheel, and rear fender moldings were eliminated. Generally, medium and dark body colors had trim of light color, and dark trim was used on light-colored cars, but there was some minor deviation from this formula. Some body colors and optional items were eliminated when the changes began. Not because of restrictions but only as points of interest are the location of door handles in line with side molding, and concealment of all door hinges except the lower rear. The last 1942 Plymouth, of unknown body type, was built on January 31st.

Often purchased for police departments, Plymouth performance and durability measured up to the job. Shown is a DeLuxe 2-Door Sedan built for the Michigan State Police. The special color treatment and extra equippage was applied by Plymouth. This view effectively illustrates the heavier and "squattier" Plymouth appearance. The horizontal front-end treatment gave an illusion of greater width and lowness.

The DeSoto DeLuxe Business Coupe, of which 469 were built, was the lowest-priced member of the DeSoto family. It carried an advertised delivered price of $1,010 at the place of manufacture. At 3,190 pounds, it was also the company's lightweight. This year's DeSoto was the S-10 series, of which the DeLuxe line was the S-10S. The interior of this 3-passenger car was the simplest of all S-10 models. The absolutely plain front seat back was vertically divided at the center, and there was a riser below the full-width seat cushion. The darker of two tones was on door bottoms, the seat riser support for the seat back, and was not applied to the top of the doors.

1942

The DeLuxe 6-Passenger Coupe was DeSoto's answer to those who wanted room for several persons, but at a sacrifice in rear legroom. It cost $1,092, weighed 3,270 pounds and was delivered to 1,968 buyers. Advertised as having "sedan-like comfort with coupe intimacy," it had a full-width rear seat and more luggage space than sedans. A choice of broadcloth or pile fabric upholstery was offered, at no cost penalty, for any DeLuxe model. Custom quality broadcloth was available at extra cost. All interiors had window garnish moldings finished in dark burl grain, which was also used on instrument panels.

DeSoto's lowest-priced sedan was the DeLuxe 2-Door Sedan, which recorded a total of 1,781 built. Weighing 3,270 pounds, it sold at the factory for $1,075. From the exterior point of view, the lowline series was identified by "DeLuxe" side nameplates and an absence of side window reveal moldings of brightwork. Interiors were in 2-tone blue, 2-tone green, and a 2-tone of tan and semi-neutral tan. Except for the Business Coupe, side panels had a band of dark tone just below the garnish moldings as well as at the bottom. Seats were in the darker tone, and were sectioned by seams with buttons.

DeSoto continued to manufacture extra-long cars though Plymouth dropped out after having offered them in eight model years. Built on a 139.5-inch wheelbase was the DeSoto DeLuxe 7-Passenger Sedan. It was powered by the same 115-horsepower 6-cylinder engine that powered all DeSotos this year. The huge car earned double distinction, as it was the least-sought and most expensive DeLuxe model. Only 49 buyers were willing to pay $1,455 plus taxes, delivery charges, etc. to get one. Though DeSoto boasted that its big models could comfortably accommodate nine persons, it continued to formally designate them as 7-passenger models.

The most popular DeSoto DeLuxe model was the 4-Door Sedan, of which 6,463 were built. Its weight was 3,315 pounds and it cost $1,103 when new. The restored car shown was owned by Guy A. Phillips of Maryland when photographed at the giant Flea Market at Hershey, Pa. A feature unique to DeSoto this year was the clever concealment of the headlamps. Called "Airfoil lights," they simplified the frontal appearance when closed. Actuated by a lever below the instrument panel, the enclosure panels retracted upward and the lights were turned on, all in one action. It was claimed that weather did not affect operation. The new grille, sometimes said to have a "cascade" or "waterfall" resemblance, curved gracefully down to the heavy low bumper. The intent of the design was to draw the observer's eye downward and promote a sense of lowness. Overall height was 67-5/8 inches.

New to the DeSoto DeLuxe line was the Town Sedan, which weighed 3,335 pounds and was factory-priced at $1,147. The formal-like model, of which 291 were built, is illustrated with optional 2-tone body colors. Four 2-tones and nine solid colors provided a broad selection to choose from. The interior of this model was of typical DeLuxe design, having armrests only at the sides of the rear seat. Standard-size DeSotos had a wheelbase of 121.5 inches.

The DeSoto Custom Coupe was the fancy version of its lowline business counterpart. The lightest and lowest-priced model in the Custom line, it tipped the scales at 3,205 pounds and asked a price of $1,046. 120 buyers took advantage of the chance to get the 3-passenger model. The very short cab, about midway of the vehicle's length, resulted in an exceptionally long deck. Cars of the Custom series, coded as the S-10C, were externally identified by "Custom" nameplates on the sides, and had side window reveal moldings of brightwork. DeSoto's "short" wheelbase models had a tire size of 16 x 6.25.

1942

Shown is the DeSoto Custom Club Coupe, which utilized the same body as the DeLuxe 6-Passenger Coupe but fitted it with a fancier interior. Because this was a fairly desirable model, the factories turned out 2,236 of them. It recorded a weight of 3,270 pounds and carried a $1,142 price tag. When extra ventilation was needed, rear quarter windows could be cranked down. Continued as an option for all DeSotos was Fluid Drive coupling and Simpli-Matic transmission. Power was transferred in a velvety-smooth flow to the gearbox, which permitted most driving to be done without using the gearshift lever or clutch pedal. The application or relaxation of pressure on the accelerator pedal was an actuating factor.

Equipped with additional ventilating wings in the rear side windows was the DeSoto Custom Brougham. This model was the counterpart of the DeLuxe 2-Door Sedan. It pressed the scales to a reading of 3,305 pounds and was offered at $1,142. Not nearly as popular as the equal-priced Club Coupe, only 913 were built. New to DeSoto was the concealment of running boards, which was accomplished in the same manner used by Plymouth. Actually, they were not true running boards as formerly known, and could have been properly termed "doorsteps." Though all DeSotos are shown with a full treatment of brightwork, the company resorted to color trim and other adjustments at the same time others did.

The Custom Town Sedan was said to be "an event in DeSoto coachcraft." With more interior luxury than the similar DeLuxe model, one of its features was a center armrest which retracted snugly into the rear seat back when not in use. The 4-door car, of which 1,084 were built, weighed 3,365 pounds and cost $1,196. At the rear, Custom cars could not be identified by extra chrome this year, as they were exactly like DeLuxe models. The center ensemble was topped by a medallion below which was the license plate fixture with integral stoplight, and at the bottom was the deck lid handle and license light assembly.

Shown with hard-to-get whitewall tires, the DeSoto Custom Convertible Club Coupe was a smart automobile, especially with the top and all four side windows down. Its standard interior of neutral whipcord and colored leather seat bolsters was of Sportsman design. 489 of them came off the assembly lines. In standard form, which included items that were optional on others, this model weighed 3,510 pounds and cost $1,317. Parking lamps on all DeSotos were located at each side of the grille. They and the tail lamps also served as direction signals when fitted with that option, an arrangement also used by Plymouth. A minor but unique extra was a light which dimly illuminated the plastic hood ornament. For unknown reasons, 79 Convertible Club Coupes were built in the DeLuxe series. A DeLuxe convertible was not listed or advertised as a public offering.

As usual, the most popular DeSoto was the Custom 4-Door Sedan, of which 7,974 were built. The 6-passenger car weighed 3,330 pounds and cost $1,152. Optional at extra cost were the rear wheel shields, which were available for other models. DeSoto joined the trend to curvature of bumper ends, which was a move toward full wraparound protection. Bumpers were more massive, and gravel shields were fitted between them and the automobile. The "alligator" type of hood was continued, and a new-design ornament of translucent plastic on a die-cast base was affixed.

1942

Shown is another of DeSoto's long-wheelbase cars, the Custom 7-Passenger Sedan. The lengthy car, of which 79 were produced, was priced at $1,504 with standard equipment. The tire size for big cars was 16 x 6.50. One of the wheel trim choices for any DeSoto was the white plastic rings shown, a substitute for the shortage and eventual lack of whitewall tires. Normally in body color, a chromed fuel tank filler cap is shown. The chrome decoration on rear wheel shields was intended to convey the impression that the bumper extended further forward than it actually did. This body was also used for the Custom 7-Passenger Limousine, which was the top of the line DeSoto at $1,580. Also, it was the model of least preference, as only 20 were manufactured.

Taxicab buyers took advantage of DeSoto's short production run to purchase 756 DeLuxe vehicles for service through the war years. The Sky-View example shown was a 7-passenger car with a limousine partition, a type not offered to the public as a DeLuxe model. Curiously, this car had no DeLuxe or Custom nameplates, but production records place taxicabs in the DeLuxe category only. This cab was equipped with auxiliary driving lamps, extra-high grille guards and a folding rear luggage rack. Also, it sported a full complement of bright wheel trim.

The Custom 4-Door Sedan exemplified what DeSoto called "Personalized Interiors." Shown is the regular Custom interior, which offered a choice of broadcloth or pile fabric at no cost penalty. Seats were sectioned by depressed seams, puffed bolsters were across the top of the backs and on the forward edge of cushions, and the intersection of seams and bolsters were deeply buttoned. Door panels simulated a square-tufted and buttoned effect between the upper and lower horizontal bands. Green, blue and tan 2-tones were offered. More expensive was the Sportsman interior which could be ordered in most Custom models. It was standard in the convertible, and was the design used in the convertible and Sportsman Club Coupe of 1941. Also offered was a special Fifth Avenue Ensemble of accessories, including Fifth Avenue nameplates.

Besides the manufacture of war goods, DeSoto lent a hand to patriotic promotions. Among them was an involvement in financing the war. A Custom 4-Door Sedan towed equipment from site to site so the "Voices for Victory" could exhort the public to buy War Bonds. Assigned to Dick Nelson, "The Freedom Man," the car was in the service of the War Finance Committee of the U. S. Treasury and bore District of Columbia license plates. Specially decorated for the role, the car was also equipped with auxiliary road lamps and a pair of extended rearview mirrors.

Shown at the Dodge truck plant in which it was built is a Fargo station wagon, of which the mechanical and sheetmetal parts were duplicates of Dodge. Though Fargo vehicles were not marketed in the U.S.A. after 1931, the Fargo Division of Chrysler Corp. continued to function as an export and fleet sales organization mostly concerned with commercial types. This wagon had Fargo identity on the grille, hood top ornament, hood sides and hubcaps, all of which were painted because of the wartime ban on brightwork. Though the builder of the wooden body is unidentified, it is likely that Cantrell did the work. The Long Island body builder had built wagons on Dodge commercials for 20 years, and it is known that contracts for export commercial bodies were made with Chrysler just before and after the war.

The entire auto industry devoted most of this period to production of war material for World War II. Having built up momentum for this effort since early 1941, total concentration began with the cessation of automobile production early in 1942. Long before New Year's Day of 1943, the industry reached full stride in the making of war goods.

Chrysler Corp. was among the earliest to receive major contracts, the first of which was for tanks. A wide variety of contracts followed with increasing frequency, and were assigned to divisions with facilities best able to handle them. In some cases, more than one division was involved in a product, each making one or more parts. Some of the machinery formerly used for auto production was not adaptable to war work, but tooling engineers found ingenious ways to convert 86% of the plant fixtures. Conversion was fast, getting some operations off to an early start. With the addition of new equipment, production of some units accelerated so fast that first deliveries to the government were well in advance of specified dates.

By January of 1943, Chrysler Corp. was employing some 145,000 people on 30 major contracts in 24 plants. As more production was needed, new plants were built and others were leased, one of which was a Detroit facility of Graham-Paige. One of the first contracts was for major fuselage sections for Martin B-26 Marauder medium bombers. Nine Chrysler plants made parts for these, which were assembled by DeSoto. Another early contract wa for Bofors anti-aircraft cannons, built by Plymouth from parts made by the other divisions and outside sources Such was the intermix of effort which reached greate magnitude as the war tempo and the need for weapon and supplies increased.

Though turning out miscellaneous small parts in larg numbers, Plymouth was primarily involved in many majc assignments. Besides the anti-aircraft guns, landing gea assemblies were made for the Corsair fighter planes bui by Chance Vought. Wing parts for the Curtiss Helldive a torpedo plane and dive bomber, were also manufacturec The welding of armor plates was an important contri bution to Chrysler's immense tank-building activity. wide variety of duralumin forgings and castings wer supplied for aircraft. Magnesium and bronze parts an ammunition of various sizes were produced in enormou quantities.

DeSoto was just as active in its own plants. Multitude of minor items were manufactured, but major involve ments were impressive. In addition to Bofors cannon part Sherman tanks got some parts from DeSoto. Gun cove were supplied for bomber planes, and wing sections wer turned out for Helldivers. In the latter part of 194 Martin Marauder production was phased out after muc DeSoto contribution to the success of this effectiv airplane. Phased in was a tremendous push for pro duction of huge sections of the newly-developed Boein B-29 Superfortress, the heavy bomber that was bigge faster and of longer range than any other nation had. Th Plymouth and Chrysler divisions provided many parts fc its construction, and Dodge produced most of the Wrigh radial engines. The superbomber was needed to hasten th end of the war, and it proceeded to accomplish tha purpose after its initial strikes in mid-1944.

At the time of the B-29 entry into the war there wa optimism that the European conflict would soon end an limited planning of postwar cars could proceed whil hostilities in the Pacific area were brought to completio However, the allied advances in Europe were somewha slowed in the latter part of the year by fierce Nazi resis ance. This caused a delay of a few months in new ca planning, which was severely restricted when it did begi Peace in Europe came on May 8, 1945, and a relaxing c controls permitted preparation for resumption of ca production. Though automakers were still committed t maintain adequate war production as long as needed, the could proceed with their own plans though procuremer of materials was somewhat doubtful.

Beset with reconversion complications because of th continuing war, Chrysler Corp. could not do much abou rearranging any plant space. Its tremendous involvemer

The Corsair single-seat fighter was built by Chance Vought, utilizing retractable landing gear made by Plymouth. Until 1945, it was a land-based plane in Navy and Marine Corps service, after which it was modified for exclusive carrier-based Navy operations. The design featured unique inverted "gull" wings. It had a Pratt & Whitney R-2800 engine, 41-foot wing span and overall length of 33 feet 4 inches. With basic designation as the F4U, it was altered in many respects. By mid-1945, more than 10,000 had been built. A late-production F4U-1D is shown.

The Martin B-26 Marauder medium bomber had nose and center fuselage sections that were DeSoto-constructed with the aid of some parts made by Plymouth. The assemblies for one plane were made up of 15,000 parts. The fuselage was of circular cross-section monocoque construction. Early models were powered by Pratt & Whitney "Double-Wasp" R-2800 18-cylinder engines of 1,850 horsepower each. It carried a 5-man crew, had a wing span of 65 feet and an overall length of 58 feet 2.5 inches. By year-end 1944, more than 5,000 were built. Used by the Army and Navy, many changes were made during production. Shown is a late version B-26F.

1943 - 1945

n war work was not much relieved until the war was
finally concluded on August 14, 1945. A few manufacturers already had cars in production. Chrysler Corp.
did not manage to get a new car off the line until very late
in the year. Part of the delay was due to new dies needed
for fairly important sheetmetal changes that most other
automakers did not make. Also, Chrysler feared that a
labor strike which closed General Motors might spread,
and start-up would not be sensible until continuous
production was assured. Furthermore, price ceilings for
the new cars must be fixed by the federal government,
which was slow in doing so.

By year-end 1945 the troubled industry managed to
produce 69,532 passenger cars, of which only 8.4% were
Chrysler-built. DeSoto accounted for 1,191, while Plymouth built 2,581, Dodge rolled out 1,210, and the
Chrysler division produced 837.

A Helldiver midwing section is shown being lifted from an
assembly jig. The lift-out was by means of a former auto
body hoist, done with extreme care to avoid even trifling
damage to the wing. Aircraft construction required ultra-
precision in parts and methods. Typical of the Chrysler
family participation in war work, Plymouth and other
divisions made parts for these wings. The scene shown was
in a DeSoto plant. On the airplane, midwing sections were
between the landing gear and the end sections.

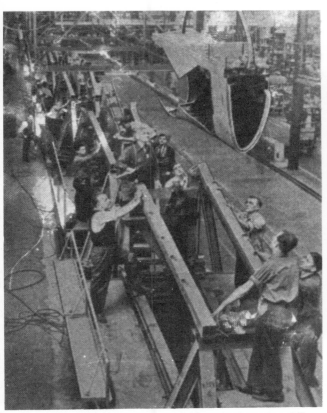

The body drop was always a milestone in automobile
assembly procedure, the point where the body was lowered
to the chassis. DeSoto modified the operation for production of Helldiver wing sections. A section of leading
edge is shown as it descended to a jig fixture in which it
would receive other parts. Unlike car-building, work could
not be done while the assembly line moved, so the line was
set up to stop at 48 stations for specific tasks. The wing
section seen would house the retracted landing gear for
which the irregular-shaped opening was provided. The far end
would fit next to the fuselage, on the airplane's right side.

Small parts for bombers were turned out on these former
automobile production machines in a DeSoto shop. These
high-speed punch presses spat out parts of intricate shapes
at the fantastic rate of tens of thousands daily. Machine tool
designers and toolmakers converted 86% of Chrysler's auto
production equipment to the manufacture of military products. Thousands of new machines were also needed to
satisfy requirements.

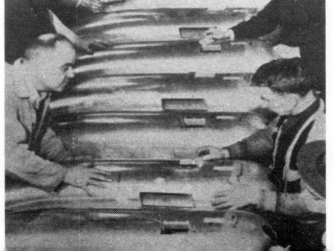

Bomber gun covers, resembling "streamlined blisters," were
formed by huge presses in the DeSoto stamping plant.
Attached to fuselages at points where guns emerged, they
shrouded the weapons and reduced wind resistance, an
important factor in the function of aircraft. They were made
to conceal 50-caliber guns. Inspectors are shown checking
for imperfections.

These automatic machines at the Chrysler Ordnance plant in Evansville, Ind., produced 30 and 45-caliber ammunition. Hundreds of machines performed individual operations. Those shown were doing a cupping job, one of the first of a hundred more processes to be done in the making of bullets. 3.25 billion rounds of small arms ammunition were made. Many of the workers were Plymouth and DeSoto employees. As was typical of factory work they could handle, women are seen operating these machines.

A skilled Plymouth worker was the first to fire Bofors anti-aircraft cannons, but not with live ammunition or procedures used in military service. A twin-unit weapon is shown in a machine for testing its function. Power was supplied by an air compressor, and dummy ammunition was used. Dials and fixtures on the machine indicated whether or not it passed the test. In military use, 2-pound projectiles were fired at a rate of 120 per minute, exploding 10,000 feet in the air.

Constructed by DeSoto, the nose section of the B-29 fuselage included many structural parts made by Plymouth and the other Chrysler divisions. The cabin was fitted with complicated flight controls and various navigational devices. Three miles of wiring and one mile of hydraulic tubing were installed in this unit alone. It was shipped in a box large enough to garage any automobile. In flight, the cabin and all crew stations were pressurized for high-altitude flying. DeSoto also fabricated engine cowlings, carburetor elbows, the leading edge of wings and many miscellaenous parts for the big bomber.

The Boeing B-29 Superfortress, with 16% of its structure manufactured and assembled by DeSoto, was a necessary factor in the ending of the war. The biggest bomber yet built, it had the extra-long range, speed, load capacity and high-flying qualities needed for its destiny. Each of its four Wright 18-cylinder radial engines, of which most were Dodge-built, delivered 2,200 horsepower. The wing span was 141 feet 3 inches, overall length was 99 feet and height at the rudder tip was 27 feet 9 inches. It had a maximum speed of about 350 m.p.h. and service ceiling of 30,000 feet, weighed about 40 tons empty and could carry 20,000 pounds of bombs. With a crew of 10 to 14, it was armed with ten 50-caliber machine guns and a tail-end 20-mm cannon. The B-29, of which 2,700 were bulit by year-end 1945, is shown with both bomb bays open. The planes that dropped the atomic bombs and ended the war had no armament or armor protection but were reinforced structurally to resist the stress of atomic blast from the ground. About four tons lighter, they depended on speed to escape enemy fighters, having no fighter escort of their own. A plane named "Enola Gay" delivered the first bomb, nick-named "Little Boy." The final mission was flown by "Bockscar," which toted the knock-out bomb "Fat Boy."

Bofors anti-aircraft guns, built by Plymouth, were necessarily adaptable to stationary or mobile mountings. A 4-wheel carriage served as an installation for many in service on land, as the unit could easily be towed to locations. The 40-mm cannon fired projectiles of slightly over 1.5-inch diameter to a height of nearly 1.9 miles. The single-barrel cannon was generally employed for land use in defending airfields, military installations and war production plants. They were used in the U. S. and its allied nations. A total of 60,000 were built in two versions.

The Curtiss SB2C-1 Helldiver, with wing sections assembled by DeSoto, was effective as a dive bomber for the Navy. Though primarily designed for that purpose, it was also used by the Army Air Force with the designation A-25. The Helldiver's radial engine was a 14-cylinder Wright "Cyclone" of 1,750 horsepower. The wing span was 49 feet 9 inches, overall length was 35 feet 8 inches and height was 16 feet 11 inches. The 2-seat airplane had four 50-caliber guns in the wings and one in the rear cockpit. Bombs were carried in the belly, and could also be hung under the wings.

For the Navy, the 40-mm Bofors was built as a twin-unit weapon with water-cooled barrels. Their alternating firing pattern quickly caused them to be called "Pom-Pom guns." Before Chrysler started work on the Bofors contract, the Swedish-designed weapon had been produced only in small numbers and largely by hand. There was no precedent of experience to serve as a guide for its production. The program required the building, laying out and tooling up of an entirely new plant. A Bofors is shown on convoy duty with loaded magazines on the turret armorplate.

DeSoto also manufactured Bofors gun collars, turning them out on a battery of newly-designed machines needed to speed up war production. Shown in process is the collar threading operation. Formerly requiring 32 minutes, it was done in eight minutes by new cutters with a speed of 15,000 r.p.m. Diamonds automatically redressed the grinding wheels, a time-saving factor in itself. This is an example of the development of methods and machines for accelerating production.

Chrysler Corp. was the largest builder of tanks, starting work in a new tank arsenal and eventually spreading it through 11 other plants. Plymouth's most important contribution to tank production was the machining and welding of armorplate, while DeSoto supplied vital assemblies of various kinds. Shown in action is an M4 General Sherman model, basis of a series of Sherman tanks. It weighed 66,500 pounds, had a top speed of 24 m.p.h. and a cruising range of 120 miles. This one had a Continental engine but earlier Shermans had a special Chrysler-built powerplant.

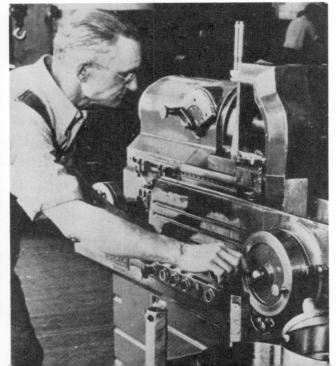

The post-war era began with frustrations and uncertainties. The sudden end of the war was not expected, and the government was caught with incomplete plans for the transition to peacetime business. Efforts to retool plants for auto production were impeded by various factors, and freedom from wartime strike restrictions brought widespread labor troubles. The struggle to attain even moderate production continued into 1946, and that year-end found the industry far short of its potential.

In the first full calendar year of post-war production, the industry produced less passenger cars than in 1934. That performance fell far short of satisfying an enormous demand created by an absence of new cars for almost four years. Of total industry production, Plymouth built almost 11.3% and DeSoto turned out over 2.8%. For 1947 the industry did much better, building 65.5% more cars than it did in 1946, with Plymouth earning a growth of nearly 44.6% and DeSoto gaining 31%. 1948 lifted the industry almost to the 1937 level with a gain of more than 9.8%. In the same year, Plymouth went up 9.9% and DeSoto rose 13.5%. For each of the three years, Plymouth held its now traditional position as the industry's third-largest producer. In that respect, DeSoto did not fare so well. In 1946 it ranked 13th, slipping to 14th in 1947 because of newcomers Kaiser-Frazer. A 1948 slide to 15th came when Packard spurted past.

Plymouth entered the post-war market with modestly redressed and mechanically refined versions of the 1942 series. New rear fenders were the most important sheet-metal change. At the front, the new grille was less ornate and the bumper wrapped around corners to the front wheel openings. All exterior moldings and ornamentation were new, and interiors were given fresh treatment.

The chassis received 34 improvements. Retaining the 117-inch wheelbase, most notable features were a more stabilizing sway eliminator, better synchronization of transmission gears and a new rear universal joint. The 6-cylinder engine with Floating Power mountings had a new compression ratio of 6.6 to 1. Horsepower remained at 95, which was developed at 3,600 r.p.m. rather than 3,400 as before. Plated aluminum pistons, a rotary-type oil pump and an oil filter with airplane-type filtration were among new features. Minor technical changes were made at various times during this 3-year period, the most obvious of them being a change in tire size from 16 x 6.00 to 15 x 6.70 in January, 1948.

No discernible exterior appearance changes were made to distinguish one year's model from another. Also, Plymouth series designations were the same for three years, as the series was continuous. Collectively designated the P-15 Series, the lower-priced DeLuxe was P-15S and the high-line Special DeLuxe was P-15C. The former comprised four body types and the latter had six. No special-appeal midyear models appeared, as extra sales lures were unnecessary in these years when a car-hungry public bought anything available.

The new Plymouths were heavier than 1942 models and prices reflected the rapidly escalating labor and materials costs. Averages for 1946 were up 47 pounds and $336. 1947 weights were unchanged but prices rose another $138. For 1948, weight curiously dropped 52 pounds but prices were $255 higher.

Announcement of the 1946 Plymouths came in March, at least three months after production slowly began, and eight months after Ford rolled first post-war models of the assembly line. Since the P-15 series was continuous, there was no reason for further introductions. For 1947 and 1948, model years began on January 1st. Serial numbers serve to identify models, which were built in Detroit (D), Evansville (E) and Los Angeles (L), and beginning numbers follow. 1946: (D) 11496001 (E) 20165001, (L) 25000001. 1947: (D) 11643104

The lowest-priced and lightest-weight Plymouth was the DeLuxe Coupe. In 1946, it cost $1,089, going up to $1,346 in 1948. Its 1946 weight was 2,977 pounds, dropping to 2,955 pounds in 1948. 16,117 examples of this model were built during the entire P-15 production run of more than three years. The 3-passenger car was especially useful for business purposes, having a large rear deck compartment. The new rear fender design, featuring more sheetmetal by having a lower wheel cutout, is clearly shown on this 1946 model. Until late 1947, all models had 16-inch wheels with 16 x 6.00 tires.

The Club Coupe in the DeLuxe line drew the least demand of any Plymouth, as only 10,400 units of total P-15 production were this model. Its weight dropped from 3,037 pounds in 1946 to 3,005 pounds in 1948. Its price took the opposite turn, beginning at $1,159 in 1946 and going up to $1,409 in 1948. Advertised as a 5-passenger model, it could accommodate six. Plymouth thought this would be a very popular model, but in low-line DeLuxe form it failed to meet expectations. The illustration is from a 1948 catalog.

E) 20185186, (L) 25009753. 1948: (D) 11854386,
E) 20233168, (L) 25035586. The P-15 series was carried
ver into 1949.

DeSoto came to the post-war market with moderately
mpressive styling changes. Not just warmed-over 1942
models, a goodly portion of the sheetmetal was new,
ncluding front and rear fenders and front doors. The
idden headlamps of 1942 were replaced by exposed
mps, and front fender modeling was smoothly extended
to the doors. Frontal design featured a smart "waterfall"
rille and a full wraparound bumper. At the rear, fenders
rouded more of the wheels, and bumper ends extended
rther forward than before. Exterior ornamentation and
terior styling was of new design.

Unchanged were the wheelbases of 121.5 and 139.5
ches, and numerous chassis improvements were made.
3-speed manual-shift transmission was standard, but
tional gyrol Fluid Drive with Tip-Toe shifting 4-speed
nge had larger gears and a non-locking device. Like
ymouth, DeSoto's new Safe-Stop brakes incorporated
vo hydraulic cylinders in each front brake. The L-head
cylinder engine, set on Floating Power mounts, had new
uminum alloy pistons, a rotary-type oil pump and an
rplane-type oil filtration method. Compression ratio and
ore and stroke were unchanged, but developed horsepower
as stated as 109 at 3,600 r.p.m., rather than 115 at
800 in 1942. Minimal engine and chassis changes came
uring these three years, and a switch from 15 x 6.50 to
5 x 7.60 tires on the short chassis came in late 1947.
ong-wheelbase models retained their 15 x 7.00 tires
roughout the period.

No exterior styling features were noticeably altered
uring the 3-year span. Basically designated the Series S-11,
eSoto offered it in two versions: The S-11S DeLuxe and
11C Custom. Included were four DeLuxe and seven
ustom body types, of which one of the latter was a late
946 addition.

Heavier than 1942 models, the new DeSotos were also
uch more costly. Calculated by averages, they were up
4½ pounds and $377 in 1946. The following year
other 10½ pounds and $105 were added. In 1948,
eight went down 38 pounds while prices went up $298.
DeSoto's public announcement of the 1946 models was

March, and no introductions followed as the S-11
tered successive years on its continuous run. It entered
w model years on January 1st of 1947 and 1948, as
rected by Chrysler Corp. Since there were no styling
anges to distinguish cars of one year from another, serial
mbers were the deciding factor when positive identi-
cation was necessary. The beginning serial number for
946 was 5784001, for 1947 it was 5825784, and for
948 it was 5885816. The Series S-11 was continued
to 1949.

This artwork of a 1948 Plymouth DeLuxe 2-Door Sedan
illustrates the complete wraparound of the front bumper on
P-15 cars. This 6-passenger model had a 1946 weight of
3,047 pounds and in 1948 fell to 2,995 pounds. Its 1946
factory retail price was $1,124, but in 1948 it cost $1,383.
Three assembly plants turned out 49,918 of these in approximately 39 months of P-15 production. All Plymouths were
look-alikes in exterior trim, but DeLuxe models were
identified by "DeLuxe" nameplates on the sides, at the rear
of the hood.

The most popular DeLuxe model was the 4-Door Sedan,
of which 120,757 were built during the 3-plus years of P-15
production. Weighing 3,082 pounds in 1946, it was reduced
to a 1948 weight of 3,030 pounds. The factory price,
beginning with a 1946 tag of $1,164, escalated to a 1948
quote of $1,441. The popular 6-passenger car is shown as
illustrated in 1948 sales literature. All P-15 body types rode
on a 117-inch wheelbase, there being no longer wheelbase or
7-passenger models. Ten P-15S chassis, as used for DeLuxe
cars, were shipped without bodies.

On display in a showroom early in 1946, a Plymouth
Special DeLuxe Coupe managed to escape immediate delivery
to an eager buyer. It weighed 2,982 pounds and was
factory-priced at $1,159, but two years later this model
weighed 2,950 pounds and had a $1,440 price tag. This was
one of the 31,399 3-passenger models built during the overall
P-15 production span. It is shown in standard equipment
form. Showroom visitors found it hard to identify the series
without looking at the "Special DeLuxe" side nameplates.

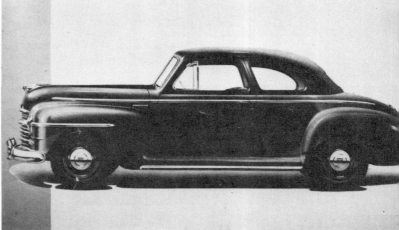

The Plymouth Special DeLuxe 2-Door Sedan was an attractive and practical automobile. The 6-passenger model was chosen by 125,704 buyers during more than three years of selling. In 1946, it weighed 3,062 pounds and cost $1,199, and its 1948 weight was 3,030 pounds and the price was $1,471. Special DeLuxe buyers had a choice of pencil-stripe broadcloth or soft pile fabric upholstery, plus extra interior fittings as standard. In lieu of unavailable whitewall tires, optional plastic wheel trim was offered. The wide off-white band had a narrow black stripe surrounding the hubcaps, as seen on the 16-inch wheels of this 1947 model.

Much more popular than its counterpart in the DeLuxe line, the Special DeLuxe Club Coupe rewarded Plymouth with the success predicted for this type. Of total P-15 production, 156,629 were this 5-passenger model. Because of its passenger capacity, it had a shorter deck than the Coupe for three passengers. This model weighed 3,057 pounds and cost $1,234 in 1946, but when this illustration appeared in 1948, its weight was 3,020 pounds and the price was $1,503. On this model, the roof met the deck abruptly instead of curving into it as shown by the 3-passenger car. Also, the longer interior and roof permitted larger quarter windows, since the two models had identical doors.

By far the best-selling P-15 Plymouth was the Special DeLuxe 4-Door Sedan, of which 514,986 were sold during more than three years of marketing. Introduced in 1946 at a price of $1,239 and weight of 3,107 pounds, it cost $1,529 and weighed 3,045 pounds in 1948. The 6-passenger car was powered by a 6-cylinder 95-horsepower engine like all other P-15 models had, and it was started by pressing an instrument panel button, a new P-15 way of doing it. Shown is a 1948 model with 15-inch wheels and 15 x 6.70 tires, a change which became standard on all cars early in 1948. The new size wheel trim, again optional, had no black stripe between the off-white and the hubcap.

Of sporty appeal was the Plymouth Special DeLuxe Convertible Coupe. The power-operated top sheltered a 5-passenger interior upholstered in soft leather. The 1946 model, shown on display with chrome trim rings on the wheel rims, weighed 3,282 pounds and was priced at $1,439. Two years later the same model weighed 3,225 pounds and was higher-priced at $1,857. 15,295 were built during this period, in which Plymouth, Lincoln Continental and Nash were the only makes still with blind-quarter convertibles. Others had the popular quarter windows.

The costliest and heaviest Series P-15 model was the Special DeLuxe Station Wagon. The 1946 car shown listed at the factory for $1,539 and weighed 3,402 pounds. In 1948, this model was priced at $2,068 and its weight was 3,320 pounds. Of total P-15 production, 12,913 were this 8-passenger body type. U.S. Body and Forging Co. continued as builder of the woodcrafted bodies, which had a choice of mahogany or light maple panels. Seats were covered with leatherette. Unlike the 1942 model, the bright beltline moldings were not extended to the body sides and rear.

This 1946 Plymouth Special DeLuxe Station Wagon was built with the optional light maple panels. The light panels offered very little contrast to the white ash wood used for the framework. Like all other wooden station wagon bodies of this period, the Plymouth body continued with a roof that was not made of steel. Willys-Overland's all-steel Jeep Station Wagon was the only wagon with a steel roof.

This view shows how Plymouth stored the station wagon's spare wheel snugly in the back of the front seat. The two rear seats were easily removable to allow cargo space, and were interchangeable, eliminating a selection process for re-installation. Interior sides and wheelhousings were neatly paneled, and the oak flooring was doubly anchored with heavy angle irons below and above the floor.

Plymouth could not place guards on the station wagon's rear bumper because their height would not allow the tailgate to open flat-out. The taillamp and license plate bracket was hinged so that it hung down when the tailgate was fully open. The tops of the two rear seat backs are visible. Plymouth continued the use of sliding glass in rear doors and quarter windows, but this was becoming obsolete.

This was a familiar vehicle in the city of Hilo, Hawaii. Somehow likened to a sampan, which is a small Chinese boat, it is called a sampan bus. The sampan shown has served through many years, but most of this type no longer exist. Accommodating ten or more passengers, it had side curtains or awnings secured to the roof rails. The unique bodies were built and installed in Hawaii, and the vehicles were painted in brilliant colors. This sampan's chassis, which included stock hood, cowl and fenders, probably was one of the 5,361 Special DeLuxe P-15C chassis-only units built for buyers who had various types of special-purpose bodies installed elsewhere.

The DeLuxe 3-Passenger Coupe was DeSoto's lightest-weight and lowest-cost car. When this 1946 illustration appeared, this model weighed 3,302 pounds and cost $1,331. In 1948, the type weighed 3,285 pounds and was priced at $1,699. During more than three years of production, 1,950 were built. The personal car had a cavernous rear deck compartment. Often referred to as a business coupe, it was not offered as a Custom model.

1946 - 1948

This 1946 DeSoto DeLuxe 4-Door Sedan weighed 3,427 pounds and cost $1,461. Two years later the same model weighed 3,435 pounds and cost $1,825. This was the most popular DeLuxe model, accounting for 32,213 units built during the continuous S-11 production run. The 6-passenger body rode on a 121.5-inch wheelbase used by all DeSotos except those of larger passenger capacity. Of unknown wheelbase length were 11,600 DeLuxe taxicabs built, designated as of California type.

The Club Coupe in the DeSoto DeLuxe line cost $1,451 and weighed 3,392 pounds in 1946, $1,815 and 3,385 pounds in 1948. 8,580 of them rolled out of the factory during the S-11 production span. The 6-passenger car is shown as a 1946 model. The DeLuxe line was specifically the Series S-11S, and was identified by "DeLuxe" side nameplates. Buyers of any DeSoto, whether DeLuxe or Custom, were offered a choice of ten solid colors and four 2-tone combinations.

The DeSoto Custom Brougham was a 2-door car with vent-panes in all side windows. The 1948 car shown weighed 3,399 pounds and cost $1,860. Its 1946 equal weighed 3,423 and cost $1,491. Total S-11 Custom Brougham production was 1,600. The comparable DeLuxe 2-Door Sedan, which had no rear vent-panes, weighed 3,397 pounds and cost $1,426 in 1946, and in 1948 registered 3,375 pounds at a cost of $1,788. Total S-11 production was 12,751 units. Whitewall tires made their postwar return as an option in April, 1947. Beginning very late in that year, all tires for short models were size 15 x 7.60, replacing the 15 x 6.50. By that time, DeSoto had begun the use of Cycleweld bonded brake linings.

Bearing a Custom nameplate on the side, this Club Coupe was shown in 1946 DeSoto sales literature. That year, it cost $1,501 and recorded a weight of 3,378 pounds. In 1948, the same model was priced at $1,874 and weighed 3,389 pounds. Total S-11 production was 38,720 units. The Custom line, S-11C, had a choice of three interior 2-tone colors.

Of all DeSoto S-11 models, the Custom 4-Door Sedan was the most popular. The 6-passenger car tallied a total of 126,226 built in about 38 production months. Shown is a 1946 example, which weighed 3,433 pounds and cost $1,511. In 1948, this model weighed 3,439 pounds and cost $1,892. The off-white plastic wheel trim was optional, used instead of unavailable whitewall tires. The exposed headlamps, replacing the hidden lamps of 1942, combined with a new grille and full wraparound bumper to give a fresh frontal look. Front fenders extended smoothly into the doors, and rear fenders were also of new design.

The least popular of all DeSotos during this period was the Custom 7-Passenger Limousine. Offered throughout the S-11 marketing program, only 120 were built. The 1946 car shown weighed 3,937 pounds and cost $2,013. Its 1948 counterpart weighed 3,995 pounds and cost $2,442. Seven passengers and the chauffeur rode in formal luxury. The rear seat had a folding center armrest, and the glass-divided front compartment was done in black with leather on the seat and cloth on the doors.

With all glass raised to show that it had quarter windows, this was a very open car with its top neatly folded down. Shown as illustrated in 1946, the DeSoto Custom Convertible Club Coupe tipped the scales at 3,618 pounds and asked a price of $1,761. Two years later the flashy sport model weighed 3,599 pounds and cost $2,296. 8,100 were built during the S-11 production span. The power-operated top was available in black and three colors to harmonize with body hues. Seats were upholstered in leather and Bedford cord.

An impressive car was the DeSoto Custom 7-Passenger Sedan, which could actually carry eight adults in comfort. As shown in 1946, its weight was 3,837 pounds and its price was $1,893. In 1948, the model weighed 3,819 pounds and was priced at $2,315. It was preferred by 3,530 buyers during the long S-11 selling span. Like all 8-passenger models, it rode on a 139.5-inch wheelbase and the 15 x 7.00 tire size did not change during its production run. All long-wheelbase cars were powered by the same 6-cylinder 109-horsepower engine used for smaller models.

Added to the DeSoto Custom line in November 1946 was the Suburban, which could seat nine adults. It had plenty of luggage-carrying space in the trunk and on the roof. The new interior layout had much flexibility. Center and rear seats had a liberal adjustment range. With no trunk partition, generous luggage-carrying space could be arranged. Seats were upholstered in Delon plastic, and interior side panels were of natural wood graining. The costliest DeSoto, it was also the heaviest. The 1946 model shown cost $2,193 and weighed 4,012 pounds, but the 1948 version cost $2,631 and weighed 3,974 pounds. 7,500 were built.

Contemplating a wood-trimmed model similar to the Chrysler Town & Country series of this period, DeSoto applied the woodcrafted look to a Suburban body. Light framework can be seen on the sides, even around the quarter window. Front door framing was not curved over the fender contour extension, but was fashioned to skirt around it. The trunk lid had wood grain on the outside as well as the inside, and the trunk floor was unlike that in the Suburban.

Through the years, DeSoto served many purposes. Family, commercial, taxicab, ambulance and wartime service were capably handled. So, too, were somber tasks. This 1948 funeral coach was a vehicle of solemn beauty. The body was by Superior Coach Corp., Lima, Ohio, specialists who also offered this type on the chassis of other automakers. The rear-loading body was mounted on a long wheelbase, one of 105 Custom S-11C chassis-only units assembled for various special purposes.

The interior of the special wooded Suburban body looked like the production Suburban except that doors had three vertical panels, with the center in darker grain. Standard Suburban seats show the split-back center seat with a fore-and-aft movement lever. The thin rear seat could be folded and flattened into a platform. The exterior wood trim of the quarter window is seen at the door opening. Perhaps DeSoto first intended the Suburban to be wood-paneled on the outside, similar to Town & Country cars.

The DeSoto instrument panel was designed for easy reading of dials and convenience of controls. A feature continued from 1942 was the color-changing speedometer indicator which was lighted to be green up to 30 m.p.h., amber from 30 to 50, and red from 50 up. Dials were edge-lighted and control knobs were crystal plastic. A new feature was a starter button on the panel, here hidden from view by the gearshift lever. The steering wheel was designed for unobstructed view of the dials.

Had it reached production, this car probably would have been a Plymouth. As Program A-106, it was developed for a 104-inch wheelbase and a weight target of 1,800 to 1,900 pounds. Begun just after the war, styling evolved from a straight-through fender design to the concept shown in half-size clay form in mid-1947. It had many new engineering ideas, including simplified framework. Seen as a 4-door sedan, a 2-door was also in the plans. Top management had little interest, and the car was never built.

With basic form similar to Chrysler's Thunderbolt "idea car" of 1941, designers finished this full-scale mockup early in 1944. Called the "Interceptor," it was projected at the immediate postwar era. With approximate dimensions of 100-inch wheelbase and 63 inches overall height, it could have become a candidate for Plymouth production. A convertible and hardtop in one package, it was ten years ahead of Ford's Thunderbird which first placed the combination on the market. The innovation was conceived by Chrysler designer Dean Clark. Made of fiberglas, the detachable hardtop was of snug blind-quarter design.

In a rough wooden mockup simulating A-106 conditions, full-scale experimental components were installed. The water-cooled 4-cylinder engine was of horizontal opposed design. Testing showed that it ran as vibrationless as a six. Foot pedals were suspended, and a high driveshaft to the rear wheels made this a 4-passenger car. Steering linkage was unusual, beginning with a vertical at the column end and criss-crossing almost above the engine. Coil springs at front and rear were uniquely installed.

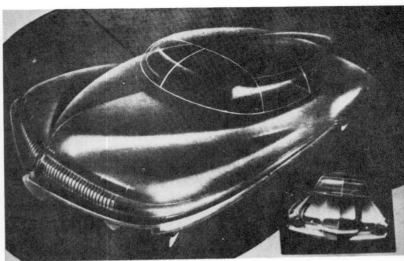

During the war, some thought was given to postwar designs. The larger of these two concepts was for DeSoto, showing a radical departure from 1942 form. Created by "Buzz" Grisinger, a Chrysler Corp. stylist, it retained the 1942 frontal flavor but curved all glass into the roof, which had a center tailfin. The front bumper seemingly extended beyond the door, and all wheels were well enclosed. It was a "dream car" on paper.

For 1946-48, DeSoto dealers outside North America offered the Diplomat as a companion car to the larger DeSotos. This Diplomat Special DeLuxe 4-Door Sedan was essentially a Plymouth with a modified DeSoto grille (unfortunately hidden in this view) and DeSoto hubcaps, medallions, and nameplates. Otherwise the car was identical to the Plymouth, including the 117-inch wheelbase. The 217.8 c.i.d. L-head six produced 95 horsepower with a 6.6 to 1 compression ratio. Similar Plymouth-based companion cars were produced before World War II but did not bear the Diplomat name.

The DeSoto, as made especially for marketing in Mexico, was another Plymouth in disguise. The most obvious alteration was the completely different grille, which conveyed some DeSoto resemblance. Parking lamps were Dodge-like, the hood top ornament and hubcaps were 1941 U.S. DeSoto, and a DeSoto medallion and nameplate were on the front. Rear end DeSoto identity included a medallion above the center stoplight (from which the Plymouth ship was removed) and the name on the chrome stoplight fixture. Inside, DeSoto identity replaced Plymouth touches. Plymouth's Special DeLuxe nameplates, both inside and outside, remained. This was a DeSoto Special DeLuxe, titled as a Diplomat model SP-15C. The 1977 photograph is by owner Carlos Heiligmann, Rowe, Mass. The compression ratio was 5.5 to 1, lower than the U.S. P-15 6.6, and a "mountain" rear axle ratio was used. A heavy-duty front and rear suspension package was incorporated. The speedometer was calibrated in kilometers and the temperature gauge was of the celsius scale.

Despite production interruptions because of labor troubles, the industry turned in a very good record. Passenger car production for the calendar year registered a gain of more than 31% over 1948, and made this the best year the industry had ever had. Some of this success was due to the wartime lack of new cars, and a fair portion was because of fresh new postwar designs introduced by some makers. The new models of Chevrolet, Pontiac and Buick contributed heavily, but so did Studebaker's slightly facelifted cars.

Springtime was almost at hand before Chrysler Corp. placed its new models on the market. Lacking the pleasing proportions and styling flair displayed by their competitors, they emphasized practicality of design and excellence of engineering. By far the best-selling was Plymouth, which produced 47.5% more in this calendar year than in 1948. This record easily held its position as the third-largest automaker. For the same period, DeSoto scored a gain of over 14.7%, rising from 15th to 13th rank by skimming past Packard.

For this model year there were actually two series. The first series Plymouth was a continuation of the 1948 P-15 lines, which became 1949 models on December 1, 1948. Beginning DeLuxe serial numbers were 15284535, 22071867 and 26017026 in Detroit, Evansville and Los Angeles assembly plants, respectively. In the same order, Special DeLuxe beginning numbers were 12066020, 20287572 and 25062783.

The second series Plymouth is generally regarded as the only 1949 series, primarily because of its new design. Publicly announced early in March, they were bannered as "The Great New Plymouth." Offered in two sizes, they were designated as the P-17 and P-18. Feeling that high production costs were pricing the regular-size cars out of the reach of some buyers, the P-17 was a 111-inch wheelbase line with a lower price. Advertised as a DeLuxe line, it comprised three body types. The P-18, on a 118.5-inch wheelbase, was divided into two DeLuxe and four Special DeLuxe types. Compared with models they succeeded,

P-18 DeLuxe models averaged 29 pounds heavier an $110 costlier, while Special DeLuxe models were u 23½ pounds and $202.

The P-17 and P-18 were powered by the familiar L-hea 6-cylinder engine which rested on Floating Power mounts Bore and stroke of 3¼ x 4-3/8 inches was the same a previously, but horsepower was increased from 95 to 9 by minor changes and a new cylinder head with 7 to compression ratio. New in design was the intake manifold and new features included an automatic electric choke and combination ignition and starter switch. Chassis components were about the same for both wheelbases, bu differed a bit between DeLuxe and Special DeLux models. New were rear shock absorbers angled towar each other. Toward year-end, some cars were give aluminum brake shoes because of a steel shortage

DeSoto's 1948 S-11 models became first series 1949 models on December 1, 1948. The beginning DeLuxe serial number was 6205976, and the Custom began with 5948453 in Detroit and 62001895 in Los Angeles

The second series DeSoto, popularly regarded as the only 1949 model, was promoted as "The Car Designed With You In Mind." Placed on the market about March 1st, they were offered in DeLuxe and Custom versions, both designated as Series S-13. Four DeLuxe and three Custom models shared a 125.5-inch wheelbase, four inches more than the previous standard-size chassis. Two Custom bodies were mounted on a 139.5-inch chassis, which was the same length as used for previous large cars. The total DeLuxe series, compared with the series it replaced, averaged 325 pounds heavier and $705 more, mostly because of new body types. The Custom average was up 316 pounds and $415.

The DeSoto 6-cylinder L-head engine was continued from the former series, but given a new cylinder head providing 7 to 1 compression ratio. The bore and stroke of 3-7/16 x 4¼ inches was unchanged, but refinements upped developed horsepower from 109 to 112. Chassis components were not changed in nature, but the rear axle was moved more rearward and a driveshaft extension was inserted just behind the transmission. Rear shock absorbers were angled as in the Plymouth, and many improvements

The first series 1949 Plymouth line was a continuation of the P-15 series as offered in 1948. The change in model year status became effective on December 1, 1948. This Special DeLuxe is typical of the lack of any visible changes. The full line, including the DeLuxe, was built until the new series went into production.

Plymouth's new economy line was based on a 111-inch wheelbase. Designated the Series P-17, it was a DeLuxe line. The 3-Passenger Coupe was lightest and lowest-priced of all new series Plymouths, weighing 2,825 pounds and having what was now a low price of $1,371. 13,715 of them were built. Placed in production soon after other new series cars, this was the first P-17 model to appear. Bumper guards and whitewall tires were P-17 extras. Rear fender trim moldings were at first optional.

ere incorporated throughout the chassis. By now, cycle-
onded brake linings were in full use, after partial use
nce late in 1947.

The new models of Plymouth and DeSoto were not new
styling concept, though they were all-new tooling.
he basic bustle-back sedan shape was begun by other
akers some years previously. The front fender form
xtended into the body much like before, though this was
ymouth's first use of it. Alongside their competitors,
e cars appeared stubby at each end, and too high and
arrow. The basic styling theme emphasized conservatism
nd practicality, and was fostered by K. T. Keller,
hrysler's president. He was not an advocate of styling as
und acceptable by the public. Principally, his objection
as to dimensional aspects of package proportions. He
elieved that sweeping length, low roofs and wide bodies
ere excessive, extravagant and impractical. Market per-
ormance would eventually prove that much of the public
d not share his point of view. The new practicality was
f good sense and purpose, but did not allow an attractive
nage.

The new approach restricted front and rear ends to short
verhang. The longer standard wheelbases were accom-
lished by moving the rear wheels back, making rear ends
ok even more stubby. Compared with previous models,
verall length was shorter despite the longer wheelbases.
hough bodies were narrower externally, interiors were
everal inches wider. Overall height was a bit lower without
eduction of vertical interior dimensions, but this was
one at the expense of a higher floor tunnel over the
riveshaft.

Somehow, first production cars of the new series were
igher than they were designed to be. During the first few
onths, Chrysler Corp. quietly took measures to reduce
e overall height by slightly shortening the front coil
prings and incorporating flatter rear springs. This lowered
e front about one inch and the rear about 1.5 inch.

The Plymouth DeLuxe 2-Door Sedan was the third and
last P-17 model to go into production, coming out of the
factories in July. It weighed 2,951 pounds and cost $1,492.
28,516 were produced. The fastback car was termed a
5-passenger model but could accommodate six with no
problem. It was the only new Plymouth model to be called
a 2-Door Sedan. P-17 cars used 6.40 x 15 tires. The engine
was a 97-horsepower six, the same as installed in all new
series Plymouths.

Appearing in June, the DeLuxe Suburban was the second
P-17 Plymouth to go on the market. The 5-passenger body,
a 2-door all-steel station wagon type without wood trim,
was mounted on the regular short passenger car chassis. This
was touted as the auto industry's first all-steel station wagon.
Weighing 3,105 pounds and costing $1,840, it chalked up a
total of 19,220 units built. The P-17 chassis without body
was not in demand, as evidenced by the fact that only four
were assembled.

Plymouth boasted of the DeLuxe Suburban as "the car
with 101 uses." There's no way of knowing how many
uses it could serve, but it was a versatile vehicle — and very
practical. Seats were upholstered in washable vinyl resin
fabric, with side panels and other interior trim just as
serviceable. With the rear seat folded down to make a flat
floor, a cargo area 5 feet and 8 inches long was provided.
The standard wheel size was 15 inches, but 18-inch wheels
were available for cars built for extra-rough country.

The Club Coupe in the Plymouth Special DeLuxe series weighed 3,046 pounds and cost $1,603. Whitewall tires, full wheel covers and rear fender stone guards were optional items. This 6-passenger model was delivered to 99,680 buyers. Front seat backs swung slightly inward as they tilted forward, making entry and exit easier. Styling of the new Plymouth bodies no longer featured side panels flared outward at the bottom, as there were no concealed door-steps. Door sills were level with the floor.

Serving the purpose of a 2-door sedan in the new Series P-18 was the Club Coupe. It is shown in the lower-cost DeLuxe version, which shared the new 118.5-inch wheelbase with the higher-priced P-18 models. Weighing 3,034 pounds, it was priced at $1,519. 25,687 of the 6-passenger cars were built. Rear fender trim moldings were optional on P-18 DeLuxe cars. Rear fenders of all new series models were easily removable, being attached by bolts and clinch nuts. Front fenders were attached by a variety of bolts, screws and studs, and were more difficult to remove.

The Plymouth DeLuxe 4-Door Sedan cost $1,551 and tipped the scales at 3,059 pounds. Factories turned out 61,021 of these P-18 6-passenger cars. Only two DeLuxe models were offered on the P-18 chassis. These had interiors of a trifle better class than the P-17 DeLuxe cars had. All P-18 Plymouths were fitted with 6.70 x 15 tires.

The heaviest and highest-priced new series Plymouth was the Special DeLuxe Station Wagon. It weighed 3,341 pounds and cost $2,372. The 4-door P-18 could carry more passengers than any other model, having room for eight on its three tandem seats. Unlike the DeLuxe Suburban, which stored its spare wheel in a rear floor well, this model enclosed it in the tailgate. 3,443 of these cars were produced. New for this body type was a steel roof. The wood-trimmed bodies were offered with dark or light panels, and were built by the U.S. Body and Forging Co. Other builders of special bodies found the Special DeLuxe chassis desirable, as 981 chassis units were shipped.

This view of the Plymouth Special DeLuxe Station Wagon with liftgate and tailgate closed shows the spare wheel enclosure on the tailgate. Actually, the wheel was semi-recessed, requiring that the circular enclosure door be superimposed on the tailgate surface, rather than flush with it. The door was hinged at the right side and fitted with a lock on the left side. This was the most convenient location for the spare wheel, which had nothing to obstruct access to it.

The most popular of all new series Plymouth models was the P-18 Special DeLuxe 4-Door Sedan, which tallied a total of 252,858 built. Its weight was 3,079 pounds and its cost was $1,629. The 6-passenger interior featured mahogany grain on the instrument panel and garnish moldings, like other Special DeLuxe enclosed bodies had. On the exterior, windshields and rear windows of Special DeLuxe models were framed in brightwork, touches not found on DeLuxe cars. The 4-door blind quarter trunkback package principle had not been used by Plymouth since the 1934 DeLuxe Town Sedan model, but the new version had proportions adapted to a more modern vehicle.

Shown with its powered top snugly folded down is the Plymouth Special DeLuxe Convertible Club Coupe. Of note is Plymouth's first use of quarter windows in this model. The 6-passenger P-18 tipped the scales at 3,323 pounds. 15,240 of the $1,982 cars were built. Stone guards on the rear fenders were optional, as were the dressy wheels and tires. All new series cars featured shortness of overhang at the ends, with the front end emphatically so. Bumpers had a corrugated character which lent strength and offered less area for scuffing and scratches.

Just in case a smaller car would be needed, Plymouth had the Cadet under development. Shown is a full-size mockup completed in 1947. The car could have entered 1949 production. Having a 105.5-inch wheelbase, it could have been a super-economy model. This design featured a front fender form extended through the body side to the rear fender. Front and rear overhang was more liberal than that of production cars. This 2-door type had a forward-slanted "B" pillar.

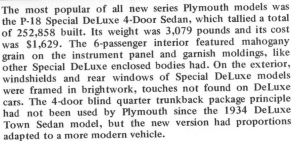

The Plymouth Cadet presented a simple frontal appearance. The hood nose form was repeated in the forward projection of the grille. Parking lamps were neatly incorporated in the outer tips of the top grille bar. Bumpers were of a concave shape like those on 1949 production Chryslers. Ford and Chevrolet had small car plans underway, too.

1949

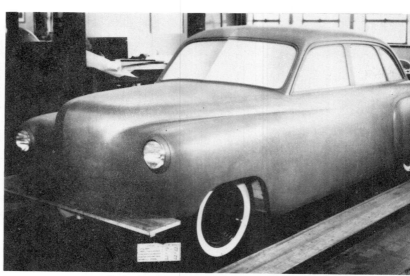

DeSoto entered the 1949 model year with a continuation of the 1946-48 Series S-11. The year change quietly occurred on December 1, 1948, when the manufacturer advised that cars produced from that date forward were designated as next year's model. The Custom, shown, and DeLuxe lines were continued without noticeable change.

Project A-92 was another consideration for 1949 Plymouth possibilities. Seen as an unfinished full-size clay exploration in 1947, it was based on a 114.5-inch wheelbase. While the wheelbase was four inches shorter than the P-18, overall length without bumpers was 8-7/8 inches less. Body width at the belt was equal to the P-18. The two sides were of different form, the nearest side rating "lukewarm" favor. The 3-window superstructure tapered well back on the trunk deck, creating a semi-fastback short deck profile at the center. Fender and body side shapes were much like the P-18.

The new 1949 DeSoto was the Series S-13, of which the DeLuxe Club Coupe is shown. This model weighed and cost the least of any new series DeSoto. It scaled 3,455 pounds and was priced at $1,976. No 2-door sedan was offered, so this 6-passenger car chalked up a production total of 6,807. Whitewall tires and full chrome wheel trim were S-13 extra-cost options. The DeLuxe line carried the definitive designation of Series S-13-1.

Included in original S-13 announcements but not in production until mid-year, the DeSoto Carry-All Sedan was classified a DeLuxe model. The rear seat of the 6-passenger car folded down to form a cargo floor length of nearly eight feet from the back of the front seat to the deck lid. The handy utility car weighed 3,565 pounds and cost $2,191. Assembly lines turned out 2,690 of them. A choice of plastic fabric or DeLuxe broadcloth/plastic fabric combination was offered for seat upholstery.

The DeSoto DeLuxe 4-Door Sedan tipped the scales at 3,520 pounds and carried a price tag of $1,986. 13,148 of them rolled from assembly lines. The example shown had off-white plastic wheel trim. The interior accommodated six passengers in comfort. Fluid Drive and Tip-Toe Shift transmission were DeLuxe options. All Series S-13 cars had a 6-cylinder 112-horsepower engine called the "Powermaster" and having Floating Power mounts.

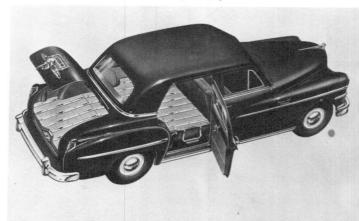

The DeSoto Custom Club Coupe, of which 18,431 were built, tipped the scales at 3,585 pounds and was priced at $2,156. Like its DeLuxe counterpart, the 6-passenger car had a luggage compartment of generous size. The Custom line, specifically designated as S-13-2, had exterior chrome trim that distinguished it from the DeLuxe line. Two short chrome strips were added to front fender lower sides, and chrome stone shields were fitted to the leading surface of rear fenders.

The Station Wagon was the first of this kind of vehicle to be offered by the DeSoto Division. It came as a DeLuxe model only. Shown with true DeLuxe exterior chrome trim, some were seen with extra fender trim as used on Custom cars. It weighed 3,915 pounds, cost $2,959 and was delivered to 850 buyers. The steel body, with real white ash framing simulated woodgrain panels, was built by Chrysler at Evansville, Ind. The 9-passenger seating arrangement was 3-in-tandem. The center seat was actually two units, since the curbside unit swung forward for access to the rearmost seat. Center and rear seats were removable to allow cargo carrying. The tailgate housed the spare wheel. This model was part of first S-13 announcements but was not in production until July.

The most-favored new series DeSoto was the Custom 4-Door Sedan, of which 48,589 were built. The 6-passenger car weighed 3,645 pounds and was priced at $2,174 when new. Now owned by Mel Franklin, Jeffersontown, Ky., the car shown is an excellent example. The 4-door blind quarter trunkback package concept was new to DeSoto. Otherwise, new series styling retained the characteristic DeSoto appearance. Compared with the DeLuxe, Custom interiors were more tasteful and of better quality. For this model, a rear center armrest was an extra-cost option.

As shown with standard wheel and tire equipment for this model only, the DeSoto Custom Convertible was priced at $2,578. 3,385 of the 3,785-pound cars were manufactured. First publicized in the initial S-13 announcement, production began three months later. New for this model was an unbreakable full-vision rear window of vinylite clear plastic. Peter De Paolo, former driver of racing cars and DeSoto endurance driver, is shown in the car. The standing gentleman is unidentified, but probably was an important race official. DeSotos were often associated with well-known personalities and events.

The DeSoto Custom 8-Passenger Sedan was an impressive automobile. It pressed the scales to a reading of 4,200 pounds and carried a price tag marked at $2,863. Only 342 of them rolled from the assembly line. It was built on a 139.5-inch wheelbase and had 8.20 x 15 tires. Smaller S-13 models had a 125.5-inch wheelbase and 7.60 x 15 tires. All Custom models, regardless of size, featured Fluid Drive and Tip-Toe Shift transmission as standard equipment.

Another model on the long 139.5-inch chassis was the DeSoto Suburban. It was the S-13 of least demand, as only 129 were built. At $3,179 it was the costliest S-13, and at 4,410 pounds it was the heaviest production DeSoto yet built. A Custom model, it was announced in March but did not get on the market until the autumn season began. The roof was fitted with luggage-supporting wood slats and chromed restraining rails.

The DeSoto Suburban seated nine persons when its three tandem seats were in use. If desired, six passengers were seated while the rearmost seat was folded flat to form a long floor for luggage. Also, the center seat could be slid against the front seat for even more luggage room, but only three persons could be accommodated. The split-back center seat allowed access for rear seat passengers. Door panels were in wood grain and seats were upholstered in plastic fabric.

This taxicab, based on a DeSoto DeLuxe chassis, was built by Derham coachbuilders in Rosemont, Pa., for service in New York. It was a trial vehicle which Derham hoped would bring orders for more, but apparently nothing developed from it. Most of the body was specially made, but it had some production sedan parts. The generously crowned roof was high at the rear, affording liberal interior headroom. A low-profile trunk was integral with the back. Not related to this vehicle were 680 California-type S-13-1 taxicabs built.

The 1949 Diplomat used the all-new Plymouth bodies with a unique DeSoto grille, hood ornament, and ornamentation to achieve a DeSoto identity. Beginning this year were wheel covers with red centers that were unique to the Diplomat. This Diplomat-Custom 4-Door Sedan shows the front fender molding extending onto the door, a treatment that did not appear on production cars. The shorter Plymouth molding was used instead.

All Diplomat-Customs, like this Convertible Coupe, rode on a larger 118½-inch wheelbase, although the overall length was reduced. The grille was a pretty close copy of the larger DeSotos' thick and thin bars, a situation that would not always be true in the future. Even though Diplomat grille-work tried to look exactly like the "real" DeSotos, completely different parts were required to fit the Plymouth sheet metal.

The best wagon in the Diplomat line was this 4-door "woodie," officially the Diplomat-Custom Station Wagon. In common with other Chrysler Corporation wagons, the spare tire was enclosed in a special compartment in the two-piece rear tailgate. With three seats in place there was room for eight people inside. The wagon featured a sliding window in the rear doors, exposed hinges, unique taillights, and a 3-piece hinged rear bumper.

The windshield of this Diplomat-Custom Club Coupe was 37% larger than last year's for improved visibility. The new Diplomats were lower, shorter, and narrower, yet boasted more room inside. Equipment on Custom models included dual air horns, steering wheel horn ring, engine vibration damper, oil filter, carburetor intake silencer, front end sway eliminator, and 15 x 6.70 4-ply Goodyear Super Cushion black sidewall tires.

This Diplomat 3-Passenger Coupe was one member of the 3-model Diplomat series, all of which were mounted on a shorter 111-inch wheelbase, 7½ inches less than the Diplomat-Customs. Both the Coupe and the 2-Door Sedan had special taillights mounted to the lower quarter panels instead of atop the fenders. Later Diplomats probably had a rear fender rub molding, since this equipment was also added to the Plymouth DeLuxe line.

DeSoto did well in foreign markets with this 6-passenger, 2-door Diplomat Utility. Its all-steel construction was a distinct advantage in humid climates where wood-bodied wagons rotted and decayed quickly. Unlike the Custom "woodie," the Utility carried its spare inside, which permitted use of a one-piece rear bumper. Interiors of all Diplomats were identical to comparable Plymouths except for instrument panel nameplate and steering wheel medallion.

In common with other Diplomats, this 2-Door Sedan used the Plymouth 217.8 c.i.d. L-head six engine (3.57 liters), developing 97 horsepower at 3600 r.p.m. Compression ratio was 7.0 to 1, but a special low-compression head was available for areas of the world where fuel quality was poor. Heavy-duty shocks were standard. Standard tire size was 15 x 6.40 4-ply, but heavier six-ply tires were optional.

This was another great year for the auto industry. The sales spurt began prematurely, before the usual springtime rush, and maintained a good pace through most of the year. At year-end, total passenger car production added up to another record year. On the heels of the record 1949 performance, this was an amazing accomplishment. The gain was a healthy 30%, and might have been 40% if Chrysler Corp. had not been shut down by a 100-day labor strike. Chrysler said the production loss was about 500,000 units and the loss of business amounted to a staggering 1.4 billion dollars. Consequently, the corporation produced just over 17.8% of the industry total, about 3.4% less than its typical showing in the previous three years. Despite the strike, which occurred early this year. Chrysler rallied to turn out almost 7.1% more cars than it did in 1949.

All Chrysler divisions registered gains, but Plymouth was the corporation's lowest gainer, mustering only about one-tenth of one percent. That almost cost Plymouth its rank as the industry's No. 3 automaker, as Buick was within very close range. DeSoto mustered a respectable increase of more than 18.9%, but dropped one notch to occupy the No. 14 spot. DeSoto's slip was because of the strike and the early entry of Kaiser-Frazer's new 1951 models which caught on fast and zoomed that combine from 16th

The Plymouth DeLuxe 3-Passenger Coupe weighed and cost the least of all Plymouths offered this year. It scaled 2,872 pounds and was priced at $1,371. The little 2-window car on the P-19 111-inch wheelbase earned enough demand to require production of 16,861. P-19 tire size was 6.40 x 15. Whitewall tires, seen on most of the Plymouths illustrated here, were an extra-cost option regardless of the model they are shown on.

Continuing the fastback profile was the Plymouth DeLuxe 2-Door Sedan, of which 67,584 were manufactured. The practical 6-passenger model tipped the scales at 2,946 pounds. It was factory-priced at $1,492. All Plymouth prices include federal taxes. This P-19 model was powered by the same 6-cylinder 97-horsepower engine used in all other Plymouths this year.

to 12th place.

Plymouth began the calendar year and the model ye with the announcement of "The Beautifully Ne Plymouth." The model line-up was the same as befor with three lines comprised of nine body types. New seri designations were P-19 for the 111-inch wheelbase DeLux and P-20 for the 118.5-inch DeLuxe and Special DeLux As a whole, weight averaged 29½ pounds heavier tha previous models, but prices were unchanged.

The Plymouth 6-cylinder 97-horsepower engine w continued with no significant changes. The transmissic and drive train components were untouched. While chass layout was as before, front tread was increased from 55 55-7/16 inches and rear tread was widened from 56 58-7/16 inches. As always, emphasis was on engineerin excellence in a car of low price. Minimum styling change were applied to the conservative shape introduced fc 1949. New sheetmetal was in the form of slightly peake rear fenders, still bolted on. Rear windows of coupes ar sedans were larger. The grille was somewhat simplifie and new bumpers were plainer. Minor touches include some new ornamentation and trim details.

The new DeSoto models, introduced in January, wei also carryover models with minimal changes. Now desi nated the Series S-14, they were again offered in DeLux and Custom versions. Wheelbases of 125.5 and 139.5 inch were retained, but the latter was not now in the Custo line only. As before, there were four DeLuxe model but an exchange was made in one instance. The Custo line had eight models instead of five, as two new on were added and one moved in from the DeLuxe lin Overall, the Series S-14 averaged 7½ pounds less weigl than its predecessor, but the price average remained stabl

DeSoto's Powermaster 6-cylinder engine again produce 112 horsepower and, like Plymouth, still featured Floatir Power mountings. Drive train components received minim changes, and chassis layout was untouched. Brake dru diameter increased from 11 to 12 inches.

Though advertised as "The New DeSoto," the S-14 wa a minor styling facelift job. Rear fenders of new peake design represented the only new sheetmetal. Coupes an sedans had larger rear windows. Grille design was new, bu distinctly DeSoto, and ornamentation was slightly r vamped. A passing glance would hardly distinguish th from the previous model. Regardless, it was a fair selle and would have done better if the long strike had nc intervened.

This year of record industry production would not t surpassed until five years later. In the interim, automake would have to contend with material shortages and minc readjustments because of the U.S. "police action" i Korea, which began this year.

Late in the year, K. T. Keller became chairman of th board of Chrysler Corp., a post that had been vacant sinc Walter P. Chrysler's death ten years before. In the interin K. T. guided the corporation, as he had been its presider since 1935. Succeeding Keller as president wa L. L. Colbert, who had been president of Dodge Divisio since 1945. Mr. Colbert would soon approve a ne direction for styling, a move that would scuttle the Kelle conservatism. Evidence of the change would appear fou years later with introduction of 1955 models.

The DeLuxe Suburban did not get the new rear fenders used on Plymouth's regular passenger cars. As a result, tail lamps remained on the rear body corners. The P-19 model was a 5-passenger car because rear wheel housings reduced seat width. It weighed 3,116 pounds and cost $1,840. The demand for this new all-steel 2-door wagon type grew rapidly since its first appearance in 1949. 34,457 of this body type were built, but not all were the regular model shown. Full wheel covers shown were an all-Plymouth option.

The Plymouth DeLuxe Club Coupe was mounted on a 118.5-inch wheelbase and was a P-20 model. The 6-passenger car, of which 53,890 were built, weighed 3,040 pounds and was priced at $1,519. Rear fender stone guards, always in chrome finish, were an option that could be had on any model. The P-20 chassis featured a front sway eliminator bar which maintained a more level keel.

A new model added to the P-19 line about September 1st was the Special Suburban. Utilizing the regular Suburban body, its distinction was in a much fancier interior and more brightwork trim on the exterior. It was further identified by Special Suburban nameplates on the sides. Its production total is unknown, since it was included with the regular Suburban total. It weighed 3,155 pounds and was priced at $1,946. For an unknown reason, one P-19 chassis-only was built.

The Club Coupe was the lowest-priced Plymouth Special DeLuxe model, being priced at $1,603. At 3,041 pounds, it was also the lightest top-line model. 99,361 of them came out of the factories. This view effectively illustrates the extended peak of the new rear fender design. Tail lamps were recessed in the fenders, a feature not used by Plymouth since 1939. Previous recessed lamps had been in the body proper.

The other of the two DeLuxe Plymouths on the P-20 chassis was the 4-Door Sedan. It accommodated six passengers, weighed 3,068 pounds and carried a $1,551 price tag. It sold well enough to require production of 87,871 units. Note that the bottom of the rear window was extended to the top of the rear deck, a new Plymouth enclosed body feature. All P-20 models, both DeLuxe and Special DeLuxe, were fitted with size 6.70 x 15 tires.

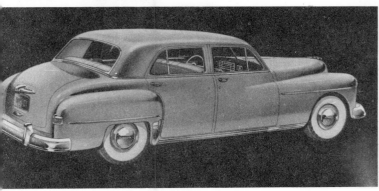

Drawing the least demand of any Plymouth model this year was the Special DeLuxe Station Wagon. Only 2,057 of these woody models were built. This was the last year Plymouth offered the smart wood-crafted type, for which bodies were built by the U.S. Body & Forging Co., Frankfort, Ind. The 8-passenger 4-door car was the heaviest Plymouth, weighing 3,353 pounds. At $2,372, it was also the costliest. Like the P-19 Suburbans, this P-20 model did not have the new-design rear fenders. A Suburban was not offered in the Special DeLuxe line. For unknown body types and purposes, 2,091 Special DeLuxe chassis-only units were shipped.

The Special DeLuxe Convertible Club Coupe was Plymouth's answer to those who liked an open car at times. Registering 3,295 pounds on the weight scale, the 6-passenger car exacted a price of $1,982. Assembly lines turned out 12,697 of them. The interior was of different design than any other model. Plymouth's new grille was quite simple, featuring generous air intake space divided by a strong horizontal bar and a set-back vertical support at the center. This was in keeping with the new trend to cavernous openings which would be prevalent for six more years.

As usual, the most popular Plymouth model was the Special DeLuxe 4-Door Sedan. 234,084 of the 6-passenger cars were manufactured. This P-20 model tipped the scales at 3,072 pounds and was priced at $1,629. Among new features on all Plymouths were bumpers of new design which reflected much more skylight, causing them to look heavier than they were. Necessarily, bumper guards were also new.

The DeLuxe Club Coupe was the lightest and lowest-priced DeSoto, weighing 3,450 pounds and costing $1,976. All DeSoto prices are factory list, including federal taxes. This 6-passenger model attracted 10,703 sales. The DeLuxe line of the new Series S-14 was known as S-14-1. All DeSotos of less than eight passenger capacity rode on a 125.5-inch wheelbase and 7.60 x 15 tires.

The DeSoto DeLuxe 4-Door Sedan, of which 18,489 were built, registered a weight of 3,525 pounds and listed a price of $1,986. Its rear window was deepened to the rear deck, an improvement all other DeSoto body types had. The 6-passenger car was powered by a Powermaster 6-cylinder 112-horsepower engine, the same as installed in all other new DeSotos. The revamped grille included a vertical center divider in body color and round parking lamps at the outer ends. Series identity script, in this case "DeLuxe," was on chrome nameplates just below the front window ventpanes.

With its side nameplates bearing the name "Carry-All," this was a model in the DeLuxe line. Introduced by DeSoto in 1949, the Carry-All Sedan continued the utilitarian dual-purpose features which made it distinctive. Its price was $2,191 and its weight was 3,600 pounds. 3,900 of these 6-passenger models were built. Another special DeSoto adaptation was the California-type taxicab, of which 2,350 were built. They were based on a DeLuxe model of unknown type. Possibly for display, an S-14-1 chassis without body was assembled.

Awaiting shipment from the factory, a DeSoto Custom Club Coupe showed dress-up items that were common to all Custom models. Two short chrome moldings on the front fender skirt teamed with the rear fender stone shield to provide exterior distinction for the higher-priced line. Inside, Custom cars were more lavish and tasteful than lower-cost models, and all had painted instrument panels and door garnish moldings instead of the woodgrain previously used. The 6-passenger car illustrated weighed 3,575 pounds and cost $2,156. 6,100 were built.

Living up to its traditional popularity rating, the Custom 4-Door Sedan was DeSoto's most sought-after model. It scored a production total of 72,664. The 3,640-pound 6-passenger car sold for $2,174. DeSoto's new rear fenders, used on all but wagon types, were slightly peaked at the crown, more horizontal in attitude, and modestly projected from the body at the rear. They housed fully-recessed tail lamps, a feature not used since 1939, after which they were housed in rear body panels until 1949. In improving its cars mechanically, DeSoto adopted two items about midyear. They were a better waterproof ignition system and a new internal expanding parking brake at the rear of the transmission.

A brand-new DeSoto body type was the Sportsman, presented only as a Custom model. Of the new hardtop convertible concept just getting a start in the industry, it utilized a convertible body on which a fixed steel roof replaced the folding top. As time has shown, this type was destined for immense popularity. Although included in first S-14 announcements, the Sportsman did not reach production until June. 4,600 were built. The classy 6-passenger car weighed 3,735 pounds and cost $2,489. It is shown with standard equipment for this model.

The Convertible Coupe was another DeSoto Custom type with a sporty flair. It registered 3,815 pounds on the weight scale and asked a price of $2,578. Assembly lines rolled out 2,900 of these 6-passenger cars. In keeping with their special appeal, whitewall tires and full wheel covers were among otherwise extra-cost items that were standard equipment on this and the Sportsman.

Not even hinted when other DeSotos were heralded in January, the new All-Steel Station Wagon was a very late addition in October. This was a brand-new body type for DeSoto. Placed in the Custom line, the 4-door body had two seats which accommodated six passengers. With the rear seat folded flat, almost ten feet of cargo space was provided. With no liftgate, the rear window lowered completely into the tailgate. The spare wheel was carried in a rear floor well. This model weighed 3,900 pounds and cost $2,717. A latecomer, only 100 were built. Thus it was the S-14 model of lowest production.

This was the last year for the DeSoto woodcrafted wagon. Announced in January, the Station Wagon did not reach the market until midyear. A Custom model, it shared its body layout with the new all-steel type. Seating, tailgate and rear window were the same. Both models had Chrysler-built bodies, and both utilized 1949 rear fenders instead of the new design. Overall length was seven inches greater than the other 125.5-inch wheelbase models. The wooden Station Wagon, of which 600 were built, weighed 4,035 pounds and was factory-priced at $3,093.

The 8-Passenger Sedan was one of three extra-long DeSoto models offered to the public. All rode on a 139.5-inch wheelbase and 8.20 x 15 tires. Shown is the Custom model, of which 734 were manufactured. The huge luxury car registered a weight of 4,115 pounds and was quoted at $2,863. For the first time since 1942, this model was also offered in the DeLuxe line. As such, it weighed 3,995 pounds and cost $2,676. The DeLuxe car had the usual DeLuxe trim treatment and registered a production total of 235.

The Suburban, based on the extra-long chassis, was the heaviest and most expensive DeSoto. It weighed a whopping 4,400 pounds, ten less than in 1949, but a base shipping weight that would not be equalled or surpassed by any future DeSoto domestic production passenger car. Its price was $3,179. A Custom model, the Suburban name appeared below the front window ventpanes. Seating nine persons when all seats were in use, it featured utility arrangements that distinguished previous Suburbans. 623 of these prestigious vehicles were built.

Built by Derham on a Custom 125.5-inch chassis, this special DeSoto utilized production parts except for the rear fenders and major portions of the body. Built around a club coupe seating plan, it had a one-piece flat windshield and new roof. Having center pillars, it was not a hardtop convertible type, but chrome-framed windows gave it a hardtop touch. Rear quarter ventpanes were a luxury feature. Rear fenders, in conformance with the modified deck, curved downward and had new tail lamps and trim. Bumpers and guards were of new design. This is assumed as a one-only example, probably built on one of the two Custom chassis-only units assembled by DeSoto.

The DeSoto name was not restricted to passenger cars. In some foreign countries a variety of DeSoto trucks were offered. Actually Dodge vehicles, they were also manufactured with Fargo nameplates affixed. Minor ornamentation details also distinguished one from another. A DeSoto Series F with stake body is shown. The Series F engine was an L-head six of 109 horsepower. This series, with wheelbases of 128 and 152 inches, offered several body choices. Of 1½-ton rating, gross vehicle wieght was 13,500 pounds.

The DeSoto Series G was powered by the 236 cubic-inch engine also used for the F and H series. For the three series, seven variations of this engine were adapted to specific models and job requirements. Series G wheelbases were 128, 152, 170 and 192 inches. Rated at 1½ tons, gross vehicle wieght was 14,500 pounds. Shown is a refrigerator model, one of a wide range of bodies. Any series could be ordered as a chassis with or without cab, or as a complete vehicle.

DeSoto cab-over-engine trucks were also offered in foreign lands. They were available in two series, GM and HM, both of which provided a wheelbase choice of 107, 131 and 161 inches. Engines were the same as those in conventional cab models. Both series were rated at 1½ tons. Gross vehicle weight was 14,750 pounds for the Series GM and 16,250 pounds for the HM. The van shown was one of a variety of body choices. Complete vehicles or the chassis with or without cab could be purchased. Records indicate first DeSoto truck production in November, 1938, continuing through succeeding years except for the war years 1942-45. DeSoto truck production for foreign markets would continue through many more years.

Shown as a tractor is the DeSoto Series H. With four wheelbases as listed for the Series G, the H was rated at 1½ tons and 16,000 pounds gross vehicle weight. Bodies for almost any purpose were available. Cabs with Standard, DeLuxe or Custom features were optional for all truck series.

This Diplomat-Custom 4-Door Sedan faithfully captured the new DeSoto grille while using two fewer vertical bars. The grille medallion on the painted center section was similar to the larger DeSotos' but the hood ornament was a continuation of the 1949 design, as were the red center wheel covers. Design of the lower hood molding above the grille was unique to Diplomat. A lower-priced Diplomat-DeLuxe 4-Door Sedan was available for the first time this year.

Sweetheart of the line was this Diplomat-Custom Convertible Coupe. Wide, chair-high seats were upholstered in Bedford cord, with upper seat backs in durable vinyl resin fabric. Doors and quarter panels were also trimmed in vinyl. The instrument panel was painted rather than wood-grained as on closed cars. Extra springs could be added to the front seat for heavier drivers. A push-button automatic top was standard equipment.

The sales success of the all-steel Diplomat Commercial Utility over its more costly and glamorous wood-bodied running mate quickly led to the demise of both wood bodies and four doors on all Diplomat wagons. Front sway eliminator was standard on the Commercial Utility and on all Diplomat-Custom models. Also standard were 15 x 6.40 blackwall tires versus 15 x 6.70 on DeLuxe and Custom models. Six-ply tires were optional.

Appearing for the last time was this Diplomat-Custom 8-passenger Station Wagon with its expensive, hard to maintain, but delightful wood body. This was to be the last Diplomat 4-door wagon until 1955. Despite the added convenience of four doors, Diplomat buyers definitely preferred the more functional all-steel Commercial Utility. Collectors, however, would disagree. The Plymouth-based "woodie" retained the tailgate-mounted concealed spare tire.

With the adoption of the new lower taillights, the Diplomat 3-Passenger Coupe used the same design as the other models — they were no longer unique. This was also true on the 2-Door Sedan. Rear window on some Diplomats was enlarged 32% for improved vision. The Coupe's full-width single seat was upholstered in dark red vinyl resin or woven fiber fabric, with broadcloth optional.

The Diplomat-Custom Club Coupe illustrates the new rectangular taillights, moved from the fender peak to the lower fender in line with the rub rail. Both front and rear fenders featured bolt-on rather than welded construction, offering easy and quick replacement in the event of damage. This was a distinct advantage overseas, where repair shops were often hard to find and repairmen were lacking in sophisticated skills.

The 97-horsepower six with a 7.0 to 1 compression ratio was continued unchanged in this Diplomat 2-Door Sedan, while a lower 6.6 to 1 ratio was optional. All Diplomat models rode on the compact 111-inch chassis while Diplomat-DeLuxe and Diplomat-Custom models used the larger 118½-inch wheelbase. If the catalog artwork is correct, Diplomat models had bright windshield reveal moldings versus black rubber on the comparable Plymouth DeLuxe models.

The sales boom of the previous two years was not repeated this calendar year, as the auto industry's passenger car production dropped almost 20%. Though some slackening of demand always follows a boom period, this time it was magnified by the U.S. military involvement in Korea. At first, the government severely restricted some materials needed for automaking, but the war scare eased and so did restrictions.

Chrysler Corp. produced 23% of all cars, bettering its industry portion with a gain of more than 5%, and registering a 2.9% increase over its own 1950 production. These gains were the fruits of a year without serious labor troubles. Of its four car divisions, Plymouth was the only gainer, going up 8.2% over 1950 and easily holding its traditional 3rd-place industry position. DeSoto production slumped more than 5% but rose from 14th to 12th position because Hudson and Kaiser-Frazer dropped from above it to places below.

The new Plymouths were moderately modified versions of previous models, but with new designations. The economy 111-inch wheelbase line, Series P-22, joined the swing to more attractive names by becoming the Concord, replacing the former DeLuxe but continuing the four models of that series. The two former DeLuxe models on the 118.5-inch wheelbase now became the Cambridge line of Series P-23. The top P-23 line, also on the longer chassis, became the Cranbrook line, replacing the Special DeLuxe. Though having four models as before, the new top line had a hardtop convertible instead of a wooden station wagon. Overall, the three lines averaged 23 pounds heavier and $203 costlier than their 1950 counterparts.

Mechanically, Plymouths were much the same as 1950. The same 6-cylinder engine still delivered 97 horsepower and featured Floating Power mountings, though minor improvements were made. The chassis was given minor changes, and new Oriflow shock absorbers provided better ride control.

Plymouth continued the body package concept introduced in 1949 but softened the front end appearance with the slanted nose of a new hood and gently-curving contours at the front of the new front fenders. In combination with bumpers and guards of new design, these changes added a bit to overall length and a better image. All ornamentation was reworked. As military needs took critical metals during the year, chrome plating became thinner, specifications changed, and some trim items became optional or impossible to get.

DeSoto's new cars were designated the Series S-15. The DeLuxe line, S-15-1, continued the four models as in 1950, with three on the 125.5-inch wheelbase and one on the 139.5-inch length. The Custom, S-15-2, now had five instead of six short-chassis models, there being no wooden station wagon this year, while the two previous models were retained on the long chassis. The Series S-15, in an overall average of comparable models, weighed 10 pounds more and was $313 more expensive than the series it succeeded.

Mechanical aspects of the new DeSotos were little different than the 1950 models. The Powermaster 6-cylinder engine retained the bore of 3-7/16 inches, but the stroke was increased from 4¼ to 4½ inches. Other modifications helped raise horsepower from 112 to 116. Floating Power engine mounts were retained. Oriflow shock absorbers were the most notable new chassis feature.

Stylewise, the new DeSotos were more than a minor change, but were not quite a major revamp. The sloped nose of the new hood and subtle use of contours in new front fenders combined with more massive bumpers and guards to improve appearance by adding a trifle to overall length. Simpler bodyside treatment made less use of ornamental brightwork. Military needs exacted penalties from DeSoto, too.

These Plymouth and DeSoto series were continued as 1952 models because of the military action in Korea. At the time tooling commitments should have been made for new 1952 models, a possibility of widescale war existed. Chrysler, heavily committed to government contracts, cautiously decided to delay any new series. An eventual relieving of tension came too late to allow new models for starting the next model year.

Among Chrysler's many military contracts was one for seaplane hulls. For the Grumman Albatross, the job was assigned to Plymouth for building in the Evansville plant.

The small fastback Plymouth was again offered, this time known as the Concord 2-Door Sedan. The 6-passenger car tipped the scales at 2,969 pounds and was priced at $1,673. The appearance of all new Plymouths was enhanced by the slanting hood nose, and front fenders curved slightly downward toward the front. These helped give a lower look to the front end.

The lightest and lowest-priced Plymouth was the Concord 3-Passenger Coupe. It weighed 2,919 pounds and was factory-priced at $1,537. The snug little car was also the least popular Plymouth. The Concord line was Series P-22 and was based on the 111-inch wheelbase. Since the Series P-22 was continued for 1952, and official production records combined both years, single model totals are placed with the 1952 models.

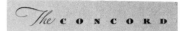

The Concord Suburban was Plymouth's economy station wagon. This was called a 5-passenger vehicle. The 2-door body had a rear seat that folded flat for extra cargo space when desired. The spare wheel was carried in a floor well, and at the rear was a conventional tailgate and liftgate. The model weighed 3,124 pounds and cost $2,064. Its interior was of simple utilitarian design.

The Plymouth Concord Savoy replaced the DeLuxe Special Suburban of 1950. Utilizing the Suburban body and seating plan, it was Plymouth's fanciest station wagon this year because there was no wooden wagon. It cost $2,182 and weighed 3,184 pounds. As standard trim, it had brightwork around the windshield, on side window dividers, the beltline and tailgate hinges. Rear fender stone shields, full wheel covers and whitewall tires were all-Plymouth options, but the latter were scarce and unavailable at times. The Concord tire size was 6.40 x 15.

The Concord Savoy interior was styled in a very special manner. Quality fabrics were used in combination with vinyl, and harmonizing 2-tone colors were employed. Features included front and rear armrests, rear assist straps on the side panels and a package compartment at each side of the rear seat.

The new Cambridge line, on a 118.5-inch wheelbase, replaced the DeLuxe line of that length. It was the lower-cost version of the Plymouth Series P-23. The Club Coupe accommodated six passengers, weighed 3,059 pounds and cost $1,703. The Series P-23 Cambridge was carried over for 1952, and production totals for its two models are recorded in the 1952 section.

This was Plymouth's lowest-priced 4-door sedan this year. Costing $1,739, the Cambridge 4-Door Sedan was fitted almost as nicely as the higher-priced version. It weighed 3,104 pounds and had room for six passengers. Cambridge models had no bright trim around the windshield and rear window. All Plymouths had narrower front pillars, while sedans and club coupes had wider rear windows curving slightly into rear quarters.

The top Plymouth line was the Cranbrook, which succeeded the Special DeLuxe. It was also the Series P-23 on the longer chassis. The Cranbrook Club Coupe, a close-coupled 6-passenger car, weighed 3,074 pounds and cost $1,796. Production totals for the Cranbrook line of four models, all continued for 1952, can be found in that year's section. The car is shown with optional wheel covers.

Unchallenged as the most popular Plymouth this year, the Cranbrook 4-Door Sedan illustrates the slightly greater front-end length given to all new Plymouths. The car weighed 3,109 pounds, could carry six passengers, and its price was $1,826 without the optional wheel covers. 1951 Plymouths had several identity clues to distinguish them from 1952. Side nameplates had block-style letters and the hood medallion was basically a 6-sided shield configuration. The hood top ornament had outstretched members at each side. At the rear, the Plymouth name was above, and not a part of, the license light fixture.

A new body type for Plymouth was the hardtop convertible, a model given to other Chrysler divisions in 1950. One of the Cranbrook models, it was called the Belvedere, a name that would escalate and decline in Plymouth model importance during the next 19 years. Utilizing the Convertible Club Coupe body, it had convertible side windows and a fixed steel roof with a 3-piece rear window wrapped well into the quarters to add a smart and airy touch. The car weighed 3,182 pounds, cost $2,114 and easily seated six persons. It was powered by the same 6-cylinder 97-horsepower engine that all other Plymouths had. This view nicely shows the wide grille and bumper guards that seemed to integrate with it.

The first of a long series of "idea cars" built for Chrysler by Ghia in Italy, the Plymouth XX-500 was custom-built on a 1951 Plymouth chassis. Only this one showpiece was built. The totally custom bodywork is quite evident. It was mounted on a stock chassis of 118.5-inch wheelbase, and the engine and drive train were also stock. The 6-passenger interior was upholstered in Bedford Cord and leather. The slab-side car with a curved-glass windshield and fastback rear treatment provided little inspiration for future Plymouth styling.

Plymouth's offering to those who liked to ride in sunshine and rushing wind was the Cranbrook Convertible Club Coupe. The car was said to be a 6-passenger model, but three on the rear seat were a bit crowded. The interior was specially designed and tailored for this model. This was the heaviest and costliest Plymouth this year, weighing 3,294 pounds and costing $2,222. Normally, this model was fitted with whitewall tires. The tire size for all P-23 models was 6.70 x 15.

The DeLuxe Club Coupe was DeSoto's least expensive and lowest-weight car. It was priced at $2,215 and weighed 3,475 pounds. Though interior length was close-coupled, it was classed as a 6-passenger car. The new DeSotos were the Series S-15, of which the DeLuxe line was S-15-1. As the S-15 was also offered for 1952, DeSoto combined the 2-year production records. Totals for individual models are provided in the 1952 section.

This view of the DeSoto DeLuxe 4-Door Sedan clearly shows some of the changes made this year. The curves and falling highlight of the front fender lowered the front end. The sloped hood nose also aided in that respect. A trifle more sheetmetal ahead of the front wheels was another move to combat the stubby look of the past two years. At the rear, the window now curved more into the quarters. This is also seen in coupes. All models had imperceptibly narrower front pillars. The car shown seated six persons, cost $2,227 and weighed 3,570 pounds.

Ready for its picture was the most popular of all S-15 DeSotos, the Custom 4-Door Sedan. It offered so much appeal that it attracted more sales than any other DeSoto this year. Weighing 3,685 pounds and costing $2,438, the 6-passenger car was powered by a 6-cylinder 116-horsepower engine like all other S-15 cars had. The wide whitewall tires were size 7.60 x 15, which was common to all regular-size DeSotos.

The DeSoto Carry-All Sedan, one of the DeLuxe models, gradually lost the sales appeal it enjoyed during the two previous years. Apparently it lost favor to the station wagon, which cost more but offered advantages. The Carry-All, shown with the rear seat folded down, seated six persons when needed. It registered a weight of 3,685 pounds and asked a price of $2,457.

The lowest-priced model in the DeSoto Custom line was the Club Coupe, which cost $2,418. The close-coupled 6-passenger car weighed 3,585 pounds. The Custom line was specifically known as the Series S-15-2. Carried over as a 1952 series, production totals for all models may be found in that section. Whitewall tires and wheel covers were optional, regardless of the model they are shown on. This model, like all DeSotos of less than 8-passenger size, had a 125.5-inch wheelbase.

The DeSoto Sportsman, handsome hardtop model in the Custom series, was now in its second year and picking up popularity gradually. It accommodated six passengers, weighed 3,760 pounds and cost $2,761. In the latest fashion, the airy hardtop roof had a 3-piece wraparound rear window. The Sportsman name was on the front fender side, where other nameplates were placed this year.

Ready for a sunny and windy drive was the DeSoto Convertible, a Custom model. It weighed 3,840 pounds, cost $2,862 and had seating for six. The new grille consisted of vertical members with an S-shape profile, and bumpers were more massive. The new hood had offset creases which swept up from the lip above the grille and stretched toward the cowl. The hood lip feature curved around the fenders and ended at the doors. 1951 DeSotos had several means for distinguishing them from 1952 sixes. On the front, the DeSoto name was of script style lettering and the hood medallion was wider than its height. At the rear, tail lamps were symmetrical in outline, and had lenses with two chrome dividers and no integral backup lights.

This was the only wagon type offered by DeSoto this year. The All-Steel Station Wagon was labeled a Custom model. Mounted on the regular wheelbase, it was a 6-passenger vehicle unless the rear seat was folded down for cargo carrying. The 4-door body continued with no liftgate since the rear window lowered into the tailgate. The vehicle registered a 3,960-pound weight and had a price of $3,047. All models in the Custom line had Tip-Toe Shift and Fluid Drive as standard equipment. These could be had at extra cost on DeLuxe models. Normally, the DeLuxe had a 3-speed manual-shift transmission.

Shown is the DeSoto Custom 8-Passenger Sedan, which weighed 4,155 pounds and cost $3,211. Also offered was a DeLuxe 8-Passenger Sedan of 4,045 pounds weight and $3,001 cost, which was the least-wanted DeSoto. On the 139.5-inch wheelbase, they had 8.20 x 15 tires and were powered by the standard engine. All DeSotos had simplified side ornamentation this year, there being no extra chrome moldings to distinguish Custom from DeLuxe cars. The side nameplates were the positive means of identification.

Maintaining its prestigious position at the top of the S-15 Series was the DeSoto Suburban. The 9-passenger body, supported by the long chassis, retained the unique interior arrangement variations which previously gave it distinction. Logically, it was at the top of the Custom line. The huge luxury car was the heaviest and costliest DeSoto this year, weighing 4,395 pounds and costing $3,566.

DeSoto served as an ambulance, too. The All-Steel Station Wagon is shown in readiness for that purpose. Presumably, the conversion was offered by DeSoto dealers, since Chrysler dealers were currently providing the Windsor in similar form. Patients undoubtedly got a smooth ride in the DeSoto, which claimed a "boulevard" ride quality with its new Oriflow shock absorbers.

Possibly an early contender for 1951 production was this design for DeSoto. The clay model, of 3/8 scale, was photographed late in 1948 when exploration was underway for a suitable concept for the early 1950s. Based on the popular 4-door sedan package, it had "pontoon" sides, a curved windshield, and lacked a typical DeSoto grille. Known only as Project AD-44-6, its approval would have given DeSoto a fresh image.

Another design that could have become the 1951 DeSoto was this 4-door sedan proposal shown in 3/8 scale clay form. Very similar to the AD-44-6, this was Project AD-44-7. AD meant Advanced Design, and these late 1948 explorations could also have vied for production later than 1951. Also of "pontoon" concept, this version's curved windshield was noticeably wrapped toward the "A" pillars.

1951 was the "year of the teeth" at DeSoto. Larger cars used nine molars, while this Diplomat-Custom 4-Door Sedan got by with just seven. The hood emblem was the same as used on the senior cars. Hernando's helmeted head made its bow on Diplomat hood ornaments this year. Diplomats also used a bright grille frame, missing on the bigger cars. The bright hood molding above the grille frame incorporated the DeSoto script.

The grafting of the DeSoto grille onto the Plymouth body was somewhat heavy-handed, as shown on this Diplomat-Custom Convertible Coupe. The DeSoto crest above the grille is missing in this illustration. A Diplomat-Custom version of Plymouth's Cranbrook Belvedere hardtop was probably added mid-year when the Belvedere appeared. Plymouth-based Diplomats and Canadian and export Dodge Kingsways were usually assembled in Detroit or Windsor for shipment, either built-up or knocked-down for local assembly overseas.

Continued was the popular DeSoto Diplomat Commercial Utility which completely replaced the 4-door "woodie" and was the only Diplomat wagon offered this year. Note the unique taillights. Standard tire size on the 111-inch wheelbase Diplomat series was 15 x 6.40 4-ply blackwall. Goodyears. Even though it resembled a metal box on wheels, the Commercial Utility was a popular Diplomat model.

Lone offering in the DeSoto Diplomat-DeLuxe line was this 4-Door Sedan. If the artwork is correct, it had neither the rear fender stone shield nor rub molding present on the Diplomat-Custom. Wheelbase on all DeLuxe and Custom models was 118.5 inches. Equipment included 15 x 6.20 4-ply blackwall tires with 6-ply and white sidewall tires optional. Both Plymouth and Diplomat used red-center hubcaps in 1951, though each hubcap design was unique.

Diplomat

Rear window of this DeSoto Diplomat-Custom Club Coupe was again enlarged, this time another 15%. Interiors were quite conventional, with vinyl scuff guards to protect the upholstery on seats and doors, grained garnish moldings, and carpet in the rear compartment, rubber mat in front. Window cranks moved the window up or down in less than two turns. Instrument panel was new this year.

The DeSoto Diplomat 3-Passenger Coupe was a pert little car whose appearance was spoiled by the buck-tooth grille compared with Plymouth's far simpler treatment. After a front-end collision, Diplomat owners might reasonably be expected to consult an orthodontist rather than a body shop. Maybe braces would have helped. A few of these coupes probably survive somewhere on the back roads of South America or Europe.

Like all DeSoto Diplomats, this 2-Door Sedan was powered by the 3.57 liter (217.8 c.i.d.) 6-cylinder engine with its 82.55 mm. (3¼-inch) bore and 111.1 mm. (4-3/8-inch) stroke. Crankcase capacity was 4.75 liters (5 U.S. quarts); radiator, 12.30 liters (3¼ U.S. gallons). The fuel tank held 64 liters in Europe, 17 gallons in the U.S., and 14.18 Imperial gallons in the Commonwealth. Any way you considered it, though, dimensions were identical with Plymouth.

The sales slump of 1951 continued through this year, cutting production schedules accordingly. For this calendar year, industry passenger car production dropped more than 18.78%. Of total industry production, Chrysler Corp. accounted for 21.96%, which was 1.04% less than it had in 1951. Compared with its 1951 production, the corporation suffered a 22.51% drop. Plymouth was down 23.74%. but held its position as the industry's No. 3 automaker. DeSoto fell 19.88%, its new V-8 softening the fall but not lifting it from its 12th position of the year before.

For the U.S. military commitment in Korea, Chrysler Corp. was supplying much. Plymouth's part, assigned last year, was the building of hulls for Grumman Albatross seaplanes, but the first one was not delivered until late this year. DeSoto got the job of making afterburners for Pratt & Whitney J-48 jet aircraft engines. Military materiel requirements eased in 1951, but too late for major changes at the start of 1952 car models. Consequently, 1951 models and their code designations were continued, but a further relaxing of government controls permitted a late introduction of DeSoto's V-8.

Plymouth and DeSoto entered the model year with ornamental and mechanical changes. These factors justified definition as new models, even though they were carryovers. Unlike the 1946-48 period in which carryovers received almost negligible change and were not advertised with model years, these were publicly proclaimed as distinct 1952 cars. Initial introduction fell within the year-end 1951-52 period of November through January, the season when most of the industry's new models appeared.

Bearing 46 improvements, Plymouth's Concord, Cambridge and Cranbrook series came on the market about January 1st. As before, the Series P-22 Concord had four body types on a 111-inch wheelbase, and the two models of the Cambridge line shared the Series P-23 118.5-inch wheelbase with the four models of the Cranbrook line. Surprisingly, the weight of the combined offerings averaged 32 pounds less than in 1951. No surprise was an average price increase of $90 for the trio.

Among Plymouth refinements were a new-design combustion chamber and several changes in the transmission to effect easier starting. Brakes, shock absorbers, starter motor and windshield wipers were also refined. Added in the spring was an overdrive transmission as optional equipment available for all models. Not offered until 1955, some cars may have been fitted with a dealer installed power brake package which was made available for Plymouths of 1951 model and later. The power brake device was not available in 1951-52.

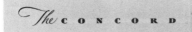

The C O N C O R D

This was the last fastback body type to be offered by Plymouth until 1964. It could not meet the competition of the bustleback design. The Concord 2-Door Sedan scored a production total of 49,139 units for its run through two model years. The 6-passenger car was factory-priced at $1,753 and swung the weight scale pointer to a reading of 2,959 pounds. This and the Concord Coupe were fitted with 15 x 6.40 tires.

The Concord 3-Passenger Coupe ranked as the lightest-weight and lowest-priced of all Plymouths this year, weighing 2,893 pounds and costing $1,610. The businesslike car also rated as the least-wanted Plymouth. This model accounted for 14,255 units built during its production span of 22 months. The Concord line was the Series P-22. Based on a 111-inch wheelbase, it had a 97-horsepower engine like all other Plymouths.

The first 1952 DeSotos were carryover 6-cylinder models which made their bow in November of 1951. The updated series S-15 continued the S-15-1 DeLuxe line of four body types and the S-15-2 Custom line of seven models. Wheelbases of 125.5 and 139.5 inches were retained. Like Plymouth, DeSoto came up with lighter weights for these new S-15 sixes, which averaged 32½ pounds less. S-15 prices averaged $136 more than the 1951 series, however. DeSoto did not enumerate the refinements incorporated in the sixes.

DeSoto's first 8-cylinder engine since 1931 came in the form of a V-8 in February this year. This car was DeSoto's big splash for the year, and nearly all publicity was concentrated on it from its inception. Named the FireDome, its series designation was S-17. Its engine was derived from the high-performance FirePower V-8 introduced in Chrysler cars for 1951. The FireDome engine featured dome-shaped combustion chambers which engineers called "hemispherical." This dome shape was said to achieve high volumetric and thermal efficiencies. The cylinders, inclined at a 90-degree angle, were topped by overhead valves of unique lateral arrangement. The large-bore short-stroke dimensions were 3-5/8 x 3-11/32 inches, respectively, which provided maximum compactness and high mechanical efficiency. The compression ratio was 7.1 to 1, and gross brake horsepower of 160 was developed at 4,400 r.p.m. This was by far the most powerful DeSoto engine yet. Since it was a smooth-running plant with no need for floating Power mountings, it was the first DeSoto engine without them since the SA Six and CF* Eight of 1931. However, the Powermaster 6-cylinder engines of the new V-8's S-15 teammates still had them, but of a different configuration than the initial version.

The FireDome 8 utilized the chassis and bodies of the S-15 Six, with adaptations for the V-8. A 3-speed manual transmission was standard, but it could be had with optional overdrive. Also optional was the automatic Tip-Toe Shift, which was available with Fluid Drive coupling or Fluid-Torque Drive, the latter being a torque converter. A larger rear axle was employed, and full-time hydraulic power steering, new to DeSoto, was optional. Only one line, rather than DeLuxe and Custom, was offered in the V-8 series. As in the S-15 Custom line, the new V-8 had five body types on the 125.5-inch wheelbase, but only one model was mounted on the 139.5-inch chassis, whereas the Custom had two. Combining comparable body types, the V-8 averaged 205 pounds heavier and $292 more expensive than the Custom six, without optional equipment. The price range placed it in direct contention with Oldsmobile's top-line 98 series.

Springtime brought announcement of the new Fluidmatic Drive as another option for the FireDome 8. This version drew its oil for the torque converter from the engine crankcase, via connecting galleries. Publicized in July was a new aluminum carburetor which DeSoto placed in production. The two-barrel design was lower in height, necessitated by the lower hood. As reported for Plymouth, some 1951-52 DeSotos may have been fitted with a power brake package made available in 1955.

The Plymouth Concord Suburban continued to be listed as a 5-passenger model. The 2-door family-utility car had a weight of 3,145 pounds and its price was $2,163. Because this body was also used by the Savoy, factory production records combined the two in one total. 76,520 of them were built during almost two years of production. The Suburban and Savoy used slightly larger tires than other Concords, being fitted with size 15 x 6.70.

The Savoy was again a dolled-up version of the Suburban. Also a 5-passenger car, its interior was treated much in the manner of a well-appointed sedan. On the outside, it had bright trim on the windshield frame, beltline and other places, and sported its own Savoy side nameplates. The Plymouth Concord Savoy scaled 3,165 pounds and was priced at $2,287. A production total is unknown, since it was included with the Suburban.

Again the middle-line Plymouth, the Cambridge series reflected its position with features from its cheaper and costlier sister cars. It was fancier than the Concord, but not as fancy as the Cranbrook. This car line was a Series P-23 with 118.5-inch wheelbase. Shown is the Cambridge Club Coupe, a 6-passenger car weighing 3,030 pounds and costing $1,784. During the 2-year span of the P-23, 101,784 of these models were built.

The Cambridge 4-Door Sedan was again Plymouth's lowest-priced car of this very popular body type. Factory-priced at $1,822, it weighed 3,068 pounds. During its extended production run through two model years, 179,417 were built. Plymouths were consistently priced above Ford and Chevrolet. This model cost about $175 more than the lowest-priced 4-door sedans of the other two, both of which were also 6-cylinder models.

Plymouth's price leader in the high-line Cranbrook series was the Club Coupe, which was marked at $1,883. This 6-passenger car tipped the scales at 3,046 pounds. It recorded a total of 126,725 units built during the 22-month stretch of P-23 production. It is interesting, and curious, that a pure 2-door sedan model was not included in the Cambridge and Cranbrook series. Of course, this was not the first year for that omission.

The favorite Plymouth model was the Cranbrook 4-Door Sedan, of which 388,735 were built during the entire P-23 production run. Weighing 3,088 pounds, the 6-passenger car cost $1,914. From the exterior point of view, 1952 Plymouths differed from 1951 models in several respects. Side nameplates had script-style lettering and the hood medallion was a circular design with side extensions. The hood top ornament was a back-swept design with no outstretched side members. At the rear, the Plymouth name was a part of the license light fixture, appearing to sit on top of it. Less obvious were new stainless steel stone shields on rear fenders. Interiors had a new variety of upholstery fabrics. A new option for all Plymouths was tinted safety glass in the windshield and windows.

Again, the most expensive Plymouth was the Cranbrook Convertible Club Coupe. It cost $2,329 without options. Prices of all other models are also quoted without options. As 1951-52 models, 15,650 convertibles were built. This second-year P-23 model weighed 3,256 pounds, which was the heaviest of all 1952 Plymouths. Full wheel covers were optional regardless of model. No Plymouths are shown with whitewall tires because the military operation in Korea stopped their manufacture until spring. The P-23 Cranbrook series rode on the 118.5-inch wheelbase and 15 x 6.70 tires. Plymouth's 3-series family of 10 body types did not offer a choice for some buyers or purposes, as indicated by a total of 4,171 unbodied P-23 chassis built during the 1951-52 span.

The Plymouth Cranbrook Belvedere sported curving rear moldings and the top color carried over the rear deck to give it added distinction. So as not to break the flowing effect of the top color to the deck, the bright beltline molding was not extended through the quarter to the rear window. Just below the roof quarter was new free-flowing script-style Belvedere lettering. The new license light fixture and integral Plymouth name, common to all models, is obvious in this view. 51,266 hardtop Belvederes were built as 1951-52 models. For 1952, the Belvedere weighed 3,105 pounds and cost $2,216.

DeSoto

The big news from DeSoto this year was the FireDome 8. The first 8-cylinder DeSoto in 21 years, it was a hot V-8 in tune with the times. Designated the Series S-17, it was presented in one line of bodies only, which can best be rated as more than equal to the 6-cylinder Custom series. The lowest-priced and lightest-weight FireDome was the Club Coupe, which in standard form was priced at $2,718 and weighed 3,675 pounds. 5,699 of these 6-passenger cars were built.

The most-wanted and most-boughten FireDome 8 was the 4-Door Sedan, of which 35,651 were built. Accommodating six passengers, it weighed 3,760 pounds and cost $2,740 in standard form. With the FireDome 8 series, DeSoto introduced a completely new hood with a functional airscoop. A new and wider medallion also graced the hood. The new 8-cylinder series was identified by FireDome 8 signatures on the front fenders, while at the rear a numeral 8 perched on top of the ornate deck centerpiece. The simple numeral 8 did not indicate whether a straight-8 or V-8 engine was under the hood, so in May a new V-8 emblem was offered as optional, but for the rear only.

Shown without a boot on its folded top is the DeSoto FireDome 8 Convertible. In standard form it cost $3,183 and weighed 3,950 pounds. 850 of these 6-passenger cars rolled from the assembly line. All FireDomes of less than 8-passenger capacity were based on the 125.5-inch wheelbase chassis which was also the base for the S-15 sixes. Even the bodies, other sheetmetal, grilles, bumpers, 15 x 7.60 tire size and many other features were shared. Note that this car had blackwall tires.

The DeSoto FireDome 8 Sportsman, of which 3,000 were produced, had a basic weight of 3,850 pounds and a basic price of $3,078. This 2-door 6-passenger hardtop model was regarded as the smartest DeSoto enclosed car. Whitewall tires became available about the time deliveries of the new V-8 were well underway, and were again made optional. First-time DeSoto options were tinted windshield and window safety glass and electric window lifts. The tinted glass was destined to become quite popular.

The FireDome 8 All-Steel Station Wagon was not a popular DeSoto model, as only 550 were manufactured. But it was a handsome vehicle, and quite utilitarian, too. Its 6-passenger interior was tailored in good taste, and it could carry quite a load of luggage or other cargo. With standard equipment, the 4-door automobile cost $3,377 and scaled 4,080 pounds. Steering this 2-ton car and other models was said to be "as easy as dialing a telephone" if buyers ordered cars equipped with DeSoto's full-time hydraulic power steering, another new option which would become very popular.

The exterior of early 1952 DeSoto sixes differed from 1951 models in only three minor respects. The DeSoto name above the grille was of bold widely-spaced block letters and the hood medallion was narrower than its height. At the rear, the tail lamp outline tapered toward the top, and the lenses had integral backup lights. Shown is the Custom Six 4-Door Sedan, which drew more buyers than any other DeSoto. For the 1951-52 demand, 88,491 were built. In standard 1952 form it weighed 3,660 pounds and cost $2,552.

DeSoto's FireDome 8 engine was an impressive powerplant. The 90-degree V-8 was a direct offshoot of the FirePower engine developed for 1951 Chrysler cars. This engine, with its unique dome-shape hemispherical combustion chambers, was one of the forebears of the fantastically high-performance "Hemi" engines which became famous within a few years. Its overhead valves were of an ingenious lateral arrangement using a new pushrod and rocker arm setup with twin rocker shafts and hydraulic tappets. Efficient carburetion and manifolding helped this engine of 276.1 cubic-inch displacement to deliver 160 horsepower. Its conservative compression ratio of 7.1 to 1 allowed use of regular-grade gasoline.

The DeSoto Custom Six Sportsman, which is illustrated with an early hood, marked up a 1951-52 production total of 8,750. Without extra equipment, the 2-door hardtop tipped the scales at 3,720 pounds and had a factory price of $2,890. All DeLuxe and Custom Six models were equipped with the Powermaster engine of 116 horsepower, and all Custom models had Tip-Toe Shift with Fluid Drive coupling as a standard feature.

The Custom Six All-Steel Station Wagon was DeSoto's answer to those who wanted plenty of room for passengers and miscellaneous items at a moderate price. It could be purchased at the factory for $3,189, without extras. In the same form, it weighed 4,020 pounds. During its production run through two model years, 1,440 came out of the factories. The 4-door 6-passenger car was indeed a practical vehicle.

The DeSoto Custom Six 8-Passenger Sedan shown weighed 4,155 pounds and cost $3,362. The 1951-52 production run turned out 769 of them. As a DeLuxe model, the big car weighed 4,035 pounds, cost $3,142 and earned a 1951-52 production of 343. Because of low demand for 8-passenger sedans, only four of the 20 domestic car makes offered them. Another huge DeSoto was the Suburban, a special 9-passenger sedan in the Custom class. It weighed 4,370 pounds, cost $3,734 and got 600 sales in 1951-52.

The 8-Passenger Sedan in the DeSoto FireDome 8 series looked like the late version of its 6-cylinder counterpart. The observer had to see the FireDome 8 name on the side to identify the model. The interior was rich and appealing, with auxiliary seats that folded snugly into the back of the front seat when not in use. The car cost $3,547, weighed 4,325 pounds and drew a demand of only 80 units. When the FireDome 8 went into production, its hood was shared with the Sixes, which got it complete with the airscoop and wider medallion.

Shown is DeSoto's lowest-priced family automobile, the DeLuxe Six 4-Door Sedan, of which 13,506 were built. Weighing 3,540 pounds, it cost $2,333. Not shown, the Carry-All Sedan was continued from 1951. Of DeLuxe class in the 6-cylinder line, it weighed 3,650 pounds, was priced at $2,572 and accounted for 1,700 built. Not related to the aforementioned models, but reported just for this record, 3,550 DeLuxe Six California taxicabs were built. All production totals are for the 1951-52 model period.

Seen here is the DeSoto Custom Six Club Coupe which weighed 3,565 pounds, cost $2,531 and attracted 19,000 sales orders. Its sister car, the DeLuxe Six Club Coupe, was the lightest and lowest-priced DeSoto this year, weighing 3,435 pounds and costing $2,319. It chalked up a production of 6,100 units. The Custom Six Convertible was continued, weighing 3,865 pounds, costing $2,996 and recording a total of 3,950 built. The production totals are for 1951-52, inclusive. Unfortunately and regretfully, a number of 1952 DeSoto models are not illustrated. An extensive search for material turned up very few.

The Diplomat-Custom Special Club Coupe was DeSoto's answer to the Plymouth Cranbrook Belvedere. The roof color was carried onto the rear deck and down to the bumper, separated from the rest of the body by a thin bright molding. The Diplomat-Custom nameplate was located on the quarter panel just under the roof pillar. The 2-tone treatment, while identical to the Belvedere, was still distinctive compared with the competition.

This 1952 Diplomat-Custom Club Coupe was practically identical to its 1951 counterpart, except that the DeSoto script and flanking horizontal bars in the hood molding were painted red. These areas were left bright in 1951. Rear fender stone shields on Custom models were of slightly different design. White sidewall tires were not available because of Korean war restrictions, a situation also true late in the 1951 model year.

Wheel discs on this DeSoto Diplomat-Custom 4-Door Sedan had a new cone-shaped section. The single-model Diplomat-DeLuxe series again contained only the 4-Door Sedan, which came without the stone shields and with black rubber moldings surrounding the windshield. All Diplomat-Custom and Diplomat-DeLuxe models rode on a 118.5-inch wheelbase. The DeLuxe series would be absent from the line in 1953.

The Diplomat-Custom Convertible Coupe was, according to Diplomat literature, "styled for enjoyment of living." It was also a virtual duplication of 1951, right down to identical technical specifications. Chrysler considered Plymouth variants like the DeSoto Diplomat and Dodge Kingsway as Plymouths for internal accounting purposes; thus DeSoto Diplomat production was included in the overall Plymouth totals.

This Diplomat 3-Passenger Coupe, with its short roof and rolling turtle deck, was the last of a long line of this once-popular Chrysler Corp. body type. After 1952, the business coupe would lose its distinctive roof and profile and emerge simply as a club coupe minus rear seat. Soon to go would be the limousines on the senior DeSoto chassis. By the mid-1950s neither model had any relevance to DeSoto buyers.

Another body style in its last year was this Diplomat 2-Door Sedan. Fastbacks like this enjoyed quite a vogue after the war but were gone by 1953. They were to reappear on sport models in the mid-1960s, but by then both DeSoto and the Diplomat were out of production. This Diplomat body style was never really attractive, and rear vision while backing was very poor.

The hubcaps had a different cross section but otherwise this DeSoto Diplomat Commercial Utility was the same as the year before, save for the addition of a rub rail molding on the rear fender. Cars in the Diplomat series used the 111-inch chassis and a 9-1/8-inch diameter clutch compared with 9¼-inch on the larger Diplomats.

For the auto industry in general, this was a good year. new rise in prosperity occurred. Bumpy conditions used by the U. S. military action in Korea were smoothed out, and more normal operations prevailed. For the calendar year, the auto industry registered a gain of almost 41.5% in passenger car production. Chrysler Corp. did not do quite as well, its four car divisions mustering a combined gain of just over 30.8%. The lower rate of gain reflected the corporation's smaller portion of industry business this year, which was 20.3%, down 1.66% from 1952. Plymouth reaped an increase of nearly 39.5% and was still the industry's No. 3 producer by a comfortable margin over Buick, which had been next in line for many previous years. This was Plymouth's biggest production year to date, surpassing its previous high in 1951. DeSoto garnered a gain of at least 33.1% but remained in 12th position.

This year's cars were of major newness, but their planning, development and eventual placing in production was not accomplished without worries. They almost missed being 1953 models because of a U. S. government order late in 1951 which banned major model changes after February 1, 1952. The order, designed to conserve materials for armaments, was later revised in time for model plans to go forward. In October this year, Chrysler purchased the Briggs Manufacturing Co. for $35,000,000. Chrysler had been taking 85% of Briggs body output for many years, and the buy would eliminate the profit formerly paid to Briggs, thereby reducing the cost of making cars. The Briggs price tag was small when compared with the $200,000,000 Chrysler reportedly spent for design, engineering and tooling the 1953 models of its four car divisions.

This was the 25th Anniversary year for Plymouth and DeSoto, who noted the milestone quietly and with no special edition cars to commemorate it. Another Plymouth milestone was the building of its 8,000,000th car in September, possibly a 1954 model. Plymouth also built its last Grumman Albatross seaplane hull for the Korean

The Club Sedan was the 2-door sedan of the Plymouth Cambridge line. The 6-passenger car had more rear seat legroom than the Club Coupe. 56,800 of these 2,943-pound cars were built. The price was $1,707. All prices quoted for individual Plymouth models were prevalent at the start of the model year, and included federal tax. In this view, Plymouth's new "two-thirds/one-third" front seat back division is apparent. Featured in all 2-door body types, it afforded rear seat access without disturbing a front center passenger.

THE *Cambridge*

The Plymouth Cambridge 4-Door Sedan, of which 93,585 were built, weighed 2,983 pounds and cost $1,745 in standard form as shown. As on other Plymouths, doors opened to a straight-out position and swung slightly upward for average curb clearance. Despite the shorter new bodies, trunk capacity was 7.6 cubic feet larger than previous models. The Cambridge line was Series P-24-1, sharing a new 114-inch wheelbase and 6.70 x 15 tire size with Cranbrook models.

The Cambridge Business Coupe, of which 6,975 were built, weighed and cost the least of any Plymouth this year. In standard form it scaled 2,888 pounds and had a factory price of $1,598. The 3-passenger car, with interior luggage space behind the seat, is shown with optional whitewall tires and wheel covers. When fitted with a rear seat for three more passengers, this model became a Cambridge Club Coupe and cost $64.50 more. The 6-passenger car drew 1,050 orders. This view superbly shows off Plymouth's new styling. So-called "pontoon" sides and one-piece curved windshield glass were finally adopted.

action late this year.

Plymouth presented only one series this year, the P-24. It was divided into two lines, the P-24-1 Cambridge and the more deluxe P-24-2 Cranbrook. Both were based on one new-design chassis of 114-inch wheelbase in which the familiar L-head 6-cylinder engine of previous years was utilized. With unchanged bore and stroke of 3¼ x 4-3/8 inches, displacement remained at 217.8 cubic inches. Two horsepower ratings were advertised, of which one was 97 with a 7 to 1 compression ratio, the same as in 1952. The other was 100 horsepower with a 7.1 to 1 compression ratio. Both power outputs were developed at 3,600 r.p.m. Floating Power mountings were featured for the 19th consecutive model year. A new radiator core, pressured cooling system and shrouded fan provided better cooling. The chassis frame featured wider and shallower siderails.

Among trim options available for the lowline Cambridge series were front and rear fender moldings which were standard fittings on the Cranbrook series. The Cambridge Suburban could nevertheless be identified by the Suburban name on front fenders, a signature that the similar Cranbrook model did not have. The 2-door Suburban was now classified as a 6-passenger car. Its rear seat back folded down to provide a longer cargo area. Without extras, this model weighed 3,129 pounds and was priced at $2,044. It garnered a total of 43,545 sales.

The Plymouth Cranbrook Club Coupe is shown with optional 2-tone roof color, wheel covers and whitewall tires. Without extras, it sold for $1,823 and weighed 2,971 pounds. It attracted 92,102 orders. This view of the 6-passenger car shows the new rear-end location of the fuel filler cap, which was toward the left side. All but the station wagons had the filler in this spot. All Cranbrook interiors were much nicer than those of the Cambridge line.

New front suspension had non-parallel control arms, and rear springs were hung inboard of the chassis siderails. The longtime layout of engine between the front wheels, allowing the rear seat to be ahead of the rear axle, continued to add to riding comfort. This layout, advertised since 1935 as providing a balanced ride, was now said to yield "a TRULY balanced ride." The overdrive transmission continued as an option, but Plymouth's headline mechanical event was the addition of Hy-Drive in April. It consisted of a torque converter coupled to a conventional 3-speed transmission, but the latter had different low and second gear ratios than the standard gearbox. Hy-Drive operation required some declutching action, thereby classifying it as a semi rather than fully automatic drive. By July, the Hy-Drive option was being built into almost 25% of Plymouth production. Not an option this year, some cars may have later been fitted with a power brake package made available for dealer installation in 1955.

Presented to the public about December 1, 1952, Plymouth's offerings were all-new in styling and size. The lowline Cambridge series included four body types, while the highline Cranbrook offered five models. Compared with the entire 1952 family of three series, these two series averaged 34 pounds less weight. At the outset of the model year, prices of some models were the same as comparable 1952 cars, while others were lower. In March, prices were revised and some trim and accessory options were made standard equipment. These price fluctuations do not permit a comparison with the previous year.

DeSoto placed its models on the market in November 1952. The new line of 6-cylinder cars did not include DeLuxe and Custom models, but was known as the Powermaster Six, Series S-18. Its companion was the FireDome V-8, Series S-16. They shared almost everything but their engines and drive train differences necessary for those engines. The new styling was not much different than 1952 models, but it required extensive new diework and tooling. Chassis lengths remained unchanged, having wheelbases of 125.5 and 139.5 inches. The Powermaster Six offered five body types which, when compared with comparable models of the former DeLuxe series, averaged 27.5 pounds heavier. The FireDome V-8 line presented six models as before, but they averaged 38.5 pounds less weight than their 1952 counterparts. DeSoto prices followed a pattern similar to those of Plymouth, and comparison with 1952 is not offered.

The Powermaster Six engine was virtually unchanged, again delivering 116 horsepower. Though boasting refinements, it still was supported on Floating Power mounts. Besides the standard 3-speed manual transmission, an overdrive unit or Tip-Toe Shift with Fluid Drive coupling were optionally available. The FireDome V-8 engine of 160 horsepower was given minor improvements, and the transmissions for the V-8 were the same types as for the Six, with an added choice of Fluid-Torque Drive. Six and V-8 chassis were refinements of comparable 1952 models. Air conditioning, made by Chrysler's Airtemp division, was shown in a DeSoto in January, to become available as soon as tooling problems could be solved. A power brake package made available to dealers in 1955 may have been applied to some 1953 models.

A new option this year was true wire wheels. Shown in chrome, they could also be had in paint. The Plymouth Cranbrook Belvedere had special Belvedere signatures on the front fenders. The chrome trim and medallion on the lower rear roof quarters were also standard on this 2-door hardtop model. Note the extra chrome on the "A" pillar which gave a square look to the windshield corners. Without options, the Belvedere cost $2,044 and weighed 3,027 pounds. Assembly lines turned out 35,185 of these Series P-24-2 hardtops. Strangely listed as Series P-24-3 were 760 similar models built, according to original production records. This stranger was the least popular Plymouth this year.

With a total of 298,976 built, the Cranbrook 4-Door Sedan was the most popular Plymouth this year. It weighed 3,023 pounds and cost $1,853 without options. An extra-cost item for this and the Cranbrook Club Coupe was the Belvedere chrome trim and medallion on the rear quarter, between the door and rear window. Chrome moldings around the grille opening were standard Cranbrook items, but could be ordered on Cambridge models. The Cranbrook line was Series P-24-2. Curiously, production records list 2,240 Series P-24-3 4-door sedans built. Other records do not include a P-24-3 series.

Formerly a Concord model, the Savoy moved up to the Cranbrook series this year. The shift was appropriate, since this car was always a step above lowline class. Now it was given Belvedere interior styling, but with more rugged upholstery and trim materials. It shared the Suburban body, carried the Savoy name above the front wheels and had typical Cranbrook exterior brightwork. Among options shown is a 2-tone color on the roof. In standard form, the 6-passenger Savoy sold for $2,187 and weighed 3,170 pounds. A production total of 12,089 was recorded. On the Savoy and Suburban, Plymouth placed the fuel filler cap on the left rear fender rather than on the rear end.

The Plymouth Cranbrook Convertible Club Coupe was the costliest and heaviest model. In basic form it was priced at $2,200 and weighed 3,193 pounds. Assembly lines turned out 6,301 of them. Among its special features was a full-width rear window of clear and pliable plastic and fitted with a zipper. The car shown had no chrome trim around the grille opening, as it was an option for all models.

Plymouth taxicab production totals were not listed in records, but they undoubtedly were hidden in totals of the models they utilized. The company was still very much involved in providing taxicabs. A Cranbrook is shown in readiness to earn fares. Plymouth's taxicab package included heavier gauge seat springs, commercial duty chassis springs, a 10-inch clutch, 100 ampere hour heavy-duty battery with a heat shield, and such other heavy-duty items as the front control arm and transmission bearing. Overdrive or Hy-Drive were not available. The paint job and special interior adaptation were not included in the package price of only $17.70. Unrelated to taxicabs was a total of 843 Series P-24-2 chassis shipped without bodies.

The Plymouth Cadet project continued the company's thinking about cars smaller than its production cars. This design, photographed in 1951, could have been considered for 1953-54 production. With a wheelbase of perhaps 105 inches, it probably would have competed with the Nash Rambler, Aero Willys, Henry J and Hudson Jet. The 3/8-scale clay model showed a marked similarity to 1953-54 production Plymouths, particularly in the frontal design, curved windshield and angled rear quarter of the roof.

This proposal for a Plymouth Cadet got as far as a full-scale clay model. At this stage in 1951, it could have reached production in 1953-54. Its wheelbase of perhaps 105 inches would have placed it in the new small car class then in production by independent automakers. The roof's rear quarter was very similar to the 1949-51 Ford 4-door sedan treatment. In the background was a full-scale clay model of a suburban which was destined to reach the production lines as a Series P-24 model.

At a glance, the newly-styled DeSotos looked about like 1952 models, but there were several notable differences. Front fender shapes extended through the body sides to join the new rear fender forms which were now integral with the body side panels, there being no separate rear fenders. From the one-piece curved windshield, the roof swept to a more pronounced slope at the rear, where the one-piece rear window was fully wrapped around. Tail lamps projected from the rear fender forms, which had a definite forward lean. All of these characteristics were common to coupes and 6-passenger sedans. Shown is the Powermaster Six Club Coupe, which weighed and cost the least of any DeSoto. It scaled 3,480 pounds and was priced at $2,334 without optional wheel covers, whitewall tires and other extras. Assembly lines turned out 8,063 of them.

The Powermaster Six Sportsman had all of the new styling except for its roof and 3-piece rear window of 1952 character. Without extras, it cost $2,604 and scaled 3,585 pounds. 1,470 of them came from the factories. The car is shown with chrome trim on the front fender and door, an extra dress-up which also appeared on other models. DeSoto's familiar grille now had 11 vertical members instead of nine, and parking lamps were integrated with the ensemble in a new manner.

This body type did not have front fenders flowing back to new rear fenders, but continued the 1952 body side panels and rear fenders. However, a new roof and cowl were required by the curved windshield. Shown is the DeSoto Powermaster Six All-Steel Station Wagon which, in standard form, weighed 3,845 pounds and cost $3,078. The 6-passenger car attracted only 500 orders. It is seen with extra trim on the front fender and door. On the rear fender, the chrome horizontal molding was placed high and in line with the sheetmetal offset on the front fender. Extra touches were the 2-tone body colors and off-white plastic wheel trim. This body type continued to place the fuel filler cap on the left rear fender.

This year's DeSoto FireDome V-8 cars carried big chrome V emblems on the front, sides and rear to tell all viewers that they had V-type engines. The 1952 unexplanatory numeral 8 had posed the possibility that the engine was a straight-eight. Such a surmise was not beyond reason, since Packard, Buick and Pontiac still had straight-eights in production. Shown is the FireDome V-8 Club Coupe which weighed 3,655 pounds and cost $2,622 in standard form. It scored a production total of 14,591. All except the station wagon and 8-passenger car now had the fuel filler cap on the rear, toward the left side.

DeSoto's Powermaster Six 4-Door Sedan rode on the same 125.5-inch wheelbase and 7.60 x 15 tires employed by all regular-size models. The reliable L-head 6-cylinder engine of the new Series S-18 delivered 116 horsepower. The 6-passenger car, of which 33,644 were built, tipped the scales at 3,535 pounds and was priced at $2,356, without extras. Prices quoted for all individual DeSoto models prevailed during the early part of the model year, and included federal tax. This view illustrates the new rake of the roof's rear quarters and the feeling of forward motion in the new rear fender outline.

The body and rear fenders of the DeSoto Powermaster Six 8-Passenger Sedan retained the 1952 styling except that the new curved windshield was incorporated. These big cars, both Six and V-8, rode on a 139.5-inch wheelbase and 8.20 x 15 tires. With standard equipment, the 6-cylinder car weighed 4,080 pounds and was priced at $3,251. Only 225 of these luxury automobiles came out of the factories. This body type may have been used for 1,700 Series S-18 California taxicabs that were built.

The FireDome V-8 4-Door Sedan was the best sales-getter in the entire DeSoto family, gathering a total of 64,211 orders. With basic equipment, its price was $2,643 and its weight was 3,720 pounds. The car shown did not have extra chrome streaming back from the front wheel, but it was equipped with air conditioning, which first appeared in January and was scarcely available. Fresh air was inducted into the conditioner through small narrow grilles located behind and in line with the door handles.

The DeSoto FireDome V-8 Sportsman is shown with continental spare wheel treatment, an option seldom seen. Supplied in kit form, dealers could install it on any model. The package included a wheel mount, cover in matching body color, special hubcap, bumper extensions and a longer splash apron to fit between the bumper and body. Without any extras, this automobile sold for $2,893 and weighed 3,740 pounds. A total of 4,700 were built. Harking back to 1952 were the hardtop roof design and 3-piece rear window. Otherwise, the styling was new.

The Convertible was the only body type that the FireDome V-8 did not share with the Powermaster Six. Without optional extras, the sporty automobile tipped the scales at 3,990 pounds and had a price tag marked $3,114. It attracted enough buyers to require production of 1,700 units. The example shown had no forward side trim, an extra until made a FireDome standard in midyear. Like Plymouth, DeSoto offered optional wire wheels which could be fitted to any model. They would have looked especially good on this model.

The least-salable DeSoto this year was the FireDome V-8 8-Passenger Sedan, which attracted only 200 sales. It was also the heaviest and costliest, weighing 4,270 pounds and exacting a toll of $3,529 when standard-equipped. The huge car on a long chassis was powered by the potent 160-horsepower hemi-head engine. Except for the curved windshield, the body was of 1952 design. Note how the front fender crown dissipated in the front door, did not stretch back to integrate with the rear. The 1952 rear fender, with its fuel filler cap, retained its thin trim molding, which did not match the pattern of the new side trim ahead.

The FireDome V-8 All-Steel Station Wagon had four doors and accommodated six passengers. When equipped and fitted in standard form, it had a factory price of $3,351 and a scale reading of 3,995 pounds. Only 1,100 of them came off the assembly lines. Like its counterpart in the 6-cylinder series, this body was largely like that of 1952. Note the rear fender horizontal trim molding placed low. This and other regular-size models of the V-8 Series S-16 shared a 125.5-inch wheelbase with the Six.

The Adventurer was DeSoto's first "idea car," one of a number of experimentals spread among the divisions of Chrysler Corp. The corporation's post-war exploration journey, begun in 1951, extended through many years. The Adventurer, of 1953 origin and first shown in the fall, starred during the 1954 model season. Conceived and designed by Chrysler in Detroit, its body was hand-crafted by Ghia, in Italy. Only 53.5 inches high, and on a 111-inch wheelbase, its overall length was 189.8 inches. The FireDome V-8 engine put out 170 horsepower, like those placed in 1954 production. The close-coupled coupe interior had seats for four. The car shown was the only one built.

Diplomat CUSTOM

Sharing Plymouth's all-new sheet metal was this Diplomat-Custom 4-Door Sedan. The narrower Diplomat sported only nine grille teeth compared with eleven in the senior DeSotos. The unique hood ornament was an attempt to simulate the air scoop present on the larger cars but the Diplomat's version was strictly a dummy. The large hood medallion was borrowed from the Powermaster Six.

The Diplomat-Custom Special Club Coupe sported different front and rear bumper guards from its cousin, the Cranbrook Belvedere. The unique design featured a bullet-shaped section on the lower half of the guards; otherwise the bumpers were identical with Plymouth. Forward visibility was considerably improved through the new one-piece windshield and over the shorter hood. The 3-piece rear window was used on this body type only.

Practically the only difference in side view between this Diplomat-Custom Club Coupe and its Plymouth Cranbrook counterpart were the red center wheel discs and the lack of the rear fender top molding present on the Cranbrook line. In common with the Business Coupe, the Club Coupe used a shorter roof than the Club Sedan. All 2-door models featured a 1/3 - 2/3 division of the front seat for easier access to the rear compartment.

Glamour car of the Diplomat line was this Custom Convertible Coupe. Note the Plymouth parking lights on either side of a grille only a DeSoto enthusiast — or a dentist — could love. All those teeth gave the Diplomat a menacing look. The convertible was upholstered in a combination of fabric and vinyl and featured new pull-type exterior door handles in common with other Diplomat models.

"DeSoto Diplomat-Custom Special Commercial Utility" was the correct name for this 2-door wagon, but the front fender nameplate said simply "Utility." As on all Diplomat models, wheelbase was 114 inches. This was a compromise between the 118½-inch and the 111-inch wheelbases used since 1949. This "Special" model featured a fabric and vinyl interior with rear seat arm rests and assist straps, amenities not present on the base model.

This Diplomat 4-Door Sedan lacked side trim and had black rubber moldings surrounding the front and rear windows. Although both the Diplomat and Plymouth shared identical 3.57 liter engines, the Diplomat continued with a 7.0 to 1 compression ratio versus 7.1 to 1 on the Plymouth. The result was that this year Diplomat had only 97 horsepower compared with 100 horsepower on the Plymouth. Canadian Plymouths, however, were also listed at 97 horsepower.

Cheapest 1953 Diplomat was the Business Coupe. Hubcaps and optional wheel covers continued to feature red centers. Black, 4-ply, 15 x 6.20 Goodyear Super Cushion tires were standard, with 4-ply and 6-ply white sidewalls and 6-ply blackwall tires optional. Only two series – Diplomat and Diplomat-Custom – were offered this year, the Diplomat-DeLuxe line being dropped for the time being.

A longer roof was featured on the Diplomat Club Sedan, which thus boasted "4-door spaciousness." Note the divider bar in the rear side window. In addition to the standard Auto-Mesh transmission, Diplomats were also available with Overdrive and mid-year with the new semi-automatic Hy-Drive. Hy-Drive-equipped Diplomats still retained the clutch pedal and would for yet another year.

The Diplomat Commercial Utility boasted all the traditional Chrysler engineering features – Floating Power, Oriflow shock absorbers, oil-bath air cleaner, Cyclebond brake linings, Oilite fuel filter, and Safety-Rim wheels. Seats, side trim panels, and the floor of the Commercial Utility could be quickly and easily cleaned with soap and water. All Utilitys were 2-seat models, with the rear seat folding flush with the cargo floor.

Following a year of excellent business, this was a year of decline in the demand for new automobiles. By the end of this calendar year, the industry accumulated a loss of almost 10.2%. If Chrysler Corp. had lost only that much, it would have been fortunate. It suffered a disastrous drop of nearly 42% in passenger car production and 7.18% of its industry share, now accounting for only 13.12% of all industry productivity. Of its four car divisions, Dodge was hit the hardest and the Chrysler car line lost the least. Plymouth, in slumping more than 39.6%, was agonized by a humiliating drop to the industry's No. 5 position. After holding the No. 3 spot since 1931, it finally gave up the cherished position to Buick. Oldsmobile shot upward from 7th to 4th post. DeSoto, down more than 46.2%, tenaciously held 12th place, a spot it held during the three previous years.

Chrysler's product image was severely damaged. Certainly not by engineering, but rather because of a product planning and styling program which had clung to a package concept and styling limitations not in line with competition and a major portion of public preference. As was the case with most of its competition, Chrysler Corp. had carryover but updated models from the previous year, but their proportions retained much of the character introduced in 1949. Others had gone more extravagant since.

The Plymouth Series P-25 was presented in October, 1953. To counter the competition, three lines were offered, a return to the similar setup of 1952. They were all based on the 114-inch wheelbase and given new series names. The lowline series was the P-25-1 Plaza which had four body types, of which one was adaptable as a fifth type. Sandwiched in the center was the Savoy, P-25-2, with three body choices. The highline Belvedere series, a step above the former Cranbrook class, had four P-25-3 offerings. Plaza and Savoy models, when compared with similar 1953 Cambridge and Cranbrook types, averaged seven pounds heavier but $5 less costly.

Advertised as having "Hy-Style," the Series P-25 had

THE Plaza

1953 bodies and sheetmetal, but with new ornamentation and subtle improvements. Excepting Suburbans, overall length was increased 4-3/8 inches. Numerous mechanical refinements were incorporated in the chassis and engine. Initially, the carryover engine of 100 horsepower was the only powerplant, but with the adoption of the new Power-Flite automatic transmission in March came the PowerFlow engine. The L-head 6-cylinder PowerFlow had the original engine's bore of 3¼ inches, but its stroke was 4-5/8 inches, an increase of ¼ inch. Displacement grew to 230.2 cubic inches, a higher compression ratio of 7.25 to 1 was used, and developed horsepower became 110 at 3,600 r.p.m. This engine, which again had Floating Power mounts, became the standard powerplant.

The PowerFlite, a torque converter and fully automatic transmission unit, was added to the Hy-Drive and Over-drive transmission options which, with the standard manual 3-speed unit, provided four drive choices. Plymouth

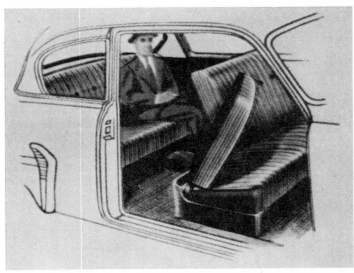

The Plaza Club Coupe was the Business Coupe with a removable rear seat, making a close-coupled 6-passenger car. The two-thirds/one-third front seat back division, introduced in 1953 models, was also a feature of other 2-door bodies. Since this model was a conversion of the Business Coupe, it was generally disregarded in records pertaining to specific models, weights and prices. However, Plymouth recorded 1,275 built.

The Plymouth Plaza Business Coupe, of which an even 5,000 were built, was the least expensive and lowest-weight Plymouth this year. In standard form, it sold at the factory for $1,618 and swung the scale pointer to a reading of 2,889 pounds. The 3-passenger car had a generous rear luggage compartment, with extra luggage space inside, behind the seat. Whitewall tires and full wheel covers were optional at extra cost.

The dark body color emphasizes the scarcity of bright trim on Plaza models. A chrome molding provided subtle relief at the beltline and the Plaza signature was simple. Advertising artwork dressed all Plymouths up with flashy wheels, but they were not standard. This model is the Plaza 4-Door Sedan, of which a total of 43,077 were built. The 6-passenger car, without options, weighed 3,004 pounds and was priced at $1,765.

This view of the Plymouth Plaza Club Sedan distinctly shows the lack of bright trim on the windshield, rear window and rear fenders. Instead, those items were of a rubber material. Also typical of all Plaza models was the absence of lower side moldings and other fancy details. With standard equipment, this particular model weighed 2,943 pounds and sold for $1,727. 27,976 of the 2-door 6-passenger cars were turned out.

The workhorse of the Plaza line was the Suburban. It could accommodate six passengers and plenty of luggage, or carry three persons and a huge load of cargo by folding the rear seat flat. With the tailgate and liftgate open, even more items could be hauled. The interior was done in long-wearing material. The 2-door car, of which 35,937 were built, weighed 3,122 pounds and cost $2,064 in basic form. Perhaps for display or a special body, one Plaza P-25-1 chassis-only was assembled.

now offered power steering, a full-time hydraulic type, as an option for the first time. Factory-installed power brakes became available at extra cost in March. A dealer-installed power brake package, offered in 1955, may have been fitted to some cars.

DeSoto's new cars were promoted as the "DeSoto Automatic," emphasizing the several automatic devices which made driving "the leisure car" quite enjoyable. Appearing in the autumn of 1953 were the Powermaster Six, Series S-20, and the FireDome V-8, Series S-19. The 6-cylinder line had only four body types this year, having dropped the Sportsman. The V-8 continued with six models, and the Coronado was added in the spring. In respect to corresponding models of 1953 sixes and eights they averaged 50 pounds heavier but registered no price difference.

Wheelbases of 125.5 and 139.5 inches were retained, but overall length increased a trifle. The chassis featured a high-roll-center front suspension system said to drastically reduce tendency to sway on curves. Many minor refinements also appeared. The 6-cylinder engine of 116 horse-power was continued, but the V-8 compression ratio was increased to 7.5 to 1, and developed horsepower reached 170. The standard transmission was a 3-speed manual unit, while Overdrive and PowerFlite were extra-cost items.

The new DeSotos had little more styling change than did the Plymouths, clinging to the previous bodies and sheet-metal, to which new dress-up touches were applied. Most notable external changes were the new grille and bumper designs. Interiors were given new treatments and fabrics. Of DeSoto's 1954 styling, advertising said it had a "forward" look, an expression that was destined to be refined and magnified as representative of the entire Chrysler product image for 1955.

The new Chrysler Engineering Proving Grounds near Chelsea, Mich., were dedicated in June. The 4,000-acre facility was opened with events which included demonstration of a turbine-powered Plymouth. Another turbine car, of unknown make, was not demonstrated.

the Savoy

The Plymouth Savoy Club Sedan was a sensible car for those who wanted more than a Plaza but less than a Belvedere. The 2-door body provided as much interior space as a 4-door model. Its 6-passenger accommodations were quite comfortable. Without the 2-tone paint scheme and any other extras, this model cost $1,835 and recorded a weight of 2,986 pounds. Production records reported a total of 25,396 manufactured.

The Savoy name was now applied to a Plymouth car line, rather than to a Suburban as before. It was the middle series, P-25-2, and had most of the exterior trim of the highline cars, but with less elaborate interiors. Shown is the Savoy Club Coupe, which attracted 30,700 sales. With basic equipment it cost $1,843 and weighed 2,982 pounds. The interior was not fitted to provide luggage space by removing the rear seat.

The overall length of all Plymouths, excepting Suburbans, was 4-3/8 inches more than in 1953, resulting from bumpers that extended further from the cars. Shown is this year's best-selling model, the Savoy 4-Door Sedan, one of three P-25-2 models offered. It weighed 3,036 pounds and cost $1,873 with no extras. A total of 139,383 were built. A fourth P-25-2 model, not advertised, listed nor offered to the general public was a Savoy Suburban, of which 450 were built, making this the model of lowest production. Also, the P-25-2 chassis was wanted for reasons now unknown, as 3,588 of them were shipped.

The hardtop of the Plymouth Belvedere line was called the Sport Coupe, though it did not have coupe "B" pillars and side window construction. This body was improved by the one-piece rear window. With no extras, it weighed 3,038 pounds and cost $2,145. It scored a total of 25,592 built. The tapered accent color on the beltline, outlined by a bright molding, was added in the spring as an option for this and the convertible. Some early convertibles had a "basket weave" in the area. Also shown are optional wheel covers which simulated wire wheels. Real wire wheels were also available for other models, and a rear-mounted continental spare could be had.

The Belvedere name, like Savoy, was now given to a car line rather than a single model. In this case, it was the highest-priced line, the Series P-25-3. The Plymouth Belvedere 4-Door Sedan cost $1,953 and weighed 3,050 pounds with standard equipment. Traditionally, this body type in the most expensive series drew the most sales, but such was not true this year. The assembly lines rolled out 106,601 of them. The car is shown without the usual medallion on the "C" pillar.

The Plymouth Belvedere Suburban had the utilitarian cargo-carrying features of the lower-cost Plaza, but with more dressy interior styling and trim materials. Its production total was 9,241. In standard form, it weighed 3,186 pounds and cost $2,288. The side trim moldings, stretching in almost unbroken line from the front to the rear of all Savoy and Belvedere cars, were intended to create an impression of greater length and lowness. A lengthier appearance was needed, since competitive cars were nine inches longer.

The heaviest and most costly Plymouth was the Belvedere Convertible Coupe, which weighed 3,273 pounds and cost $2,301 without extras. 6,900 were built. A medallion, as used on the "C" pillars of Belvedere 4-Door Sedans and Sport Coupes, was located on the rear fenders of this model, trailing the tip of the vertical stone shield. Other typical Belvedere touches were chromed sill moldings and miniature fins above the tail lamps, but the latter was not given to the Suburban. These fins were offered as optional for Savoy models. The P-25-3 chassis, as used for the Belvedere series, was bought for other purposes, as indicated by a total of 2,031 units shipped.

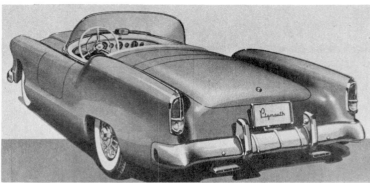

The Plymouth Belmont was another "idea car" experiment. Its fiberglass body, made in Chrysler's Briggs facilities, was a roadster type, having no side windows. The detachable fabric top stowed in the rearmost compartment with the spare wheel. A compartment behind the individual seats was for luggage. Door sills were level with the seat cushions. Built on a Dodge chassis of 114-inch wheelbase, it had a Dodge 150-horsepower V-8 engine coupled to a Plymouth Hy-Drive automatic transmission. Loaded with fuel, oil and water, it weighed 3,315 pounds. Overall height at the windshield top was 49¼ inches. This lone example was first shown early in the year.

The Plymouth Explorer was designed by Chrysler stylists and custom-built by Ghia in Italy. The "idea car" was a 2-passenger sports coupe with individual aviation-type seats, behind which was a compartment with two matched suitcases. The instrument panel had radio controls that slid out of sight when not in use. The bodywork was of "sculptured sheetmetal" with a minimum of chrome trim. It was based on the regular Plymouth 114-inch wheelbase chassis equipped with the stock 6-cylinder 110-horsepower engine and Hy-Drive. Overall height was 54.5 inches. Appearing early this year, the single Explorer drew much public attention and opinion during many showings.

The first gas turbine-powered automobile built by Chrysler Corp. is shown as it whooshed along on a rainy day. The Plymouth Belvedere Sport Coupe was chosen for installation of the new engine which stemmed from serious experiments begun in 1945. The post-war jet airplanes excited public interest in gas turbine engines, which spurred experiments with smaller versions which applied the tornadic power to the wheels of earthbound vehicles. Chrysler first confirmed its own automotive application in March and demonstrated this car to the press in June. Chrysler's selection of the popular production car was logical. It showed that the corporation was aiming the turbine at general public use, and that it was feasible for the average driver in city and highway traffic. In contrast, General Motors' projectile-like Firebird could only be driven by experts on a test track. Ford had research quietly underway, testing a Boeing unit in a production Fairlane model.

The powerplant fitted snugly in the Plymouth Turbine car. The gas turbine was said to have many advantages over a conventional piston engine. Among them were instant warm-up, no water or antifreeze required, and only a small fraction of the moving parts. Also, a turbine could use a wide variety of fuels, and with efficiency. The Chrysler GT-1001 had a fuel consumption rate of 14.9 miles per gallon of unleaded gasoline at 40 miles per hour, the best mileage that had been reported for a turbine engine. The key component was a heat exchanger, or regenerator, which extracted heat from the exhaust to pre-heat the fresh incoming air. At the tailpipe, exhaust was only mildly warm. The turbine revved at a high rate when idling, and at fantastic rates through acceleration to full power, requiring reduction gears to translate the revs to an acceptable rate at the rear wheels. At peak, the GT-1001 whipped up 120 shaft horsepower.

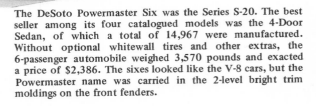

This year saw the last production of DeSoto sixes, at least on the domestic U.S. scene. In the final series was the Powermaster Six Club Coupe, which was the lightest and least costly of all models offered by DeSoto this year. When equipped only in standard form, it registered a scale reading of 3,505 pounds and carried a factory price tag marked at $2,364. The assembly lines rolled out 3,499 of the close-coupled 6-passenger cars. An early 2-tone effect is shown.

The DeSoto Powermaster Six was the Series S-20. The best seller among its four catalogued models was the 4-Door Sedan, of which a total of 14,967 were manufactured. Without optional whitewall tires and other extras, the 6-passenger automobile weighed 3,570 pounds and exacted a price of $2,386. The sixes looked like the V-8 cars, but the Powermaster name was carried in the 2-level bright trim moldings on the front fenders.

The Powermaster Six All-Steel Station Wagon did not attract much attention this year, as only 225 were built. Weighing 3,855 pounds, its price was quoted at $3,108, both of which did not include any extra equipment. This body, used also for the V-8, dated from 1949 except that its curved windshield with new roof and cowl appeared on 1953 models. All sixes delivered 116 horsepower, and regular-size models were on a 125.5-inch wheelbase.

The 8-Passenger Sedan was the lone DeSoto Powermaster Six model on a 139.5-inch wheelbase. In basic form, it weighed 4,100 pounds and cost $3,281. The factories turned out a mere 263 of them. This body was another that dated from 1949, but with updated windshield, roof and cowl. Note the difference in rear fender shape and fittings, as compared with other cars. This body was probably used for the 2,000 S-20 California taxicabs built.

The DeSoto FireDome V-8 again shared its 125.5-inch wheelbase with the Six. Shown is the FireDome V-8 Club Coupe which, without extra-cost whitewall tires and other options, recorded a scale reading of 3,735 pounds and a factory price of $2,652. This model accounted for 5,762 units of DeSoto's total production. Among DeSoto's new features were the new-style bumpers and guards, which made these cars a bit longer than in 1953. Shown is the second version of 2-toning.

The most popular DeSoto was the FireDome V-8 4-Door Sedan. The production total for this body type was 45,095 units, but not quite all of them were the standard model illustrated. Production records did not break down the total to show how many of this and the Coronado were built. The model shown, when equipped in standard form, recorded a weight of 3,790 pounds and a price of $2,673. The car seated six passengers comfortably.

Added to the DeSoto FireDome V-8 line in the spring, the Coronado was a high-fashion 4-door sedan. Though it had other special features, it was distinguished on the outside by Coronado signatures on the rear fenders and small medallions on the "C" pillars. The Coronado was not acknowledged in some automotive trade records. Its production total, weight and price are unknown, but the latter was higher than that of the standard sedan.

Looking very sporty with its top and windows down was the DeSoto FireDome V-8 Convertible, of which a total of 1,025 were built. With standard equipment, this car with a youthful flair cost $3,144 and weighed 4,015 pounds. Its 170-horsepower engine was like other models had. Bold V emblems were on the rear fenders of most V-8 models, and on the hoods of all. The FireDome name on front fender trim was also common to all V-8 cars.

The DeSoto FireDome V-8 All-Steel Station Wagon, of which 946 were built, cost $3,381 and weighed 4,045 pounds in basic form. As used also for the Six, this body and rear fenders dated from 1949, but with windshield, cowl and roof updating. The fuel filler cap remained on the carryover fender, which is shown with a different trim arrangement than other illustrated models. The V-8 insignia was not applied to these fenders. An export model is shown.

The DeSoto FireDome V-8 Sportsman had a new one-piece rear window this year. Shown with extra-cost wire wheels and whitewall tires, the 2-door hardtop weighed 3,815 pounds and cost $2,923 when not equipped with extras. DeSoto produced 4,382 of these V-8 Series S-19 models. Curiously, 250 Series S-20 Sportsman models were also built, but the Powermaster Six line was not known to include the hardtop. Perhaps it was a special order.

This model was the least popular, costliest and heaviest DeSoto. The FireDome V-8 8-Passenger Sedan got only 165 orders. Without extras it cost $3,559 and weighed 4,305 pounds. It shared its long chassis and modified 1949 body with the similar Six. No V-8 emblems were on the rear fenders. This and the Six's big sedan had 1953 bumpers and guards. Probably for display, one V-8 chassis of unknown length was assembled.

DeSoto proudly showed off another "idea car" this year, the Adventurer II. Designed by Chrysler and built by Ghia, it was trotted out in midyear. Though larger than the 1953 Adventurer, the sport coupe seated only two persons. On a stock chassis of 125.5-inch wheelbase, it was another adventure in sculptured sheetmetal. The aerodynamic shape was powered by the FireDome 170-horsepower V-8 hooked to a PowerFlite transmission. The bumperless car was 55.5 inches high, and its rear window retracted into the deck. A central control console divided the passenger compartment, which had a fitted luggage area behind the seats. The Adventurer II was a one-only example.

This year, both the "real" DeSoto and the Plymouth-based Diplomat had the same number of grille teeth – nine in all – as illustrated on this Diplomat-Custom 4-Door Sedan. The shorter teeth had a less aggressive look than last year. "Frenched" headlights and park and turn lights were pure Plymouth, as were the bumper guards. The unique guards of 1953 were discontinued in favor of a strictly Plymouth design.

The Diplomat-DeLuxe Club Coupe was available with Hy-Drive, Overdrive, and the standard 3-speed transmission. DeLuxe cars lacked the sill molding and rear fender ornaments compared with the Custom models. Interior trim was considerably improved this year with all appointments color-keyed. Chair-high seats were still a major Diplomat selling point.

This Diplomat-Custom Special Commercial Utility – quite a mouthful – was available only as a 2-door wagon. Interiors were luxurious compared with the Commercial Utility. The 2-tone treatment illustrated may be incorrect since later Belvedere Suburban advertisements show the 2-tone confined to the window area only and the roof in the same color as the lower body. All wagons had a concealed compartment for personal articles at each end of the rear seat.

The Diplomat Commercial Utility was indeed a plain-jane car. Still, as a DeSoto, it outclassed its Plymouth counterpart, the Plaza Suburban, even though it apparently lacked the Suburban's chrome belt molding. The spare tire was concealed in a well beneath the cargo floor. Interior was sturdy and practical, since everything was washable.

Riding on a 114-inch wheelbase, this Diplomat-DeLuxe 4-Door Sedan was again powered with Plymouth's sturdy L-head six, developing 100 horsepower this year in the Diplomat with the adoption of the higher compression ratio of 7.1 to 1. The Diplomat-DeLuxe series was limited to just two body types, as there was no DeLuxe Club Sedan. Overall length was 193½ inches.

This side view of the Diplomat-Custom Convertible Coupe shows little change from the standard 1954 Plymouth. Note, however, the DeSoto medallion atop the rear quarter stone shield, rear fender fins minus the Plymouth flag, and the unique wheel covers. Their red centers contained a DeSoto crest this year compared with the DeSoto script used previously. The 2-tone interior featured doeskin and basket weave vinyl trim.

This Diplomat-Custom Sport Coupe is shown in 2-tone dress and lacks the square-cornered windshield trim shown in Plymouth literature. Presumably the 2-tone painted belt treatment added mid-year to the Belvedere Sport Coupe and Convertible were also added to the Diplomat, but this cannot be confirmed. A DeSoto medallion graced the roof sail panel.

Diplomat's last short-roof Business Coupe lacked a rear seat; instead, a twelve square-foot area was provided for carrying sample cases and the like. However, a 2-section rear seat could be fitted at extra cost if desired. The 15x6.70 4 or 6-ply white sidewall tires were strictly optional, as were 6-ply black tires. All Diplomats continued on the 114-inch wheelbase.

Diplomats used the same hood and hood ornament as in 1953, but the smaller DeSoto medallion was the same as used on the larger 1954 FireDomes (minus the "V"), as were the hood letters. Note that this Diplomat Club Sedan lacked the black rubber rear quarter scuff guards that were present on the comparable Plymouth Plaza models. Power steering was optional this year on all Diplomats.

This was a year of exceptional prosperity which brought the industry out of the mild sag of 1954 and boosted it to a record high. The best year since its previous record was set in 1950, a better one would not come until 1965. When the passenger car production totals of all manufacturers were added up at the end of this calendar year, an increase of more than 44.1% over 1954 was shown. Chrysler Corp. rebounded from its disastrous slump with the fury of a rocket, attaining a fantastic rise of almost 83.6% for its combined divisions. That thrust increased its industry share by 4.02%, which gave it 17.14% of the business. Plymouth and DeSoto each shot upward to a whopping gain of over 85.8%. The ascent gave Plymouth the industry's No. 4 spot by dumping Oldsmobile out of it and into Plymouth's former No. 5 resting place. Despite DeSoto's new energy, it could not budge from its No. 12 position because the ambitious new American Motors Corp. had its compact Rambler bounded over it.

Chrysler's new success was due to a drastic restyling and updating of its cars, and to a new corporate and product image called "The Forward Look." Slipping sales had caused top management to dump the short, high and narrow concept offered since 1949 and order the creation of exciting new cars of longer, lower and wider proportions. Talented designer-stylist Virgil Exner, with Chrysler since 1949, took charge of the styling program.

For design, development and tooling, the corporation spent 250 million dollars. An incomprehensible sum, but it was a good investment in the future of what was now five makes of cars, since the Imperial was separated from the Chrysler car line and declared a distinct make of car. All five captured the hearts and fancy of the public, each with its own special kind of appeal. In appearance, Plymouth and DeSoto differed widely from each other, but had a sameness in the superstructure's wraparound windshield and roof lines.

Mechanically, Plymouth's new Hy-Fire V-8 engine was the highlight of the year. This was the first 8-cylinder powerplant offered by Plymouth. Similar to DeSoto's V-8, it was designed for Plymouth's needs. Cylinders were banked at 90 degrees and combustion chambers of polyspheric shape had overhead valves of diagonally opposite arrangement. It was built in three variations which delivered 157, 167 and 177 horsepower, all at 4,400 r.p.m. The PowerFlow L-head 6-cylinder engine was carried over from 1954, but with compression ratio up to 7.4 and horsepower increased to 117 at 3,600 r.p.m. The six retained its Floating Power engine mountings, which surprisingly were adopted for the new V-8.

All Plymouths were based on a new 115-inch wheelbase. Notable chassis improvements included front shock absorbers mounted within the coil springs and the widening of rear spring leaves to 2.5 inches. Three transmissions were offered: Standard 3-speed manual and optional overdrive and PowerFlite. For the latter, the drive selector was now mounted on the instrument panel. All models featured suspended foot pedals, and tubeless tires also made their first appearance. A new encased heating system was mounted on the dash, and a new option was air conditioning. Other extra-cost items were powered devices for the brakes, steering, windows and front seats. Overall length of the new Plymouths was 10.3 inches greater than 1954 models, measuring 203.8 inches. Overall

height was lowered to 60.1 inches for sedans and 59.3 inches for the hardtop. Width of 74.6 inches was a maximum increase of only 1.1 inches. The lowline Plaza was offered in five models, the Savoy in two and the highline Belvedere in five. All but two models were available as a six or a V-8, the former being the Series P-26 and the latter the P-27. To those series designations, suffixes of -1, -2 and -3 were added for Plaza, Belvedere and Savoy, respectively.

DeSoto abandoned its 6-cylinder series, devoting itself to the V-type eight. The six was replaced by the flashy Firedome line, which even got a de-emphasized letter "d" in its name. The carryover V-8 engine was modified for two power outputs. Both versions had a bore and stroke of 3.72 x 3.344 inches (approximately 3-23/32 x 3-11/32, which mainly represented a larger bore) and a displacement increase to 290.8 cubic inches, while the compression ratio remained at 7.5:1. Fitted with a 2-barrel carburetor, the engine produced 185 horsepower at 4,400 r.p.m. and was installed in the Firedome series. With 4-barrel carburetion it developed 200 horsepower at 4,400 r.p.m. and

The Plaza Business Coupe weighed and cost the least of any Plymouth model this year. It tipped the scales at 3,025 pounds and chalked up a factory delivered price of $1,639. This model was offered only with the 6-cylinder engine. A total of 4,882 of the 3-passenger cars were built. Utilizing the same body as the Club Sedan, it had plenty of luggage and merchandise space behind the seat as well as under the rear deck.

The Plymouth Plaza Club Sedan is shown with 2-tone paint and side trim moldings which were added as options in mid-year. This model attracted enough buyers to score a production total of 53,610. Offered as a Six and a V-8, this point of view obscures any clue as to which engine this particular car had. As a V-8, this model swung the scale pointer to a reading of 3,202 pounds and carried a price tag marked $1,841. The 2-tone was also a Savoy option.

A very popular Plaza was the 4-Door Sedan, of which Plymouth built 84,156. Available as a Six or V-8, it is shown as the former, which was priced at $1,781 and weighed 3,129 pounds. The 6-passenger car is shown with optional 2-tone roof color, whitewall tires and wheel covers. The Plaza Six was the Series P-26-1, the V-8 P-27-1.

Arriving after other models had a good start was the Plymouth Plaza 4-Door Suburban. The 6-passenger vehicle offered buyers a choice of Six or V-8 engines. They bought 15,422 of the practical cars. Those who selected the 3,408-pound V-8 version paid $2,262 for it. By June, Plymouth was installing one-piece plastic headlining in Suburbans, the first automaker to do so. Made of rubber resin alloy, the linings were of no cost differential to buyers.

was the new Fireflite series powerplant. Floating Power engine mountings were not mentioned as a feature, a DeSoto had never related the vibration-ridding princip to the V-8.

Only one chassis was offered by DeSoto, who no long could cater to the very small market for long-chass 8-passenger models on a factory-offered basis. The ne chassis was of 126-inch wheelbase, had a wider tread ar suspension changes similar to Plymouth. Transmission features and options were also much as noted fo Plymouth. A dual exhaust system was introduced, bu could not be had on the station wagon.

DeSoto's overall dimensions did not change as much Plymouth's, the length being increased only 3.4 inches become 217.9, while width grew a mere fraction of a inch. Overall height reduction corresponded to Plymouth The Firedome, which was the lowline Series S-22, offere a choice of five models. The highline Series S-21 was t Fireflite, a new series with three models, to which Coronado was again added.

An averaged comparison of weights and prices wit those of the previous year is no longer feasible as capsulated record of the physical growth and rising co of Plymouth and DeSoto from year to year. Beginning th year, the increasing complexity of series and the variatio within them do not allow simple comparisons. Particular is this true of Plymouth and its range of engines in a broa variety of models.

Henceforth, picture captions will continue the practic of quoting weights and prices as applying to standar equipped models only, but without specifically stating s By this year the demand for options and accessories wa so great that most models were illustrated with ext equipment, which amounted to a sales pitch aimed at a option-loving public. Wherever possible, models shown wi continue to be specifically identified and related to weigh and price. But production totals, especially in regard Plymouth, will report the overall volume for the serie and body type shown and, except for specific instance will disregard engine types. With reference to the diffe ential between this year's Plymouth sixes and eights, th sixes averaged about 129 pounds less weight and $10 less cost.

Sold as a Six or V-8 was the Savoy Club Sedan. Plymouth factories turned out a total of 74,880. The V-8 example illustrated weighed 3,224 pounds and had an asking price of $1,940. The fender and door trim was standard for the Savoy line, which as a Six was Series P-26-3, and as a V-8 was P-27-3. This smart automobile accommodated six persons.

The Plymouth Plaza 2-Door Suburban is shown with side trim moldings not usually associated with the Plaza series. The 6-passenger car accounted for 31,788 units built. V-8 models weighed 3,389 pounds and were priced at $2,180. It could also be had as a 6-cylinder car. As shown, the car did not disclose whether it had a PowerFlow Six engine or a Hy-Fire V-8. All Plymouths had 6.70 x 15 tubeless tires.

The Plymouth Savoy 4-Door Sedan shows off the forward lean of the new front end styling. This was Plymouth's most popular automobile, recording a total of 162,741 built. The V-8 model shown sold at $1,983 and weighed 3,265 pounds. It also could be had as a Six. Perhaps for display, one 6-cylinder P-26-3 chassis-only was assembled.

The Belvedere Club Sedan, offered with a Six or V-8 engine, drew enough domestic demand to require production of 41,645 of them. The V-8 Series P-27-2 model shown cost $2,039 and weighed 3,228 pounds. The 6-cylinder Belvedere line was Series P-26-2. In Canada, the Belvedere Six was Series P-26-4, in which version 100 Club Sedans were built.

Plymouth produced a total of 160,984 Belvedere 4-Door Sedans for the domestic market, including both Six and V-8 models. Shown is a V-8, which scaled 3,267 pounds and cost $2,082. This V-8 had an identifying emblem above the rear wheel, a mark not seen on all V-8 cars. The new wraparound windshield is obvious, as is the fully-wrapped rear window. The pronounced forward thrust of the front fender was followed by a swept-back profile at the rear, which gave an impression of more length than the cars actually had. For Canada, 786 Belvedere 4-Door Sedans were built as Series P-26-4 6-cylinder models.

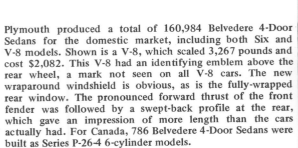

The advertising theme promoted the new Plymouths as the cars for the "Young in Heart." The most youthful-looking Plymouth was the Belvedere Convertible Coupe, especially with its top and windows down. Supplied only as a V-8, the sporty 6-passenger car tipped the scales at 3,409 pounds and required $2,351 for its purchase. It attracted 8,473 buyers. The lowered top helped this model to look longer than any other Plymouth.

The Belvedere Sport Coupe, of which Plymouth built 47,375 examples for U.S. buyers, is shown with a 2-tone side treatment that also appeared on other models. Its miniature windshield visor could also be had on certain other models. Also offered as a Six, the 8-cylinder model shown, identified by its V-8 hood emblem, weighed 3,261 pounds and cost $2,217. For Canadians, this model was supplied as a P-26-4 Six, of which 93 were built.

The Belvedere 4-Door Suburban was an 8-passenger car available with a Six or V-8 engine. Plymouth built 18,488 of them for U.S. buyers. Shown is a V-8 model which, as Plymouth's heaviest and most expensive car, weighed 3,475 pounds and cost $2,425. Like all Plymouths, this P-27-2 model had a 115-inch wheelbase. For Canada, this car was built as a 6-cylinder P-26-4 only, of which 21 were produced. For unknown purposes, ten U.S. Series P-27-2 chassis-only units were shipped.

The Plymouth Hy-Fire V-8 engine, featuring polyspheric-shape combustion chambers and overhead valves, had a 5-bearing crankshaft. It was offered in three versions, all with 7.6:1 compression ratio allowing use of regular-grade fuel. With bore and stroke of 3.44 x 3.25 inches, 241 cubic inch displacement and 2-barrel carburetor it was the standard 157-horsepower V-8. With bore increased to 3.563 inches and a displacement of 259.2 cubic inches, 167 horsepower was developed. By adding a power package with 4-barrel carburetor to the middle version, it became a top-performance 177-horsepower engine.

Chrysler continued to blaze the turbine trail, this year placing a turbulent powerplant in a Plymouth Belvedere 4-Door Sedan. Called the Turbine Special, it had distinctive nameplates and insignia as well as an engine which was essentially the same as the 1954 unit. Chrysler's gas turbine experiments were aimed at practicality, demonstrating that the fiery power was adaptable to a common car in which the family could go about the city or cruise the highways.

DeSoto's attractive new styling and proportions are quite apparent in this pose of the Firedome 4-Door Sedan. This was the most sought-after and lowest-priced DeSoto, as evidenced by the fact that 46,388 buyers each paid $2,498 to get one. The smart 6-passenger automobile weighed 3,810 pounds. The constant-width side moldings were standard Firedome trim. Standard Fireflite moldings were similar, but were tapered toward the rear.

Called the Special Coupe, this Firedome model was a lower-cost version of the 2-door hardtop. It was priced at $2,541 and, at 3,790 pounds, was the least-heavy DeSoto this year. Despite its lower price, it had a very attractive interior, almost as nice as its Firedome Sportsman sister car, with which it was registered in production totals. The Firedome line, Series S-22, was powered by a V-8 engine which developed 185 horsepower.

This illustration of the Firedome Sportsman shows the evolution of the DeSoto grille design, which now was integrated with the bumper guards. The Sportsman was a handsome automobile with a weight of 3,795 pounds and a $2,654 price tag. The specific number built cannot be reported because the record of total Firedome hardtop production, which was 28,944 units, was not broken into individual totals for this and the Special Coupe.

The Firedome Convertible rated the least demand of any DeSoto this year, collecting a total of only 625 sales. Those who bought the 4,010-pound car paid $2,824 for it. In price, it compared with the Oldsmobile Super 88 Convertible, but was heavier and less powerful.

The special edition Coronado again came as a springtime addition to the Fireflite line. Shown with standard 3-tone color styling, it was identified by special Coronado nameplates below the Fireflite signatures. Common to this car were a host of fancy features, mostly in the interior. Not usually recognized in model listings, neither was the Coronado production total defined, since it was included in the Fireflite sedan total.

A very substantial medium-priced automobile was the Fireflite 4-Door Sedan. DeSoto priced the 3,935-pound car at $2,727. The sweeping 2-tone side treatment was optional, adding a flamboyant flair that many buyers wanted. This model's production total is unknown, since all Fireflite sedans were recorded in a single sum of 26,637 units, including the Coronado. The standard Fireflite sedan shown accounted for most of the total.

The DeSoto Firedome Station Wagon shows off the wraparound windshield that was typical of all body types. It also sported optional 2-tone colors and trim moldings in a pattern that suggested forward thrust. It had seating for six passengers and was the heaviest and costliest DeSoto, weighing 4,175 pounds and selling for $3,170. A total of 1,803 were manufactured. It shared a 126-inch wheelbase with all other models.

Posed on a new expressway overpass yet unopened to traffic was a DeSoto Fireflite Convertible, looking eager to demonstrate its flashy performance among other cars. Buyers bought 775 of them to enjoy the superlative characteristics. Tipping the weighing scales at 4,090 pounds, the Convertible exacted a price of $3,151. In advertising its fresh new designs, DeSoto strangely resorted to the time-worn phrase "Styled for Tomorrow."

The DeSoto Fireflite Sportsman, of which 10,313 were built, weighed 3,885 pounds and was priced at $2,939. Its miniature "Sun Cap" visor was also seen on some of the other models. Among extra trim items that all Fireflite models had as standard were slender chrome diecastings above the headlamps and chrome moldings on the body sills. The Fireflite line was the Series S-21, and was powered by a 200-horsepower hemi-head V-8.

The Falcon was one of three Chrysler Corp. idea cars first publicized late in the summer of this year, but their showings were most prevalent during the 1956 model year. Actually, the car shown was preceded by two similar Falcons, all Chrysler-designed and Ghia-built. The sheetmetal body was of unit construction with an integral cellular platform frame based on a wheelbase of 105 inches. A 1954 DeSoto V-8 engine of 170 horsepower was coupled to a PowerFlite drive which was controlled by a centrally-mounted floor lever. Dual external exhausts were used. Called a sports roadster, the Falcon had electric window lifts and a spring-balanced manually-operated fabric folding top that withdrew into a lidded deck well. Overall, the 2-passenger car was 51-1/8 inches high, 68¼ inches wide and 182 inches long.

Flight Sweep I was a true convertible with electrically-operated curved glass windows and seating for four persons. Except for its convertible features and colors, it was precisely like its sister idea car. Designed by Chrysler and built by Ghia, many extraordinary features were incorporated. The body, cowl and front fenders were welded to the chassis frame in a unitized manner. The deck was uniquely enclosed by two lids with the spare wheel mounted on the lower panel and the tire cover on the upper. The cars had modified 1954 DeSoto 170-horsepower V-8 engines and chassis, the latter being shortened to a 120-inch wheelbase.

Flight Sweep II, except for its colors and hardtop construction, was exactly like the convertible. Between the bucket front seats was a console upon which were controls for the PowerFlite drive, radio, heater and turn signals. Cockpit styling featured a sweeping instrument panel with large round dials. On the exterior, headlamps were visored in a clamshell fashion, side treatment forecast the future in its sweep to a finlike rear, and wheel covers simulated exposed brake drums with cooling fins. A sports car look prevailed. Overall dimensions included a height of 53½ inches, width of 70-3/8 inches and length of 207 inches.

Sweetheart of the all-new Diplomat line was this Custom Sport Coupe. All those DeSoto teeth in the Plymouth sheetmetal opening gave the car a bit of a "Flying Tiger" look. Note the numeral "8" above the hood medallion, which appeared on all 8-cylinder Diplomats. The hood ornament continued to resemble an air scoop. Wheelbase was increased one inch to 115 inches. Color sweep panel was standard.

In side view, this Diplomat-Custom Convertible Coupe was practically identical to the comparable Plymouth Belvedere. Subtle differences included the DeSoto emblem in the Sportone color sweep panel and unique wheel covers. Gone were the red centers used since 1949; instead, the centers of the starkly simple covers were gold with a black and chrome DeSoto crest.

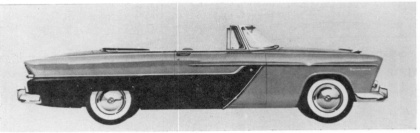

This DeSoto Diplomat-Custom 4-Door Sedan illustrates the full-length body molding used on Custom sedans and wagons. The Sportone color sweep was optional on Belvedere sedans and wagons, so this was probably true for the Diplomat, too. A Custom 2-Door Club Sedan was also offered. New options included Airtemp air conditioning and clutchless (finally!) PowerFlite automatic transmission with its shift lever located on the instrument panel.

This DeSoto Diplomat Utility 2-door wagon has the front fender door molding that was standard on the Diplomat-DeLuxe series but optional on the Diplomat. Standard powerplant was a 230 c.i.d. Six, an engine that was phased in during the latter part of the 1954 model year. Overall length was 208.6 inches for the wagons, 203.8 inches for other body styles, both a substantial increase from a year earlier as Diplomats shed their dowdy look in favor of "The Forward Look."

In common with Plymouth, Diplomat finally got a 4-door wagon this year, the first since 1950. The toothsome grille on this Diplomat-Custom 4-Door Suburban sported eleven teeth versus seven on the larger DeSotos. Available for the first time were two new V-8 engines with 241 and 260 c.i.d.'s respectively, though like Plymouth, the smaller eight was phased out during the model year. Added mid-year was a low-line 4-door Diplomat Suburban.

Following a year of fantastic sales, this was a fall-off year for every automaker. At calendar-year end, the industry showed a passenger car production total that was more than 26.9% short of the record high set in 1955, but it was still better than 1954. All divisions of Chrysler Corp. accumulated a loss of nearly 36.6%, which brought the corporation's industry share down to 14.8%. Plymouth dropped more than 37% from 1955 but remained in the industry's No. 4 position. DeSoto's performance was more pleasant, since it lost only about 23.8% but advanced to the No. 11 spot, relinquishing No. 12 to the Chrysler car lines.

Stylewise, Plymouth and DeSoto offered modifications to the concepts introduced for 1955. Most notable were the new rear fenders with fins which swept a new trend into the industry and eventually evoked much controversy about their esthetic worth as an automotive design feature.

Plymouth entered the model year with continuations of the Plaza, Savoy and Belvedere lines and a new Suburban line which drew its models from the other three and gave them new names. All models within the four lines were available with a Six or V-8 engine, except for the Belvedere Convertible which was a V-8 only. Withheld for its own special debut about two months after the others bowed was the Fury, a special hardtop with a high-performance V-8 only. All 6-cylinder cars were designated as Series P-28 and all V-8 models were Series P-29, with suffixes of -1, -2 and -3 added for Plaza, Savoy and Belvedere in that order. The Fury was also P-29-3 and the Suburban line had no suffix numeral. The Plaza and Savoy lines each comprised three body types, the Belvedere had five and the Suburban line offered four choices.

Plymouth's expansion of models offered was accom-

panied by a wider choice of engines. Of four Hy-Fire versions, the most brilliant was reserved for the Fury o It had a bore and stroke of 3.81 x 3.31 inches, displa ment of 303 cubic inches, 9.25:1 compression ratio, su 4-barrel carburetion and a maximum output of 240 ho power at 4,800 r.p.m. The two middle versions, also wh new, had a bore and stroke of 3.75 x 3.13 inches, 2 cubic-inch displacement and 8:1 compression ratio. top middle engine had a 4-barrel carburetor and c exhaust system, produced 200 horsepower at 4,400 r.p and was optionally available for all four lines. The ot middle version, with 2-barrel carburetor and single exha turned up 187 horsepower at 4,400 r.p.m. and was standard V-8 for Belvedere and Suburban models. junior member of the V-8 family, not a new design, ha bore and stroke of 3.63 x 3.256 inches, 270-cubic-i displacement, 8:1 compression, 2-barrel carburetor, si exhaust system and put out 180 horsepower 4,400 r.p.m. It was the standard V-8 for Plaza and Sa cars.

The carryover Plymouth PowerFlow L-head 6-cylin engine continued with bore and stroke of 3.25 x 4 inches and 230-cubic-inch displacement, but got a 7.6:1 compression ratio and was offered in two po outputs. In basic form, 125 horsepower was delivered, with 2-barrel carburetion and special intake manifol the horsepower was 131. Both power outputs w developed at 3,600 r.p.m.

Floating Power engine mountings were not mentione publicity, but they appeared in final versions on carryover Six and 270-cubic-inch V-8. Inaugurated on Plymouth Model PA in 1931, the vaunted principle engine suspension, said to keep engine vibration from rest of the car, spread to all Chrysler Corp. cars. Thro the years, modifications gradually obliterated the orig concept and Floating Power, as a coined term and en eering feature, slowly lost importance. DeSoto admitted to its use on the 1954 Six, and Plymouth g it obscure mention in 1955. Perhaps the quarter-cent span of use is, and may forever be, a record for distinc termed automotive features.

The Plymouth chassis continued with a 115-inch wh base. A 3-speed manual transmission was offered, could be had with optional Overdrive. The extra-PowerFlite automatic transmission now was actuated pushbuttons and had a 90-90 Turbo-Torque conve which gave quick action in acceleration. A 12-volt electr system was introduced and ammeter and oil press registration was by means of red flasher lights on instrument panel. Safety belts were again available front and rear seats, and a Hi-Fi record player was a option. In May, a new factory process for optional u coating was offered.

This year, the Plaza Business Coupe was not restricted to a 6-cylinder engine. Like most other Plymouths, it gave buyers a choice of a Hy-Fire V-8 or a PowerFlow Six. In either case, the 3-passenger car was the lightest-weight and lowest-priced Plymouth. As a V-8, it weighed 3,170 pounds and cost $1,888. The practical car was also the least popular model, as only 3,728 were built.

The Plymouth Plaza Club Sedan registered a total production of 43,022 units. It was offered as a Six or V-8. In the latter form it weighed 3,250 pounds and asked a price of $1,986. The 2-door 6-passenger car is shown with optional wheel trim and whitewall tires. All Plymouths had a 115-inch wheelbase, and all except the Fury had a standard tire size of 6.70 x 15.

eSoto again entered the model year with Firedome and
Fireflite lines, now registered as Series S-23 and S-24,
respectively. One V-8 design was used, but with different
horsepower ratings for each series. The basic engine
continued the 3.72-inch bore but increased the stroke to
inches. Displacement rose to 330 cubic inches and a
8.5:1 compression ratio was used. The Firedome
line had a 2-barrel carburetor and produced 230
horsepower, while the 4-barreled Fireflite revved up
horsepower. Both developed peak power at 4,400
r.p.m. and were available with dual exhaust system.
eSoto's chassis retained the 126-inch wheelbase. New
features were a 12-volt electrical system and Center-Plane
brakes with 25% more braking surface. Transmission
choices for the Firedome line included a 3-speed manual as
standard and an Overdrive and PowerFlite as optional,
while all Fireflite cars were equipped with the PowerFlite
automatic, which in all installations had pushbutton controls.
Numerous refinements were made in chassis components,
lines and bodies. Among new accessories this year were
high-fidelity record player and a gasoline-burning interior
heating outfit which was completely independent of the
engine and coolant system. Again available were safety seat
belts, and safety padding on the instrument panel was
added in the spring.

The Firedome series consisted of seven models and the
Fireflite line had four regular choices and a special
convertible. In February, DeSoto added the Adventurer
to the S-24 series. A special hardtop built for extraordinary performance, it had the mightiest engine DeSoto
had ever produced. A modified Fireflite powerplant, the
stroke was left untouched but the bore was increased to
3 inches and displacement went up to 341 cubic inches.
Upping the compression ratio to 9.25:1 and adding twin
four-barrel carburetors, new distributor timing, a high-lift
camshaft and revised intake manifold, 320 walloping
horsepower was produced at 5,200 r.p.m. Among other
special engine items were enlarged ports, stiffer valve
springs, modified slipper pistons, heavy-duty rods and
and a shot-peened crankshaft. A dual exhaust system
was the finishing touch.

The 2-door hardtop was so popular that Plymouth made it
available to more buyers by including it in the Savoy line.
Known as the Sport Coupe, it is shown as a V-8 which
recorded a weight of 3,275 pounds and a price of $2,233.
Total Six and V-8 production was 16,473 units. In 2-tone
coloring and dressed-up wheels, it was a smart automobile.
The Savoy line was a price and quality compromise between
the Plaza and Belvedere.

The V-8 Plymouth Plaza 4-Door Sedan tipped the scales at
3,275 pounds and posted a price of $2,030. Also available
as a Six, the combined production total was 60,197. It is
shown with a 2-tone paint scheme featuring contrasting
color on the lower areas and the roof. The lower treatment,
conservative in contrast to the Belvedere, was optional for
Plaza and Savoy models as well as for DeLuxe and Custom
Suburbans.

Shown with extra-cost 2-tone paint is the Plymouth Savoy
Club Sedan. Production of this model, in both Six and V-8
form, amounted to 57,927 units. The V-8 model shown
recorded a weight of 3,255 pounds and carried a $2,086
price tag. Plymouth provided no means of distinguishing Six
from V-8 cars when viewed from the side. However, Sixes
had a horizontal bar through the trunk lid medallion, which
was graced with a V-like bar on V-8 cars. At the front, an
outstretched V in the grille centerpiece identified V-8s.

Winning 151,762 orders, the Savoy 4-Door Sedan was
Plymouth's best seller. Also available as a 6-cylinder car, it is
shown as a V-8 which weighed 3,295 pounds and exacted
a price of $2,129. It is seen with a minimum 2-tone paint
treatment which provided only the roof in a contrasting
shade. A full-length side molding was also a Savoy option.

The price leader in the Belvedere line was the Club Sedan, but that did not make it the Belvedere breadwinner. Only 19,057 of them came off the assembly lines. As a V-8, it weighed 3,285 pounds and cost $2,170. Throughout the four Plymouth series, a Six cost $104 less than a V-8 but the weight differential ranged from 120 to 190 pounds less.

This view permits a good appraisal of the 1956 Plymouth image. All Belvedere models featured the zig-zag side moldings, but the contrasting colors they outlined were optional. The Belvedere 4-Door Sedan accounted for 84,218 units. The V-8 model shown weighed 3,325 pounds and cost $2,213. Because of its V-8 engine, the car sported a broad V in the grille centerpiece. It was also offered as a Six.

A smart-looking automobile was the Plymouth Belvedere Sport Coupe, of which 24,723 were built. When built as a V-8, it cost $2,317 and weighed 3,320 pounds. Unusual 2-tone side configurations were not uncommon among the offerings of other automakers at this time. This Plymouth example created an impression of forward thrust. The Belvedere name was within the reverse angle at the door center.

A new body type for Plymouth was the 4-door hardtop. Called the Sport Sedan, it was available only in the Belvedere series. A total of 17,515 were built. When powered with a V-8, it sold for $2,385 and weighed 3,415 pounds. The rear door glass, of two sections, pivoted downward as one unit disappearing completely. Plymouth's new tailfins show up well in this view. They were a conservative omen of more daring fins to follow.

The Fury name was introduced to the automotive world with Plymouth's entry into the specialty high-performance class. The heaviest and costliest Plymouth this year, it weighed 3,640 pounds and cost $2,866. Offered only as a 2-door hardtop with a 240-horsepower V-8 engine, it broke two U.S. stock car records on the sands of Daytona. For the flying mile it averaged 124.01 m.p.h., and its flashy acceleration put it through the standing start mile at an average of 82.54 m.p.h. To preserve the Fury as a prestige car, production of only 1,500 was originally set, but by introduction time in January, a limit of 5,000 was established. The sharp Sport Coupe ended its production run at 4,485 units, all built at Evansville, Ind. All of them were painted off-white, had gold-anodized aluminum side appliques and other gold-like touches in trim details. Tire size was 7.10 x 15.

The Belvedere Convertible was Plymouth's offering to those who liked sunny motoring and were willing to accept wind with it. The factory asked them $2,478 for the 3,435-pound car, and they got a V-8 engine. This model, because of its sports appeal, was not available with a 6-cylinder powerplant. The flashy car was chosen by 6,735 buyers. Those who wanted more than the standard Belvedere V-8 of 187 horsepower paid more and got a 200-horsepower engine.

1956

This year, Plymouth grouped all Suburbans in a separate series. The economy model, which was of Plaza class, was the DeLuxe Suburban, of which 23,866 were built. The 2-door 6-passenger car, when built as a V-8, weighed 3,460 pounds and was priced at $2,300. These models had Suburban script, rather than Plaza, on the rear fenders.

The Plymouth Custom 2-Door Suburban, which accounted for 9,489 units built, was offered as a 6-passenger car only. It could be had as a Six or V-8, and in the latter form tipped the scales at 3,500 pounds and posted a price of $2,371. Custom Suburbans, related to the Savoy series, had their own distinctive nameplates on the rear fenders. A full-length side molding was an option for both Custom Suburbans.

The Custom 4-Door Suburban was the most popular Plymouth station wagon type this year, marking up a total of 33,333 units built. As a V-8 6-passenger vehicle it weighed 3,565 pounds and was offered for $2,417. Buyers could choose a 6-cylinder engine, and could order a third seat to make it an 8-passenger car.

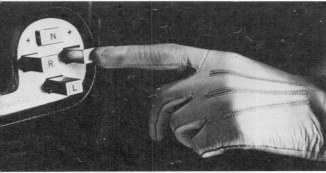

All Chrysler-built cars introduced pushbutton controls for the automatic transmission this year. Shown is Plymouth's adaptation for the PowerFlite. Mounted at the extreme left of the instrument panel, it shows a finger about to press the Drive button which moved the car from standstill to cruising speed. At the bottom, the Low button kept the car in that gear as long as desired, and a Reverse button was at the left. The top, or Neutral, button was for parking, in which case the parking brake had to be separately set. DeSoto had the same layout, but with different styling of the housing.

Suitable for many uses was the Plymouth Sport Suburban, which had a roof rack as standard equipment. It weighed 3,605 pounds and cost $2,587 when fitted with a V-8 engine and seats for six passengers. A total of 15,104 of these Belvedere-class vehicles were built as Sixes and V-8s. It is shown as a V-8 with optional third seat to provide 8-passenger capacity. It bore Sport Suburban side nameplates where Belvedere models had their name. This was an impressive automobile amongst its low-priced contemporaries.

Chrysler came up with another gas turbine engine this year, again installing it in a Plymouth. The Chrysler Turbine Special utilized a Belvedere 4-Door Sedan to show that the turbine engine was aimed at practical common use. This was the first turbine-powered automobile to make a transcontinental run. It made a 3,020-mile endurance run from New York City to Los Angeles in four days to test the engine under actual traffic and climatic conditions. Maintaining speeds of 40 to 45 m.p.h., fuel consumption averaged 13 to 14 m.p.g., using white gasoline. The engine performed flawlessly through atmospheric temperatures of 18 to 89 degrees and altitudes up to 7,700 feet. The refined version made first use of automatic control of turbine temperature, idling and top speeds, making it feasible for an average driver. It idled at 20,000 r.p.m., and attained a maximum of 50,000 r.p.m.

Joining Chrysler's family of "Idea Cars" was the Plainsman. It was a corporate experimental, rather than a Plymouth or DeSoto sponsorship. First shown about the turn of this year, it used a 1955 Plymouth engine and chassis as the basis for its unusual concept. Designed and built by Chrysler, its finish and interior trim were keyed to a Western Plains motif. Among the 8-passenger 2-door vehicle's innovations were some that eventually reached production. The third seat faced the rear and the spare wheel was carried within the right rear fender, accessible by a long panel which enclosed the driving wheel. The roof canopy was padded and covered with vinyl. The wheelbase was 115 inches and the 167-horsepower V-8 was coupled to a PowerFlite transmission. Overall height and length measured 60.2 and 208 inches, respectively.

DeSoto entered the model year and the tailfin era in appropriate form. Styling, engineering and performance gave it top value in its class. The Firedome 4-Door Sedan was the lightest, lowest-priced and most-wanted DeSoto this year. It scaled 3,780 pounds and exacted a price of $2,678. A total of 44,909 of them came out of the factories. It is shown with the side molding which was a standard DeSoto trim item.

The camera did not make the DeSoto Firedome 4-Door Seville look as long and low as catalog and advertising artwork did. This view is more in accordance with the car's actual proportions, but it was an attractive automobile regardless. This model weighed 3,920 pounds and was priced at $2,833. Its production total of 4,030 was about 2.5 times more than the similar Sportsman model marked up. The side trim gave an impression of forward thrust, with mass at the rear wheels to emphasize the propelling force at that point.

New lower-priced hardtops were added to the DeSoto Firedome series this year. Known as the Seville, they were slightly less pretentious than the Sportsman hardtops, particularly in respect to interiors. Externally, they were identified by Seville script on the rear fenders. Shown is the 2-Door Seville, which had less decor on the roof rear quarters than the similar Sportsman. It weighed 3,800 pounds, cost $2,734 and marked up a total of 19,136 built. Its popularity was more than four times that of its sister car.

The DeSoto Firedome 2-Door Sportsman recorded a weight of 3,835 pounds and had a price tag marked at $2,854. The total number of these cars built was 4,589. The most obvious external difference between this and its Seville counterpart was in the roof rear quarters, where extra chrome swept in a V-like manner below round medallions.

The talent of an artist gave a look of lowness and sweeping length to the DeSoto Firedome 4-Door Sportsman. The smart hardtop registered 3,945 pounds when weighed and required payment of $2,953 when purchased. This model's production total was an unimpressive 1,645 units. Its roof quarter decor was not like the 2-door. Sportsman script on the rear fenders identified all Sportsman models.

1956

Of all DeSoto models offered this year, the Firedome Convertible drew the least buyer acceptance. Only 646 persons found it attractive enough to pay $3,081 for the pleasure of owning it. They got a 4,080-pound car with plenty of sport-flavored class to show off. The Firedome's flashy V-8 engine provided 230 horsepower for the playful car.

The heaviest of all DeSotos this year was the Firedome Station Wagon, which weighed 4,095 pounds. The 4-door 6-passenger car was priced at $3,371 and drew a total of 2,950 purchase orders. This model had rear fenders carried over from 1955, updated with large diecast fins and tail lamps of different design.

Exaggerated artwork gave pronounced importance to the fins of the DeSoto Fireflite 2-Door Sportsman. The handsome hardtop's price was $3,346 and its weight was 3,905 pounds. A combined production total again occurred in this case, with 8,475 Fireflite 2-door hardtops reported as built, while the same record disclosed no Adventurer cars. Fortunately, an unusual finding eventually occurred. It brought to light the number of Adventurers built. Probably for convenience, they had been added to the Fireflite total in an all-model record prepared later. A deletion of the Adventurers produced a Fireflite 2-Door Sportsman total of 7,479. Searching for old records is usually not so fruitful.

This view of the Fireflite 4-Door Sedan shows the DeSoto front end quite well. The mesh grille was a refreshing change from the vertical members. Parking lamps were in the bumper/grille guards. The overall frontal design was quite pleasing. Fireflites had chrome decor on top of the front fenders. This model, of which 18,207 were built, weighed 3,860 pounds and cost $3,119.

Poised for a windy dash through the countryside was a new DeSoto Fireflite Convertible. Its 4,075-pound weight was handled quite well by the 255-horsepower V-8 which powered all Fireflites. The spirited sportster was available for $3,544. The factories turned out 1,485 of these cars, but a relatively few of that total were Pace Car replicas.

The 4-door hardtop was a new body type for DeSoto this year. Anticipated popularity caused it to be offered in three versions, of which the most expensive was the Fireflite 4-Door Sportsman shown. Following years did not bring the expected demand, which was based on an assumption that it would approach or exceed 4-door sedan popularity. The new Fireflite model, of which 3,350 were built, weighed 3,970 pounds and cost $3,431.

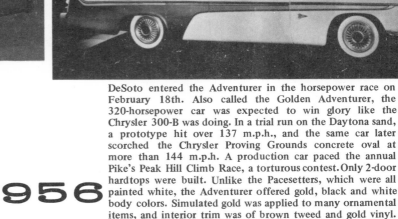

DeSoto was honored when selected to pace the Indianapolis 500-Mile Race this year. A Fireflite Convertible was the lucky car. Because it had no convertible, the Adventurer was not considered, and anything else was not acceptable for this event. The Pace Car, driven by DeSoto president Irv Woolson, hit 100 m.p.h. while leading the pack. But on the previous January 11th, DeSoto announced the Pacesetter, a limited-production replica. Dressed up with many special touches that would appear later on Adventurers, Pacesetters had beefed-up suspension but the engine and transmission were standard. Power front seats, electric windowlifts, a clock and windshield washer were included unless otherwise specified. The Pacesetters, which did not have lettering as shown on the Pace Car, weighed 4,070 pounds and cost $3,615. The unknown production total was probably only a few hundred. One of them paced the race on the well-known track at Langhorne, Pa. this year. DeSoto earned high respect with its ability in performance events.

1956

DeSoto entered the Adventurer in the horsepower race on February 18th. Also called the Golden Adventurer, the 320-horsepower car was expected to win glory like the Chrysler 300-B was doing. In a trial run on the Daytona sand, a prototype hit over 137 m.p.h., and the same car later scorched the Chrysler Proving Grounds concrete oval at more than 144 m.p.h. A production car paced the annual Pike's Peak Hill Climb Race, a torturous contest. Only 2-door hardtops were built. Unlike the Pacesetters, which were all painted white, the Adventurer offered gold, black and white body colors. Simulated gold was applied to many ornamental items, and interior trim was of brown tweed and gold vinyl. Standard equipment included power brakes, whitewall tires, dual exhausts with tailpipe extensions, dual side mirrors, dual rear manual radio antennae, instrument panel padding and the items listed for Pacesetters. Priced at $3,728, the Adventurer was the costliest DeSoto this year. Only 996 of the 3,870-pound cars were built.

DeSoto did not offer this model to the public, but it was available to commercial buyers through the Fleet Sales Department. The Memphis Coach Co. stretched Fireflite 4-Door Sedans three feet and added two doors and a seat in the center. The 9-passenger vehicle was suitable for airport cab service and sightseeing tours, also as a courtesy car at conventions, etc. Not necessarily Memphis-built were station wagons, police vehicles and sedans of 7 and 12-passenger capacity, all obtainable through the fleet office.

The Diplomat line received a modest facelift to bring the grille in line with the changes on the larger DeSotos. Gone were the famous teeth, replaced by a wide mesh screen surrounded by a bright frame. Centered on the screen was a gold "V", though perhaps only on 8-cylinder cars. The new hood ornament no longer resembled an air scoop. In side view, Diplomats were identical to comparable Plymouths, even to the wheel covers. Only the series nameplates were different. Even the catalog art and format were identical with Plymouth, changed only where necessary. A new Diplomat body type was the Custom 4-Door Hardtop (Sport Sedan).

When the DeSoto Retailer magazine published this picture, the caption was headed by "Get a Hearse!" Dealers were informed that such vehicles could be ordered, but the builder of the hearse was not identified. They were also advised that funeral flower cars, ambulances and ambulance conversions were available. It was said that several well-known body companies were involved in these offerings.

Diplomat rear ends received considerably more attention than the fronts. DeSoto called it "Aero Sweep Styling," but the fins, taillights and bumpers were strictly Plymouth. DeSoto identification at the rear was limited to a nameplate and the deck lid ornament. Diplomat-Custom, Diplomat-DeLuxe, and Diplomat series were identical to comparable Plymouths, except that there were no 2-Door Club Sedans in the Diplomat-Custom and Diplomat series. Technical specifications were identical to Plymouth, except some options like the Highway Hi-Fi record player were not offered. Pushbutton PowerFlite was available in left-hand drive cars only!

For the automobile industry, this year was but little better than last. Of the 19 passenger car brand names on the market, only 10 enjoyed better business, and half of those were Chrysler's family of five. Total passenger car production for the calendar year was a meager 5.4% better, but the percentage would have been less if Chrysler Corp. had not scored a huge gain of 41.7% over 1956. That jump, and the slump of others, gave the corporation a 5.18% bigger slice of the industry's total, for a comforting portion of 19.98%.

Plymouth, with a 44.3% gain in output, stepped up from 4th place to retake honors as the industry's 3rd biggest producer, a pleasure not enjoyed since 1953. The No. 3 spot was vacated by Buick, whose cars were not selling so well. DeSoto was Chrysler's weakest member this year, mustering a 16% gain, which was pokey in contrast to the strides of its sister car. Regardless, DeSoto remained in 11th position, aided by the addition of a lower-priced series and the fast flop of Nash and Hudson in their final year.

Introduced in the fall of 1956, the new Plymouth Series K was a complete styling departure without being radical. The frontal aspect was wide and low. Headlamps and parking lamps were well sheltered by fender "brows" which were made large enough to accommodate smaller diameter dual headlamps to come in 1958. The six wide cooling slots below the bumper were early production. No screening was used behind the slots, and too many stones got through, resulting in a revision that appears on the Fury shown elsewhere. The ornament at the grille center was an abstract form of a sailing ship, oriented in a head-on view. It also appeared on the deck lid ornament. Of course, the ship symbolized the Mayflower vessel which was identified with Plymouth until 1958.

THE Plaza

The resurgence of Chrysler Corp. was due to overwhelming public acceptance of its new models, which displayed daring styling and advanced engineering. More than 300 million dollars were spent for design, development and production tooling before the public got a glimpse of the five car brands. By midsummer, Chrysler was so elated by the sales-winning appeal of the fresh styling that Virgil Exner, boss of all styling, was elevated to the newly-created corporate post of Vice President, Director of Styling. At last, those at the corporate top level had fully recognized styling as a prime activity, much as engineering, manufacturing, sales and other major operations had long been regarded.

Outstanding engineering talent came up with important technical advances in addition to finding structural ways to accomplish the low silhouettes established by the styling concept. Among the new achievements, torsion-bar front suspension was the most notable. Basically, it featured two torsion bars which served a springing function. Combined with leaf-type rear springs that were outside the chassis frame and trailing the rear axle by two-thirds of their length, a more level ride was provided, especially in cornering. Also at the front, a new mounting of the upper control arms prevented nose-diving in quick stops. All of those features were incorporated in all cars. A notable advancement in comfort was the optional air conditioning and heating unit, now combining both functions and using common ductwork.

Declaring "Suddenly it's 1960," Plymouth claimed to be three full years ahead. All the newness was wrapped up in four basic car lines, as before, and with the same names. The Plaza had three models, the Savoy first had three and added one later, the Belvedere continued with five and the Suburbans expanded to six. The Fury continued as a special hardtop only. Except for the Belvedere Convertible and the Fury, which were exclusively V-8, all were available with a Six or V-8 engine. The 6-cylinder cars, in all cases, were Series P-30 and all V-8 cars were Series P-31. The Plaza line was sub-designated with the series suffix -1 (such as P-30-1), the Savoy was -2 and the Belvedere -3, but the Fury and Suburban line had no suffix.

Plymouth's PowerFlow Six was carried over with modifications including a new 8:1 compression ratio which gave it 132 horsepower. While the Six was reduced to one version only, V-8 engine variations remained at four. The standard V-8 for Plaza cars was a HyFire carryover now rated at 197 horsepower. For Savoy, Belvedere and Suburban models, the standard V-8 was the Fury 301 with a bore and stroke of 3.91 x 3.13 inches, displacement of 301 cubic inches and 8.5:1 compression ratio which produced 215 horsepower at 4,400 r.p.m. The Fury 301 Quad, with 4-barrel PowerPak, delivered 235 horsepower and, except for the Fury hardtop, was an all-series option. The Fury hardtop was powered by a Fury V-800 engine with bore and stroke of 3.91 x 3.31 inches,

Plymouth's entry in the lowest price category was again the Plaza series. The Business Coupe was the lowest-priced and least-heavy Plymouth this year, in either Six or V-8 form. As the latter, it cost $1,999 and weighed 3,315 pounds. In both forms, 2,874 were built. The 6-cylinder version is shown in early artwork which divided rear side windows into two panes. Later, this was corrected to show one pane for this model.

318-cubic-inch displacement, 9.25:1 compression, 8-barrel carburetion and other applications which provided 290 horsepower at 5,400 r.p.m. Concurrent with the addition of the Fury hardtop in January, the V-800 engine became optionally available for all other models which, for that engine, were fitted with special high-performance chassis details.

Two chassis lengths were now utilized by Plymouth. A new and longer wheelbase of 118 inches carried all but the Suburbans, which were mounted on 122 inches. Overdrive and PowerFlite transmissions continued as options for all but the Fury, and a new Torque-Flite 3-speed automatic was an added option for Belvedere and Suburban V-8s and the Fury hardtop. Also new this year were smaller wheels with fatter tires, the new size 7.50 x 14 being standard for all but the Fury and 9-passenger Suburbans, which had 8.00 x 14.

The Plaza Club Sedan, of which 49,137 were built, shows the 2-piece rear side windows this model always had. The V-8 shown tipped the scales at 3,330 pounds and posted a price of $2,109. Plymouth also offered it as a Six. The forward-thrusting lower side moldings, which defined a 2-tone paint treatment, were optional.

The Plymouth Plaza 4-Door Sedan had enough sales appeal to require the building of 70,248 of them. When built as a V-8, it recorded a weight of 3,405 pounds and a price of $2,155. A Six is shown. Regardless of the model, a Six cost $100 less than a V-8. Weights of the Sixes, however, ranged from 105 to 205 pounds less.

DeSoto entered the season with a new lower-priced Firesweep series added to the Firedome, Fireflite and Adventurer. They were the Series S-27, S-25, S-26 and S-26A, in the same order as named. The Firesweep series had five models, the Firedome had four and the Fireflite had six. The Adventurer started in January as a hardtop only, but a convertible was added later.

The new Firesweep was on a 122-inch wheelbase and its V-8 engine had a bore and stroke of 3.69 x 3.8 inches, displacement of 325 cubic inches, an 8.5:1 compression ratio and a horsepower output of 245 at 4,400 r.p.m. With optional power package, the 325 engine produced 260 horsepower. The Firedome, which shared its 126-inch wheelbase with the Fireflite and Adventurer, was powered by a V-8 with a bore and stroke of 3.78 x 3.8 inches, 341-cubic-inch displacement, 9.25:1 compression and a 270-horsepower output at 4,600 r.p.m. The Fireflite V-8 was the same as the Firedome but its 4-barrel carburetion gave it 295 horsepower. The Adventurer V-8, with bore and stroke of 3.8 x 3.8 inches, displaced 345 cubic inches, had 9.25:1 compression and dual 4-barrel carburetion and delivered 345 horsepower at 5,200 r.p.m.

DeSoto did not offer an overdrive transmission this year. The PowerFlite option could only be had for the Firesweep, which also shared the new Torque-Flite with others. The Torque-Flite unit had made its first appearance on Chryslers and Imperials for 1956. New to DeSoto this year were 14-inch wheels and larger tires that carried 10% more air volume. Firesweep tire size was 8.00 x 14, the Adventurer had 9.00 and the others wore 8.50.

Plymouth reached another milestone in January when its 10-millionth car was built. The specific model on which the distinction fell is not known. At midyear, Chrysler Corp. began preliminary exploration work on a new and smaller car which would become the 1960 Valiant

Shown under controlled studio lighting is the Savoy 4-Door Sedan, the most popular Plymouth model this year. A total of 153,093 were built, of which almost 70% were V-8s similar to the example shown. In standard form, the V-8 weighed 3,415 pounds and cost $2,294. Among other options seen here are the upswept extensions at the bumper ends.

The 2-tone paint scheme gave some life to the otherwise standard Plymouth Savoy Club Sedan. Cars are not usually shown with small hubcaps and blackwall tires. The V-8 shown weighed 3,335 pounds and exacted a price of $2,364. The 2-door car accounted for a total of 55,590 Sixes and V-8s built.

THE SAVOY LINE

The Plymouth Savoy 2-Door Hardtop is shown with the standard Savoy side trim. Sometimes called the Sport Coupe, this model attracted a total of 31,373 sales. Also offered as a Six, the V-8 shown was priced at $2,329 and weighed 3,335 pounds. Excepting the Fury and 9-Passenger Suburbans, the standard Plymouth tire size was 7.50 x 14.

Added to the Savoy line in March was the 4-Door Hardtop, otherwise known as the Sport Sedan. Built in Six and V-8 form, 7,601 were turned out. The V-8 shown weighed 3,480 pounds and cost $2,417 in standard form. Among options shown are the upswept bumper ends. Plymouth added this car to the Savoy line because of price resistance to the similar Belvedere model, not because of a significant increase in hardtop demand.

The Plymouth Belvedere Club Sedan attracted 55,590 sales orders. It recorded a weight of 3,340 pounds and a price of $2,364 when built as the V-8 shown. All Plymouth V-8 cars were externally identified by a V emblem on each front fender, forward of the wheels. The standard V-8 engine for Plaza cars was a 197-horsepower job, while a 215-horsepower plant served as standard for the Savoy, Belvedere and Suburban models.

Effectively displaying the styling that excited the public was the Belvedere 2-Door Hardtop as it sat for a portrait. The new concept exemplified aggressive motion in every line, terminating in even more upswept tailfins. This model, called a Sport Coupe at times, attracted 67,268 sales. When built as the V-8 shown, it cost $2,449 and weighed 3,415 pounds. All Plymouth 2-Door Hardtops, except the Fury, measured a loaded overall height of 54 inches, which was 4.5 inches lower than previous models. The lowness made them look much longer than they were. Though the new wheelbase for all but Suburbans was 118 inches, three inches longer than before, overall length was two-tenths of an inch less than previously.

Sitting serenely and stylishly was the Belvedere 4-Door Sedan, of which 110,414 were built in Six and V-8 form. The V-8 shown weighed 3,475 pounds and cost $2,410. The single full-length side trim molding was a Belvedere standard, but the wide and bright molding above the roof drip rail was among other options shown. All Plymouth 4-Door Sedans and Club Sedans had an overall height of 56.5 inches when loaded, much lower than 1956 models.

The tapered full-length stretch of 2-tone paint on the side made the Belvedere 4-Door Hardtop, also called a Sport Sedan, appear long and fast. Sold as a Six or V-8, the smart automobile won 37,446 orders, of which one for a V-8 as shown was placed by the author. The 3,505-pound V-8 was priced at $2,519. All Plymouth 4-Door Hardtops had an overall height of 55.5 inches when loaded. Considering all body types, overall width was greater by as much as 4.8 inches. The new styling introduced windshields swept back at a more rakish angle and having 58% more glass area. Windshield pillars were also slanted more and were uniquely bent near the top as they curved to meet the smartly chopped roof header.

Built only as a V-8 was the Plymouth Belvedere Convertible, of which 9,866 were produced. The 3,585-pound car sold for $2,638. Not visible here, this model's windshield had a compound upper curvature which curved the glass toward the header. This racy-looking car seemed to be eager to get out of the auto show and onto the highway. Another Plymouth won honors on the road this year, but not for speed. In the annual Mobilgas Economy Run, this time from Los Angeles to Sun Valley, a Belvedere V-8 took top laurels in the low-price class by averaging 21.3907 miles per gallon. A teammate Belvedere V-8 finished ninth with 20.8968 m.p.g.

The high-performance Plymouth Fury was introduced in January, about two months after the others, thereby gaining special attention for itself. In accordance with its prestige position, it was the most costly Plymouth this year, being priced at $2,925. The 3,595-pound 2-Door Hardtop drew 7,438 orders. Its V-8 engine delivered 290 horsepower and it rode on 8.00 x 14 tires. This was the lowest Plymouth, having an overall height of only 53.5 inches when loaded. Many special decorative items, including anodized aluminum side inserts, distinguished this model. Also standard for the Fury were the upswept bumper end extensions, which were called wing guards. Shown below the bumper are the revised cooling slots, or louvers, which entered production on all Plymouths about the time the Fury appeared.

Plymouth again offered the DeLuxe Suburban as the economy station wagon model. It recorded a total of 20,111 built. The 2-door 6-passenger car is illustrated as a Six. As a V-8, it weighed 3,685 pounds and cost $2,430. The DeLuxe related to the Plaza series in class. This year, Suburbans were longer than the regular passenger cars, riding on a 122-inch wheelbase. Also, they were fitted with 8.00 x 14 tires.

The Plymouth Custom 2-Door Suburban was not especially popular, scoring a total of 11,196 built. It accommodated six passengers and, when built as the V-8 shown, tipped the weighing scale at 3,755 pounds and posted a price of $2,540. Suburbans had different rear fenders than the passenger cars, tailfins beginning well forward, rising much more gradually and having the trailing edge slanted forward instead of toward the rear.

The Plymouth Custom 4-Door Suburban was offered with optional seating capacity as well as a Six or V-8 engine. In V-8 form the 6-passenger vehicle cost $2,594 and weighed 3,840 pounds, while the 9-passenger version cost $2,749 but its weight is not available. Of overall Six and V-8 production, 40,227 were 6-passenger cars and 9,357 were 9-passenger. Custom Suburbans ranked with the Savoy series.

Showing its Belvedere characteristics was a Plymouth Sport Suburban. As V-8s, the 3,840-pound 6-passenger cost $2,722, while the 9-passenger job cost $2,877 and, though no weight figure is available, was undoubtedly the heaviest of all Plymouths this year. Production was 15,414 6-passenger and 7,988 9-passenger cars. All 9-passenger Suburbans, both Custom and Sport models, had a rear-facing third seat and the spare wheel was carried upright in the right rear fender, both features being new this year. The seat folded flat into the floor when not in use. Another new feature, optionally available for all Suburbans, was an electrically-operated rear window that retracted into the tailgate at the touch of a button by the driver or a rear seat passenger.

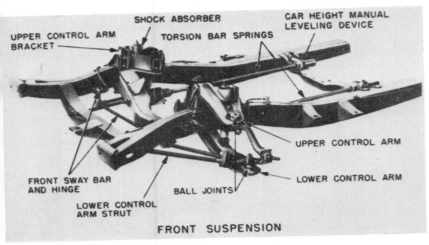

UPPER CONTROL ARM BRACKET

SHOCK ABSORBER

TORSION BAR SPRINGS

CAR HEIGHT MANUAL LEVELING DEVICE

UPPER CONTROL ARM

LOWER CONTROL ARM

FRONT SWAY BAR AND HINGE

BALL JOINTS

LOWER CONTROL ARM STRUT

FRONT SUSPENSION

The significant engineering feature for Plymouth, DeSoto and all domestic Chrysler-built cars this year was torsion bar front suspension. Though called torsion bar springs, they were not springs in the usual sense. Replacing coil springs, the bars reacted to bumps and road irregularities with a twisting action which absorbed the roughness. The system, which included ball joints, did not allow much tilt or sway when rounding curves or corners. Also virtually eliminated was vehicle nose-diving in stopping. The torsion bar suspension was destined for a successful future.

Demand for Plymouth police cars was almost four times that of 1956. Savoy Sedans and Suburbans were offered in 2-door and 4-door versions especially equipped with many heavy-duty parts. The full variety of engines was available. Also booming was the demand for Plymouth taxicabs. For that purpose, Plaza and Savoy sedans got 30 special factory-installed items, leaving only the top light and meter for local installation. Among them were parts and trim made for hard usage, as well as items for the convenience of fare-paying passengers.

Probably considered for production this year was the Cabana, a Plymouth special suburban shown in full-scale clay mockup form. A rear canopy was added to a 4-door hardtop roof for an effect similar to the Plainsman Idea Car of 1956. The severely slanted tailgate and rear glass gave prominence to the tailfinned passenger car rear fenders. Perhaps the unfinished car was to be a prestige wagon similar to Chevrolet's early Nomad.

New for DeSoto was the Firesweep series, of which the 4-Door Sedan is shown. At $2,777, this was the lowest-priced DeSoto this year. A total of 17,300 of the 3,675-pound cars were manufactured. The Firesweep series was introduced to provide DeSoto with market coverage in the low-medium price field. Shorter than other DeSotos, it was based on a 122-inch wheelbase.

DeSoto offered the Firesweep 4-Door Sportsman at $2,912. The 3,720-pound car brought a total of 7,168 sales orders. The shorter length of the Firesweep series was in the front end, from the body forward. The hood and front fenders were shared with Dodge, as was the chassis also. Fenders had a prominent visorlike "brow," of much different character than other DeSotos had. In fact, Dodge built the Firesweep cars.

The Firesweep 2-Door Sportsman was DeSoto's lightest car, weighing 3,645 pounds. The attractive hardtop, of which 13,333 were produced, was available at $2,836. The standard Firesweep engine was a 245-horsepower V-8, while an optional powerplant of 260 horsepower could be had. The tire size for this series was 8.00 x 14.

The lowest-priced Firesweep station wagon was the Shopper. A 4-door 6-passenger vehicle, it sold for $3,169 and recorded a weight of 3,965 pounds. All DeSoto station wagons had rear fenders like those of the Plymouth Suburbans, definitely unlike those of the regular passenger cars. In profile, their main difference was in the forward slant at the rear, not backswept like the others. A total of 2,270 Firesweep Shoppers were built.

The most popular of all DeSotos this year was the Firedome 4-Door Sedan. A total of 23,339 were produced. Weighing 3,955 pounds, it asked a price of $2,958. The car shows off the new styling well, particularly at the rear. The vertical 3-light arrangement included a backup light as the center unit, cleverly disguised as a taillight to maintain the continuity. The horizontal elliptical shapes between the taillights and bumper were a new engine exhaust port concept. All Firedome cars had 8.50 x 14 tires.

DeSoto's Firesweep Explorer was a 9-passenger station wagon featuring the rear-facing third seat as shown. The 3,970-pound car sold for $3,310. It accounted for 1,198 units manufactured. Third-seat access was fairly convenient by means of safety steps and the tailgate. This model's interior was smartly trimmed.

In basic form, DeSoto styling was a combination of simple design elements skillfully merged into an artistic automotive shape. The result was a functional mass with graceful simplicity, molded with a definite feeling of motion. Since simple form was not salable, ornamental details were applied. In front end design, years of evaluation had phased the long familiar grille-above-bumper configuration into the ultimate blend of cooling and protection in one massive assembly. Parking lamps were sensibly placed in the ends of the impact bar slot, and a screen in the lower opening was a necessary barrier to stones and insects. Displaying these characteristics is the Firedome 4-Door Sportsman, of which 9,050 were built. It weighed 3,960 pounds and cost $3,142.

The DeSoto Firedome 2-Door Sportsman is shown as stretched by an artist, who did similar trickery with certain other models he illustrated. This attractive model was priced at $3,085 and weighed 3,910 pounds. A total of 12,179 of these hardtops were produced. The Firedome series utilized a 126-inch wheelbase. The engine for Firedome cars was a 270-horsepower V-8, there being no option with more horsepower.

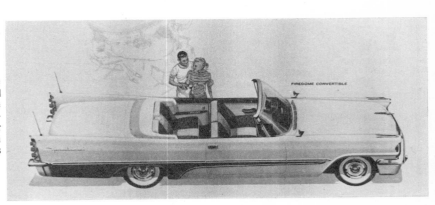

The DeSoto Firedome Convertible presented an attractive 2-tone interior that was typical of the times. This model is shown with twin radio antennae on the tailfins, while some DeSotos had a single antenna mounted on the center-line of the deck. Not all Firedomes had the front fender top ornaments. This sporty Firedome model, of which 1,297 were built, scaled a weight of 4,065 pounds and was quoted at $3,361.

This Fireflite 4-Door Sedan, photographed at the Chrysler Proving Grounds, was probably a pre-production prototype. It had no hood ornament, but otherwise it was very production-like. The front fender top ornaments were seen on most Fireflites. This car had the standard side trim, a single molding with a medallion toward the front. DeSoto priced this 4,025-pound car at $3,487 and built 11,565 of them.

This view of the DeSoto Fireflite 2-Door Sportsman effectively displays the rakish forward thrust that was characteristic of 2-door hardtop roofs. They had an airy fleetness that could not be duplicated in any other models. DeSoto's lower 2-tone design symbolized forward motion which originated at the rear wheels. This flashy Fireflite, of which 7,217 were built, sold for $3,614 and weighed 4,000 pounds.

The DeSoto Fireflite 4-Door Sportsman displays the roof style that was typical of 4-door hardtops. Because of rear door entrance and exit requirements in relation to rear seat position, its quarters could not slant forward as much as those of the 2-door models. The sedan roof was yet another design, providing more headroom and general interior space required by that model. The attractive Fireflite shown, of which 6,726 were built, weighed 4,125 pounds and cost $3,671. The car had the standard headlamp setup of two single units, also a single antenna mounted toward the right side of the deck.

The compound curvature of windshield glass, as used for convertibles only, is obvious in this view of the Fireflite Convertible. Curiously, it curved into the header, adding more distinction to this body type. This dashing automobile was available upon payment of $3,890. Only 1,151 buyers took advantage of the opportunity to get one of the 4,085-pound cars. All Fireflites were fitted with 8.50 x 14 tires.

The DeSoto Fireflite Shopper was a very stulish vehicle that was equally suited to normal family use or the carrying of miscellaneous items. The 6-passenger 4-door car tipped the scale at 4,290 pounds, which made it the heaviest of all production DeSotos this year. It cost $3,982 and was delivered to 837 buyers.

Entering the automotive scene two months after other DeSotos, the Adventurer was given an introduction befitting its prestige. Again built on the 126-inch chassis, its big V-8 engine delivered 345 horsepower this year. Featuring many items of equipment and decor that were exclusive to its lofty rank, it was wanted by many, but only a relative few got it. First offered was this 2-Door Hardtop, which only 1,650 persons were privileged to buy. The car weighed 4,040 pounds and exacted a price of $3,997. It is shown with dual headlamps, which the last holdouts of the 48 states had made legal in time for the Adventurer to make them standard equipment.

The Fireflite Explorer is shown with third-seat passengers facing the rear of the 9-passenger station wagon. They entered by stepping on circular step pads on the bumper at the sides of the tailgate, upon which they also stepped. This model, of which 934 were built, weighed 4,250 pounds and cost $4,124. With the introduction of Goodyear's new dual-chamber tires, which provided reserve air pressure for a considerable distance after a tire puncture, DeSoto became the first automaker to eliminate the spare tire. All Explorers were equipped with the Goodyears, which were said to render a spare tire unnecessary.

DeSoto added the Adventurer Convertible after the hardtop took its bow. As only 300 were built, this was the lowest-production factory-offered DeSoto this year. One of them is shown with its top raised, a state in which convertibles are usually not shown. The high-powered car, which weighed 4,235 pounds, cost $4,272 and was the most expensive car offered by the DeSoto factory.

DeSoto continued to cater to the fleet sales market. Among the offerings was the Firedome police or fire chief car shown. A Fireflite model was also available. They were built with heavy-duty torsion bars, rear springs and shock absorbers, also a 70-ampere battery and 40-ampere generator. Another fleet offering was Firesweep taxicabs, which could be had with 6-cylinder as well as V-8 engines. The cabs also had a full complement of heavy-duty equipment, and were otherwise specially fitted for their purpose. The DeSoto factory had built no taxicabs during the previous two years.

Another DeSoto fleet offering was this 9-passenger sedan which left the DeSoto factory as a production Fireflite 4-Door Sedan. Shipped to Armbruster & Co., Inc., Fort Smith, Ark., it was given the 6-door stretch job shown. When completed, it was given Memphian nameplates on the front fenders. An undetermined number of these were built for companies providing airport, sightseeing and taxicab services, etc.

A 7-passenger car also was offered by DeSoto's fleet sales department. Shown is a Firedome conversion, accomplished by stretching the chassis and body. The rear doors were made extra-wide for this 4-door sedan version. The conversion was probably by Armbruster. DeSoto also offered two station wagon conversions as police and industrial ambulances. Fleet orders could be placed through DeSoto dealers, who could sell to any operator of five or more vehicles owned by a business, and whose business use of the vehicles exceeded 50% of the total annual mileage.

This DeSoto ambulance bore Memphian nameplates in addition to Firedome signatures. The conversion shops made these vehicles with high roofs for plenty of interior headroom. They had built-in tunnel-type lights above the windshield and roof-mounted warning lights at the rear. The pod-like fixture high on top was a combination siren and light.

1957 was an all-new ball game for Diplomat. In addition to its radically changed body, Diplomats for the first time did not carry Plymouth front end sheetmetal. Instead, the line used the front end from the DeSoto Firesweep, thus enabling the Diplomat and senior DeSotos to have identical grilles and bumpers for the first time. Shown is the Diplomat-Custom V-8 Sport Coupe; other Custom models included the Convertible Coupe and the Sport Sedan (4-door hardtop).

Although the grille and bumper were the same as the larger DeSotos, the front end sheetmetal was practically identical with Dodge. This was also true of the domestic Firesweep cars. The heavy chrome lip around the single headlights and leading edge of the hood was somewhat bizarre. Because of a higher front wheel opening, the Sportone color sweep stopped short on the front fender, as on this Diplomat-Custom V-8 4-Door Sedan.

This Diplomat-DeLuxe Club Sedan shows the optional 2-tone treatment available on the lower-priced Diplomats. The Plymouth deck lid ornament sported a DeSoto crest. Other DeLuxe models included the 4-Door Sedan and a Sport Coupe. Diplomat wheel covers were no longer unique but were identical with Plymouth. Production records (available for 1957-59 only) indicate that 4,572 1957 Diplomats were built: 3,337 Sixes and 1,235 V-Eights.

This Diplomat Commercial Utility (also available as a DeLuxe model) carries the optional rub molding which was standard on the Diplomat-DeLuxe line. Diplomats were available with a 301 c.i.d. V-8 (Power-Pak optional) or the sturdy 230 c.i.d. Six. Special low-compression ratios were offered on each. New this year were TorqueFlite, torsion bar suspension, and 7.50 x 14-inch wheels.

Available as a 6 or 9-passenger model, this DeSoto Diplomat-DeLuxe Custom Suburban was also offered in the Custom line as a Sport Suburban. All Diplomat wagons had a wheelbase of 122 inches while all other Diplomats rode on a 118-inch chassis. Every Chrysler Corp. wagon used the same bodies this year. The Firesweep front end meant that Diplomats were from 2 to 4.2 inches longer than comparable Plymouth models.

This year brought no cheer to the automobile industry in general. A nasty recession set in and sent all but one automaker into a severe slump. Only American Motors was happy, since its Rambler demand nearly doubled. By midyear, the growing popularity of compact-size cars caused Chrysler Corp. to order a speed-up of its Valiant development program.

This calendar year registered a sharp drop of 30.6% in industry passenger car production. Chrysler Corp. suffered a sickening production loss of more than 47.4% and slipped to only 13.65% of the industry total. Plymouth paid a penalty of over 44% but clung to its honors as the 3rd biggest automaker because others in the top level also slumped. DeSoto took the most damaging dive, landing at a 69.9% lower level than it held a year before. The plummet put DeSoto in 13th position, a drop of two notches on the industry scale. With production the lowest for any full year since 1938, DeSoto, except for a feeble lift to come in 1959, was now in its terminal drop.

In overall engineering and styling, this year's models were a modest updating of the successful 1957 cars. Though sales did not reflect it, the public still acclaimed the styling theme. New engineering contributions even failed to excite many to buy. Two new options were offered by Plymouth and DeSoto. They were an electronic fuel injection system for Plymouth's new Golden Commando engine and DeSoto's Adventurer and a sure-grip differential that could only be applied to cars with certain axle ratios. Four headlamps, of smaller diameter, were now featured on all cars.

Plymouth lined up its cars like before, but used a new code system of series designations. Series LP2-L was the Plaza V-8 line of three models, LP2-M was the Savoy V-8 line of four, and LP2-H was for the five Belvedere V-8 models and the Fury hardtop. The Suburban V-8 line of seven was simply LP2. For 6-cylinder models, designations had a numeral 1, such as LP1-L. The Six was available for all models but the Fury hardtop and Belvedere Convertible.

Wheelbases remained at 118 and 122 inches, the latter for Suburbans, of which 9-passenger models were now fitted with 8.00 x 14 tires. Plymouth's PowerFlow Six engine was continued with no basic changes, and the Hy-Fire V-8 did not show up this year. The standard V-8 for all models but the Fury hardtop was the Fury V-800 engine which, with a 2-barrel carburetor and compression reduced to 9:1, gave 225 horsepower at 4,400 r.p.m. The same engine, with 4-barrel Super-Pak, produced 250 horsepower and was optional for all but the Fury automobile, for which it was the standard engine known as the Dual Fury V-800. The Dual version was the same engine, in all respects, as used in the Fury car of 1957, and was not available for any other models this year. In fact, the V-8s named thus far were all variations of one basic engine, the carryover V-800 of 318-cubic-inch displacement. Plymouth got a new V-8 again this year and called it the Golden Commando. Featuring a deep-skirt block and wedge-shape combustion chambers, it had a bore and stroke of 4.062 x 3.375 inches, displacement of 350 cubic inches and a 10:1 compression ratio. With dual 4-barrel carburetors it produced 305 horsepower at 5,000 r.p.m., and with fuel injection it delivered 315 horsepower. This brute powerplant was available for all Plymouths, including the Fury hardtop.

The standard transmission for all models was a 3-speed manual, but Plymouth now spread the TorqueFlite option to all V-8s. PowerFlite was available for all cars with standard chassis, and Overdrive could be had on all but those with high-performance chassis.

DeSoto, like Plymouth, gave its car lines new code designations. The Firesweep was Series LS1-L and offered six models this year, one more than last. The Series LS2-M Firedome came in four models, the Fireflite LS3-H had six and the Adventurer LS3-S had two choices. Wheelbases were unchanged, with the Firesweep on 122 inches and its sister cars on 126. Tire sizes were the same as those noted for the previous year.

The new Turboflash V-8 engines for DeSoto were actually four variations of one design. For the Firesweep, it had the same specifications as Plymouth's Golden Commando, but in standard form it had a 2-barrel carburetor and a horsepower output of 280 at 4,600 r.p.m., while optional 4-barrel equipment provided 295 horsepower. By increasing the bore to 4.125 inches and displacement to 361 cubic inches, horsepower went up to 295 and the engine was used for the Firedome series. Equipped with a 4-barrel package, the 361 job was the Fireflite engine of 305 horsepower. For the Adventurer standard plant, compression was raised to 10.25:1, a dual 4-barrel power package was used and horsepower became 345 at 5,000 r.p.m. With optional fuel injection the Adventurer was a 355-horsepower car.

A 3-speed manual transmission was standard for the Firesweep and Firedome. The PowerFlite was a Firesweep option, as was the TorqueFlite which was also a Firedome option and was the only unit with which the Fireflite and Adventurer were equipped.

This was the last year DeSoto built cars in its own factories. By midsummer, production ended and the division's properties were turned over to other Chrysler Corp. activities. The main facilities at Wyoming Ave. and Ford Road on Detroit's far west side eventually were used for glass-making and export operations. Plants on West Warren Ave. in the neighboring city of Dearborn became the new source of Imperials. Formerly built with Chrysler cars, Imperial production was segregated in order to provide better custom car quality for the prestigious car which was aiming to establish a new pinnacle of perfection. In effect, DeSoto switched with Imperial and began production of 1959 models in the Chrysler plant.

The Plymouth Plaza Business Coupe held three distinctions: It was the lightest, lowest-priced and least-wanted Plymouth in the respective Six and V-8 standard categories. The practical automobile weighed 3,320 pounds and was priced at $2,136 when built as a V-8. Its overall production total was a mere 1,472 units. The 2-door body was the same as the Club Sedan, but had one-piece rear side windows and no rear seat. A Six is shown.

The Plaza Club Sedan, a 6-passenger car with divided rear side window glass, is shown with a simple side trim molding. A total of 39,062 came out of the factories in Six and V-8 form. The V-8 illustrated weighed 3,315 pounds and had a factory delivered price of $2,225. This year's Plymouths were the Series L, which retained all of the principles so successful the previous year.

Plymouth built this Plaza 4-Door Sedan as a very simple automobile. It was a 6-cylinder car in standard form except for whitewall tires and full wheel covers. With no side trim moldings, it was indeed plain. This model was also offered as a V-8, in which form it weighed 3,415 pounds and listed at $2,277. The combined Six and V-8 production total was 54,194 units.

Added as a spring sales tonic and marketed in selected areas was the Plymouth Silver Special. Not officially a Plaza, it was of that class, but with certain extras included at a bargain price. Offered as a Club Sedan and 4-Door Sedan, it had the Forward Look emblem rather than Plaza nameplates on the rear fenders. Trim moldings were placed high on the front fenders and doors, and the low side trim design, normally a Plaza option, had an anodized aluminum insert of a contrasting paint color. The roof was painted metallic silver and wheels were deluxe-fitted. Turn signals, windshield washers and electric wipers were included. The all-inclusive price at Detroit dealerships, with nothing more to pay, was $1,958. Information did not specify the engine, but the car shown was a V-8. The unknown number built was hidden in the Plaza Club Sedan total.

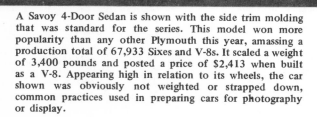

A Savoy 4-Door Sedan is shown with the side trim molding that was standard for the series. This model won more popularity than any other Plymouth this year, amassing a production total of 67,933 Sixes and V-8s. It scaled a weight of 3,400 pounds and posted a price of $2,413 when built as a V-8. Appearing high in relation to its wheels, the car shown was obviously not weighted or strapped down, common practices used in preparing cars for photography or display.

The Club Sedan in the Savoy line is shown with optional 2-tone paint treatment. The low thrusting pattern, which Plymouth called Sportone, was almost an exact copy of the treatment used by DeSoto the previous year. The car shown cannot be identified as a Six or V-8, since a broadside view provided no clue this year. As a V-8, this model weighed 3,360 pounds and cost $2,362. The overall production total was 17,624.

Appearing very low in this view was the Plymouth Savoy 2-Door Hardtop, of which 19,500 were built. The sporty automobile, when built as a V-8, registered a weight of 3,400 pounds and carried a price tag marked at $2,436. From this viewpoint, it is impossible to define this car as a Six or V-8. This year's changes included placing the tail lamps at the base of the tailfins and mounting a single backup light unit in the bumper's auxiliary underpiece.

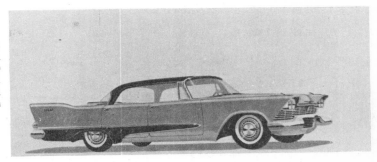

The Plymouth Savoy 4-Door Hardtop was not nearly as popular as its fancier Belvedere counterpart. Offered as a Six or V-8, it managed to gather a total of only 5,060 purchase orders. The V-8 shown sold for $2,507 and tipped the scale at 3,475 pounds. The standard V-8 engine for all but the Fury was a 225-horsepower job, up from 215 in 1957. The optional engine delivered 250 horsepower.

The Club Sedan was the price leader of the Belvedere series. There seemed no other reason for inclusion of the 2-door car in the top line. Its price and other appeal brought a total of 4,229 sales, less than half as many as the Convertible garnered. Most buyers who wanted an enclosed 2-door Belvedere selected the hardtop model. Also built as a Six, the V-8 Club Sedan shown cost $2,496 and weighed 3,370 pounds.

Plymouth built this Belvedere 4-Door Sedan with the single trim molding that was standard for the series. This car was prepared for the pose, snuggled closer to the wheels than the corresponding Savoy model shown elsewhere. In overall Six and V-8 production, a total of 49,124 Belvedere 4-Door Sedans were manufactured. As a V-8, the handsome automobile weighed 3,430 pounds and sold for $2,547.

Appearing eager to move, but resting serenely in a photographic atmosphere, the Plymouth Belvedere 2-Door Hardtop exemplified motion in metal. Plymouth letters on the off-white deck lid were not apparent under the bright lighting. This Six or V-8 model scored a production total of 36,043 units. The V-8 version weighed 3,410 pounds and cost $2,564. Note the wing guards on the bumper ends.

An automobile with much appeal was the Plymouth Belvedere 4-Door Hardtop, of which 18,194 were built in Six and V-8 form. The V-8 shown registered 3,520 pounds on the weighing scale and was sold on deposit of $2,635. Available for all Belvederes was the Sportone side treatment, which normally was of 2-tone body color but could be ordered with silver-anodized aluminum inserts instead.

Again exclusively built as a V-8 was the Plymouth Belvedere Convertible. With its top neatly folded down, this automobile expressed speed in every line. The fast-looking car excited 9,941 persons so much that they paid $2,762 to get it. The sun-and-wind job weighed 3,545 pounds. Like all Belvedere models shown, it is seen with bumper wing guards at the front and rear.

The Plymouth DeLuxe 2-Door Suburban chalked up a total of 15,535 units built. The 6-passenger car, when built as the V-8 shown, weighed 3,645 pounds and cost $2,539. Added in February as a Six or V-8, the DeLuxe 4-Door Suburban accounted for 15,625 manufactured. The V-8 4-door vehicle, which was also a 6-passenger, recorded a weight of 3,740 pounds and a price of $2,593. These models were Plaza-related.

By now the Fury had brought much fame and prestige to Plymouth. The high-performance car retained its exclusiveness as a V-8 2-Door Hardtop. The 3,510-pound car, of which 5,303 were built, cost $3,067, making it the most expensive Plymouth this year. Among other special appointments, it had gold-anodized aluminum Sportone inserts. New to all Plymouths were dual headlamps, squeezing parking light units in above them. New under-bumper sheetmetal included a grille pattern matching that of the main unit above. The V emblem at the grille center was the only means by which any Plymouth V-8 could be identified externally.

Shown is a Plymouth V-8 Custom 2-Door Suburban. Also available as a 6-cylinder car, this model ran up a total of 5,925 units built in both forms. With a V-8 engine it registered a 3,690-pound weight and was affixed with a $2,661 price tag. This was a 6-passenger vehicle. The three Custom Suburban models bore a class relationship to the Savoy series.

The Plymouth Custom 4-Door Suburban, shown as a V-8, was also built as a Six. In V-8 6-passenger form it weighed 3,755 pounds and was priced at $2,715. As a 9-passenger V-8 its weight was 3,840 pounds and its price was $2,854. Overall Six and V-8 production amounted to 38,707 6-passenger cars and 17,158 of the 9-passenger vehicles. The V-8 9-passenger model was this year's heaviest Plymouth. Optional front wing guards are shown on the car illustrated.

As a V-8 vehicle of 6-passenger capacity, the Plymouth Sport Suburban weighed 3,745 pounds and cost $2,868. The 9-passenger V-8 weighed 3,830 pounds and was priced at $3,008. Six and V-8 production totalled out at 10,785 of the 6-passenger cars and 12,385 of the 9-passenger carriers. Sport Suburbans ranked in the Belvedere category. In respect to any Plymouth model, a Six cost $108 less than a V-8 and weighed anywhere from 120 to 190 pounds less.

Continuing to cater to the expanding taxicab market, Plymouth offered some very practical models for the operating companies to choose from. All-around adaptability and economy of operation were important assets. Comfort was also a factor. Cars were specially fitted for this purpose. A Plaza Six is shown, and Savoys were also offered.

A new entry in the "Idea Car" fleet was the Cabana, a Plymouth 9-passenger station wagon. Built by Ghia on a 1958 Plymouth chassis, it had no engine or drive train. Chrysler-conceived and designed, it met three design objectives: Combine all desirable wagon features, make it adaptable to ambulance or hearse conversions, and reduce the conventional boxy wagon appearance. The 4-door body, with hardtop windows, had doors that center-locked to floor-height pillars, providing maximum side access. A full-width side-opening power-hinged door replaced the tailgate. Two sliding clear plastic roof panels aided rear seat entry and added to usable cargo height, and the steel roof had a skylight at the front. All seats but the driver's seat folded down to allow a carpeted floor from the front toeboard to the rear-end door. Measured in inches, the wheelbase was 124, overall length 215.8, height 55.9 and width 80.0.

The Custom Suburban was not only useful in hauling police officers, as shown, but in service as an emergency ambulance and general utility vehicle. Specially built to meet the needs, Plymouth built many of them for police departments and emergency agencies.

The Plaza 4-Door Sedan was one of the police car versions offered by Plymouth. The Plaza Club Sedan, as well as similar Savoy models, were also provided. The full range of Six and V-8 engines was available to the officers of the law, who got Plymouths that were fully capable of every automotive job from cruising to chasing and overtaking.

The Firesweep 4-Door Sedan was the least expensive DeSoto this year, being priced at $2,819. At 3,660 pounds, this and the Firesweep 2-Door Sportsman shared honors as DeSoto's lightweights for the year. This attractive model chalked up a production total of 7,646 units. On all sedans and wagons the 2-tone option included the lower bright molding, as the upper molding was standard. Other models had all moldings, whether 2-toned or not.

Looking very bright under studio light was this DeSoto Firesweep 2-Door Sportsman. The smart hardtop, of which 5,635 were built, weighed 3,660 pounds and cost $2,890. Having gone to a simplified bumper and cooling arrangement in 1957, DeSoto adulterated it this year by applying a stepdown to the looped impact bar which now had a textured screen insert. Parking lamps were removed to the lower opening, which now had no screenwork. These changes were all for the sake of change, and DeSoto would begin a return to the more conventional grille-above-bumper front end layout next year.

This view shows the compound curvature windshield, slightly "domed" at the top, featured on all Sportsman as well as Convertible models this year. It was introduced on convertible cars in 1957. With wheels appearing quite conspicuous against its dark body color, a DeSoto Firesweep 4-Door Sportsman got its picture taken. This model, of which 3,003 were built, cost $2,953 and weighed 3,720 pounds.

This sleek and dashing body type was new to the Firesweep series this year, as DeSoto sought to gather more sales in the low-medium market. The Firesweep Convertible attracted only 700 buyers, but was the best seller of the four DeSoto sun-and-fun cars. The flashy automobile pressed the weight scale pointer to a reading of 3,850 pounds and carried a price tag marked $3,219.

Though the DeSoto Firesweep Shopper was not nearly as long as the catalog artwork made it appear, it was a roomy station wagon. The 6-passenger automobile recorded a weight of 3,955 pounds and posted a price of $3,266. Of total DeSoto production, it accounted for 1,305 units.

DeSoto said this automobile was styled for the country club and built with ruggedness for the ranch, and certainly it could serve well in either place. DeSoto was commenting about the Firesweep Explorer, a 9-passenger station wagon based on the same 122-inch wheelbase as the Firesweep Shopper. The 3,980-pound Explorer, of which 1,125 were built, was priced at $3,408.

Again the most popular DeSoto for the year, the Firedome 4-Door Sedan recorded a total of 9,505 units built. Most sedan buyers made a middle-class choice, not wanting the lowest-priced model nor selecting the most expensive. This car weighed 3,855 pounds and cost $3,085. Firedome and Firesweep cars ended the top molding just above the front wheel.

The DeSoto Firedome 2-Door Sportsman attracted more buyers than any Sportsman model. The handsome 3,825-pound car caused 4,325 buyers to part with $3,178 to get it. Part of its attraction was due to the smartness of its interior, which was trimmed in richly textured Frontier Homespun fabric and grained vinyl. Colors were carefully selected to harmonize with exterior paint schemes.

In reality, most any young man would have found the DeSoto Firedome 4-Door Sportsman quite alluring. It had plenty of both feminine and masculine appeal, but only 3,130 buyers found they could not live without one. They each paid $3,235 for the 3,920-pound car. Firedome Sportsman and Sedan interiors were available, at additional cost, for Firesweep Sportsman and Sedan models.

Among the array of models that came out of the DeSoto factory was the Firedome Convertible. Its 295-horsepower V-8 engine, shared with other Firedomes, gave it spirited performance. The youthful-looking model, of which 519 were built, weighed 4,065 pounds and cost $3,489. In these early years of the wraparound windshield era, DeSoto called this compound curvature type a "wrap-over."

This factory-fresh DeSoto Fireflite 4-Door Sedan was photographed while awaiting shipment to one of the 4,192 persons who became proud owners of this model. It needed a bit of cleaning up, especially a scrubbing of its whitewall tires. The car weighed 3,990 pounds and cost $3,583. This model's interior featured metallic damask and vinyl. Integrated armrests had aluminum recesses above.

Dual headlamps were standard equipment on all DeSotos this year. The cavity surrounding them was sometimes painted black. Shown in a rather formal all-white atmosphere, the Fireflite 2-Door Sportsman assumed an air of magnificence, but it looked well under less sophisticated circumstances. This model recorded a weight of 3,920 pounds and a price of $3,675, and was delivered to 3,284 buyers.

Shown is a Fireflite 2-Door Sportsman with a spring dress-up group that was available for all DeSotos but the Adventurer series. Included were thinly-fluted anodized aluminum inserts within the sidesweep moldings, eight stainless steel accent strips on the deck lid and sill moldings of stainless steel. To further attract buyers in the spring market, new body colors were introduced.

The DeSoto Fireflite Convertible was probably wanted by many more than the 474 persons who bought it. In this year of economic recession, the public was not in a proper mood for buying much, if anything. This model weighed 4,105 pounds and had a price of $3,972. The severely stretched dart-like shape of the side color pattern suggested a long, fast and fleet automobile.

In this view, the DeSoto Fireflite looked impressive and powerful. With its 305-horsepower V-8 engine, it was not inferior to many. Shown is the 4-Door Sportsman, which was chosen by 3,243 buyers who paid $3,731 for the 3,980-pound automobile. On all Fireflite and Adventurer models, the top molding of the sidesweep extended to the headlamp and a round medallion was fitted to it near the door.

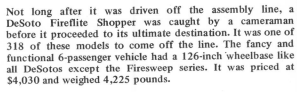

Not long after it was driven off the assembly line, a DeSoto Fireflite Shopper was caught by a cameraman before it proceeded to its ultimate destination. It was one of 318 of these models to come off the line. The fancy and functional 6-passenger vehicle had a 126-inch wheelbase like all DeSotos except the Firesweep series. It was priced at $4,030 and weighed 4,225 pounds.

The exclusive Adventurer was presented at least two months after other DeSotos bowed. The 2-Door Hardtop, of which 350 were built, weighed 4,000 pounds and cost $4,071 in standard form. The car shown was equipped with fuel injection, as indicated by the special nameplate above the round medallion on the front fender. This was the only year DeSoto used the injection system, which boosted horsepower to 355 and made cars so equipped the mightiest production DeSotos of all time. Shown are the wheel covers with simulated knock-off hubs.

The heaviest of all production DeSotos this year was the Fireflite Explorer. It scaled a weight of 4,295 pounds without any of the nine passengers it could accommodate. This fashionable model was as fitting in sumptuous surroundings as at the railway station or produce market. With center and rear seats folded down, it had 92 cubic feet of floor space. The $4,172 car drew 609 sales.

Cost and demand usually go hand-in-hand. Accordingly, the most expensive and lowest-production DeSoto this year was the Adventurer Convertible. It cost $4,369 and only 82 were built. The car shown had dual 4-barrel carburetion providing 345 horsepower, standard for both Adventurer models. Typical for the series were the decorative deck bars and the dart-shape insert on the tailfin, which included the Adventurer namescript. This series continued the use of many gold-like accents which had become synonymous with its distinctive identity.

Some of DeSoto's station wagons were diverted to conversions such as this. A Fireflite is shown as a hearse, the work of the National Body Corp. in Detroit. The same company provided ambulance conversions. In both cases, Fireflite and Firesweep Shoppers and Explorers were available. They could easily be reconverted to normal station wagon use by making only minor adjustments.

For this conversion, a stock Fireflite Shopper was given a "ballooned" roof to allow additional vertical space inside. The builder of this hearse conversion is unknown. Conversion orders were placed through DeSoto dealers, who ordered the stock vehicles from the factory, instructing that they be shipped directly to the conversion company. Production totals for conversion units are not available.

This DeSoto Diplomat Business Coupe illustrates the reworked front end for 1958. In common with U.S. Firesweeps, Diplomats now had dual headlamps and a facelifted bumper-grille. Note the grille texture now appeared in the restyled upper mouth, while in 1957 the texture was confined to the lower opening. Wheelbase was 118 inches; overall length, 204.6 inches.

Except for its Firesweep front end, the Diplomat Commercial Utility was a stock Plymouth right down to its wheel covers. The hood medallion was new, but the hood ornament and gold DeSoto letters were carryover. DeSoto production dropped this year and Diplomat was no exception; 3,250 Diplomats were assembled, 2,286 Sixes and 964 V-Eights.

Because of the higher Firesweep wheel opening, it was necessary to shorten the lower molding of the color sweep on this DeSoto Diplomat-Custom Sport Sedan. This modified molding treatment thus bore a striking resemblance to the body moldings used on the senior U.S. Fireflite series. The 55.5-inch high 4-door hardtop shows the new wheel cover design shared with Plymouth.

This DeSoto Diplomat Club Sedan is shown with the optional color sweep similar to that used on the Plymouth Plaza. For the first time, the Diplomat color sweep was different from that used on the Diplomat-DeLuxe series. Both the 230 c.i.d. Powerflow six and the Fury V-800 engines were available with special low-compression ratios for use overseas where high octane fuels were often not available. Other base Diplomats included the Business Coupe and the 4-Door Sedan.

Available for the first time in the DeSoto Diplomat-DeLuxe series was this 4-Door Sport Sedan, advertised as the lowest-priced 4-door hardtop in DeSoto history. The color sweep panel was similar to that used on the 1957 Fireflite. Large chrome rear bumper wing guards were an attractive option. Taillights were new, as was the single centered back-up light. Other models in the DeLuxe line included a 4-Door Sedan, Club Sedan, Sport Coupe, and Custom Suburban.

This 9-passenger Diplomat-Custom Sport Suburban was mounted on a 122-inch wheelbase in common with all other Chrysler Corp. wagons. Features included a rearward-facing "observation seat" with electric tailgate window, plus a spare tire concealed in the right rear fender under a removable panel. A 2-seat 6-passenger version was also available. In the senior export DeSotos, the only wagons offered were in the Firesweep series.

Long and low was this Diplomat-Custom Convertible Coupe. Three V-8 engines were available, including the 318 c.i.d. Fury V-800 with and without the "Super Pak" (4-bbl. carburetor). Ultimate power came from the 350 c.i.d. Golden Commando V-8 with its 4-bbl. carburetor and 10 to 1 compression ratio. The DeSoto Diplomat-Custom series also included the equally sleek Sport Coupe and the ever-present 4-Door Sedan.

Fair weather prevailed throughout the industry this year, but not quite every manufacturer enjoyed it. Buick was the only automaker who could not garner a gain in production. All of the others combined to push passenger car output to a 31.8% improvement over the gloom year 1958. The calendar year was not quite so good to Chrysler Corp., which was hit with complaints of poor quality. Regardless, the corporation's productivity was more than 27.3% better, though its portion of the industry's total dropped slightly to 13.19%.

With an uplift of only 11.6%, Plymouth was Chrysler's weakest gainer. Its position as the nation's No. 3 automaker was almost grabbed by Rambler, whose production nearly doubled again this year. This was the last year Plymouth would rank as high as 3rd position until 1970. Rambler's success got competition late this year, however, when Chrysler, Ford and Chevrolet put their compacts into production. DeSoto had problems of its own, mainly a softening of demand for cars of its middle price class. Ford's Edsel, among others, faced the same trend. But surprisingly, DeSoto ended the year with an 18.2% better record than the previous year and easily held its 13th position.

Chrysler spent 150 million dollars to prepare its five facelifted cars for the market. Plymouth received more styling change than any of them. Worried about keeping Plymouth in 3rd place, Chrysler strongly admonished dealers that it was their No. 1 car and should be treated accordingly in the overall sales effort. Plymouth had fairly extensive changes in front and rear end styling, but the 2-year-old vehicle basics did not look a great deal different. The styling changes were accompanied by a number of mechanical refinements and innovations. Optional air suspension was introduced for the rear end only, and was used in conjunction with conventional but lighter leaf springs. Front torsion bars were shortened and the system was redesigned. New options included swivel front seats, an electronic headlight dimmer and a self-dimming rear view mirror.

Plymouth realigned its series, eliminating the Plaza, making the Fury a series and adding a Sport Fury top-line bracket. The V-8 Savoy, Series MP2-L, offered only two models while the Belvedere V-8, MP2-M, presented five choices. The Fury Series MP2-H had three models and the Sport Fury MP2-P offered only two types. As V-8s, the Suburban line was Series MP2 and comprised seven models. As 6-cylinder cars, the Savoy MP1-L had three models, the Belvedere MP1-M had four and the Suburban MP1 could be had in only three types. All Fury and Sport Fury cars, as well as some Suburban models, were exclusively V-8.

Wheelbases continued at 118 and 122 inches, the latter for Suburbans. Standard tire sizes remained at 7.50 x 14 for all but 9-passenger Suburbans, which had 8.00 x 14, a size that was optionally available for all other cars. Plymouth's PowerFlow Six engine got no notable change as public demand for V-8s was overwhelming. The Fury V-800 engine with 2-barrel carburetor, upped to 230 horsepower, was the standard V-8 for all but the Sport Fury line. With 4-barrel Super-Pak, the V-800 was increased to 260 horsepower and was the standard Sport Fury powerplant which was also optional for all other V-8 models. The Golden Commando V-8, again the premium engine, was given new dimensions. With a bore and stroke of 4.12 x 3.38 inches, displacement of 361 cubic inches and unchanged 10:1 compression, its many high performance characteristics now combined to produce 305 horsepower at 4,600 r.p.m. Only one 4-barrel carburetor was used, and fuel injection was no longer available. Designated the Golden Commando 395 (for 395 ft/lbs. of torque at 3,000 r.p.m.), it was an option for all models but the Savoy Business Coupe.

Plymouth still offered a 3-speed manual as the standard transmission for all models. Optional PowerFlite and Overdrive versions were available for all models but those with Golden Commando engines, and TorqueFlite could be had in all V-8 cars.

The DeSoto Division, which borrowed production space from other Chrysler divisions during the first eight years of its existence and had its own exclusive headquarters in Detroit for the next 22 years, was again housed with someone else. This time, its main management and production operations were with the Chrysler car division. All of this year's models but the Firesweep line, which always was assembled by the Dodge Division, were built alongside Chrysler cars in that division's Jefferson Ave plant in Detroit. DeSoto continued in that relationship as long as it functioned as a domestic entity of Chrysler Corp.

Business Coupe 6

Rating the least demand of all Plymouths this year was the Savoy Business Coupe, of which 1,051 were built. It also was the lightest and lowest-priced Plymouth, weighing 3,130 pounds and costing $2,143. This year it was not offered as a V-8, and that made it the only model restricted to the 6-cylinder engine. It was a 3-passenger car, had interior as well as rear compartment luggage space, and had 1-piece rear side windows.

This car had a body like the Business Coupe but had a rear seat, nicer interior and 2-piece rear side windows. It was the Plymouth Savoy 2-Door Sedan, of which 46,979 came from the assembly lines as Sixes and V-8s. In V-8 form, it weighed 3,425 pounds and cost $2,352. Externally, the only means of distinguishing any model as a V-8 or Six was on the deck lid or tailgate. A V-8 had a small chrome V following the Plymouth script, while a Six had only the script.

DeSoto's facelifted family was again comprised of four series members. The Firesweep Series MS1-L had six models at first, later added two Seville hardtops. The Firedome Series MS2-M first had four choices, adding two Seville hardtops later. The Series MS3-H was split into the Fireflight line of six models and the Adventurer offering of two. Wheelbase and tire sizes were the same as those of 1957-58.

Engines were changed for the new DeSotos, which again had Turboflash V-8 versions as standard for each series but the Adventurer. The Firesweep engine was like Plymouth's Golden Commando 395 except that it had a 2-barrel carburetor and produced 295 horsepower. The Firedome had a bore and stroke of 4.25 x 3.38 inches, displacement of 383 cubic inches, 10.1:1 compression and a 2-barrel carburetor which combined to deliver 305 horsepower. The same engine, with 4-barrel carburetion, developed 325 horsepower for the Fireflite. The Adventurer engine, which was optional for all other models, had Firedome/Fireflite basic specifications but was equipped with dual 4-barrel carburetion and other special details which provided 350 horsepower. The Adventurer's output was developed at 5,000 r.p.m., the other versions at 4,600. Fuel injection was not offered. Transmission types and their relationship to series were like those noted for 1958.

Instrument panel padding, formerly standard on the Adventurer, now became standard on the Firedome and Fireflite as well. Safety seat belts were again available. A new option was air suspension which was installed only at the rear, and was in conjunction with new-design semi-elliptic springs. The front torsion bar suspension setup was revised. Notable among new options were a self-dimming rear view mirror, electronic headlight dimmer and swivel front seats.

By far the most popular Plymouth model was the Savoy 4-Door Sedan. It registered a combined Six and V-8 total of 84,274 units built. As a V-8, it cost $2,402 and tipped the scales at 3,390 pounds. A Plaza line was not offered this year, the Savoy line being downgraded to take its place. Savoy models were available with optional side trim as shown on the DeLuxe 4-Door Suburban.

The Plymouth Belvedere 4-Door Sedan was popular enough to attract a total of 67,980 sales orders. Available as a Six or V-8, in the latter form it weighed 3,430 pounds and was quoted at $2,559. Typically, a V-8 cost $119 more than a Six, but the weight difference varied widely, ranging from 100 to 200 pounds heavier.

Shown is a Plymouth Belvedere 2-Door Sedan, identified as a V-8 by a small V at the right of the Plymouth script on the deck lid. This model sold for $2,509 and recorded a weight of 3,395 pounds. A total of 13,816 Sixes and V-8s came off the assembly lines. Like the Savoy, the Belvedere series was downgraded. The purpose was to make room for the new 3-model Fury series, which assumed the former Belvedere rank.

Low and rakish in appearance, the Plymouth Belvedere 2-Door Hardtop was a dashing automobile. The factories turned out a grand Six and V-8 total of 23,469 of the handsome vehicles. The V-8 version registered a weight of 3,405 pounds and posted a price of $2,581. For all but Sport Fury models, the standard V-8 engine was the Fury V-800 of 230 horsepower. It was optionally available as a 260-horsepower job.

This view of the Belvedere 4-Door Hardtop shows the creased brow above the headlamps, a sort of double-roll effect which was a new Plymouth design feature this year. Built as a Six or V-8, this model accumulated a production total of 5,713. The V-8 version reported a weight of 3,475 pounds and a price of $2,644.

The simulated spare wheel cover on the deck lid was a sporty touch that Virgil Exner, Vice-president and Director of Styling, loved to apply. It served only a decorative function. The Belvedere Convertible, available only as a V-8, weighed 3,580 pounds and cost $2,814. The Plymouth plants turned out 5,063 of them.

The Plymouth Fury 2-Door Hardtop, of which a total of 21,494 were produced, again shows Exner's beloved spare wheel impression on the deck lid. The feature brought criticism. Some felt that a spare wheel should not be simulated; others thought it should be above the bumper in a continental manner, if at all. However, the controversy was not of great import, and the desirability of the automobile was not affected. The car weighed 3,435 pounds and cost $2,714.

The Fury name no longer meant a specialty high-performance car. It was now a series which included the 4-Door Sedan shown. This model, of which 30,149 were built, weighed 3,455 pounds and carried a $2,691 price tag. The Fury series did not make a 6-cylinder engine available. The fuel filler door is quite obvious in this view.

Plymouth's new tailfins were much more prominent, sweeping in a graceful curve from the body "C" pillar. The Fury 4-Door Hardtop is shown with upswept front corner guards and a wide sill molding, options that appear on some other models. In standard form, this model weighed 3,505 pounds and cost $2,771. A total of 13,614 were built. Plymouth introduced a new emblem this year. Seen on the grille, it was an abstract shape.

The Plymouth Sport Fury Convertible weighed 3,670 pounds and cost $3,125. A total of 5,990 were manufactured. The standard Sport Fury engine was a 4-barrel V-8 of 260 horsepower, which was an option for other models. A new 305-horsepower Golden Commando 395 could be ordered in any Plymouth, except for the Savoy Business Coupe.

The new top-line Plymouth was the Sport Fury, which was designated as a premium line. The official code was MP2-P, of which the suffix letter denoted premium. The less-costly Fury series was MP2-H, which meant high-line. The Sport Fury 2-Door Hardtop, of which 17,867 came out of the factories, recorded a weight of 3,475 pounds and a price of $2,927. Sport Fury models did not have Sport Fury name-plates, using only the Fury stylized script, but they had distinctly different side decorative treatment.

Again, Plymouth grouped all Suburbans into a special Suburban series, not calling them Savoy, Belvedere or Fury. The low-line was the DeLuxe series, which was in the Savoy class. Shown is the DeLuxe 2-Door Suburban, a 6-passenger vehicle of which 15,074 were built. Offered as a Six or V-8, it weighed 3,690 pounds and cost $2,694 as a V-8.

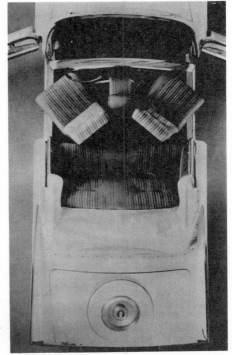

New this year were the swivel-action front seats. Standard in the Sport Fury Convertible and Hardtop, the innovation provided easier entrance and exit. The touch of a finger actuated the seats — they were not linked to the doors. In riding position they locked firmly in place. Shown with the center armrest folded down, three front passengers could be accommodated by swinging it upward, flush with the seat backs.

The Plymouth DeLuxe 4-Door Suburban was a practical 6-passenger vehicle which accounted for 35,086 built. It was the most popular Suburban, but by a margin of only 62 units. As a V-8, the weight was 3,725 pounds and the price was $2,761. It also could be had as a Six. 4-Door Suburbans differed from 2-door types in the design of the body "C" pillars. 4-door models had wider and tapered pillars, whereas 2-door cars had narrow pillars of uniform width.

Custom Suburbans were middle class, relating to the Belvedere. The Plymouth Custom 2-Door Suburban easily accommodated six passengers and, strangely, was built only as a V-8. The car attracted only 1,852 sales, making it the least-wanted Suburban model. It registered a weight of 3,690 pounds and asked a price of $2,814.

Closely related to the Fury series, the Plymouth Sport Suburban was exclusively V-8, regardless of seating capacity. In 6-passenger form it weighed 3,760 pounds, cost $3,021 and accounted for 7,224 units built. As a 9-passenger car, of which 9,549 were built, it weighed 3,805 pounds and cost $3,131, making it the heaviest and costliest Plymouth this year. Shown is a 9-passenger model.

The Plymouth Custom 4-Door Suburban offered ample choices to buyers. As a 6-passenger car, they could get it as a Six or V-8. Those who wanted it as a 9-passenger vehicle got it as a V-8 only. As a 6-passenger V-8 it weighed 3,730 pounds and cost $2,881, while the 9-passenger version was a 3,775-pound car costing $2,991. Assembly lines turned out 35,024 6-passenger types and 16,993 9-passenger models.

The Plymouth Patroller 6 was one of several police specials. It was a 2-door model with the PowerFlow Six 132-horsepower engine. A 3-speed manual transmission was standard, but the car was available with 2-speed PowerFlite. Typical of police cars and taxicabs, it was built with many heavy-duty components.

Shown is the Plymouth Savoy Taxicab, one of three taxicab models. The others were a Special and a Belvedere. They were available with the PowerFlow Six or 230-horsepower Fury V-800 engines. Even the PowerFlite automatic transmission could be had. The cabs were built with an oversize clutch, heavy-duty transmission, heavy-duty wheels, special battery with heat shield, heavy-duty generator, heavy-duty suspension, extra-strong Herculite door glass, heavy-duty seat construction and many other special items.

Chrysler revealed some new gas turbine developments this year, again wrapped in a Plymouth package. A Fury 4-Door Hardtop became the Chrysler Turbine Special. The experimental car made a 576-mile cross-country run, averaging over 19 m.p.g. of Diesel fuel at an average highway speed of 38.3 m.p.h. On the 618-mile return trip on turnpikes, at an average 51.65 m.p.h. speed, fuel consumption was over 17 m.p.g., using Diesel and turbo-jet fuel and leaded gasoline. The fuel economy improvement over previous turbine engines was due to compressor, burner and regenerator refinements. The engine used two new Chrysler-developed metals in critical components, a significant breakthrough in the effort to make turbines more efficient in operation and more economical and feasible for mass automotive production.

Breadwinner Plymouth, also in its 30th year, far outnumbered DeSoto in milestones by rolling out its 11-millionth car about the time DeSoto reached its own milepost. The significant Plymouth is shown as it neared the end of a final inspection line in Detroit. On hand for the event were men well qualified to be there. At the left was Plymouth General Manager Harry E. Chesebrough, and behind him was Williard Sloan, a Detroiter who bought one of the first Plymouths and had followed it with 13 others. At the right was Plymouth Plant Manager William C. Cawthorn, and beyond him was William Cox, an inspector of the early Plymouths.

Shown is the Plymouth Patroller Special 8, a 4-door car. Either the standard 230-horsepower or the optional 260-horsepower engine could be had. Two optional automatic transmissions were offered, the PowerFlite and the 3-speed TorqueFlite. Plymouth also built 6 and 9-passenger suburbans for police departments, emergency services, etc.

The price leader of the entire DeSoto family was the Firesweep 4-Door Sedan at $2,904. It also rated more demand than any other, marking up a total of 9,649 built. The 3,670-pound car was offered with the standard Firesweep 295-horsepower V-8 or an optional 350-horsepower job. The Firesweep series continued on a 122-inch wheelbase.

The lightweight of the DeSoto family was the Firesweep 2-Door Sportsman, which weighed 3,625 pounds. It was priced at $2,967. The factory reported 5,481 Firesweep 2-door hardtops built, but not all of them were the Sportsman. An undisclosed number were the Firesweep 2-Door Seville, which entered production early in March. No weight or price figures are available for the Seville, which looked very much like the Sportsman.

The DeSoto Firesweep 4-Door Sportsman was priced at $3,038 and recorded a weight of 3,700 pounds. A total of 2,875 Firesweep 4-door hardtops were recorded as built. However, an unknown portion of that total were the Firesweep 4-Door Seville, for which a price and weight record is also lacking.

DeSoto's lowest-priced sun-and-wind offering was the Firesweep Convertible, for which a $3,315 price was asked. The sporty car, which weighed 3,840 pounds, was the most popular DeSoto Convertible this year. The factory assembly lines turned out 596 of them.

The FireDome 4-door Sedan was a fairly popular member of the DeSoto family. It registered a total of 9,171 units built. Weighing 3,840 pounds, it was priced at $3,234. All Firedome models were on a 126-inch wheelbase, and the standard Firedome engine was a 305-horsepower V-8. The Adventurer 350-horsepower engine was available on special order.

Shown is the Firesweep Explorer, a 4-door station wagon with accommodations for nine passengers. Priced at $3,508, it weighed 3,980 pounds and recorded a production total of 1,179. DeSoto also offered the same car as the Firesweep Shopper, a 6-passenger vehicle costing $3,366 and weighing 3,950 pounds. A total of 1,054 Shoppers were built.

The DeSoto Firedome 2-Door Sportsman is shown with a simple side trim molding, rarely seen and quite conservative in comparison with the more popular elaborate trim. The car weighed 3,795 pounds and was priced at $3,341. Records report that 2,862 Firedome 2-door hardtops were built. Not all of them were the Sportsman, however, as the total included the similar Seville model.

Recording a weight of 3,895 pounds was the DeSoto Firedome 4-Door Sportsman, which also posted a price of $3,398. The factory production sheet showed a total of 2,744 4-door hardtops built, but it combined Sportsman and Seville models in the one sum. DeSotos were now built in the Chrysler factory, having had to give up the plants in which they had been built since 1936.

The DeSoto Firedome Convertible, of which 299 were manufactured, weighed 4,015 pounds and cost $3,653. The car displays items that were also options for others. The elaborate side trim, chrome sill molding, side mirrors, wheel covers, whitewall tires and snubby rubber-tipped bumper guards were only some of the many choices available.

Added as a spring sales tonic were four Seville models, which were in honor of DeSoto's 30th Anniversary. The new cars had certain features of their own, but generally looked like the others. The Firedome 2-Door Seville is shown with the swivel front seat in position for entrance, or perhaps in this car it had facilitated exit. DeSoto, like Plymouth, featured the swivel seats in some sport models. Seville weights, prices and production totals are not available.

An attractive automobile was the DeSoto Firedome 4-Door Seville. Standard features of this and other Sevilles included the special side decorative treatment, plaid interior trim, a padded instrument panel and special steering wheel. Sevilles were externally identified by Seville namescript on the rear fenders where the Sportsman name normally appeared. The cars were named for the Spanish city where explorer Hernando DeSoto began his expedition to the New World.

Perhaps the lady was just returning from a pleasant drive in the DeSoto Fireflite 4-Door Sedan. Its 126-inch wheelbase and 3,920-pound weight added to riding pleasure, and if it were equipped with the new air suspension option at the rear, even more comfort was enjoyed. In standard form this model, of which 4,480 were built, cost $3,763.

With its side trim giving an impression of fleetness and extraordinary length, the DeSoto Fireflite 2-Door Sportsman looked ready to go places. The side insert of anodized aluminum added a flashing touch to any DeSoto. This spirited model, of which 1,393 were turned out, registered a weight of 3,910 pounds and posted a price of $3,831.

Fireflite models were powered by the standard Fireflite 325-horsepower engine unless they were ordered with the optional 350-horsepower walloper. Shown is DeSoto's attractive Fireflite 4-Door Sportsman, a 3,950-pound car with a $3,888 price. Its attractive quality was not persuasive to many buyers, however, as only 2,364 were sold.

The Fireflite Convertible was one of DeSoto's last convertible offerings. Declining DeSoto popularity took a heavy toll, and DeSoto did not build convertibles after this year. The Fireflite model registered a weight of 4,105 pounds and sold for $4,152. It excited only 186 persons enough to buy it.

The junior Fireflite station wagon was the Shopper, which was provided only as a 6-passenger vehicle. It sold at a price of $4,216, while its weight was 4,170 pounds. Only 271 of them rolled out of the factory. This was the last year that DeSoto offered a station wagon. The company could only market more salable models from here on.

Taking honors as the heaviest of all DeSotos this year was the Fireflite Explorer. The impressive 4,205-pound car, which had three seats for nine passengers, was DeSoto's prestige station wagon. It earned enough respect to bring 433 purchase orders. The swanky vehicle was priced at $4,358.

Sticking to tradition, the DeSoto Adventurer was introduced later than its less prestigious mates. The intent was to keep it in a lofty position. However, this was the last year it would be given such high respect. Its mighty 350-horsepower engine was installed in a high-performance chassis of 126-inch wheelbase. The engine was now optionally available to buyers of the lesser series, so the car's exclusiveness was already weakening. The hardtop, weighing 3,980 pounds and costing $4,427, had textured paint on the roof to give it a grain leather effect. Its production total was 590.

The DeSoto Adventurer Convertible shows the swivel front seats that all Adventurers had. At $4,749, this was the most expensive DeSoto this year. It ranked as the DeSoto of least demand, since only 97 were built. The 4,120-pound car shows the chrome deck lid accent strips that were options for other models. Adventurer standard equipment included TorqueFlite transmission, power steering, power brakes, backup lights and whitewall tires. Exterior body colors were black and pearl white. Generous use of simulated gold accents continued to be an Adventurer trademark.

A milestone was reached during DeSoto's 30th Anniversary year when the two millionth DeSoto was built. Chrysler Corp. President L. L. Colbert, left, and DeSoto General Manager J. B. Wagstaff reportedly applied final touches to the honored car, which came off the line early in 1959. DeSoto built its first million in 20 years and required only half that long to build the second million.

For the first time ever, the Diplomat sported the same front end (and wheel covers) as the senior DeSotos. This was true because the domestic Firesweep front end sheetmetal was identical to the larger cars. This Diplomat-Custom 4-Door Sedan shows the new twin air scoop front styling. The basic body, however, was unchanged from 1957. The body molding was also used on the Custom 2 and 4-Door Hardtops and the Sport Suburban.

Looking into the future, DeSoto probed the use of electro-chemical fuel cells for automotive power. The vehicle proposed for the exotic power was the Cella I, shown as a 3/8-scale model. The serious investigation involved the principle of electrical energy produced by the chemical interaction of hydrogen and oxygen within a cell. The power thus generated would drive four high-speed lightweight traction motors individually geared to the wheels through universal-jointed shafts. Independent wheel suspension and a system of differential speed governors were to coordinate the wheel revolutions. Spent power would be recovered by dynamic braking, which would regenerate current in the cell during normal brake usage. Reversing the field current flow would reverse car direction. Advantages were silent operation, maximum acceleration and traction, fewer moving parts, a flat floor and the conservation of petroleum products, the latter of which is of critical importance today. Project Cella I, which indicated a possible Cella II later, never reached a prototype stage.

The Diplomat Club Sedan sported a brand-new fin and rear deck treatment, plus larger oval taillights — all, of course, identical to comparable Plymouth models. The five other DeSoto Diplomat body types included the Business Coupe, 4-Door Sedan, 4-door DeLuxe Suburban, 2-door Commercial Utility, and Taxicab. A single horizontal rub molding was standard. V-8 models had a gold "V" on the deck lid next to the DeSoto script.

With the change in the fin angle on wagon models, this DeSoto Diplomat-DeLuxe Custom Suburban now more closely resembled the other cars in its rear end styling, although the taillights were unique. This molding treatment was also used on the DeLuxe Convertible Coupe, 4-Door Sedan, Club Sedan, 2-Door and 4-Door Hardtops, and Commercial Utility. Just 2,364 Diplomats were built in 1959: 1,309 Sixes and 1,055 V-Eights.

The most glamorous Diplomat ever was this Adventurer Convertible Coupe, DeSoto's version of the Plymouth Sport Fury. This beauty boasted a spare tire imprint on the deck lid and individual front seats which swiveled outward when either door was opened. Alas, only 22 of these cars — 8 Convertibles and 14 2-Door Hardtops — were built, the first and last Adventurers in the Diplomat line. Standard engine was the 318 c.i.d. Fury V-8 with Power-Pak, with the 361 c.i.d. Golden Commando V-8 optional.

The big news from Chrysler Corp. was the Valiant compact car, which helped to improve the corporation's respectability in an industry which produced over 19.7% more passenger cars during this calendar year than it did in 1959. Chrysler's share of the industry total rose to 15.22%, reflecting a production increase of more than 38.1%. In overall computations, Valiant production was combined with Plymouth's, which scored a gain of better than 17.1% over the previous year. The rise was not enough to keep Plymouth in the industry's 3rd position, which was lost to the Rambler by a margin of only 1,776 cars, pressing Plymouth down to 4th place. DeSoto suffered a smothering compression caused by a shocking drop in demand which cut its production to 51.5% less than its 1959 total and lowered it to the industry's 14th position.

Chrysler's experiments with small cars of its own design began at least 26 years before the Valiant went into production, but the development program which produced the Valiant did not stem from any earlier exploration. Begun as Project A-901 in May of 1957, concentrated effort to bring the little car to reality got underway in mid-1958. During the final surge of development, 32 prototypes were handbuilt for testing which rolled up a total of more than 750,000 miles. In addition, 57 engines were built and rigorously tested.

During the final detailing phase, a name was sought. Within styling and engineering activities, "Falcon" had been used in verbal references to the car, but eventual word of Ford's selection of that name for its own compact ended its use. Finally, five names, including "Valiant," were chosen from a list of thousands and submitted to 2,017 automobile owners across the country, and the majority preference ended the search for a name. For this first year only, the Valiant was a distinct brand, emphasized by Chrysler Corp. publicity which boasted six separate brands of passenger cars built in the U.S.: Plymouth, Dodge, DeSoto, Chrysler, Imperial and Valiant.

Further pointing up its independence, promotional media boldly stated that it was "Nobody kid's brother, this one stands on its own four tires—." So it was not a Plymouth Valiant, nor any other brand's Valiant. And it rated equal status with others when the new Plymouth-DeSoto-Valiant Division was created.

Built in Dodge plants, Valiants were sold by dealers who sold Plymouths. Valiant was the answer to domestic and export demands for compact-size cars. Since 1955, sales of imported small cars had risen at an alarming rate while exports of American cars dropped off sharply. Valiant sales success was immediate. In step with its individuality styling was distinctive and unlike any other car. It bore an abundance of engineering newness, too. Unitized body construction was based on a wheelbase of 106.5 inches. Sedans, when measured in overall inches, had a length of 184, height of 53.3 and width of 70.4. Suburbans were generally a trifle larger.

One 6-cylinder engine design, first intended to be made mostly of aluminum, was common to all Valiants and could be had with the standard 3-speed manual transmission with floor shift or an optional pushbutton-operated 3-speed automatic similar to TorqueFlite. Torsion bar front suspension and asymmetrical leaf-type rear springs were used. Tire size was 6.50 x 13, fitted to 13-inch wheels. Power steering and power brakes were options. Valiant was presented in two series known as V-100 and V-200, each having a 4-door Sedan and a 4-door Suburban, the latter available in 2 and 3-seat versions. The V-100 was designated Series QX1-L and the V-200 was QX1-H.

Plymouth presented all-new designs with unitized body front-end structures but kept former wheelbases of 118 inches for all but Suburbans, which rode on 122 inches. A new Fleet Special series, with 6 and V-8 engines and 2 and 4-door sedans for taxicab companies, was inserted at the bottom of the series roster. Next above it was the Savoy line, which in V-8 form was the Series PP2-L with

The first production Valiant is shown as it neared the end of the line in the Dodge Hamtramck plant. It was greeted by L. L. Colbert, Chrysler's finger-pointing board chairman, and other executives. Chrysler called the Valiant a distinct brand of car, not related to Plymouth, DeSoto, Dodge or the others. However, the new baby remained in that status for this year only. The center-confined grille idea would be common by 1977.

The V-100 series was Valiant's economy line. The V-100 4-Door Sedan was Valiant's lowest-priced and lightest model, being priced at $2,053 and weighing 2,635 pounds. A total of 52,788 were built. Externally, the series was identified by a lack of bright trim molding on the lower body sides and the rear fenders. Deliberately, the new Valiant styling concept was created to make it different from any other car of its time.

two models. The Belvedere V-8, PP2-M, had three models and the V-8 Fury PP2-H offered four. The V-8 Suburban line, PP2, comprised six models. A Sport Fury series did not appear this year. All but the Fury Convertible, Sport Suburbans and 9-passenger Custom Suburbans were available with 6-cylinder engines, for which the primary series designation was PP1. It is interesting that the economy six could be had in more models this year.

After many years of service, Plymouth offered the familiar L-head 6-cylinder engine no more. In its place was the new 30-D Economy Six, the same slanted design as used by Valiant but with a 4.125-inch stroke and 225-cubic-inch displacement which produced 145 horsepower at 4,000 r.p.m. A new V-8, the SonoRamic Commando, was added as the top engine option. Featuring sweeping 30-inch intake manifolding and dual 4-barrel carburetion, its bore and stroke of 4.25 x 3.38 inches, displacement of 383 cubic inches and 10.1:1 compression ratio provided 330 horsepower at 4,800 r.p.m. The Golden Commando 395 and Fury V-800 with Super-Pak were continued unchanged and were again optional. The standard V-8 engine remained the Fury V-800, which was not changed in specifications or power.

Plymouth no longer had an overdrive transmission. Manual 3-speed units were standard for all models, but a new heavy-duty design was specified for SonoRamic and Golden Commando engines. TorqueFlite was now an all-model option and PowerFlite could be had for all V-8s except the two Commandos.

DeSoto, experiencing rough going in its struggle for survival, could offer only two series for 1960. Gone were the Firesweep and Firedome. The Fireflite, Series PS1-L, was now the low-cost series, priced about where the Firesweep would have been. The Adventurer, Series PS3-M, no longer a luxury/sports specialty, was in a price bracket just below the Fireflite of 1959. Each series had three like models, and no convertibles or station wagons were offered. All cars rode on a 122-inch wheelbase and 8.00 x 14 tires. Styling and construction were completely new, featuring Chrysler's new Unibody structural design which joined the body unit to the front frame assembly in a unitized manner. It was featured by all but Imperial.

The Fireflite's standard engine was the Firesweep Turbo-flash V-8 of 1959, while the standard Adventurer power-plant was the same as the former Firedome had. The latter engine was now available with two power-packing options. One was called the Adventurer Mark I, utilized a 4-barrel carburetor, developed 325 horsepower at 4,600 r.p.m. and could be ordered in all models. The other, known as the Ram Charge, used dual 4-barrel carburetion with long ram induction manifolding, delivered 330 horsepower at 4,800 r.p.m. and was available for Adventurer cars only.

DeSoto now required a special order when a buyer wanted a car with manual-shift transmission. Obtainable on Fireflite cars only, it was not at extra cost. Unless ordered with the manual, Fireflites were built with either of two extra-cost units, PowerFlite or TorqueFlite. The latter continued as the only unit used in the Adventurer series. Neither DeSoto nor Plymouth repeated the rear-end air suspension option of 1959.

A new body rust and corrosion preventative method was used by Plymouth, Valiant and DeSoto. It involved a multi-step spray-and-dip process of alkaline cleanings and phosphate and zinc emulsion coatings. Sill innards were additionally coated with a virtually unmeltable wax. The system's development was spurred by excessive rusting of cars built during the past few years.

To bring its cars to the point of production, Chrysler Corp. spent 350 million dollars for design, development, new tooling and plant rearrangement necessary for new assembly techniques required by the Unibody designs. The Valiant program alone was said to have cost 100 millions.

Shown is the Valiant engine, which was shared with Plymouth, whose specifications differed from Valiant. Engineers approached this development program from a new angle, giving the engine a 30-degree slant toward the car's right side. The tilted block, first of cast-iron but changed to aluminum in midyear, allowed a long-branch intake manifold and accessories on the left side, in turn presenting a lower hood potential. The in-line Six overhead valve engine had wedge-shape combustion chambers. As the standard for Valiant, it had a bore and stroke of 3.4 x 3.125 inches, displacement of 170 cubic inches, compression ratio of 8.5:1 and developed 101 horsepower at 4,400 r.p.m. For a V-200 option, 4-barrel carburetion and 10.5:1 compression provided 148 horsepower at 5,200 r.p.m. Also new this year was the alternator, which obsoleted the generator. Obscured by the fan in this view, it was not featured by Plymouth or DeSoto.

The Valiant V-100 Suburban was available in two versions. The 2-seat vehicle, of which 12,018 were built, weighed 2,815 pounds and cost $2,365. The 3-seat model was priced at $2,488, weighed 2,845 pounds and was Valiant's least popular model, totalling 1,928 built. Valiant Suburbans were not placed in a separate category, such as the Plymouth practice, but shared the V-100 and V-200 series designations with the Sedans.

Valiant styling was distinctive and attractive, and did not include the use of tailfins. The simulated spare wheel cover on the deck was calculated to add class. Of the three new compact cars introduced this year, some industry observers opined that the Ford Falcon was conservative and practical, Chevrolet's Corvair rated special note because of its rear engine, while Valiant was the stylish one. Seen is Valiant's best seller, the V-200 4-Door Sedan, of which 106,515 were built. It weighed 2,655 pounds and cost $2,130.

Doors opened to a full 70 degrees, allowing plenty of access to any Valiant interior. The V-200 4-Door Sedan shows styling that was typical of all Valiants, differing only in minor respects. Six persons could be seated and seat cushions were a comfortable height from the floor. Headroom was about 33.5 inches. Three color choices were available for V-200 interiors, in which seat material was nylon faced while bolsters and doors were of grained vinyl. V-100 interiors were only in shades of gray.

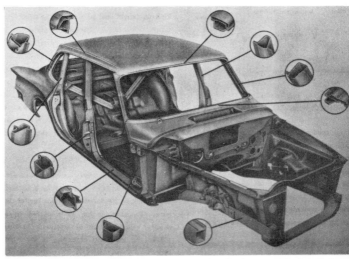

Valiant's unitized body construction is shown with detailed cross-section cuts to define significant structural members and points. Since this all-welded concept eliminated a chassis in the conventional sense, it was designed to allow lowering the unit over the engine, drive train and suspension components on the final assembly line. Over 5,300 spot and seam welds were used in this "monocoque" construction. The result was a unit of exceptional strength, in accordance with the Valiant name which was derived from the Latin word "valere," meaning strong. Plymouth and DeSoto employed a similar concept known as Unibody, in which the welded front end structure was bolted to the body proper.

The Valiant V-200 Suburban shows the bright side moldings typical of all V-200 Valiants. The 2-seat model, of which 16,368 were built, cost $2,433 and weighed 2,855 pounds. The 3-seat car, of which 4,675 were built, was the heaviest and costliest Valiant, weighing 2,860 pounds and selling for $2,566. In references to Suburban seating capacity, Valiant always noted the number of seats rather than the number of passengers. This fact hinted that Valiant would not admit that passenger capacity, particularly in the 3-Seat Suburban, was a bit shy of the nine that a Plymouth Suburban could carry. Valiant's rear-facing third seat was adequate for two adults, making the vehicle an 8-passenger car. With all but the front seat folded down, cargo space was 72 cubic feet. Suburbans shared a 106.5-inch wheelbase with the Sedans.

One of the early Valiants was turned into an interesting semi-fastback coupe. The 4-passenger 2-door car, created by Ghia in Italy, was of unusual design. Unique were the forward-thrusting parking lamps, from which the front fender crowns flowed rearward. The windshield and pillars were severely backswept. Louvers were applied to the depressed hood center. Above the grille center were what appear to be the numerals 250, and offside was a Chrysler nameplate.

The Valiant-based Ghia creation, which showed no evidence of a Valiant name, had a Chrysler nameplate on the rear as well as the front. The sleek coupe had two rear windows widely separated by sheetmetal and extensively wrapped around the sides. Rear lamps were in the sculptured housings that abruptly terminated the peaked rear fender crowns. The rear bumper stretched almost to the wheels, and was given further emphasis by means of a concave sheetmetal treatment above it.

This was Plymouth's most popular car this year, amassing a total of 51,384 units built. In V-8 form the Savoy 4-Door Sedan weighed 3,500 pounds and cost $2,429. It was also available as a Six. Savoy models had no nameplates. The dart-like ornament on the tailfin was the new Plymouth emblem introduced in 1959 and destined for at least a 19-year run. Shown here tipped on its side, it normally pointed upward when on the grille and other places. The abstract shape symbolized Plymouth, replacing the Mayflower ship.

The Plymouth Belvedere 2-Door Sedan was built as a Six or V-8 and marked up a total of 6,529 units produced. The V-8 car weighed 3,505 pounds and cost $2,508. The three tailfin ornaments did not symbolize anything, but were part of the Belvedere decor. Other Belvedere trim included extension of the tailfin peak molding to the car's front, plus a molding on the frontal brow and diagonal "hook." For all Plymouths of less than 9-passenger capacity, the standard tire size was 7.50 x 14, with 8.00 x 14 optional.

Called "The Solid Plymouth" because of its new Unibody construction, the four series had fresh styling. The most predominant newness was at the front end, where winglike brows swept back to hook around odd-shaped wheel openings in the front fenders. Shown is the Savoy 2-Door Sedan, the lightest and lowest-priced Plymouth offered to the public. Offered as a Six or V-8, 26,820 were built. The V-8 weighed 3,490 pounds and cost $2,379.

This view of the Plymouth Belvedere 4-Door Sedan shows the more integrated rear bumper design. At the ends, it was shaped to conform to the rear lamp assemblies. The new tailfins were higher than previously, and rear fender wheel cuts were lower, giving even more mass to rear fender appearance. Production of this model amounted to 42,130 units. When built as a V-8, it weighed 3,520 pounds and cost $2,559.

The Belvedere 2-Door Hardtop is shown with an optional Sky-Hi rear window that extended well forward. The huge piece of glass was also featured on the similar Fury model. Total Six and V-8 production of this model was 14,085 units. As a V-8, it weighed 3,505 pounds and was priced at $2,580. Like all Plymouths, except Suburbans, it rode on a wheelbase of 118 inches.

All slicked up for its picture was the Plymouth Fury 4-Door Sedan. Offered as a Six or V-8, it attracted a total of 21,292 sales orders. As a V-8 it weighed 3,550 pounds and cost $2,694 in standard form. It is shown with accessory bumper grille bar, side mirrors and a chrome stone shield behind the front wheel. The 2-tone paint scheme, with roof and front fender areas in contrasting color, was also optional.

The Plymouth Fury 2-Door Hardtop drew a total of 18,079 orders. In V-8 form its weight was 3,535 pounds and its price was $2,718. It also could be had as a Six. No Plymouth model offered any external means of identifying it as a Six or V-8. The car shown had what was called a Sport Deck, including the spare wheel impression. Also shown is a standard rear window which was unsuual for this car. The high-back driver's seat was a standard Fury feature, and swivel front seats were available.

A total of 9,036 orders were filled by the Plymouth Fury 4-Door Hardtop, which was available as a V-8 only. The car tipped the weighing scale at 3,610 pounds and exacted a price of $2,775. It featured a rear window glass that extended rather high. Plymouth offered four V-8 engines of 230, 260, 305 and 330 horsepower.

Just the car for a drive to the sandy shores was the Plymouth Fury Convertible. Offered only as a V-8, the 3,630-pound car sold for $2,967. It drew a total of 7,080 sales. It sported the standard Fury side trim which, in addition to Belvedere trim, included sill moldings, much chrome on rear fender skirts and large round medallions on the tailfins. Curiously, the car shown had no Fury namescript on the front fender. Perhaps it was a pre-production prototype car for which the item was not yet available.

Parked in the snow was a Plymouth DeLuxe 2-Door Suburban. Available with a Six or V-8 engine, the Savoy-like vehicle accounted for a production total of 5,503 units. The V-8 model recorded a weight of 3,870 pounds and a price of $2,721. It was built only as a 6-passenger car. All Suburbans rode on a 122-inch wheelbase and 8.00 x 14 tires.

Appearing rather standard was the Plymouth DeLuxe 4-Door Suburban, of which a total of 18,482 came out of the factories in Six and V-8 form. It was provided only as a 6-passenger vehicle. When built as a V-8, it recorded a weight of 3,890 pounds, while a price of $2,787 was asked. The DeLuxe Suburban series offered a choice of 15 colors.

Shown is a Plymouth Custom 4-Door Suburban. In 6-passenger form, of which 17,308 were built, it could be had as a Six or V-8. The V-8 version weighed 3,890 pounds and cost $2,880. Built as a V-8 only was the 9-passenger version which weighed 4,000 pounds, cost $2,990 and accounted for 8,116 units manufactured. The example shown had the top V-8 engine option, the 330-horsepower SonoRamic Commando, indicated by the special nameplate on the front fender. Other extras seen on the Belvedere-class vehicle are a bumper grille bar, a side mirror and a chrome stone shield behind the front wheel.

The third seat of Plymouth's 9-passenger Suburbans was fairly easy for adults to get in and out of, especially with the aid of the handgrips on the rear pillars. Shown is a Sport Suburban. A high-back driver's seat was standard in all Sport Suburbans, and swivel front seats could be ordered. Note the fuel filler cap just below the nearest pillar. All Suburbans had them in that location, while passenger cars placed them behind the rear license plate.

Available in V-8 form only were the Plymouth Sport Suburbans. The 6-passenger model was the least-popular Plymouth this year, drawing a total of 3,333 sales. Its weight was 3,895 pounds and its price was $3,024. As a 9-passenger, it was Plymouth's heaviest and most costly vehicle for the year, weighing 4,020 pounds and costing $3,134. The 9-passenger version accounted for a production of 4,253 units. The Sport Suburbans were Fury-class vehicles.

Demand for Plymouth taxicabs had grown so large that a new Fleet Series was set up this year to include them. Known as the Plymouth Special Cab, they were built as a Six or a V-8 with special factory-installed taxi requirements and features. If buyers did not want the Special Cab, they could get more regular Plymouths with one of three equipment packages. Plymouth tried to have something for everyone.

Shown is a Plymouth 4-Door Suburban equipped with two cots for police emergency use. When not needed, the cots could be removed and the vehicle's three seats used in a normal manner. Suburbans were not part of the Fleet series, but 2-door and 4-door sedans for police use were included. Police vehicles, for which a full range of engines and equipment were offered, did not have the Savoy name but were of that class.

Plymouth again lent itself to Chrysler's unrelenting gas turbine experiments. The newest Chrysler Turbine Special utilized a Fury 4-Door Hardtop to show turbine feasibility for normal passenger car use. Chrysler also displayed its turbine-powered futuristic Turboflite show car and Dodge 2½-ton truck when the Turbine Special was first publicly demonstrated early in 1961. A new CR2A engine powered the Turbine Special. Its major advance was a variable nozzle system that helped fuel economy, provided engine braking power and greatly improved acceleration. The 140-horsepower turbine provided vehicle performance comparable to that of a 200-horsepower piston engine, and with equal fuel consumption. It also was smaller and lighter than a conventional engine of like power.

A new Idea Car this year was Plymouth's XNR, for which the designation was derived from the name of Exner, Chrysler's chief stylist. On a modified Valiant chassis, the styling was asymmetrical, having the upper design feature off-center and in line with the driver. The main mass, of fuselage shape, was topped by a gently rounded form that tapered to become a tailfin, interrupted only by the cockpit. The bumper-grille idea would reappear on 1971 Plymouths. The car seated two, having a flush cover and pop-up racing windshield for the passenger seat. It had a 106.5-inch wheelbase and 46-inch overall height. It was first fitted with a Valiant 101-horsepower engine, to which later modifications resulted in 250-horsepower. On the test track it hit 150 m.p.h.

After showings and test runs, the Plymouth XNR eventually was sold to a butcher in Geneva, Switzerland. Reportedly, it later went to the Shah of Iran. Thanks to the National Geographic magazine for May, 1969, it is shown while then owned and driven by auto distributor Anwar al-Mulla in Kuwait, a small Middle East oil-producing country. The XNR was more fortunate than some experimentals, which were destroyed after their purpose was served. However, others also were sold, generally in foreign countries.

DeSoto presented only two series and a total of six models this year. The most popular car was the Fireflite 4-Door Sedan, of which 9,032 were built. At $3,017, it also was the least expensive, and it shared low-weight honors with another model, weighing 3,865 pounds. DeSoto suffered a general down-grading this year. The two surviving series had less class importance than previously, and no convertibles or station wagons were offered.

The DeSoto Fireflite 2-Door Hardtop, which attracted 3,494 orders, weighed 3,885 pounds and cost $3,102. Hardtops were no longer known as Sportsman models. Any DeSoto could be ordered with the optional swivel front seats and 2-tone paint. The bright moldings on the sill and wheel cutouts, however, were a Fireflite option but were standard on Adventurer models. The Fireflite and Adventurer series were reduced to a 122-inch wheelbase this year.

This was the least popular DeSoto this year. The Fireflite 4-Door Hardtop went to only 1,958 buyers. They paid $3,167 for it. The 3,865-pound car was adequately powered when equipped with the standard Fireflite engine of 295 horsepower, and was an agile performer with the extra-cost 325-horsepower engine. DeSoto offered an array of options of all kinds. Certainly no prospective buyer turned away from DeSoto because of a lack of tempting choices.

The Adventurer was no longer a high-performance specialty car with prestige. Now a 3-model series, it included the 4-Door Sedan, which brought 5,746 orders. DeSoto priced the 3,895-pound car at $3,579. The small round objects on the lower bumper were rubber-tipped guards, an Adventurer standard that was optional for Fireflites. The Adventurer moved quite well with the standard 325-horsepower V-8, a bit better with the optional 330-horsepower job.

The Adventurer 2-Door Hardtop was the heaviest DeSoto this year, weighing 3,945 pounds. Upon payment of $3,663, it went to 3,092 buyers. The car shown should have had bumper guards. Adventurers were identified by nameplates on the tailfins, Fireflites had no series signatures. DeSoto's all-new styling expressed much motion in the long sweeping tailfins which now started near the windshield. However, the grille height and sag-center bumper gave a heavy appearance to the front end.

The costliest DeSoto this year was the Adventurer 4-Door Hardtop, priced at $3,727. The attractive automobile, of which 2,759 were built, weighed 3,940 pounds. Wheel covers were standard on Adventurers, optional for Fireflites. Both series had 8.00 x 14 blackwall tires as standard, 8.50 x 14 whitewalls at extra cost. After five years of production, during which it held a cherished position, this year saw the last of the DeSoto Adventurers.

EC-1108-5
12-9-57

This DeSoto styling exploration in clay was underway late in 1957 as a possible design theme for 1960 production. Its side treatment had some of the character of the Cella I, DeSoto's Idea Car proposal shown in 1959. The tailfin was an extension of a line that began at the hood front. The front end was extensively projected ahead of the wheels, providing a very long hood, a feature that would be popular throughout the industry some 15 years later. The uninterrupted highlight from the headlamp cavity to the rear end gave an illusion of considerable vehicle length. Elliptical concave sculpturing of the wheel areas beautifully emphasized the wheels but would have been mud and stone catchers on the road. A number of other theme explorations were underway at the same time.

No, it's not a Dodge Dart – it's a DeSoto Diplomat-Custom 4-Door Hardtop. This year the Diplomat was not based on the Plymouth, but instead on Dodge's all-new Dart. Except for nameplates and side trim, the Diplomat line was identical to the Dart. For the first time, no attempt was made to incorporate any DeSoto identity into the front end styling. The Custom line included a 2-Door Hardtop, neat Convertible Coupe and a 4-Door Sedan.

The Diplomat-DeLuxe 4-Door Sedan illustrates the one place where the designers threw in a little DeSoto feeling – the body side molding treatment, which closely resembled that used on the 1957 DeSoto Fireflites. This area could also be painted a contrasting color if desired. All DeLuxe and Custom models featured a raised seat back behind the driver. A 2-Door Hardtop, Club Sedan, and 4-Door Station Wagon were also available in the DeLuxe series.

Except for the body side moldings, this Diplomat 4-Door Station Wagon was a Dart all the way. No 2-door wagons were offered. New this year were unitized body construction and a 225 c.i.d. inclined Six. A special engine, the 383 c.i.d. Super D500 V-8 with Ram Induction, was optional on Diplomat police cars and the Diplomat-Custom series. Diplomat, Dart, DeSoto, and Dodge all shared the same basic instrument panel in 1960-61.

After two years of going upward, this was a year of decline which dropped the industry volume to a level about equal to 1959, representing a reduction of 17.6% in passenger car production. Chrysler Corp. fared twice as poorly, having a production loss of almost 36.4% and falling to 11.76% of the industry total. Plymouth, even with Valiant included, lost nearly 35.9% and sank to 7th position. DeSoto production did not extend into this calendar year.

This year, Valiant became a sub-series under the Plymouth name, erasing its initial status as a separate brand. Reportedly, the step was taken so that Valiant production figures would be included in overall totals regularly reported by Plymouth, which needed them to bolster its position. In 1960, Falcon production was added to Ford car line totals and the Corvair was a part of Chevrolet's reports, since both of the compacts bore their parents' nameplates. Chrysler had proudly placed Valiant on an independent pedestal in 1960, so the transition to a junior series Plymouth was made quietly and tactfully. Chrysler never directly admitted to the status change, but this year's Valiants appeared with Plymouth namescript on their deck lids where the Valiant name used to be.

The Plymouth Valiant showed few styling and mechanical changes. The compression ratio was reduced from 8.5 to 8.2:1 for better use of regular-grade fuels. The standard engine was yet 101 horsepower and the 148-horsepower 4-barrel V-200 option continued. Appearing in the spring, the Super 225 option was the 145-horsepower engine used by larger Plymouths. Dealer-installed air conditioning was added to the option list. New body types were the 2-Door Sedan and Hardtop. The Valiant family, designated the Series RV, included the V-100 and V-200 lines, each with three models riding on a 106.5-inch wheelbase and 6.50 x 13 tires.

Plymouth's larger series carried the same names they had in 1960 but were now tagged the Series RP. The Fleet Special, Savoy, Belvedere, Fury and Suburban groups each supplied the same body types as in 1960, even to 6 and V-8 engine distribution. Wheelbases remained at 122 inches for Suburbans and 118 inches for others. Standard tire sizes ranged from 7.00 x 14 to 8.00 x 14, subject to the needs of specific car models. The engine line-up was not changed, nor were dimensions and power output, but some got a reduction in compression ratio. The 30-D Economy Six was cut to 8.2:1, the standard Fury V-800 and the Super Fury V-800 (formerly the Fury V-800 with Super-Pak) were untouched, the Golden Commando 395 was cut to 9:1 and the SonoRamic Commando was shaved a mere trifle to 10:1. The transmission line-up was not altered.

In its last stand, DeSoto was unable to offer much for this model year. Struck down by sagging middle price car demand and unkind rumors of discontinuance since 1957, DeSoto had no strength for survival. The booming market for smaller and lower-priced cars was syphoning buyers from the next higher level. Rumors of an impending DeSoto dropout ran rampant after the homesite was abandoned for less costly quarters in 1958. Placed on the market October 14, 1960, the new 1961 models failed to attract many buyers. A gloomy 30-day watch of sales reports warranted a decision nobody wanted to make. After judicious consideration of all factors, Chrysler reluctantly concluded that production must end by November 30th.

DeSoto had been in business more than 32 years and confidently expected to continue. The 1962 model was in final form and metal prototypes were under construction. In the styling studios were full-size clay proposals from which a 1963 design was to be selected. On paper, stylists had projected DeSoto into 1964 and beyond. Necessarily, engineering had gone forward accordingly. But though domestic passenger car production and planning stopped, DeSoto commercial vehicles continued to be built elsewhere for foreign markets, an operation begun 22 years earlier.

For 1961, DeSoto was reduced to only one series which was designated RS1-L. It was known simply as the DeSoto, having no distinctive series name such as Fireflite, etc. In that sense, DeSoto ironically returned to the basis of its original offering for 1929. The final series was priced the

Becoming a sub-series of Plymouth this year, Valiant was now classified as the Plymouth Valiant. Therefore, the lightest and lowest-priced Plymouth was the Valiant V-100 2-Door Sedan, which weighed 2,565 pounds and cost $1,955. This was a new body type for the Valiant series, and it attracted a total of 22,230 sales. The previous grille was used this year, but was selectively painted black to give it the effect shown.

The Plymouth Valiant V-100 4-Door Sedan, of which 25,695 were built, shows the almost total absence of bright side trim that was characteristic of the economy V-100 line. The side mirror, wheel covers and whitewall tires were options. The standard Valiant tire size was 6.50 x 13. In standard form, this model recorded a weight of 2,590 pounds and a price of $2,016.

same as the Fireflite of 1960, but its model variety was cut to two hardtops only. Exner's stylists worked out a new frontal theme for the basically 1960 cars but it was scorned by many who came to the marketplace to see the Plymouths and Valiants. There was no change in wheelbase and tire dimensions, and no engine options were available. The Turboflash V-8, which powered both hardtops, had the lowest power output of any DeSoto since 1957. Basically the same as that in the previous Fireflite series, its compression was cut from 10:1 to 9:1 and horsepower was down to 265 at 4,400 r.p.m. A 3-speed manual transmission was standard and Torqueflite was the only option.

Recurrent rumors of a DeSoto departure were probably more responsible for its demise than were its price and size. Many observers doubted that DeSoto would enter this model year, and a great many felt that it would be in the form of a luxury compact, if any. But a smaller DeSoto was not seriously contemplated by Chrysler's top management, which was in a shifting movement caused by ill winds at that level.

Now that DeSoto was defunct and Valiant was adopted by Plymouth, the Plymouth-DeSoto-Valiant Division was transformed into a revival of the Plymouth Division. Imperial had problems with its independence, too, and was moved back into Chrysler's Jefferson plant for production of 1962 models, after which its former DeSoto plant was eventually sold.

This year was loaded with top management trouble which were first exposed in 1960 when William C. Newberg was involved in a conflict-of-interest scandal. He was relieved as Chrysler's president after holding office only 63 days. The office was unfilled until midway of this year when Lynn A. Townsend was promoted to it. At the same time L. L. Colbert, under pressure, resigned as board chairman and a committee of top business leaders headed by Pittsburgh banker-industrialist George H. Love assumed the direction of corporate affairs. Late in the year, after the poor reception of 1962 models, Virgil M. Exner resigned as vice-president and director of styling. The famed styling executive, who had sold management a mixture of pleasing and controversial design elements for ten years, fell victim to the lack of enthusiastic public acceptance of his newest creations. After influencing much corporate success and moderate distress as well, he was no longer regarded as an asset. Elwood P. Engel, a Ford executive stylist whose design philosophy was compatible with Chrysler's turn toward less daring artistry, got the job. Engel's safe and sound use of line and form, not fully evident in production until 1965, would prevail into the 1970s.

The Valiant V-200 4-Door Sedan was the most-demanded Plymouth model this year, scoring a total of 59,056 built. The 2,600-pound car cost $2,112. Bright side trim typical of the V-200 line this year is easily apparent. The scene was at the Detroit Zoo, to which Chrysler Corp. had donated two railroad trains some 20 years before the Valiant was built. The locomotives were designed and built by Chrysler, using industrial engines for power. The locomotive shown was named for Walter P. Chrysler.

As seen broadside, Valiant styling had strong horizontal character with a racy touch provided by the curving line ahead of the rear wheel. This year, Valiants of the type shown were called Station Wagons, plain and simple. The renaming was a bit strange, since similar models in other Plymouth series continued as Suburbans. Shown is the Plymouth Valiant V-100 4-Door Station Wagon, of which 6,717 were built. The 6-passenger car cost $2,329 and weighed 2,745. The rear seat was now 4.5 inches wider.

Another new body type for the Valiant series this year was the 2-Door Hardtop. Presented only as a V-200 model, its weight was 2,605 pounds and its price was $2,139. This body was an adaptation of the 2-Door Sedan, which was not available as a V-200 car. The rear side window glass was divided into two parts to allow out-of-sight lowering. A single glass would not have lowered much because of the rear wheel housing. The same conditions applied to the 2-Door Sedan. Hardtop production totalled 18,586 units.

Shown under controlled lighting is the Plymouth Valiant V-200 4-Door Station Wagon. The smart little automobile recorded a weight of 2,770 pounds, a price of $2,425 and a production of 10,794. Valiant Station Wagons, both V-100 and V-200, were built only as 2-seat 6-passenger cars this year. However, some were fitted with a third seat at dealerships. This was a factory arrangement, the bodies and seats having been factory-built for the purpose.

The Plymouth Savoy series offered only two body types, both of which were available as a Six or V-8. Shown is the 2-Door Sedan, of which 18,729 were manufactured. As a V-8 it sold at $2,381 and weighed 3,440 pounds. The front end styling of larger Plymouths reached the ultimate of complexity this year. Uniqueness was the goal and ornateness was supplementary.

This was the most-wanted of the large Plymouths. The Savoy 4-Door Sedan was delivered to 44,913 buyers. In V-8 form it was priced at $2,432 and recorded a weight of 3,465 pounds. Again this year, no Plymouth V-8 had external insignia to distinguish it from a Six. The illustration shows the rear quarter trim molding extended well past the door handles. It is not seen on the Savoy 2-Door Sedan.

The Plymouth Belvedere 4-Door Sedan shows the pronounced concave form at the rear which gave prominence to the plateau-like appearance of the deck. Taillamps, having been recessed since 1939, were once again separate units, this time as long projectile shapes mounted outboard. Backup lamps were located near the license plate. This model, of which 40,090 were built, weighed 3,470 pounds and cost $2,561 when built as a V-8.

This view illustrates Plymouth's approach to the long hood and short deck package concept that would be common to the industry within 15 years. The longer front end had a pronounced forward thrust, emphasized by the strong horizontal character line and a forward-curving wheel opening. The horizontal "ledge" effect was repeated at the rear, where no tailfins were in evidence this year. Shown is the Belvedere 2-Door Sedan, of which 4,740 were built. When built as a V-8, it weighed 3,450 pounds and cost $2,510.

Belvedere exterior trim was mainly constituted in tapered decorative applications on the rear quarters. Belvedere signatures were placed just ahead of them. Plymouth was not extravagant with exterior trim this year. Posing as a sample was the Belvedere 2-Door Hardtop. The factories turned out 9,591 of them as Sixes and V-8s. In V-8 form it recorded a weight of 3,460 pounds and carried a price tag marked at $2,582.

Sitting pretty for the photographer was the Plymouth Fury 4-Door Sedan. It was popular enough to win 22,619 sales orders. Available as a Six or V-8, it registered a weight of 3,515 pounds and posted a price of $2,696 when built in the latter form. It is shown with optional whitewall tires but no dressy wheel covers. It was unusual for any model, especially a Fury, to be seen with standard hubcaps.

The Fury series made use of the tapered rear quarter decor similar to the Belvedere, but added a slanted detail to it and extended a molding to the front quarter panel. Just to the rear of the front wheels, Fury models had distinctive signatures that included the Plymouth symbol. This is the 2-Door Hardtop, of which 16,141 Sixes and V-8s were built. The V-8 car weighed 3,520 pounds and cost $2,720. It was fitted with an accessory bumper grille bar.

Built as a Six or V-8 was the Plymouth Fury 4-Door Hardtop which drew a total of 8,507 orders. The 3,555-pound V-8 was priced at $2,777. All Fury models sported brightly decorative design features applied to the center of the deck and were fitted with chromed taillamps. The high rear glass was standard for this model. Fury 2-Door Hardtops also had an extra-large glass as standard, and it seemed to reach further forward than this one.

The most unwanted domestic Plymouth this year was the DeLuxe 2-Door Suburban. The 6-passenger vehicle accounted for 2,464 units of the total Plymouth production. Available as a Six, or V-8, it recorded a weight of 3,845 pounds and asked a price of $2,723 in the latter form. The DeLuxe Suburban line was classified in the Savoy category.

Since 1958, 2-tone paint schemes had grown more conservative, and Plymouth began this year with the familiar practice of making the roof the predominant feature when 2-toning was wanted. In that respect, Plymouth was consistent with the prevailing industry trend. While most automakers lost sales in an economic cutback this year, Plymouth suffered severely. Dealers asked for something flashy to spark sales. The answer was this 2-tone, called a split-level Sportone, introduced June 1st as an option for Fury models only. A Fury 2-Door Hardtop shows what it looked like.

The Plymouth Fury Convertible, built only in V-8 form, had a production run of 6,948 units. The sporty car weighed 3,535 pounds and cost $2,969. It is shown with some of the options that were also available for other Plymouths. Besides a bumper grille bar, it was prettied up with headlamp trim plates. Made of bright aluminum, they sheathed the upper concave areas around the lamps. Bright moldings extended from the outboard lamps, pointing toward the front wheel openings. Swivel front seats were not offered this year.

Again this year, all Suburbans had a 122-inch wheelbase, while passenger cars employed a 118-inch chassis. Shown is the Plymouth DeLuxe 4-Door Suburban, which reported 12,980 units built as 6-passenger vehicles and with Six and V-8 engines. The V-8 model weighed 3,885 pounds and cost $2,790. Built for Canada only were 74 DeLuxe 4-Door Suburbans as 9-passenger models with Six and V-8 engines. The 9-passenger model was, therefore, the least popular of all Plymouths this year.

1961

Appearing long, substantial and adequate for its purpose, the Plymouth Custom 4-Door Suburban was related to the Belvedere series. The 6-passenger model, of which 13,553 were built as a Six or V-8, cost $2,882 and weighed 3,885 pounds in V-8 form. It was also provided as a 9-passenger car with V-8 engine only, in which case the price was $2,992, weight was 3,985 pounds, and 5,898 were built.

As usual, Plymouth's heaviest and most costly model for the year was the Sport Suburban of 9-passenger capacity, which weighed 3,995 pounds and billed each sale at $3,136. A total of 3,088 were built. The 6-passenger version, which went to 2,844 buyers, registered 3,890 pounds and a $3,026 price. Sport Suburbans were built only as 4-door models with V-8 engines and were regarded as a branch of the Fury series. All 9-passenger Custom and Sport Suburbans were built with V-8 engines because the 145-horsepower Six was not quite adequate for the vehicles when they were fully loaded. For all Plymouths but the exclusively 6-cylinder Valiants, a choice of four V-8 engines was offered. The standard V-8 developed 230 horsepower, while extra-cost versions delivered 260, 305 and 330 horsepower.

The regular-size Plymouth taxicab used the Savoy as a base, with a Six or standard V-8 engine. The cabs, which were part of the Fleet Series, offered operating companies a choice of two equipment "packages" similar to those set up for the Valiant. In all cases, the cabs were specially built, as Plymouth was a master in the art of cab building.

A Plymouth Police Special in the service of the Kentucky State Police is shown at an entrance to the Kentucky State Police Academy. The Fleet Special series tendered three 2-door models. The Patroller 6 had the regular Economy Six engine and 3-speed manual transmission and was standard-equipped with a police-calibrated speedometer and such heavy-duty items as springs and shock absorbers, 40-ampere alternator, 70-ampere battery, seats and floor mats, wheels and a 3.31 ratio maximum duty rear axle. Many options were also offered. The Patroller Special 8 had 230 horsepower as standard, 260 optional. The Pursuit Special had the 305-horsepower V-8 as standard and a special 325-horsepower job as optional, both with a heavy-duty Torque-Flite transmission. Otherwise, all V-8 cars had features like those noted for the Patroller 6.

Plymouth included the Valiant in its taxicab offerings, giving them the standard Valiant 101-horsepower Economy Six engine. The cabs were supplied in two versions. One included the clutch, springs, shock absorbers and seat construction of heavy-duty design, plus a host of other special mechanical and convenience items. The other did not offer the heavy-duty chassis components but provided many other cab necessities.

Plymouth built the Emergency Police Wagon as a 4-door 6-passenger model only. Ideal for a Civil Defense unit or as an emergency ambulance, its second seat folded down to provide over 95 cubic feet of space for carrying supplies and equipment or two regulation-size cots. It was powered by the 230-horsepower V-8 and was otherwise equipped like the Patroller 6.

The last DeSotos built in the U.S.A. presented a new frontal appearance. The "stacked" grille arrangement utilized outstretched headlamp configurations to cradle the upper grille. Parklamps were angularly crowded in between the headlamps and bumper wings. The bumper, of predominant horizontal lines, was pleasing. Some observers found the upper grille distasteful. However, no controversy was aroused and whatever distaste existed was not an important factor in the lack of public acceptance of this model.

The DeSoto 4-Door Hardtop, of which 2,123 were built, weighed 3,820 pounds and cost $3,167. It did not have a high rear window this year, and swivel front seats were not available for this or the 2-door type. This model served double duty, since a sedan was not offered. The full-length side trim now narrowed midway of the vehicle. The car shown was not fitted with optional brightwork on the sill and wheelcuts.

DeSoto presented a single nameless series which offered two models. The lightest, lowest-priced and least popular was the DeSoto 2-Door Hardtop. It recorded a weight of 3,760 pounds, a price of $3,102 and a production total of 911 units. The V-8 engine of 265 horsepower was mounted in a chassis of 122-inch wheelbase. The standard tire size was 8.00 x 14, but optional whitewalls were 8.50 x 14.

This clay exploration, shown when underway in 1958, was one of a number of approaches. As often done in styling, the model served dual purpose by presenting a different version on each side. If one side was selected as a favorite, it was duplicated on the opposite side. The concept shown could have become 1961 DeSoto production had extensive new tooling been planned for the year. Its predominant feature was the long dihedral fin flowing from the front rather than rising toward the rear.

This striking touring coupe was built by Nardi in Turin, Italy for Mr. Simpson of Miami, Fla., who specified its design. Styling of the one-only car called the Silver Ray was executed by Michelotti, famed Italian auto designer. Nardi built the chassis around a Plymouth 305-horsepower V-8 engine and TorqueFlite transmission. It had framework of rectangular-section tubing and independent front suspension employing large coil springs and shock absorbers in oil-bath enclosures. Rear springs were semi-elliptic, front brakes were disc and wheels were 16-inch diameter. The interior featured an adjustable steering wheel and two anatomically-shaped bucket seats. In section, the body was of pronounced dihedral shape. The extremely low car required one and a half years to build.

The Plymouth XNR Idea Car was first shown early in 1960 and continued its showings this year. The car illustrated is not the XNR, but probably was inspired by it. Ghia designed and built this creation, calling it the Asimmetrica. Though based on a Valiant chassis, it was not built for Chrysler. With no Chrysler, Plymouth or Valiant nameplates, it had a Ghia signature on the deck. As evidenced by the conventional windshield and side ventpanes, it was a fabric-top convertible. It had one tunnel-like feature on the driver's side of the hood, though windshield reflection causes an illusion of two. The "tunnel" shape was not resumed at the rear to form a high fin, there being a low fin in line with it. The narrower bumper-grille had two headlamps, the other two lamps being outboard with parklamps below them. Rear end design was much-altered. There is evidence that another Asimmetrica of longer wheelbase was built.

1961 saw the end of both the DeSoto car and the Diplomat series. As in 1960, the Diplomat was simply a Dodge Dart with different trim and nameplates. As with the Dart, the Diplomat received a major front and rear facelift. The result was hardly an improvement, as shown on this Custom 4-Door Hardtop. The Custom line included a 2-Door Hardtop and a 4-Door Sedan, but convertibles were absent in this last year.

In common with Dodge Dart wagons, DeSoto Diplomat wagons were mounted over a 122-inch chassis as on this DeLuxe 4-Door, 3-Seat Wagon. Styling of the rear fin and taillight was identical to that used on the Dodge Polara. The body side molding was unique to Diplomat-DeLuxe and export Dart Pioneer wagons. Only two Diplomat wagons were offered, both 4-doors. The 225 c.i.d. Slant Six developed 145 horsepower.

The Diplomat 4-Door Sedan was also offered as a 2-door model. The rear end design was distinctive, to say the least. Note the DeSoto nameplate plaque just above the license plate, and the Diplomat name on the fins. Without the extra body molding, the Diplomat series looked identical to the Dart. Two V-8s were available, a 318 c.i.d. Red Ram V-8 with 230 horsepower and a 361 c.i.d. Super Red Ram V-8 developing 265 horsepower.

The only other wagon in the 1961 Diplomat lineup was this 2-Seat 4-Door Wagon. The jet-tube taillights were also used on Dart wagons and the entire Dodge Polara series. This fin and taillight treatment looked much better than the smaller fins used on regular models. Diplomat was not the only export DeSoto. There were also the senior cars and the DeSoto "Rebel" based on a Dodge Lancer built in South Africa, plus a full line of DeSoto trucks.

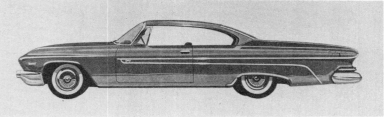

This Diplomat-DeLuxe 2-Door Hardtop sports the unusual reverse fins and aggressive wheel openings. A DeSoto identity was implied by the lower chrome body side molding which angled sharply downward aft of the rear wheel. The resulting area, though resembling the DeSoto color sweeps of the 1950s, was never 2-toned. Note the special medallion on the front door. A DeLuxe 4-Door Sedan was also offered.

For the auto industry as a whole, this was a good year. Passenger car production for the calendar year recorded a rise of more than 25.7% over 1961, bringing it about equal to the 1960 total. Chrysler Corp. did not enjoy such a gain, however, mustering only a 10.5% improvement through the combined efforts of its divisions. Regardless of the modest increase, the corporation's share of total industry production slipped to 10.34%, a loss of 1.42%.

Plymouth's production performance was poor, showing a gain of only about 6.7%. The dismal showing dropped Plymouth from 7th to 8th place in the industry. This was in sharp contrast to the leaders it hoped to emulate. The Ford car line boosted itself over 16% and had no threat to its 2nd position. Chevrolet shot upward almost 35% and retained its No. 1 spot with no challenge. Plymouth's slump in rank was partly due to new Buick popularity which brought the Flint automaker up from 8th to capture 6th place.

The Plymouth Valiant series continued basically as before, with minor styling modifications to identify it as for a new model year. Designated the Series SV, the V-100 and V-200 lines again offered three models each. However, the Hardtop was singled out for special attention and was called the Signet 200. All rode on the unchanged wheelbase of 106.5 inches and had 6.50 x 13 tires as standard. The slanted engine was built in two versions: The standard cast-iron Economy Six of 101 horsepower and the extra-cost aluminum block 145-horsepower Super 225. Revised

camshafts and new engine mounts added to smoothne[ss]

The regular Plymouths were all-new models this ye[ar]. The new styling was more simple than the 1961 series ha[d] shown. Designated the Series SP, three lines were intr[o]-duced in the autumn of 1961. The Savoy line offere[d] three body types, the Belvedere had five and the Fury li[ne] presented six types. Station wagons were not placed in [a] separate group, but were models within the Savo[y,] Belvedere and Fury lines. Added a few months later we[re] two Sport Fury models. Nine models offered Six or V[-8] engines, while seven were built in V-8 form only. This yea[r] all models utilized a new 116-inch wheelbase, two inch[es] shorter than 1961 passenger cars had and six inches le[ss] than the former Suburbans employed. Standard tire si[ze] varied from 14 x 6.50 for 6-cylinder Sedans and Hardto[ps] to 14 x 7.00 for V-8 Sedans, Hardtops and Convertibl[es] and all Six and V-8 Station Wagons. All models could [be] fitted with 14 x 7.50 tires as optional.

Plymouth entered the market with powerplants th[at] should have brought more sales. The inclined 30[°] Economy Six had a bore and stroke of 3.4 x 4.125 inche[s,] 225-cubic-inch displacement, 8.2:1 compression ratio a[nd] 2-barrel carburetor which provided 145 horsepower [at] 4,000 r.p.m. Three V-8 engines were announced. T[he] standard V-8 was the Fury V-800 with bore and stroke [of] 3.91 x 3.31 inches, 318-cubic-inch displacement, 9[:1] compression, 2-barrel carburetor and an output of 2[30] horsepower at 4,400 r.p.m. The same engine became t[he]

For a drive through the country or a leisurely ride on city boulevards, the Valiant V-100 4-Door Station Wagon looked appropriate and served well. Chrysler claimed that any Valiant was more stylish than other compact cars, and that was the opinion of some industry observers, too. Plymouth priced this model at $2,285 and sold 5,932 of them. The smart little 6-passenger car weighed 2,660 pounds.

The least costly Plymouth this year was the Valiant V-100 2-Door Sedan which cost $1,930. It was also Plymouth's lightest model, weighing 2,480 pounds. A total of 19,679 of these economy sedans came off the assembly lines. From this point of view, the new V-100 did not appear to differ from its counterpart of the previous year.

Again, the Plymouth Valiant V-100 line was characteristically devoid of bright trim on the sides. The short molding on the rear quarter panel peak served the practical purpose of hiding a necessary but unsightly panel fabrication area. Shown is a V-100 4-Door Sedan, one of 33,769 to come out of the factories. It weighed 2,500 pounds and cost $1,991.

per Fury V-800 when a 4-barrel carburetor was used,
~~ving 260 horsepower and being an all-model option. The
~~lden Commando had a bore and stroke of 4.12 x 3.38
~~ches, 361-cubic-inch displacement, 9:1 compression,
~~barrel carburetion, delivered 305 horsepower at 4,800
~~.m. and was also optional for all models. The high
~~rformance SonoRamic Commando engine was not avail-
~~le this year.

A new pushbutton automatic 3-speed transmission with
~~uminum case was optionally available for all cars with
~~8 engines. Lighter and more compact, it allowed a lower
~~nt tunnel. All cars, including Valiants, now featured
~~,000-mile chassis lubrication, a new starter motor with
~~eater torque and a printed electrical circuit. Many other
~~inor improvements were built in.

The Unibody structure for Series SP Plymouths now was
~~lled "one-piece," meaning that the welded unit included
~~e front-end section ahead of the cowl. The Unibody
~~inciple, as had been applied to regular-size Plymouths
~~r 1960-61, had secured the separately-welded forward
~~ction to the main unit with bolts.

The predominant Valiant appearance change for the year was
in the grille, which featured a refined texture within a more
costly-looking frame that gave an illusion of more grille
height. The bright-trimmed headlamp frames had an argent
finish rather than the former black. Parklamps were located
in the ends of the under-bumper panel opening, where they
had been on earlier models. Shown is the Plymouth Valiant
V-200 2-Door Sedan, of which 8,484 were built. It weighed
2,500 pounds and cost $2,026.

Valiants had never been offered with a 2-tone paint scheme,
so the old standby device was resorted to as a spring sales-
getter. The measure of success this move achieved is
unknown, but the resulting appearance was tolerable. A
V-200 4-Door Sedan showed off the scheme, which gave
emphasis to the upward curve and flair of the rear quarters.

Valiant rear end styling was altered, presenting a deck with
no spare wheel impression. Lower taillamps were of circular
design and neat caps tipped the rear quarters where taillamps formerly were located. The V-200 4-Door Sedan
shown was the most popular Plymouth this year, drawing
55,789 orders. The 2,510-pound car cost $2,087. V-200
standard trim included the deck ornamentation shown. V-100
models had only the horizontal name plaque on the deck.
Options seen are bumper guards and wheel fittings.

Plymouth differentiated the Valiant Hardtop this year, giving
it a special designation and a number of exclusive features.
Called the Signet 200, its special interior had bucket front
seats. Externally, the grille and headlamp frames were painted
black, the grille having a large medallion at the center.
Bright side trim was minimum, while painted accent strips
toward the front were outlined with thin bright moldings.
The car shown was without a small Signet 200 medallion
normally appearing between the front wheel and door. This
model, of which 25,586 were built, weighed 2,515 pounds
and cost $2,230.

The Plymouth Valiant V-200 4-Door Station Wagon serves to illustrate the side trim that was typical of all V-200 models. The wide lower molding was in contrast to the thinner molding that curved up and flowed to the rear. The 6-passenger car tipped the scale at 2,690 pounds and sold for $2,381. A total of 8,055 were built. Again this year, no 9-passenger Valiants were built.

Shown at the International Automobile Show in Geneva, Switzerland, was this unusual hardtop designed and built by Ghia, who called it the St. Regis. It was based on a Valiant chassis, but was not a Chrysler Idea Car. Most unique was the front end, with the bumper grille well ahead of the wheels to provide a long hood of sports car flavor. Outboard headlamps and parklamps were sheltered by the wing-like front quarters, whose edges flowed uninterruptedly through to the rear end.

All models of the Plymouth Savoy series were offered in Six or V-8 form. Shown is the Savoy 2-Door Sedan, of which 18,825 were built. The V-8 model weighed 3,080 pounds and cost $2,313. The new Series SP almost went into production with an asymmetrical styling flavor. Until tooling-up time, the windsplit "ridge" features on the deck and hood were offside, in line with the steering wheel. When Lynn Townsend became Chrysler's new president, he thought the offside location was too unusual and ordered the features moved to the centerline of the vehicle, where they are seen in the illustrations shown.

SAVOY 4-DOOR SEDAN

The new body side styling of the Series SP featured strong horizontal shapes superimposed on a "no-belt" body form. The "no-belt" term applied to a belt without the familiar "bulge" curving outward and down from the windows. As seen here on the rear door, the sheetmetal surface immediately below the belt was slanted to appear as a continuation of the plane of the window glass. The treatment had appeared on Valiants since 1960. Shown is the Plymouth Savoy 4-Door Sedan, which scored a total of 49,777 built. When built as a V-8 it weighed 3,115 pounds and cost $2,369.

The Plymouth Savoy 4-Door Station Wagon, sold in the U.S. as a 6-passenger car, posted a total of 12,710 built. When built in V-8 form, it cost $2,717 and weighed 3,390 pounds. For Canada, 13 of these were built in 6-cylinder 9-passenger form. All Series SP wagons had impressive length, even though they were on a much shorter wheelbase than were the wagons of 1961. This view clearly shows the extra length behind the rear wheels.

The 2-Door Sedan in the Plymouth Belvedere series chalked up a production total of 3,128 built in Six and V-8 forms. The V-8 model tipped the scale at 3,070 pounds and carried a price tag marked $2,450. This body type seemed to bear the appearance of a coupe rather than a sedan, but this was only an illusion, since it had a 4-door sedan roof and the interior space of that model.

The front end of the Series SP, or regular-size, Plymouth was a horizontal scheme with a pronounced concave delicate-textured grille that incorporated the inboard headlamps and was flanked by large tunnel-like housings for the outboard lamps. Bumpers, no longer massive, were quite thin in appearance. Shown is the Belvedere 4-Door Sedan, of which 31,263 were built as Sixes and V-8s. The V-8 model, of which one was delivered to the author, cost $2,507 and weighed 3,095 pounds.

Posed against a background of solid rock in character with Plymouth's solid construction was a Belvedere 2-Door Hardtop. The Unibody structure of all Plymouths was quite sturdy. This model, offered as a Six or V-8, accounted for a total production of 5,086 units. In V-8 form it recorded a weight of 3,075 pounds and a price of $2,538.

Series SP Station Wagons were eight inches longer than other models, but all shared a 116-inch wheelbase. By comparing this model with the illustration of the Fury 2-Door Hardtop, it is obvious that the extra length was from the rear wheels back. Shown is the Belvedere Station Wagon. In the 9-passenger form shown, the Plymouth Belvedere 4-Door Station Wagon was built only as a V-8 weighing 3,440 pounds, costing $3,071 and accounting for a total of 4,168 units built. As a 6-passenger model, it was offered as a Six or V-8 model, scored a total of 9,781 produced in both versions and recorded a weight of 3,390 pounds and a price of $2,815 in V-8 form.

This view of the Fury 2-Door Hardtop presents the basic Series SP Plymouth passenger car package in profile. The concept, oriented toward a long hood and short deck, was another step in the approach begun by Virgil Exner with the 1961 models. This was at a time when the more successful competitors were going the opposite direction, with hoods that appeared shorter in relation to the extensive length of the decks. The model shown, when built as a V-8, weighed 3,105 pounds and cost $2,693. A total of 9,589 were built as Sixes and V-8s.

The Plymouth Fury 4-Door Sedan was offered with the 145-horsepower Six and a choice of the standard 250-horsepower V-8 or the extra-cost 260 and 305-horsepower V-8 versions. This model's appeal was enough to require production of 17,231 units to meet the demand. The production total included Six and V-8 cars. In 8-cylinder form, the car weighed 3,125 pounds and was priced at $2,670.

Supplied only as a V-8 was the Plymouth Fury 4-Door Hardtop. This attractive model was sold to 5,995 buyers. It tipped the scale at 3,190 pounds and posted a price of $2,742. Plymouth called the new Series SP styling "Forward Flair Design," adding that the accent had moved toward the front of the car, where the longer hood gave an impression of immense power.

Ready for any road was a Plymouth Fury Convertible when caught by a cameraman. The sporty automobile was available only as a V-8. It was one of 4,349 built. The 3,210-pound car was priced at $2,924. Quarter panels of all Series SP cars featured more circular wheel openings, of which those at the rear provided more wheel exposure than the 1961 Series RP had.

After an absence of two years, the Sport Fury series was reinstated about four months later than other Plymouths. Shown is the 2-Door Hardtop, of which 4,039 were built. It weighed 3,195 pounds and cost $2,851. Illustrated are bright trim moldings which extended the belt trim to each end of the car. Placed along the sides of the hood and deck, their purpose was to accentuate the length of the car in one unbroken sweep of brightwork. Earliest Sport Fury models lacked the long belt trim, since it appeared a little later. The 6-lamp arrangement seen on the rear appeared on all Sport Furys and was applied to Fury models, which also received the long belt trim about midyear. Early Furys had a rear lamp setup like that shown on the Savoy 2-Door Sedan, which was also used for Belvedere models. The dress-up was in response to the demands of dealers who complained about the skimpy rear lamps and the lack of a strong car-length design feature.

Built only with a V-8 engine was the Fury 4-Door Station Wagon. The 6-passenger version, of which 2,352 were built, scaled a weight of 3,395 pounds and asked a price of $2,968. As a 9-passenger car, it was the heaviest model offered by Plymouth this year, weighing 3,455 pounds. A price of $3,071 was asked for the 9-passenger model, which went to 2,411 buyers.

The least-popular Plymouth sold in the U.S. this year was the Sport Fury Convertible, for which a low total of 1,516 was recorded as built. This was also the most costly Plymouth for the year, the 3,295-pound car having a price of $3,082. The Sport Fury series was exclusively V-8. An early production example is shown, since no car-length belt moldings are apparent. Sport Furys had special features. Interiors had bucket seats and a front center console. Grilles had black-painted margins to set off the bright vertical ribs. Medallions and wheel covers were of special design, as were many other items. Sport Fury nameplates were placed on the front quarters ahead of the wheels, as well as on the deck lid.

Shown as if doing night duty is a sample Patroller 6, its taillights seeming to glow white. The car had no backup lights. This model offered a 101 or 145-horsepower 6-cylinder engine and was one of the Plymouth Police Specials. Another was the Patroller Special 8 with the 230-horsepower V-8. The top offering was the Pursuit Special, a high-performance 305-horsepower V-8. All were factory-fitted for their respective work.

The Emergency Police Wagon was supplied as a Six or V-8 this year, but again was built only in 6-passenger form. Either a 101 or 145-horsepower 6-cylinder engine could be ordered, while V-8 choices were the 230 and 305-horsepower jobs. All Police Specials were based on the Savoy series. For this body type, the fuel filler cap was located on the left rear quarter, just below the window. A sample vehicle is shown.

Chrysler excited the automotive world with two gas turbine experimental cars this year. One was the Plymouth Turbo-Fury shown and the other was the Dodge Turbo-Dart, both hardtops. Since several Plymouths had been used for turbine testing and publicity in previous years, the Dodge Turbo-Dart was given the starring role this year. It made a cross-country run from New York City to Los Angeles, averaging 52 m.p.h. speed and 17 m.p.g. fuel consumption. From a standing start, the Turbo-Dart accelerated to 60 m.p.h. in less than eight seconds, and its top speed was 115 m.p.h. Since the Turbo-Fury had equal power and drive components, it performed as well. It is seen with car-length belt trim and other side moldings like the Sport Fury series. Signatures on the front and rear quarter panels were distinctive, as were the wheel covers and other special touches. The 140-horsepower CR2A turbine engine required minimal air intake, as evidenced by less air-admittance area above the bumper. The headlamps were of larger diameter than the dual size.

Shown at a railroad station is a Plymouth taxicab sample, one which was built with many special cab features. Also offered was cab equipment for cars that were not so specially built for the purpose. In this view, the Series SP front end is shown to good advantage. The large housings for the outboard headlamps, combined with dominant horizontal character, gave an impression of exceptional width.

Photographed in January of 1959, this styling exploration could have become the DeSoto design for 1962. It had evolved through critical advance phases and become this yet-unfinished full-scale clay model, a stage that many concepts never reached. At this point, the opposite side of the clay form had another version underway for study. The long fin of the concept shown was canted outward, while rear quarters had fins that curled inward toward the fastback rear end. This early step in the movement toward a 1962 design was halted at this stage, outmoded by a decision to abandon fins.

While stylists in the DeSoto studio were working out their own ideas, corporate styling boss Exner had a small group doing secret work in another room. Their express purpose was to develop a basic styling theme to which alterations for individual product identity could be applied by the various car line studios. Shown is Exner's corporate concept when presented in May, 1959. A full-scale clay model of a convertible type, it bore a rear placard with the designation DS-62. The long hood/short deck package featured shallow-V lower lines at the front and rear, the front end form extended well into the doors, odd folded-back rear quarters with intrusions into the window area, and very thin bumpers. For this basic purpose, foil was not applied to simulate brightwork.

By September of 1959 the "parent" concept had undergone changes in the rear quarters and DeSoto stylists had given distinctive identity and a finished appearance to the mockup automobile. However, numerous ideas had been tried on the concept before reaching the final detailing shown. Junior stylists called the double-sweep rear quarter design a "chicken wing." In this final form, the upper sweep tapered and diminished toward the deck, as seen on the sedan which also shared its front end design with this convertible. Contrary to the long horizontal attitude of the front end, the short deck sloped at an approximate angle of 18 degrees. Small round rear lamps were in groups of three and the bumpers, made heavier, were horizontal with a center step-down. The convertible had Starflite series signatures and insignia.

DeSoto intended to offer this Adventurer 4-door sedan for 1962. It is seen in mock-up form as it appeared in February, 1960. Details that differed from the Starflite were the smartly unique 2-toned roof, a bright molding on the front quarter and door, special wheel covers, Adventurer signatures and distinctive medallions. The 1962 frontal design arranged the headlamps in an offset and canted manner. The grille had thin horizontal vanes between the bright members seen. Parklamps, invisible here, were in the bumper's outer and lower sections. Nine months after this photo was made, Chrysler terminated DeSoto passenger car production only weeks after 1961 models appeared. The DeSoto name continued on foreign commercial vehicles, however. One 1962 metal prototype was built before the stop order ended the program. The basic concept was to be shared with 1962 Chrysler and Imperial cars, but the whole plan was cancelled by top management.

The momentum gained by the automobile industry in 1962 gradually lost speed this year. Regardless of the slowing down, the industry rose to its second best year to date. Passenger car production was over 10.1% greater than 1962, making this the best year since 1955. The industry was now in the middle of a 4-year period of rising fortunes.

After registering only meager gains in 1962, doing less than half as well as the industry, Chrysler Corp. turned the tables this calendar year. Its improvement was well over four times greater than that of the industry. The corporation zoomed to a whopping increase of more than 5.1%, moving its share of industry production from 10.34% to 13.72%. Plymouth did even better, pushing itself up almost 50%. In doing so, the corporation's breadwinner climbed from 8th to 5th position on the industry ladder, scrambling over Rambler and Buick, who were not climbing as fast.

The fantastic measure of success enjoyed by Chrysler Corp. was due to several factors. President Lynn Townsend and an aggressive top management team won much new public respect for the corporation. An important move was the creation of a new corporate image, symbolized by a 5-sided Pentastar hallmark. A new 5-year/50,000-mile warranty was given with new cars, the first time any automaker had backed up his products so strongly. The Plymouth Valiant, Dodge Dart and Chrysler cars appeared in all-new styling that was more palatable to public taste. Other car lines, basically carryovers from the previous year, were given extensive facelifting that was more in conformity with public demand.

The format of the new styling was necessitated by competitive requirements. No longer could the corporation afford to risk designs that were aimed at setting new trends. The new and more conventional direction, seeming to reflect a "me too" intention, was tuned to the taste of the buying public but allowed some room for innovation. Virgil Exner, after setting aside some of the design principles he loved so dearly, directed the development of these new cars in 1960-61. He gave them his characteristic finesse as well as some elements that were not quite of "me too" flavor. After Exner's resignation late in 1961, successor Elwood Engel had time to apply some finishing details to the cars.

The new Valiant was designated the Series TV (T for the model year and V for Valiant). The economy line was again the V-100 with three models. The V-200 now had four models rather than three, and the Signet 200 came in two versions rather than one. Of unitized construction, all rode on a 106-inch wheelbase and 6.50 x 13 tires. Continued was the slanted 6-cylinder engine, which in 101-horsepower form was again the standard powerplant. It was also available as the Super 225, a 145-horsepower option.

The "parent" Plymouths, designated the Series TP, continued the previous four lines. The Savoy line was increased from three to four models, while the Belvedere remained at five. Six choices were again offered in the

Seen in the all-new styling garb for the year is the Valiant V-100 2-Door Sedan. The new design had a beltline crease that extended through the length of the car. At the front, the crease folded and trailed back at an odd angle. The body form now had a definite "ledge" at the bottom of the windows and, in fact, through the entire belt. The lightest and lowest-priced Plymouth this year, this model weighed 2,515 pounds and cost $1,910. A total of 32,761 were built.

The Plymouth Valiant V-100 4-Door Station Wagon, of which 11,864 were manufactured, was again supplied only as a 6-passenger vehicle. It recorded a weight of 2,700 pounds and was listed at $2,268. All Valiants had a Valiant name plaque at the front center of the hood, but only Station Wagons and Convertibles had a similar piece on the side, as seen between the front wheel and door.

Shown in absolutely standard form is the Valiant V-100 4-Door Sedan. No fancy wheel covers, no whitewall tires or any other extras. It tipped the weighing scale at 2,535 pounds and posted a price of $1,973. The practical little automobile accounted for a production total of 54,617 units. The new Valiants presented a functional appearance that was quite appropriate for a compact car.

This was the most-sought and most-bought Plymouth model this year, but only by a slim margin. The Valiant V-200 4-Door Sedan attracted a total of 57,029 sales. The popular car exacted a price of $2,097 for each sale. The bright applique between the deck lid and bumper was part of the standard V-200 trim. Bumper guards were an all-Valiant option, as were the whitewall tires. It scaled 2,555 pounds.

New for Valiant this year was the convertible body type. The first example is shown as it rode on conveyor belts through the final inspection line. This V-200 Convertible led a flow of 7,122 of its particular kind from the factory. On the market, the 2,640-pound car sold for $2,340. For the first time, Valiant this year had only two headlamps and they were larger than the dual size.

The Signet 200 was again the high-class Valiant, having special features of its own. The 2-Door Hardtop, of which 30,857 were built, weighed 2,570 pounds and was priced at $2,230. DeLuxe wheel covers and backup lights were among standard Signet 200 items of equipment. Made available after December 1, 1962, was a textured vinyl roof option for this model. It was Plymouth's first offering of a vinyl roof.

Fury line and the Sport Fury was again available in on two models. Nine models could be ordered with Six V-8 engines and eight were exclusively V-8 cars. The 11 inch wheelbase was retained, but all cars now were fitt with 14 x 7.00 tires as standard, while 14 x 7.50 w optional.

Only one 6-cylinder engine was offered for the Seri TP. It was the slanted 30-D Economy Six of 145 hor power. The V-8 engine line-up was altered for this ye but the standard remained the Fury V-800 of 318 c.i. and 230 horsepower. The lowest-cost option was known the Commando 361, having a bore and stroke of 4.12 3.38 inches, 361 c.i.d., 9:1 compression, 2-barrel carburet and an output of 265 horsepower at 4,400 r.p.m. T top V-8 option was the Golden Commando 383 with bore and stroke of 4.25 x 3.38 inches, 383 c.i.d., 10 compression and 4-barrel carburetion, which turned o 330 horsepower at 4,600 r.p.m. The extra-cost V-8 engin were available for any TP model.

Among new features this year were amber turn sign lights as standard equipment and fully transistoriz radios as optional.

In this instance, the catalog artwork did not make the V-200 side trim clear. A thin bright molding capped the beltline crease from front to rear, but not the whipped-back extension above the front wheel. Shown is the Valiant V-200 2-Door Sedan, which accumulated a total of 10,605 sales. When equipped in standard form it registered a weight of 2,515 pounds and carried a $2,035 price tag.

Plymouth built 11,147 of these Valiant V-200 4-Door Station Wagons. Weighing 2,715 pounds, they were priced at $2,392 and were of 6-passenger capacity. Station wagons had a small V-100 or V-200 plaque on the pillars between the rear doors and quarter windows. All Valiants had horizontal taillamps, but the wagon lamps were not like others, the reason being that they had to be located clear of the tailgate.

1963

Posing for a Chrysler Corp. picture that included new Dodge cars was a Plymouth Valiant Signet 200 Convertible. The flashy little car, of which 9,154 were built, weighed 2,675 pounds and cost $2,454. This and the V-200 Convertible were built with manually-operated tops unless ordered with the optional powered top. Not visible in this view, Signet 200 nameplates were within the "hairpin" turn of the crease line on the front quarter panels.

The new regular-size Plymouths, designated the Series TP, were basically a new "skin" over the 1962 framework structure. All models with a rear deck seemed to be noticeably longer than 1962 models, especially from the rear wheels back. However, overall length was only three inches greater. The lengthy impression was created by two design factors. First was the rearward slant of the rear end to make the deck longer and thereby depart from the former long hood/short deck concept. Secondly was the crease line that swept through the full length of the vehicle, becoming more pronounced toward the rear in order to further emphasize length at that end. Showing off these characteristics is the Plymouth Savoy 2-Door Sedan, of which 20,281 were built in Six and V-8 form. The V-8 model weighed 3,200 pounds and cost $2,313.

The Savoy 4-Door Sedan illustrates the stark simplicity of the Savoy series. Devoid of bright moldings for distinction, this was the only series with a Plymouth signature on the side. Other series placed their series signatures there. The short bright molding on the tip of the rear quarter panel concealed a panel fabrication seam. This model nearly captured honors as Plymouth's most popular car for the year, recording a production total of 56,313 units. Offered as a Six or V-8, it weighed 3,220 pounds and cost $2,369 when built in the latter form.

Series TP wagons were only one-tenth of an inch longer than 1962 wagons and were 4.9 inches longer than other 1963 models, the latter dimension relating to the area aft of the rear wheels. The Savoy 4-Door Station Wagon was offered as a Six or V-8 in both 6 and 9-passenger form. This was the first year for a 9-passenger offering in the least-expensive regular-size series. The 6-passenger car, of which 12,874 were built, weighed 3,475 pounds and cost $2,717 when built as a V-8. As a 9-passenger, the production total was 4,342, while the weight and price of a V-8 model was 3,560 pounds and $2,318.

The Plymouth Belvedere 2-Door Sedan is shown in purely standard form. The long bright trim molding, characteristic of all Belvederes, served to accentuate length without the aid of color within the molding. Note the Belvedere signature just ahead of the door. Not all Belvedere models offered a choice of Six or V-8 engines, but this one did. A total of 6,218 were built in both forms. As a V-8 it weighed 3,215 pounds and cost $2,450.

With their high performance and agile handling qualities, Plymouths were winning laurels in stock car racing events. This California car was fitted with special wheels and wide tires at the rear and was without hubcaps. Seen accelerating in a trial run is a Belvedere 2-Door Hardtop. For normal use, this model was supplied as a Six or V-8. A total of 9,204 were built. In standard form, a V-8 cost $2,538 and weighed 3,190 pounds.

The Plymouth Belvedere 4-Door Sedan displays its roof in a manner favorable to comment. Its rear quarters were of "blind" character, not featuring a wraparound rear window as had been the practice for several previous years. The rear glass was curved, however. This roof was used for all Series TP sedans and hardtops. The model shown, of which 54,929 were built in Six and V-8 form, weighed 3,235 pounds and cost $2,507 when built as a V-8.

Offered only as an 8-cylinder automobile this year was the Belvedere 4-Door Station Wagon. As a 6-passenger vehicle it weighed 3,490 pounds, cost $2,815 and brought a total of 10,297 purchase orders. The 9-passenger version, which scaled a weight of 3,585 pounds and listed a price of $2,917, recorded a production total of 4,012 units. All wagons had exhaust tailpipes that projected low, as seen here.

Seen in a lumber yard is a Fury 4-Door Sedan. This fancy-fitted car was offered to fleet buyers as well as to everyone else. Plymouth assembly lines turned out 31,891 of them to meet the total demand. It was built with either a Six or V-8 engine, according to the buyer's choice. An overwhelming majority of buyers chose a V-8 which, if ordered in standard form, cost $3,265 and weighed 2,670 pounds.

The Fury 2-Door Hardtop displays trim that was common to Fury models. The band of brightwork across the rear and the wide side molding was similar to Sport Fury treatment. This model, of which 13,832 Sixes and V-8s were built, weighed 3,215 pounds and cost $2,693 as a V-8. Taillamps for the Series TP were of distinctive squarish shape and backup lights flanked the license plate recess. Obvious in this view, especially in the door panel, is the concave sculpturing of the belt.

The grille and headlamp assembly of Series TP Plymouths was neatly nestled in a recessed manner. The projecting front quarters were slightly canted and were fitted with elliptical housings for the parking and turn signal lights. The Fury Convertible, of which 5,221 were built, weighed 3,340 pounds and cost $2,924 in standard form. It was exclusively a V-8 car. The example shown was fitted with the top-option Golden Commando 383 engine, as indicated by a small plaque below the Fury signature on the side.

The Plymouth Fury 4-Door Hardtop is seen here at a roadside picnic table. It appeared equally appropriate when parked at the entrance to an exclusive shop or concert hall. This car was not available with a 6-cylinder engine. It recorded a weight of 3,295 pounds, a price of $2,742 and a production total of 11,887 units. This body type was available only in the Fury series.

An impressive vehicle was the Fury Station Wagon, built only in V-8 form. The 9-passenger version, shown with optional roof rack, rear pillar assist handles and wind deflectors, was the heaviest Plymouth this year. In standard form it weighed 3,590 pounds and was priced at $3,071. It went to 3,368 buyers. As a 6-passenger car it weighed 3,545 pounds, cost $2,968 and was the least popular Plymouth for the year, garnering only 3,304 sales orders.

Appearing long and lovely was this Sport Fury 2-Door Hardtop when a cameraman came by. The three "marks" on the roof blind quarter were individual diecastings with chrome framing for red, white and blue paint. Those and the bright sill molding were among special touches applied to the Sport Fury series. The model shown, of which 11,483 were built, weighed 3,235 pounds and listed at $2,851. All Sport Fury cars were built only as V-8 automobiles.

The Sport Fury Convertible was Plymouth's most expensive offering for the year, listing at $3,082. The 3,385-pound car had a production run of 3,836 units. The example shown had the lowest-cost V-8 engine option, the Commando 361, identified by a special plaque below the Sport Fury signature just ahead of the door, at the narrowing of the side molding. Series TP convertibles had power-operated tops as a standard feature. The distinctive hood ornament on all Series TP cars was fixed in the vertical position shown.

Shown under way in a typical stock car race sponsored by USAC (United States Auto Club) is a car driven by Norm Nelson, who entered two Plymouths in the USAC racing circuit this year. In the 16-race season, Plymouths won six, finished second seven times and had the fastest qualifying time in six races. For that record, Chrysler-Plymouth Division was given the annual USAC Manufacturers' Award. A new 426 hemi-head maximum-performance V-8 engine was supplied in limited numbers by Plymouth, who was out to capture honors in speed and acceleration events. The 426 c.i.d. engine delivered up to 425 horsepower when fitted with 13.5:1 compression, dual 4-barrel carburetion and short ram manifolding. It was not available to average buyers.

Plymouth offered a wide variety of models to fleet owners. Especially built for the various jobs to be done, they were purchased by taxicab companies, police departments and an endless variety of commercial firms. Shown is the Fleet Special Savoy, a very basic offering. Other Savoy models, as well as Belvedere, Fury and the three Valiant series were offered for special services. Engine types were as required for specific models and tasks.

This car is seen in a hard turn at the Riverside International Raceway in California. The event was sponsored by the Nationwide Consumer Testing Institute, which made the rules, hired the drivers, supplied the officials and supervised the competition. For the testing event, the Insittute purchased comparably equipped Plymouth Fury, Ford Galaxie 500 and Chevrolet Impala V-8 models directly from dealer showrooms. They were made test-ready by dealer mechanics. The Plymouth's performance won more points than the others. Plymouth had already established a hard-to-beat track reputation in 1962.

Placed on display in February was the Plymouth Satellite, a one-only show car. The 4-place convertible had an array of interesting features. Front and rear seats were of bucket design, and a full-length center console had a tachometer up front. A hard-finish plastic cover for the top well fitted flush with the rear deck and was formed into twin nacelles for the rear seat headrests which appeared to be faired into the deck. The car was painted iridescent blue, with pearlescent blue and shell white leather upholstery and all-wool deep pile carpeting.

The Valiant was tested in competition with other car makes of its class. A stock V-100 is shown on the course at the Riverside Raceway. On its door is the insignia of the Nationwide Consumer Testing Institute, sponsor of the event. The purpose was to find out what comparable models, selected at random from dealer showrooms, could and could not do. A comparison with factory claims was also made. The Valiant fared well.

For the calendar year, the automobile industry was stabilized in its production of passenger cars, registering an increase of 1.33%. Chrysler Corp. did much better, its car divisions piling up a production gain of more than 27.8% over the previous year. The surge of vitality was largely responsible for moving the corporation from 13.72% of the industry total to 15.82%, a share it had not enjoyed since 1957. However, some of Chrysler's gain was due to the losses of Chevrolet, Cadillac, Rambler and Studebaker. Plymouth scored a production gain of about 15.1%, rising from 5th to 4th place in the ranks of automakers. In so doing, Oldsmobile was ousted from 4th because it mustered a very small gain for the year. In the 1-2-3 spots were Chevrolet, Ford and Pontiac, in that order.

The continued success of Plymouth rode on corporate measures taken the previous year, plus a performance image that had been taking shape on race tracks and drag strips across the country. Also of assistance, though moderate, was the expansion of the Valiant series by adding the Barracuda and a V-8 engine.

The Valiant cars, now designated the Series VV, were modified versions of the design introduced new for the previous year. Placed on the market in the autumn of 1963 were the three familiar lines. The economy V-100 line presented three body types, the V-200 had four and the Signet 200 offered two. Continued was the slant-6 engine of 101-horsepower standard and 145 optional, both with compression raised to 8.5:1. The 106-inch wheelbase and 6.50 x 13 tire size were also retained. New options were a "4-on-the-floor" transmission with Hurst linkage and a Sure-Grip differential.

Placed in production in December of 1963 was a V-8 engine for the Valiant series. It was an option for all models. Not actually a new design, it was a hybrid of Plymouth's 318 c.i.d. engine, modified with changes to adapt it to the limitations of compact-size cars. An important factor was engine weight, which was reduced 90 pounds by various means. Of the total reduction, about 40 pounds were taken from the block alone by the use of thin-wall casting techniques. A new intake manifold concept cut off 12 pounds. The manifold, having intake chambers on one level rather than the conventional over-and-under layout, also reduced engine height. Chromium alloy cast iron cylinder heads, the same as those used on the 361, 383 and 426 c.i.d. engines, were employed primarily because of their space-saving size.

The Barracuda made its appearance about April 1st. For this first model year of the compact fastback, it was definitely a Valiant, though having much character not shared with the others. In addition to the Barracuda and Plymouth names, it bore the Valiant signature and V-shaped blue/red Valiant emblem. Also designated the Series VV, it was based on the Valiant wheelbase and chassis components. Its standard and optional engines were like those offered for other Valiants, as were its transmission choices.

Registered as the Series VP, the parent Plymouths were the second revision of the basics that were introduced for '62. This year's sheetmetal alterations were not as extensive as those of 1963, as that year established a theme that was a sales success, so it was continued. The model line-up was exactly the same as for 1963. Respective series and number of models were: Savoy, four; Belvedere, five; Fury, six; Sport Fury, two. Six or V-8 engines could be had in nine models, while a V-8 was the only power for eight models. All rode on the previous wheelbase of 116 inches and tires of 14 x 7.00 standard size or 14 x 7.50 optional.

The Series VP retained former engines and catalogued a new super-version. At the low end of the line was the 30-D Economy Six of 145 horsepower. The 230-horsepower 318 was again the standard V-8. The 265-horsepower Commando 361 and 330-horsepower Commando 383 were continued as V-8 options, while at the top of the catalogued list was the new Commando 426 of 365 horsepower for "street" or normal use. Not catalogued nor offered to the public were two hotter versions of the 426 engine. These maximum-performance powerplants were among the mightiest stock engines in the land. Revving up 415 and 425 horsepower, they could be termed "the wild ones." Sold only to qualified performance specialists, they were for the competition cars that brought fame to Plymouth.

The transmission line-up for the Series VP was expanded. The 3-speed manual continued as standard, with the push-button automatic 3-speed TorqueFlite optional for all models. New for the Sport Fury only was an optional floor-mounted stick selector for the TorqueFlite. The big news was the extra-cost "4-on-the-floor" manual gearbox designed and built by Chrysler, utilizing Hurst linkage.

Among mechanical changes were a self-cleaning valve for the closed crankcase ventilation, a variable-speed fan for V-8 engines in air-conditioned cars and a 2.1-inch wider rear track to make it about equal with the front.

Retaining its traditional rank as Plymouth's lightest and lowest-cost model was the Valiant V-100 2-Door Sedan, which weighed 2,540 pounds and cost $1 921 in 6-cylinder form. The overall Six and V-8 production total for this model was 35,403 units. All V-100, V-200 and Signet 200 models offered a 6-cylinder engine as standard and a V-8 as optional. Weights and prices of those models are quoted for 6-cylinder cars only, since such records of comparable V-8 cars were not found in available research material. However, it is certain that any model equipped with a V-8 cost $131 more than a Six.

The new Valiant grille was a simple horizontal design constituting one assembly and extending from headlamp to headlamp. The plain motif was relieved by the slightly forward-offset center portion and a fairly large circular frame for the emblem. The V-100 4-Door Sedan accounted for a production total of 44,208 units, of which a 101-horsepower Six went to the author to serve as a second car. This model weighed 2,575 pounds and cost $1,992 when built in standard 6-cylinder form.

The Plymouth Valiant V-100 4-Door Station Wagon, of which 10,759 were built, weighed 2,725 pounds and cost $2,273 in standard Six form. Cars of this body type had the Valiant signature on the front quarter panel, since there was not room on the body "C" pillar, where sedans and hardtops carried the name on a trim strip. Wagons had small V-100 or V-200 plaques on their narrow "C" pillars.

Of middle-class Valiant appeal was the V-200 2-Door Sedan, which recorded a weight of 2,545 pounds and a price of $2,044 as a standard Six. It attracted a total of 11,013 sales orders. This year, full wheel covers were standard equipment on V-200 as well as Signet 200 models, optional for V-100. Whitewall tires were an all-Valiant option.

Plymouth's most popular car was the Valiant V-200 4-Door Sedan, which had a production run of 63,828 units. In standard Six form it cost $2,112 and weighed 2,570 pounds. All Valiant sedans and hardtops had a new roof which featured a bevel edge from front to rear, but the former overall vehicle height of 53.4 inches was unchanged. New bumpers of deeper section extended further from the vehicle, making all Valiants two inches longer this year. Seen here as a white dot just under the lower bright trim molding on the front quarter panel is the Pentastar, the new emblem of Chrysler Corp. Of 5-sided shape and gold-like finish, it was placed on the curb side only. It appeared on all Chrysler-built automobiles until the 1973 series.

The Valiant V-200 Convertible, of which 5,856 were built, shows off the vertical taillamps that were typical of all Valiants this year. Also seen is the Valiant emblem at the center of the deck. This emblem was introduced with the 1960 Valiant. Instrument panel trim and the bright applique above the bumper were standard on all V-200 and Signet 200 cars. Front and rear bumper guards were an all-Valiant option. This model weighed 2,670 pounds and cost $2,349.

The Valiant V-200 Station Wagon was as useful for a fishing trip as for other pleasures and tasks. In standard form it weighed 2,730 pounds and was priced at $2,388. It had a production run of 11,146 units. The vehicle shown was made more practical by having an optional roof rack. All Valiant Station Wagons were built in 6-passenger form only.

Shown as a V-8 car is the Valiant Signet 200 Convertible. From the external point of view, only a V-8 emblem identified V-8 cars. It was located on the sides near the cowl, on all models but the Barracuda. The new engine began finding its way into cars about January 1st, about four months after 6-cylinder Valiants went on sale. By the end of the 1964 manufacturing program, it had accounted for 15.5% of total Valiant production, including Barracuda. The Signet 200 Convertible, of which 7,636 were built as Sixes and V-8s, weighed 2,690 pounds and cost $2,473 in standard 6-cylinder form.

The smartly different Barracuda took its bow in the springtime. It bore the Valiant signature at the lower right corner of the deck lid, and an encircled Valiant emblem was at the top center of the deck lid, besides having Plymouth and Barracuda names located elsewhere. Therefore, it was in fact a Plymouth Valiant Barracuda, but for this model year only. Aimed at the sports-minded youth market, it was designed and fitted accordingly. The 5-passenger interior had bucket seats in front and a bench-type rear seat of simulated bucket design. The foldable rear seat and other innovations provided a long flat floor for cargo. The fastback design was a daring step for Plymouth, as fastbacks had lost public favor some years before. The rear glass, of 14.4 square feet area, was the largest of its kind ever used on a standard production car. The hardtop shown was a V-8, indicated by the V-8 emblem which, on the Barracuda, was located near the headlamps. The V-8 car weighed 2,905 pounds and cost $2,496 in standard form. The wheels shown cost extra. A total of 23,443 Barracudas were built. About 90.5% of them were V-8s.

Seen with one of two roof options is the Signet 200 2-door Hardtop. A vinyl-covered roof, offered in 1963, was again available in black or off-white, and for this model only. New to the Valiant this year was the offering of 2-tone roof paint colors for this and other models. Part of the Valiant's facelift for the year was a new hood which provided design detail to which the new grille was related. In standard form the model shown weighed 2,600 pounds and cost $2,256. Its production run was 37,736 cars. Not offered in the U.S.A. was a V-200 2-Door Hardtop, of which 3,312 were built and recorded as Canadian.

Valiant Signet Convertible

In addition to a new roof and fastback deck, the Barracuda had new front quarter panels which brought the belt crease forward in a more level attitude and folded it back in a nearly parallel fashion. The crease change forecast the pattern for 1965 Valiants. The front end featured a center grille flanked by wide openings in which a single bar and turn signal lamps were set. The overall height of the 6-cylinder car shown was 53.7 inches and the V-8 was 53.9, a bit higher than Valiant's 53.4-inch sedans and hardtops and 53.1-inch wagons. Overall length was 188.2 inches, equal to the sedans and hardtops and 6-tenths of one inch less than wagons. Shown are Barracuda standard wheel covers with simulated knock-off hubs.

The parent Plymouths, Series VP, appeared noticeably longer than those of the previous year, but their overall length was only about 1.5 inches greater. Shown is the Savoy 2-Door Sedan. Like all cars of the Savoy Series, it was available with 6-cylinder or V-8 engines. This model had a production run of 21,326 units. In V-8 form its weight was 3,205 pounds and its price was $2,332.

Plymouth boasted that Valiants equipped with the V-8 engine were America's lowest-priced V-8 cars. The overhead-valve engine had modified wedge-shape combustion chambers. It had a bore and stroke of 3.63 x 3.31 inches, displaced 273 cubic inches, had a compression ratio of 8.8:1 and was fitted with a 2-barrel carburetor. The perky powerplant delivered 180 horsepower at 4,200 r.p.m. Cars equipped with this engine also had a higher-output alternator, 7.00 x 13 tires and heavy-duty construction of standard or automatic transmissions, torsion bars, rear springs, shock absorbers, driveshaft and rear axle.

All Plymouths but the Barracuda featured a car-width grille/headlamp frontal appearance, which was the prevailing industry trend. It was based on the design philosophy that the excessive use of brightwork across the front gave a wider and more impressive appearance, which also was an important sales factor. Shown is the Savoy 4-Door Sedan, of which 51,024 were built. As a V-8, it weighed 3,210 pounds and cost $2,388.

Shown rounding a corner on a rain-swept street is a Plymouth Belvedere 2-Door Sedan. The improved torsion bar front suspension would keep it nearly level in the turn. A total of 5,364 examples of this model came from the factories. As a V-8 it had a weight of 3,210 pounds and a price of $2,466. Excepting wagons, the Belvedere series offered a choice of Six or V-8 engines. The new and more massive front bumpers on Series VP cars had built-in turn signal lamps. Likely the new bumper accounted for the slightly increased overall length of this year's big Plymouths.

Any Plymouth, and particularly Series VP models, was capable of towing sizable boats, trailer homes, etc. Because of their ability to carry many extra things, wagons were especially useful for towing. Shown with options is the Savoy 4-Door Station Wagon. A total of 12,401 6-passenger types were built, of which those built as standard V-8s weighed 3,495 pounds and cost $2,728. The 9-passenger version, which drew 3,242 sales, was the least popular Plymouth this year. When built as a basic V-8 it weighed 3,600 pounds and cost $2,829. All Series VP wagons had a new roof, windshield and cowl.

After having wide blind quarters on all hardtop models in 1963, this tapered design for 2-door cars was quite a departure. It gave a light and airy appearance to the sporty cars. From this point of view, the Belvedere 2-Door Hardtop shows off the new roof quite well. This model accounted for a total production of 16,334 Sixes and V-8s. The V-8 version sold for $2,551 and recorded a weight of 3,190 pounds.

All Series VP sedans were given a new roof with a bevel-edge design feature through the length of the roof. The bevel added crispness that is obvious in this view. Also, the roof had no slight visored effect above the rear glass, as had been featured in 1963. It was an inch higher, increasing overall vehicle height to 55.1 inches. This Belvedere 4-Door Sedan weighed 3,225 pounds and cost $2,524 in V-8 form. Total Six and V-8 production was 57,307 units.

The Plymouth Belvedere 4-Door Station Wagon is seen in standard form except for the dressed-up wheels. The lengthy-looking vehicle was available only as a V-8, and was offered with two seating arrangements. As a 6-passenger car it weighed 3,510 pounds, cost $2,826 and was delivered to 10,317 buyers. The 9-passenger version, of which 4,207 were built, cost $2,928 and tipped the scale at 3,605 pounds.

Shown with standard side trim for the series is the Fury 4-Door Sedan, which could be ordered with a 6-cylinder or V-8 engine. A total production of 34,901 was recorded. As a V-8 model it sold for $2,680 and recorded a weight of 3,230 pounds. Series VP cars were offered in optional 2-tone colors, the roof being done in a harmonizing hue. In that case, the chrome trim at the bottom of the blind quarter provided a nice cover-up for the color division line.

The Fury 2-Door Hardtop gave buyers a choice of Six or V-8 engines. They placed 26,303 orders for both kinds. The V-8 model swung the weighing scale pointer to a reading of 3,215 pounds and posted a price of $2,706. The new roof appeared quite thin from this angle. Series VP 2-door hardtops were of 54.4-inch overall height, 7-tenths of an inch lower than 4-door models. Rear bumper guards were accessories.

The Fury Convertible certainly gave its occupants much more and longer-lasting pleasure than they were about to get from the ice cream vendor's product. The car was offered only in V-8 form. Costing $2,937 and weighing 3,345 pounds, a total of 5,173 came out of the factories. This car is shown with an accessory bumper guard. Unlike the rear guards, which were vertical, it was a horizontal rail with a rubber insert serving as an impact buffer.

The new roofs for all large Plymouths were in conjunction with a new windshield and cowl. The slightly more vertical windshield glass was curved more like a true arc. Cowl sheetmetal did not curve up to meet the windshield, which now extended down to meet the normal cowl surface instead. The rear window was also brought down to meet a revised deck panel. The Fury 4-Door Hardtop, built only as a V-8, had a production run of 13,713. Its weight was 3,300 pounds and its price was $2,752.

The Fury 4-Door Station Wagon was built as a V-8 only. Shown in addition to other accessories is a roof rack, rear assist handles and wind deflectors. In 6-passenger form it weighed 3,530 pounds, cost $2,981 and had a production run of 3,646 vehicles. As a 9-passenger car it recorded a 4,482-unit production total and sold for $3,084, and at 3,630 pounds was Plymouth's heaviest model for the year.

The new hardtop roof for 2-door models had a definite forward thrust. Unlike 4-door models, on which rear quarter panels rose to join the blind quarters in a flush mating, the 2-door's tapered quarters were slightly offset, seeming to sit on top of the modified rear quarter panels which permitted a clean sweep of line through the car's entire length. All Series VP cars had new quarter panels at the front. The exclusively V-8 Sport Fury 2-Door Hardtop, which weighed 3,270 pounds and cost $2,864, had a production run of 23,695 units.

Again the most expensive Plymouth for the year was the Sport Fury Convertible, which sold for the sum of $3,095. Like its hardtop mate, it was presented only as a V-8 automobile. A total of 3,858 of these 3,405-pound beauties came off the assembly lines. Sport Fury models were fitted with simulated knock-off wheel hub attachments.

Shown in a manner emphasizing the manual 4-speed transmission for this and other engines is the Commando 426, a "street" version offered as optional for the Fury and Sport Fury series. It had wedge-shape combustion chambers, bore and stroke of 4.25 x 3.75 inches, 426 cubic inch displacement, 10.3:1 compression and one 4-barrel carburetor. Developing 365 horsepower at 4,800 r.p.m., it was Plymouth's most powerful offering to the general public this year.

Announced in February were Plymouth's Super-Commando 426 maximum-performance V-8 engines. Featuring hemispherical combustion chambers, dual rocker-arm shafts and an entirely new valve train, they had a bore and stroke of 4.25 x 3.75 inches, were of 426 c.i.d. and had more effective ram induction manifolding. Shown is the engine for sanctioned closed-circuit stock car racing. Having a single 4-barrel carburetor and 12.5:1 compression, it produced 400 horsepower at 5,600 r.p.m. At top track speed, racing observers claimed this engine put out at least 600 horsepower. A similar engine for supervised drag racing had two 4-barrel carburetors and was supplied in a choice of two power outputs. One had 11.0:1 compression and a horsepower rating of 415, while the other with 12.5:1 compression rated 425 horsepower. Both power ratings were at 6,000 r.p.m. The Super-Commandos were so powerful that Chrysler had to have new dynamometers which could absorb 600 horsepower at 10,000 r.p.m. in order to test them.

One of the maximum-performance V-8 engines for competition events only was the Super Stock 426. Having wedge-shape combustion chambers, bore and stroke of 4.25 x 3.75 inches, 426 c.i.d., two 4-barrel carburetors and short ram intake manifolding, it was offered in a choice of two power outputs. One had 11.0:1 compression and developed 415 horsepower at 5,600 r.p.m. The other had 12.5:1 compression and delivered 425 horsepower at 5,600 r.p.m. These engines had overhead valves with conventional tappets.

With the fury of a bomb, the Super-Commando engine flashed to fantastic victories in its debut in the NASCAR Daytona 500 race in February. Plymouths finished 1-2-3, driven by Richard Petty, Jimmy Pardue and Paul Goldsmith, in that order. That ended a string of 10 consecutive Ford victories in NASCAR races of 500 miles or longer. Petty and his No. 43 car, in winning by more than a lap, set a new 500-mile stock car record of 153.34 m.p.h. He lapped the field twice, setting a new stock car lap record in excess of 175 m.p.h. and for the last 50 miles averaged nearly 170 m.p.h.

Another Plymouth bomb hit in February, this one at Phoenix, Ariz. The event was the Winternational Drag Championships sponsored by the American Hot Rod Association. Hayden Proffitt drove a Super Stock 426 to a top speed of 122.64 m.p.h., with an elapsed time of 11.8 seconds for the quarter mile. He won the title of "Mr. Top Stock Eliminator" in this first half of the "Winter World Series" of drag racing.

Plymouth's spectacular February onslaught to rock the stock car racing world included a hammering blow delivered in the second half of the "Winter World Series" of drag racing at Pomona, Calif. Tom Grove rammed a Super Stock 426 to win the annual National Hot Rod Association Winternational Drag Championship. Sizzling to a top speed of 124.13 m.p.h. and a quarter-mile elapsed time of 11.63 seconds, he somehow managed to beat out another 1964 Plymouth Super Stock.

In a 4-event series called "Test Track, U.S.A." staged by the Nationwide Consumer Testing Institute, Plymouth took nearly all honors. Against comparable Ford and Chevrolet models, Furys won 10-out-of-10 at Sebring Grand Prix Course and 9-out-of-10 at Indianapolis Raceway Park, Watkins Glen Grand Prix Race Course and Riverside International Raceway. For testing things that consumers buy cars for, like acceleration, handling, fuel economy, braking, etc., the Institute bought cars at random from dealer showrooms and had dealer mechanics ready them for testing. The Institute supplied all test personnel.

Not all Plymouth victories were for speed, acceleration, endurance, handling, etc. For the 8th consecutive year, Plymouth won a class championship in the annual Mobil Economy Run. But this year it was a double victory. In Class E, for full-size 6-cylinder cars, a Savoy finished on top with an average fuel consumption of 29.2955 m.p.g. Top honors in Class F, for full-size 8-cylinder low-priced cars, went to a Savoy V-8 for averaging 22.1963 m.p.g.

Plymouth's show car for the year was the Satellite II. Built on a standard production chassis, the car featured a black vinyl-covered roof section which could be removed, leaving a chic landau rear canopy. The interior was fitted with four bucket seats, was trimmed in leather and nylon fabric and had hand-rubbed walnut appointments and a full-length center console.

This was a tremendous year for the automobile industry, which rocketed to an all-time production record. At the end of the calendar year, a gain of better than 20.5% was registered for passenger cars. Chrysler Corp. also had a record year, earned with a production increase of about 7.2%. Chrysler slipped a bit in its industry standing, however, losing 0.31% to end up with 15.51% of the industry total. The share loss was due to vigorous activity of General Motors and Ford.

Plymouth production was up almost 19% over 1964, giving it the second-best year in its history. Chrysler's breadwinner just could not come within reach of its best record, which was set in 1955. But Plymouth easily held its No. 4 rank among all automakers.

An extensive marketing plan was instituted by Plymouth, providing broader coverage with more models. At the low end of the price list was the Valiant Series AV, of which the 100 line had three models, the 200 had four and the Signet had two. All continued the 101-horsepower Slant-Six engine as standard, with the 145-horsepower Six optional. Two V-8 options were available. The previous 180-horsepower V-8 was offered for all models. A hot new Commando 273 could be had only in 200 and Signet models. It had the standard V-8's bore and stroke of 3.63 x 3.31 inches and 273 c.i.d., but utilized 10.5:1 compression, a 4-barrel carburetor and other features to develop 235 horsepower at 5,200 r.p.m. The facelifted Valiant continued on the 106-inch wheelbase and standard tire sizes of 6.50 x 13 for Sixes and 7.00 x 13 for V-8s.

The Barracuda, in a transitional move toward self-identity, discarded the Valiant name but retained the Valiant emblem and shared the AV series designation. The standard Barracuda offered a choice of the 145-horsepower Six, 180-horsepower V-8 and the 235-horsepower Commando 273. A new Barracuda Formula S competition package was added. It included special chassis components, the Commando 273 engine and distinctive decor.

The former 116-inch wheelbase cars were facelifted to become a middle-sized Plymouth series this year. Designated the Series AR, they were aligned as the Belvedere I line of three models, the Belvedere II line of five and a new Satellite offering of two. In standard form, Belvedere I and II models had the 145-horsepower Six or 180-horsepower V-8, while four V-8 options were available to the public. The weakest was the 318 (numerical designations mean c.i.d.) of 230 horsepower. Next was the Commando 361 with bore and stroke of 4.12 x 3.38 inches, 9:1 compression, 2-barrel carburetion and 265 horsepower developed at 4,400 r.p.m. Putting out 330 horsepower at 4,600 r.p.m. was the Commando 383 with bore and stroke of 4.25 x 3.38, 10:1 compression, a special camshaft and one 4-barrel carburetor. The top public offering was the Commando 426 with 4.25 x 3.75 bore and stroke, 10.3:1 compression, special cams, one 4-barrel carburetor and 365 horsepower developed at 4,800 r.p.m.

The Satellite line offered no Six, had the 273 V-8 as standard, plus the 318, 361, 383 and 426 options. The Series AR also could be built with a maximum-performance 426 Hemi engine. Available only to speed specialists for competition stock car racing, etc., it had hemispherical combustion chambers. Its bore and stroke of 4.25 x 3.75 inches, 12.5:1 compression and twin 4-barrel carburetors produced 425 mighty horsepower at 6,000 r.p.m.

New for the year was a larger series which included a new line-up of Fury models plus the Sport Fury. Designated the Series AP, it presented the Fury I line of three models, the Fury II line of four and the Fury III group of six, while the Sport Fury had only two. They rode on wheelbases of 119 and 121 inches, of which the latter was for station wagons. Standard tire sizes for 6-cylinder cars were 7.35 x 14 for sedans and hardtops, 8.25 x 14 for wagons; for V-8 cars they were 7.75 x 14 for sedans, hardtops and convertibles, 8.55 x 14 for wagons.

Not all Series AP models offered a 6-cylinder engine, but all were available in various V-8 forms. Standard engines for the Fury I, II and III lines were the 225 (145-hp) Six and 318 V-8, while a choice of three V-8 options was listed. For this series, the Commando 383 engine was provided in two versions. The weakest had 9.2:1 compression, a 2-barrel carburetor and an output of 270 horsepower at 4,400 r.p.m., while the more powerful version as listed for the Series AR was the second-best option. The top choice was the Commando 426. The Sport Fury line was not offered as a Six, had the 318 as standard, plus the Fury options. The 426 Hemi could not be ordered in Series AP cars.

Pushbutton automatic transmission controls were abandoned and the conventional steering column-mounted shift lever and quadrant were installed unless optional console-mounted shifting was ordered. The change applied to all Plymouth series. A new feature this year was curved side window glass for the all-new Series AP cars.

The 14-millionth Plymouth, a 1966 model, was built late this year.

The Valiant 100 2-Door Sedan was again the lowest-priced and lightest-weight Plymouth for the year, costing $2,108 and weighing 2,740 pounds in standard 8-cylinder form. A total of 40,434 were turned out as Sixes and V-8s. All 100, 200 and Signet models were available with a Six or V-8 engine. Prices and weights for all Valiants are quoted for standard V-8 models. Standard Sixes cost $128 less.

Except for the whitewall tires, this Valiant 100 4-Door Sedan is shown in very standard form. As a V-8, the little car registered a weight of 2,770 pounds and carried a price tag marked $2,178. The assembly lines turned out a total of 42,857 of them as Six and V-8 cars. All Valiants were designated Series AV.

The new Valiant grille was a more delicate design than was featured for 1964. The model illustrated is the 2-Door Sedan in the 200 line. When built as a V-8, it asked a price of $2,229 and recorded a weight of 2,750 pounds. Considering its family roominess at an economical price, it was not a very popular car, drawing only 8,919 sales.

Offered only as a 6-passenger vehicle was the Plymouth 100 Station Wagon, but it was available with a choice of Six or V-8 engines. With standard V-8 engine, it weighed 2,930 pounds and cost $2,458. A total of 10,822 Sixes and V-8s came out of the factories. In addition to the wheel dress-up shown, the roof rack was optional.

A very attractive compact car was the Valiant 200 4-Door Sedan. Its appeal was great enough to draw a total of 41,642 sales. In standard 8-cylinder form it tipped the weighing scale at 2,795 pounds and required payment of $2,295. The side mirror and bumper guards were options. Shown is a V-8 car, identified by the V-8 emblem near the headlamp.

This view of the Valiant 200 Convertible conveys an impression of greater overall height than other models, but it actually was no higher. The effect was caused by the dark top fabric, which did not pick up overhead light like painted surfaces did. As a V-8, this model weighed 2,875 pounds and cost $2,532. A total of 2,769 were built in Six and V-8 form. The wheel covers on this car were an extra-special option.

Shown with extra-cost wind deflectors on the rear pillars is the Valiant 200 Station Wagon, of which 6,133 were built. The 4-door 6-passenger car was available in Six or V-8 form. When built as a standard 8-cylinder vehicle it scaled a weight of 2,935 pounds and posted a price of $2,570.

Shown is the Valiant Signet 2-Door Hardtop, of which 10,999 were built for the U.S.A. Offered as a Six or V-8, it weighed 2,820 pounds and cost $2,437 in the latter form. Note the accessory bumper guards. According to production records 1,844 Valiant 200 Hardtops were built for Canada. Also on record are 2,457 Valiant 100 Hardtops indicated as built for the U.S.A., but possibly built for Canada instead. Series 100 and 200 Hardtops were not among factory catalogued domestic models.

Obvious in this view is the front quarter panel crease treatment featured by all Valiants this year. The body belt crease folded back tightly, almost parallel. This quarter panel was introduced on the 1964 Barracuda. Shown is a Valiant Signet V-8 Convertible, which chalked up a weight of 2,905 pounds and a price of $2,654. Also built as a Six, the overall production of this model totalled 2,578 units.

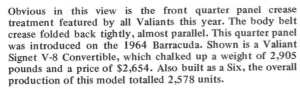

The most popular Plymouth this year was the Barracuda, of which 64,596 were built with Six or V-8 engines. In standard form the V-8 cost $2,535 and weighed 2,930 pounds. The rallye stripes were extra-cost treatment. This year, Plymouth began a 2-year strategy for divorcing the Barracuda from the Valiant. The Valiant signature did not reappear at the lower corner of the deck lid, but the Valiant emblem remained at the lower center of the rear glass. With no Valiant name on it, the car now was properly the Plymouth Barracuda, rather than the Plymouth Valiant Barracuda, but was a Series AV model.

The Barracuda was provided with a Formula S competition package for rallies and road races. Cars so-equipped were identified by special circular Formula S medallions just back of the headlamps, and by wider wheels with special Goodyear Blue Streak tires. Other package features were a Commando 273 V-8 engine of 235 horsepower, heavy-duty front torsion bars and rear springs, firm-ride shock absorbers, sway bar and rallye stripes. The cost is unknown and the number built was hidden in the regular Barracuda production total. The Barracuda's entry into competition events was inevitable.

The Belvedere series, a modified version of the 1964 cars, was split into two car lines. The lowest-priced line was the Belvedere I, of which the 2-Door Sedan is shown. Offered as a Six or V-8, it weighed 3,130 pounds and cost $2,292 in the latter form. Total production amounted to 12,536 units. The simple side molding was standard Belvedere I trim. Plymouths of this size were designated the Series AR.

Except for its optionally dressed-up wheels, a 6-cylinder Belvedere I 4-Door Sedan looked like a rather standard vehicle as it sat for a photographer to take its picture. This model tipped the scale at 3,200 pounds and posted a price of $2,330 when built in standard V-8 form. The Plymouth factories turned out a total of 35,968 of them in various forms.

The Series AR facelift included new front quarter panels, hood, grille and front bumper. Single headlamps were used, duals having been reserved for the further distinction of the new Fury cars. Turn signals were again in the bumper, below the headlamps. The bumper guards shown were accessories. Also built as a Six, the Belvedere II 4-Door Sedan shown was a V-8 which weighed 3,155 pounds and cost $2,415. Total Six and V-8 production was 41,445.

Shown is a 6-cylinder Plymouth Belvedere I Station Wagon. This model was built only as a 6-passenger vehicle. With a standard V-8 engine, the 4-door car weighed 3,465 pounds and cost $2,621. An overall total of 8,338 units were built. The Series AR continued the former 116-inch wheelbase for all body types. The standard tire size for AR wagons was 14 x 7.75, while 14 x 8.25 was optional.

Plymouth said of this car, "A sense of adventure and fun in the air become part of the standard equipment when you get behind the wheel" to drive it. Illustrated is a 6-cylinder Belvedere II Convertible. This model weighed 3,265 pounds and cost $2,655 in standard V-8 form. Overall production totalled 1,921. Excepting wagons, the standard tire size for Series AR cars was 14 x 7.35, while options were 14 x 7.75 and 14 x 8.25.

When built in standard V-8 form, the Belvedere II 2-Door Hardtop weighed 3,170 pounds and cost $2,441. Total production was 24,924 Six and V-8 cars. The V-8 example shown was like the car purchased by the author, except for the dark-colored roof. The car-length side trim distinguished all Belvedere II models. It was wide, with a bold center stripe and bright borders.

The Belvedere II Station Wagon, of which a V-8 is shown, could be had with a 6-cylinder engine and with 6 and 9-passenger seating capacities. The 6-passenger model, of which 5,908 were built, weighed 3,465 pounds and cost $2,706 in V-8 form. The 9-passenger vehicle, which had a 3,294-unit production run, weighed 3,525 pounds and cost $2,802 as a V-8. The vehicle shown was without the bright sill molding seen on other Belvedere II models.

Also part of the Series AR, the new Plymouth Satellite line borrowed everything but minor trim and 6-cylinder engines from the Belvedere cars. Satellites shunned flashy car-length side trim moldings in favor of wide sill trim, wheelhouse moldings and louver-like decor near the taillamps. The exclusively V-8 Satellite 2-Door Hardtop, of which 23,341 were built, weighed 3,220 pounds and cost $2,612 in standard form.

The least popular domestic Plymouth model for the year was the Satellite Convertible, of which 1,860 were built, all V-8s. With standard equipment, it weighed 3,325 pounds and cost $2,827. In total, the Series AR represented the last vestige of the long hood/short deck vehicle package concept begun by Virgil Exner with 1961 models. In 1963, the deck became longer in a move away from the concept. When Chrysler Corp. phased out the concept, however, it was introduced elsewhere and went on to become an industry-wide trend within a few years.

The new Series AP presented Elwood Engel, Chrysler vice-president and director of styling since late 1961, with his first opportunity to direct the styling of a wholly-new Plymouth line of cars. The basic styling theme is most apparent in the Fury I, which was the basic Series AP line. Shown is a 6-cylinder Fury I 2-Door Sedan. This model weighed 3,605 pounds and cost $2,452 when built in standard V-8 form. Total Six and V-8 production was 17,294 cars.

The Plymouth Fury I 4-Door Sedan, of which total production was 48,575, is shown as a 6-cylinder car. The same model, when built as a standard V-8, recorded a weight of 3,655 pounds and a price of $2,505. All Series AP sedans, hardtops and convertibles were built on a 119-inch wheelbase and had a 209.4-inch overall length. Tire sizes varied according to the requirements of specific Six and V-8 models. Fury I and II sedans had an overall height of 56 inches.

Shown as a 6-cylinder vehicle is the Fury I Station Wagon. The 4-door car was offered in the U.S.A. as a 6-passenger model only. The standard V-8 version sold for $2,844 and weighed 4,120 pounds. A total of 13,360 were built in Six and V-8 forms. The roof rack was an extra-cost item. Built for Canada only were 79 Fury I 9-passenger Wagons. All Series AP wagons had different basic dimensions than other models. The wheelbase was 121 inches, overall length was 216.1 inches and overall height (without rack) was 57 inches. Tire sizes varied as needed for Six and V-8 and 6 and 9-passenger models.

The 2-Door Sedan of the Fury II line is shown as a 6-cylinder car. Combined Six and V-8 production amounted to a total of 4,109 cars. When built in standard V-8 form it registered a weight of 3,605 pounds and listed a price of $2,552. The rear window and roof quarters of Series AP sedans and 4-door hardtops did not have quite as much slant as similar AR models. Built for Canada only were 2,714 Fury II 2-Door Hardtops.

The new Series AP cars appeared to be large and heavy, and they were. Shown is a V-8 Fury II 4-Door Sedan, which listed at $2,604 and had a weight of 3,660 pounds. The removable rear fender skirts were optional. Total Six and V-8 production was 43,350 cars. Series AP and AR cars equipped with V-8 engines had V-8 emblems on the front quarter panels, near the bumper. Cars with 6-cylinder engines had no emblems to identify the type of powerplant.

The Fury II Station Wagon was available only as a V-8, though the example shown had no V-8 insignia on the front quarter. The 6-passenger model, of which 12,853 were built, weighed 4,135 pounds and cost $2,908. The 9-passenger version registered 4,160 pounds, had a $3,009 price tag and a production run of 6,445 units. All AP wagons were 4-door models and had much more length from the rear wheels back than other AP models had. From the front seat back, folded rear seats provided a cargo floor length of 95.7 inches with the tailgate closed, 128.9 inches with it opened flat-out.

The Fury III 2-Door Hardtop is seen as a V-8. In basic V-8 form this model cost $2,760 and weighed 3,640 pounds. The production total was 43,251 Six and V-8 cars. Series AP 2-door hardtops continued the roof styling of similar Series AR models, having much more slant in the rear glass than sedans had. The roof was lower than sedans, too, giving this model a 54.9-inch overall height. A vinyl-covered roof was an optional goodie.

Built only as a V-8 was the Plymouth Fury III 4-Door Hardtop, which ran up a production total of 21,367 units. In basic form it tipped the scale at 3,690 pounds and asked a price of $2,825. This model, having the same roof as the 4-door sedans, also shared a 56-inch overall height. Quite obvious in this view is the new proportioning given to Series AP sedans and hardtops. It was a complete rejection of the long hood/short deck concept. The opposite ends now appeared to be much more equal in length.

Chrysler's product planning department specified a large vehicle package for the new Series AP. Styling's directive was to design a fittingly heavy and impressive appearance. Engineers followed through with appropriate sturdy construction. Shown is a V-8 Fury III 4-Door Sedan. When built with a standard V-8 engine, and without any options, it weighed 3,685 pounds and cost $2,754. Total Six and V-8 production was 50,725 cars.

The car shown did not display a V-8 insignia, but the Fury III Convertible was exclusively a V-8 model. In basic form it weighed 3,710 pounds and was priced at $3,006. Plymouth factories manufactured 5,524 of them with various engines. With the top and windows lowered, the automobile looked extra-long. The Series AP styling, with strong horizontal lines through the length of the vehicles, was intended to convey a lengthy effect.

An impressive vehicle was the Fury III Station Wagon. Built in V-8 form only, it is shown with no V-8 identity. The hump seen inside the rear was a hood over the spare wheel, which was carried upright behind the right rear wheelhouse. When built in 6-passenger form, this model weighed 4,140 pounds, cost $3,047 and attracted 8,931 sales. As a 9-passenger vehicle weighing 4,200 pounds, it was the heaviest Plymouth this year. The 9-passenger model cost $3,148 and was delivered to 9,546 buyers.

The exclusively V-8 Sport Fury line featured special interiors and appointments. Shown is the 2-Door Hardtop, which could be ordered with a vinyl-covered roof. This model recorded a weight of 3,715 pounds and a price of $2,920 when equipped in basic form. A total of 38,348 came out of the factories. All new Series AP bodies were fitted with curved side window glass, a new feature for Plymouth.

The most expensive Plymouth for the year was the Sport Fury Convertible, which cost $3,164. The 3,755-pound car was purchased by 6,272 buyers, some of whom added options that increased the cost and weight. The styling for Series AP models featured a ledge-like form through the belt, obvious here in the door area. A gentle crispness of form was apparent in the new cars.

Chosen to pace the 49th annual Indianapolis 500-Mile Race was a Plymouth Sport Fury. The selection was made by Tony Hulman, the speedway's president, who said Plymouth deserved the honor because of its excellent showing in stock car competition events. The car was driven by P. N. Buckminster, general manager of the Chrysler-Plymouth Div. Plymouth had never before been given this envied honor.

Plymouth's show car for the year was the XP-VIP, based on a Series AP. Its interior was fitted to the needs of a V.I.P. of the business world. Up front were a telephone and tape recorder, while an entertainment and refreshment center in the rear featured television, stereo and a beverage cabinet. An electronic rear-view device utilized a compact closed-circuit TV set. The transparent roof sections were of photochromic glass, which could "squint out" bright sunlight and "open up" when natural light faded. Except for the side portions, the glass was completely retractable into the trunk area.

Shown is the Plymouth Fury Patroller, one of the Police Specials. Another was the Belvedere Patroller. Both offered a choice of 2-door or 4-door sedan models and, in standard form, were built with the 6-cylinder 145-horsepower engine. V-8 options were available. All Police Specials were factory-built with varying equipment to fit them for their special kinds of police work.

Familiar on the streets of Detroit were the Plymouths of the Tactical Mobile Unit, a special squad for instant emergency action. Plymouth's Police Specials included several Pursuit models. The Fury Pursuit Special was fitted with a 330-horsepower Commando 383 engine and the Fury Pursuit had the 230-horsepower 318 job, both using the Fury I as a base. The Belvedere Pursuit Special had the 383 engine and the Belvedere Pursuit used a 273 V-8 of 180-horsepower, both models based on the Belvedere I. Those were the standard engines, all but the Fury Pursuit Special being optionally available with more power. The Pursuits and Pursuit Specials were offered in 2-door and 4-door sedan form.

Plymouth continued to enjoy a huge taxicab business, attracted by a wide variety of equipment and options. Shown is a Fury I, while other series were also offered. Plymouth claimed that its cars were preferred by cab companies because of special taxi equipment at no extra cost, exceptional passenger-mile profits and the fact that Plymouths attracted more passengers.

The Police Special series included two Emergency Wagons. Shown is the Fury, and the other was a Belvedere. For these cars, a choice of two standard powerplants was offered, the 145-horsepower Six and the 230-horsepower 318 V-8. They were also available with more powerful V-8 engines. Factory-built with special equipment like other police cars, they served equally well as patrol vehicles or ambulances.

Following record production in 1965, this was a year of adjustment in which the industry lost 7.8%. Chrysler Corp. total passenger car production dropped very little, sagging only 1.3% for the calendar year. However, the corporation's share of industry productivity rose 1.10% to give it a 16.61% slice. The share increase was due to a substantial gain registered by the Chrysler car lines and a modest rise in Imperial output. While Plymouth production

Plymouth gave the previous Valiant skeleton framework much new "skin." Sedans and hardtops were given crisp new roofs. The rear window extended to the deck, made possible by a new upper deck panel. A new deck lid extended down to the top of a new and heavier bumper, requiring a new lower deck panel. New rear quarter panels did not have a lower bulge feature as formerly, since the bumper form was not carried forward in the sheetmetal. Shown is a 6-cylinder Valiant 100 2-Door Sedan, which was the lightest and lowest-priced Plymouth for the year. The V-8 version weighed 2,800 pounds and cost $2,153. A total of 35,787 were built.

The Plymouth Valiant 100 4-Door Sedan accounted for 36,031 units of the total Valiant production for the model year. Shown as a 6-cylinder car, it registered a weight of 2,820 pounds and posted a price of $2,223 when built in standard V-8 form. All Valiants continued on a 106-inch wheelbase.

Again available only as a 6-passenger vehicle was the Valiant 100 Station Wagon. The 4-door car won enough popularity to require production of 6,838 units. It is shown as a 6-cylinder model. When built in basic V-8 form it tipped the weighing scale at 2,970 pounds and carried a $2,515 price tag.

slipped a little more than 5.7%, the breadwinner slightly increased its industry portion because of Chevrolet and Rambler losses. Plymouth easily held its No. 4 industry rank.

Chrysler Corp. spent 300 million dollars for development of all of its new models and placing them in production. Plymouth was the beneficiary of a goodly portion of the money, which was spent judiciously. New design, mechanical features and tooling expense were applied where needed. Since the big Fury line was new for 1965, it received a fairly minor facelift this year. The mid-size Belvedere-Satellite series needed a complete styling overhaul, and got it. The 3-year-old Valiant package was given a major, but not complete, styling revamp. Nearly major appearance changes were made in the Barracuda. The change pattern staggered completely new designs from year to year so as to spread the cost burden.

The Valiants, designated the Series BV, again came in three lines. The 100 continued with three models, the 200 was reduced to two and the Signet again offered two. All were built on the previous 106-inch wheelbase. Standard tire sizes remained at 6.50 x 13 for Sixes and 7.00 x 13 for V-8s. The engine line-up was the same as for 1965, having a 101-horsepower Six and 180-horsepower V-8 as standard, plus a 145-horsepower Six and 235-horsepower V-8 for options. The latter V-8 was not available for wagons.

The Barracuda, which was also part of the Series BV, moved a bit closer to self-identity by discarding the Valiant triangular emblem for a fish symbol. The fish was appropriately a barracuda, a vicious and voracious breed from the tropical seas. This was the last year the Barracuda automobile used the Valiant series designation and the Valiant appearance likeness. The standard version again shared the Valiant wheelbase and tire sizes, and retained the 145-horsepower Slant-Six as the standard Six, while standard and optional V-8s were the same as for Valiant. The Formula S again appeared in 235-horsepower and competition chassis form.

The new mid-size Plymouth Series BR included two Belvedere lines and the Satellite. The model line-up was the same as for 1965, with three in the Belvedere I line, five Belvedere II types and two Satellites. Belvedere I and II cars continued to offer the 145-horsepower Six and 180-horsepower V-8 as standard engines. Former V-8 options retained were the 318 of 230 horsepower, the Commando 361 of 265 horsepower and the Commando 383 which developed 325 horsepower at 4,800 r.p.m. instead of the former 330 at 4,600. The top public option offering was the new 426 Hemi "street" engine. Strictly for competition events was the awesome Hemi maximum-performance powerplant. Hemi engines are described in photo captions.

The Satellite cars were not available in 6-cylinder form, but offered the complete Belvedere V-8 engine line. The three new Series BR lines utilized fully-unitized construction. Oddly, station wagons rode on a new 117-inch wheelbase, while other models retained a 116-inch wheelbase. Standard tire sizes varied from 6.95 x 14 for 6-cylinder sedans and hardtops, 7.35 x 14 for 6-cylinder convertibles and V-8 sedans, hardtops and convertibles to 7.75 x 14 for 6-passenger wagons and 8.25 x 14 for 9-passenger wagons.

Largest of the Plymouths was the Series BP. Models were distributed like they were for 1965: The Fury I had three, Fury II had four, Fury III had six and the Sport Fury was available in two forms. New this year was a VIP team of two models. The former 119-inch wheelbase was used for all except station wagons, which again had a 121-inch chassis. Standard tire sizes for 6-cylinder models were 8.35 x 14 for cars and 8.55 x 14 for wagons. V-8 cars had 8.75 x 14 and wagons used 8.55 x 14. Some BP models were offered in Six or V-8 form, and all were available with a variety of V-8 engines. Standard Fury I, II and III engines were the 145-horsepower Six and 318 V-8, while the 318 was the only standard for the Sport Fury and VIP. Series BP V-8 options were the Commando 383 2-barrel 270-horsepower and 4-barrel 325-horsepower, plus a new Commando 440. The 440 had a bore and stroke of 4.32 x 3.75 inches, 440 c.i.d., 10.1:1 compression, one 4-barrel carburetor and a developed horsepower of 365 at 4,600 r.p.m. A 426 engine was not available for Series BP cars. This year, all Plymouths built for California were equipped with a Cleaner Air Package for exhaust emission control to aid in overcoming smog conditions. Plymouth introduced several new options this year. A Tilt-a-Scope steering wheel could be tilted and telescoped in several positions, and caliper-type front disc brakes provided safer braking. An emergency light-flashing device utilized the normal turn signal light system. To increase driver awareness of the turn being signalled, auxiliary turn signal indicators were provided for the front fender tops. Significant changes occurred at the top of the corporate ladder at the end of this calendar year. Lynn A. Townsend stepped up from the presidency to become chairman of the board of Chrysler Corp. Virgil E. Boyd became president after advancing through executive ranks since joining Chrysler as vice president and general sales manager in 1962. Previous to that, Mr. Boyd had been with American Motors Corp. in an executive sales capacity nearly eight years.

All Valiants featured complete newness at the front end. A new hood, distinctive 3-section grille treatment, quarter panels and bumper gave them a fresh appearance. Shown is a 6-cylinder Valiant 200 4-Door Sedan. As a V-8, this model cost $2,354 and weighed 2,820 pounds in basic form. Combined production was 39,392 units. When built in standard 6-cylinder form, any Valiant model cost $128 less than the basic V-8 counterpart.

Valiant wagons were not given a new roof, new rear quarter panels and a new rear bumper. The 200 Station Wagon, of which 4,537 Sixes and V-8s were produced, was built only as a 6-passenger car. The V-8 shown was priced at $2,630 and weighed 2,985 pounds without extras. The roof rack, side mirror, bumper guards and dressy wheel fittings were extra-cost items. The bright side trim molding was standard for the 200 series.

A young lady smiled prettily as she posed in a Plymouth Valiant Signet Convertible. Apparently, the car was as pleasing to her as it was to the 2,507 persons who bought this model. They had a choice of Six or V-8 engines as power for the youthful car. The example shown had a small plate just behind the front wheel, signifying that it had a V-8 engine. Valiant Sixes had no similar plate or mark. Seen are optional wheels with extra-special class. A standard V-8 weighed 2,925 pounds and cost $2,655.

Shown as a 6-cylinder car is the Valiant Signet Hardtop. Combined with V-8s, the 2-door model rolled up a production total of 13,045 units. The 2,835-pound V-8 version sold for $2,389. A distinctive Signet feature was the lower body side treatment in satin-silver metallic paint. Turn signal indicators on the front quarter tips were new this year. A vinyl-clad roof, not shown, was optional for the hardtop only.

Plymouth again offered the Barracuda with a Formula S Package. It included a Commando 273 V-8 engine of 235 horsepower, heavy-duty rallye suspension, special wheels and Blue Streak tires, a tachometer and other special items. Circular Formula S medallions appeared below the Barracuda signatures on the front quarter panels. The package price is unknown, as is the Formula S production total which was included with the regular Barracuda. In the circular medallion at the center of the grille was Barracuda's new symbol, a barracuda fish sculptured in miniature. The symbol also appeared in other locations and on all Barracuda automobiles.

A Plymouth Barracuda V-8 is shown when spanking new and awaiting delivery to one of the 38,029 buyers who selected this model in either Six or V-8 form. The basic V-8 price was $2,637 for 2,930 pounds of car. The Barracuda did not have a new roof and deck lid, as did the Valiants. New this year was lacquered striping just below the beltline crease. Also new for this model was an optional vinyl-covered roof, not shown. The Barracuda was designated as Series BV, the same as Valiants.

The Plymouth Belvedere I 4-Door Sedan chalked up a total of 31,063 units built during the model year. It is illustrated as a 6-cylinder car. When built in standard V-8 form it registered a weight of 3,210 pounds and listed a price of $2,409. The mid-size Plymouths were designated the Series BR.

The new mid-size Plymouth styling was a pleasing combination of chiseled crispness and gentle sculpturing with strong horizontal lines from any viewpoint. Curved side window glass, introduced by the Fury cars of 1965, now appeared in the mid-size bodies. The auxiliary inboard grille lamps were park/turn signals. Displaying a small V-8 plate near the forward point of the front quarter is a Belvedere I 2-Door Sedan, which in basic form sold for $2,371 and weighed 3,175 pounds. Total Six and V-8 production was 9,381.

Production of the Belvedere I Station Wagon, a 4-door 6-passenger vehicle, amounted to 8,200 units. The basic V-8 cost $2,699 and weighed 3,575 pounds. The 6-cylinder car shown illustrates the standard Belvedere I side trim, a bright molding on the lower crease line, beginning with a Belvedere I nameplate at the front wheelhouse. Series BR wagons were on a 117-inch wheelbase, while other BR models had a 116-inch chassis.

For the model year production run, Plymouth factories turned out 49,941 examples of the Belvedere II 4-Door Sedan, which is shown as a Six. The V-8 model, when built in standard form, listed a price of $2,499 and registered a weight of 3,195 pounds. The circular medallion on the left rear quarter served as the fuel tank filler cap.

This was the only Series BR body type on which a vinyl-clad roof could be ordered, the vinyl being either black or off-white. The 2-Door Hardtop in the Belvedere II line, shown as a Six, weighed 3,205 pounds and cost $2,524 in basic V-8 form. A total of 36,644 were built. In regard to each Belvedere I and II model, a standard Six cost $94 less than a standard V-8.

Just right for buyers who wanted a sun-and-wind car of this size and price class was the Belvedere II Convertible. It attracted 2,502 buyers, and that total was the lowest of all domestic Plymouth models this year, but by a margin of only one car. In standard V-8 form this model weighed 3,285 pounds and cost $2,738. It was also built in 6-cylinder form. The V-8 car photographed had optional rub strips on the bumpers.

This smart Plymouth was available only as a V-8. When built with the lowest-cost enigne and none other than standard equipment, the Satellite 2-Door Hardtop was listed as weighing 3,320 pounds and costing $2,910. Assembly lines turned out 35,399 of them in all V-8 forms. The example shown was fitted with accessory rub inserts on the bumper and turn signal indicators on the front quarter tips.

Without the optional roof rack and dressed-up wheels, the 9-passenger V-8 Belvedere II Station Wagon shown weighed 3,670 pounds and cost $2,898 if equipped with the standard engine. The 9-passenger model accounted for a production total of 4,726 Sixes and V-8s. The 6-passenger version, which had a Six and V-8 production run of 8,667, cost $2,789 and weighed 3,585 pounds when built in basic V-8 form. The wide and bright side molding was standard trim for all Belvedere II models.

Catalog artwork gave the Satellite Convertible much different proportions than its Belvedere II counterpart, but they were the same automobile with different trim and names. The exclusively V-8 Satellite Convertible, of which 2,759 were built, displays the bucket front seats that were standard for both Satellite models. It weighed 3,320 pounds and cost $2,910 when standard-equipped.

Shown throwing much dirt and dust as it bit at the road in fast cornering is a Satellite powered by a 426 Hemi engine of "street" form made available to the public this year. Cars equipped with the brute powerplant were identified by "HP2" emblems on the lower portion of the front quarter panels, just to the rear of the wheels. Transmissions were a 4-speed manual or heavy-duty 3-speed TorqueFlite automatic. Total Hemi-powered car production is unknown, as are car prices, but the engine cost about $1,000. All Hemi engines were custom-built by Chrysler's Marine/Industrial Div. at Marysville, Mich.

This is a cutaway view of the "street" version of the 426 Hemi engine. Its hemispherical-chamber cylinder heads, made of cast iron, had widely-spaced intake ports and abbreviated water jackets. The cylinder block, of tin-alloy cast iron, had extra support for No. 2, 3 and 4 main bearing caps and first had 4, later 5, special cylinder head studs on each cylinder bank. Pistons were domed to provide a 10.25:1 compression ratio. Valve heads were of tulip shape for minimum air flow resistance. Mechanical tappets and push rods were lightweight to reduce valve train inertia, and rocker arms were of forged steel for high-speed endurance. Camshafts were designed with valve duration and timing for smooth low-speed operation, while also allowing efficient high-speed breathing and power output. Two special 4-barrel carburetors were connected by a staged throttle linkage and fitted with a single large air cleaner of low air restriction. The exhaust manifold supplied heat to the intake manifold. at the base of the rear carburetor. New exhaust headers allowed minimum exhaust escape restriction. The engine incorporated many other special features. With bore and stroke of 4.25 x 3.75 inches, the 426 c.i.d. power-packer developed 425 horsepower at 5,000 r.p.m. and a maximum torque of 490 lb -ft at 4,000 r.p.m.

After a year of absence because of the NASCAR ban on Hemi engines, Richard Petty won new racing honors for himself and Plymouth. The ban was because the Hemi was not a production engine; hence the "street" offering this year to qualify Plymouth for the NASCAR events. Petty won the Daytona 500 with a record average speed of 160.627 m.p.h., but the record did not stand because the race ended at 495 miles because of rain. He qualified at 175.165 m.p.h. and zoomed to 176.817 m.p.h. in a single race lap, both of the marks setting new records. The Petty car, prepared by Richard's father and brother, was powered by a 404-cubic-inch hemi, a de-stroked version of the 426, and cranked out about 550 horsepower. The 404 engine had a different crankshaft as well as longer connecting rods and various other adaptations. Chrysler went all-out to develop hemi engines that would win in various racing circuits. After several years of sponsoring and factory team participation, Chrysler Corp. ended its corporate involvement in stock car racing at the end of the 1966 season.

On drag strips across the nation, Plymouths continued to score victories with various maximum-performance engines. With each performance, the public became more aware of Plymouth potency. The thundering 426 Hemi engines, heard by thousands of spectators who thrilled to the spectacular action, were especially fitted for certain kinds of competition. A compression ratio of 12.5:1 and dual 4-barrel carburetors were essential ingredients of the winning formula.

While some Plymouths were making a big show of power and speed on race tracks and drag strips, this one made a "light-foot" trip from coast to coast. Winning economy laurels in its class was a 6-cylinder Belvedere I 4-Door Sedan. Entered by the Dick Green Chrysler-Plymouth dealership, of Detroit, the car is shown at the end of the 3,301-mile leisurely drive from Los Angeles to Boston as a contestant in the Mobil Economy Run. Its engine was the standard 145-horsepower Slant-Six.

The Plymouth Fury I 2-Door Sedan, of which 12,538 were built, displays the new deck lid, rear quarter panels and rear bumper given to all Series BP models except wagons. The deck lid was marked by center sculpturing which divided the horizontal treatment into dual features. The bumper top, with Plymouth letters spread across it, was higher than previously. Shown is a 6-cylinder car. A basic V-8 weighed 3,610 pounds and cost $2,531.

The Fury I 4-Door Sedan was a fairly good seller, attracting a total of 39,698 sales. The appearance of the 6-cylinder car illustrated was exactly like its V-8 counterpart. In standard V-8 form, this model cost $2,584 and weighed 3,655 pounds. The Fury I, II, III, Sport Fury and VIP lines were designated the Series BP. Excepting wagons, the BP wheelbase was 119 inches.

The Fury I Station Wagon was available in the U.S.A. as a 6-passenger vehicle only, its production run amounting to 9,690 units. The 4-door model, shown as a Six, cost $2,941 and weighed 4,130 pounds as a standard V-8. Production records list 102 Fury I 9-passenger wagons built, indicated as for Canada. Series BP wagons did not have new rear quarter panels and a new rear bumper. The standard side trim for all Fury I models was a simple bright molding through the midsection of the body.

The 2-Door Sedan of the Plymouth Fury II series was a very unpopular model. Its production run of 2,503 cars was only one unit more than the least popular domestic model, which was the Belvedere II Convertible. The 6-cylinder car shown was obviously retained as a Fury II price leader. With standard engines, Series BP Sixes cost $105 less than V-8s. In V-8 form, this model cost $2,631 and weighed 3,630 pounds.

Built only with V-8 engines were the Fury II Station Wagons. The 6-passenger model, of which 10,718 were built, registered a weight of 4,145 pounds and a price of $2,986 when built in standard form. A total of 5,580 9-passenger models were manufactured, of which those built in standard form weighed 4,175 pounds and cost $3,087. The 9-passenger car was the heaviest Plymouth vehicle this year. All Series BP wagons rode on a 121-inch wheelbase.

The Plymouth model that won the most demand this year was the Fury II 4-Door Sedan, which had a production run of 55,016. Shown as a Six, it was also offered as a V-8 which, in standard form, weighed 3,665 pounds and cost $2,684. Fury II standard side trim consisted of a bright molding along the upper crease line. The Series BP divided grille treatment related to the design forms on the deck lid.

Added as a spring sales-getter was the Plymouth Fury Silver Special, which is shown as a 6-cylinder Fury II 4-Door Sedan. It had special features as standard, and at a special low package price. The body was painted in solid silver metallic and the interior was all-vinyl of an exclusive blue shade. Whitewall tires, deluxe wheel covers and bright-framed door windows complemented the standard Fury II exterior trim. The production total for this special model is unknown, since records simply included it in the regular Fury II 4-Door Sedan total.

The Plymouth Fury III Convertible was manufactured only as a V-8 car. When built with the standard engine, it tipped the scale at 3,720 pounds and carried a price tag marked $3,074. A total of 4,326 of these attractive automobiles came off the assembly lines.

This is a Fury III 2-Door Hardtop, which was powered by a 6-cylinder engine. The same model was supplied as a V-8, which in standard form recorded a weight of 3,675 pounds and posted a price of $2,829. The total Six and V-8 production was 41,869, which may have included similar VIP models. Not available in the U.S.A. was a Fury II 2-Door Hardtop, of which 2,433 were built for Canada, according to factory production records.

Shown as a 6-cylinder car is the Plymouth Fury III 4-Door Sedan. Also available as a V-8, this model scored a substantial production record of 46,505 Six and V-8 cars. When built with a standard V-8 engine and no optional equipment, it weighed 3,715 pounds and cost $2,823.

The new rear quarter panels of Series BP cars were more level, having less downward curve from the doors back. Also, their rearmost point was higher than previously. The new rear bumper's top was higher than that of 1965, and was trimmed vertically at the ends, not slanted as before. Vehicle overall length was not materially changed. The Fury III 4-Door Hardtop, exclusively a V-8 model, had a production run of 33,922 units, some of which may have been similar VIP cars. In basic form it cost $2,893 and weighed 3,730 pounds. The hooked bright molding and louver-like group were standard Fury III trim.

The Fury III Station Wagons were V-8 vehicles only. As a 6-passenger vehicle, of which 9,239 were built, its basic-form weight and price were 4,155 pounds and $3,115. The 9-passenger version, which had a production run of 10,886, weighed 4,165 pounds and cost $3,216 when standard-equipped. Obvious in this view of a 9-passenger car is the enclosure for the spare wheel, which stood upright behind the right rear wheelhouse and was higher than the bottom of the window. All Series BP wagons were given a new tailgate outer panel.

A Sport Fury 2-Door Hardtop received the honor of being the 14-millionth Plymouth. Built in Detroit late in the 1965 calendar year, it is shown with Robert Anderson, general manager of the Chrysler-Plymouth Div. This exclusively V-8 model, which is shown with an optional vinyl roof, weighed 3,730 pounds and cost $3,006 in basic form. Its production total of 32,523 units possibly included similar VIP models.

Again the most expensive Plymouth for the year was the Sport Fury Convertible. The exclusively V-8 car, when built in standard form, cost $3,251 and weighed 3,755 pounds. The factories turned out 3,418 of them. The fender skirts were among Sport Fury standard items, and were optional for lower-cost Fury models. Typical Sport Fury side trim featured a bold molding design that capped the entire crease line. The three bars on the door were another "earmark" of the series.

Added about January 1 was the VIP 2-Door Hardtop, which had a production run of 5,158. Factory records indicate that this model's production total was included with another series, but they do not clarify whether the Fury III or Sport Fury were involved. This handsome prestige model recorded a weight of 3,700 pounds and listed a price of $3,069 when fitted as a standard-equipped vehicle. Shown with an optional vinyl-covered roof and standard rear fender skirts, it was available with none other than V-8 power.

Introduced with other models at the beginning of the model year was the Plymouth VIP 4-Door Hardtop. It sold for $3,133 and weighed 3,780 pounds in basic form. Though the factory recorded 12,058 built, it indicated that they were included in an unspecified model's total. Logically, that total would be the Fury III 4-Door Hardtop, since it was the only Series BP car of similar type. This premium class VIP model, built only in V-8 form, is shown with the vinyl-clad roof option. The prestigious VIP cars had vinyl inserts of simulated walnut grain in the body side moldings and "C" pillar brightwork.

Shown is the VIP 4-Door Hardtop interior, which was similar to the 2-door model. They were 6-passenger cars, but with center armrests swung down they appeared to accommodate only four. The tufted seat pattern enhanced the look of luxury. Simulated walnut grain inserts gave a rich appearance to the hardware and front seat sides. A number of special appointments included reading lamps, of which one is seen on the "C" pillar trim.

Plymouth's offerings to the taxicab trade were the Fury I shown and the Belvedere I. Both were available with a 145-horsepower 225 Six or a 230-horsepower 318 V-8 engine and a choice of manual or TorqueFlite transmissions. They were built with many special cab chassis and body features as standard, while a long list of cab extras gave fleet buyers the kinds of vehicles they needed. Plymouth also continued its line of Police Specials.

The automobile industry's moderate downward adjustment of 1966 took on a complication this year. It was made more serious by a shallow drop in the national business climate and economy. The decline was not severe, however, but industry passenger car production fell nearly 3.9% for the calendar year. Chrysler Corp. weathered the cooler climate better, having a production loss of just over 7%. But its share of industry productivity rose 1.56%, giving it an 18.17% slice. The larger portion was mainly due to a severe slump suffered by the Ford family of cars. Plymouth's 4.7% drop for the calendar year would have been worse if it had not bitten into Ford, Chevrolet and Rambler business. Plymouth's rank as the No. 4 automaker did not change.

Plymouth readjusted certain areas of its product groups this year, giving most attention to a realignment of its compact cars while adding some models to the mid-size series and applying new styling to the senior cars. The Valiant family was drastically overhauled, getting a thoroughly new design from the inside out and a revision of models offered. The new Valiants were the Series CV. The economy 100 line had only two body types. The 200 was not continued as a distinct line, but was reduced to a 200 Decor Option that was available for the 100 line. The Signet line had the same body types as the 100, but with more deluxe trim and fittings than the 200 Option. Hardtops, convertibles and wagons were not included in the Valiant series, which now had a new 108-inch wheelbase, two inches longer than before. Standard tire sizes remained at 6.50 x 13 for Sixes, 7.00 x 13 for V-8s. Among optional tires and wheels was the extra-wide with D70 x 14 Red Streak tires.

The standard 6-cylinder engine for the Valiant 100 was the Slant-Six of 170 c.i.d., which was now up to 115 horsepower at 4,400 r.p.m. by using the 225 camshaft and modifying the combustion chambers. The 100 optional Six was the 225 c.i.d. of 145 horsepower. V-8 engines for the 100 were the 273 c.i.d. 2-barrel 180-horsepower job as standard, while the 273 4-barrel of 235 horsepower was optional. The Signet offered the 225 Six as standard, while the 170 Six could be ordered; standard and optional V-8s were the same as for the 100.

The Barracuda was given status as a car line, even with its own designation as the Series CB. Now divorced from the Valiant, it took on the convertible and hardtop body types formerly offered by Valiant. The fastback reappeared, making a 3-model series. The Formula S high-performance option was again on the scene. Much of the undercarriage came from the Valiant, including the 108-inch wheelbase. Tire sizes included the standard 6.95 x 14 or optional D70 x 14. Standard engines were the 225 Six and 273 2-barrel V-8. Optional V-8s were the 4-barrel 273 and a 383 c.i.d. job having a bore and stroke of 4.25 x 3.38 inches, 10:1 compression, 4-barrel carburetion and a 280-horsepower output at 4,200 r.p.m.

The mid-size Plymouths were the Series CR, which had slightly modified styling. At the bottom of the CR list was a new economy wagon. Called the Belvedere, with no I or II, it was added to replace the former Valiant wagons. Repeating the 1966 line-up was the Belvedere I with three models, the Belvedere II line of five and the Satellite selection of two. A new GTX pair of models was added to top the CR list. Belvedere, I and II standard engines were the 225 Six and 273 2-barrel V-8, the latter also serving as

the lone standard for the Satellite, which did not offer the Six. Three optional V-8s were available for all CR cars but the GTX. The smallest was the 318, which was given major updating with wedge chambers and other details without altering basic dimensions or its 230-horsepower output. Next was the 2-barrel 383 of 270-horsepower, and at the top was the 4-barrel 383 with 325 horsepower.

The GTX cars were built as high-performance vehicles with appropriate chassis and engine fittings. The standard powerplant of the exclusively V-8 series was the Super Commando 440 with bore and stroke of 4.32 x 3.75 inches, 10.1:1 compression, one 4-barrel carburetor and a horsepower output of 375 at 4,600 r.p.m. Optional for the GTX only was the 426 Hemi "street" engine, which was essentially the same as offered for 1966. Though Chrysler did not back racing this year, competition Hemis continued to be built for independent racing teams.

Holding its rank as the lightest and lowest-priced Plymouth for the year was the Valiant 100 2-Door Sedan. A V-8 weighed 2,830 pounds and cost $2,245. Total production was 29,093 units. Shown is a Six with the 200 Decor Option which consisted of full-length bright side moldings and "Valiant two hundred" nameplates on the outside, an interior class that was midway between the 100 and Signet, plus a greater choice of paint and interior colors than the standard 100 offered. The 200 Decor Option for the 100 was in lieu of a regular Valiant 200 series.

Except for the dressed-up wheels, a 6-cylinder Plymouth Valiant 100 4-Door Sedan is shown in standard form. It had no side moldings and carried "Valiant 100" nameplates on the rear quarter panels. This model, of which 46,638 were built in various forms, was also available with the 200 Decor Option. A standard V-8 cost $2,291 and weighed 2,850 pounds. For any Valiant model, a standard V-8 cost $128 more than a standard Six. The new Series CV Valiants were on a longer 108-inch wheelbase but overall length was unchanged. Overall height went up one-half inch.

Series CR wheelbases were 117 inches for wagons a[nd] 116 for other models. Tire sizes were a complex m[ix] Sedans, hardtops and convertibles with a Six, 273 or 3[83] engine had 7.35 x 14; with the 383 engine they had 7.7[5 x] 14, which also was for wagons with a Six and the G[T] with 440 or Hemi power.

The senior Plymouths, Series CP, had almost totally n[ew] styling based on the previous inner structure and chas[sis] layout. The Fury I offered three models, the Fury II h[ad] four, the Fury III had six while the Sport Fury provid[ed] three and the VIP offered two. Wheelbases remained [at] 121 inches for wagons, 119 for others. Wheel and tire siz[es] were so varied according to models and equipment th[at] data material advised readers to consult dealers for speci[fic] information. Nearly as complex was the distribution [of] engines. The three Fury I models, Fury II sedans and Fu[ry] III sedan and 2-door hardtop had the 225 as the standa[rd] Six and the 318 as the standard V-8. The 318 was t[he] only standard engine for other Fury II and III models [as] well as the Sport Fury and VIP cars. The 2-barrel a[nd] 4-barrel 383 V-8s were optional for all Series CP mode[ls] while a 4-barrel 440 of 350 horsepower could be order[ed] in any CP wagon and the 375-horsepower 440 was availab[le] for all CP models except wagons.

Safety was becoming ever more important, and Plymou[th] provided standard and optional features for it. Instrume[nt] panels were well padded, with instrumentation and contr[ols] designed for safety. An energy-absorbing steering colum[n] was crushable. Front seat passengers could have headres[ts] and safety shoulder belts. A remote-control side mirror w[as] provided for the driver. For entertainment, a stereo 8-ta[pe] cartridge player was available. For comfort, some mode[ls] were built with Flow-Through ventilation.

On the corporate level, the major news this year w[as] Chrysler's purchase of controlling interest in Root[es] Motors Ltd., in England. Chrysler put up 56 million dolla[rs] for the ailing company, and an agency of the Briti[sh] government bought 4.2 million dollars worth of shar[es] from Chrysler to retain a British voice in the firm['s] affairs. Rootes was making Hillman, Humber and Sunbea[m] passenger cars and Commer and Dodge trucks. Eventuall[y] some of the cars to come from Rootes would bear t[he] Plymouth name.

Shown as a V-8 is a Valiant Signet 2-Door Sedan, which scaled 2,835 pounds and cost $2,390. The Six and V-8 production total was 6,843. The body brightwork shown was standard for Signets. Interiors were fancy, offering a choice of bucket or bench front seats. Included with the bucket seat option was striping on the body sides. Valiant's divided grilles were distinctive, unlike any other Plymouth. The tasteful new styling concept was a combination of crisp bevelled edges, angular but gently-crowned planes and subtle contour sculpturing.

The V-8 Plymouth Valiant Signet 4-Door Sedan shown recorded a weight and price of 2,855 pounds and $2,436. Exactly 26,395 of these cars came from assembly lines in Six and V-8 forms. The extra-cost vinyl-clad roof could be had on both Signet sedans. This was the first year for sedans in the Signet series. The new Valiants continued the unitized construction principle. Curved side window glass finally reached the compact cars, blending well with the smooth contours. The new styling did not have a fast or powerful "look," but was graceful.

The new Barracuda styling had an Italian custom sports car flavor, but no Italian talent was responsible for its creation. Designed by the stylists at Chrysler Corp., the cars did not look crisp, had more flowing lines and surface curvature than other Plymouths. The hardtop roof had a pronounced forward thrust and a rear glass that was "dished in" near the top, rather than having a slight outward curve. All Barracudas had unitized body structure and curved side window glass. This model's overall height was 53.5 inches, about equal to Valiant's. Shown is a 6-cylinder Barracuda Hardtop. A V-8 weighed 2,855 pounds and cost $2,530. A total of 28,196 were built.

The fastback, known as the Sports Barracuda, had less rear glass area this year. The roof contours swept back to a neat marriage with the deck plane. Overall height was 53.4 inches for V-8s, 53.7 for Sixes. The Sports Barracuda shown had a 6-cylinder engine. Its V-8 counterpart registered a weight of 2,940 pounds and posted a price of $2,720. A total of 30,110 were built in all forms. In standard form, a Barracuda V-8 cost $81 more than a Six. The new Barracuda line, designated Series CB, was introduced about three months later than other Plymouths.

The Sports Barracuda is shown in Formula S trim, signified by the circular medallion behind the front wheel. The option offered extra appearance, interior and instrumentation items teamed with heavier sports car chassis features. Or all of those things could be combined with the high-performance V-8 engine to make it a hard-to-beat performer. With or without the Formula S package, the Sports Barracuda had a folding rear seat for convenience in carrying luggage, etc. All Barracudas had the pit-stop fuel filler cap as seen on the rear quarter panel.

The Plymouth Barracuda Convertible is shown as a 6-cylinder car. When built as a V-8, it tipped the weighing scale at 2,965 pounds and carried a price tag marked $2,860. With its top raised, it was 54.1 inches high. The classy little automobile attracted a total of 4,228 sales orders. The Barracuda wheelbase of 108 inches was the same as the Valiants had. Overall length, however, was 192.8 inches, which was 4.4 inches longer than the Valiants and 4.5 inches more than the 1966 Barracuda.

Plymouth's show car for the year was the Barracuda Formula SX. Designed by Plymouth and built by Chrysler Corp., it was not a running automobile. Built on a stock wheelbase with non-functioning chassis components, its bodywork was of fiberglass reinforced plastic. The semi-fastback design featured flush-fitting bumpers at front and rear, and no door handles were in sight. Windshield pillars were unusually thin and would not have been practical for production cars.

Built in Italy under an arrangement with Chrysler Corp. was the Ghia 450ss. It was priced at $11,800, was available as a 2-plus-2 convertible or the hardtop shown, or as a 2-seater roadster with a removable steel cover over the small rear seats. Based on a Barracuda Formula S with a 273 4-barrel engine, it had special tubular framework with torsion bar rallye suspension, disc power brakes, power steering and an automatic TorqueFlite transmission. The interior was of genuine leather and was air conditioned. Luxury sports car appointments were everywhere, including the Borrani chrome wire wheels with premium Pirelli "Cinturato" high-speed tires.

Introduced to fill the void left by the lack of Valiant wagons was the Belvedere Wagon. It was of lower class than the Belvedere I. Shown as a Six, it also was built as a V-8 weighing 3,610 pounds and costing $2,673. It won 5,477 buyers. Built on the Series CR 117-inch wagon wheelbase, it was supplied in 2-seat form only. Note the lack of bright side moldings. No longer was this body properly called a Station Wagon, it was a Wagon, very simple. And seating capacity was not 6 or 9-passenger anymore, but was 2 or 3-seat.

The price leader of the mid-size Plymouths was the Belvedere I 2-Door Sedan. In V-8 form it cost $2,412, which was only $22 more than the Valiant Signet V-8 of similar model. The V-8 Belvedere I weighed 3,180 pounds, 345 more than the Signet, and was 12.1 inches longer. The sharp-looking model, shown as a Six, chalked up a total of 4,718 units built in all forms.

The mid-size vehicle styling was a continuation of the 1966 sheetmetal, there being no noticeable sheetmetal changes for the year. Therefore, the series identification had to be by means of applied parts only, mainly ornamentation and trim. A 6-cylinder Belvedere I 4-Door Sedan displays typical Belvedere I side trim, which consisted of wide bright sill moldings only. As a V-8, this model weighed 3,210 pounds and cost $2,450. In all forms, it won 13,988 sales.

The Plymouth Belvedere II 4-Door Sedan, of which 42,694 were built, is seen as a 6-cylinder car. When built as a V-8 it had an asking price of $2,528 and tipped the scale at 3,205 pounds. Not visible on this car is the bright molding that was standard Belvedere II trim. Near the peak of the belt and quarter panels, it extended from front to rear. Window frames were also bright. The bright sill and wheelhouse moldings were optional.

Shown is a Plymouth Belvedere I Wagon in 6-cylinder 2-seat form. The V-8 counterpart was priced at $2,746 and weighed 3,620 pounds. Assembly lines turned out 3,172 of them in Six and V-8 forms. This model was not available as a 3-seat vehicle. For Belvedere, Belvedere I and II wagons and passenger cars, the price of a standard V-8 was $94 more than a standard Six.

The Belvedere II 2-Door Hardtop had a production run of 34,550 Sixes and V-8s. A V-8 model weighed 3,215 pounds and cost $2,551 in standard form. The example shown was a "Bonus Special" offered as an extra sales punch. It lumped special trim and certain accessories into an attractive price package. Included was the regular-option vinyl roof, but unusual to the Belvedere II was the Satellite paint stripe at the belt, rather than the normal bright molding. The Series CR regular option list had a variety of wheels and wheelcovers.

The new grille of the mid-size cars incorporated dual-unit headlamps. The park/turn signals, formerly inboard on the grille, were in the bumper, which was given openings for them. The Belvedere II Convertible drew the least demand of any domestic Plymouth model this year, having a Six and V-8 production run of 1,552 units. As a V-8 it sold for $2,789 and weighed 3,290 pounds. All Plymouth convertibles had real rear window glass.

The Plymouth Satellite series was available only with V-8 engines. Standard side trim included full-length belt paint stripes, plus satin-silver paint on the lower areas with bright moldings to top it off. The Satellite 2-Door Hardtop weighed 3,265 pounds and cost $2,747. Its 30,328-unit production total probably included the similar GTX model, which was also a Series CR premium car.

The exclusively high-performance GTX was properly known as the Plymouth Belvedere GTX, since it carried all of those names in chrome. The 2-Door Hardtop shown was powered by the Super Commando 440 375-horsepower V-8 that was standard for both GTX models. The car cost $3,178 and weighed 3,545 pounds. The twin paint stripes on the deck were optional, the dark silver finish in the recess between the lamps was standard, as were the bright moldings on the sill and wheel openings. The factory did not get around to record this new model's production separately, so it was probably lumped into the Satellite hardtop total.

The Belvedere II Wagon was again presented as two models, both available with a Six or V-8 engine. The 2-seat model, of which 5,583 were built, had a V-8 price of $2,823 and weight of 3,620 pounds. Shown is the 3-seat model, which had a V-8 price and weight of $2,930 and 3,705 pounds. The 3-seat vehicle had a 3,968-unit production run. The sill molding was standard for this model, the roof rack was extra.

Satellites had silver paint on the rear like that on the lower body sides. The wide chrome framing and narrow taillamps were shared with the GTX. Shown is the Satellite Convertible, which registered a weight of 3,335 pounds and listed a price of $2,986. The exact number built is unknown, since the production total of 2,050 units probably included the GTX Convertible, another CR premium model.

To enhance the GTX high-performance appearance, stylists applied two simulated air scoops to the top of the hood. This car shows the Belvedere plaque, which had GTX letters just below it, on the front quarter panel upper area, ahead of the wheel. Much more significant is the Hemi plaque on the lower panel area, behind the wheel. This car was powered by the optional 426 Hemi "street" engine, a fantastic 425-horsepower V-8. When built with the 440 engine and other standard fittings, this model cost $3,418 and weighed 3,615 pounds. The number built is unknown, as it likely was combined with the Satellite convertible total.

Although the camera in this instance grossly distorted proportions as it recorded a rear view for catalog artwork, the new Series CP cars were wide. Plymouth wanted impressive bigness in the top series, and they were designed and illustrated to appear even larger than they were. Shown is a Fury I 2-Door Sedan, which in V-8 form weighed 3,550 pounds and cost $2,598. Including Sixes, 6,647 were built.

Sales promotion touted the new Series CP groups as the big cars in the low-price field. They were big, but no bigger than the comparable models of primary competitors. In fact, the CP wheelbases and overall length dimensions were equal with the competition, excepting the longer CP wagons. The Fury I 4-Door Sedan, shown as a Six, weighed 3,590 pounds and cost $2,622 as a V-8. Exactly 29,354 were built.

Shown is a V-8 Fury I 2-Seat Wagon. The 4,055-pound automobile was priced at $2,989. Including Sixes, a total of 6,067 were built. A 3-seat model was not available in the U.S.A., but 77 were built for Canada or export. In standard form, no Fury I model had any bright side trim moldings or distinguishing features other than the signatures. All Series CP wagons were on a 121-inch wheelbase, other CP models rode on 119 inches.

A 6-cylinder Plymouth Fury II 2-Door Sedan displays the standard Fury II side trim. The body side molding, of bright finish, was of simple section. Roof drip rails were clad in bright stainless steel. A total of 2,783 were built. A V-8 weighed 3,545 pounds and cost $2,676. For all Series CP models with a choice of such engines, a standard V-8 cost $105 more than a standard Six.

Shown as a 6-cylinder car is a Fury II 4-Door Sedan. This model attracted a total of 45,673 Six and V-8 sales. When built as a standard V-8, and with no extras, it tipped the scales at 3,580 pounds and posted a price of $2,719. Excepting wagons, all Series CP models had an overall length of 213.1 inches, 3.3 more than the similar 1966 series. The 56.1-inch overall height exceeded 1966 by 8-tenths of an inch.

Offered only as a V-8 model was the Fury II 3-Seat Wagon shown. Priced at $3,122, it weighed 4,110 pounds and chalked up a production total of 5,649. It was also built in 2-seat V-8 form which cost $3,021, weighed 4,045 pounds and amassed a 10,736-unit production total. Series CP 2-seat wagons were 216 inches long overall, 3-seaters were 217.3, both were about equal to the 1966 jobs. Their 57.8-inch height was one inch more.

The Fury III 4-Door Sedan was the most popular Plymouth this year, having a production run of 52,690 Sixes and V-8s. The V-8 price was $2,851 and the weight was 3,615 pounds. The new Series CP styling covered the previous skeleton with a completely new appearance below the belt. The superstructure of sedans and wagons was not changed, but all hardtops were given new roof designs.

The exclusively V-8 Fury III 4-Door Hardtop, with a weight of 3,650 pounds and price of $2,922, accumulated a production total of 43,614 units. Its new roof completely framed the rear glass, a step toward more formal appearance. In general, Series CP body styling was a combination of clean surfaces and crisp edges. This was one of the models featuring Flow-Through ventilation.

Shown as a V-8 is the Fury III 2-Door Hardtop which weighed 3,595 pounds and cost $2,872. Including Sixes, total production was 37,448. Not offered in the U.S.A. were 2,405 Fury II 2-Door Hardtops built for Canada or export. This Fury III model had a new roof with nearly constant-width "C" pillars. The car is seen with optional bright sill moldings, part of a "Bonus Special" sales package that included vinyl on the roof.

The Plymouth Fury III Convertible, of which 4,523 were manufactured, was built in V-8 form only, weighed 3,670 pounds and cost $3,118. Shown is standard Fury III side trim. Beginning at the front, a thin bright molding on the panel crease line swept back to cap the rear quarter peak. It accentuated the subtle rise that brought the line up to belt level. Bright moldings on the wheel openings completed the dress-up.

A massive Fury III 3-Seat Wagon is shown with optional roof rack and rear pillar assist handles. This was the heaviest Plymouth for the year. In basic form, it weighed 4,135 pounds and cost $3,245. A total of 12,533 were built. The Fury III 2-Seat Wagon had a production run of 9,270, weighed 4,080 pounds and cost $3,144. Both wagon models were built only with V-8 engines.

This is the Sport Fury 2-Door Hardtop, having the new roof seen on the Fury III. The "C" pillar was characterized by nearly parallel front and back lines. The V-8 car's weight was 3,630 pounds and its price was $3,033. The exact number built is unknown. Production records listed one 28,448-unit total for this model and the new Fast Top. The Series CP presented only two roof designs for 2-door hardtops. However, another was also shown in sales literature and press release photographs. It was the tapered "C" pillar design used for the big Series BP 1966 cars. Until fairly late in the 1967 model development program, CP hardtops were to retain the previous year's roof, as was done with other models. The late change decision, plus the advance release of model details to advertising and artwork agencies, resulted in the error.

The new Sport Fury Fast Top was another 2-door hardtop design. Shown with optional vinyl covering, the roof featured a blind triangular "C" pillar. This roof was introduced to expand the choice of hardtops. The exclusively V-8 car weighed 3,705 pounds and was priced at $3,062. Its unknown production total was combined with the other Sport Fury hardtop. Flow-Through ventilation was a feature.

This year's most expensive Plymouth was the Sport Fury Convertible. It sold for $3,279 and weighed 3,645 pounds in basic form. Exactly 3,133 were built. The Sport Fury series, built only with V-8 engines, had a paint stripe extending the full length of the upper character line, plus bright moldings on the sill and wheel openings as standard side trim. The unique flanks of the Series CP front end design crowded the headlamps a bit, but the extended outer edges provided a longer front appearance when viewed from the side.

In the VIP series, this model was called the 2-Door Hardtop, not Fast Top. It was priced at $3,182 and it weighed 3,705 pounds. Its production run was 7,912 cars. Vinyl roofs were a VIP option, as were super-luxury interiors. On this model, the deck curved up to meet the rear glass. In that curve was a wide span of louvers which were escape vents for the controlled Flow-Through ventilation system which was standard on this and other specified CP models. With windows closed, fresh air admitted at the front passed through the interior and exited through a rear package shelf vent and these louvers. Circulation was forced by car movement only. At 60 m.p.h. the interior air changed four times a minute. The system proved less effective than expected and was abandoned with this model year. Perhaps buyers preferred the refrigerated air conditioning system.

The luxury-laden Plymouth VIP series continued as an exclusively V-8 line. The 4-Door Hardtop, which shows the tapered blind quarter of the new roof, recorded a weight of 3,660 pounds, a price of $3,117 and a production run of 10,830 cars. Standard VIP side trim included a stripe to accent the upper character line, wide lower stretches of brushed aluminum and bright moldings outlining the front wheel openings. This model had Flow-Through ventilation.

The Fury I taxicab was for operators who felt that the big car's comfort was important to their business. They could have a 225 Six or 318 V-8 in this one, too. And it was factory-built with dozens of special cab features as standard, many others optional. An all-vinyl interior was a standard cab feature.

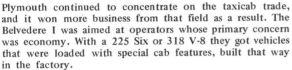

Plymouth continued to concentrate on the taxicab trade, and it won more business from that field as a result. The Belvedere I was aimed at operators whose primary concern was economy. With a 225 Six or 318 V-8 they got vehicles that were loaded with special cab features, built that way in the factory.

Becoming ever more popular with law enforcement agencies were Plymouth's factory-built police cars. Shown is the Belvedere Pursuit, and there was a Belvedere Pursuit Special, both offering 318, 383 2-barrel and 383 4-barrel V-8 engines. For tamer work, but capable of more exciting jobs if ordered with the Pursuit engines was the Belvedere Patroller which normally had a 225 Six for power. The three Belvederes were available in 2-door and 4-door models.

The Fury Pursuit, shown as a 2-door, could also be had as a 4-door model. Engines were the 318, 383 2-barrel and 4-barrel, plus the 440 plants of 350 and 375 horsepower. For routine neighborhood cruising, the Fury Patroller with a 225 Six was on hand, or it could be hopped up with any of the Pursuit V-8s. Any could be had as a 2-door or 4-door.

Plymouth's Police Specials included emergency vehicles. The Fury Emergency Wagon shown could be ordered with a 225 Six or V-8s in 318, 383 2-barrel and 4-barrel and 440 350-horsepower form. Also on the available list was the Belvedere Emergency Wagon, which could have any of those engines but the 440 job. The wagons were double-duty vehicles, fitted for police and ambulance use.

With the return of more flourishing business conditions, total industry passenger car production increased about 19.4% for the calendar year. Chrysler Corp. car divisions combined to amass a production gain of nearly 16.3% but dropped to 17.24% of the industry's total productivity. The .93% share loss was mostly due to the vigorous rebound of the Ford Motor Co. Plymouth improved by more than 12%, more than recovering its losses of the previous two years but dropping a bit of its share of the industry total. Though retaining its rank as the nation's No. 4 automaker, Plymouth's position was facing a threat.

The new Series DV Valiants had superficial styling changes and minimal mechanical improvements. The economy 100 line continued with two models to which a 200 Decor Group option could be added, and the Signet again offered two types. They continued to ride on a 108-inch wheelbase. The standard engine was the 170 Slant Six 115-horsepower job. Except for the 145-horsepower

225 Slant Six, Valiant optional engine choices got some changes. The 273 2-barrel V-8 was upped to 9:1 compression and 190 horsepower at 4,400 r.p.m. and the 273 4-barrel engine was not available. The 318 V-8 of 230 horsepower was a new option for Valiant.

The Barracuda line, now the Series DB, also received very minor appearance and mechanical changes and retained the 108-inch chassis. The model line-up was unaltered, remaining at three, and the Formula S options were available for all three. The standard Six was again the 225, but the standard V-8 was now the 318. The two V-8 options were supplied only for cars with Formula S equipment. New to Plymouth was the 340-S, which had a bore and stroke of 4.04 x 3.31 inches, 340 c.i.d., 10.5:1 compression, a 4-barrel carburetor and a 275-horsepower output at 5,000 r.p.m. A 383 option was again present, but as a special 383-S engine not available for other Plymouths. For the S version, the former 383 was given new cylinder heads and a new 4-barrel intake manifold which provided 300 horsepower at 4,200 r.p.m.

The intermediate class was freshly styled. Split into five groups, Plymouth referred to them collectively as "The Mid-Size 5." There were no 2-door sedans, but coupes were introduced. The economy group was the Belvedere, with three models. Next up was the Satellite line, which was expanded to seven models including Sport wagons. New was the Road Runner, first offered as a coupe and later adding a hardtop. Also new was the Sport Satellite with two body types. Again at the top was the GTX pair of models.

The Series DR engine list offered about as many choices as the menu of a 24-hour restaurant. The 225 Six and 273 V-8 were standard for all Belvedere and Satellite models, except that the Satellite Sport Wagon did not offer the Six. The 318 V-8 was standard for the Sport Satellite, optional for the Belvedere and Satellite lines, all three also offering 383 engines of 2-barrel 290-horsepower and 4-barrel 330-horsepower as optional. Standard for the Road Runner was a 383 4-barrel job which turned out 335 horsepower for these cars only. The GTX standard was the 440 375-horsepower V-8 as used for 1967. Optional for the Road Runner and GTX was the renowned 426 Hemi street engine of 425 horsepower. Again provided for specialized racing and drag strip teams, the fantastic 426 Hemi competition engines were available for the Barracuda as well as the Series DR cars. The mid-size series again placed wagons on a 117-inch wheelbase and others on a 116-inch chassis.

The big Plymouths, designated the Series DP, were given a partial restyling, using some of the 1967 sheetmetal and the basic structure introduced for 1965. The model line-up was altered, placing wagons in a separate group and calling them Suburbans. Therefore, excluding Suburbans the Fury I and Fury II each offered two models, the Fury III had five, the Sport Fury offered three and the VIP

Plymouth Valiant styling for the year was confined to changes in minor detail and ornamentation on the exterior, new seat and side trim design inside. All major sheetmetal parts were the same as for 1967, possibly excepting hidden detail changes. The Valiant 100 2-Door Sedan is shown as a Six. The car weighed 2,655 pounds and cost $2,254. Its weight and price were the lowest of any Plymouth this year. Total Six and V-8 production was 31,178, of which some were dressed with the optional 200 Decor Group.

Except for optional wheel dress-up, the Valiant 100 had a very plain appearance in standard form. There were no bright side moldings or stripes to pretty it up. The 4-Door Sedan, seen here as a Six, was also provided in V-8 form. The Six cost $2,301 and weighed 2,675 pounds. Total production, including those with the 200 Decor Group, was 49,446 units. Any Valiant model cost $127 more when fitted with the standard 273 V-8 than when equipped with the standard 170 Slant Six.

had two body choices. All rode on a 119-inch wheelbase. One standard Suburban was offered, while the Custom and Sport Suburbans each provided two models, all mounted on a 121-inch wheelbase.

Not quite as impressive as the DR engine list was the Series DP powerplant roster. Fury I, II and III sedans and hardtops, plus the standard Suburban, offered the 225 to buyers who wanted a Six. The 318 was the standard V-8 for all Series DP models, which were also available with the optional 383 engines of 290 and 330 horsepower. A 350-horsepower 440 could be had in DP Suburbans only, while the 375-horsepower 440 could be ordered for any DP model except Suburbans.

Bowing to federal government ideas relating to safety, all Plymouths were fitted with small side marker lights on the four corners, and none had hood top ornaments that stood upright. A new option for Wagons and Suburbans was a rear window washing system concealed in the tailgate. The washing was done while the glass was down.

A 6-cylinder Valiant 100 2-Door Sedan is shown with the 200 Decor Group option. It included bright belt moldings indented with a red stripe, "Valiant two hundred" name-plates on the front quarter panels, vinyl-and-cloth or all-vinyl seats, a 3-spoke steering wheel with partial horn ring, color-keyed floor mats, a cigar lighter and dual horns. The vinyl roof, fancy wheels and bumper guards were not part of the 200 Decor. The new Valiant grilles were divided by a color panel that tapered narrower at the bottom.

In this and other years, special sales campaigns offered various Plymouth models with special trim and equipment at "bargain" prices. Often the cars had combinations of trim and other items not normally specified as standard or optional for the specific models so-equipped. They were factory-built that way. The car shown had "Valiant 100" nameplates, bright belt moldings like the 200 Decor, bright drip moldings like the Signet, plus other extras. In this case, both series 100 models were offered, and were advertised as "Valiant Value Specials."

The Valiant Signet 2-Door Sedan, shown as a V-8, won 6,265 Six and V-8 sales. The price of the Six was $2,400 and its weight was 2,660 pounds. The car shown had optional wheelcovers, whitewall tires, a vinyl-clad roof and a full-length accent stripe through the body midsection. Barely discernible in this view are the small circular side marker lights near the bumpers. New this year, all Plymouths had to have them because they were felt necessary for indicating a moving vehicle's length at night.

A 6-cylinder Plymouth Valiant Signet 4-Door Sedan displays standard Signet trim such as the brightwork across the rear and around the side windows, plus bright moldings on the sill, wheel openings and lower edges of the front and rear quarter panels. Signets had extra-class interiors, too. In standard Six form, this model recorded a weight of 2,680 pounds and was offered at a price of $2,447. A total of 23,906 were built.

Shown as a Formula S car is the Barracuda Hardtop Coupe. Any Barracuda could be ordered with Formula S equipment. The option included a choice of 275 or 300-horsepower V-8s and other goodies. Heavy-duty suspension with anti-sway bar, firm-ride shock absorbers, heavy-duty wide-rim wheels with E70 x 14 Red or White Streak wide-oval tires and a low-restriction dual exhaust system were among the chassis features. Body side trim included Formula S medallions and wide bright sill moldings.

The V-8 Barracuda Hardtop Coupe weighed 2,895 opunds and cost $2,711 with basic equipment and trim. It is shown with such extra-cost items as the vinyl roof, sport stripes and wire wheelcovers. The car purchased new by the author did not have those extras. However, its factory order specified the sport stripes but the assembly scheduling system skipped the item and the car came out of the factory without them. Exactly 19,997 of these cars were built in various Six and V-8 forms.

A 6-cylinder Barracuda Sports Fastback is shown fitted with a trailer hitch for towing the race car in the background. Barracudas could easily tow a 1500-pound load. Bright sill moldings are among extras seen on this car. In standard form, a V-8 Sports Fastback cost $2,868 and weighed 2,980 pounds. Exactly 22,575 were built in various forms.

The Plymouth Barracuda Convertible Coupe, which had a production run of 2,840, was especially sharp-looking with its top folded down. When built as a standard V-8, it weighed 3,010 pounds and cost $3,013. Any Barracuda model cost $105 more as a standard V-8 than as a Six. The car shown is a V-8 model. Some of the Barracudas had a continuous beltline stripe from front to rear, others had narrow sill moldings. The Barracuda line was continued with no new sheetmetal this year.

The Barracuda was popular as a basis for add-ons. Well-known customizer George Barris of North Hollywood, Calif., provided a Spoiler kit that was sold by Plymouth dealers in the southwest. Shown on a Formula S car, it consisted of five basic bolt-on parts, of which four were for looks only. The spoiler on the rear might have been useful at very high speeds. The eyewash items were dual hood scoops, rear quarter window air scoops, extruded rocker side exhaust headers and brushed alloy wheels. The kit cost $523.70.

Ready to do its "thing" on a California strip was a Hemi-powered Barracuda. The Chrysler-Plymouth Div. offered these cars for Super Stock competition in sanctioned drag racing and they were sold through the division's dealers. In testing on this strip, the car cut consistent times below 11 seconds and ET's of better than 130 m.p.h. Besides the 426 Hemi competition engine and special drag underpinnings, the car was fitted with fiberglass front end components.

The smoothly-flowing contours of the new mid-size Plymouths were a complete departure from the rigid crispness of 1966-67. Showing its new sculpturing is a Belvedere Coupe, which had a Six and V-8 production run of 15,702. A V-8 model had a weight of 3,130 pounds and a price of $2,538. A true coupe with "B" pillars and a 6-passenger seating capacity, it replaced the former 2-door sedan. Oddly, this car had no sill molding.

Shown with its tailgate opened like a door is a 6-cylinder Plymouth Belvedere Wagon. Built as a 2-seat model only, it easily accommodated six passengers. The V-8 price was $2,867 and the weight was 3,605 pounds. Precisely 8,982 came out of the factories in various forms. Standard Belvedere side trim was a narrow bright sill molding. The mid-size Series DR wagons continued on a 117-inch wheelbase, other models on 116.

The Belvedere 4-Door Sedan, seen as a Six, weighed 3,155 pounds and cost $2,577 as a V-8. Total production was 17,214. A mystery to the author is an entry in the official factory production records listing 39,488 Belvedere 2-door sedans and indicating that they were built in and for the U.S.A. There are no known records of the disposition of these cars. Perhaps they were built on special order for a fleet-operating buyer or two.

A very smart-looking family-size car was the Plymouth Satellite 4-Door Sedan. Apparently, that is what 42,309 buyers thought. Some of them bought the 3,160-pound V-8 for $2,666, others bought Sixes. In the Series DR line, any model with a standard V-8 was priced $94 higher than a Six. All Satellites had bright finish on the side window frames, full-length belt moldings and wheel opening moldings. The attractive car shown had optional wide sill moldings and rubber bumper strips.

Satellite Hardtop

The Satellite Hardtop shows typical Satellite trim stretching from taillamp to taillamp. It also shows optional vinyl on the roof and rubber scuff strips on the bumper. The V-8 weighed 3,150 pounds and had a purchase price of $2,688 in standard form. A total of 46,539 came from the factories in Six and V-8 forms. This car was 52.5 inches high.

Ready for a sunny and windy drive was this Satellite Convertible. Not many people wanted such a ride in this car, however, as only 1,771 Six and V-8 examples were built. The standard V-8 models weighed 3,270 pounds and sold for $2,918. Some mid-size vehicle dimensions differed from 1967. Hardtops were 1.6 inches lower overall, other models were about as high as formerly. In overall length, wagons did not change but others were 2.2 inches longer.

The Satellite Wagon was built in two models, 2-seat and 3-seat, both offered in Six and V-8 forms. The V-8 2-seat model weighed 3,605 pounds and cost $2,985, while the V-8 3-seat vehicle weighed 3,675 and cost $3,092. Factory production records combined the Satellite Wagon and Sport Wagon, providing separate totals for 2 and 3-seat models only. Therefore, the Satellite Wagon production was listed as 12,097 of the 2-seat models and 10,883 of the 3-seaters. There is no way of knowing how many were standard Wagons and how many were the higher-class Sport Wagons. The standard Wagon is shown with a narrow bright sill molding.

Two-way tail gate as tail gate

New to Plymouth was the 2-way tailgate that opened flat-down or swung like a door. It offered dual convenience and was easily operated. It was a feature on Series DR wagons only, and was standard equipment on all models. Note the step pads on the tailgate inner panel and the sill, located toward the curb side.

The Satellite Sport Wagon had wood-grain vinyl on the sides and tailgate, plus other niceties that made it the top Series DR wagon. It was available only as a V-8. The 2-seat model scaled 3,610 pounds and cost $3,131, while the 3-seat version weighed 3,685 pounds and sold for $3,239. Unknown production totals were combined with the standard Satellite Wagons. The Satellite Sport Wagons were not part of the Sport Satellite car line. All Series DR wagons continued to use the 1966-67 superstructure, which included the roof and upper frames of the doors.

One of the new series added this year was the Sport Satellite. It filled the spot held by the Satellite in 1967, while the new Satellite series was slightly downgraded and expanded to replace the former Belvedere II. The phasing down of existing series was a means of making way for fresh new series as needed for changing public tastes and market conditions. The Sport Satellite Hardtop was a V-8 weighing 3,155 pounds, costing $2,822 and recording a production total of 21,014 units. The standard side trim for Sport Satellite models included full-length belt striping, bright trim on the wheel openings and wide bright sill moldings. Making its bow this year was the Road Runner, a high-performance series named for the famed animated cartoon bird character. Chrysler obtained rights from the Warner Bros.-Seven Arts movie firm to use the name and the cartoon image. Even the bird's "beep-beep" warning sound was duplicated by the car's horn. The Coupe, of which 29,240 were built, weighed 3,390 pounds and cost $2,896 in standard form. The car shown was powered by the 383 Road Runner V-8, a 335-horsepower engine that was standard and exclusive to the "cartoon" series. The stretch of black across the hood top was optional. In standard form, no side decor was used, only the Road Runner name and cartoon appearing near the windshield pillars.

The Road Runner Hardtop, added some time after the Coupe appeared, weighed 3,400 pounds and cost $3,034 in the standard form shown. It had a 15,359-unit production run. The car shown had a 383 engine, indicated by bright 383 numerals on the simulated air scoops on the hood. Cars powered by the 426 Hemi street engine, which was the Road Runner's only optional powerplant, had the Hemi name in bright letters on the scoops. Wide-rim wheels and Red Streak wide-oval F70 x 14 tires were standard.

This view of the Sport Satellite Convertible displays the thin-vaned grille design which it shared with the GTX. Also obvious are the angular frontal planes and the "beverage bottle" shape of the body sides, characteristics of all mid-size cars. Sport Satellite models were exclusively V-8. The Convertible, which had a production run of 1,523, recorded a weight of 3,285 pounds and posted a price of $3,036.

The Plymouth GTX was the top offering in the mid-size series. Like the Road Runner, it was a high-performance series, but was fitted more expensively. Shown is the GTX Hardtop with standard side trim and the Super Commando 440 375-horsepower engine that was the GTX standard. The Hardtop's appeal was strong enough to score a total of 17,914 cars built. In standard form, the 3,470-pound car was priced at $3,355.

The GTX Convertible drew the least demand of any domestic Plymouth model this year, as only 1,026 of them were built. The price was $3,590 and the weight was 3,595 pounds, standard-equipped. The fast and powerful-looking car shown was fitted with the standard 440 V-8. The GTX series also had the distinction of boasting the 425-horsepower street version of the 426 Hemi. The Hemi was its only engine option.

The price leader in the big Plymouth Series DP family was the Fury I 2-Door Sedan, which sold for $2,722 as a 3,540-pound V-8 car. Being the lowest-priced of the series did not make it the most popular, however, as its Six and V-8 choices garnered a mere total of 5,788 sales. The senior cars, again modified designs, continued as large and impressive automobiles.

The basic forms incorporated in the new Series DP rear end styling are obvious in this view. The deck was platform-like, flanked by smooth-surfaced quarter panels that curved slightly inward toward the peaks. The concave recess from side to side emphasized vehicle width and provided a relieving feature. As a V-8, the Fury I 4-Door Sedan cost $2,765 and weighed 3,580 pounds. Including Sixes, 23,208 were built.

The Fury II 4-Door Sedan is shown with standard side trim for this series. The full-length bright molding was of constant width and the roof drip rail was of bright finish. Also standard was a satin-finish aluminum insert across the rear, in the concaved recess area. When built as a V-8, this 3,595-pound model quoted a price of $2,862. Total Six and V-8 production amounted to 49,423 cars.

For all of the big Plymouth models, the entire front end sheetmetal remained the same as 1967. Also unchanged were the superstructures, front doors and front bumper. The new grille's screened lower section appears as an opening in this view. The Fury II 2-Door Sedan shown cost $2,820 and weighed 3,545 pounds as a V-8. The Six and V-8 production total was 3,112. Built only for Canada or export were 3,449 Fury II 2-Door Hardtops.

Sedans, hardtops and convertibles of the big Series DP were given much new sheetmetal at the rear. All had new quarter panels and deck lids, and the rear doors of 4-door bodies were new from the belt down. A new rear bumper was also given to all. The Fury III 4-Door Sedan, of which 57,899 Sixes and V-8s were built, also shows the rear end decor typical of its series. A V-8 weighed 3,605 pounds and cost $2,995.

The Fury III 2-Door Hardtop was registered as weighing 3,600 pounds and costing $3,017 in V-8 form. It also was built as a Six. The exact number built is unknown, since the factory combined this car and the Fast Top model in an overall Fury III 2-door hardtop production total of 60,472 units. This was the highest single production total for the year, but it actually was a double entry.

The Fast Top was a new entry in the Fury III line. The 2-door hardtop car offered a choice of Six or V-8 engines. As a 3,590-pound V-8 it cost $3,037. For Series DP models having the choice, a standard V-8 cost $105 more than a Six. The Fast Top production total is unknown. Shown is the regular Fury III side trim. The full-length paint-filled molding was wider through the rear quarter panel. Rear wheel skirts were extra.

Looking low, wide and handsome was the Plymouth Fury III Convertible. The big sport car was built only with the V-8 choices available. In basic form it tipped the weighing scale at 3,680 pounds and had an asking price of $3,236. Its popularity required production of 4,483. In this view, the finely-textured screening in the lower grille shows up well in the light body color.

The Plymouth Fury III 4-Door Hardtop was built only in V-8 form. It registered 3,635 pounds of weight, a $3,067 price and a 45,147-unit production run. The big series cars retained the former 119-inch wheelbase. The new styling of the rear end added no length to that area. Vehicle overall dimensions, meaning length, height and width, remained about the same as those of 1967.

The new rear quarter panels on the big cars neatly executed a transition from the carryover doors and front quarters. The creased character lines of the forward sections were quickly blended and terminated, and new upper and lower lines emerged to sweep to the rear. The lower character line was enhanced by the use of the optional rear wheel skirts. Shown is the Sport Fury 2-Door Hardtop which weighed 3,620 pounds, cost $3,206 and drew a 6,642-unit demand.

The Sport Fury Fast Top, of which 17,073 were built, weighed 3,615 pounds and was priced at $3,225. It shows the standard side trim for all Sport Furys. Appearing as a midsection molding, the full-length striping was actually triple stripes. Bright moldings were applied to the sill and wheel openings. Seen near each bumper are small side marker lights like all Plymouths had. The front lights were amber and the rear were red.

The Sport Fury series was exclusively V-8, having engines ranging from the standard 230-horsepower 318 to the optional 375-horsepower Super Commando 440. With the biggest engines, they were performance cars with lots of luxury. Illustrated is the Sport Fury Convertible. With the 318 engine and no optional extras, this 3,710-pound car was listed at $3,425. In all forms, it attracted a total of 2,489 sales.

The luxury-loaded Plymouth VIP Fast Top, of which 6,768 were built, weighed 3,615 pounds and cost $3,260 with a 318 V-8 and other standard equippage. This year, the Series DP Fast Tops and 4-Door Hardtops had no flow-through ventilation system as featured for 1967. Therefore, no louvers were required in the upper deck panels, just below the rear windows of these bodies.

None of the big Suburbans had new sheetmetal for the year, continuing as was for 1967, even to the rear bumper. And the 2-way tailgate feature of the mid-size wagons was not incorporated in the big vehicles. The Plymouth Custom Suburban was available only in V-8 forms. The 2-seat model, of which 17,078 were built, cost $3,252 and weighed 4,045 pounds. Shown is the 3-seat model, a $3,353 car weighing 4,090 pounds and having a production run of 9,954 units. Custom Suburbans had interiors of Fury II design, exterior trim borrowed from Fury III cars.

The sophisticated VIP 4-Door Hardtop was Plymouth's topline 6-passenger car. It weighed 3,655 pounds, cost $3,326 and had a 10,745-car production run. The VIP series was exclusively V-8, with engines of 230, 290, 330 and 375 horsepower. Interiors were sumptuous. Standard exterior body side dress employed rich satin-finish bright moldings to define the lower lines. Rear wheel skirts were standard for this series.

The big Series DP wagons were called Suburbans and were not known as Fury I, II and III vehicles. The lowest-priced was the Plymouth Suburban, a 2-seat model which in V-8 form cost $3,153 and weighed 4,030 pounds. Exactly 6,749 Sixes and V-8s were built. It had typical Fury I interior design, but exterior trim was Fury II. Not offered in the U.S.A. was a 3-seat Suburban, of which 65 were built for Canada or export.

All of the big Suburbans retained the 121-inch wheelbase. The Plymouth Sport Suburban, built only with V-8 engines, was provided in two models. The 2-seat model cost $3,442 and recorded a 4,055-pound weight and 9,203-unit production total. The 3-seat model was the heaviest and most expensive Plymouth this year, weighing 4,100 pounds and listing at $3,543. A total of 13,224 were built. Interiors of the Sport Suburbans utilized the Fury III design theme. On the exterior, body sides were adorned with wood-grain vinyl, and ornamentation between the taillamps was similar to the VIP.

Plymouth's Police Specials continued in good demand by the law enforcers. The factory-built offerings were well-known to policemen and citizens alike. Shown is the Belvedere Pursuit, which was offered with a 318 or Commando 383 2-barrel V-8. When powered by the big Super Commando 383 4-barrel job it was known as the Pursuit Special. For mild work, the Belvedere Patroller with a 225 Six was adequate, but it could be built with any of the V-8s for handling anything requiring speed. Belvedere police cars were available as coupes and 4-door sedans.

Many a motorist has seen the rear end of a Fury Pursuit as it flashed by in a hot chase or emergency run. The engine list began with the 318, next were two 383 jobs of 2 and 4-barrel varieties, plus the Commando 440 4-barrel, and more. With the Super Commando 440 high-performance 375-horsepower job it became the Fury Pursuit Special and could outrun almost anything but another like it. As a town car, there was also the Fury Patroller with a 225 Six or any of the V-8s. All could be had in 2-door and 4-door sedan forms.

Police could also have Plymouth Emergency Wagons. Shown is the Belvedere model. It could have any of the engines available for other Belvedere Police Specials. If a bigger vehicle was wanted, a Fury Emergency Wagon could be ordered with any Fury engine but the Super Commando 440. These vehicles were useful for police and ambulance duty.

Familiar vehicles on the streets of every city and metropolis in the nation were Plymouth taxicabs. This year's Fury provided a comfortable ride for the passengers who hailed it. The more economical Belvedere model, which was no slouch in the comfort department, was ideal for small town cab operators. Plymouth outfitted the cabs in a very special way, offering a choice of engines and all kinds of interior and chassis features.

This was an adjustment year, but in a downward direction. At the end of the calendar year, industry passenger car production totalled out at more than 7% less than 1968. About one-third of the makers gained rather than lost, however, as a surge of demand for some medium-priced and most all expensive cars was underway.

Excepting Imperial, all Chrysler car lines dropped for a collective corporate loss of about 12.1%. The corporation's share of industry activity was scaled down to 16.76%. Plymouth production slumped only about 4.8%, but the company fell from 4th to 6th position in the industry ranks. It was dislodged by Buick and Oldsmobile, who zoomed from below to take 4th and 5th, respectively. But Plymouth would recover nicely the next year.

Plymouth's overall model offerings increased in number, mostly in the mid-size and larger series. But the basic compact car line-up remained unchanged. The Valiant group, Series EV, included the 100 and the Signet, each with two body types. With minor styling changes, they continued on the 108-inch wheelbase. Engine choices were the same as for 1968, with the 170 Slant Six and 273 V-8 as standards and the 225 Slant Six and 318 V-8 as options. Horsepower and basic specifications were unchanged, but Sixes provided better fuel economy than before.

The Barracuda Series EB retained the successful styling and three body types on a 108-inch chassis. New option packages emerged as the performance craze boomed, warranting a variety of decor and engine advertising on the body sides. Standard engines were the 225 Six and 318 V-8. Extra choices were the 340 V-8 as offered for 1968 and the former 383 V-8 which was now rated at 330 horsepower at 5,200 r.p.m. The Formula S performance chassis was available with the 340 and 383 engines. A special performance package was the 'Cuda, which had the 340 as standard and the 383 for extra kicks.

The mid-size Series ER was given mild new styling touches and an expansion of models offered. The economy Belvedere line again had three models but the Satellite was reduced to five because the Sport wagons joined the Sport Satellite line which also added a sedan for a total of five models. The Road Runner, adding a convertible, now had three models and the GTX continued with two. Unchanged were the wheelbases they rode on: 117 inches for wagons and 116 for the others.

The engine list for the mid-size cars eliminated the 273 V-8 and shuffled the 318 around. Belvederes and Satellites had the 225 Six and 318 V-8 for standards, while the 318 was the only standard for Sport Satellites. All three of those lines again offered the two 383 V-8 options as they were for 1968. Road Runners retained their exclusive 335-horsepower 383 as standard and GTX cars were the only Plymouths to give that status to the 375-horsepower 440 V-8. The sole option for Road Runner and GTX cars was the brute 425-horsepower 426 Hemi street engine. Super-powered Hemi competition engines were again available for ER cars and Barracudas to be used by independent racing and drag teams.

Since their first appearance in 1965, big Plymouths had acquired a classification as "standard-size" rather than "big" cars. The term also applied to the big cars of Ford, Chevrolet, Dodge, etc. But regardless of whether standard-size or not, the big Plymouths got bigger this year. After four years of use, the 1965 basic car and wagon packages were replaced with longer, wider and heavier vehicles as Plymouth sought more sales from the lower fringes of the medium-price market.

The Series EP was new in styling and structure, as well as in dimensions. The unitized construction principle continued as a feature. Wheelbases were one inch longer, with suburbans on 122 inches and other models on 120. The roster of models registered two each in the Fury I and Fury II lines, with coupes replacing 2-door sedans. The Fury III had five models and the Sport Fury continued with three, but each had a replacement hardtop. The VIP line was expanded to three models. Suburbans remained aloof from the car lines, with no change in the list which offered one standard Suburban and two each in Custom and Sport Suburban forms.

The Series EP engine list was a duplicate of 1968. The 225 Six was supplied when wanted for Fury I, II and III hardtops and sedans, also for the standard Suburban. For all Series EP models, the standard V-8 was the 318 and optional V-8s were the 383 engines rated at 290 and 330 horsepower. A 375-horsepower 440 was available for all models except the suburban series, for which a 350-horsepower 440 was reserved.

Numerous new items and refinements related to fuel economy, human safety and health were built into Plymouths this year. Among them were improved brakes and better control of exhaust emissions. To design, develop and tool all of its cars for this year, Chrysler Corp. spent 365 million dollars.

The Valiant 100 2-Door Sedan is shown in absolutely standard form. It was even fitted with the 170 Slant Six engine. Its new low price of $2,094 was boldly painted on the windshield. The 2,656-pound car weighed and cost the least of any Plymouth this year. Including V-8s, 29,672 examples of this model were built. Standard V-8 Valiants cost $111 more than standard Sixes. Valiant prices were lower this year, but other Plymouth models were higher than in 1968.

The Valiant 100 4-Door Sedan also displays the practical appearance of the economy series, but optional deluxe wheel fittings are shown. As a Six, this model cost $2,154 and weighed 2,676 pounds. Assembly lines turned out 49,409 of them as Sixes and V-8s. Production totals for both 100 models include those built with the 200 Decor.

Continuing the practice of the previous two years, a 200 Decor Group option was available for both Valiant 100 sedans. Deluxe cloth-and-vinyl or all-vinyl seats, plus other extras were interior features, while on the exterior were full-length bright moldings and "Valiant two hundred" nameplates on the body sides. Wire wheelcovers, whitewall tires and bumper guards were all-Valiant options, not part of the 200 Decor package.

A V-8 Signet 2-Door Sedan displays the new full-width grille and the styling of the new hood given to all Valiants. The hood was the only new major sheetmetal part. The front end design, with park/turn signals in the grille, was cleaner and gave a wider appearance to the cars. As a Six, this model weighed 2,656 pounds and cost $2,253. Its Six and V-8 production run was 6,645 cars.

The Valiant Signet 4-Door Sedan weighed 2,676 pounds and cost $2,313 in standard Six form. A total of 21,492 were built in all forms. This V-8 model had a mixture of trim features. Standard Signet touches included bright moldings on the drip rails, window frames, "B" pillars, body sills, wheel openings and deck lid. The vinyl roof, belt stripes and attractive wheel fittings were extra-cost items.

The Plymouth Barracuda Sports Coupe shown was built with a 340 engine and Formula S chassis components. It had 340-S designations on the front quarters. The 340 V-8 had bore and stroke of 4.04 x 3.31 inches, 340 c.i.d., 10.5:1 compression, a 4-barrel carburetor and a horsepower output of 275 at 5,000 r.p.m. The Formula S package included heavy-duty torsion bars and rear springs, front stabilizer bar, firm-ride shock absorbers, wide-oval tires and Formula S ornamental identification. This was just one of the numerous Barracuda variations.

This Barracuda model had two names — Sports Coupe and Hardtop. This photo from a sales catalog was captioned as a Sports Coupe. The vinyl roof was optional, as was the wheel dress-up, but the thin body stripes were generally seen on any Barracuda that was not decorated in a performance-oriented manner. With no extras, this model was called the Hardtop, and in that form a V-8 cost $2,780 and weighed 2,899 pounds. Under both names, total Six and V-8 production was 12,757 cars, including all performance varieties.

Colorful flower-patterned vinyl was offered in several ways. On the roof, it was called the Mod Top option. One package included matching seat and interior side trim panels with the roof. And it could be ordered for the roof only, or the interior only. The floral decoration was in shades of yellow and black for the Barracuda Sports Coupe, hues of blue and green for the Satellite Hardtop.

A new Barracuda performance package was the 'Cuda option, provided with 340 or 383 engines. Other goodies were a 4-speed transmission with Hurst shifter, twin scoops on top of the hood, two wide black hood stripes, lower body contrasting paint treatment all-around, and minor additives. Shown is a 'Cuda 340 version which had its designation in black, just behind the front wheel.

The Barracuda Fastback is shown with an optional vinyl panel on the roof. This was the only manner in which vinyl was offered for the Fastback, since extending it to the drip rails and around the rear glass was not regarded as tasteful. In standard V-8 form the Fastback weighed 2,984 pounds and cost $2,813. The production total for this body type was 17,788 cars, including all Six and V-8 variations. This body no longer had the folding rear seat and unique trunk feature as standard, but continued the practical novelty on an optional basis.

This version of the sleek Barracuda was called the Sports Fastback, but it was not actually another model, and its production total was included with the standard Fastback. It is shown as a 383-S with a bold side stripe that did not necessarily accompany the Formula S chassis under this body. The stripe was available for cars with the 383 engine, which had a bore and stroke of 4.25 x 3.38 inches, 383 c.i.d., 10:1 compression, a 4-barrel carburetor and a 330-horsepower output at 5,200 r.p.m. The 383-S designation appears just below the Barracuda signature at the front.

The mid-size cars were given new deck lids. A Belvedere Coupe shows the panel with no superficial adornment, only the Plymouth name within the recessed design feature. The deck lid was the only sheetmetal change in the Series ER. Large squarish taillamp assemblies were end caps fitted to the quarter panels. This model, of which 7,063 were built as Six or V-8 cars, had a V-8 price and weight of $2,599 and 3,126 pounds.

The Barracuda Convertible is shown in standard form except for the sporty wheel trim. The V-8 price was $3,082 and the weight was 3,034 pounds. Including Sixes and all variations, 1,442 were built. Any Barracuda standard V-8 model cost $106 more than a Six of similar model. All Barracudas had new hood and grille panels, the only sheetmetal changes made for the Series EB.

The Belvedere 4-Door Sedan sold for $2,638 and weighed 3,156 pounds as a V-8. Including Sixes, a total of 12,914 came out of the factories. Standard Belvedere side trim consisted of a narrow sill molding of bright finish. The Series ER offered 14 or 15-inch wheels. Tire sizes varied according to model and equipment.

The Plymouth Satellite 4-Door Sedan recorded a weight of 3,161 pounds and posted a $2,725 price when built as a V-8. Its total Six and V-8 production run was 35,296 cars. Bright moldings as shown on the lower body side and wheel areas were standard Satellite treatment. Any mid-size model with a standard V-8 cost $90 more than the similar Six.

Costing $2,749 and weighing 3,151 pounds in V-8 form was the Satellite Hardtop, which had a 38,323-unit production run, including Sixes. This model's roof, shown with black vinyl, was also optionally available as a flowered Mod Top as offered for the Barracuda. On Satellites, the recessed deck lid area was framed with a thin bright molding. All mid-size cars had backup lights in the rear bumper this year.

Shown is the Satellite Wagon, which had a 2-way tailgate that sung down or sidewise like all mid-size wagons. The 2-seat model, of which 5,837 were built, weighed and cost 3,586 pounds and $3,087 as a V-8. Weighing 3,656 pounds and costing $3,196 was the 3-seat V-8. The 3-seater had a production run of 4,730. Not shown is the Belvedere Wagon, which was built only in 2-seat form and as a V-8 weighed 3,591 pounds and cost $2,969. Exactly 7,038 Belvederes were built. All production totals include Sixes.

Of special appeal to 1,137 buyers was the Satellite Convertible. Built as a Six or V-8, it weighed 3,276 pounds and cost $2,965 in the latter form. Many new options were offered for mid-size cars as buyers demanded ever more choices. Among them were a manually-adjusted bucket seat for the driver, allowing a multitude of fore and aft, up and down and tilting positions.

The Sport Satellite Hardtop drew 15,807 buyers who could get it only as a V-8. The 3,156-pound car was listed at $2,883. Offered for mid-size cars was a Performance Axle Package inclduing a 3.55 axle ratio, Sure-Grip differential, viscous drive fan, an extra-wide 26-inch radiator, fan shrouds and suspension as used for Road Runner Hemis. Including those features, but with a 3.91 axle, was a High-Performance Axle Package available only for cars with 383 4-barrel engines.

New to the Sport Satellite series was the 4-Door Sedan, of which 5,836 were built. Supplied only as a V-8, it cost $2,911 and weighed 3,196 pounds. For standard side decor, Sport Satellites had bright sill and wheel opening trim, plus full-length striping on the lower character line, including over the wheels. A new option for mid-size cars was the Turnpike Cruising Package. It included a 383 2-barrel engine, automatic speed control, power front disc brakes, a 2.76 axle ratio, undercoating and a signal to warn of turned-on headlights.

The Sport Satellite Convertible, built only as a V-8, weighed 3,276 pounds, cost $3,081 and had a production run of 818. Obvious is the applied ornamentation between the taillamps, typical of the Sport Satellite series. Another option for mid-size cars was the Super-Performance Axle Package. Available only with a 440 4-barrel engine or Hemi automatic, it had a 4.10 axle and items included with the 3.55 and 3.91 axle packages.

For 1968, this was called the Satellite Sport Wagon because it was related to the Satellite series. This year the words were shifted because the vehicle was placed in the expanded and slightly down-graded Sport Satellite series. The Sport Satellite Wagon, exclusively V-8, was built in two models. The 2-seat version was a 3,596-pounder, was priced at $3,241 and had a 3,221-unit production run. Weighing 3,666 pounds and costing $3,350 was the 3-seater, of which 3,152 were built.

The Road Runner series was so popular that production was nearly double that of the 1968 series. In standard form, the Road Runner Coupe cost $2,945 and scaled 3,435 pounds. In all forms, 33,743 were built. The car shown was powered by the 440 4-barrel V-8 and was fitted with a special competition-type hood with a large functional air scoop and lock-pin fastenings. Wheels with extra-wide rims are seen with no trim.

In standard form the Road Runner Hardtop weighed 3,450 pounds and cost $3,083. It had an all-forms production run of 48,549 cars. A 383-powered car is shown with such extra-cost items as a pair of very wide flat black paint bands on the hood, full-length striping on the body side belt and a bright sill molding. The driver was using a shoulder strap for safety, straps being standard for front seat passengers. A new option for all Plymouths except convertibles was shoulder straps for the rear seat.

The Convertible, of which 2,128 were built, was new to the Road Runner series. The car weighed 3,790 pounds and listed at $3,313 in standard form. The car shown had a 383 4-barrel 335-horsepower V-8 which was again standard and exclusive to the Road Runner series. Appearing as a light stripe on the hood scoop, red paint accented the grilles of the ducts, which faced the sky. In standard form the scoops were dummies, but were available in functional form for Road Runner and GTX models with standard engines. The functional type, which could be opened or closed at the driver's will, was standard on all cars having the 426 Hemi street engine.

The Plymouth GTX Hardtop weighed 3,465 pounds and cost $3,416 in standard form, including the 375-horsepower 440 engine. Its 14,902-unit production total included those powered by the 426 Hemi. Standard GTX body side decor consisted of black paint on lower areas, edged by bright moldings with a red or white reflective tape stripe just below them. New was a Track Pak option with a Hurst 4-speed shifter, extra-heavy-duty 3.54 axle, 9.75-inch ring gear diameter, Sure-Grip differential, viscous drive fan and a dual breaker distributor. Except for a 4.10 axle and the addition of power front disc brakes, an extra-special Super Track Pak had the same items. Both Paks were for GTX and Hemi-powered Plymouths.

Ready for a dash on a drag strip was a Road Runner of Plymouth's Super Stock team, Sox & Martin. Besides putting the cars through competitive events, Ronnie Sox and Buddy Martin operated the Plymouth Supercar Clinic tour of dealerships across the nation, giving advice and demonstrations to drag racing amateurs. Among the cars they used were a special "Project-Wedge" Road Runner 440 and a 'Cuda with a 426 competition Hemi. GTX cars were also used by the team, which first swung to Plymouth in 1965 and went on a winning binge through the next several years. Plymouths did not compete in NASCAR racing this year.

Drawing the least demand of any Plymouth model offered to U.S. buyers this year was the GTX Convertible, which had a production run of only 700 cars. When built with no extras, the sporty automobile gave a scale reading of 3,590 pounds and carried a $3,635 price tag. The car shown was powered by a 440 engine.

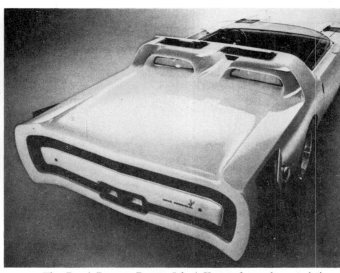

Plymouth's show car for the year was the Duster I, which had a vastly modified Road Runner base. The wheelbase was shortened to 100 inches and tires were large H60 x 15 prototypes. A 426 street Hemi was under the low dual-scooped hood. Headlamps were rectangular and the front rock shields had spoilers to reduce frontal lift. The car had no roof, and the windshield and side glass were low. The car was developed by Chrysler stylists and engineers, and was built for show only.

The Road Runner Duster I had Kamm form characteristics at the rear. Dual exhaust ports were at the center. Taillamps were in the seat headrest nacelles. Spoilers in the rear quarter panel sides were adjustable to prevent side-to-side yaw when slipstreaming. Spoilers in the roll bar were also adjustable. Hinged quick-fill fuel tank caps were on each side and there was no deck lid.

The Plymouth Fury I Coupe was the lowest-priced of the new Series EP big cars. As a V-8, the 3,548-pound car was listed at $2,806. Not very many people preferred this large but very practical automobile, as only 4,971 Sixes and V-8s were manufactured. For Series EP models offering the choices, a standard V-8 cost $105 more than a Six.

Shown is the Fury II 4-Door Sedan, which cost $2,946 and weighed 3,583 pounds as a V-8. Including Sixes, 41,047 were built. It has the basic Fury II body side trim, which was a full-length bright molding on the same level as the grille top. Not shown is the Fury II Coupe which had a V-8 weight and price of 3,553 pounds and $2,918, and of which 3,268 were built in Six and V-8 forms. Not available in the U.S.A. was a Fury II 2-Door Hardtop, of which 3,299 were built for Canada or export.

The Fury I 4-Door Sedan shows the standard Fury I body side appearance, which had no bright moldings or striping. A V-8 model weighed 3,538 pounds and cost $2,849. Total Six and V-8 production was 18,771. Series EP cars had 15-inch wheels, up from the 14-inchers of 1968. Tire sizes varied according to model and equipment. This year, all Plymouths had rectangular side markers, again amber at the front and red at the rear, but the rear marker is not obvious in this view.

Accounting for a Six and V-8 production total of 44,168 was the Fury III 2-Door Hardtop shown. As a V-8 it weighed 3,563 pounds and sold for $3,105. Not shown is the Fury III 2-Door Formal Hardtop with different roof styling like the VIP Formal model. It weighed 3,653 pounds and cost $3,125 as a V-8 and had a 22,738-car production run, including Sixes. Also unavailable in photo form is the Plymouth Snapper, a spring sales special based on the above. It was identified by the Snapper name on a turtle image within an oval-shaped "camp" emblem on the "C" pillars. The roof vinyl was of a distinctive turtleshell texture and a number of options were included as standard. Since the Snapper was a sort of option package rather than a distinctive catalogued model, the factory did not record its production separately.

The Plymouth Fury III 4-Door Sedan recorded a weight of 3,588 pounds and listed at a price of $3,084 when built with the standard V-8 engine and no optional extras. This big automobile was easily the year's most popular Plymouth model, having a Six and V-8 production run of 72,747 units. Of all the newly-styled Series EP cars, the Fury III line was by far the best seller, scoring substantial gains over the 1968 Fury III.

The new styling of the big Plymouths had more curvature than previously. Chrysler's styling vice president Elwood Engel likened the shape to that of a jet aircraft fuselage. He was in reference to a cross-section through the body at the "B" pillars. Even the side glass was more curved. Some of the character is obvious in this view of the Fury III 4-Door Hardtop, which was built only as a V-8. The 3,643-pound car cost $3,155 and had a production run of 68,818. Shown is the standard Fury III side treatment, which included a full-length bright molding heavier than that of the Fury II, plus bright trim on the wheel openings. Rear wheel skirts were optional on all but VIP models.

The Plymouth Fury III Convertible, exclusively a V-8 model, registered a weight of 3,704 pounds, a price of $3,324 and a production total of 4,129. Placing the headlamps in a horizontal attitude gave a lower appearance to the grilles of the new big cars. Another feature of all Series EP cars was the concealment of windshield wipers, which were parked in a gap between the hood and windshield. This gave a cleaner appearance to the area, since exposed wipers are not attractive.

Continuing its special kind of appeal was the exclusively V-8 Plymouth Sport Fury series, of which the 2-Door Hardtop is shown. Selling at $3,283, the 3,603-pound car won a total of 14,120 sales. It shows the Sport Fury body side dress without options, having bright moldings on the wheel openings and sill, plus dual striping that extended from the front quarter tip to just beyond the door, trailed by red, white and blue bars. Not shown is the Sport Fury 2-Door Formal Hardtop which replaced the 1968 Fast Top model. The Formal cost $3,303, weighed 3,678 pounds and had a production run of 2,169.

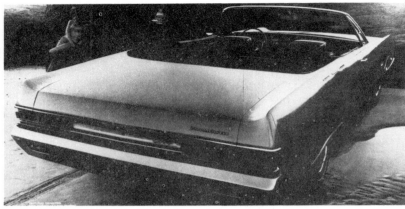

The strong horizontal treatment emphasized the width of the big Plymouths, which at 79.6 inches were 1.9 inches wider than the big cars of 1968. The 214.5-inch overall length was 1.5 inches longer. All but the Suburbans rode on a 120-inch wheelbase which was one inch longer than before. Shown is the 3,729-pound Sport Fury Convertible which sold at $3,502 and chalked up a production total of 1,579.

The 2-Door Formal Hardtop of the exclusively V-8 VIP series weighed 3,668 pounds, cost $3,402 and attracted 1,059 sales. Added to the Fury III, Sport Fury and VIP lines after other models appeared, the Formal Hardtop used the Series EP coupe roof design which had decidedly different styling of the blind quarters. In optional vinyl-covered form it had a padded appearance. The car shown was air conditioned, as indicated by the absence of front ventpanes.

The Plymouth VIP 2-Door Hardtop scaled 3,583 pounds of weight, marked its price at $3,382 and scored a production total of 4,740. It is seen with no ventpanes on the doors, as they were eliminated from Fury III, Sport Fury and VIP 2-door hardtops with air conditioning. The deletion would shortly become widespread, air conditioning or not. Standard VIP side treatment included bright trim on front wheel openings, wide bright-edged paint-filled lower moldings, rear wheel skirts and built-in front cornering lights in line with the lower moldings. The rectangular feature between the front wheel and door, seen on all big Plymouths, was a series name plaque.

Shown on the turntable in a walled outdoor area of Chrysler's Highland Park engineering and styling complex is a VIP 4-Door Hardtop. The prestigious luxury automobile sold for $3,433 and weighed 3,663 pounds. A total of 7,982 rolled off the assembly lines. Vinyl roofs were optional for all VIP models, but most, if not all, were built with the formal-like touch. All big Plymouths could be ordered with the Turnpike Cruising Package as noted for the mid-size cars.

The Plymouth Suburban was regarded as of Fury I class. Its interior was of Fury I design and the exterior trim was also Fury I, except for the use of Fury II body side moldings. The side name plaques bore the name "Suburban." The 2-seat vehicle weighed 4,103 pounds and cost $3,336 as a V-8. Including Sixes, 6,424 were built. Not shown, and not available in the U.S.A., 111 3-seat Suburbans were built for Canada. All Series EP suburban models were built on a 122-inch wheelbase, one inch longer than for 1968.

1969

When viewed from the rear, the big suburbans had a hoop-like shape, consistent with the "fuselage look." The raised portion at the extreme rear of the roof was the new integral wind deflector. The bridge-like span, with air passage slots between it and the roof, deflected air downward past the tailgate window, keeping the glass free of dust. Shown is the Plymouth Custom Suburban, built only in V-8 form. Of Fury II class, it had Fury II design inside and across the rear outside, but the exterior body side trim was Fury III. Side name plaques were labelled "Custom Suburban." The 2-seat model, of which 15,976 were built, weighed 4,103 pounds and cost $3,436. The 4,148-pound 3-seat model, priced at $3,527, had a production run of 10,216.

With downtown Detroit's skyline in the background, a Plymouth Sport Suburban shows off its wood-grained vinyl-clad side. This model had an interior of Fury III design and carried "Sport Suburban" on its side plaques, plus being an exclusive V-8 variety. The 2-seat vehicle cost $3,651, weighed 4,123 pounds and won 8,201 buyers. The 3-seat model again took honors as the costliest and heaviest Plymouth for the year, selling for $3,718 and weighing 4,173 pounds. The 3-seater garnered a total of 13,502 sales. All of the Series EP suburbans featured a tailgate that opened either flat-out or swing-out.

The expanding taxicab market warranted increasing attention from Plymouth, who had even bigger Furys to offer this year. They provided more room for passengers. In the rear seat area there was 2.8 inches more shoulder room and almost one inch more headroom than 1968 Furys had. And trunks had 1.8 more cubic feet of space for carrying luggage. Except for the roof signlight and side lettering as seen on the Fury shown, Furys and Belvederes were factory-prepared in taxicab varieties, even with special paint treatments. They were sold through Plymouth dealerships, just as the regular passenger cars were.

As the market for police cars was strong enough to sustain a constant demand, Plymouth was busily engaged in going after a substantial share of the business. For some years past, special catalogs and sales promotion effort had been devoted to police cars. But Plymouth's reputation for building quality cars to meet the exacting and often extra-ordinary demands brought many sales without the use of sales media as an introduction. Shown is the Belvedere Pursuit, one of the complete line of Plymouth Police Specials that included Pursuits, Pursuit Specials, Patrollers and Emergency Wagons in Fury and Belvedere types.

Intending to race them in the Indianapolis 500 this year, Andy Granatelli, president of STP Corp., built two of these Plymouth-powered racers. The design, called the Super Wedge, was as wedge-shaped to a bird in flight as it appears in this view. Engines were the 318 V-8, highly modified by STP and a Chrysler engineer. Using stock blocks, bore was increased from 3.91 to 4.00 inches and the stroke cut from 3.31 to 3.18 inches. Of stock design, new crankshafts were made of high-stress alloy. Fuel injection, dry sump lubrication, gear-driven camshafts and tuned exhaust headers were applied. The standard 4-speed transmission was in front of the 4-wheel-drive central gearcase. Hoped-for horsepower was 525 to 550. Somehow, the cars did not get into the famed 500 race, but one later won at Dover, Del.

This calendar year ended with almost every automaker in the losers column on the industry passenger car production sheet. Only Plymouth, Lincoln's Continental Mark III and the American Motors group were in the gainers column. While the industry dropped nearly 20.4%, the Chrysler Corp. family sagged only 8.9%. However, Chrysler's share of industry activity picked up 2.35%, which gave the corporation a 19.10% slice, a portion not enjoyed since 1957.

Plymouth was the prop that kept Chrysler from sagging lower. Volume was almost 7.4% greater than for 1969, boosting the breadwinner up into 3rd position, a rank it had not held since 1959. Those in the two top positions changed places, too, as the Ford cars regained No. 1 spot from Chevrolet, who had held it since 1960.

The vitality of Plymouth was centered in the new Duster cars that were introduced to compete with the Ford Maverick. The economy compact was tremendously successful in its mission, as reflected in the Valiant production total which more than doubled this year. Carrying all three names, it was properly called the Plymouth Valiant Duster. The offspring Duster inherited its basic package from the parent Valiant, but its body proper appeared in a new form.

The Valiant family, designated the Series FV, continued on the former 108-inch wheelbase. The Duster was presented only as a coupe, first offered in standard and 340 versions but later adding the Gold Duster option. The parent Valiant was reduced to one 4-door sedan model, there being no 100, 200 Decor and Signet varieties. For Duster and the regular Valiants, the standard 6-cylinder engine was the Slant Six, updated with 3.40 x 3.64 inches bore and stroke, 198 c.i.d., lower 8.4:1 compression and horsepower up to 125 at 4,400 r.p.m. The 145-horsepower 225 Slant Six was continued as optional for Duster and Valiant. The reliable 230-horsepower 318 was the standard

Duster V-8, and was the only V-8 offered for the Valiant. New to this series, and powering the Duster 340, was the 275-horsepower 340 V-8. A new fully-synchronized 3-speed column-shift manual transmission was standard with the 318 engine. A floor-mounted 3-speed manual was standard with the 340, optional for other Dusters. TorqueFlite 3-speed automatics were available for all.

The Barracuda Series FB was a completely new design and unitized body structure, but was again based on a 108-inch wheelbase. So popular was this series that it registered a 73% production gain over 1969. The fastback

The year's most popular Plymouth model was the Duster Coupe, of which 192,375 were built in all Six and V-8 forms except the 340. As a Six in standard form it weighed 2,790 pounds and cost $2,172, which made it the lightest-weight and lowest-priced Plymouth for the year. The pre-production prototype shown was without Valiant Duster signatures on the side and a Plymouth emblem at the grille center. The vinyl-clad roof, highback bucket front seats, sporty wheels and bumper guards were optional. Duster body design featured a sweeping roof and deck silhouette, was almost semi-fastback. Pillars and side glass curved inward more than the Valiant sedan.

Added in the spring was the Gold Duster, which featured a special option package at a special savings price. With a 225 Six or 318 V-8 engine, it had dual horns, whitewall tires, unique wheelcovers, bright drip moldings, an argent painted grille, gold side and rear tape stripes, bucket-style seat trim and a cigar lighter. The 5-passenger car was further identified by Gold Duster signatures. All Dusters had ventless door glass and no upper frames on the doors. Normal Duster overall height was 52.6 inches and overall width was 71.6 inches. Front track was 57.4 inches and the rear was 55.6 inches.

Part of Plymouth's campaign to win buyers away from the Ford Maverick was the offering of the Valiant Duster Coupe in this form. With the standard 198 Six engine were options such as the TorqueFlite transmission, deluxe wheel-covers, whitewall tires and AM radio. Four of these items cost less than similar Maverick items, but vehicle retail price was $90.75 more than a similar Maverick. Regardless, the Duster's superior interior and trunk space had sales appeal. Many Dusters had dual black tape stripes across the rear, connecting the 2-level taillight openings. Structure of all Duster bodies, from the hood and front quarters back, was new. Front end sheetmetal was like the Valiant sedan.

model was no longer around, but the year began with a hardtop and convertible, and a coupe was added later. The series was divided into three sub-series: The low-line, the Gran Coupe and the 'Cuda, of which the 'Cuda was provided in several versions.

The 225 Six and 318 V-8 were standard engines for the Barracuda low-line and Gran Coupe, which had two 383 V-8 versions of 2-barrel 290-horsepower and 4-barrel 330-horsepower as optional engines. Rated at 335 horsepower was another 4-barrel 383 which was standard for the 'Cuda. Optional for the 'Cuda were four V-8s. For 'Cuda buyers who wanted less than the standard 'Cuda 383, the 340 as used by the Duster was available. The 4-barrel 440 of 1969 mid-size and bigger Plymouths was given lower 9.7:1 compression but still delivered 375 horsepower for the 'Cuda. A new 440 with 10.5:1 compression and three 2-barrel carburetors put out 390 horsepower at 4,700 r.p.m. A public offering in compact cars for the first time, the 426 Hemi street engine with its customary 425 horsepower was provided for buyers who felt they had enough guts to handle the hairy beast in a car of 'Cuda size. A 3-speed manual transmission was standard for the 225, 318, 340 and both 4-barrel 383 engines. Standard for both 440 engines was a 4-speed manual, which was optional for the 318, 340 and 4-barrel 383 plants. The only transmission for the 2-barrel 383 and the Hemi was the TorqueFlite, which was optional for the 225, 318, 340 and both 4-barrel 383 engines. Six rear axle ratios were provided.

Demand for the mid-size cars was lower this year, even the Road Runner falling to almost half its 1969 production. Modified from the previous year, the Series FR continued the 117-inch wheelbase for wagons and 116 for others. The Belvedere line continued with three models and the Satellite again had five. The Sport Satellite was reduced to four models by elimination of a convertible. Three models were retained in the regular Road Runner series, and the aerodynamic SuperBird was added. The GTX was offered only as a hardtop.

The Belvedere and Satellite lines had the 225 Six and 318 V-8 as standard engines, while the 318 was the only standard for the Sport Satellite. Those three sub-series had the 290 and 330-horsepower 383 engines for options. The 335-horsepower 383 was again standard for the Road Runner regulars, while the 4-barrel 440 was standard for the SuperBird and GTX. The 6-barrel 440 and the 426 Hemi were optional for the regular and SuperBird Road Runners and the GTX. The standard transmission for the 225, 318 and both 4-barrel 383s was the 3-speed manual. Standard for both 440s and the Hemi was the 4-speed manual, which was optional for 4-barrel 383s. TorqueFlite was offered for all engines and was the only gearbox for the 2-barrel 383. Seven rear axle ratios were distributed among those combinations.

Given minor appearance changes was the big Series FP, in which a model shake-up occurred in some areas. Retained was the 120-inch wheelbase for all but suburbans, which continued on the 122-inch chassis. The Fury I and Fury II each had two models and the Fury III offered five. The Sport Fury line became a family of six and the VIP did not appear. Continuing as separate, the suburban group now had two models each in standard, Custom and

The Duster 340 was a performance version of the regular coupe. Its powerplant was the V-8 with bore and stroke of 4.04 x 3.31 inches, 340 c.i.d., 10.5:1 compression, 4-barrel carburetion and a 275-horsepower output at 5,000 r.p.m. Its standard transmission was a 3-speed manual with shift-stick on the floor. Front brakes were disc and tires were wide tread. The front track was 58.2 inches, rear 55.6. It had Duster 340 signatures and the side tape shown. The 3,110-pound car, of which 24,817 were built, was priced at $2,547.

Plymouths continued to give an excellent account of themselves in exhibition and competitive events. Shown is Tom McEwen's Duster "funny car" called the Mongoose, which was capable of more than 200 m.p.h. The typical "funny car" modifications included removal of the coupe "B" pillars and installation of roll-over reinforcement inside.

Carried over with minor styling detail changes, the Plymouth Valiant 4-Door Sedan brought 50,810 Six and V-8 sales. The standard 6-cylinder version weighed 2,709 pounds and sold for $2,250. It had no exterior sheetmetal changes, but shared its entire front end with the Duster. The grille design was more interesting than that of 1969. A host of interior and exterior options were available for this carryover Valiant, which was offered only as the model shown. The Valiant line, including Duster, was designated the Series FV.

The new Plymouth Barracuda Series FB was an all-new design, again of sports car flavor and sharing none of its structure with Valiant. The standard Barracuda Hardtop, shown with optional full-length colored rub strips at the midsection, sold for $2,865 and weighed 3,025 pounds in V-8 form. It also was built as a Six. Total production was recorded as 25,651, of which some probably were the standard coupe. All Barracudas had ventless front windows and concealed windshield wipers.

Sport Suburban forms, but they were upgraded a step in their relation to Fury car lines. Those were the offering at the start of the model year, and the engines for them follow.

For those models offering a Six, the 225 was standard for the Fury I, II and III, and for the standard Suburban. The 318 was the standard V-8 for all Series FP models but the Sport Fury GT, and the 383 engines of 290 and 330 horsepower were optional for all that offered the 318. The 4-barrel 440 was optional for all FP cars but the Sport Fury 2-Door Hardtop and was standard for the Sport Fury GT, which had the 6-barrel 440 as its option. The 3-speed manual transmission was standard for the 225, 318 and 2-barrel 383 engines, which offered the TorqueFlite automatic as extra. The only transmission for the 4-barrel 383 and the 440 engines was the TorqueFlite. Only three rear axle ratios were available.

The Series FP, introduced with the others in the early fall of 1969, did not draw as much demand as the big cars of the previous year, even with the broader model coverage. While no significant changes were added to lower-range Furys, a new model was entered at the top in February. Known as the Fury Gran Coupe, its prime purpose was to compete more effectively with the Ford LTD and Chevrolet Caprice. Bearing Fury III and Sport Fury characteristics, it included numerous options as standard, including the 2-barrel 383 V-8 engine.

Though this summary of all the new models is extremely basic and brief, it registers the complex variety of cars and equipment. The tremendous demand for performance and luxury features, plus safety and emission control requirements, brought a flood of new items that cannot be included in this limited report. To develop all of its new cars and trucks and put them in production, Chrysler Corp. spent 425 million dollars.

Another of Plymouth's spring additions was the Barracuda Coupe with fixed quarter windows. Standard equipment included the 198 Six and highback bucket front seats. Sales promotion stressed more features at a lower price than the Ford Mustang, Chevrolet Camaro and Pontiac Firebird. It helped Barracuda popularity to boom, requiring 73% more production this year. The Coupe also offered optional engines and other extras. The unknown number built probably was included in the standard hardtop total. Also, the model was not listed in the weight and price records usually published.

This view illustrates Chrysler's return to the long hood/short deck vehicle package concept approached by Virgil Exner in 1961 and brought to full fruition on 1962 standard-size models. The public did not accept it for family-size cars, and Chrysler soon phased it out. However, Ford's new sporty-flavored Mustang introduced the concept in 1964 and it went on to establish a trend. Shown is the Barracuda Convertible, of which the total Six and V-8 production was 1,554 cars. As a V-8 it weighed 3,100 pounds and cost $3,135. For any Barracuda model offering the choice, a standard V-8 cost $101 more than a standard Six.

The Barracuda Gran Coupe Hardtop garnered a total of 8,183 sales. Also offered as a Six, it weighed 3,040 pounds and sold for $3,035 in V-8 form. Seats were genuine leather with bolsters and backs of vinyl, and an overhead consolette was standard. The vinyl roof, wire wheelcovers and F70 x 14 white letter tires were optional. Gran Coupe models had a special medallion on the sides and rear, near the Barracuda signatures. In overall dimensions in inches, all Series FB models were 186.7 long and 74.9 wide, with hardtops being 50.9 high. All were on a 108-inch wheelbase and had a 59.7-inch front track, while the rear track was 60.7 inches for 'Cudas and 61.3 for others.

Having the lowest production total of any Plymouth model this year was the Barracuda Gran Coupe Convertible, which had a Six and V-8 production run of only 596 cars. When built in standard V-8 form, it registered a weight of 3,115 pounds and listed a price of $3,260. The term "Gran Coupe Convertible" seems contradictory and improper for this model until the reader realizes that the convertible was actually a convertible coupe.

The 'Cuda Hardtop is shown with 340 tape decor on the rear quarter, indicating that the car was fitted with a 340 V-8 engine. 'Cudas were not offered as Sixes. In standard form, this model weighed 3,395 pounds and cost $3,164. A total of 18,880 were built in various forms, including all of the engine and performance combinations. The 'Cuda Convertible, not shown, cost $3,433 and weighed 3,480 pounds in basic form and had an all-forms production total of 635. The tape design on the rear quarter panels was humorously called "the inverted hockey stick."

A 'Cuda Hardtop was selected to pace the annual Tournament of Roses Parade in Pasadena, Calif., on New Year's Day, preceding the famed annual Rose Bowl football game, at which the car also appeared. The feminine beauty with the car is Parade Queen Pamela Dee Tedesco. Shown is the hood used for 'Cudas with engines of lesser power than the 6-barrel 440 and the Hemi. It had two air scoops with the slots oriented in an oblique manner, opposite to each other. This car had a 440 4-barrel engine and appropriate designations on the hood scoops and rear quarters to advertise it.

Shown in Hemi form is the 'Cuda Hardtop. The unique through-hood housing for the cold air induction system was standard for Hemi 'Cudas and optional for 6-barrel 440 'Cudas, which otherwise used the 2-scoop hood. The housing was known as "the shaker" because it was attached directly to the engine and shook with every engine quiver. The name of this particular model appeared as "hemicuda" on each side of the shaker and as "Hemi" on the rear quarters. 'Cudas were fitted with twin high-intensity road lamps below the bumper. Urethane-skinned bumpers were optional and were available in nine body colors.

The AAR 'Cuda was added in the spring as a special edition. The engine was a special version of the 340 V-8 with three 2-barrel carburetors, Edelbrock aluminum intake mani-folding, special cylinder heads and a modified block and valve train. Suspension changes included raising the rear end 1.75 inches to allow clearance for the side-exit exhaust system and the extra-large G60 x 15 rear tires. Front tires were E60 x 15. The special fiberglass hood had a large functional scoop and was painted flat black, as was the grille. The rear spoiler was standard and a front one was optional. Planned production was 2,800, but the exact number built is unknown. The number probably was combined with the 'Cuda Hardtop in an all-inclusive total.

Swede Savage, racing driver on the Trans-Am circuit, is shown with the second AAR 'Cuda prepared for that competition. The first was driven by international racing star Dan Gurney, whose All-American Racers team provided the AAR for the car's name. For its Trans-Am participation, the car was fitted differently than those offered for sale. At the rear end of the strobe side treatment was "CUDA" and the Gurney team crest with the AAR letters, details that also appeared on the sales versions. Sales cars were offered with 4-speed manual or TorqueFlite transmission and a Sure-Grip differential with 3.55 or 3.91 axle ratio. Power disc front brakes, 11-inch rear drums and 7-inch-wide wheels were standard. Special front and rear anti-sway bars were among other items fitted to the particular needs of this "package."

The Series FR mid-size cars had extensive outer sheetmetal changes. At the rear were new quarter panels, deck lid and full-width panel for the taillamps. A new bumper also appeared. Shown is the Belvedere Coupe, a 6-passenger car that recorded 3,140 pounds of weight and a $2,693 price as a V-8. Including Sixes, 4,717 were manufactured.

At the front, mid-size cars were given newness in the quarter panels, hoods and grille panel. The bumper was also new, as were the outer panels of the rear doors of 4-door models. The hood shown was applied to all models except Road Runner and GTX cars. Showing these features off is a Belvedere 4-Door Sedan, of which 13,945 were built in Six and V-8 forms. A V-8 cost $2,731 and weighed 3,180 pounds.

The Plymouth Satellite 4-Door Sedan shows the smooth sides typical of the mid-size cars this year. Eliminated were the creased design features near the highlight of the quarter panels and rear doors. The car is shown with an optional full-length side molding featuring a puffy vinyl insert. As a V-8, this model sold for $2,831 and weighed 3,175 pounds. Its production amounted to 30,377 cars, including Sixes.

Shown as a Police Emergency Wagon is the Plymouth Belvedere Wagon. As offered to the public, this was built only as a 2-seat model and was fitted with a Six or V-8 engine according to the buyer's preference. The 4-door vehicle tipped the weighing scale at 3,655 pounds and listed a $3,075 price when built as a V-8. Its total production run turned out 5,584 units.

The Satellite Hardtop was much more attractive than it appears in this picture. The 2-door automobile attracted a total of 28,200 sales. Buyers had a choice of Six or V-8 engines. Those who bought a standard V-8 got a 3,155-pound car for $2,855, plus taxes and delivery costs, etc. Any mid-size standard V-8 model cost $90 more than a Six.

The Satellite Wagon, built in Six and V-8 forms, presented a choice of two models. The 2-seat model, of which 4,204 were built, cost $3,191 and weighed 3,660 pounds as a V-8. The 3-seat model shown had a total production of 3,277. Its V-8 weight and price were 3,730 pounds and $3,301. Among options shown are the roof rack, car-length side molding and a bright sill molding. Mid-size wagons had no new sheetmetal from the cowl back.

Suffering from the general decline in convertible popularity was the Plymouth Satellite Convertible. Offered as a Six or V-8, it mustered only 701 sales in both forms. The V-8 version scaled a weight of 3,260 pounds and posted a price of $3,096. This and the Satellite Hardtop are shown with an optional molding extending from end to end through the beltline. This was the last year a mid-size convertible would be offered.

Appearing quite attractive in this view is the Plymouth Sport Satellite Hardtop. The dual striping at the beltline and the bright moldings on the lower outline were standard for Sport Satellite cars. This 2-door automobile, available only as a V-8, registered 3,170 pounds of weight and was priced at $2,988. Exactly 8,749 of them came out of the factories.

Shown with accessory rub strips through the midsection is the Sport Satellite 4-Door Sedan. Like all other Sport Satellites, it was built only as a V-8. Selling at $3,017, it weighed 3,205 pounds. The least popular Plymouth 4-door sedan this year, its production run was 3,010. It was fitted with a combination ignition/steering lock on the column. This device was standard on all Plymouths and was required by the government.

Dressed up in the wood-grained vinyl that was standard for this car, the Sport Satellite Wagon was a handsome utility vehicle. Only V-8 engines were available. The 2-seat Wagon, which attracted 1,975 sales, cost $3,345 and weighed 3,675 pounds. Costing $3,455 was the 3-seat model, which weighed 3,750 pounds and recorded a total of 2,161 built.

Shown is the Plymouth Road Runner Hardtop, of which 24,944 came out of the factories in all V-8 forms. With standard engine and equipment, its weight was 3,475 pounds and its price was $3,034. It is seen with optional side tape which simulated a spiral dust trail from the bird to the decorative scoop just back of the door. All Road Runners except SuperBirds had a "power bulge" on the hood. Not shown is the Road Runner Convertible which had a production run of only 824. It weighed 3,550 pounds and cost $3,289 in standard form.

The Road Runner Coupe, which weighed 3,450 pounds and cost $2,896 in standard form with the 335-horsepower 383 engine, had an all-forms production run of 15,716. The Air Grabber hood scoop, standard with the Hemi and optional for other engines, was opened at the driver's discretion and was said to be more efficient than the 'Cuda "Shaker." The black hood paint was optional. The car is seen with the standard Road Runner body dress, which was simple. The cartoon bird was near the headlamps and Road Runner nameplates were near the rear wheels. Both identity marks were also on the rear end.

To facilitate Plymouth's return to NASCAR superspeedway racing this year, 1,920 fantastic Road Runner SuperBirds were built. Those governing the racing ruled that Plymouth must build half as many of these cars as the total number of dealers. So SuperBirds were built in the street form shown which, excepting minor details, looked like those that won new laurels on the tracks. And Richard Petty was back with Plymouth to drive the racing cars. The nose extension, made of steel for the street version, had hidden headlamps and a spoiler and added 17.2 inches to the standard Road Runner's 203.8 inches of length. A special hood was flanked by vents on the quarter panels and aerodynamic moldings were on the windshield posts. The standard engine was the 4-barrel 440, optional were the 6-barrel 440 and the 426 Hemi. TorqueFlite was standard and 4-speed manual was optional.

In standard street form, the SuperBird weighed 3,785 pounds and listed at $4,298. Built only as a hardtop with vinyl roof, the rear window was modified with convex glass. The rear stabilizer was 24 inches above the rear quarters. Special axle ratios were in accordance with transmission choices. Wheel rims were of 7-inch width. Standard tires were F70 x 14 wide-profile and F60 x 15 extra-wides were optional. Seven body colors and bench or bucket seats were offered. The aerodynamic features were carefully determined and developed by Plymouth engineers, aided by stylists. Decor as shown was standard. Announced in October, SuperBird production was completed by mid-January this year. In racing trim, the car was said to be capable of speeds in excess of 220 m.p.h. SuperBirds were factory-built with custom-like care given to special details during construction.

The Plymouth Fury I 4-Door Sedan shows the massive bumper/taillamp assembly and the offside medallion/trunk lock typical of all but the suburbans of the senior Series FP line. This model weighed 3,655 pounds and cost $2,930 as a V-8. Its total production was 14,813. Not shown, the Fury I 2-Door Sedan weighed 3,630 pounds and cost $2,895 in V-8 form and had a total production run of 2,353 units. Fury I cars were offered with Six or V-8 engines. When FP models offered the choice, a standard V-8 cost $105 more than a Six.

The Plymouth GTX Hardtop was the only entry to carry the GTX mark this year. The V-8 car weighed 3,515 pounds, cost $3,535 and drew 7,748 sales. Standard body side trim is shown. Simulated airscoops were on the rear quarter panels of all mid-size 2-door models. GTX hoods had a "power bulge" design feature, in which the end toward the driver could have optional turn signal blinkers. The Air Grabber scoop hatch, shown closed on the bulge, was a Hemi necessity and was optional with other engines. Plymouth publicized the GTX, Road Runner, 'Cuda, Duster 340 and Sport Fury GT as part of "The Rapid Transit System." The R.T.S. also provided performance information and aids. Don Grotheer and Sox & Martin conducted Plymouth Supercar Clinics. The ultimate R.T.S. Supercars were the Trans-Am racers, Super Stockers and AA/Fuel dragsters.

The Plymouth Fury III 2-Door Hardtop was offered with a choice of Six or V-8 engines. In both forms, it attracted a total of 21,373 sales. As a V-8 it listed at $3,196 and registered 3,620 pounds of weight. The roof had different blind quarter styling than the Formal model.

The Fury II 2-Door Sedan shown was offered as a Six or V-8. Its V-8 weight and price were 3,620 pounds and $3,008. The 21,316-car total probably included Fury Gran Coupes, since they had identical model designation codes. Not shown is the Fury II 4-Door Sedan which had a V-8 weight and price of 3,650 pounds and $3,027 and a production total of 27,694. Also not shown is a Fury II 2-Door Hardtop listed in factory production records but not catalogued as a domestic offering in the U.S.A. According to the records, 2,044 were built for the U.S.A. and 780 were built for Canada.

The full-length body side molding with vinyl insert was standard for all Fury III models, but the vinyl roof and rear wheel skirts were options. The Fury III 2-Door Formal Hardtop, strictly a V-8 car, was preferred by 12,367 buyers. Those who bought it in standard form got a 3,635-pound car for $3,217. The rear of the roof was raked back at a pronounced slant.

From this point of view, the roof of the Fury III 4-Door Hardtop looked quite low on the immense sheetmetal form. The big car, exclusively V-8, tipped the scale at 3,690 pounds and was listed at $3,246. Exactly 47,879 of them came out of the factory. Unavailable in photo form for this book was the Fury III 4-Door Sedan, which was offered as a Six or V-8. As the latter, its price was $3,174 and its weight was 3,655 pounds. The sedan's total production run was 50,876 units.

The Fury III Convertible was the last of the sun-and-wind cars built in the big Plymouth size. Popularity was so low that only 1,952 were built to meet the demand. Again available only as a V-8, it weighed 3,770 pounds and cost $3,415. Conversion to the massive bumpers on the senior Plymouths did not require visible changes in the front and rear quarter panels. However, the panels had new caps, or extensions, applied at the ends to blend them with the bumper designs. The cars were only 4-tenths of an inch longer than their 1969 counterparts.

New to the Sport Fury series was the 4-Door Sedan, as Plymouth reorganized models in the upper price echelon. This was the highest-priced Plymouth sedan this year, listing at $3,291. Its registered weight was 3,680 pounds. Offered only as a V-8, it had a 5,135-car production run.

New outer sheetmetal at the front end of the big Plymouths consisted of the hood and a panel below the bumper. Not visible in this view, the lower panel had an air opening with park/turn signals in the ends. The twin bulges on the hood appeared on all big Series FP models. Some cars were fitted with optional turn indicator lights recessed in the top and near the front of each bulge, easily seen by the driver. The loop bumper/grille assembly incorporated the headlamps, which on Sport Fury models were concealed by retractable doors. Shown is the Sport Fury 2-Door Hardtop, a V-8 weighing 3,630 pounds and costing $3,313. The 8,018-unit production total included GT and S/23 cars.

Another new body for the Sport Fury was the 4-Door Hardtop. In basic V-8 form it weighed 3,705 pounds and cost $3,363. Exactly 6,854 were built. The car shown had a Brougham interior option, available for any Sport Fury but the standard 2-Door Hardtop. Interior trim design was special. In 4-door models, front seats were a split bench type with individual center armrests. For 2-door models, individual front seats had a narrow center section and folding armrest between them. In all models, the passenger seat had a reclining feature. Cars with the option were externally identified by a small Brougham medallion on the roof blind quarters.

The GT was a luxury Sport Fury with high performance equipment. The standard engine was the 4-barrel 440 and the 6-barrel 440 was optional. Suspension was heavy-duty, as were the brakes. The axle ratio was 3.23 unless 2.76 was ordered. H70 x 15 tires were fitted to road wheels, and chrome-plated dual exhaust tips were an added touch. Hood and body decor were shared with the S/23, but GT letters appeared at the front ends of the strobe stripes. The standard version of the Sport Fury GT 2-Door Hardtop weighed 3,925 pounds and cost $3,898. The factory lumped its production with the standard Sport Fury 2-Door Hardtop so the number of GT cars built is unknown.

The 2-Door Formal Hardtop displays standard Sport Fury body side ornamentation. The full-length bright molding had a puffed vinyl insert. Wheel openings and sills were fitted with bright moldings. The V-8 automobile registered a reading of 3,645 pounds on the weight scale, carried a $3,333 price tag and won 5,688 sales. Series FP cars, excepting suburbans, had a 62.1-inch front track and a 62-inch rear track, compared with 1969 tracks of 62 front and 60.7 rear.

The S/23 was sort of a junior Sport Fury performance car, having some performance chassis features, but not as many as the GT. Its engines ranged from the standard 318 through the two 383 versions. In standard form, the Sport Fury S/23 2-Door Hardtop cost $3,379 and weighed 3,660 pounds. The unknown number built was hidden in the standard Sport Fury 2-Door Hardtop total. The car had hood "runner" stripes like the GT, and a strobe tape stripe extended the length of the sides and across the rear, also like the GT. The S/23 designation appeared on the rear, between the Sport Fury signature and the bumper. Excepting suburbans, all big Plymouths had a new sheetmetal panel below the rear bumper.

The Plymouth Fury Gran Coupe, added in February, was based on the Fury II and given many options as standard. They were the Sport Fury grille and hidden headlamps; vinyl-insert side trim; deluxe wheelcovers; whitewall tires; vinyl roof in standard or a new patterned design; ventless door glass. Also a 2-barrel 383 V-8; TorqueFlite; power steering; power brakes; tinted glass; air conditioning and many interior and convenience features. All were in an "A" package costing $4,216, vehicle price. Without tinted glass and air conditioning it was a "B" car at $3,833. Gran Coupe signatures were on the blind quarters and Fury (script only) was on the sides. Production, not recorded separately, likely was lumped with the Fury II 2-Door Sedan on which the Fury Gran Coupe was based. Coded as a low-line car but fitted and priced as a premium, it defies specific classification.

Plymouth advanced the Custom Suburban to Fury III class. Again it appeared in two models and only as a V-8. Weighing 4,155 pounds and priced at $3,527 was the 2-seat Custom Suburban, of which 8,898 were built. Garnering 6,792 sales, the Custom Suburban 3-seat model tipped the weighing scale at 4,215 pounds and was offered at $3,603. Normally at the center of the grille, the Plymouth emblem was missing from the car shown.

Given equal status with the Sport Fury standard passenger cars was the Sport Suburban, which was fitted with a Sport Fury grille and hidden headlamps. Exclusively V-8, it was offered in two versions, of which the 3-seat model shown took honors as the heaviest Plymouth of the year. The 4,260-pound vehicle, of which 9,170 were built, was priced at $3,804. The other Plymouth Sport Suburban was a 2-seat model listing at $3,725, weighing 4,200 pounds and winning 4,403 buyers. Though all Series FP Suburbans had new front end styling like the passenger cars, they could not have a huge rear bumper like the cars had. The body sheet-metal and rear bumper were continued without change from 1969, with the body getting minor ornamentation detail alterations.

For this year, the Plymouth Suburban was upgraded to Fury II rank and a 3-seat model was added. The 2-seat Suburban had a Six and V-8 production run of 5,300 units. It weighed 4,160 pounds and cost $3,408 as a V-8. Presented only as a V-8 was the 3-seat Suburban priced at $3,518, weighing 4,205 pounds and recording a production total of 2,250. Headlamps on Fury I, II and III cars were fixed in the exposed position.

Continuing to please taxicab companies, drivers and fare-paying passengers with their operating economy, reliability and comfort were the Belvedere (left) and Fury taxicabs. As usual, Plymouth popularity in that field was extraordinary. Plymouth Police Specials again were favorites with those who enforced the law. Belvedere coupes, sedans and wagons teamed with Fury sedans and suburbans to provide a specialized line of Pursuits, Pursuit Specials, Patrollers and Emergency Wagons.

While the calendar year saw total industry passenger car production go up 31% over 1970, Chrysler Corp. gained a puny 2.9% in production while cutting itself a smaller 15.01% piece of the industry pie. Plymouth failed to repeat its upswinging 1970 momentum, building 9% less cars and plopping itself out of 3rd and into 6th position. Oldsmobile, Buick and Pontiac took 3rd, 4th and 5th spots, while Chevrolet regained the No. 1 rank from Ford.

Plymouth's waning activity was not for want of new products and a broad market coverage. Product planners gave most of their attention to reorganizing the mid-size cars while adding a new compact and making a gesture at the sub-compact field. The baby car was built in England by Chrysler United Kingdom, Ltd., formerly Rootes Motors, and had been marketed there as the Avenger. It was slightly modified for sale in the U.S.A. and was renamed the Plymouth Cricket. Built only as a 4-door sedan on a 98-inch wheelbase, it was of unitized construction with coil spring suspension all around. The 4-cylinder in-line engine had overhead valves and gross/net horsepower ratings of 70 and 57. Power was delivered to the rear wheels through a standard 4-speed manual on the floor or a 3-speed automatic transmission. Disc brakes were used at the front, with drums at the rear.

The Valiant group, Series GV, got a new Scamp hardtop on 111 inch wheelbase. Continued with detail changes were the Duster coupe and Valiant sedan on 108 inches. For all three cars, standard engines were the 198 Six with gross/net horsepower of 125/105 and the 318 V-8 with compression reduced to 8.4:1 and gross/net horsepower of 230/155. Optional was the 225 Six of 145 gross horsepower which netted 110. The performance Duster 340 model was exclusively fitted with the 340 V-8 with lower 10.3:1 compression and horsepower at 275 gross and 235 net.

Horsepower underwent some changes this year as automakers were saddled with ever-increasing government pressure for more effective emission controls. Lower compression ratios and other factors began a trend to less power. In the transition, the previous practice of advertising dynamometer, or gross, horsepower was superceded or accompanied by the net horsepower of engines installed in cars. After all, power available to the driver was most important. The looming urgency of fuel conservation was a further threat to power, as economy devices would take their toll. Generally and basically, engines would be known by cubic inch displacement and the number of cylinders and carburetor barrels.

The Series GB Barracuda retained the former styling basics, again on a 108-inch wheelbase. The basic Barracuda line had three models, the Gran Coupe was a hardtop only and the 'Cuda was presented in two body types. The 198 Slant Six was standard and available only for the basic coupe. The 225 Slant Six was optional for the basic coupe and standard in the other two basic models. The 318 was the standard V-8 for basic models and the Gran Coupe, all of which offered two 383 V-8s as optional. The 383 engines were a 2-barrel job with gross/net horsepower of 275/190 and a 4-barrel 300/250 version, both with lower compression of 8.5:1. 'Cuda models used the 4-barrel 383 as standard while offering the 340, 6-barrel 440 and 8-barrel 426 Hemi street engine for options. The 440 compression was down to 10.3:1 and gross/net horsepower

was cut to 385/330. Hemi compression was slightly reduced to 10.2:1, gross horsepower remained at 425 and net was 350.

The Cricket was Plymouth's entry in the new sub-compact field. Built in England in the former Rootes plants now owned by Chrysler, the car was sold there as the Hillman Avenger. For exporting to the U.S.A., it was given left-hand drive, a few minor changes and the Plymouth Cricket name. In Detroit, Chrysler's Project R-429 had a sub-compact car under development, but it was not completed. So the British baby was a convenient and quick way of getting one. The Cricket 4-Door Sedan, which was the only model offered, was a 5-passenger car designated as Model 4B21. Weighing 1,963 pounds and costing $1,915, its exact production total is unknown, but a press release indicated about 40,000 built.

As a family car of small size, the Plymouth Cricket had acceptable styling. Its other characteristics were suitable, too, The front-mounted 4-cylinder engine of 91.4 c.i.d., and 8.0:1 compression was rated at 70 gross horsepower. Independent front suspension had coil springs and a Mac-Pherson strut, rear suspension was 4-link with coil springs and a live axle. In inches, wheelbase was 98, front and rear tracks 51, overall width 62.5, overall height 54.6 and overall length 162. Radial-ply tires were 155 x 13. A 4-speed floor-mounted manual shift was standard, a 3-speed automatic was available. Options included air conditioning and a number of convenience and dress-up items.

Mid-size cars were all-new, but again featured unitized construction and torsion bar independent front suspension. A new dual package concept placed 2-door coupes and hardtops on a 115-inch wheelbase, 4-door sedans and wagons on 117. The separation provided individual distinction for 2-door and 4-door models which shared little other than names, engines, chassis and interior components.

The Series GR mid-size spread was divided into eight ranks. Six ranks were Satellites, with the basic low-line rank followed by those with the sub-titles Sebring, Sebring-Plus, Custom, Brougham and Regent. Not carrying the Satellite name were the Road Runner and GTX. The basic Satellite rank had a coupe, sedan and wagon; the Sebring and Sebring-Plus were in hardtop form; a sedan and two wagons were of Custom rank; the Brougham was a sedan and Regent applied to two wagon models. The Road Runner and GTX were hardtops. The 225 was the standard Six, applying to the Satellite low-line, Custom and Sebring only. The 318 was the standard V-8 for all Satellites, which also had the 383 2-barrel and 4-barrel engines to offer. The 383 4-barrel was standard on Road Runners and a 4-barrel 440, now with lower 9.5:1 compression and gross/net horsepower at 370/305, was the GTX standard. Road Runner and GTX also had the 6-barrel 440 and 426 Hemi for extras. Added by spring was a 340 option for the Road Runner.

The big Plymouths were the Series GP, which received a very minor styling facelift and continued to mount suburbans on a 122-inch wheelbase and other models on 120. Excepting a couple of additions later, the year began and continued with the Fury I and Fury II presenting two models each, the Fury III and Sport Fury each had four choices and a Sport Fury GT hardtop was at the top. The big suburbans were again grouped separately, with standard, Custom and Sport versions having two models each. The 225 Six engine was available for the Fury I, Fury II and certain Fury III models. Excepting the Sport Fury GT, big cars and suburbans had the 318 V-8 as standard, while options were the 383 2-barrel, 383 4-barrel, a 440 4-barrel with reduced 8.8:1 compression and lower gross/net horsepower of 335/250, plus a new 360 V-8 with 8.7:1 compression, 2-barrel carburetor and a horsepower of 255 gross and 175 net. The Sport Fury GT was powered only by the 4-barrel 440 used as standard by the mid-size GTX.

Appearing about three months after the model year began were some new members of the Plymouth Series GP family. The Fury Custom, regarded as a distinct line with two models, was based on the Fury I and standard-equipped with extras at special package prices. It offered a choice of 225 Six or 318 V-8 engines. Not regarded as a distinct series, but rather as an option package, the Fury Gran Coupe was available in two models based on the Fury III. The Gran Coupe package incorporated many optional features, including a 360 V-8 as the smallest powerplant. Larger engines were available.

Changes in specifications probably occurred during the year, as Plymouth adapted to varying regulations and conditions. Particularly during the 'Sixties and 'Seventies, models with various combinations of equipment and trim were offered as sales-getters. Generally factory-built, they often were for a seasonal sales campaign of national scope, but sometimes were for certain areas, and on occasion were only for specific distributors or purposes. Plymouth cautioned that some production cars may differ from prescribed standards.

In the corporate news was Chrysler's acquisition of a 15% equity interest in Mitsubishi Motors Corp. of Japan this year. The arrangement between the two companies called for Chrysler to make additional 10% investments in 1972 and 1973. The move eventually provided Plymouth with new products. Chrysler introduced the Mitsubishi-built sub-compact Dodge Colt in the U.S.A. this year.

Shown in standard body side appearance except for bright moldings on the wheel openings and sill is the Plymouth Duster Coupe. In standard 6-cylinder form it weighed 2,825 pounds and cost $2,313. In all Six and V-8 forms it chalked up a production total of 173,592. The standard Duster grille was the design seen on the Valiant Sedan. The 1972 deck lid, with a subtle peak at the center, was advanced to 1971 Duster production in mid-year. Added in the spring was a sun roof option.

The body side stripe shown, which had "340" at the rear end, identified the Plymouth Duster 340 Coupe. Built only with the 340 V-8 engine, it weighed 3,140 pounds and listed at $2,703 in standard form. The 340 had a 12,886-car production run. The grille design, featuring vertical bars, differed from basic Dusters and was standard for the 340. This year, Dusters bore no Valiant nameplates, therefore were not Plymouth Valiant Dusters. However, they shared the Series GV designation with Valiant.

A Plymouth Duster 340 is shown with options that gave it a performance car appearance. Flat black paint stretched across the hood to the peaks of the front quarter panels and extended along the belt to the roof blind quarters. In the numeral 4 of the bold 340 on the hood was the word "Wedge," in reference to the engine's wedge-shape combustion chambers. The hood was fitted with lockable fastening pins. The rallye wheels and wide tires with white letters were options for any Duster.

Announced in February was the Twister package option, for those who wanted a regular Duster with a "hot machine" look. Engine choices were the 198 and 225 Sixes and the 318 V-8. Flat black covered most of the hood width and extended to the windshield. A strobe stripe pattern adorned the hood center. The simulated airscoops were applied extras. A flat black 340 grille was used, and black body side tapes had Duster Twister identification. Rallye wheels and whitewall tires, bright drip rail and wheelcut moldings, racing mirrors, bench seat, lower deck lid stripes and special identity decals were other package items.

Continued with insignificant changes was the Plymouth Valiant 4-Door Sedan. Among tiny detail differences was the omission of a Plymouth emblem at the grille center. The 5-year-old basic body design was still a good seller with extra resale value. Its Six and V-8 production total was 42,660. As a Six it sold for $2,392 and weighed 2,835 pounds.

New to the Plymouth compact group was the Valiant Scamp Hardtop, built as a Six or V-8. The 2-door car, larger than Dusters and the Valiant Sedan, differed in the roof and rear end styling from the doors back. Front end appearance was like the Sedan. This model was brought in to expand Plymouth market coverage with a car between the compact and mid-size varieties. It was adapted from the successful Dodge Dart Swinger. The Plymouth Valiant Scamp, of which 48,253 were built, weighed 2,900 pounds and cost $2,561 in standard 6-cylinder form.

The Plymouth Barracuda Coupe is shown in standard Barracuda form except for the dressed-up wheels. Available were full-length vinyl rub strips and thin tape stripes extending from the vehicle's front to the rear corner of the fixed side glass, at the belt. Many other options were listed for the basic Barracuda line. In V-8 form the Coupe cost $2,780 and weighed 3,070 pounds. Also built as a Six, total production is unknown because it was recorded with the Barracuda Hardtop.

The last convertibles built by Plymouth were Barracuda and 'Cuda models. Shown is the Barracuda Convertible, which is seen with an optional elastomeric bumper color-keyed to the body color. This model attracted 1,014 buyers who had a choice of Six or V-8 engines. Truly a smart little car, it scaled 3,165 pounds and cost $3,124 in V-8 form.

All Series GB cars had a new vertical-sectioned grille design with dual-unit headlamps, grille finish differing between models. The sheetmetal below the front bumper also was new. Shown is the Barracuda Hardtop which in V-8 form cost $2,867 and weighed 3,090 pounds. Total Six and V-8 production, recorded as 9,459, included an unknown number of Coupes. For the Barracuda Hardtop and Convertible, a standard V-8 cost $101 more than the standard 225 Six. For the standard Coupe, the difference was $134 because its basic Six was the 198. Regular Barracudas and Gran Coupes had a plain hood as shown.

The Plymouth Barracuda Gran Coupe was available only as a V-8 hardtop. Built for 1,615 buyers, it scaled a weight of 3,105 pounds and listed at $3,029. It was identified by Gran Coupe medallions near Barracuda signatures on the sides and rear. It is seen with an optional vinyl roof, bright sill and wheelcut moldings and a thin tape stripe from the front to the roof blind quarter.

Plymouth turned out 6,228 'Cuda Hardtops with a variety of V-8 engines, performance and appearance features. In standard form it cost $3,155 and weighed 3,475 pounds. It is seen as a 'Cuda 340 with optional elastomeric bumpers, road lamps, hood with a "shaker" airscoop, the 340 designation integrated with a dull black rear quarter pattern, a vinyl roof and decktop luggage rack, plus other items. A 383 4-barrel engine was standard, while a 6-barrel 440 and the 426 Hemi were provided for the 'Cuda series.

Probably ranking as the lowest-production Plymouth this year was the 'Cuda Convertible, as only 374 were built. In standard form it weighed 3,550 pounds and cost $3,412. It offered the same engines and features as were available for the 'Cuda Hardtop, except that the vinyl roof option was replaced by a power top option that also was available for the Barracuda Convertible. The car shown was fitted with the twin-scoop hood as seen on the 1972 'Cuda Hardtop. Among Barracuda and 'Cuda options were spoilers and backlight exterior louvers, plus a 'Cuda AAR package with 6-barrel 340 engine.

The Plymouth Satellite Coupe was a practical model with a sports car look. Available as a Six or V-8, it weighed 3,295 pounds and sold for $2,758 when built as a V-8. The number built is unknown, since factory production record-keepers entered this model in the Satellite Sebring Hardtop column. For mid-size models offering a Six and V-8, a standard V-8 was priced at $95 more than a standard Six.

A quick glance from this point of view saw mid-size sedans in the same image as 2-door models. The general styling flavor was quite similar from this angle, but 4-door and 2-door cars shared no sheetmetal, not even deck lids. Bumpers differed, too. Sedans were larger, of a family car concept with different proportions, and were on a longer 117-inch wheelbase. Shown is the Satellite 4-Door Sedan which had a Six and V-8 production run of 11,059 cars. A V-8 cost $2,829 and weighed 3,340 pounds.

Mid-size sedans shared their wheelbase, doors, front end sheetmetal and front appearance characteristics with mid-size wagons. Necessarily, wagons had different rear quarter panels and a rear bumper to fit the body package. All wagons were on a 117-inch wheelbase with 60.1-inch front track and a 63.4-inch track at the rear. Overall length was 210.9 inches. Illustrated is the Plymouth Satellite Wagon, supplied only as a 2-seat model. Six and V-8 production totalled 7,138 vehicles. The V-8 weighed 3,790 pounds and carried a $3,153 price tag.

A Satellite Sebring Hardtop displays the long front section and loop bumper typical of all mid-size 2-door cars. The hood, with two ridges curved toward the center at the front, was used on all 2-door cars but the Road Runner and GTX. The model shown was offered as a Six or V-8. The V-8 price and weight were $3,026 and 3,320 pounds. Total production logged for this car was 46,807, but all were not this model because an undisclosed number of Satellite Coupes were combined with it in factory records. A 318 V-8 Satellite Sebring, one of the many thousands built in Canada for sale in the U.S.A., was purchased new by the author of this book. It gave exemplary service for six years.

The front end styling of mid-size sedans, as well as wagons, is well-shown in this view. Bumper and grille were not integrated, the hood had two ridges stretching straight back from the front, and front quarter panels featured a peaked crispness at the top. From a broadside viewpoint, the front end had a profile of more horizontal attitude than 2-door cars had. Showing these features is a Plymouth Satellite Custom 4-Door Sedan which had a Six and V-8 production run of 30,773. A V-8 cost $3,003 and weighed 3,340 pounds. It was on a class level with the Satellite Sebring.

The Plymouth Satellite Custom Wagon offered a choice of Six or V-8 engines in two models. The 2-seat model attracted a total of 5,045 sales, scaled a weight of 3,795 pounds and listed a price of $3,330 in V-8 form. Found irresistible by 4,626 buyers was the 3-seat version, which tipped the scale at 3,865 pounds and posted a price of $3,410 as a V-8.

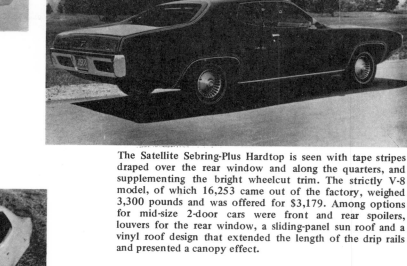

The Satellite Sebring-Plus Hardtop is seen with tape stripes draped over the rear window and along the quarters, and supplementing the bright wheelcut trim. The strictly V-8 model, of which 16,253 came out of the factory, weighed 3,300 pounds and was offered for $3,179. Among options for mid-size 2-door cars were front and rear spoilers, louvers for the rear window, a sliding-panel sun roof and a vinyl roof design that extended the length of the drip rails and presented a canopy effect.

A Plymouth Road Runner Hardtop shows off the standard hood for Road Runner and GTX cars, which could be had with a hood featuring a large "power bulge" with an Air Grabber scoop rising from the center. The purely V-8 Road Runner Hardtop weighed 3,640 pounds and cost $3,147 in basic form. Exactly 14,218 were built in all forms. All mid-size cars, including coupes, hardtops, sedans and wagons, featured concealed windshield wipers and ventless front windows.

The Satellite Brougham 4-Door Sedan, more luxuriously fitted than other mid-size sedans, was built only as a V-8. Weighing 3,330 pounds, it was priced at $3,189. Exactly 3,020 buyers found they could not get along without one. The car compared with the Satellite Sebring-Plus in class level. Bright trim rose from the front bumper and capped the peak through the belt to the rear deck. More bright trim outlined wheelcuts and sills. Overall and in inches, mid-size sedans were 204.6 long, 54.5 high and 78.6 wide. Front track was 59.7 inches, rear 61.6.

A Road Runner Hardtop is illustrated with a pair of options worth noting. The unique broken color pattern, wrapping over the roof and angling toward the rear wheels, was a Road Runner exclusive. Color-keyed elastomeric bumpers were available for the Road Runner, GTX and Satellite Sebring-Plus. Ever since it first appeared as a 1968 model, the Road Runner was often characterized as "The poor man's high performance car."

Replacing the 1970 Sport Satellite Wagon was the Plymouth Satellite Regent. The purely V-8 wagon ranked with the Satellite Sebring-Plus and Brougham. As a 2-seat model it cost $3,558, weighed 3,815 pounds and had a 2,161-unit production run. The 3-seat vehicle weighed 3,885 pounds, cost $3,638 and went to 2,985 buyers. Bright moldings defined a lower area on which a wood-grain effect was applied.

GTX 2-Door Hardtop

Plymouth's luxury high-performance car again was the GTX Hardtop, offering none but V-8 engines of brute power. With the weakest engine and no extras or frills, it listed at $3,733 and weighed 3,675 pounds. Exactly 2,942 were built. Bold stripes wrapped over the front quarters were unique. Tape stripes emphasized the "layered" lower side effect that stretched from front to rear. A pronounced outward flare above each wheel added a "power" touch to the mid-size sports car concept. The package featured a short deck that was higher than the long sloping front, and the roof swept downward from a severely-raked windshield. This package was based on a 115-inch wheelbase, had a 59.7-inch front track, 61.6 rear track. Overall and in inches, length was 203.2, height 52 and width 79.1.

Richard Petty continued to ram Road Runners with his famed No. 43 to victories in the NASCAR circuit. In 1970 he won 18 races, outdoing all other NASCAR drivers. And in 1971 he went on to win more honors for himself, and for Plymouth. Other well-known drivers roared Plymouths around ovals, zoomed and twisted them through road courses and streaked them on drag strips. Maximum-performance engines were given "the works." For pro drag cars, the 426 Hemi got 16-plug heads.

The Plymouth Fury I Coupe, available in Six and V-8 forms, cost $3,223 and weighed 3,750 pounds as a V-8. Recorded production was 5,152, but an unknown number of Fury Custom Coupes were included. This model utilized a 2-door hardtop roof, rather than the 2-door sedan roof of 1970. Except for the roof change, this car was basically like the 1970 Fury I 2-Door Sedan. Plymouth juggled the designation of this body package, calling it a sedan in 1968, a coupe in '69, sedan in '70, and now a coupe. The switching applied to Fury I and Fury II models. Not shown is the Fury I 4-Door Sedan built as a Six or V-8, weighing 3,780 pounds and costing $3,256 in V-8 form. Its 16,395-car production total included an unknown number of Fury Custom Sedans.

Plymouth shared honors with Petty at a White House reception. He stood with clasped hands as President Richard M. Nixon confronted the fabulous No. 43 racing machine. Seeming to be in a pensive mood, Petty probably was awed by the occasion and personal honors. And rarely is an automobile, of any kind, given such presidential recognition. Petty won his third Grand National championship this year, and Plymouth carried him to it.

The Fury Custom series, whipped up as a special-equipment offering at attractive prices, was a tardy addition to the big Plymouth family. Offering a choice of the 225 Six or 318 V-8 engines, Customs were fitted for special sales appeal. A paisley-accented interior, 2-tone paint and some 20 other items constituted standard equipment. Lumping a 318 engine, air conditioning, power devices, vinyl roof, many goodies and free TorqueFlite made up another version. The cars had Fury Custom nameplates. Shown is the Coupe, which weighed 3,750 pounds and cost $3,318. A 4-Door Sedan cost $3,351 and weighed 3,780 pounds. Figures quoted are for V-8 standard versions. Unknown production totals were combined with similar Fury I models, since the Customs had a Fury I base.

A Fury II 4-Door Sedan displays the new rear bumper featured by all big Plymouths except Suburbans. For a 3,785-pound V-8, $3,372 was asked. Exactly 20,098 were built, including Sixes. Not shown is the Fury II 2-Door Hardtop, of which 7,859 were built in Six and V-8 forms. The V-8 weight and price were 3,750 pounds and $3,393. This model, which replaced the Fury II 2-Door Sedan of 1970, had a roof like the Fury I Coupe.

The big Plymouths, Series GP, continued the general styling concept of 1970, and all were fitted with ventless front windows. The Plymouth Fury III 4-Door Sedan recorded a weight of 3,790 pounds and posted a price of $3,547 when built as a V-8. Including 6-cylinder cars, a total of 44,244 came out of the factory. For Series GP models offering both engines, a standard V-8 cost $110 more than a Six.

Illustrated is the Plymouth Fury III 2-Door Hardtop, which had a Six and V-8 production run of 21,319. V-8 weight and price were 3,755 pounds and $3,568. Not shown, the exclusively V-8 Fury III 2-Door Formal Hardtop listed at $3,600 and weighed 3,760 pounds. The Formal's 24,465-car total included an unknown number of cars built in Fury Gran Coupe form. The Formal roof was as seen on the Sport Fury Formal.

All new senior Plymouth models had a new hood, which was the only major change in outer sheetmetal. It was very simple, having only a subtle "windsplit" ridge to define the center. The Plymouth Fury III 4-Door Hardtop, offered only as a V-8, sold for $3,612 and recorded a weight of 3,820 pounds. Factory records list 55,356 as built, but all were not this model, an undisclosed number being of Fury Gran Coupe form.

The Plymouth Sport Fury 4-Door Sedan went to 2,823 buyers, who bought them in V-8 form because a Six was not available. Probably nobody wanted a Six in this luxury car, anyhow. If there had been enough demand for a Six, Plymouth would have offered it. The car weighed 3,845 pounds, and exacted a price of $3,656. This year, there was not much difference in body side trim moldings between the various Fury series.

Plymouth built exactly 3,957 Sport Fury 2-Door Formal Hardtops, all V-8s. This model weighed 3,810 pounds and cost $3,710 in standard form. The car is shown with rear wheel skirts that were optional for all Fury I, II, III and Sport Fury models but the GT, for which they were not available. It is also shown as having the extra-cost Brougham interior luxury package available for all Sport Furys, but not for others. The package had special seats, fabrics and appointments, including Brougham signatures on the roof blind quarters as shown.

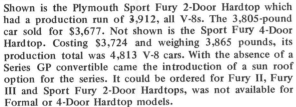

Shown is the Plymouth Sport Fury 2-Door Hardtop which had a production run of 3,912, all V-8s. The 3,805-pound car sold for $3,677. Not shown is the Sport Fury 4-Door Hardtop. Costing $3,724 and weighing 3,865 pounds, its production total was 4,813 V-8 cars. With the absence of a Series GP convertible came the introduction of a sun roof option for the series. It could be ordered for Fury II, Fury III and Sport Fury 2-Door Hardtops, was not available for Formal or 4-Door Hardtop models.

Of luxury-performance appeal was the Plymouth Sport Fury GT, which was built only with a 4-barrel 370-horsepower 440 V-8 engine. Only a 2-Door Hardtop was offered, having a standard rather than a Formal roof. Among special decor for this model were tape strobe stripes on the sides and rear, tape stripes and GT letters on the hood, plus three die-cast bars at each side of the hood. The $4,111 car weighed 4,090 pounds. Only 375 were built, which was just one more than the least popular Plymouth for the year. Sport Furys again featured concealed headlamps.

Appearing this year in optional package form rather than "main billing" as a distinct model was the Fury Gran Coupe, now a "special attraction." And it now was based on the Fury III rather than the Fury II, and was offered on two body types instead of one. As previously, the Sport Fury grille and a multitude of extras were standard at special prices, and in two packages. On a 2-door, the option cost $1,125.45 with air conditioning, $796.40 without; cost was $2.35 more on a 4-door. A 360 V-8 and TorqueFlite were standard, larger engines extra. The Gran Coupe option applied to a 2-door hardtop with formal roof, shown, and a 4-door hardtop. Fury script was on the sides, Gran Coupe script on roof blind quarters. Treating this like other options, the factory did not log Gran Coupe production. Cars so-equipped were recorded with similar Fury III models.

On a class level with Fury II models was the Plymouth Suburban, the "economy" version of the big Series GP wagon offerings. Two models were tendered, both with V-8 engines only. The 2-seat model, of which 4,877 came out of the factory, was listed as weighing 4,245 pounds and costing $3,758. Priced at $3,869 was the 3-seat model, which registered 4,290 pounds on the weight scale and had a 2,662-unit production run.

Ranking with Fury III models but not designated as one of them was the Plymouth Custom Suburban, offered in two V-8 models. Weighing 4,240 pounds was the 2-seat model, which sold for $3,854 and went to 10,874 buyers. Exactly 11,702 orders were filled by the 3-seat model, which weighed 4,300 pounds and cost $3,930. As usual, roof rack and rear assist handles were extras. This model was also provided with a Brougham interior option package having special seats and extra luxuries. Vehicles with the fancy interior advertised it with Brougham signatures on the rear-end pillars.

With status equal to Sport Fury models, the Plymouth Sport Suburban was also built only as a V-8. Wood-grained vinyl adorned the sides as standard, and a Brougham interior was optionally available. Registering 4,290 pounds, the 2-seat model cost $4,071 and attracted 5,103 sales. Selling at $4,146 and weighing 4,370 pounds, the 3-seat model upheld its reputation as the costliest and heaviest Plymouth for the year. The impressive 3-seat automobile was just what 13,021 buyers wanted.

Shown is the Plymouth Satellite Pursuit, offered to police departments along with the Satellite Patroller, both in 4-door form only. Also in the Plymouth Police Special line-up were the Fury Pursuit and Patroller 4-door models, plus Satellite and Fury Emergency Wagons. Engines ranged from the 225 Six to the 370-horsepower 440 V-8. Plymouth taxicab offerings were the Satellite and Fury I 4-door sedans with a choice of 225 Six or 318 V-8 engines. As usual, the factory mixed production of these cars into the grand totals reported for similar models built for public consumption.

Plymouth continued to promote performance cars in a "Rapid Transit System" manner. This year, the System made a caravan tour of the country, showing at shopping centers, etc. Appearing with the "regular" performance offerings was a special Road Runner custom-built by Chuck Miller's Styline Custom shop in Detroit. The design was created by Harry Bradley, not a Chrysler Corp. stylist. The only items not altered were the roof, doors and interior. The molded front end extended more than six inches and had a built-in roll pan to accentuate a hand-formed steel mesh grille. The hood featured two depressed areas for directing air to twin ram-air induction scoops at the cowl.

The R.T.S. caravan Road Runner's deck lid had a slanted surface that passed under an integral spoiler. The roll pan across the rear concealed red, green and amber taillight lenses. Under the pan were twin dual exhaust ports for the modified 383 engine's increased horsepower. Goodyear G60 tires were fitted. Unique were the 3-dimensional vacuum-formed Road Runner "chicken heads" that served as side marker lights. The car was painted a vibrant candy-over-pearl orange with white pearl applied to the sides, front and rear for accent. The cross-country caravan was handled by Promotions, Inc. of Lake Orion, Mich.

Following the big spurt in 1971, industry passenger car production relaxed a bit this year, as if to catch its breath for a new record attempt in 1973. The calendar year-end found that a gain of just over 2.8% had been achieved. Doing a little better, Chrysler Corp. showed a production improvement of nearly 3.2% and edged up to 15.05% of the industry's total activity. Plymouth continued its slide of the previous year, dropping another 3.7% but still holding its rank as the nation's No. 6 automaker.

While Plymouth substantially reduced the number of offerings, the Cricket now had two models instead of one. In styling and mechanics, it was as before except for optional twin carburetors. Unchanged was the Series HV group of compacts, though an engine option was added. Duster and Duster 340 coupes and the Valiant sedan again rode on a 108-inch wheelbase, and the Scamp retained its 111-inch chassis. The 198 Six, with net horsepower cut to 100, was standard for Duster, Valiant and Scamp, which had the unchanged 225 Six as optional. The 318 V-8, with net horsepower down to 150, was standard for all but the Duster 340 coupe. The 340 V-8 engine, with compression reduced to 8.5:1 and net horsepower at 240, was the Duster 340 coupe's only powerplant, but now was made optional for Duster, Valiant and Scamp.

Severely cut in model range was the Barracuda Series HB, which was in familiar form on its 108-inch wheelbase. Only a hardtop appeared this year, and in Barracuda and 'Cuda forms only. Barracuda standard engines were the 225 and 318, with the 340 extra. The 'Cuda, suffering badly from the power purge, now had the 318 for its standard and the 340 as its only option. No longer did it offer the 426 Hemi, 440 or 383 engines. The cut in models and engines reflected a general decline in the popularity of all compact sports cars. Extremely high insurance rates and government pressure for better emission control were contributing factors, especially in regard to high-performance engines.

Mid-size Plymouths, new for 1971, appeared in the same separate 2-door and 4-door concepts this year. Logically, 2-door cars again were on a 115-inch wheelbase and 4-door types, including wagons, rode on 117 inches. Designated as Series HR, the middle group was slightly altered in make-up. The standard Satellite had three models, while the Satellite Sebring and Satellite Sebring-Plus were hardtops. Three models comprised the Satellite Custom line and the Satellite Brougham did not appear in model status this year. The Satellite Regent was again offered as two wagon models and the Road Runner was a hardtop. No longer around was the GTX high-performance car, as sagging 1971 sales and other conditions brought doom this year.

The 225 Six and 318 V-8 were standard for Satellite, Custom and Sebring cars, which had two versions of a new 400 V-8 for extras. Replacing the former 383, the 400 had bore and stroke of 4.34 x 3.38 inches, 400 c.i.d. and 8.2:1 compression. In 2-barrel form the 400 put out 190 net horsepower, while the 4-barrel job produced 255 net. The Sebring-Plus had the 318 as standard, both 400 engines as extras. The 4-barrel 400 was standard for the Road Runner, which had as options the 340, the 4-barrel

440 with compression cut to 8.2:1 and net horsepower down to 280, plus a 6-barrel 440 with unchanged 10.3:1 compression and 330 net horsepower. For Satellite, Custom and Regent wagons, engine choices were the same as noted for the Sebring-Plus.

The tooling cycle brought the senior Plymouths into focus, giving them a major revamp. As a result, the new Series HP appeared in a smoother skin. Most unseen basics remained, however, and wheelbases continued at 122 inches for suburbans and 120 for others. A series change occurred at the top, where the Sport Fury was cast out in favor of the Gran Fury. On the bottom of the big stack, the Fury I was reduced to one model. As for 1971, the Fury II had two models and the Fury III offered four. Presenting three models, the Gran Fury had one less than the former Sport Fury, there being no high-powered GT. The suburban line again listed two standard, two Custom and two Sport models.

Appearing in the styling form it had for 1971 was the Plymouth Cricket 4-Door Sedan. It weighed 1,958 pounds and was priced at $2,017. New options this year were a vinyl roof and dual carburetors. As previously, a decor option included full-length body side tape stripes. The production total for the Model 4B41 is unknown.

Added in the Spring was the Plymouth Cricket Station Wagon. Intended to capture a goodly portion of the emerging mini-wagon market, it was priced at $2,399. In its first months, it was marketed only in selected areas of the country. The little car's weight is not available, nor is its English production total.

The Plymouth Cricket Station Wagon, Model 4C45, was adapted from the sedan by use of a new roof and a new rear-end structure. Wheelbase, like the sedan, was 98 inches. The twin-carburetor 4-cylinder engine, standard for this model, put out 70 net horsepower. The one-piece vertical-swing tailgate gave access to 60 cubic feet of cargo space.

Shown with optional vinyl roof, vinyl rub strips and Rallye wheels is the Plymouth Duster Coupe. In standard 6-cylinder form, this model registered a weight of 2,780 pounds and posted a price of $2,287. Offered in a variety of interior and exterior decor and fittings, it was Plymouth's most popular car this year, attracting 212,331 sales, including V-8 models. Not offered in the U.S.A., 2,001 Duster Hardtops were also built.

The engine roster for senior Plymouths listed only fou varieties, whereas seven were present the previous year A Six was not offered, nor was the 383, and the 440 offering was cut from two to one. The 318 was standard for all models, which provided three other engines fo extra wallop. A 360, which late in the year was standard on suburbans, had 8.8:1 compression and 175 net horse power. The new 400, as used in 2-barrel form for mid-size cars, was the middle option. The premium option was a 4-barrel 440 with 8.2:1 compression and ratings of 225 and 230 net horsepower.

A new electronic ignition system first offered by Chrysler on a very limited basis in 1971 was at first optional on certain Plymouth V-8 engines early this year later became standard on all V-8s. The new device eliminated breaker points and condenser, simplified tune-ups improved fuel burn and thereby aided exhaust emission control.

Though the 426 Hemi street engine was not offered to the public, the competition Hemi was available on special order. Supposedly, it was purchased for supervised and sanctioned racing and drag use only.

During the year, some changes in specifications may have occurred and are not noted here. Sometimes, records of a change are not available or discovered during historical research. Also, some cars with a different item or two may have been "guinea pigs" for market testing, or to test public use and reaction to something tentatively planned as a general offering the following year.

Opened this year was the new Walter P. Chrysler Building in the Chrysler Center at Highland Park, the "captive" Detroit suburb. The building houses styling, engineering, sales and other operations. On the styling level, Elwood P. Engel, vice-president, retired and his responsibilities were given to Richard G. Macadam, who was appointed director of design, an interim position. Macadam had come up through the styling ranks at Chrysler, and the author worked closely with him at times.

The Plymouth Duster 340 Coupe, as indicated by its 340 designation, was powered only by the engine of that size. But the 340 V-8 was available for other Dusters, and for the Valiant Sedan and Scamp as well. The bold side tape stripe was standard on the 340 Coupe, which scaled a weight of 3,100 pounds, listed at $2,742 and was built for 15,681 buyers.

Back again as an option was the Gold Duster. Its canopy-style vinyl roof was of gold reptile grain for body colors compatible with gold, black boar grain for other colors. Special Gold Duster decals near the front wheels identified the car, which also had gold tape across the rear. Whitewall tires on 5.5-inch wide wheels, special wheelcovers, bright drip rails and special interior trim also went with the package price. All Dusters had a deck lid with a center ridge as shown. First scheduled for this year, the lid made its appearance on 1971 models as a running change in mid-year.

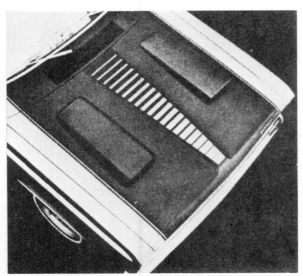

The Twister option was again available for the Duster. Hood decor treatment was like that of 1971. This bird's eye view of the hood shows twin add-on simulated airscoops and a center strobe stripe effect. The body side tape pattern was as shown on the 340 Coupe, except that the Twister name replaced the 340 numerals. Other special items were included in the package.

Still a sporty-looking small car was the Plymouth Barracuda Hardtop. A total of 10,622 came out of the factory in various Six and V-8 forms. The standard V-8 cost $2,822 and weighed 3,330 pounds. A standard Six cost $112 less. The car shown was prettied up with optional body side tape. Not offered this year were a convertible or coupe.

From this point of view, the Plymouth Satellite Coupe could easily be mistaken for its 1971 counterpart. Except for wheel dress and single-window side markers, they were alike, but only until their rear bumpers could be seen. This model weighed 3,300 pounds and cost $2,716 as a V-8. Including Sixes, 10,507 were built. For mid-size cars, a standard V-8 cost $107 more than a Six.

Once more, the Plymouth Valiant 4-Door Sedan appeared in the form that had made it a sales success for several years. And this year its popularity demanded a higher production rate than ever before. A total of 52,911 Sixes and V-8s were built. It was the answer to those who wanted a very sensible small sedan. In standard 6-cylinder form it weighed 2,800 pounds and cost $2,363.

Picking up more customers for Plymouth this year was the Valiant Scamp Hardtop, which required production of 49,470 cars to satisfy the demand. Offered as a Six or V-8, the good-looking modest luxury car recorded a weight of 2,825 pounds and a price of $2,528 when built in 6-cylinder form.

Although much-tamed in power, the 'Cuda continued with the twin-scoop performance hood, shown with an optional "3-runner" flat black pattern. Another application reversed the scheme, placing black or off-white on the scoop stretches. The exclusively V-8 'Cuda Hardtop sold for $3,029, weighed 3,195 pounds and went to 7,828 buyers. The grille design, shared with the standard Barracuda, was a simple concept much like that of 1970, even to the use of single-unit headlamps.

The Plymouth Satellite 4-Door Sedan looked like its 1971 counterpart from this point of view since, unlike 2-door cars, the rear bumpers were not different. However, side marker lens design differed, and wheels were not dressed the same, but those are very minor details. When built in V-8 form, this practical mid-size economy model weighed 3,345 pounds and cost $2,785. Including Sixes, 12,794 were built.

This model was as much like its 1971 counterpart as was the Satellite Sedan. All mid-size Plymouth wagons and sedans featured a grille of new design. Illustrated is the Plymouth Satellite Wagon, built only as a 2-seat model and offered only in V-8 form this year. It registered 3,785 pounds on the weight scale, carried a $3,167 price tag and chalked up 7,377 built. This and the Satellite Sedan ranked with the Satellite Coupe.

The new Satellite Sebring Hardtop was fitted with bright moldings on the "layered" lower body character line. This very sporty-looking automobile was offered with a choice of Six or V-8 engines. A grand total of 34,353 came off the assembly lines. The car weighed 3,315 pounds and listed at $2,978 when built as a V-8.

As in 1971, the air deflector at the rear-end of the roof was an extra-cost feature for all mid-size wagon models. The Plymouth Satellite Custom Wagon was a V-8 vehicle offered in two models. The 2-seat model weighed 3,825 pounds, cost $3,340 and went to 5,485 buyers. Listed at $3,418 was the 3,780-pound 3-seat wagon, of which 5,637 were built. In class, the Satellite Custom Wagon and Sedan equalled the Satellite Sebring Hardtop.

The Satellite Custom 4-Door Sedan was so attractive to 34,973 individuals that they bought it. They had a choice of Six or V-8 engines, and those who chose a V-8 got a 3,350-pound car for $2,955. The example shown was fitted with a Brougham interior option, signified by a Brougham signature on the roof blind quarter, and available only for this model.

Though not apparent on this light-colored car, Satellite Sebring-Plus Hardtops featured argent metallic paint below the lower body side moldings. The canopy vinyl roof was optional. This model tipped the weighing scale at 3,320 pounds and asked a price of $3,127. Assembly lines turned out 21,399 of them, all with V-8 engines. The car shared a class level with the Satellite Regent Wagon.

The Plymouth Road Runner Hardtop, weighing 3,495 pounds and costing $3,095, was exclsuively V-8. Exactly 7,628 were built. Shown is the standard Road Runner hood. Available was a tape pattern of closely-spaced stripes, parallel with and as long as the hood "vents," that wrapped over the sides. The strobe stripe pattern over the roof was similar to, but not exactly like, the wrap-over decor of 1971.

A Road Runner shows optional tape stripes on the deck, and the outline ahead of the windshield denotes an optional performance hood with a "power bulge" and Air Grabber scoop. Within the loop bumper, Road Runners had a distinctive grille design with air admitted only through a central opening with a vertical divider strut at the center. Shown is the new rear bumper typical of all mid-size 2-door models.

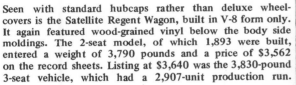

Seen with standard hubcaps rather than deluxe wheelcovers is the Satellite Regent Wagon, built in V-8 form only. It again featured wood-grained vinyl below the body side moldings. The 2-seat model, of which 1,893 were built, entered a weight of 3,790 pounds and a price of $3,562 on the record sheets. Listing at $3,640 was the 3,830-pound 3-seat vehicle, which had a 2,907-unit production run.

The Plymouth Fury I 4-Door Sedan provides a good view of the new bumper design applied to all big sedans and hardtops. More expensive models had larger taillamps, and the Fury Gran series added decor between the lamps. The car illustrated was priced at $3,464, weighed 3,840 pounds and had a 14,006-unit production run. All senior Plymouths were V-8 cars this year. Since horsepower was reduced, the big cars needed a V-8. Also, a V-8 was preferred by a large majority of buyers.

The more massive front bumper had a recessed center, giving it a dual-loop appearance. The grille inserts shown were typical of all but the Fury Gran cars and Sport Suburbans. Extensive re-styling also required a new hood, front and rear quarter panels and doors. Displaying the new characteristics is the Fury II 4-Door Sedan. It was a 3,830-pound car selling at $3,583. Chrysler-Plymouth dealers sold 20,051 of them.

Long and impressive were the big Plymouths, as this photograph of a Fury II 2-Door Hardtop shows quite well. At 217.2 inches overall, hardtops and sedans were 2.1 inches longer than their 1971 counterparts. This big beauty, priced at $3,605 and weighing 3,790 pounds, was delivered to 7,515 buyers.

This model was chosen by 46,731 buyers. It is the Plymouth Fury III 4-Door Sedan, which registered a weight of 3,830 pounds and posted a price of $3,763. The car, like numerous others shown in this book, was photographed on a turntable in a private display area within Chrysler's Highland Park engineering and styling complex. While working for Chrysler, the author viewed, many cars, mostly proposals and prototypes, in this area.

This car shows two styling features that appeared only on "informal" 2-door hardtops. One was the roof, with a nearly-vertical leading edge on the blind quarter and a crisp, sharply-raked rear window. It had a convertible-like character. The other feature is in the rear quarter panels, where sculpturing gave prominence to the wheel area. The angular form transition ahead of the wheel was repeated in reverse at the rear of the wheel. Other models did not have the return transition at the rear. The Fury III 2-Door Hardtop, of which 21,204 were built, weighed 3,790 pounds and cost $3,785.

Shown is the Fury Gran Coupe, a 2-door hardtop with roof and rear quarter panels like the Fury III 2-Door Hardtop. Note that the sculpturing in the rear wheel area returned to the panel's normal surface after clearing the wheel. Shown are optional wheel skirts. This model, which was delivered to 15,840 buyers, weighed 3,735 pounds and was priced at $3,941. The Gran series featured a grille of thin bright vertical bars closely-spaced. Sections of the grille opened to reveal hidden headlamps. This was the last year for concealed headlamps.

The roof for this model was also new this year, but was not like that of the "informal" 2-door model. The car illustrated is the Plymouth Fury III 2-Door Formal Hardtop, of which 9,036 rolled off the assembly lines. The 3,790-pound car listed at $3,818. The Formal Hardtop was discontinued at the end of this model year.

Ranking fourth in Plymouth popularity this year was the Fury III 4-Door Hardtop, which had a 48,618-car production run. It was outranked by the Duster Coupe, Valiant Sedan and Scamp Hardtop, in that order. This big automobile weighed 3,855 pounds and sold for $3,829. Like all senior Plymouths this year, it was offered in V-8 form only.

The Fury Gran Coupe 2-Door Formal Hardtop shared its roof and rear quarter panels with the comparable Fury III model. Note that the sculpturing ahead of the rear wheel formed a new surface that continued to the rear bumper. This rear quarter design also was used on all senior sedans and 4-door hardtops. The luxury automobile shown, of which 8,509 came out of the factory, sold for $3,974 and recorded a weight of 3,805 pounds.

Sharing its new roof with the comparable Fury III 4-Door Hardtop, the Fury Gran Sedan also was a 4-door hardtop model. This beautiful car swung the weight scale pointer to a reading of 3,865 pounds and posted a price of $3,987. Beginning ahead of the rear wheel, the rear quarter panel lower surface character is apparent in this view. A total of 19,377 were built.

The Plymouth Suburban again was on a class level with Fury II models. The 2-seat Suburban cost $4,024, weighed 4,315 pounds and had a production run of 5,368 cars. The 3-seat Suburban, of which 2,773 came out of the factory, had a weight of 4,360 pounds and listed at $4,139. Standard, Custom and Sport Suburbans were built only with V-8 power.

Ranking with Fury III models was the Plymouth Custom Suburban. Weighing 4,315 pounds, the 2-seat model cost $4,123 and went to 11,067 buyers. Exactly 14,041 orders were filled by the 3-seat model, which listed at $4,201 and weighed 4,365 pounds. A new option for suburbans was a vinyl roof, which is shown. The roof rack and rear assist handles were continued options. All suburbans featured lower rear side sculpturing similar to that seen on all but "informal" 2-door hardtops.

The Plymouth Sport Suburban, ranking with the Fury Gran series, had the same grille as used for Gran cars. Wood-grain vinyl was applied to the upper body sides. The 2-seat model weighed 4,335 pounds, cost $4,389 and recorded a production total of 4,971. Maintaining its tradition of long standing, the 3-seat model was the costliest and heaviest Plymouth for the year. It listed at $4,466, weighed 4,395 pounds and chalked up a 15,628-unit production total. The 3-seater was the most popular Plymouth station wagon type this year.

Raring to go was the Motown Missile, a Pro Stocker driven by Don Carlton, one of a 5-man crew that modified, maintained and managed the car and its public appearances. It continued the amazing performance of 1970-71 Motown Missiles. The 'Cuda had a specially prepared 426 Hemi engine to blast it down the strips. Many stock chassis parts were duplicated in titanium and magnesium to reduce front end weight. Not part of the Plymouth Supercar Clinic or associated with Sox & Martin, the team operated independently, but served as a test bed for Chrysler Drag Program engineers. Many innovations were passed on to other Chrysler competition machines. Inevitably, the tricks were acquired or duplicated by competitors.

As usual, Plymouth met the exacting demands incurred in offering automobiles specially built for law enforcement agencies. Production records logged them separately, rather than merging them into totals listed for similar models built for public sale. Shown is a Fury Police Special, one of 13,045 4-door sedans built in several versions. Also, 657 Fury Police Emergency Wagons, all 2-seat models, were built. The wagons were fitted with the usual complement of stretchers and emergency gear.

When the operators of taxicab companies needed new Plymouths this year, most of them found the Satellite 4-Door Sedan to be a desirable vehicle. Their choice was reflected on the production records, which listed 2,146 built. The illustration is a photograph of a regular production car, given a taxi resemblance by a photo retouch artist.

With the same photograph as used for the Satellite taxicab as a base, a photo retouch artist simulated the Satellite Police Special. As a police vehicle replacement this year, this model was not regarded as nearly so desirable as the big Fury. It drew a modest total of 2,632 orders from the law enforcers.

Another creation of the photo retouch artist was this illustration of the Fury taxicab. This model attracted a total of 1,925 orders from the taxicab companies. The cars had various distinctive markings to advertise the businesses they served, just as they also were equipped and fitted in a special manner.

The DeSoto name did not terminate with cessation of domestic DeSoto passenger car production in 1960, but continued on foreign commercial vehicles, which first used it in the mid-thirties. This year's models were built by Chrysler Sanayi, Istanbul, Turkey. The DeSoto Town Panel, shown as a Model D100, was also built as a D200. The D100 chassis had a 114-inch wheelbase, I-beam front axle, semi-floating rear axle and semi-elliptic springs. Tires were 6-ply 6.50 x 16. The engine was a 140-horsepower 225 Slant Six, coupled to a 3-speed transmission with column shift. Gross vehicle weight was 5,381.2 pounds.

Advertised as farm trucks were the DeSoto W100 and W200 Pick-Up vehicles. In appearance and general dimensions, they were like the D-series pick-ups, but featured 4-wheel drive. They bore the Power Wagon name on the cowlsides. Shown is the W100, which was on a 114-inch wheelbase and 6-ply 7.00 x 15 tires. The 140-horsepower 225 Six, a 4-speed transmission and semi-floating rear axle were employed. Gross vehicle weight was 5,588 pounds. The W200 was the same, except that its wheelbase was 127.9 inches, the rear axle was full-floating, 8-ply tires were 7.50 x 17 and gross vehicle weight was 7,981.6 pounds.

The DeSoto Pick-Up is shown in D100 size, but it also was available in D200 form. The D200 series had a 127.9-inch wheelbase, I-beam front axle, full-floating rear axle and semi-elliptic springs. Tires were 8-ply 7.50 x 17. The engine was the 225 Six, but the transmission was a 4-speed type. The gross vehicle weight rating was 7,480 pounds. Chrysler advertised the D100 and D200 lines as light trucks, and said they were strong and dependable. They were of a strictly functional and simple design formula. The use of flat surfaces and angular shapes made metalwork much less costly than the manufacturing cost of similar U.S. vehicles.

The largest DeSoto trucks were the PD-600 series, with a 6-cylinder Perkins Diesel 6-354 engine of 130 horsepower at 2,800 r.p.m. The transmission was a 5-speed unit, and the drive was to a rear axle. Service brakes were fully air-operated. The wheelbase was 196.8 inches and gross vehicle weight was 23,680 pounds. DeSoto truck reference material for this book was in the Turkish language, and a translator interpreted terms and details for the author. Chrysler opened the Istanbul plant in 1964, and has been producing these same light and medium-duty vehicles with DeSoto, Dodge and Fargo names since. The vehicle concepts were continued into 1978.

Good times were enjoyed by the industry, which established a new passenger car production record. For the calendar year, the total industry gain was 9.5% over 1972. Chrysler Corp. turned out 13.1% more cars and boosted its industry share to 15.55%. Plymouth did exceptionally well, registering a 21.2% improvement. But the vigorous activity did not budge Plymouth from its position as No. 6 automaker.

Plymouth's series line-up, and sub-series within them, was unchanged. Cricket, the adopted English baby, was still with the family, but this was the last year. Again offered on a 98-inch wheelbase were the sedan and wagon. A 4-cylinder 91.4 c.i.d. engine with single carburetor and a rating of 55 net horsepower was standard for the sedan. With twin carburetors it produced 70 net horsepower, was

The Plymouth Cricket was on the U.S.A. domestic scene again this year, but this was its last appearance. Sales volume was encouraging in 1971, its first year, but a 1972 recall for corrective measures was damaging to its future in this country. Shown is the Cricket 4-Door Sedan. Cricket weights, prices and production totals are not available.

Despite numerous improvements made almost constantly since its 1971 inception, the Plymouth Cricket could not strengthen its position in the U.S.A. The little English car just did not "catch on." Shown is the Cricket Station Wagon, a very practical sub-compact car. Its 70-horsepower 4-cylinder engine was optional for the Sedan, which offered a 55-horsepower engine as standard.

optional for the sedan, and was the only engine for the wagon.

The compact group was now the Series JV. Duster coupes continued on a 108-inch wheelbase with the Valiant sedan, and the Scamp hardtop remained on a 111-inch chassis. The 198 Slant Six, with net horsepower now reported as 95, and 318 V-8 were standard for all but the Duster 340 coupe, which was the only JV car with a 340 V-8. The only engine option for all but the Duster 340 coupe was the 225 Slant Six.

The Barracuda Series JB was again a hardtop in standard and 'Cuda versions on a 108-inch base. For these cars engine availability was cut again this year. The 318 was standard and the 340 was optional for both models.

In the mid-size Series JR, extensive styling changes were made in 2-door 115-inch wheelbase models, while 117-inch sedans and wagons remained relatively untouched. Bearing the Satellite name were three standard models, three Customs, a hardtop in Sebring and Sebring-Plus versions, plus two Regent wagons. Not called a Satellite was the Road Runner coupe. Excepting wagons, the 225 Six was standard for Satellite, Custom and Sebring models which with the Sebring-Plus and wagons, also had the 318 V-8 as standard. All offered two 400 V-8s as extra. One with 2-venturi carburetion was listed at 175 net horsepower, while the other, a 4-venturi job, still rated 260 net. Road Runners had the 318 as standard, with the 340, 4-venturi 400, and 440 of 280 net horsepower for options.

The senior Series JP received a partial styling revamp and continued on a 122-inch wheelbase for suburbans and 120 for others. As for 1972, the Fury I was a sedan, and the Fury II was reduced from two models to a sedan. The Fury III was cut from four models to three and the Fury Gran was pared from three to two. The standard Suburban was reduced from two versions to a 2-seat model only, while Custom and Sport Suburbans were again offered in two models each. The 360 V-8 engine, with compression cut to 8.4:1 and net horsepower reduced to 170, was standard for all suburbans and optional for all other models, which had the 318 as standard. Options for all big Plymouths were a 2-venturi 400 of 185 net horsepower and a 4-venturi 440 of 220 net.

Plymouth introduced new emission control and safety features as standard this year. An exhaust gas recirculation system routed a varied volume of exhaust gas to the incoming fuel-air, lowering peak burn temperatures. An orifice spark advance and electric assist choke also aided reduction of air pollution. Without doing significant damage, front bumpers were capable of impacting a fixed barrier at 5 m.p.h., while rear bumpers had a 2.5 m.p.h. protection factor. By mid-year, steel beams were built into doors for side-impact protection. A new option for discouraging theft was a security alarm system that blew the horn intermittently while flashing the headlights, taillights and side marker lights. Available only with the power door lock option, the system was armed by locking either front door, and was triggered if someone tampered with the doors, hood, trunk or ignition. For big-size 4-door models only, a new option was vent windows, last used on those models in 1970 when they were standard.

For changing conditions or special purposes, Plymouth may have made substitutions, additions or deletions not recorded in this summary.

Again establishing itself as the unchallenged winner of Plymouth's top popularity prize was the Duster Coupe, of which 249,243 were built in various Six and V-8 equipment and trim combinations. In standard Six form, it also was Plymouth's lightest and lowest-priced domestic-built model, weighing 2,830 pounds and costing $2,376. It is shown with optional Rallye wheels and canopy-style vinyl roof. Not shown is a Duster Hardtop, of which 2,614 were built for Canada.

One of the numerous Duster variations was the Special Coupe option, which included certain extras in an attractive package price. Shown are full-length vinyl-insert side moldings, full vinyl roof, whitewall tires and deluxe wheel-covers. Inside was a pleated vinyl front bench seat with high backs and center armrest, a Spacemaker Pak with folding rear seat for added carrying space, plus other popular items. This was a good combination of practical and luxury features.

The Plymouth Duster 340 Coupe is shown with optional tape decor on the body side and rear. This model featured the 340 V-8 engine. It recorded a weight of 3,175 pounds, a price of $2,822 and a production total of 15,731 cars. Also optional were the Rallye wheels and whitewall tires. All Dusters had a new sheetmetal panel to incorporate the more attractive taillamps.

The Space Duster conversion option was another Duster variation. The rear seat back could be folded flat forward and the safety panel behind it could be folded backward to provide a fully-carpeted cargo area 6.5 feet long. With a sliding sun roof, it was claimed that tall items could be carried by projecting them through the roof. However, the roof opening was above the front seat only.

The Gold Duster was again available at extra cost. It was not limited to gold body color, but offered a variety of color choices. The canopy vinyl roof was of golden reptile pattern, or could be had in black or white, whichever was compatible with the body color. Body side and rear end tape decor was in gold, black or white. Gold Duster decals were on the sides for identification. A host of interior and other features was included.

VALIANT

Continuing to cater to those who preferred cars with a performance image, Plymouth again offered the Duster Twister option. Design features of the new hood permitted a pleasing application of dull black. Though they were not functional, twin "airscoops" added to the hood magnified the power image. Bumper guards shown were part of the new impact-absorbing bumper protection standard on all cars. Despite the Valiant sign, the car was not a Valiant.

The Plymouth Valiant 4-Door Sedan turned in another good sales performance this year, requiring production of 61,826 Six and V-8 cars. As a standard Six, it cost $2,447 and weighed 2,865 pounds. It is shown with a number of dress-up options. Body side, superstructure and rear end styling was unchanged, but a new hood, grille and front bumper was shared with Duster and Scamp models.

Winning even more popularity this year was the Plymouth Scamp Hardtop. The car went to 53,792 buyers, who had a choice of Six or V-8 engines. It is doubtful that any of them bought it as a standard Six with no extras, but in that form it scaled a weight of 2,885 pounds and asked a price of $2,822. The rear end design was the same as it had been since its inception as a 1971 model.

The 'Cuda Hardtop is shown with the functional airscoop hood that was fitted to 'Cuda and Barracuda cars powered by the 340 V-8 engine. For those with 318 engines, the plain hood as used for 1970-72 was installed. The body side tape pattern was optional for Barracuda and 'Cuda models. A flat black hood pattern also was available. This model, of which 10,626 were built, cost $3,120 and weighed 3,235 pounds.

This was the fourth year for the sleek Barracuda styling concept, which was still regarded as quite attractive. But appearance was not enough to improve its sales appeal. However, in the general sales upswing this year, it did a trifle better. Shown is the Barracuda Hardtop, available only as a V-8, weighing 3,140 pounds and costing $2,935. Its production total was 11,587 cars.

Mid-size Plymouth 2-door cars underwent an extensive styling change this year. This view provides a look at the new rear quarter panel and bumper designs. Body sides were smoother, without a "layered" effect through the lower portion. Displaying these characteristics is the Satellite Coupe, which in V-8 form weighed 3,440 pounds and cost $2,867. Exactly 13,570 were built, including Sixes.

No sheetmetal changes were made for mid-size Plymouth sedans and wagons, nor was bumper styling altered. The sensible-looking Satellite 4-Door Sedan had a Six and V-8 production run of 14,716. When built as a V-8, it tipped the weighing scale at 3,515 pounds and listed at $2,936. The quite acceptable body styling was in its third year without change.

Again offered only as a V-8 engined 2-seat model was the Plymouth Satellite Wagon. The 3,950-pound vehicle was priced at $3,272. Production amounted to 6,906 units. This was the only mid-size model that did not enjoy an increased demand this year. Its production was down about 6.3%.

The Satellite Custom 4-Door Sedan had a production run of 46,748 Sixes and V-8s. In V-8 form it sold for $3,086 and recorded a weight of 3,510 pounds. The new grille design for mid-size sedans and wagons had a more unified appearance in the headlamp areas. All Plymouths were standard-equipped with elastomeric front and rear bumper guards as part of the bumper protection system necessary this year.

An unidentified vendor's new Satellite Sebring Hardtop was used for transportation to the giant old car flea market at Hershey, Pa., where it is seen. It is one of 51,575 built in Six and V-8 forms. The V-8 cost $3,109 and weighed 3,460 pounds. For mid-size models offering the choice, a standard V-8 cost $112 more than a Six. Note the curving body side molding used on this model.

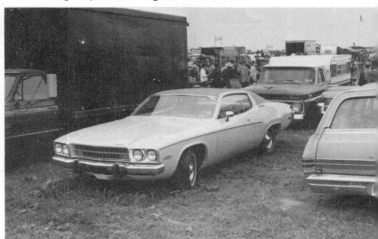

Built only as a V-8 was the Satellite Custom Wagon, which was offered as two models. The 2-seat model attracted a total of 6,733 buyers, registered a weight of 3,945 pounds and listed at $3,400. As a 3-seat vehicle it was priced at $3,518, chalked up a weight of 3,990 pounds and amassed a production total of 7,705 units.

New Satellite 2-door models lacked the front end uniqueness of their 1971-72 predecessors. With no loop bumper, frontal design was conventional. The hood, quarter panels and doors were less interesting from a styling standpoint. Shown is the Satellite Sebring-Plus Hardtop, an exclusively V-8 model that 43,628 buyers found they could not get along without. The 3,455-pound car listed at $3,258.

In keeping with its reputation as a performance car, the Road Runner offered a choice of V-8 engines only. Built only as a hardtop since 1970, it was now a coupe. The performance hood and fancy tape stripes shown were optional. In standard form, the Road Runner Coupe registered a weight of 3,525 pounds and was listed at $3,115. A total of 19,056 were built in all forms.

Again this year, all of the big standard-size Plymouth models were powered by V-8 engines. Shown in wide and impressive form is the Plymouth Fury II 4-Door Sedan. It recorded a reading of 3,845 pounds on the weight scale and carried a $3,694 price sticker. A total of 21,646 of them were produced. Not shown is a Fury II 2-Door Hardtop, of which 3,176 were produced, probably for Canada. This model was not offered in the U.S.A.

Maintaining its dignity as the top mid-size wagon was the Satellite Regent. Again it sported wood-grained vinyl on the sides, as well as an especially handsome interior. Appropriately, it was offered only as a V-8. The 3,950-pound 2-seat model cost $3,621 and had a 2,781-unit production run. The 3-seat model weighed 4,010 pounds, cost $3,740 and was delivered to 4,786 buyers.

This rather unattractive illustration is a copy of a commercial artist's basic kind of rendering. The automobile is the Plymouth Fury I 4-Door Sedan, the "economy" leader of the senior Plymouth family. With the 318 V-8 engine and other standard equipment, the 3,865-pound automobile asked a price of $3,575. It ranked sixth in senior model popularity, drawing a total of 17,365 sales.

The massive new rear bumper seemed to clutch the new upstanding taillamps, but actually was not attached to them. The big cars had plenty of protection here. The Fury III 4-Door Sedan was so attractive to 51,742 individuals that they bought it. It weighed 3,860 pounds and cost $3,866. Excepting 2-door hardtops, all big Plymouths had a sculptured diagonal transition ahead of the rear wheels, bringing the lower surface out and continuing it smoothly to the bumper.

The Fury III 2-Door Hardtop was recorded as weighing 3,815 pounds and costing $3,883. The factory also recorded a production total of 34,963, of which one was selected from the showroom floor by the author's wife. Fitted with many extras, it had a cloth-and-vinyl interior featuring fabric with a special feminine appeal. Overall, the car was a shade of beige that made it even more attractive to women. Powered by the optional 360 V-8, it was especially nice for road trips.

The loop front bumper/grille was discarded for big Plymouths, too, which brought back a conventional front layout. The new hood, grille, bumper and headlamp housings did the trick. The Fury III 4-Door Hardtop, of which 51,215 were built, had a weight of 3,880 pounds and was priced at $3,932. Though this view indicates dual sculpturing in the rear wheel area, as featured on 2-door hardtops, this model did not have it. Perhaps this was a photo retouching error.

The Fury Gran Coupe, actually a hardtop, listed at $4,064 and weighed 3,845 pounds. The impressive automobile attracted 18,127 sales. Like the Fury III 2-Door Hardtop, it had dual diagonal sculpturing that emphasized the wheel area of rear quarter panels. Sculpturing at the rear of the wheel is vaguely perceptible in this view. Seen on the hood is a new stand-up hood ornament that would tip backward if bumped, thereby minimizing possible injury to persons. It was common to the Fury Gran series.

Another example of Plymouth limited production offerings was the Fury Special, so-named in advertising only. A combination of options and special features, it was a special package rather than a full-rank model, as it carried Fury III signatures. Among its goodies were a special dark chestnut metallic paint, parchment vinyl roof, color-keyed body side moldings, bright sill moldings, stand-up hood ornament, vinyl interior with tapestry-cloth seat inserts and shag carpeting. These were considered standard for this edition. The Fury Special was available as a Fury III 2-Door Hardtop or 4-Door Hardtop.

Loaded with elegance and luxury, the Fury Gran Sedan proved irresistible to the 14,852 individuals who bought it. The attractive 4-door hardtop weighed 3,890 pounds and was available upon payment of $4,110. The Fury Gran series was available with an optional Brougham interior that offered a choice of seat style and trim, individual front seat adjustment and a reclining feature for the front passenger. The Fury Gran series truly was a pair of prestigious passenger cars.

The Plymouth Satellite Taxicab offered a choice of green or black interiors, while engines were the 225 Six or 318 V-8. TorqueFlite transmission and power disc brakes were heavy-duty. The front seat back was recessed for additional rear-seat knee room, typical of the many taxi touches incorporated by Plymouth. Belvedere Taxicab production was 2,140 units. Police departments bought 2,397 Belvedere Sedans specially built for their use.

Distinguished by wood-grained vinyl on its sides was the Plymouth Sport Suburban, ranking with the Fury Gran series. The 2-seater weight was 4,435 pounds, price was $4,497 and production total was 4,832. The 3-seat model was Plymouth's costliest and heaviest for the year, asking $4,599 and weighing 4,495 pounds. It attracted exactly 15,680 buyers. Custom and Sport Suburbans again were available with Brougham interiors, but the vinyl roof option failed to return. Suburbans did not have a new rear bumper this year, but the carryover design was adapted to the new protection standard partly by means of the elastomer-padded guards shown.

Shown is the Plymouth Suburban, the economy vehicle of the Suburban series, but it was on a level with the Fury II Sedan, rather than the Fury I. This year, it was built only as a 2-seat model weighing 4,410 pounds, costing $4,150 and having a 5,206-unit production run. Not shown is the Plymouth Custom Suburban, of Fury III rank. The 2-seat Custom, of which 9,888 hit the market, listed at $4,246 and weighed 4,420 pounds. Weighing 4,465 pounds and priced at $4,354, the 3-seat Custom brought in 15,671 sales.

Shown is the Plymouth Fury Taxicab, of which 2,326 were built. Its equipment compared with the Satellite, except that all interiors were gray. The Fury was also built for police use this year. A total of 480 Emergency Wagons, in 2-seat form, and 13,461 Sedans were turned out for enforcers of the law. They were provided with more powerful engines and necessities for varied police work.

Industry passenger car production fell more than 24.5% this calendar year, and the total Chrysler Corp. plummet was a sickening 25.6%. The corporation's 16.14% share of industry output was down only slightly from 1973, however. Though its total output was 18% lower, Plymouth again was the nation's No. 3 producer, an honor not held since 1970. The advance in position was caused by the tumble of Buick, Oldsmobile and Pontiac, whose demand was sharply cut by a severe shortage of gasoline this year. Like Ford, Chevrolet and American Motors, Plymouth had compact economy cars that sold exceptionally well during the fuel crisis.

Plymouth's breadwinners were the Duster, Valiant and Scamp, Series 4V. This was the only series to register an increase. The Duster continued as a coupe on the 108-inch wheelbase, but with minor changes. The Valiant sedan was lengthened to the Scamp hardtop 111-inch chassis, and a late introduction added two Valiant Brougham models. The former 340 V-8 engine was replaced by the 360, which powered the Duster 360 Coupe. In this version, the 360 had 4-venturi carburetion and reported 245 net horsepower. Other Series 4V models had the 198 Six and 318 V-8 as standard engines, offering the 225 Six as optional.

Now coded as the Series 4B were the Barracuda and 'Cuda, which made their final appearance this year. Of familiar hardtop-only form on the 108-inch chassis, they were fitted with the 318 as standard and 360 as optional. The 360 was as built for the Duster.

The mid-size cars, Series 4R, were carried over with very minor changes. They continued with 2-door models on a 115-inch wheelbase and 4-door cars, including wagons, on 117. Three models comprised the Satellite offerings and a like number were Satellite Customs. Satellite Sebring and Sebring-Plus hardtops, plus two Satellite Regent wagons and the Road Runner coupe rounded out the mid-series. Excepting the Sebring-Plus, Road Runner and wagons, the 225 was the standard Six, while all listed the 318 as the standard V-8. The 360 and 400, both 4-venturi, were optional V-8s for all, while the Road Runner provided a 4-venturi 440 for extra-special 275-horsepower punch.

Big Plymouths were an all-new design concept with sedans and hardtops on a 122-inch wheelbase and suburbans on 124, which were two inches longer than previously. They averaged 327 pounds heavier at a time when big cars, unless very expensive, were not attracting many sales orders. Coded the Series 4P, they were the Fury I and Fury II sedans, the Fury III group of three models, plus two Fury Gran types. Appearing for the last time without Fury nameplates were the big wagons, which were the standard 2-seat Suburban and two models each in Custom and Sport Suburban varieties. The 2-venturi 360 V-8 engine was standard for all 4P models but the Fury Gran and all suburbans, for which the 2-venturi 400 was standard. A 205-horsepower 400 and a 230-horsepower 440, both with 4-venturi carburetion, were available for the entire Series 4P.

All 4V, 4B, 4R and 4P vehicles were given new fuel economy, emission control and safety features and refinements. A 2-stage electric assist choke and an emergency device for closing the throttle were added. Rear bumpers, like those at the front, had a hydraulic impact-absorbing

system affording damage protection at speeds up to 5 m.p.h. Hardtop roofs were given new crush resistance. The passenger restraint system of lap and shoulder belts was interlocked with the ignition switch.

Plymouth decided to enter the expanding market for multi-purpose and sports/utility vehicles this year. So the Voyager and Trail Duster were introduced in time for the spring sales push. The Voyager series of wagons was offered in several body types, and in standard, Custom and Sport

Again, one of the Duster option packages was the Gold Duster shown. It included such things as the vinyl canopy roof, wheelcovers and whitewall tires, special exterior trim, a deluxe insulation package, pleated all-vinyl seats and wall-to-wall carpeting. Plymouth did not alter Duster styling this year, not even a new grille design to identify it as a new model. Lack of change did not hinder Duster sales, which hit an all-time high this year.

By far the most popular car in the Plymouth family this year was the Duster Coupe, which enjoyed a Six and V-8 production run of 277,409 units in various forms. As a standard Six, it also was the least-heavy and lowest-priced Plymouth, weighing 2,975 pounds and costing $2,829. Shown are options such as a vinyl canopy roof, highback seats, racing mirrors and Rallye wheels with white-letter tires. Dusters were 1.7 inches shorter despite the shock-absorbing rear bumper this year.

trim and equipment versions. They were built as the PB100 and PB200, each with wheelbases of 109 and 127 inches, and the PB300 on 127 inches only. All were of 5-passenger standard seating capacity, while optional capacity was 8 for the PB200, with seating for 8, 12 and 15 available for the PB300. The 225 Six was standard for PB100 and PB200 models which, with the PB300, also had the 318 V-8 as standard. Voyagers had independent front suspension that utilized coil springs rather than torsion bars. Among many options were TorqueFlite automatic transmission, power front disc brakes, power steering and air conditioning.

The Trail Duster sports/utility on-and-off-the-road vehicles had full-time 4-wheel drive. They had only the driver's seat unless front passenger seat and rear bench seat options were ordered. With full seating, they were advertised as having 5-passenger capacity. Buyers had a choice of a vinyl soft top or a steel roof. Standard and Sport

exterior/interior trim versions were offered. Known as th Model PW100, the vehicles were on a 106-inch wheelbas and had a gross vehicle weight rating of 4,900/6,00 pounds maximum. The standard engine was the 318 while extra choices were the 4-venturi 360, 2-venturi 40 and 4-venturi 440. Many extra-cost items included thos noted for the Voyager.

On the corporate executive level, Richard G. Macadar was elected vice-president in charge of design (styling) i June, and continues in that capacity at this writin; This was a most fitting reward for "Dick," who has all c the qualities needed for the position and its immens responsibilities.

Despite a general economic decline that swept acros the nation in the latter part of this year, Valiant (includin Duster and Scamp) set new records, outselling all othe compact cars. This, of course, was due to the gasolin shortage earlier in the year, which created a preferenc for small cars.

The Space Duster Pak continued to attract buyers who wanted utility features in a sporty little automobile. Its rear seat and security panel offered various ways to utilize interior space. With seat and panel up, the concealed trunk space was conventional. With the seat down and panel up, there was more interior load space. With seat up and panel down, trunk capacity was greater. With seat and panel down, a carpeted cargo area 6.5 feet long was provided. The metal sliding sun roof panel was a Duster extra.

Showing its special name on the rear quarter panel is the Twister, which again was a Duster option package. It was for those who wanted good handling and a sporty looking car with less engine displacement. It looked like the Duster 360, had a front sway bar to aid handling characteristics and was fitted with Rallye wheels. The vinyl canopy roof gave Dusters a smart appeal.

The Duster 360 Coupe was powered by a 245-horsepower V-8 engine that was not available for other Dusters, or the Valiant or Scamp. It had a front sway bar and heavy-duty strength in the suspension, shock absorbers and wheels. Tires were E70 x 14, an 8.25-inch rear axle was featured and the transmission was a 3-speed manual with a floor-mounted gear selector. The wide tape stripe was shared with the Twister, but this model had Duster 360 signatures on the front quarter panels. It weighed 3,315 pounds and cost $3,288, but the unknown production total was merged with the regular coupe total.

Valiants were longer this year, due to adoption of the Scamp 111-inch wheelbase. The extra length was in the body proper, as the front end was unaltered. It provided 1.2 inches more leg and knee room for rear seat passengers. Shown with dress-up on the wheels, wheelcuts, window areas and roof is the basic Valiant 4-Door Sedan. It weighed 3,035 pounds and cost $2,942 as a Six. The Six and V-8 production total, including the Brougham, was 127,430 cars. The Valiant side signature was too high on this prototype.

Valiant 4-Door Sedan popularity was more than twice that of 1973. Part of the reason was in the offering of many options to discriminating buyers. The car is seen with a vinyl-covered roof, highback front seats, vinyl-insert side rub strips, plus bright trim on the drip rail, window frames, "B" pillar, wheel openings and sill. Wheel fittings and bright bumper guards complemented the smartness. Most of these items were grouped in a Custom Exterior Trim option.

A late addition was the Valiant Brougham series, of which the Hardtop model is shown. As a Six, it cost $3,794 and weighed 3,180 pounds. The Six and V-8 production run was 2,545 units. The special interior was of parchment crushed velour cloth and vinyl, with other luxury appointments. Also among other standard goodies were color-keyed wheelcovers, whitewall tires, bright wheel opening and sill moldings, chromed grille, a hood molding and stand-up ornament, upper bodyside stripes and a vinyl-clad roof. As a Valiant, the hardtop was not available in other than Brougham form.

The Valiant Brougham series offered the 225 Six or 318 V-8 engines, TorqueFlite, power steering, front sway bar and other "standardized extras." Brougham script was on the roof blind quarters and the usual Valiant signatures on front quarter panels were replaced by small Valiant name plaques invisible in this view. Shown are wheelcovers that simulated wire wheels. The Plymouth Valiant Brougham 4-Door Sedan cost $3,819 and weighed 3,195 pounds when built as a Six. Total production is unknown because the factory mixed it in with the regular Valiant Sedan.

The Plymouth Scamp Hardtop shows new rear end styling which was like that of the Valiant Brougham series. Actually, the Valiant Brougham Hardtop was this car with equipment differences. In standard Six form the Scamp was priced at $3,077 and registered a weight of 3,010 pounds. It had a Six and V-8 production run of 51,699 cars, not quite as high as the 1973 total. For Duster, Scamp and the regular Valiant, the standard 198 Six cost $151 less than the 318 V-8.

Throwing plenty of dust for this action picture was the Plymouth Barracuda Hardtop. It stirred up no wave of buying, however, as its production total of 6,745 was the lowest ever recorded for this model. Once eagerly sought, it was now forsaken and in its last year. Built only as a V-8, it recorded a weight of 3,210 pounds and posted a price of $3,067.

Although Barracuda styling had remained basically unaltered since this concept was introduced for 1970, the car still had an abundance of smartness. Certainly, styling obsolescence was not the reason for the car's lack of popularity this year. Rather, the reason was the soft-pedaling of the sports/performance image which the Barracuda had always exemplified. Also, public attention was now drawn to the Duster/Valiant/Scamp group because of the popularity of economy cars during the period of gasoline shortage. The basic Barracuda is shown with standard black wheels and hubcaps.

Posing placidly by the rolling seaside surf was a Plymouth 'Cuda Hardtop, which also made its final appearance this year. Once mighty for its size, it was now much weaker and had lost its sales appeal. Only 4,989 were built, the lowest total it had ever posted. The exclusively V-8 car cost $3,252 and weighed 3,300 pounds. 'Cuda and Barracuda styling was unchanged.

Continued without styling change were the mid-size 2-door Plymouths. The rear bumper, carried over from 1973, was mounted in a shock-absorbing manner to qualify it for damage protection at speeds up to 5 m.p.h. All Plymouths had the feature, which was applied to front bumpers on 1973 models. The Plymouth Satellite Coupe, weighing 3,510 pounds and costing $3,271 as a V-8, had a Six and V-8 production run of 10,634 cars.

Shown is the Plymouth Satellite 4-Door Sedan, which had a Six and V-8 production run of 12,726 cars built for public sale. When built in V-8 form, it tipped the weighing scale at 3,590 pounds and listed at $3,342. This model was a basis for special vehicles built for taxicab and police use, as Plymouth continued to concentrate on those markets. Taxicab production was 2,631 units, while 5,274 Police Specials were built.

Showing the new front bumper featured on mid-size 4-door cars is the Satellite Custom 4-Door Sedan, which was offered as a Six or V-8. It scaled a weight of 3,585 pounds and sold for $3,445 in V-8 form. Like other mid-size models offering both engines, its standard V-8 price was $116 more than a standard Six. Mid-size sedans and wagons also sported a new grille of slightly more refined character.

Illustrated is the Plymouth Satellite Custom Wagon, built only in V-8 form and offered in two models. The 2-seat model, of which 4,354 were produced, weighed 4,065 pounds and was priced at $3,839. Weighing 4,110 pounds was the 3-seat model, which cost $4,152 and had a 5,591-unit production run. Not shown is the base Satellite Wagon, also all-V-8, which was a 2-seat vehicle weighing 4,065 pounds and costing $3,654. It recorded a 4,622-unit production total. All mid-size wagons featured a new bumper design at the rear, as well as at the front. New taillamp design incorporated the backup lights.

Appearing eager to get going was a Plymouth Satellite Sebring Hardtop as it posed for the photographer. Again, this was the only mid-size hardtop that gave buyers a choice of a Six or V-8 engine. When built as a V-8, it asked a price of $3,468 and recorded a weight of 3,530 pounds. Factory production records, listing 22,002 units, included an undetermined number of Sebring-Plus cars.

The Plymouth Satellite Sebring-Plus Hardtop was exclusively a V-8 automobile. Registering 3,555 pounds on the weight scale, it was listed as costing $3,621. This attractive model, with tape stripes smartly accenting the sweeping character of its front-to-rear length, is shown with chrome-styled road wheels, an option. The production total is unknown, since it was mixed with the Satellite Sebring.

Introduced to spark spring sales was the Sundance option package for the Satellite Sebring. The interior featured yellow-gold/white/black cloth set off with white vinyl. Outside, a pattern of ornate yellow-gold design swept back from the front end and arched over the rear of the roof, just behind the vinyl canopy. A sunburst design on the roof blind quarters was repeated on the hood enclosure panel and rear deck lid, where it was accompanied by the Sundance name. Premier wheelcovers, whitewall tires and regular bright trim touches completed the package. Body color was Aztec Gold Metallic or Spinnaker White.

The newly-designed big Plymouths continued the Unibody construction principle, having more than 4,000 welds to bring one body all together. All big cars were built with a V-8 engine. Lowest-priced of the senior series was the Plymouth Fury I 4-Door Sedan, which was marketed at $4,101. Exactly 8,162 of the 4,185-pound cars were built for public marketing. This model was adapted to other purposes, too, as 757 were built as Taxicabs and 9,351 saw duty as Police Specials.

As shown, the Road Runner was not running, and was not properly oriented on the road. The "power bulge" hood was standard on this exclusively V-8 car, but the sliding sun roof panel was optionally available for all mid-size 2-door models. The bold tape decor was standard. The Plymouth Road Runner Coupe, which had a production run of 11,555, listed a price of $3,545 and a weight of 3,615 pounds when in standard form.

Again at the top of the mid-size wagon list was the Satellite Regent, which could only be had with a V-8 engine. As a 2-seat model it was a 4,065-pound vehicle with a $4,066 price tag which brought Plymouth 2,026 sales. Listing at $4,381 and scaling 4,130 pounds was the 3-seat model, which attracted 3,132 buyers. The luggage rack on the roof was on the mid-size wagon option list.

The Plymouth Fury II 4-Door Sedan shows the massive rear end design of the big cars. Shown with the vinyl-covered roof option, this model was fitted in a trifle more deluxe manner than the Fury I. Priced at $4,223, it weighed 4,165 pounds. A total of 11,649 buyers signed on the dotted line for it.

The most popular model of the big-size Plymouths was the Fury III 4-Door Sedan. It attracted a total of 27,965 buyers. They got a car that listed a base price of $4,400 and registered a base weight of 4,180 pounds. The grille of the big cars was of thin horizontal bars spaced close together and having bright frontal edges.

This Plymouth was so impressive that it attracted more buyers than any other model in its series. It is the Fury Gran Coupe, actually a 2-door hardtop, which marked up a total of 9,617 built. The luxury automobile swung the weight scale pointer to a reading of 4,300 pounds and asked each buyer for $4,627 as the advertised delivered price at the factory.

Shown is the Fury III 2-Door Hardtop, which weighed 4,125 pounds, cost $4,418 and had a production run of 14,167. Not shown is the Fury III 4-Door Hardtop, a 4,205-pound car that sold for $4,468 and went to 18,778 buyers. Also not shown is a Fury II 2-Door Hardtop, of which 1,826 were built. Not offered in the U.S.A., probably all or most of the Fury II Hardtops were sold in Canada.

Joining the trend to the new styling innovation, springtime brought the formal opera window option to the Fury Gran Coupe. It was enhanced by a complete vinyl covering of the roof and quarters, adding dignified elegance. For this, Gran Coupe medallions were moved from the roof quarters to the sheetmetal just below. The window option had no special interior, but the car shown was fitted with a separate Brougham interior option that was extra-plush. The Brougham trim, available in the Fury Gran series, included Brougham signatures just above the rear side marker lenses.

The Fury Gran Sedan, a 4-door hardtop, weighed 4,370 pounds, cost $4,675 and went to 8,191 buyers. The example shown had a Brougham interior. Compared with 1973, the beltline of the big cars was two inches lower. Possibly of interest is the following comparison of overall dimensions, given in inches, of the big 2-door hardtops of 1973/1974: Length 223.4/219.9, height 54.9/54.2 and width 79.8/79.9. The 4-door stood 0.6 of an inch higher. Wheelbase was 122 inches, two inches longer than in 1973. The new bodies had side glass of less curve and larger area.

The standard Plymouth Suburban, built only as a 2-seat model, listed at $4,669 and weighed 4,745 pounds. For the public, 2,490 were built. Law enforcement agencies bought an additional 285 specially built as Police Emergency Wagons. Standard, Custom and Sport Suburbans rode on a 124-inch wheelbase, a stretch of two inches over that of 1973. Stated in inches are the following overall dimensions for comparing suburbans of 1973/1974: Length 227.5/223.3 and width 79.8/79.4. Available records did not quote 1973 overall height, but the 1974 dimension was 58.5 inches.

This illustration from sales literature was captioned as the "Fury Custom Suburban with Trailer-Towing Package in Action." The vehicle was fitted with the Heavy Package for towing up to 7,000 pounds. It included heavy-duty suspension and other necessities built into the vehicle. A Light Package for loads up to 2,000 pounds required less modification. Similar packages were available for all Plymouths but the Barracuda series, and had been offered for some years previously. The Custom Suburban 2-seat model, of which 3,877 were built, weighed 4,755 pounds and cost $4,767. The 3-seat model, costing $4,878 and scaling 4,800 pounds, recorded a total of 5,628 built.

The Plymouth Sport Suburban cost $5,025 and weighed 4,795 pounds in 2-seat form. Exactly 1,712 were built. The 3-seat model, for many years ranked as the heaviest and costliest Plymouth, bowed this year to the new Voyager. However, it weighed 4,850 pounds, cost $5,130, and listed 6,047 sales. Custom and Sport Suburbans offered optional Brougham interiors. In the family of big Plymouths, suburbans continued as a group apart from the sedans and hardtops, which carried Fury nameplates. For unknown reasons, planners had not identified suburbans with the Fury name for some years. This year, however, advertising added the Fury name to suburban names (such as Fury Custom Suburban), though the vehicles were without the Fury name. This was a transition move toward complete integration of the Fury and suburban names for 1975 models.

Below at right is the Voyager Custom version of the Model PB200 127-inch wheelbase vehicle. The V-8 cost $4,294 and weighed 4,025 pounds net. PB200 models were: Six or V-8, 109 and 127-inch chassis, 5 or 8-passenger, standard and Custom forms; Six or V-8, 127-inch chassis, 5 or 8-passenger extended body, standard and Custom; V-8 127-inch chassis, 5 or 8-passenger regular or extended body, Sport version. Shown at left is a 127-inch PB100 standard Voyager, which in V-8 form weighed 3,820 pounds net and cost $3,973 without the optional sliding side door.

The new Plymouth multi-purpose vehicle line's economy model was the Voyager 109-inch wheelbase Model PB100. Of 5-passenger capacity, it was offered as a Six or V-8. As a V-8, net weight was 3,685 pounds and the factory price was $3,855. This PB100 was also available as a Voyager Custom. The PB100 could also be had on a 127-inch wheelbase as a Six or V-8 in standard or Custom trim, and as a V-8 in Sport form. Production totals for individual models were not available, but a grand total of 11,701 Voyagers were built for this model year. These and similar Dodge Sportsman models were built on the same assembly lines.

A Voyager Sport is shown as a PB300 with regular-length body. Without the sliding side door option, its net weight was 4,315 pounds and the price was $4,934. All PB300 models had a V-8 engine and 127-inch wheelbase. PB300 models were: 5-8-12-passenger regular body in standard, Custom and Sport forms; 5-8-12-15-passenger extended body in standard, Custom and Sport versions. Of interest are Voyager dimensions, given in inches to relate wheelbases to overall lengths (wb/oal): 109/176, 127/194 regular body, 127/212 extended body. They apply to PB100, PB200 and PB300 models.

A Plymouth Voyager with extended body (at the rear) is shown as a Sport model. This particular vehicle had seats for 15 passengers, of which seating for ten was provided at extra cost. Without options, this PB300 in Sport trim weighed 4,435 pounds net and cost $5,130. Since Voyagers were classified as commercial vehicles, they had designated gross vehicle weights (GVW). PB model/GVW (pounds) ratings were: PB100/4,800; PB200/5,500; PB300/6,700. For Voyagers offering the choice of a 225 Six or 318 V-8: The V-8 cost $117 more in PB100 models, $85 more in PB200. Power was delivered to the rear wheels, and all Voyagers also had independent coil-spring front suspension.

A Trail Duster in standard monotone paint is shown with optional steel roof, which was of inner and outer double-walled construction. The roof enclosure included a fixed-glass liftgate to complement the body's standard tailgate. The Trail Duster was designated Model PW100. In standard form, it registered a net weight of 3,910 pounds and was factory-priced at $3,964. Gross vehicle weight ratings were 4,900/6,000 pounds maximum. A total of 5,015 units were built in all versions. They were built by Dodge, on the same assembly lines that turned out similar Dodge Ramchargers.

For those who wanted more than the basics, and most buyers did, Plymouth offered many style, comfort and convenience options for the smart and husky Trail Dusters. This one is a Sport model featuring wide bright-edged lower side moldings with simulated woodgrain inserts, similar bright and woodgrain tailgate trim, bright windshield molding and bumpers, vinyl full-foam bucket seats for the driver and passenger, color-keyed door inner trim panels with map pockets, a front center console and other goodies.

The new Plymouth Trail Duster, classified as a truck, was a sport/utility vehicle with versatility for on-or-off-the-road use. Offered was a choice of four V-8 engine sizes to power the rugged vehicles, which featured full-time 4-wheel drive. Only one basic body was manufactured, available with a vinyl folding top as shown, or with a hardtop enclosure. The 106-inch wheelbase chassis had individual leaf springs for front and rear wheels. Shown is an optional 2-tone paint combination, including narrow bright moldings on the 2-tone break line.

Showing its optional roll bar is a Trail Duster without a top. When soft tops were wanted, they were dealer-installed. In standard form, Trail Dusters had a driver's seat only. Optional were a front passenger seat, and if wanted, a rear bench seat for three. Seat design had a plain utility appearance. Normally, the spare wheel stood between the rear seat and tailgate, but it could be mounted on the outside, at the rear. For protection from possible damage in negotiating rough terrain, optional skid plates provided shielding for the fuel tank and transfer case.

The business decline continued, and at calendar year-end a passenger car production loss of more than 8% was registered by the industry. Combined Chrysler Corp. car output suffered a much greater loss of over 24%, cutting the corporation's share of industry productivity to only 12.6%. Faring even worse with total vehicle output down 26.5%, Plymouth fell to the industry's No. 6 position.

Popularity of compact cars dropped sharply, but the Duster/Valiant/Scamp group won twice as much demand as Plymouth's mid-size family and three times more than the big car series. The compacts, all designated Series 5V, continued with a minimum of change, but some models were added. The Duster was presented as a basic, Custom and 360, each as a Coupe on a 108-inch wheelbase. Valiant offered a sedan in basic and Custom versions, plus two Brougham models. The Scamp, sharing its 111-inch wheelbase with Valiant, again appeared in a single hardtop version. The 198 6-cylinder engine was not continued this year, so the previously optional 225 Six was now teamed with the 318 V-8 as engine choices for all but the Duster 360, which was exclusively powered by a 360 V-8 with 4-venturi carburetion.

Mid-size Plymouths, Series 5R, were now known as "the small Fury." Newly-styled 2-door models were on a 115-inch wheelbase, while sedans and wagons rode on a 117.5-inch base. The basic line was the Fury, with three models. The Fury Custom offered four models and the Fury Sport presented three. Of Fury form but without Fury nameplates, the Road Runner continued as a single model, but it was a hardtop this year. The 225 Six engine was standard for all but the Road Runner and wagons. Also standard was the 318 V-8, which applied to all models. Optional V-8 engines were the 360 and 400 in 2 and 4-venturi versions.

Given very minor modifications were the big Plymouths, Series 5P, known as the Gran Fury. Suburbans, now identified as Gran Fury models and bearing that signature, were again on a 124-inch wheelbase, while other models scaled the base at 121.5 inches. At the bottom of the group was the basic Gran Fury, which was a pair of models. The middle line was the Custom with five models, while at the top were two Broughams and two Sport Suburbans. The entire Gran Fury family was powered by V-8 engines. For basic and Custom models,

except Suburbans, the 2-venturi 360 was standard and the 318 was optional. For Broughams and all suburbans, the standard was the 2-venturi 400, which was optional for basic and Custom sedans and hardtops. The 2-venturi (2V) 360 was optional for Broughams, while a 4V 360, 4V 400 and 4V 440 were available for certain models. Engine offerings, as related to particular models, are too complex to be defined in a simple manner. As was the practice during the previous few years, certain engines

Showing details of the Duster/Valiant/Scamp front end is the Plymouth Duster Custom Coupe. The Custom was a new Duster offering this year. Its main claim to distinction was its interior, which provided a choice of seat designs and trim and color variations. As standard, it also had bright drip rails, sill and wheelcut moldings, plus bumper guards and a few other extras. As a Six, it weighed 2,970 pounds and cost $3,418. Total Six and V-8 production was 38,826 Customs.

The Duster presented a pleasing appearance from the rear, as well as from other points of view. A minor detail is the bumper guards, which were of a less bulky design this year. The basic Duster Coupe is shown with a number of options, including the fully vinyl-clad roof, bodyside vinyl-insert rub moldings and whitewall tires. Plymouth said the Duster was what most small cars were trying to be.

In standard form with the 225 Six engine, the Duster Coupe was Plymouth's lowest-priced model for the year, having a factory delivered price of $3,243. In the same form it shared honors with the Custom as the lightweight, recording a shipping weight of 2,970 pounds. In all forms, including Six and V-8 models, a total of 79,884 were built, making this year's most popular Plymouth. The illustration shows the car in absolutely basic trim and equipment.

were not available in California.

Plymouth Voyager multi-purpose station wagons were continued without notable change. PB100, PB200 and PB300 models were offered in a mixture of body lengths on wheelbases of 109 and 127 inches, provided in standard, Custom and Sport trim and equipment versions. Standard engines were the 225 Six and 318 V-8 for PB100 and PB200 models. The 318 was the only standard for the PB300 which, with the PB200, had a 360 V-8 available.

The Trail Duster continued as a single body type on a 106-inch wheelbase, but added a 2-wheel drive model to the previous full-time 4-wheel drive vehicle. The 2-wheel reardrive vehicle was Model PD100 and the 4-wheel drive was Model PW100. Both series listed the 318 engine as standard, the 2V 360 and 4V 440 optional. Also made available this year was the 225 Six.

Because of emphasis on unleaded fuel and other factors that restricted power output, published horsepower ratings were seldom available, especially for passenger cars. Some engines were accompanied by a catalytic converter, an emission control device in the exhaust system. It cut hydrocarbon emission 90% and carbon monoxide emission 83%, and required that the engines use lead-free fuel. Other engines had air pumps rather than converters, and used leaded fuel. Some technical changes may have quietly entered production during the year. If so, they may not have been noted in published matter used as reference for this book.

On Chrysler's top management level, big news broke this year. Lynn Townsend, chairman of the board, retired in October and was succeeded by John J. Riccardo. Stepping into the president's office vacated by Riccardo was Eugene A. Cafiero. Actually, the change became effective on January 1, 1976.

The special-edition Duster 360 Coupe was again provided for those who wanted a compact car with performance features. Among other things, it had dual exhausts, heavy-duty suspension and shock absorbers, a 3-speed automatic transmission and a front sway bar. It sported new tape stripes on the bodysides to identify it. Logically, it was built only with a 360 V-8 engine. Priced at $3,979, it tipped the weighing scale at 3,315 pounds. Only 1,421 of them were built.

A Duster 360 is shown without the decorative bodyside tape stripes that were standard for this model. The prototype car builders had not yet got around to apply the stripes to this one. But they did fit it with a sun roof, an option that was available for the Duster, Duster Custom, Duster 360, Scamp and Valiant Brougham Hardtop, as well as larger Plymouths.

This rendering of the Plymouth Duster 360 Coupe shows the performance car in absolutely standard form, including the bodyside tape stripes. No vinyl roof, no deluxe wheelcovers or rallye wheels, no whitewall or white letter tires, no bright sill or wheelcut lip moldings, all of which were options. The standard blackwall tires and black wheels with small hubcaps illustrate why most cars are shown with wheel dress-up.

The Gold Duster continued as a package option found desirable by many buyers. Its production total is unknown, as this was not classified as a separate model, so its output was included with the basic Duster Coupe. The package included the vinyl canopy roof and a number of interior luxury and exterior decor features. At no cost difference, buyers could choose full-length bright-edge bodyside moldings with gold vinyl inserts, or the side tape pattern shown. The Gold Duster package cost $181 above vehicle price.

This illustration shows the Gold Duster with full-length bodyside moldings rather than the tape decor pattern. Thus, buyers had a choice of moderate protection or a strictly decorative design. The tape design across the rear of the Gold Duster was much like that of the Duster 360, but they were not alike. Gold Dusters had the name on the front quarter panels, but not on the rear end.

To make it more attractive, this basic Valiant 4-Door Sedan was fitted with extra-cost wheelcovers and whitewall tires. Standard blackwall tires, black wheels and small hubcaps would not be pretty. Otherwise, it appears very standard. In this and very similar equipment, the basic car attracted a total of 44,471 Six and V-8 sales. In standard Six form it cost $3,247 and weighed 3,040 pounds. In the Duster/Valiant/Scamp family, a standard Six cost $121 less than a standard V-8, excepting Valiant Broughams.

With features offered as a package option for 1974, the Valiant Custom was a new model this year. Inside, it had a choice of seat styles and materials, plus loop-pile carpeting and other niceties. Most of the bodyside brightwork shown was not included. The single model had small Custom designations just below the Valiant signatures on the sides. The Valiant Custom 4-Door Sedan had a Six and V-8 production run of 56,258 cars. The Six weighed 3,040 pounds and cost $3,422.

The Plymouth Valiant Brougham 4-Door Sedan displays the smart appearance that attracted a total of 17,803 Six and V-8 sales. The interior was even more appealing and expensive-looking, with rich velour cloth and vinyl trim, premium fittings, simulated wood accents and other luxury touches. The simulated wire wheel fittings were not standard equipment. As a Six, the car weighed 3,250 pounds and cost $4,139. The cost difference between a Brougham Six and V-8 was $96.

Again provided for the luxury compact car market was the Valiant Brougham series. Shown is the Hardtop, which recorded a weight of 3,240 pounds and listed at $4,232 when built as a Six. Exactly 5,781 came from the factory in Six and V-8 forms. Not shown is a model listed in factory production records as a Valiant Hardtop, of which 1,302 were built, presumably for Canada. Since this was something other than a Brougham model, it was not a known U.S. offering.

Appearing to be of a luxury level common to more costly cars, this interior belongs to a Valiant Brougham 4-Door Sedan. Rich velour cloth and vinyl trim were used throughout. The heavily-hooded instrument panel featured simulated woodgrain inserts of a warm tone. Premium fittings included a full complement of courtesy lights, convenient pockets on the front seat backs, and other niceties.

Drawing its usual share of attention at the marketplaces was the Plymouth Scamp Hardtop, of which the factory turned out 23,581 examples with Six and V-8 engines. In 6-cylinder form, it asked a price of $3,518 and tipped the scale at 3,020 pounds. As usual, the Scamp was available in one version only, having no Custom, Brougham or other variation. Classed above the Valiant at its beginning in 1971, it now was sandwiched between the Valiant Custom and Brougham.

For operators who were watchful of the high fuel costs, Plymouth added the Valiant to its taxi offerings this year. It was built only with the 225 Six engine, which was specially adapted to taxi use and fitted with a catalytic converter. In addition, the vehicles were factory-built with nearly all of the special features found on larger Plymouth taxi models. Apparently, Plymouth's assessment of the Valiant Taxi market potential was not so good, as only 123 were built.

The basic series of the mid-size Plymouth group was the new Fury line, of which one of the models was the 2-Door Hardtop illustrated. In the absolutely standard form shown, it was devoid of trim moldings and superfluous ornamentation. The bright Fury signature just ahead of the door is not distinct in this view. This model, offered as a Six or V-8, was delivered to 8,398 buyers. In terms of a V-8, the list price was $3,672 and the weight was 3,670 pounds.

Presenting a severely plain appearance in its strictly standard form, the Fury 4-Door Sedan was not particularly attractive in this basic illustration. However, when seen in 3-dimensional reality, and in color, it was a good-looking automobile. The same is true of the Fury Hardtop. The Sedan, built as a Six or V-8, attracted 11,432 buyers. Probably most of them bought it with optional dress-up items. It weighed 3,700 pounds and cost $3,720 in V-8 form.

Newly-styled mid-size 2-door Plymouths had an interesting design form on the deck lid that was repeated inversely on the bumper. Inward-slanted taillamps reflected the similar slope of the upper bodysides. The Fury Custom 2-Door Hardtop cost $3,840 and weighed 3,750 pounds as a V-8 and had a production run of 27,486, including Sixes. For mid-size models offering both, a standard V-8 cost $129 more than a Six.

Mid-size sedan styling differed from 2-door models from the front door pillars to the rear bumper. They shared a 117.5-inch wheelbase with Fury suburbans. Overall dimensions (given in inches) were: Length 217.9, height 53.9, width 77.7. In comparison with their 1974 counterparts, they were (in inches) 9.0 longer, 0.3 higher and 0.9 narrower. Shown is the Fury Custom 4-Door Sedan, which in V-8 form weighed 3,750 pounds and cost $3,834. A total Six and V-8 production run of 31,080 was recorded for it, but some were the Fury Salon Sedan.

Station wagons in the mid-size group were now called Suburbans, rather than the former designation as Wagons. They were much like 1974 models, except from the windshield forward. All were built with V-8 engines. Shown is the Fury Custom Suburban. The 2-seat model, weighing 4,230 pounds and costing $4,512, had a 3,890-unit production run. The 3-seat Custom cost $4,632, weighed 4,285 pounds and went to 5,430 buyers. Not shown is the basic Fury Suburban, built in 2-seat form only, weighing 4,180 pounds, costing $4,309 and recording a total of 4,468 built.

The Fury Salon was an option that was priced $230 above the Fury Custom Sedan. It was the plushest of all the new small Furys. In addition to the standard interior, there were two optional interiors with soft velour and vinyl choices. Floor carpeting was of deep-pile shag, and the trunk was lined with woven carpeting which also was used for a spare wheel cover. Distinctive Salon signatures were applied to the roof blind quarters.

The Fury Sport 2-Door Hardtop, built only as a V-8, is shown with optional 15-inch urethane road wheels and raised white-letter tires. In standard form, it weighed 3,790 pounds and cost $4,105. Exactly 17,782 were built in all forms. Actually, small Fury 2-door cars were not small. On a 115-inch wheelbase, their overall measurements (in inches) were: Length 213.8, height 52.6, width 77.4. Compared with the 1974 mid-size hardtops, they were (in inches) 1.8 longer, 0.4 higher and 1.4 narrower.

This mid-size model was selected by 7,183 buyers. Those, if any, who bought it in standard form got a 3,760-pound car with a $3,973 price tag. It is the Plymouth Road Runner 2-Door Hardtop, which offered a choice of five variations of V-8 engines. For the Road Runner grille only, the texture was painted black, which made the chrome verticals prominent. Also standard and exclusive to this model was the tapered bodyside stripe that arched over the roof rear quarters.

Exclusively V-8, the Plymouth Fury Sport Suburban was presented in two versions. The 2-seat version was priced at $4,770, weighed 4,230 pounds and chosen by 1,851 buyers. Built to fill 3,107 orders was the 3-seat model weighing 4,295 pounds and costing $4,867. The "small" Fury suburbans were on a 117.5-inch wheelbase and measured (overall in inches) 225.6 long, 56.5 high and 79.2 wide. Also in inches, they were 8.5 longer, 0.1 higher and equally as wide as the 1974 mid-wagons.

For owners who wanted others to be sure of what kind of car they had, this deck lid graphic decor was available on order. The bold and unusual design depicted Road Runner lettering heading into a tunnel, just as the cartoon bird often did. But when the car zoomed past others, the identity of the fast automobile could hardly be mistaken. Built with heavy-duty suspension and other performance features, the top engine option was a 4-venturi 400 V-8 with dual exhausts.

For operators who felt that the mid-size sedan was adequate for their localities and needs, Plymouth built 1,627 Fury Taxis. With the experience gained during many years of producing specialty vehicles, they were built specifically to do the job. The same can be said of the Fury Police Specials, of which 6,877 were manufactured. They utilized the same model as a basis.

The basic line in the big "standard-size" Plymouth group was the Gran Fury, with no follower name. Shown is the Gran Fury Suburban, built only as a 2-seat vehicle weighing 4,855 pounds and costing $5,067. Its production total was 2,295. No pictures were available for showing the following models. The Gran Fury 4-Door Sedan, which cost $4,565, scaled 4,260 pounds and scored a total of 8,185 built. Not offered in the U.S.A. was a Gran Fury 2-Door Hardtop, of which 1,433 were built, presumably for Canada.

The grille design and grille enclosure panel of Gran Fury Custom models differed from the Gran Fury Brougham. The assembly included dual-unit headlamps, and park/turn signal lamps were fitted into the bumper opening. Shown is the Gran Fury Custom 4-Door Hardtop, a 4,290-pound car that cost $4,837 and had a production run of 11,292. Lack of a picture prohibits showing the Gran Fury Custom 2-Door Hardtop which sold for $4,781, weighed 4,205 pounds and recorded a total of 6,041 built.

From this point of view, the big standard-size Plymouths looked much as they did in 1974. Only minor details were changed for this year. Offering itself for study is the Gran Fury Custom 4-Door Sedan, which drew a total of 19,043 sales. The attractive but heavy-looking automobile weighed 4,260 pounds. Its price tag was marked $4,761. All Gran Fury, Gran Fury Custom and Gran Fury Brougham cars and their teammate suburbans were powered by V-8 engines.

The Brougham was an option package in 1974, but this year it acquired full-rank model status. The Gran Fury Brougham 4-Door Hardtop, weighing 4,400 pounds and costing $5,067, was the choice of 5,521 buyers. It displays the distinctive Brougham front end design. The grille enclosure panel separated the grille from the lamps by means of form deviation and body color. Single-unit headlamps were in housings that also incorporated vertical park/turn signal lamps positioned inboard. Also seen on this car is a ventpane in the front door glass. Manual ventpanes had been optional on big series 4-door sedans, hardtops and suburbans since their return on 1973 models.

Plymouth presented the Gran Fury Custom Suburban in a double image. One form was the 2-seat model, of which 3,155 were turned out. The 2-seater recorded a weight of 4,870 pounds and listed a price of $5,176. The other image was the 3-seat vehicle, which tipped the weighing scale at 4,915 pounds and showed a $5,294 price on the sale invoice. Exactly 4,500 buyers selected the 3-seater.

With grace and dignity, the Plymouth Gran Fury Brougham 2-Door Formal Hardtop displayed impressive length and a very expensive appearance. However, its $5,146 price was competitive with its rivals. The 4,310-pound car posted a production total of 6,521. The Brougham series did not offer a 2-door hardtop without formal opera windows. Since the three Gran Fury series of hardtops and sedans were of the 1974 vehicle package, wheelbase and overall dimensions were unchanged this year.

As the flagship of the Plymouth fleet for this year, the Gran Fury Brougham series probably was the finest line of Plymouths built up to this point in the company's long history. Among its many fine features were the die-cast grille and jewel-like hood ornament. A Gran Fury Brougham 2-Door Formal Hardtop exemplifies what Plymouth said was a proud-looking automobile, built for people with distinctly individual motoring needs.

Having a class rank equal to the Brougham series, the Plymouth Gran Fury Sport Suburban also featured the Brougham front end design. The 2-seat model recorded a 4,885-pound weight, $5,455 price and a 1,508-unit production total. The 3-seat model was the heaviest Plymouth this year, weighing 4,930 pounds. It cost $5,573 and went to 4,740 buyers. The three Gran Fury suburban series retained the wheelbase and vehicle package of 1974 big suburbans, but differed in two overall dimensions. Quoted in inches, they were 2.6 longer and 0.4 higher, but width was unchanged.

Exactly as shown for 1974, the basic Voyager illustrated is a Model PB100 in 109-inch wheelbase form. As a V-8, its net weight was 3,715 pounds and its factory price was $4,568. Total production was 2,261 units, including Six and V-8 vehicles in basic and Custom versions. This vehicle package also was built in Voyager basic and Custom Six and V-8 forms as a Model PB200, which had a production run of 399 units. All Voyager sizes and their model, trim and engine relationships were exactly as noted for 1974.

Based on the Gran Fury 4-Door Sedan, which is not shown elsewhere, was the Gran Fury Police Special, of which Plymouth built 14,208 in various forms. The Gran Fury Sedan also served as a Taxi basis, as records show that 742 were built for that purpose. The Gran Fury 2-seat Suburban was offered as a Police Emergency Wagon, but only two were assembled. Perhaps those two were prototypes or sample vehicles built in anticipation of orders that failed to materialize.

This illustration, common to 1974-77 Voyager sales literature, is of the Voyager Custom version of the regular-length body on a 127-inch wheelbase. As a Model PB200 V-8, it cost $5,102 and weighed 4,025 pounds net. In this package, total PB200 Six and V-8 production was 4,237. The package also was offered as a PB100, of which 1,103 were built in Six and V-8 forms, and as a PB300 V-8 which had an 802-unit production run. All three PB series were built in basic, Custom and Sport versions.

Shown is a Plymouth Voyager Sport with contrasting color above the beltline of the extended-length body, which rode on a 127-inch wheelbase. This PB300 model was the most expensive Plymouth this year, being priced at $5,811. Its net weight was 4,435 pounds. In this extended body form, a total of 1,441 PB200 and 3,305 PB300 vehicles were manufactured. They were Custom and Sport versions, and were powered only by V-8 engines. Viewed from this side of the vehicles, Voyagers had only a door for the driver.

With an extended body, which was available on the long wheelbase, a Voyager Sport is shown with contrasting color through the midsection. The following items relate to this and other models. A sliding side door, single rear-end door and seating for 8, 12 and 15 passengers were options. GVW ratings were as noted for 1974, except that PB200 Custom and Sport extended body models had a GVW of 6,100. For models with this choice of engines, a 318 V-8 cost $161 more than a 225 Six. In total, the complexity of Voyager offerings defies simple and comprehensible definition.

A Trail Duster Sport 4-wheel drive model is shown with a hardtop enclosure. Soft tops were provided at no cost difference, and were installed at dealerships. The Sport package again included a special interior with front bucket seats and a center console, plus exterior brightwork and other items. Plymouth provided a good selection of convenience, comfort, appearance and performance options for Trail Dusters.

Plymouth added a 2-wheel drive model to the Trail Duster line this year. Known as Model PD100, it offered Six or V-8 engines on a 106-inch wheelbase. Drive was through a rear axle, and independent front suspension utilized coil springs. Shown is a Sport model. In basic trim, the V-8 vehicle had a net weight of 3,570 pounds and cost $3,640. Total PD100 production, including all varieties, was only 666 vehicles.

Shown with soft top and 2-tone paint options is a Plymouth Trail Duster 4-wheel drive vehicle. Designated the Model PW100, it had a 225 Six added to its V-8 engine offerings this year. In standard V-8 form, it was priced at $4,546 and registered a net weight of 4,085 pounds. PW100 production amounted to 3,877 units, including all forms. GVW ratings for 2 and 4-wheel drive models were 4,900/6,000 pounds maximum.

This year brought a brighter business picture into focus. At the end of the calendar year, the industry summed up a passenger car production improvement of more than 26.6% over 1975. Chrysler Corp. accounted for 14.84% of the industry total, and at the same time scored a remarkable increase of nearly 49.2% over its own performance of the previous year. Plymouth did nearly as well as the corporation, marking up a gain of more than 48.2%, and remaining as the industry's No. 6 automaker.

Demand for the Duster/Valiant/Scamp group took a bad tumble, but the new Volare series more than made up the loss. Besides Volare, Plymouth added another name to the roster this year — the Arrow. The little sub-compact car was built in Japan by Mitsubishi Motors Corp., in which Chrysler had begun acquiring a financial interest in 1971. The Arrow entered the U.S. market with three versions of a basic model, on a 92.1-inch wheelbase. Coil springs were used at the front, semi-elliptics at the rear. Engines were a 4-cylinder hemi-head cam design with a 5-bearing crankshaft. A 1600-cc engine was standard, while a 2000-cc was optional.

The Duster/Valiant/Scamp group was designated the Series 6V. All were continued without notable styling or mechanical change. On a 108-inch wheelbase, the Duster offered trim option packages for the coupe, but a specially-treated performance 360 model was not available. Valiant was now a sedan only, with trim options on a 111-inch wheelbase. Again sharing the Valiant wheelbase, the Scamp presented the hardtop in two models this year. For the three Series 6V car lines, the 225 Six and 318 V-8 were standard, and the 360 V-8 was available.

The exciting news of the year was the new Volare, designated Series 6H. It was presented in three distinct lines: The basic line of three models, two Custom models and three Premier offerings. Plymouth chose the familiar two-wheelbase pattern for the new cars, basing 2-door models on 108.5 inches and others on 112.5. Engine choices were the same as listed for the Series 6V group.

The mid-size Fury was carried over without notable changes in styling and mechanics, but some adjustment of model line-up occurred. The new Series 6R had four basic models, and the Salon and Sport was a highline group of four. There was no Custom, and the Road Runner was now a Volare option. Retained were the two wheelbases: 115 inches for 2-door cars and 117.5 for others. Engine availability was changed in relation to models. The 225 Six and 318 V-8 were standard for all but suburban models. A 2-barrel 360 V-8 was the suburban standard, and was optional for others. Extra-cost for all models were 4-barrel 360 and 400 V-8 engines, while a 2-barrel 400 was offered for all but suburbans.

The standard-size Gran Fury was the same package as offered for 1975, but the number of models was reduced. Tagged as the Series 6P were two basic models, four Customs, two Broughams and one Sport Suburban. Again, all suburbans were mounted on a wheelbase of 124 inches, with other models on a 121.5 length. Excepting suburbans, standard engines for the basic and Custom lines were the 318 and 2-barrel 360, respectively. For the Brougham line and all suburbans, the 2-barrel 400 was standard. Optional engines were offered in a complicated manner, for select models, but they were the 360 and 400, both in 2 and 4-barrel versions, and a 4-barrel 440. The optional engine/model mix was so complex that it cannot be detailed in simple form.

Appearing the same as previously were the Plymouth Voyager PB100, PB200 and PB300. Again on 109 and 127-inch wheelbases were the regular and extended bodies in basic, Custom and Sport versions. Standard powerplants were the 225 Six and 318 V-8, while a 360 and 440 were on the option list.

The Trail Duster followed the pattern of other carryover Plymouths by not having any notable newness. PD100 and PW100 models on a 106-inch chassis had the 225 and 318 engines as standard, but the option list added the 400 V-8 to the 360 and 440 this year.

Plymouth continued to apply engineering refinement and innovations to the need for better fuel economy, emission control and safety measures. A variety of rear axle ratios for various engine/transmission combinations was offered to promote increased gasoline mileage.

The lightweight of the entire Plymouth family was the Arrow 160 Hatchback Coupe, which weighed 2,110 pounds. The sleek little car was also Plymouth's lowest-priced model, being tagged at $3,175. Built in Japan by Mitsubishi, the Arrow was imported to fill the need for a sub-compact car. It rode on a 92.1-inch wheelbase, had an overall length of 167.3 inches, was 52.5 inches high and 63.4 inches wide. Its track was 51.2 inches at the front and 50 inches at the rear.

The Plymouth Arrow GS was an option package applied to the basic 160, and costing $208 more. It included such things as styled road wheels, flipper quarter windows and chrome-plated bumpers, plus bright moldings on the rear, sills and wheelcut lips. Inside was woodtone on the instrument panel, and carpeting extended through the cargo area. The Arrow could seat five passengers, and was powered by a 4-cylinder engine which was available in two versions.

The Plymouth Arrow GT was a premium model with all of the features of the 160 and GS, plus other goodies. It had a center floor console, rallye cluster with tachometer, sporty soft-trim steering wheel, dual sport mirrors in black, an overhead console and exterior tape stripes that crossed over the hatchback door. The GT cost $3,748 and weighed 2,290 pounds. No production totals were available for the Arrow series, which was known as the Model 7.

Now in its final year, the Duster series was pared down, insofar as variations are concerned. The basic Duster Coupe is shown with roof, bodyside and other extra-cost dress-up. In standard form, and with a 225 engine, it registered a weight of 2,975 pounds and posted a price of $3,241. The recorded production of 34,681 cars included Sixes, V-8s and the optional trim and equipment packages known as the Feather Duster and the Silver Duster.

Identified by Feather Duster lettering on the front quarter panels, this car was fitted with the fuel economy option package known by that name. It is seen with optional whitewall tires on standard wheels. The package included such aluminum parts as the intake manifold and inner panels for the hood and deck, plus a special rear axle ratio for the specially-tuned 225 Six. A manual transmission with overdrive and an aluminum case was available.

In lieu of a Gold Duster, a Silver Duster trim option package was offered this year. Unique bodyside and deck stripes in red and black were among distinguishing features that set the Silver Duster apart from other Dusters. Also included was a red interior. And for those who wanted even more stylish appeal, the interior could be handsomely done in a Boca Raton cloth and vinyl combination. The Silver Duster package was priced at $178.

A Brougham signature on the roof blind quarter identifies this Valiant 4-Door Sedan as fitted out with the Brougham trim option. The vinyl-covered roof was not a standard part of the option package, which included the exterior trim shown, plus an attractive interior that offered a choice of seat design. Plymouth did not offer a hardtop in the Valiant series this year. This was the last year for the Plymouth Valiant.

The basic Valiant 4-Door Sedan is shown in one of its dress-up forms. This model, when built as a Six with basic equipment, registered a weight of 3,050 pounds and a price of $3,276. Total Six and V-8 production, including basic, Custom and Brougham versions, amounted to 40,079 units. Since Customs and Broughams were options applied to the basic car, and not distinct models, they did not rate separate production counts.

Also in its last year was the Plymouth Scamp Hardtop, which now was offered in two models. Shown is the highline Scamp, which listed at $3,510 and weighed 3,020 pounds as a Six. Together with V-8s, 6,908 were built, including an unknown number with the Brougham trim option. Not shown is the Scamp Special, a new lowline model, of which the Six weighed 3,020 pounds and cost $3,337. Exactly 4,018 Six and V-8 Specials were built.

The Plymouth Volare 4-Door Sedan weighed 3,315 pounds and was marked at $3,524 when built in standard V-8 form. The Six and V-8 production run was 23,058 units. It is shown with such extra-cost items as a vinyl roof, bright door window trim, bright belt moldings at the window base and thin rub strips on the body side, plus wheel dress-up and bumper guards. Volare body construction was of the popular unibody type.

The new Plymouth Volare series was declared "Car of the Year" by Motor Trend magazine. All 2-door models were shorter than others. Measured in inches, the wheelbase was 108.5, overall length was 197.5 and overall height was 53.1. Shown is the standard Volare Coupe which listed at $3,489 and weighed 3,285 pounds as a V-8. Total Six and V-8 production amounted to 37,024, of which an indefinite number sported the Road Runner trim and equipment.

The basic Volare Wagon is shown with a roof rack and rear air deflector, both of which were extra-cost items. In standard V-8 form, this model registered 3,650 pounds and was price-tagged at $3,759. Exactly 46,065 were built. All Volare wagons were 4-door 6-passenger vehicles, as a third seat was not offered. A liftgate door permitted rear access to the cargo area.

The Road Runner was no longer in the mid-size Plymouth series. It was now an option package for the Volare Coupe. The brilliant color of the lower bodyside stripe was emphasized by a wide band of black below it. In the black band was the Road Runner name and cartoon bird. The package had a number of other features, including the 318 V-8 as the only standard engine, heavy-duty suspension, and a 3-speed manual transmission with floor shifter. A 2-barrel 360 V-8 was available, as it also was for other Volares.

This view of the regular Volare Road Runner shows the band of black stretching between the taillamps. Added in mid-year was the Road Runner Super Pak, with features the regular option did not have. Body color was Spitfire Orange, and there were three interior choices. Quarter windows were semi-enclosed with louvered panels. Spoilers were at the front and rear, and dual racing mirrors were in chrome. Plymouth aimed the performance-type appearance package at the youth market, calling it the "Super Beep-Beep."

Plymouth introduced the Volare cars to replace the Duster/Valiant/Scamp group, which had served well for several years but was ready to bow to a fresh new series. The Volare Custom 4-Door Sedan shows the lower bodyside moldings that were standard on Custom and Premier cars. It weighed 3,325 pounds and cost $3,706 in V-8 form. Including Sixes, 36,407 were built. Basic and Custom sedans and coupes with the standard 318 V-8 cost $165 more than similar cars with the 225 Six.

The Volare Custom Coupe is shown with a smartly unusual 2-tone paint treatment that was optionally available on this model only. Normally, the car was monotone, and with wide moldings on the lower bodysides such as seen on the Premier Coupe. As a V-8 in standard form, the Custom Coupe scaled a weight of 3,295 pounds and carried a $3,671 price tag. Exactly 31,252 Sixes and V-8s came off the assembly lines.

Shown with its liftgate door raised with the aid of a cylinder-assist device is the Volare Wagon. This was the only basic model for which the wide moldings on the lower bodysides could be ordered as an option. As a standard V-8, this model cost $113 more than it did as a Six. Dimensions of Volare and Volare Premier Wagons, given in inches, were: Wheelbase 112.5, overall length 201.5, overall height (without roof rack) 54.8, cargo area length 81.7 with the rear seat folded down. A Custom wagon was not offered.

The vinyl-covered roof was a standard feature of the Plymouth Volare Premier 4-Door Sedan. This car recorded a weight of 3,530 pounds and posted a price of $4,502 when built in standard V-8 form. The total Six and V-8 production run amounted to 37,131 cars. Volare sedan package dimensions were the same as those given for the wagons, but logically did not include a cargo area.

The simulated wire wheelcovers added a sporty touch to the Plymouth Volare Premier Coupe. The stand-up hood ornament, from which a chrome molding trailed back, was a Premier standard feature. Offered as a Six or V-8, this model was found imperative to the needs and tastes of 31,475 buyers. In V-8 form, it registered a reading of 3,490 pounds on the weight scale and had a price tag marked $4,515. This was the costliest of all Volares.

The vinyl roof with opera windows, in this case known as a Landau roof, was standard on the Volare Premier Coupe. Also standard were the lower bodyside moldings, which emphasized the curving character line that was on the rear quarter panels of all coupes. The line was not applied to sedans and wagons. Premier coupes and sedans with the standard V-8 engine cost $113 more than similar Premier models equipped with the 225 Six.

The Volare Premier Wagon was coded as a highline model, rather than the premium model code given to the Premier coupe and sedan. This wagon featured simulated woodgrain on the exterior. It was the most popular Volare, as well as the most popular Plymouth, this year, drawing a total of 49,507 buyers. With a standard V-8 engine, it weighed 3,695 pounds and cost $4,210. Surprisingly, this price was $234 more than the same model with a 225 Six.

The California Cruiser, a limited-production customized version of the Plymouth Volare and Dodge Aspen Coupe, is shown as a Volare. It utilized the hood and front bumper of the Aspen, and the grille was of tube construction. The padded roof featured broad blind quarters and a small rectangular rear window. Non-functional side pipes were fitted below the sills. Wide-whitewall tires, "baby moon" hubcaps and wide trim rings dressed the wheels, and the cars had many regular extras as standard. The 2-barrel 318 engine was fitted with a single exhaust and California emission package. Chrysler Corp. sanctioned the offerings, and suggested a retail price of $1,892.15 for the Cruiser package.

The Volare introduced a new transverse front suspension system. The assembly shown was called a "cross member," which was located just under the engine. The configuration of transverse torsion bars and other elements was a different kind of independent suspension. Liberal use of rubber mountings at strategic points isolated the assembly from the vehicle. Also isolated were the semi-elliptic rear springs. The isolation provided smoother ride qualities.

Plymouth continued the mid-size cars in the same form they had for 1975. Looking ready and eager to go somewhere is the Fury 2-Door Hardtop, which was available as a Six or V-8. When built as a V-8, this handsome automobile weighed 3,830 pounds and cost $3,937. Total Six and V-8 production amounted to 16,415 cars. Wherever applicable, a Fury standard V-8 cost $238 more than a Six.

In its sales promotion to an economy-conscious public, Plymouth said the Fury "is proving once again that you can have your economy and enjoy it, too." But even this mid-size car was a bit too large to woo buyers who wanted real economy. However, the Fury 4-Door Sedan won 22,654 buyers who got a Six or V-8 car that was economical in its class. The V-8 model cost $3,971 and weighed 3,860 pounds.

Shown is the Fury Sport 2-Door Hardtop, which normally had quarter windows like those seen on the lower-priced Fury model. But Plymouth added the smart opera window option for the Sport model this year. The novel slotted window design provided an attractive semi-blind quarter appearance. In standard V-8 form, the car weighed 3,835 pounds and cost $4,226. Including Sixes, 28,851 were built.

Drawing a goodly portion of attention in the intermediate field was the Fury Salon 4-Door Sedan. This year, the Salon was given status as a highline model, rather than as a plush option package applied to a lesser model. It now was on a class level with the Fury Sport Hardtop. The Salon reported a weight of 3,875 pounds and a price of $4,260 as a V-8. The Six and V-8 production run was 20,234.

Almost as impressive as its Gran Fury counterpart, the Fury Sport Suburban appears to be large enough for anyone's wagon needs. The 2-seat model listed at $4,986, weighed 4,285 pounds and went to 2,175 buyers. Attracting 3,482 sales with its $5,128 price and other factors was the 4,360-pound 3-seat model. Not shown is the basic Fury Suburban. The 2-seat basic model scaled 4,285 pounds, asked $4,597 and got it from 4,624 buyers. The 3-seat model, of which 4,412 were built, was a 4,350 pounder costing $4,739. All suburbans were powered by V-8 engines.

This is a view of the Plymouth Gran Fury Custom 4-Door Sedan, of which 14,738 were built. The 4,305-pound automobile listed at $4,715. Not available for illustration, a basic Gran Fury 4-Door Sedan was offered at $4,349, registered a weight of 4,140 pounds and chalked up a production total of 8,928. All Gran Furys, including basics, Customs, Broughams and Suburbans, were powered by V-8 engines.

The Gran Fury Brougham series presented the grandest Plymouths of the year. Although these cars were losing favor to smaller and more economical models, they were still wanted by those who loved luxury. In reference to the series, Plymouth urged prospective buyers to enjoy "the pleasure of its company." Exactly 2,990 persons bought that pleasure in the form of the Gran Fury Brougham 4-Door Sedan, which cost $5,162 and weighed 4,435 pounds.

This is the Gran Fury Custom 2-Door Hardtop, a $4,730 car that weighed 4,265 pounds and had a 2,733-car production run. This year, the Brougham front end design was applied to the lower-priced Gran Fury models, which did not have that distinction in 1975. Not illustrated, and not offered to the U.S. public, 951 basic Gran Fury 2-Door Hardtops were built. Possibly all of them were for Canada.

Shown is the Gran Fury Sport Suburban, which was offered only as a 3-seat model. Listed at $5,761, the 4,975-pound vehicle drew 2,484 sales. Not shown is the basic Gran Fury Suburban, which was a 2-seat model that weighed 4,880 pounds, cost $4,909 and went to 1,587 buyers. Also not shown is the Gran Fury Custom Suburban, which was marketed in two versions: 2-seat and 3-seat. The 2-seat model, of which 1,433 were built, weighed 4,895 pounds and was priced at $5,193. Weighing 4,940 pounds, the Custom 3-seat model listed at $5,316 and had a production run of 1,998 units.

The Gran Fury Brougham 2-Door Formal Hardtop exemplified elegance in every detail. The opera windows were standard on this model, and the interior was trimmed, fitted and appointed in a most tasteful manner, just as the Gran Fury Brougham Sedan also was treated. The Formal Hardtop was delivered to 2,619 buyers. It weighed 4,400 pounds and listed at $5,334.

Plymouth offered the Valiant sedan as a police vehicle, but according to production records, none were built. The artist's illustration shows the Valiant Pursuit with full equipment. It offered a choice of the 225 Six, 318 V-8 and 360 V-8 engines. Special suspension and chassis components, specifically adapted to each engine, were to be built-in. Apparently, the car never made it to the precinct station.

This is the Gran Fury Pursuit, shown as a 4-door sedan which brought Plymouth 10,296 orders from police departments. Also offered was the Fury Pursuit, of which the 4-door sedan drew 4,593 orders. Hardtops, sedans and suburbans were available to the police, who could get them in Fury, Fury Salon, Gran Fury and Gran Fury Custom forms. However, production records show that only sedans were in demand. The engine range included everything that Plymouth had to offer, the top engine being the 4-barrel 440. Plymouths were the best-selling police cars in the U.S.A.

This is the third consecutive year for this picture, which means that the Voyager's design details did not change. It is the basic Voyager PB100 on the 109-inch wheelbase. The V-8 cost $4,939 and its net weight was 3,715 pounds. This package also was produced as the PB200, and in that form the V-8 price was $5,027 and the net weight was 3,905 pounds. Regardless of vehicle size, a PB100 standard V-8 cost $170 more than a Six, while the PB200 difference was $164.

127" WB models

Also used previously, this picture reaffirms the lack of Voyager change. Shown is a regular-length body on a 127-inch wheelbase. This package in PB100 V-8 form cost $5,047 and weighed 3,860 pounds net. As a PB200 V-8, it had a net weight of 3,930 pounds and a $5,120 price tag. Both series were also available as a Six. Built only as a V-8 was the PB300, which in this size scaled 4,140 pounds net and was priced at $5,644. All weights and prices are for Voyagers in basic trim.

The ultimate-size Voyager was the extended body on the 127-inch wheelbase. It was built in PB200 and PB300 forms. The PB200, offered as a Six or V-8, recorded a net weight of 4,105 pounds and listed at $5,340 as a V-8. Price-tagged at $5,841 was the exclusively V-8 PB300, which registered a net weight of 4,280 pounds. This illustration shows the vehicle in Sport trim form. Besides this and the basic Voyager, Custom and Premium trim options were also available.

A long-wheelbase Voyager Custom is shown towing a boat trailer. For trailer towing, Voyagers were specially built with light or heavy-duty packages. Both included a 52-ampere alternator, 70-ampere-hour battery, increased cooling, plus heavy-duty variable load flasher and wiring harness. The heavy-duty package added 15-inch heavy-duty rims and heavy-duty shock absorbers.

For this year, Voyager production records were not available in breakdown form. Therefore, totals for individual models are not given. However, the grand total for this model year was 10,819 vehicles. A Voyager with regular-length body on the long wheelbase is shown with the optional Premium trim package. Not very obvious in this view, the most notable Premium feature was the special interior with seats and side panels done in vinyl and a cloth of decorator stripe pattern. Vehicles with Premium trim had Voyager Sport nameplates on the front doors.

Plymouth supplied the extended body on the 127-inch wheelbase only. It is seen with the optional sliding side door, and in Sport trim. With a choice of two interiors, the Sport package had other goodies. Among them were bright-finish items, such as a molding around the grille opening; belt moldings extending along the sides and across the front and rear; windshield, side and rear window moldings; taillamp bezels, bumpers and hubcaps.

A long-body Voyager Sport is shown with the standard 3-door arrangement on the side and an optional single rear door. Long bodies had a 5-passenger standard seating arrangement, but could be ordered with seating for 8, 12 or 15. Regular-length bodies on the long chassis had the same seating plan, but with a 12-passenger limit. Voyagers of short-chassis size were 5-passenger vehicles unless ordered with an extra 3-passenger rear seat.

A Voyager Sport with Premium trim is shown with an added option: Distinctive gold tape stripes to decorate the midsection belt area. The stripes were available for basic Voyager and Custom trims with certain moldings, as well as for Sport and Premium versions. Also, they were applicable to PB100, PB200 and PB300 models, to body sizes on both chassis, and to single and 2-tone colors. Voyager models, sizes and trims continued as a complex mix, making them most difficult to define in simple and comprehensible terms.

A Trail Duster 4-wheel drive model, designated as the PW100, is shown in Sport form. This model's net weight was 4,085 pounds and its price was $4,834 when built in basic form with the 318 V-8. The low-cost engine was the 225 Six, while at the top was a walloping 4-barrel 440 V-8. The 4-wheel drive was full-time. The steel hardtop enclosure was optional. Available production records did not define specific models, but a grand total of 4,255 Trail Dusters were built for this model year.

Continued with the style and size that distinguished it previously was the Plymouth Trail Duster. This view is of the PD100 2-wheel drive model in Sport trim. As a standard V-8 with basic trim, it scaled a net weight of 3,570 pounds and listed at $3,896. For PD100 and PW100 models, the standard 318 V-8 cost $194 more than a Six. The gross vehicle weight rating for the Trail Duster range was 4,900/6,100 pounds maximum.

Trail Dusters were again available with the soft vinyl top. The option was not factory-installed, as that was the job of Plymouth dealerships. The windows could be rolled up and fastened in place. A sturdy roll bar was available for all models. Unless ordered with an extra-cost 3-passenger rear seat, Trail Dusters carried two persons. The rugged sports/utility vehicles were built in basic and Sport versions.

The rising tide of good business in 1976 continued into his calendar year, but only a modest improvement was hown at the year's end. The industry settled for an ncrease of almost 9.1% in passenger car production. Not o lucky was Chrysler Corp., whose combined output of passenger cars was more than 7.1% less than in 1976, and ts portion of the industry total dropped to 12.64%. Plymouth suffered a severe fall, its passenger car and multi-purpose vehicle production declining to a level nearly 24.8% lower than that of 1976. The plummet lowered Plymouth to the industry's No. 8 production position.

Chrysler said that the bulk of the loss was in the fourth quarter of the calendar year, and that there were two main reasons. One was the early beginning and continuation of subnormal winter weather, cutting public traffic to dealerships. The other was an inability to get 1978 Horizon and Voyager models into production before this year ended, a delay that resulted from late vehicle design completion caused by the cutback in engineering and development programs during the 1974-75 recession. However, Plymouth's 1977 model production was above the 1976 total.

For this model year, Plymouth's family size was smaller because of absence of the Duster/Valiant/Scamp group. But the adopted Japanese-import Arrow was again the subcompact segment. The little fastback appeared much the same as previously, offered in three versions on a 92.1-inch wheelbase. The 4-cylinder engine with hemispherical combustion chambers was provided in 1600-cc form as standard, and a 2000-cc was optional.

Volare offerings, designated the Series 7H, retained the immensely successful 1976 image on the two wheelbases of 108.5 inches for coupes and 112.5 inches for other types. The model line-up also was unchanged, with the basic line having three offerings, while the Custom had two and the Premier line consisted of three. Standard 6-cylinder engines were a single-barrel 225 Six for all but the wagons, which had a 2-barrel 225 Super Six. For all models, the standard 8-cylinder engine was a 318 V-8. Optional engines were the 225 Super Six (excepting wagons) and a 360 V-8 in 2 and 4-barrel versions.

Showing up with minor styling alterations was the intermediate Fury group, Series 7R. There were four basic lowline Fury models, while a highline group of four were Salon and Sport models. Wheelbases were 115 inches for hardtops, 117.4 for sedans and 117.5 for wagons. The 225 Super Six and 318 V-8 were standard engines for all but suburbans, which had the 2-barrel 360 V-8 as the only standard. The latter engine was optional for all other models, and additional extras for all Furys were the 4-barrel 360 and a 4-barrel 400 V-8.

Making their final appearance this year were the large, or so-called standard-size, Plymouths. Because of the trend to a general down-sizing of passenger cars, this size had no place in Plymouth's future. The Chrysler Cordoba and LeBaron models were smaller than this. As a result, demand for the big Plymouths slumped sharply this year. The definition of "standard size" automobiles would be altered for future models.

Appearing with no visible change were the big Gran Fury cars, registered as the Series 7P. The number of models was again reduced, as there was no Custom line. Offered in basic Gran Fury form were three models, while the Brougham line had two models and the Sport Suburban also had two. For sedans and hardtops, the wheelbase was now 121.4 inches, and suburbans continued on a 124-inch base. Standard engines ranged from the 318 for

The Arrow continued to represent Plymouth in the subcompact car market, as Plymouth's planned domestic subcompact was in its final development wrap-up stage and would not be ready for the market until the 1978 model year. This is the lowline, or basic, Plymouth Arrow. Its engine was the regular 1600-cc 4-cylinder. Built by Mitsubishi in Japan, this car weighed 2,110 pounds and was priced at $3,379 at the U.S. port of entry. This was the lowest-priced Plymouth this year.

Shown with an optional vinyl roof is the Arrow GS. With the Arrow 160 engine, it also weighed 2,110 pounds, but its P.O.E. price was $3,654. The GS optional engine was a 2000-cc "Silent Shaft" 4-cylinder featuring two counterbalancing shafts at different heights on each side of the crankshaft. Rotating in opposite directions, they were said to reduce engine vibration and noise. This engine, like the regular 1600, had hemispherical combustion chambers and an overhead camshaft.

the basic sedan and hardtop, to the 2-barrel 360 for Broughams, to the 4-barrel 400 for all suburbans. The 2-barrel 360 was optional for the basic sedan and hardtop which, like the Broughams, could also have a 4-barrel 360, a 4-barrel 400 or a 4-barrel 440. The latter was the only extra-cost engine for both suburban series.

As listed, the Gran Fury array of V-8 engines was truly a selective mix. Following the practice of the previous few years, some engines could not be had in cars sold in California, and now some were not available in areas with an altitude of over 4,000 feet. These and other restrictions applied in varying ways to all Plymouth engines and vehicles.

Continued with little change were the Voyagers. As previously, they were a complicated assortment of PB100, PB200 and PB300 models, two wheelbases of 109 and 127 inches, three body lengths offering four seating plans, and a choice of basic, Custom and Sport trim and equipment versions. Standard engines were the 225 Six and 318 V-8, while a 360, 400 and 440 were available. This extensive variety of vehicle combinations was necessary for the kind of market Voyagers catered to.

Carried over with slight changes were the Trail Duster PD100 and PW100 on/off-road vehicles, again on a 106 inch wheelbase. Standard were the 225 and 318 engines with the 2-barrel 360 and 400, and the 4-barrel 440 available.

Chrysler's Electronic Lean Burn System, introduced for 1976, was now standard on 4-barrel 360, 400 and 440 V-8 engines, and may have been installed on some of the popular 318 powerplants. The system employed a 200 component analog computer located near the carburetor. Monitoring signals from sensors placed at strategic engine points, it measured inlet air temperature, water temperature, throttle position, vacuum and ambient air determined the exact instant of combustion and accordingly fired spark plugs at a precise time. The better air/fuel ratio resulted in lower emission levels. The system also provided better fuel economy, smoother engine operation and more responsive acceleration.

For high-altitude operation, engines were fitted with a compensating carburetor that supplied the same relative air/fuel mixture at varying altitudes by means of a sensing valve that sampled the atmospheric pressure. Also new were a fresh air induction system for all engines, and an air aspirator valve for most engines. The former made inlet air cooler on hot days, while the latter admitted air to the exhaust system at idling speed to aid emission control. A new innovation for California cars was the air switching system, which injected air into the exhaust near the valve ports during engine warm-up, then switched to an injection point behind the catalytic converter of 6-cylinder engines or at the base of the right exhaust manifold on V-8s. Switching was controlled by the same temperature-sensing switch that actuated the power heat valve.

All of these features are typical of the thorough design attention given to Plymouths, and others may have eluded the author's research for inclusion in this brief report.

In standard form, the Arrow GT was the lightest Plymouth this year, if the reported weight of 2,090 pounds is true. Its P.O.E. price was $4,008 with the standard 1600-cc Silent Shaft engine, which was not installed in other models. Silent Shaft engines were also a feature of 1976 Arrows. Again this year, Arrows were known as the Model 7, and were 5-passenger 2-door hatchback coupes. Production totals were not available for the little cars.

A Volare 4-Door Sedan is shown with optional bright moldings on the wheelcut lips, as well as extra-cost bumper guards and dressed-up wheels. Without extras, this model weighed 3,345 pounds and cost $3,789 with a standard V-8 engine. Exactly 44,550 buyers got this car as a Six or V-8. It also was the basis for Taxi and Police Pursuit cars. There is no record of any Taxis built, but 965 Police Pursuits were produced. The Volare Custom Sedan was also available with Police Package equipment.

Shown in standard form except for wheelcovers, whitewall tires and bumper guards, is the Volare Coupe, lowest-priced model in the Volare family. This model in the basic Volare series weighed 3,290 pounds and cost $3,740 in standard 318 V-8 form. Also offered as a Six, total production was 42,455 cars, of which an unknown number were built as Road Runners, Sun Runners, etc. As a standard V-8, basic coupes and sedans cost $170 more than a standard 225 Six.

Amassing a production total of 80,180, this was the most popular Plymouth of the year. The Volare Wagon, built only as a 2-seat vehicle, carried a $4,025 price tag and scaled a weight of 3,540 pounds in standard form with 318 V-8 power. When built with the standard 225 Super Six, the price was $95 less. Among other extras, Rallye wheels are shown. The gas-cylinder-assisted liftgate door provided ample access to a cargo area of 72.8 cubic feet.

The Volare Coupe is shown with a 2-tone paint treatment that was offered in a choice of nine color combinations. A similar treatment was offered for 1976, but this year's pattern was slightly different. As can be seen, the bottom line of the dark bodyside color stretches in an apparently straight line from the top of the front bumper to the rear, except for wheelcut interruptions. Previously, the line was a bit lower, and dipped slightly downward on the rear quarter panel. The option was available on basic, Custom and Premier Coupes. Plymouth called it one of the "Fun Runner" options.

This is the "Front Runner," a Volare Coupe with Road Runner and Super Pak option packages. The Road Runner decor was like that of 1976, featuring bold tape stripes on the lower bodysides and on the rear end, plus Road Runner identification within the stripe on the lower area. The Super Pak added spoilers at the front and rear, flared wheelcut openings and louvered quarter windows. The "Front Runner" was termed one of the "Fun Runner" group.

Another member of the Volare group of "Fun Runners" was called the "Sun Runner," which actually was two separate options. One was the T-bar roof shown, which made its Plymouth debut this year. It featured lift-out glass panels. The other was the more conventional sun roof, which had a manually-operated panel and no glass. Both of these options were available on basic, Custom and Premier Coupes. The T-bar roof is shown on a "Front Runner."

Attracting a generous portion of popularity was the Volare Custom 4-Door Sedan. A total of 50,859 persons found it to be just the right model for their needs, and signed on the dotted line for it. They got Sixes and V-8s with an assortment of options, one of which was the vinyl-clad roof shown. With no extras, a standard V-8 registered a weight of 3,350 pounds, and the manufacturer's suggested retail price was $3,971 plus destination charges. All Plymouth prices, excepting the Arrow, are quoted on that basis.

The optional canopy vinyl roof gave a distinctive smartness to the Volare Custom Coupe, and the optional simulated wire wheelcovers added a sports car flavor. This model was preferred by 34,196 buyers. In basic form, and with the standard 318 V-8 engine, it swung the weight scale pointer to a reading of 3,295 pounds and posted a price of $3,922. In the Volare Custom series, the 318 engine cost $170 more than the standard 225 Six.

The Volare Premier Coupe is illustrated with no extra trim or equipment. In this form, Plymouth reported the standard V-8 as weighing 3,480 pounds and costing $4,418. Total Six and V-8 production amounted to 21,979 cars, including those with a Landau roof and other extra-cost features. For coupes and sedans in the Premier series, the standard 318 V-8 cost $113 more than the standard 225 Six. A 225 Super Six was optional for these and Custom and basic coupes and sedans.

Plymouth again offered the smartness of the Landau vinyl roof as an option for the Volare Premier Coupe. The opera quarter windows complemented the appearance of a custom roof treatment. Normally, the interior featured a 60/40 split-bench vinyl front seat with folding center armrest and dual reclining seat-backs. The same interior and seat design could be had in cashmere-like cloth, or highback bucket front seats were available in an all-vinyl interior.

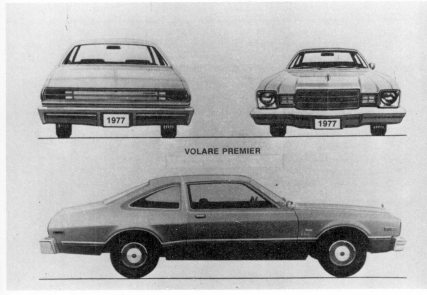

VOLARE PREMIER

1977

This model was so attractive to 31,443 individuals that they felt they just had to have one. They had a choice of the 225 Six, 225 Super Six, 318 V-8 or 2-barrel 360 V-8 engines, like the Volare Premier Coupe and Volare basic and Custom coupes and sedans offered. It is the Volare Premier 4-Door Sedan. Plymouth recorded this model's weight as 3,545 pounds and priced it at $4,467 in standard form with the 318 engine.

The flagship of the Plymouth Volare fleet was the Premier Wagon, which was built only as a 2-seat model. Its popularity was so high that the factory turned out 76,756 to satisfy the demand. As a 318 V-8 with no extras, it scaled a weight of 3,585 pounds and posted a price sticker listing $4,476 as the base. This model, like the basic Volare Wagon, did not offer the 225 Six, had the 225 Super Six and 318 V-8 as standard engines and the 2-barrel 360 V-8 for an option. The price differential between the 225 Super Six and 318 V-8 was $205, applicable to this model only.

From this point of view, the intermediate-size Plymouth Fury 2-Door Hardtop looks like its 1976 counterpart, but there were minor design differences at the rear, and more extensive changes at the front. This automobile weighed 3,855 pounds and cost $4,154 when built as a standard V-8. Total Six and V-8 production was 16,410 cars. Standard engines for intermediate hardtops and sedans were the 225 Super Six and 318 V-8, while 2-barrel 360 and 4-barrel 400 V-8s were available. The Six cost $261 less than the 318.

Of special appeal to 25,172 buyers was the Fury 4-Door Sedan. As a 318 V-8, it was listed as costing $4,205 and weighing 3,890 pounds. Plymouth also used this model as a basis for some of its Taxi and Police Pursuit offerings. Apparently, no taxicab operators placed orders, since none were recorded built. The reverse was true of law enforcement agencies, however, as 8,095 Fury Police Pursuits were built. The total was in addition to Fury Sedans built for public sale. All other intermediate models could be ordered with Police Package special equipment.

Plymouth again provided the basic Fury Suburban as two models, 2-seat and 3-seat, and powered them with V-8s. The 2-seat model, of which 6,765 were built, cost $4,687 and weighed 4,335 pounds. Priced at $4,830 was the 4,390-pound 3-seat model, which went to 5,556 buyers. Prices and weights relate to the 2-barrel 360 engine, which was standard for basic Fury and Fury Sport Suburbans. For these models, the 4-barrel 400 was the only extra-cost engine.

FURY SUBURBAN

The Fury Sport 2-Door Hardtop shows the new Fury front end well. Dual-unit rectangular headlamps were stacked beside a new grille of rectangular theme, and park/turn signal lamps were set in the bumper. With the 318 V-8 and no extras, this model weighed 3,865 pounds and was price-tagged at $4,394. Total Six and V-8 production was 30,075. The example shown sported the optional canopy vinyl roof and opera quarter windows, plus wheels that Plymouth called "styled road wheels."

This is the Fury Sport 2-Door Hardtop purchased new by the author, who is shown beyond the trunk. In Golden Fawn color, the car is fitted with Rallye wheels, the canopy vinyl roof with opera windows, and a lot of other extras. The engine, however, is the standard 318 V-8. The camera-work is by William L. Bailey, who added many to the hundreds of pictures made for this book by publisher George H. Dammann. The locale of this view is a parking lot on the grounds of the Detroit Public Library, where much research for this book was done in the National Automotive History Collection. Not well-shown here are minor rear-end changes made in Fury and Fury Sport Hardtops. Backup lamps were removed from the taillamps and placed within the bumper, resulting in a new taillamp lens design.

Showing a new taillamp lens design and the new placement of the guards near the ends of the bumper is the Fury Salon 4-Door Sedan. When built with the 318 engine and no extra frills and gadgets, its weight was 3,900 pounds and its price was $4,446. Including Sixes, a total of 25,617 came off the assembly lines. Normally, the optional bodyside protective moldings had vinyl inserts that were color-keyed to match the vinyl roof, and so the white inserts shown were not in accordance with the roof.

The exclusively V-8 Fury Sport Suburban was Plymouth's answer to those who wanted an intermediate-size wagon with a capacity for making people exceptionally comfortable. Its foam-padded seats provided that comfort in 2-seat and 3-seat models. The 2-seater, which attracted 2,502 buyers, cost $5,192 and weighed 4,330 pounds in standard form. Winner of 4,065 sales, the 3-seat model registered 4,400 pounds and listed at $5,335 when standard-equipped.

This scene, in which a Gran Fury was being washed, could have forecast the fate that was to fall upon the big Plymouth series at the end of this model year. It was "washed up" – terminated – would not remain in production for 1978. The washing also might have signified the importance of tender loving care for Gran Furys, since they would be the last of their kind. This is the basic Gran Fury 4-Door Sedan, which went to 14,242 buyers. In standard form it weighed 4,145 pounds and cost $4,677. This was the basis for the Gran Fury Police Pursuit, of which 8,204 were built for law-enforcing agencies. All Gran Fury models, including Broughams and Sport Suburbans, were available with special Police Package equipment.

For their final year, the big Plymouths received almost no appearance changes. Shown is the basic Gran Fury 2-Door Hardtop, which in standard form scaled 4,070 pounds and was priced at $4,692. Exactly 2,772 came out of the factory. All of the big senior Plymouths were V-8s. Standard for Gran Fury hardtops and sedans was the 318, with the 2-barrel 360 and 4-barrel 400 and 440 optional.

GRAN FURY SUBURBAN

Except for the air deflector on the rear end of the roof, the basic Gran Fury Suburban is shown in absolutely standard form. This vehicle, of which 2,055 were built, was built only with two seats. It weighed 4,885 pounds and cost $5,315 with the standard 4-barrel 400 V-8. The 4-barrel 440 V-8 was optional.

Displaying its elegance in a grand manner is the Gran Fury Brougham 4-Door Sedan, for which the demand required a production run of 17,687 examples. In standard form, this luxury automobile registered a weight of 4,250 pounds and posted a price of $4,948. The car illustrated has front window ventpanes, an option that was also available for the basic Gran Fury Sedan and Suburban, as well as the Gran Fury Sport Suburban.

This year, opera windows were an option on the Gran Fury Brougham 2-Door Formal Hardtop. Without any extras, this was a 4,190-pound car that was marketed at $4,963. The qualities of this model were so appealing that 4,846 individuals signed sales orders for it. They had an ample choice of engines for the big car. Gran Fury Brougham models offered the 2-barrel 360 V-8 as standard, and the 4-barrel 400 and 440 engines as optional.

GRAN FURY SPORT SUBURBAN

The big Gran Fury Sport Suburban is illustrated with standard fittings, including the rear air deflector. Weighing 4,880 pounds and costing $5,558, the 2-seat model went to 1,631 buyers. Priced at $5,681, the 4,925-pound 3-seat model had a 4,319-unit production run. Prices and weights are for cars with the 4-barrel 400 engine, which was the standard powerplant. For buyers who wanted more power, the 4-barrel 440 was provided at extra cost.

A basic Voyager on the 109-inch wheelbase is shown with a custom paint pattern and side pipes that were not Plymouth originals, but the wheels were Plymouth's optional wide sport road wheels. This vehicle package size was available in Model PB100 and PB200 forms. The PB100 had a net weight of 3,715 pounds, a $5,372 price tag and a production run of 1,843. The PB200 listed at $5,473, weighed 3,805 pounds net and went to 583 buyers. Weights and prices are for vehicles with the standard V-8 engine and basic features. Production totals represent overall Six and V-8 assemblies.

The Plymouth Voyager with regular-length body on a 127-inch wheelbase is shown as a Voyager Sport in 2-tone color option No. 2. This vehicle size was offered in all three PB series. As a PB100, the price was $5,482, net weight was 3,860 pounds and the production total was 975. The PB200 cost $5,593, weighed 3,930 pounds net, and its 7,740-unit production run made this the most popular Voyager package combination this year. Priced at $6,048, the PB300's net weight was 4,140 pounds and its production total was 821. Prices and weights are for standard V-8s and basic vehicle features. Combined Six and V-8 production is quoted, except for the exclusively V-8 PB300.

Painted in 2-tone color option No. 1, the extended body on the 127-inch chassis is shown as a Voyager Sport. This extra-long vehicle size was not available in PB100 form. The PB200 standard V-8 with basic vehicle specifications sold for $5,772 and weighed 4,105 pounds net. Including Sixes, 2,265 were built. When built in standard form in all respects, the PB300 version scaled a net weight of 4,280 pounds and posted a $6,245 price, which is the highest price quoted for any Plymouth this year. The PB300 package of this size was chosen by 5,173 buyers. The PB300 package featured V-8 engines only.

This Voyager Sport has fancy stripes on the belt color, a sliding side door and darkly-tinted "Sunscreen" glass, all optional. Seen with a single rear door, dual doors were available. All Voyagers had 5-passenger seating as standard, with optional seating for 8, 12 and 15, depending upon the PB series and body length. As in previous years, PB numerical designations related to load/weight/chassis factors. PB100 and PB200 standard engines were the 225 Six and 318 V-8, with the latter standard for the PB300. The 360 V-8 was available for all, while the 400 and 440 were for PB200 and PB300 chassis. The Six-to-318 price differential was: PB100 $173; PB200 $208; PB200 w/extended body $233.

Wearing 2-tone color option No. 3 is a Voyager Sport. The color options are not in reference to red, blue, green, etc., but to the placement of 2-tone colors in respect to certain areas on the vehicle. Plymouth offered 14 colors for Voyagers, and vehicles were painted in a single color, or in one of three 2-tone option schemes. Voyagers again were available in basic, Custom and Sport trim and interior versions, plus the extra-fancy Premium interior. These were not firmly linked to PB designations.

The Plymouth Trail Duster Model PD100 2-wheel drive sports/utility vehicle was finding sales hard to get. Only 727 of them were turned out. It registered a net weight of 3,570 pounds and listed at $4,526 as a standard V-8 vehicle in basic trim, and with the optional steel roof. The price of the roof enclosure, in body color, was $470. The spunky car is shown in basic trim except for sporty wheels and whitewall tires.

New styling was applied to the Trail Duster grille and lamp units. Grille design was suggestive of long narrow slots arranged in a stacked manner, but secondary vertical members joined them together as a unit. Park/turn signal lamps, formerly between the grille and bumper, were placed within the headlamp housings, in a vertical attitude. Shown is the 4-wheel drive Trail Duster, Model PW100, of which 5,813 were built. It cost $5,523 and weighed 4,085 pounds net when fitted with the standard V-8, hardtop roof and basic trim. It is seen as a Sport model with optional 2-tone paint and 8-spoke white-painted wheels fitted with white-lettered wide tires.

Trail Dusters ordered with the optional soft vinyl top were shipped from the factory without them installed, and they were fitted to the vehicles at Plymouth dealerships. This 4-wheel drive Trail Duster Sport is equipped with chrome-styled slotted wheels. As had been the practice, many comfort, convenience and other options were available. Trail Dusters were offered in gross vehicle weight packages of 4,900, 5,200, 5,600 and 6,100 pounds.

This 4-wheel drive Plymouth Trail Duster Sport, seen frolicking in the surf, has an optional roll bar for added protection. The high front seat backs indicate that this vehicle was fitted with the optional high-back Command Seat interior in cloth and vinyl. Another option was the all-vinyl Sport interior with different seat design. The basic interior was of simple design, and in vinyl. Standard seating provided only the two front seats. Trail Dusters never had a bench front seat, but the optional rear seat was a bench type of 3-passenger width.

For extra front end protection, a sturdy guard framework was available for Trail Dusters. The structure featured a ladder-like center with side extensions to guard the lamps. The 4-wheel drive functioned on a full-time basis, not requiring the driver to decide which wheels should be driven. For 2 and 4-wheel drive models, standard engines were the 225 Six and 318 V-8, optional engines were the 2-barrel 360 and 400. The big 4-barrel 440 V-8 was available for 4-wheel drive models only.

As this final chapter is being written, the auto industry is halfway through the 1978 model production run. At this point, it appears that the industry will report a high, but not record, production total at the end of this calendar year. As usual, a portion of the total will be 1979 models, which rumors indicate will be an interesting array of cars. But Plymouth has placed a very interesting range of vehicles on the market for 1978, offering an exceptionally wide variety of models.

The headline news from Plymouth was the Horizon, which represented a bold and confident step into the sub-compact field. The car, boldly differing from any ever offered by Plymouth, was confidently placed in a market that already was highly competitive. Horizon and its Dodge Omni twin won like "Car of the Year" awards from Motor Trend magazine upon their introduction in January, and drew wide public acclaim as well. They were the first sub-compact cars to be built by Chrysler in the U.S.A.

The Plymouth Horizon, designated Series M, was offered only as a 4-door sedan of unitized construction. Its transversely-mounted 4-cylinder engine, coupled to a front-wheel drive, had a cast-iron block, aluminum head, overhead camshaft, 104.7 cubic-inch displacement and a 2-barrel carburetor, plus the Electronic Lean Burn System. The standard transmission was a 4-speed manual. The wheelbase was 99.2 inches, and all four wheels were independently suspended by an unusual arrangement of coil springs.

Another new Plymouth was the Sapporo, designed by Chrysler and built by Mitsubishi as a sophisticated luxury sub-compact car for the U.S. market. Named for the Japanese city where the 1972 Winter Olympics were held, the car was offered only as a 2-door hardtop on a 99-inch

wheelbase. Engines were 4-cylinder Silent Shaft, with a 1600-cc version as standard and a 2600-cc optional, both incorporating a new MCA-Jet system. The system employed a small valve near the top of the hemispherical combustion chambers. This valve, actuated simultaneously with the regular intake valve, sends a jet air stream into the chamber, causing a swirling movement in the regular fuel/air mixture for maximum fuel burn and economy. Mitsubishi continued to build the Arrow fastback for Plymouth's U.S. market, fitting them with Silent Shaft 1600-cc and 2000-cc engines with the MCA-Jet system.

The popular Volare Series 8H reflected previous characteristics of this very successful car line. Custom and Premier no longer denoted sub-series however, but were optional trim packages available for the three Volare body types. Dual wheelbases were 112.7 inches for sedans and wagons, 108.7 inches for coupes. The single-barrel 225 Six was standard for coupes and sedans, while the 2-barrel 225 Super Six was a base engine for wagons. The standard V-8 for all models was the 2-barrel 318. The option list included the 225 Super Six, plus 2 and 4-barrel 360 V-8s. Such were the engines for areas except California and altitudes of 4,000 feet or more, which required engine assignments that differed in some respects.

The Series 8R Fury offered four basic and four highline models, of which the latter were in Salon and Sport forms. Wheelbases were 114.9, 117.4 and 117.5 inches for hardtops, sedans and suburbans, respectively. Standard engines for sedans and hardtops were the 225 Super Six and 2-barrel 318. The only base engine for suburbans was the 2-barrel 360, which was optional for other models. All Fury options were 4-barrel 360 and 4-barrel 400 V-8s. Here again, cars for California and high altitudes differed in engines offered, as was the case for all Plymouths.

For certain areas, a 4-barrel 318 V-8 was available for all

The Plymouth Horizon, built only as a 4-door car, weighed 2,145 pounds and had a factory delivered price of $3,706 when introduced. The figures apply to vehicles with standard equipment only. The car is shown in nearly standard form. Bumper guards, Rallye wheels and the rightside rearview mirror were extra-cost items. Whitewall tires and black vinyl-insert bodyside rub moldings were among bonus items included as standard. The basic package concept was styled in a fittingly functional and attractive manner.

Shown with Custom exterior trim is a Plymouth Horizon with its liftgate open and the lockable luggage compartment security panel raised. All Horizons had a rear seat with a fold-down back, providing more space for carrying luggage or whatever. The Custom exterior trim package included bright moldings on the sills, wheelcut lips, drip trough and hood front, plus narrow vinyl-insert bodyside strips. A Custom interior package had seats and door panels of distinctive Custom design, plus trim choices and other goodies.

1978

Plymouth vehicles, except sub-compacts. This year, the Electronic Lean Burn System, standard on most other V-8s for 1977, was added to the 318 engine, except in some areas.

The Plymouth Voyager introduction, delayed until February, revealed some newness in body design. However, 109 and 127-inch wheelbases, plus PB100, PB200 and PB300 versions again were offered. And buyers had a choice of basic, Custom, Sport and Sport Premium trims, plus three body lengths and four seating plans. The 225 engine was standard, while the 318, 360, 400 and a big 440 were available.

The Trail Duster was a continuance of the former PD100 and PW100 models on a 106-inch wheelbase. In addition to the standard 225 Super Six, V-8s of 318, 360, 400 and 440 displacements were offered.

All new was a lock-up torque converter, providing direct mechanical linkage between the engine and rear axle when the automatic transmission shifted into drive. This resulted in lower engine speed and better fuel mileage.

Information reported for this year was based on releases in the early months of model year production. Undoubtedly, changes will have occurred by the time this is published. In regard to the DeSoto name, it continued this year on vehicles built in Turkey, and they were quite similar to those reported for the 1972 model year.

This Horizon has Custom exterior trim and multicolor sport stripes bordering the lower bodyside blackout paint treatment. Horizon offered 14 colors and five 2-tone combinations. Many options were also available, including air conditioning, power steering, power front disc brakes and an automatic transmission. The sub-compact Horizon's interior was so spacious that the government's EPA records classified the car as of compact size. The seating plan utilized two front bucket seats and a 2-passenger rear bench seat.

In addition to woodgrain on the bodysides and liftgate, the Premium Woodgrain exterior trim package included bright moldings on the hood edge, belt, upper door frames, drip trough, fenders, bodysides, liftgate and sills, plus bright rallye hubs and lug nuts. A Premium trim, without woodgrain, had all of this brightwork, plus bright wheelcut lip moldings. A Premium interior package featured exclusive seat and side panel styling, trim choices, a shift-lever console and other extra-nice touches. For solid-color cars, Horizon even offered a vinyl roof covering that extended down over the quarters. The car shown has an optional roof luggage rack featuring adjustability for carrying luggage, skis, camping gear, a canoe or bicycle, etc.

With high-fashion styling and appointments throughout, the new Sapporo was created to fit a very special sub-compact market niche. Designed by Plymouth and built in Japan by Mitsubishi, it was offered in 2-door hardtop form only, and in a single trim version. Standard equipment included almost everything a buyer could want, but there were a few options, including a choice of engines. In basic form as shown, the car weighed 2,455 pounds and was priced at $5,498 at the start of the model year.

The Sapporo concept differed completely from the Horizon and Arrow, but the chassis and drive train layout was very similar to the latter. A larger car than the Arrow, it also offered an engine of higher power output. Among options for the 4-passenger car were air conditioning, an automatic transmission, 4-wheel disc brakes and power devices for steering and windows. Vinyl was fitted over the rear of the roof in a yoke fashion, and the quarters had opera lamps. Three body colors were offered.

The Arrow continued as Plymouth's only car with fastback styling. A standard version of the sub-compact car is shown. Plymouth said it was "basically smart, nicely priced." At introduction time, its price was $3,691 and its weight was 2,175 pounds, without options. Among items of standard equipment were reclining front bucket seats, a folding rear seat, an adjustable steering column, power front disc brakes and a locking fuel filler door.

Again, the middle model of the Arrow line was the GS. To basic Arrow features, the GS added woodgrain on the instrument panel, carpeting throughout, flipper quarter windows, an electric defroster for the rear window, a right roof rail grip and several other items. Of course, the car was identified with distinctive bodyside stripes and GS letters, had a Plymouth grille medallion and sported chrome on the wheelcut lips and sills. Initially, the 2,180-pound car was priced at $3,978.

The Plymouth Arrow GT fittingly added more to the GS features. A rallye cluster with tachometer, a floor console, sports steering wheel and dual racing mirrors were among the inclusions. Also, decor was different. An unusual gradation of stripes was applied to the lower bodysides, hood and rear end, and bold GT letters were on the sides. The standard black grille and optional black bumpers and cast aluminum wheels enhanced the image. The introduction price of the 2,175-pound GT was $4,552.

The Arrow Jet was an option package for the basic Arrow. The youthful assemblage featured 2-tone orange and black body paint, an orange-colored grille, black bumpers, dual racing mirrors, cast aluminum wheels and radial tires with raised white letters. The Arrow Jet name was boldly spelled out on the lower bodysides. For extra details, 12 optional decals of small sign size, for application at strategic points, named the function or advised caution and proper respect in the usage of some areas.

In basic form, the Plymouth Volare Coupe was the economy model of the popular Volare series. When built as a V-8, its initial price was $3,905 and its weight was 3,255 pounds. All three Volare models were available as a Six or V-8. With the standard 225 Six engine, the coupe and sedan cost $170 less than those with the standard 318 V-8. The wagon, for which the standard 6-cylinder engine was the 225 Super Six, had a $130 price differential between the Six and 318.

Shown with Custom exterior trim is the Plymouth Volare Coupe, which also has an optional vinyl roof known as the Halo design. Halo was in reference to the area covered by the vinyl, which stretched from the windshield header to the juncture of the rear pillars and quarter panels. Distinct Volare Custom and Premier models no longer were offered, these class levels now replaced by Custom and Premier trim packages as options for the three basic models.

Continuing as an attractive option was the Landau vinyl roof with opera quarter windows, shown on a Volare Coupe with Premier exterior trim. The vinyl did not extend over the roof to the windshield, as it did on the Halo roof. In this view, the lower bodyside appears to be in black or a dark color, but the car was painted a single solid color. This model, in different colors and equipped with the Lean-Burn 318 V-8 and many extras, was selected by the author's wife for her personal car.

The Volare Coupe in Premium exterior trim appears to be a duplicate of the Custom version, but it is not. Besides having Custom items, the Premier list included a stand-up hood ornament, a long bright molding on the hood center, plus selective use of delicate tape stripes. As in the case of the Custom package, Premier trim did not include the Halo vinyl roof shown. On the Volare Coupe, trim versions were identified by Custom or Premier nameplates just above Volare signatures ahead of the doors.

The Road Runner again was an option for the Volare Coupe. This was the eleventh year for the Road Runner name on a Plymouth. The name no longer represented a power-packed fireflash supercar, but it continued to denote a special performance image. For distinctive identity, lower bodysides were accented by bright yellow stripes, from which an extension stretched across the rear. The car is shown with Rallye wheels and white-lettered RWL radial tires.

One of Plymouth's means of maximizing the performance image was the Road Runner Sport Pak on the Volare Coupe. Spoilers were at the front and rear, and flared wheel openings ended in flaplike shapes. Louvers partially obscured the quarter windows. Brilliant tricolor stripes stretched in a stacked manner around bodies that either were white or black. This dazzler was powered by a 4-barrel 360 V-8, which was the most powerful engine available for a Volare.

Another example of Plymouth's strong appeal to the youth market was the Fun Runner option, for those who couldn't afford many specialty extras on the Volare Coupe. In addition to the louvered quarter windows, bodysides were 2-toned on a line at bumper-top level, and narrow stripes stretched from headlamps to taillamps. And to identify the Fun Runner from the rear, a distinctive tape applique was applied above the taillamps, appearing to link them together.

A new Volare performance option was the Super Coupe, featuring heavy-duty suspension, a rear anti-sway bar, special wide-stance wheels and the 4-barrel 360 V-8 engine. Front and rear spoilers, flared wheelcuts and louvered windows added youth appeal to the form. Most brightwork was blacked out, the hood and front fender tops were dull black and the remainder of the body was a rich brown. Vivid stripes reached from the front corners to the "B" pillars, which carried them up to arch over the roof. Volare also offered an exclusive Street Kit Car for performance enthusiasts. And the Sun Runner, with a T-bar roof and lift-out glass skylights, was again available.

The Plymouth Volare 4-Door Sedan is illustrated with Custom exterior trim, but the sporty wire wheelcovers and whitewall tires were not included with the option. Volare continued in much the same styling form as previously. No new sheetmetal was apparent, but some details were changed. Among them was a new grille design that lacked the delicate and refined finesse of the former grille. Park/turn signal lamps took the opposite turn and were of more simple design.

The basic Volare 4-Door Sedan is shown with optional whitewall tires and deluxe wheelcovers. With a standard V-8 engine and no extras, this model's introduction price was $4,023 and its weight was 3,295 pounds. This practical family car was the basis for sedans with Custom and Premier trim options.

In this view, the Plymouth Volare 4-Door Sedan is shown prettied up with the Premier trim features. When applied to the Sedan, the Premier package had bodyside stripes that extended along the full length of the beltline. On the Coupe's different shape, they stretched from the headlamp to the rear edge of the door, then streaked up over the roof. The Volare Sedan and Coupe had rear-end lamps in a new arrangement, plus fresh new styling in that area.

Shown with Custom trim is the Plymouth Volare Station Wagon, which is also seen with a roof rack and rear air deflector, both of which were extra-cost items. Of course, the Rallye wheels and whitewall tires also cost extra. In basic trim and equipment form, but with a standard V-8 engine, the Volare Station Wagon registered a weight of 3,490 pounds and posted a price of $4,325 when first placed on the market. Volare Wagons were built only as 2-seat 6-passenger vehicles.

When sporting the Premium Woodgrain trim shown, the Plymouth Volare Station Wagon was an impressive vehicle. Woodgrain was also applied to the rear liftgate. This woodgrain package was available only for the Station Wagon. However, it is conceivable that experienced bodymen could apply the side woodgrain and moldings to sedans in what could be termed a "suburban sedan" effect. But if there had been a worthwhile market for such a specialty, Plymouth probably would have built it.

Plymouth's expertise in the building of taxicabs continued to attract a major portion of that market. In addition to an interior that was designed, trimmed and fitted for taxicab service, the Volare Taxi had other special equipment as standard. Heavy-duty design and toughness was applied to the suspension system and many components to withstand hard and constant taxicab usage. The standard engine was the single-barrel 225 Six, and the 2-barrel 318 V-8 was available in heavy-duty form.

Plymouth called the Volare Pursuit "a dependable law enforcer," and said that the car was engineered for this particular kind of duty. Truly, it was. Heavy-duty components served important functions, and special attention was given to many areas. Even the front seat was specially constructed to make it comfortable for the lawman's long hours of duty. Power choices were the single-barrel 225 Six and 2-barrel 318 V-8, plus 2 and 4-barrel 360 V-8s, all heavy-duty.

Plymouth's new Fury series offered no newness in styling. Formerly classified as the intermediate series, the Fury was now Plymouth's largest passenger car, without getting any notable change in dimensions. In fact, overall length was shortened a fraction of an inch. Shown is the basic Fury 2-Door Hardtop. As a standard V-8 without extras, its introductory price was $4,388 and its weight was 3,855 pounds. The canopy vinyl roof was one of the options shown.

Shown is the basic Fury 4-Door Sedan, which in standard V-8 form registered a reading of 3,885 pounds on the weight scale and was affixed with a $4,468 price tag when introduced. The Fury Sedan and Hardtop, the Fury Sport Hardtop and Fury Salon Sedan were available as a Six or V-8. Any model with a 6-cylinder engine was base-priced $176 less than the same model with a standard V-8. The 6-cylinder was the 2-barrel 225 Super Six, and the standard V-8 was the 2-barrel 318.

Plymouth offered the basic Fury Suburban with a choice of V-8 engines only. The 2-seat model reported a weight of 4,310 pounds and a price of $5,024. As a 3-seat model, the price was $5,167 and the weight was 4,370 pounds. Weights and prices are as listed at the beginning of the model year, and are for basic vehicles with the standard 2-barrel 360 V-8 engine. This 360 was also standard for Fury Sport Suburbans. The 225 Super Six was a bit too weak for these big vehicles with heavy load capabilities.

This view shows the Plymouth Fury Sport 2-Door Hardtop with optional vinyl roof and opera quarter windows. This model could also be had with a full-length vinyl roof treatment and no opera windows, or with no vinyl. The basic car with a standard V-8 weighed 3,860 pounds and listed at $4,628 when placed on the market. The V-8 options for this model and for the Fury Salon and Fury Hardtop and Sedan were the 2-barrel 360, 4-barrel 360 and 4-barrel 400.

The most luxurious sedan among Plymouth's offerings, at least at the start of this model year, was the Fury Salon 4-Door Sedan. As a standard V-8 with no extra equipment, its weight was 3,900 pounds and its starting price was $4,703. A Saxony cloth-and-vinyl interior with bench seat and fold-down center armrest was standard. For those whose taste was more expensive, the Oxford super-soft all-vinyl interior with a similar bench seat was available.

The exclusively V-8 Sport Suburban in the Plymouth Fury series offered just about everything a buyer could want in this kind of vehicle. Plenty of passenger space or lots of cargo area — whatever the need might be. In 2-seat form, it scaled a weight of 4,300 pounds and listed at $5,482. As a 3-seat vehicle, it recorded a weight reading of 4,375 pounds and asked a price of $5,625. These figures are early releases, and are for standard V-8 cars with no options.

Plymouth Pursuit offerings included the full line of Furys. Shown is the basic Fury Sedan, but the basic Hardtop and Suburban, Fury Sport Hardtop, Salon Sedan and Sport Suburban were also available with Pursuit A38 equipment. Typically, thorough attention was given to special features needed for such service, and they were built-in by Plymouth. The 225 Six, plus 318, 360, 400 and 440 V-8 engines were offered, most of them fitted for heavy-duty service.

Because of its larger size, extra comfort and better ride qualities, the Fury Taxi was likely to be a better-selling cab than the Volare Taxi. Experience had proved that smaller cars were unpopular in the taxicab trade, but changing conditions might cause a reversal. As was Plymouth's practice in taxi-building, special features were built-in at the factory. Engines for the Fury Taxi were the 225 Six and 318 V-8, both built for heavy-duty service.

From the latest sales literature, this illustration appears to be a carryover from earlier years, but it shows new details on the latest Voyager. This 109-inch wheelbase package, shown in basic Voyager trim, was offered in two PB forms. The PB100 weighed 3,715 pounds net and had a $5,725 price tag. With net weight at 3,805 pounds in PB200 form, the price was $5,873. The figures are for standard V-8 vehicles, as first announced. For the PB100 package, a Six cost $218 less, while the PB200 Six was $169 less.

Reflecting the newest details is the Plymouth Voyager Wagon on a 127-inch wheelbase, dressed in 2-tone color option No. 1. This size was available in all three PB forms. PB100 net weight was 3,880 pounds and price was $5,883. The PB200 registered 3,930 pounds net and cost $6,030. Priced at $6,569 was the PB300, which had a net weight of 4,140 pounds. All quotations relate to a standard V-8 in the early marketing period. A PB100 Six cost $219 less, a PB200 was $169 less. The PB300 was V-8 only.

A Voyager Wagon on the long wheelbase shows off color option No. 3, with extra striping. Among other options shown are Sunscreen glass (from the front door back) and a sliding mid-door. Not apparent here is a new extra, the Sunscreen Skylight above the front compartment. This Voyager is in Sport trim. Also available were Custom and Sport Premium option packages. Voyagers were new from the front doors back, and had new roofs. The grille was revised, and taillamps were vertical rather than squarish.

The new Voyager Maxiwagon's rear end was eight inches longer than the earlier extended body, but the wheelbase remained at 127 inches. Wraparound quarter windows were a new feature. The vehicle is shown in Sport trim with 2-tone color option No. 2. Maxiwagons were not built in PB100 form. The basic V-8 PB200 net weight was 4,105 pounds and its price was $6,311. A PB200 Six cost $169 less. The PB300, offering V-8s only, weighed 4,280 pounds net and cost $6,893 in basic form. These figures prevailed at introduction time. All Voyagers had standard 5-passenger seating and, depending on body size, could carry 8, 12 or 15 with optional seats. Gross vehicle weights were 4,800, 6,100 and 6,700 for PB100, PB200 and PB300 models, respectively.

Plymouth, the taxicab specialist, added the Voyager Taxi to the list, pointing out that Voyagers offered "big taxi or shuttle bus" sizes. The entire complex variety of PB models, sizes, trims and engines was available. Shown is a Maxi-wagon in Sport trim. Since passenger cars were becoming smaller, perhaps Plymouth felt that many taxicab buyers would prefer the Voyager's greater capacity.

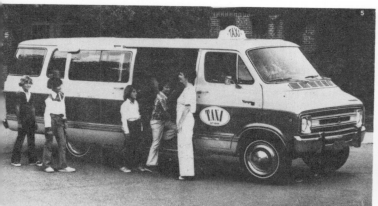

To show the Trail Duster PD100 rear-wheel drive model, 1978 sales material contained this retouched photograph of the 1977 vehicle. The updating shows the PD100 in Sport trim with black paint-filled lower moldings. A basic V-8 model weighed 3,570 pounds net and initially cost $4,866. A Six was $219 cheaper. Trail Dusters were offered only in basic and Sport trims, and could be ordered with a soft folding top. Gross vehicle weight ranged from 4,900 to 6,100 pounds.

Further emphasizing Plymouth's concentration on the police vehicle field, the full range of Voyagers was offered to that particular market. Advertised as the Voyager Law-Enforcer, Plymouth said these wagons offered maximum versatility for that purpose. To allow longer use periods and fewer fuel stops, an optional 36-gallon fuel tank was available. The Law-Enforcer shown is a Maxiwagon Sport with 12-passenger seating.

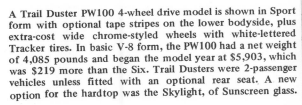

A Trail Duster PW100 4-wheel drive model is shown in Sport form with optional tape stripes on the lower bodyside, plus extra-cost wide chrome-styled wheels with white-lettered Tracker tires. In basic V-8 form, the PW100 had a net weight of 4,085 pounds and began the model year at $5,903, which was $219 more than the Six. Trail Dusters were 2-passenger vehicles unless fitted with an optional rear seat. A new option for the hardtop was the Skylight, of Sunscreen glass.

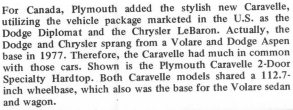

For Canada, Plymouth added the stylish new Caravelle, utilizing the vehicle package marketed in the U.S. as the Dodge Diplomat and the Chrysler LeBaron. Actually, the Dodge and Chrysler sprang from a Volare and Dodge Aspen base in 1977. Therefore, the Caravelle had much in common with those cars. Shown is the Plymouth Caravelle 2-Door Specialty Hardtop. Both Caravelle models shared a 112.7-inch wheelbase, which also was the base for the Volare sedan and wagon.

Shown is the Plymouth Caravelle 4-Door Sedan, a car that would make many Canadians proud to own, and others want to buy. The Caravelle offered buyers many choices. Those who wanted performance not offered by the standard 225 Super Six could get a 2 or 4-barrel 318 V-8 or a 2-barrel 360 V-8. Power steering and power front disc brakes were standard, and power-assist was available for several other functions. Two interiors provided a choice of luxury.

1929 MODEL Q.

CHRYSLER
PLYMOUTH

1930-31 MODEL 30-U

1932 Model PB

1933 PD
PC

1934
PE

1935

MODEL PJ

Production Totals

AUTO INDUSTRY — Passenger Cars

Cal. Yr.	Units
1929	4,794,898
1930	2,910,187
1931	2,038,183
1932	1,186,185
1933	1,627,361
1934	2,270,566
1935	3,387,806
1936	3,669,528
1937	3,915,889
1938	2,000,985
1939	2,866,796
1940	3,717,385
1941	3,779,682
1942	222,862
1943-44	none
1945	69,532
1946	2,148,699
1947	3,558,178
1948	3,909,270
1949	5,126,060
1950	6,672,132

PLYMOUTH — North American Production

Cal. Yr.	Units	Model Yr.		Units
1928-29	146,019	1929	Q	62,444
1930	67,658	1929-30	U	108,350
1931	106,259	1930-31	30-U	75,510
1932	121,468	1932	PA, PB	186,106
1933	442,281	1933		298,557
1934	351,113	1934		321,171
1935	442,281	1935		350,884
1936	527,177	1936		520,025
1937	514,061	1937		566,128
1938	297,572	1938		285,704
1939	350,046	1939		423,850
1940	509,735	1940		430,208
1941	429,869	1941		522,080
1942	25,225	1942		152,427
1943-44	none	1943-44		none
1945	2,581	1946-47-48 model year		
1946	244,846	production totals		
1947	353,848	not available		
1948	378,048	1946-48 total		1,059,489
1949	574,734	1949		520,385
1950	375,009	1950		610,954

DeSOTO — North American Production

Cal. Yr.	Units	Model Yr.		Units
1928-29	98,256	1929-30	K	93,202
1930	34,889	1930-31	CK, CF	32,275
1931	29,835	1931-32	SA, CF*	32,580
1932	27,441	1932	SC	24,496
1933	20,186	1933		22,736
1934	15,825	1934		13,940
1935	34,276	1935		27,581
1936	52,789	1936		43,710
1937	86,541	1937		82,000
1938	32,688	1938		39,203
1939	53,269	1939		55,699
1940	83,805	1940		67,790
1941	85,980	1941		99,999
1942	4,202	1942		24,771
1943-44	none	1943-44		none
1945	1,191	1946-47-48 model year		
1946	62,374	production totals		
1947	82,232	not available		
1948	93,357	1946-48 total		252,995
1949	107,151	1949		95,051
1950	127,435	1950		136,203

Year	Auto Industry	Plymouth	Plymouth (1951–52 combined)	DeSoto	DeSoto (1951–52 combined)
1951–52 combined total			1,007,662		193,999
1951	5,338,820	622,667		120,781	
1952	4,337,481	474,836		97,558	
1953	6,134,534	662,510	650,451	129,918	132,104
1954	5,509,550	399,785	463,148	69,831	78,580
1955	7,942,132	743,001	705,455	129,767	115,485
1956	5,801,864	462,269	571,634	97,809	109,442
1957	6,115,458	667,166	726,009	113,473	126,514
1958	4,244,045	373,725	443,799	33,853	49,445
1959	5,593,707	417,306	458,261	40,058	45,734
1960	6,696,108	483,969	483,969	19,411	26,081
1961	5,516,317	310,445	356,257	none	3,034
1962	6,935,182	331,079	339,527		
1963	7,637,173	496,412	488,448		
1964	7,739,034	571,339	551,633		
1965	9,329,104	679,539	728,228		
1966	8,598,917	640,450	687,514		
1967	7,406,788	610,098	638,075		
1968	8,843,031	683,678	790,239		
1969	8,219,463	651,124	751,134		
1970	6,545,908	699,031	747,508		
1971	8,578,349	636,592	702,113		
1972	8,821,737	612,997	780,937		
1973	9,660,821	742,926	908,790		
1974	7,290,258	609,385	745,805		
1975	6,705,837	447,403	507,338		
1976	8,537,759	663,257	550,876		
1977	9,312,207	499,223	589,336		
Grand Total			22,862,171		2,024,629

Plymouth calendar year column does not include commercial vehicles or foreign imports.

Plymouth model year column includes all vehicles except foreign imports.

DeSoto model years do not include the Diplomat.

All Plymouth and DeSoto totals are obtained from the Chrysler Historical Collection and Chrysler Corp. Production Programming Dept.

Auto Industry pre-war totals are from original records of the industry. Post-war totals are from Ward's Automotive Reports.

About the author

Few automobiles were rambling the roads of Paulding County, Ohio, when farmers Edward and Eva Butler welcomed the birth of Donald, the last of six children, on March 11, 1911. Only he and his sister, Mrs. Alice Gaunt of Napoleon, Michigan, remain to share the memories of their parents and brothers. Alice recalls the earliest years more vividly. In 1914, the Butlers moved to Hillsdale County in southern Michigan. Father loved farming and horses, not cars or motor-driven things, but he bought the family's first automobile in 1919. That used Chevrolet 490 provided young Donald's first close association with a car; it introduced him to the age of motoring, and that was about all it meant to him. When father got a new Model T Ford in 1923, 12-year-old Donald was quite impressed.

Left fatherless at 15, Donald had to give up schooling to share support responsibilities with his mother and youngest brother, as the older children were married. In 1927, Donald had his first experience at the controls of a moving automobile. Maybe he didn't actually drive it - - and maybe he did - - but perhaps it was "borderline" driving. It came about when a relative with a new Chrysler 60 had to make long walking inspections of roadside drainage ditches, accompanied by the car. It was placed in first gear, and it moved slowly under Donald's light foot-touch and straight guidance. That turtle-pace experience, though lacking any performance characteristics, endeared Chrysler to the boy, but he soon settled for learning to drive the Butler's rattly Model T.

Farming was not liked by the brothers, so in 1928 they found factory jobs in the county seat city of Hillsdale, which is today beloved by Donald as his hometown. But they didn't move to the hilly city until 1930, after spending 1929 in the nearby pleasant village of Jonesville. It was in 1929 that Donald, by then popularly known as Don, bought his first car, a new Model A Ford Tudor Sedan. The great depression began late that year and Don joined the unemployed ranks. Occasional no-skill jobs were found until he was hired by a Hillsdale manufacturer of trousers for men and boys, where he worked 11½ years as a cutter. World War II then changed the course of his life to a new direction in peacetime.

Born talented, Don had always drawn pictures, and his love for cars generally decided the subject of his drawings. While serving in the western states, he drew imaginary car designs during off-duty hours. They impressed other men, who thought he had been a professional designer of cars before the war. Told not, they urged him to make a post-war go for it. It was difficult for this descendant of the farm and factory to conceive of being paid for doing what he had always done for fun, and without specialized education, but he decided to take the step. Interviews at Ford and Chrysler were encouraging, but the Hudson Motor Car Co. didn't hesitate to put him on the styling staff. Excited and proud, awed and a bit scared, Don began his new career soon after re-becoming a civilian in 1946, and helped finish the design of the 1948 "step-down" Hudson.

Going next to Willys-Overland, he worked on the Jeepster, Jeep station wagons, and a later-aborted Willys car. He entered Nash in 1948, was delighted with the Nash-Hudson merger and birth of American Motors Corp. in 1954, but had to look for a new employer when AMC hit rough economic roads in 1956. Opportunity was found at Chrysler Corp., where his 18-year employment was filled with body and ornamentation styling for all cars, plus an unauthorized bonus of looking into Chrysler's historical past. Work forces were cut sharply late in 1974, and Don was among those idled. Retirement followed on January 31, 1975. Later that year, Chrysler called him back as a historical specialist for three months.

Since then, he has been quite busy with research and writing, and as a consultant for various publications devoted to automobiles. Though often utilizing sources elsewhere, he has an extensive reference collection in his home. Begun in 1927 with sales literature and advertisements, trade journals and other media have been added to the ongoing collecting "trip". The material relates to most American automobiles since pre-1900, as Don's interest was never confined to Chrysler Corp. The collection was strictly for pleasure, but events of recent years have cast a very different light upon it. Don speculates that perhaps a career in automotive history is under way - - and he hopes that it is.

Don has never owned a car of historical significance, at least while in his possession. His first Chrysler-built car was a new Dodge in 1941, replaced by another new Dodge in 1947. Next was a new 1957 Plymouth, which has been followed by eight more Plymouths. He is a member of the Society of Automotive Historians, the Antique Automobile Club of America, Autoenthusiasts International and the Classic Car Club of America.

Formally addressed as F. Donald Butler, he prefers the informality of the pen name Don Butler. Married in 1948 to Avis M. Elliott, of Jackson, Michigan, their home has been in the city of Detroit ever since. Son Dean also lives there, but daughter Patricia and son-in-law Douglas Wasama reside in Kansas City, Missouri.